Developing Critical Reading Skills

When you sell a man a book, you don't sell him twelve ounces of paper and ink and glue—you sell him a whole new life.

—Christopher Morley

Developing Critical Reading Skills

Sixth Edition

Deanne Spears
City College of San Francisco

Boston   Burr Ridge, IL   Dubuque, IA   Madison, WI   New York   San Francisco   St. Louis
Bangkok   Bogotá   Caracas   Kuala Lumpur   Lisbon   London   Madrid   Mexico City
Milan   Montreal   New Delhi   Santiago   Seoul   Singapore   Sydney   Taipei   Toronto

McGraw-Hill Higher Education 🐝

A Division of The **McGraw-Hill** Companies

DEVELOPING CRITICAL READING SKILLS
Published by McGraw-Hill, a business unit of The McGraw-Hill Companies, Inc., 1221 Avenue of the Americas, New York, NY, 10020. Copyright © 2003, 1999, 1995, 1991, 1987, 1983 by The McGraw-Hill Companies, Inc. All rights reserved. No part of this publication may be reproduced or distributed in any form or by any means, or stored in a database or retrieval system, without the prior written consent of The McGraw-Hill Companies, Inc., including, but not limited to, in any network or other electronic storage or transmission, or broadcast for distance learning.
Some ancillaries, including electronic and print components, may not be available to customers outside the United States.

This book is printed on acid-free paper.

1 2 3 4 5 6 7 8 9 0 DOC/DOC 0 9 8 7 6 5 4 3 2

ISBN 0-07-249132-9 (student edition)
ISBN 0-07-255458-4 (annotated instructor's edition)

President of McGraw-Hill Humanities/Social Sciences: *Steve Debow*
Executive editor: *Sarah Touborg*
Editorial assistant: *Anne Stameshkin*
Senior marketing manager: *David Patterson*
Project manager: *Rebecca Nordbrock*
Production supervisor: *Carol A. Bielski*
Designer: *Matthew Baldwin*
Producer, media technology: *Todd Vaccaro*
Supplement associate: *Kate Boylan*
Photo research coordinator: *Judy Kausal*
Photo researcher: *Elsa Peterson*
Cover design: *Argosy*
Cover image: The Window, *by Pierre Bonnard, 1925, Copyright Tate Gallery, London/Art Resource, NY*
Interior design: *Mary Christianson*
Typeface: *10/12 Stone Serif*
Compositor: *Shepherd Incorporated*
Printer: *R. R. Donnelley & Sons Company*

Library of Congress Cataloging-in-Publication Data

Spears, Deanne.
    Developing critical reading skills/Deanne Spears.—6th ed., Annotated
instructor's ed.
        p. cm.
    Includes index.
    ISBN 0-07-255458-4 (Annotated instructor's ed.: alk. paper)—ISBN 0-07-249132-9
    (Student ed.: alk. paper)
    1. Reading (Higher education) 2. Reading comprehension. I. Title.
LB2395.3 .M55 2003
428.4'071'1—dc21   2002067750

www.mhhe.com

ABOUT THE AUTHOR

After receiving a B.A. and an M.A. in Comparative Literature from the University of Southern California, Deanne Spears worked for a management consultant firm as a junior editor. A few months of delivering mail, typing, and correcting the consultants' grammar convinced her that a business career was not for her. She found a long-term substitute teaching job at Los Angeles Valley College, then taught at Rio Hondo Community College, and in 1968 joined the English Department at City College of San Francisco. She has done postgraduate work at San Francisco State University, studying logic, anthropology, and literature. At City College of San Francisco she teaches reading and composition. In addition to this text, she is the author of an intermediate reading book, *Improving Reading Skills* (4th ed.), also published by McGraw-Hill. She is married to a fellow English teacher, David Spears.

IN MEMORY OF

Edward Stephen Koziol, M.D.
and Dorothy Granter Koziol

BRIEF CONTENTS

CONTENTS

PART II
Discovering Meaning: The Importance of Form 95

CHAPTER 9

Evaluating Arguments: Problems in Critical Reading   302

CHAPTER 10

Critical Reading and the World Wide Web   350

PART V
Reading Essays and Articles   361

PART VI
Reading Short Stories   511

PREFACE

Developing Critical Reading Skills continues to evolve. Instructors new to this text will reap benefits from the cumulative changes in the earlier editions. I hope that these changes will satisfy the needs of both students and instructors. The terrorist attacks on the United States and in other parts of the world—and their repercussions—have made it even more crucial for us to be an educated populace, able to read with accuracy, skilled in detecting propaganda and jingoistic slogans, and interested in acquiring knowledge about cultures that behave in seemingly incomprehensible ways or that have different worldviews.

Accordingly, I have again increased the attention given to critical reading, both by adding the word *critical* to the title in the previous edition and by expanding the treatment of the many elements subsumed under that term. The book proceeds from the assumption that good reading and clear thinking go hand in hand. It seeks to remedy teachers' and employers' legitimate concerns: Increasingly, students in the classroom and employees in the workplace demonstrate weaknesses in reading perceptively, following directions, and thinking critically. Perhaps this book can do a small part to help students—indeed, all of us—be better thinkers and better-read citizens.

The text emphasizes practice in sustained, analytical reading. Students first work with high-quality short passages before moving on to practice with longer pieces of greater complexity. A glance at the table of contents shows the variety of skills taken up in the book and the order imposed on them. As in the earlier editions, the readings explore diverse subjects: anthropology, sports, human behavior, politics, social policy, education, ethics, autobiography, personal reminiscence, the minority and the immigrant experience, humor, satire, and so forth. The passages also reflect diverse writing styles, thereby giving students the experience of reading high-level prose by its best practitioners. Finally, because learning to read analytically requires concentration and an intense engagement with the text, this edition, like its five predecessors, deliberately omits a discussion of speed-reading techniques.

The book succeeds if students become more self-assured about their reading and if they recognize that reading well—with confidence, fluency, and enjoyment—is a significant part of their emotional and academic lives. My hope is that students will feel genuine excitement when they encounter a writer who shows them a new way of looking at their lives and at the world. It is this feeling—inspiration, perhaps, for lack of a better word—that I always hope to impart to my students in my teaching and in this book.

I am indebted to the thoughtful and practical suggestions reviewers gave me, which I have incorporated almost without exception. I hope that these new features make the sixth edition attractive and pedagogically useful. Here are the major changes I have made:

- Coverage of topics is more accessible and less dense; the treatment of the skills has been pared down. Although the scheme is almost identical to that of the earlier editions, the chapters in Parts 2, 3, and 4 are delineated more clearly.

- Besides suggestions for improving vocabulary and some brief notes on punctuation, the introduction now contains a review of online dictionaries and several word-of-the-day sites on the World Wide Web.

- Each chapter begins with an explanation of the chapter objectives and a list of topics covered in the chapter. Important information and terms throughout the text are boxed for convenient reference.

- Each chapter in Parts 1 through 5 includes one or more annotated excerpts demonstrating the art of reading with a pencil in one's hand. Learning to annotate leads to better comprehension, concentration, and retention.

- Short practice exercises are interspersed throughout Chapters 1 through 9, allowing the student to practice a particular skill before proceeding to the next one.

- As before, each chapter ends with exercises providing practice in reading and analyzing short passages and an essay. In this edition, in Parts 1 through 3, answers for the first selection's exercises follow the exercise section, allowing students to check their answers immediately.

- Each long essay in Parts 1, 2, 3, and 5 ends with suggestions for further exploration: Features called "On the Web," "In the Bookstore," or "At the Movies" point the student to relevant websites, books, and films thematically connected to the reading.

- The section on reading critically (Part 4) has been completely reorganized. In Chapter 8, students practice breaking down an argument into its constituent elements: the writer's authority, the claim, unstated assumptions, definitions, and supporting evidence. Chapter 9 takes up problems associated with reading argumentative prose, including errors in reasoning, emotional appeals, logical fallacies, bias, and other deceptive techniques. Examples in both chapters have been chosen from a wide variety of newspapers and magazines; they concern contemporary political, social, educational, and ethical problems and assorted events, some humorous, most of some consequence. Last, both chapters end with newspaper and magazine editorials on timely issues for analysis and evaluation. Three of these pieces deal with the aftermath of the terrorist attacks of September 11, 2001.

- Chapter 10 (in Part 4), new to this edition, is titled "Critical Reading and the World Wide Web." This brief chapter consists of an overview of reading on the World Wide Web and the particular problems online reading entails, a list of useful search engines, websites for improving critical reading skills, and five exercises for evaluating websites and doing simple research activities. These exercises include researching an environmental or health issue; evaluating the websites of the Democratic, Libertarian, and Republican Parties; and analyzing Richard Nixon's "Checkers" speech.

- Of the 22 longer essays and articles throughout the text, 10 are new; of the short stories in Part 6, all four are new.

- Black-and-white thumbnail photographs of many of the major authors precede their essays, articles, or short stories.

- In keeping with the trend of increasing globalization (for better or for worse), the sixth edition includes more major international writers: Salman Rushdie and Pico Iyer (India and England); Margaret Atwood and Bruce McCall (Canada); Virginia Woolf (England); Ryszard Kapuściński (Poland); Andrei Codrescu (Romania and the United States); and Leo Tolstoy (Russia). Throughout the text, both the short and long readings represent a diverse group of American writers, including many women and people of color.

■ ANCILLARY MATERIALS

- The World Wide Web site for the text has been completely redone. The address is *www.mhhe.com/spears*. There, students can click on "Student Resources" to find an extensive array of practice exercises accompanying each chapter. Instructors also will find multiple forms of the major tests covering Parts 1 through 4 for convenient downloading and class duplication. For ease of correction, a separate version of the test with boldfaced answers is provided.

- The annotated instructor's manual for the sixth edition, in addition to the usual apparatus, includes answers for the text, making the tedious process of transferring answers from the instructor's manual to the text no longer necessary. For further information, instructors should consult the manual's introduction. As before, a test booklet is available for instructors who adopt the text.

A word of caution about websites: Please be sure to preview any websites used in class to avoid untoward problems. Sometimes hackers have entered a site and substituted unwanted or embarrassing content. This warning applies particularly to teachers who have access to the World Wide Web in their classrooms.

■ ACKNOWLEDGMENTS

I am grateful for the generous help I received from many sources—first from my colleagues at City College of San Francisco who have used the text: Carol Fregly, Pamela Gentile, Michael Hulbert, Abdul Jabbar, Robert Stamps (emeritus), Susan Zimmerman, and Rosalie Wolf (emeritus). Special thanks to my friend and colleague, Joan Wilson, for her helpful ideas during our many conversations about argumentation. Meryl Corwin-Udell of Diablo Valley College and Dorothy Scully of Modesto College made some valuable suggestions as I was preparing this revision, and my friend and former student, Jill Ramsay, ensured the book's accuracy on Canadian matters. I am also grateful to the following people for recommending new writers for me to explore: my daughter, Charlotte Milan, of San Francisco; Monilou Carter, of Half Moon Bay, California; Naomi Mann, of San Francisco; Geri McCauley, of Napa, California; and Jennifer Ruddy, of Camden, Maine.

Additionally, the book's many reviewers deserve special mention for their careful reading and judicious recommendations:

Maureen Connolly, Elmhurst College
Alan Smolka, Leeward Community College/University of Hawaii
Janice Horn, Irvine Valley College
Janice Hill-Matula, Moraine Valley Community College
Jessica Stephens, Eastern Kentucky University
Denise Chambers, Normandale Community College
Ruth Becker, Pensacola Junior College
Loreen Inman, Fullerton College
Alice Perrey, St. Charles County Community College
Jesus Adame, El Paso Community College
Shirley Brownfox, Seattle Central Community College
Marybeth Ruscica, St. John's University
Sharon Snyders, Ivy Tech State College
Patricia Grega, University of Alaska—Anchorage
Christy Rishoi, Jackson Community College

Warmest thanks to Sarah Touborg, my editor at McGraw-Hill, for her abiding encouragement and enthusiasm; to Anne Stameshkin, for her prompt handling of countless details; to Rebecca Nordbrock, project manager, for her efficient overseeing of the production process, and to Alice Jaggard, whose copyediting immeasurably improved the book's writing style. And special thanks go to my husband, David, for recommending Katherine Anne Porter's fine story, for his unerring eye and extensive knowledge of grammar, and most of all, for his understanding and boundless good humor.

Students and instructors who have comments, suggestions, or questions are invited to contact me via e-mail. The address is *dspears1@mindspring.com* or *dkspears@ccsf.edu*. I will do my best to answer within a day or two of receiving messages.

Deanne Spears
City College of San Francisco
San Francisco, California

TO THE STUDENT

A few years ago I was shopping in downtown San Francisco with the man who is now my husband and his 12-year-old daughter. A street musician, whom my husband was acquainted with from his own musician days, was playing the tenor saxophone on a street corner. His name is Clifford, and he had attracted a crowd with his wonderful performance. After he finished, my husband introduced him to me and to Sarah, his daughter. Clifford asked Sarah if she played an instrument, and when she replied that she was taking trumpet lessons and played in her junior high school band, he said, "That's fine, little lady. Learn your instrument well and you can play anything."

Somehow these simple and wise words struck me as fitting not only for an aspiring trumpet player but also for a reader. When you learn to read well, you can read anything you want—not just the daily newspapers and mass-circulation magazines, but more difficult reading, such as philosophy, anthropology, film criticism, particle physics, military history—whatever interests you. You will not be limited in any way. Assuming you have the vocabulary—or at least a good dictionary at your side—you can pick up a book or an article, concentrate on it, and make sense of the writer's words.

Reading is an almost magical process that involves more than merely decoding print. It requires internal translation. In other words, you internalize the writer's words so that you take them in, not only to understand their surface meaning but also to understand what they suggest beyond that. Rather than reading passively, sitting back and letting the writer do all the work, in this course you will learn to interact with the text. You will learn to read with a pencil in your hand. When you read, you enter into a peculiar relationship with the writer, a two-way process of communication. Although the writer is physically absent, the words on the page are nonetheless there to be analyzed, interpreted, questioned, perhaps even challenged. In this way, the active reader engages in a kind of silent dialogue with the writer.

Sadly, reading instruction in American schools often ends in elementary school, and students may have difficulty as they progress through school. The reading material becomes harder, yet they must tackle their assignments still armed with elementary school reading skills. The result, too often, is frustration and loss of confidence. And the assigned readings in your college courses will be even more demanding than the readings were in high school—in complexity of content and in the amount of reading assigned. *Developing Critical Reading Skills* is designed to accomplish several tasks: to teach you the skills that will enable you to read with greater comprehension and retention, to help you undertake reading assignments with confidence, and to show you how to become an active, fluent reader.

This is the sixth edition of *Developing Critical Reading Skills.* With each edition and with each semester using the text, I have learned a great deal. You will be the recipient of the many excellent suggestions, which, along with various reviewers' and colleagues' remarks, I have incorporated. Take some time to look through the table of contents to become familiar with the book's layout and scope. You will begin with basic comprehension skills and gradually move toward the more difficult skills associated with critical reading.

As you glance through Parts 1, 2, and 3, you will see that these seven chapters treat the paragraph extensively, including explanations, illustrative passages, and exercises. At first it may seem odd—and perhaps artificial—to devote so much time to single paragraphs that, after all, are seldom read in isolation. Yet my students have found that concentrating on short passages promotes careful reading. The paragraph is the basic unit of writing and, in fact, is often referred to as the main building block of the essay. Studying paragraph structure closely and examining short passages for placement of the main idea, inferences, methods of development, patterns of organization, language (especially connotation and figurative language), and tone will teach you how to analyze on a small scale. Certainly, it is less intimidating to practice with a hundred-word paragraph than with a five-page essay. Once you become proficient with paragraphs, you will apply the same analytical skills to longer works.

Specifically, you will learn to identify the main idea and, more important, to put it into your own words; to see relationships between ideas; to determine the writer's tone and purpose; to make accurate inferences; to recognize arguments; to weigh evidence; to detect bias, unstated assumptions, false appeals, logical fallacies, distortions, lack of balance, and the like. Because the bulk of the reading you must do in college is expository—that is, prose writing that explains, shows, and informs—the readings in this book reflect mostly that kind of writing, although editorials and short fiction are also included.

Much emphasis has been placed on increasing reading speed, on skimming and scanning, on zipping through material simply to get the drift of what the writer is saying. These techniques have their place: A football fan skims through the sports pages to find out if the Green Bay Packers beat their archrival, an employee scans the help-wanted columns to look for a new job, and a student looks through the electronic card catalog for likely research sources. But skimming is inappropriate for the major part of the reading you will have to do in college. For this reason, *Developing Critical Reading Skills* does not include a discussion of speed-reading techniques.

During the course, as you sharpen your skills, your work should have two results. The first will be an improvement in your own writing. Good reading skills and good writing skills are most certainly interrelated. When you understand how professional writers organize, develop, and support their ideas, you will become more aware of how to deal with your own writing assignments. But more important, you will learn to be a better thinker as well. These skills will serve you well for the rest of your life.

If you have comments, suggestions, or questions, you are invited to contact me via e-mail. The address is *dspears1@mindspring.com* or *dkspears@ccsf.edu*. I can also be reached through the McGraw-Hill Higher Education website at *www.mhhe.com/spears*. I will do my best to answer within a day or two of receiving messages.

Deanne Spears

Developing Critical Reading Skills

Introduction

- An Overview of the Text and the Reading Process
- Improving Your Vocabulary
- Punctuation

■ AN OVERVIEW OF THE TEXT AND THE READING PROCESS

Becoming a good reader, rather than merely a competent one, is crucial if you are to do well in your college courses. In my teaching experience, some students find their first academic experiences bewildering: They may not know what to look for when they read, nor are they sure what their instructors expect of them. *Developing Critical Reading Skills* will help you with both matters. You will learn how to look critically and analytically at short passages, essays, and articles, and how to discern the parts, the substance, and the strengths and weaknesses of the writer's prose. As you work through this text, you will find your ability to comprehend difficult prose, your confidence, and most important, your enjoyment in the experience of reading gradually improving. These are admittedly ambitious goals, requiring a closer look at how they can be accomplished.

Defining the Reading Process

The reading process begins with decoding words, that is, deciphering the letters that make up individual words. But reading is more than merely processing letters and sounds. The real meaning of a text lies in the relationships the words have with each other. Reading well requires us to recognize these relationships and to put together the meaning of the text. When you think about everything that goes on simultaneously in the human mind as one reads, the process not only defies easy explanation but also takes on almost magical qualities. Isolating the steps makes the process seem mechanical or reducible to a formula. But nothing about reading is mechanical or formulaic.

In this passage from his book on the modern media, *Amusing Ourselves to Death,* Neil Postman sums up the problems reading poses for the reader:

> [A language-centered discourse] is serious because meaning demands to be understood. A written sentence calls upon its author to say something, upon its reader to know the import of what is said. And when an author and reader are struggling with semantic meaning, they are engaged in the most serious challenge to the intellect. This is especially the case with the act of reading, for authors are not always trustworthy. They lie, they become confused, they over-generalize, they abuse logic and, sometimes, common sense. The reader must come armed in a serious state of intellectual readiness. This is not easy because he comes to the text alone. In reading, one's responses are isolated, one's intellect thrown back on its own resources. To be confronted by the cold abstractions of printed sentences is to look upon the language bare, without the assistance of either beauty or community. Thus, reading is by its nature a serious business. It is also, of course, an essentially rational activity.

Beyond Decoding—The Requirements of Reading

Reading involves—far beyond decoding the words and knowing their meanings in context—paying attention to these and other elements all at once. Following are the major requirements of reading (with the chapters where each element is discussed in the text):

- Identifying the main idea, the focus or controlling idea, and the writer's purpose (Chapter 1).
- Discerning the relative importance of supporting ideas (major and minor support) as they relate to the main idea (Chapter 1).
- Making accurate inferences; reading between the lines and identifying what the writer does not explicitly say but surely suggests (Chapter 2).
- Identifying the methods of development, the logical connections between the parts of a passage, and the arrangement of ideas the writer imposes on the subject (Chapters 3, 4, and 5).

- Understanding the denotative and connotative values of words (Chapter 6).
- Perceiving the writer's point of view and tone, or emotional feeling (Chapter 7).
- Recognizing strategies—both fair and unfair ones—in argumentative and persuasive writing; learning not to believe everything you read just because someone published it (Chapters 8, 9, and 10).

The reading process is quite different from watching television, where the images wash over us as we sit like passive automatons. Note that the pejorative term *couch potatoes* applies only to TV watchers, never to readers! The good reader is engaged with the text and participates fully in the world the writer recreates on the page. However—and this is the magical part—the good reader is unaware of these elements as she reads. They occur involuntarily and effortlessly, the sweep and flow of the words transporting her along and down the page.

Becoming a First-Rate Reader

Each semester I begin the course by asking students to evaluate their past experiences with reading. We try to determine what makes some readers really good and others merely adequate—decoders of print but not much more. The session helps them focus on what they need to do in the course (as well as over the course of their lives) to become the very best readers they can. Students often write or e-mail me after they have transferred to a four-year university, such as San Jose State University or UC Davis, typically saying that they are stunned by the amount of reading they are expected to do in their upper-division courses. They report that some courses require them to read as many as 8 or 10 books over a semester. Clearly, unless you are exceptional, the skills that got you through high school won't be up to this job.

College reading instructors might list these habits as characteristic of good readers:

Good Readers
- Preview the assignment to get an overview of its content (not just to count the pages or the pictures).
- Are actively involved with the text; they read with pencils in their hands, annotating main points and writing question marks next to puzzling material.
- Identify relationships between ideas and examine how the parts of an essay fit together.
- Read important assignments twice.

- In the first reading, underline or circle vocabulary words to look up and then look them up in the second go-around.
- Question the writer; they look beneath the surface for implications.
- Anticipate questions for quizzes, discussion, or in-class writing assignments.
- Maintain focus and block out distractions as much as is humanly possible.
- Start reading assignments early enough to complete them (not at 10 P.M. the night before class or on the morning bus ride to campus).
- Consider each reading assignment a challenge and a way to learn, even if the subject matter is not particularly interesting, not an unpleasant task to be put off until the very last minute.

If you have not developed these habits yet or if they sound too daunting and formidable, keep in mind that you will not have to learn everything at once. You will undertake each element singly, with lots of opportunities for practice. And unlike Postman's lonely reader, you will have your instructor to guide you through the rough patches. In the meantime, get as much practice as you can outside class. Most reading teachers recommend that students try to fit in at least an hour of reading on their own every day—not required assignments for classes, but reading for pleasure.

An even more compelling reason to read a lot derives from the results of a recent study by Dr. Robert Friedland, a professor of neurology at Case Western Reserve University School of Medicine, published in the *Proceedings of the National Academy of Sciences*. Friedland found that "adults with hobbies that exercise their brains—such as reading, jigsaw puzzles or chess—are 2½ times less likely to get Alzheimer's disease, while leisure limited to TV watching may increase the risk."[1]

Reading with a Pencil

Let us illustrate an important skill mentioned earlier: how to annotate a text. If you have trouble concentrating or are easily distracted by the passing world around you, reading with a pencil in your hand will go a

---

[1]Paul Recer, "Brain Teasers May Delay Alzheimer's," Associated Press, March 6, 2001. The abstract of this study is worth reading; both it and the complete text of the study's research methods and results are available by searching the archives for March 2001 at *www.pnas.org, Proceedings of the National Academy of Sciences.*

long way toward helping you comprehend better and maintain focus. Annotating means making brief marginal notations, specifically, writing questions to raise in class, underlining important points, circling words to look up.

Reprinted here is a short excerpt from a book that caused a stir in zoological circles and in the popular press when it was published in 1995. The thesis of *When Elephants Weep,* by Jeffrey Masson and Susan McCarthy, is that animals feel emotions and that we can observe these feelings. (Hard scientists usually reject human attempts to interpret animal behavior in anthropomorphic terms.) The chapter from which the excerpt is taken is entitled "Grief, Sadness, and the Bones of Elephants," which is a fair indication of its contents; the subsection is called "Imprisonment."

Captive animals are sad

[1]Even when captive animals are not confined in solitude, their imprisonment may make them sad. It is often said of zoo animals that the way to tell if they are happy is to ask whether the young play and the adults breed. Most zookeepers would not accept this standard of happiness for themselves. As Jane Goodall noted, "Even in concentration camps, babies were born, and there is no good reason to believe that it is different for chimpanzees."

Goodall—chimps breed in captivity?

[2]Captivity is undoubtedly more painful to some animals than others. Lions seem to have less difficulty with the notion of lying in the sun all day than do tigers, for example. Yet even lions can be seen in many zoos pacing restlessly back and forth in the stereotyped motions seen in so many captive animals. The concept of *funktionslust,* the enjoyment of one's abilities, also suggests its opposite, the feeling of frustration and misery that overtakes an animal when its capacities cannot be expressed. If an animal enjoys using its natural abilities, it is also possible that the animal *misses* using them. Although a gradual trend in zoo construction and design is to make the cages better resemble the natural habitat, most zoo animals, particularly the large ones, have little or no opportunity to use their abilities. Eagles have no room to fly, cheetahs have no room to run, goats have but a single boulder to climb.

Animals suffer b/c can't do natural activities, even in good zoos

"Possible" suggests speculation, not fact

Most likely sad, not grateful for good care

Negative side effects— no breeding, stress causes illness or death; may starve on purpose

Gorilla in 1913 died of "broken heart"

Marine mammals in captivity—high death rate: not enough room to roam

[3]There is no reason to suppose that zoo life is not a source of sadness to most animals imprisoned there, like displaced persons in wartime. It would be comforting to believe that they are happy there, delighted to receive medical care and grateful to be sure of their next meal. Unfortunately, in the main, there is no evidence to suppose that they are. Most take every possible opportunity to escape. Most will not breed. Probably they want to go home. Some captive animals die of grief when taken from the wild. Sometimes these deaths appear to be from disease, perhaps because an animal under great stress becomes (vulnerable) to illness. Others are quite obviously deaths from despair—near-suicides. Wild animals may refuse to eat, killing themselves in the only way open to them. We do not know if they are aware that they will die if they do not eat, but it is clear that they are extremely unhappy. In 1913 Jasper Von Oertzen described the death of a young gorilla imported to Europe: "Hum-Hum had lost all joy in living. She succeeded in living to reach Hamburg, and from there, the Animal Park at Stellingen, with all her caretakers, but her energy did not return again. With signs of the greatest sadness of soul Hum-Hum mourned over the happy past. One could find no fatal illness; it was as always with these costly animals: 'She died of a broken heart.' "

[4]Marine mammals have a high death rate in captivity, a fact not always apparent to visitors at marine parks and oceanariums. A pilot whale celebrity at one oceanarium was actually thirteen different pilot whales, each successive one being introduced to visitors by the same name, as if it were the same animal. It takes little reflection to see the great difference in a marine mammal's life when kept in an oceanarium. Orcas grow to twenty-three feet long, weight up to 9,000 pounds, and roam a hundred miles a day. No cage, and certainly not the swimming pools where they are confined in all oceanariums, could possibly provide satisfaction, let alone joy. They are believed to have a life expectancy as long as our own. Yet

Can't move naturally, esp. hard on large species

Note other "hedge" words ("probably")

1913? Why no recent ex?

Note obvious anthropomorphic slant

What is life span for orcas in wild?

at Sea World, in San Diego, the oceanarium with the best track record for keeping orcas alive, they last an average of eleven years.

[5]If a person's life span were shortened this much, would one still speak of happiness? Asked whether their animals were happy, a number of marine mammal trainers all said yes: they ate, engaged in sexual intercourse (it is extremely rare for an orca to give birth in captivity), and were almost never sick. This would mean that they were not depressed, but does it mean they were happy? The fact that people ask this question again and again indicates a malaise, perhaps profound guilt at subjecting these lively sea travelers to unnatural confinement.

Would we want this for ourselves? No!

> Jeffrey Masson and
> Susan McCarthy,
> *When Elephants Weep*

Three words in this excerpt might be unfamiliar to you: "*funktionslust*" in paragraph 2; "*vulnerable*" in paragraph 3; and "*malaise*" in paragraph 5. Notice that the German word *funktionslust* is defined by the phrase that follows it: "the enjoyment of one's abilities."

Similarly, the meaning of *vulnerable* should be evident from the context. Of these four dictionary definitions, which best fits the way the writers use the word?

1. _____ capable of or susceptible to being wounded or hurt physically or emotionally.
2. _____ susceptible to temptation or corrupt influence.
3. _____ open to or defenseless against criticism or moral attack.
4. _____ open to assault; difficult to defend.

For this context, the best answer is number 1.

The dictionary lists two definitions for *malaise*. Again, in context, which of the two definitions seems to fit? (Remember that the writers are discussing *human,* not animal, reactions to keeping marine mammals in captivity.)

1. _____ a vague feeling of bodily discomfort, as at the beginning of an illness.
2. _____ a general sense of depression or unease.

The better choice seems to be number 2.

Now, list two or three questions that occurred to you as you read the excerpt.

_____

_____

_____

_____

Here are a few that occurred to me, along with some tentative answers:

1. *Have the writers proved their point that captive animals are sad? What evidence is offered? Is it sufficient, relevant, and up-to-date?* Certainly, some of the behaviors exhibited by zoo animals (pacing, repetitive actions, infrequent breeding) suggest unhappiness and stress. The fact that zoos often resort to artificial insemination to breed their captives adds credence to the writers' observation, though they do not mention this. The discussion in paragraph 2 is more speculative or theoretical, and the authors admit as much by using the "hedge" word *possible* in explaining that an animal misses using its natural abilities.

2. *Why haven't the writers used a more current example of an animal's having "died of a broken heart" than that of the gorilla observed in 1913, nearly a century ago?* This question is unanswerable but still justified. Does the use of this example suggest that the writers couldn't locate one more recent than almost nine decades old? Also, the phrase "to die of a broken heart" is anthropomorphic; while we can surely identify with the emotion, the diagnosis is emotional, not scientific. Additionally, one's interpretation of this passage depends a great deal on one's world view. Readers who avoid zoos because the sight of caged animals depresses them would probably be more likely to accept Masson and McCarthy's observations than would readers who think zoos are important educational institutions.

3. *The writers suggest that zookeepers would not accept for themselves the level of happiness afforded captive animals. Does the Jane Goodall quotation at the end of paragraph 1 support this contention?* Since no one is proposing that zookeepers be "confined in solitude" as zoo animals are, the statement about an unacceptable level of happiness is moot. Goodall's quotation is more puzzling, however. If babies were born in concentration camps—to prisoners who lived in unspeakable conditions—isn't that an indication of rising above one's misery rather than giving in to it? If Goodall's remark

is supposed to reinforce the idea that chimpanzees can breed in captivity, then Masson and McCarthy contradict themselves in paragraph 3 when they write that most captive animals "will not breed."

4. *Is the evidence based on fact or on speculation, or is it a combination of both?* Notice that most evidence is general rather than specific: "Eagles have no room to fly, cheetahs have no room to run"; "Most take every possible opportunity to escape"; and so on. The writers cite only one example of a specific animal at a specific zoo. I noted the adjective *possible* in paragraph 2; paragraph 3 uses similar words, suggesting that these remarks are theoretical: "*Probably* they want to go home"; "these deaths *appear* to be from disease"; "Wild animals *may* refuse to eat," and so forth. These words suggest that the writers are trying to protect themselves from attack.

Despite the flaws and the absence of hard scientific research, the discussion is nonetheless compelling because Masson and McCarthy make us feel empathy. If we would not like to live in such conditions, as they say, why do we suppose that animals would?

This exercise illustrates the analytic method of reading undertaken in this text. As you work through it, you will be asked to read passages, longer ones than this, using these techniques. But critical analysis and questioning on this level are possible only as a result of careful reading and annotation. Skimming through a passage quickly will allow you to get its drift but not to have full understanding.

■ IMPROVING YOUR VOCABULARY

A good vocabulary is probably the single most important prerequisite for good reading. Every other skill—comprehending, retaining information, making inferences, drawing appropriate conclusions, evaluating—depends on whether you know what the words on the page mean in relation to each other and in their context. After all, if you don't know what the words on the page mean, you cannot know what you are reading. Sometimes it is possible to wing it, getting the general idea without complete clarity. Most often, however, and especially with the analytical reading you will do in this course, your understanding of a passage may hinge solely on the meaning of a single word, a situation in which guessing is hazardous.

Ignoring new words, hoping that they don't really matter, may impair your comprehension. A recent incident that occurred in one of my classes illustrates what can go wrong when a reader assumes he or she knows what a word means and fails to look it up. The class had been discussing a *New York Times* editorial written by an Orthodox Jewish student at Yale University. The writer was defending a lawsuit he had filed against the university; he argued that Yale should exempt him and a few other Orthodox Jewish students from the requirement that freshmen and sophomores live in dormitories. He and his fellow students objected to the permissive sexual environment of the dorms. In one sentence the student quotes the president of Yale, who states that the university is proud of not having any "parietal rules." When I asked a student in the class what *parietal* meant, he responded that it meant that Yale didn't have any rules such as parents might make.

Despite their similar appearance, *parietal* and *parental* have nothing to do with each other. *The American Heritage Dictionary* defines parietal rules as those "governing the visiting privileges of members of the opposite sex in college or university dormitories." In other words, Yale has *no rules* governing its students' sexual conduct or visiting privileges. The student's inaccurate guess resulted in his misconstruing Yale's position and thus misinterpreting an important part of the editorial.

In the real world, failing to check the meaning of words in the dictionary may have serious financial repercussions. In 1997, Reebok, the athletic shoe manufacturing company, had to discard 53,000 pairs of a new line of women's running shoes called "Incubus," even though the shoes had been on the market for a year with no customer complaints. ABC, upon learning about the name of the shoe line, put the story on the evening news. It seems that no one at the company had bothered to check in the dictionary to see that an incubus is a male demon who comes to a woman and makes love to her while she sleeps. Reebok suffered a corporate red face and lost a lot of money.

Vocabulary in Perspective

The task of improving your vocabulary is inescapable, and it is a lifelong one. At first, learning dozens of new words may seem like a discouraging, maybe even an overwhelming, prospect, but it *is* possible. Everyone has to start somewhere, and even the best reader's vocabulary can be improved. The number of words in the English language is sufficiently vast to make even the best reader occasionally reach for the dictionary. (The 2000 edition of the *Random House Webster's College Dictionary* lists 180,000 entries or words; the third edition of *The American Heritage Dictionary,* also published in 2000, contains 350,000 words, 16,000 of them new.)

To put these numbers into perspective and to see the dimensions of acquiring an adult-level vocabulary, consider the findings of Richard C. Anderson and William E. Nagy, authorities in reading and educational theory. They estimate that there are approximately 88,000 words in what they call "school English" (compiled from 1,000 items of reading materials from elementary through high school).[2] When they added proper nouns, compound words, multiple meanings of homonyms (words that sound alike but that have different spellings and meanings), and idioms, they estimated that "there may be 180,000 distinct vocabulary items in school English and that an average high school senior may know eight thousand of them."[3] The sheer number of words in the language partly explains why acquiring a good vocabulary takes so long. Obviously, a college student is expected to know even more than the figures Anderson and Nagy cite, since college reading assignments are more difficult than those in high school. Many studies point to American students' diminished vocabulary; such findings demonstrate the importance of getting your level up to par at the beginning of your college career.[4]

An exhaustive treatment of vocabulary acquisition is not within the scope of this book, and many excellent vocabulary guides are available. Simply memorizing lists of words in isolation is tempting but inefficient. You won't remember many of them, nor will you understand the subtleties in their meaning or their meanings in various contexts. The very best way to learn new words is to read as much as you have time for. Most of the words you recognize in your reading you know because of prior exposure. New words are best learned—and retained—when you encounter them in your reading.

Suggestions for Vocabulary Improvement

My students have benefited from implementing these ideas:

- *Invest in a new hardback dictionary.* If you do not have an unabridged dictionary published recently, buy one. It will be money well spent. A new dictionary will last well beyond your college years. Some suggestions are provided in the next section.

- *Develop an interest in words and their origins.* When you look up a new word in an unabridged dictionary, look at its **etymology,** or history; many English words have unusual origins. The etymology of a word—often printed in brackets following the definitions—explains and traces the derivation of the word and gives the original meaning in the language or languages the word is derived from.

---

[2]Richard C. Anderson and William E. Nagy, "The Vocabulary Conundrum," *American Educator* (Winter 1992), 16.
[3]Anderson and Nagy, 19.
[4]From *Harper's* Index for August 2000: "Average number of words in the written vocabulary of a 6- to 14-year-old American child in 1945: 25,000. Average number today: 10,000." The source for these sobering figures is Gary Ingersoll of Indiana University.

For instance, one dictionary traces the history of the word *villain* like this: [Middle English *vilein,* feudal serf, person of coarse feelings, from Old French, from Vulgar Latin *villanus,* feudal serf, from Latin *villa,* country house]. You can easily see how far this word, now denoting a bad guy, has deviated from its earlier meanings.

Here is another example. The word *curfew* comes from medieval French. Because most houses in France during the medieval period were made of wood and had thatched roofs, the danger of fire was always great, particularly at night. Every evening residents had to put out their candles when a bell was rung, signaling the order to "cover fire." The French word *couvre-feu,* meaning "cover fire," brought to England by the Norman French conquerors, later evolved into today's word *curfew.*

- *Learn the most common prefixes and roots.* Approximately 60 percent of the words in English come from Latin and around 15 percent come from Greek. Therefore, learning Latin and Greek prefixes and roots can add to your vocabulary stock.[5] For example, the Greek prefix *mono,* meaning "one," can be seen in *monogamy* (sexual relations or marriage with only one person at a time); *monotheism* (the belief in one god); *monocle* (a single-lens eyeglass); *monolingual* (speaking one language); and *monopoly* (control over producing and selling by one group). The Latin root *specere,* meaning "to look," gives us the English words *spectacle, spectacular, introspective, inspect, speculate, spectrum, spectrograph,* and so on.

- *Devise a system for learning important new words.* Some students like to write such words in a small notebook or on index cards. Some instructors recommend the three-dot method, which works like this: When you look up a new word in the dictionary, with a pencil, place a small dot next to it. The next time you look it up, add a second dot. The third time, add a third dot and learn the meaning of the word.

- *Subscribe to one or more word-of-the-day websites.* These sites offer a painless, entertaining way to learn new words. Try two or three of those listed in the box below to see which you prefer. You can either visit the sites every day, or more conveniently, subscribe to their service, which sends the word of the day to your e-mail address. Most offer interesting, relatively challenging words; most include—besides the obvious definitions—the etymology and some illustrative sentences using the word. All are free, though most do have banner ads. The following list includes a representative word from each site.

[5]The website that accompanies this text provides a comprehensive list of these prefixes and roots. Click on "Student Resources" at *www.mhhe.com/spears6e.*

NAME OF SITE	WORLD WIDE WEB URL	SAMPLE WORD
Dictionary.com	*www.dictionary.com/wordoftheday/*	cataract
Cool Word of the Day	*www.edu.yorku.ca/wotd/*	abeyance
Merriam-Webster OnLine (click on "Word of the Day")	*www.m-w.com/*	undulate
WordCommand Word of the Day	*www.wordcommand.com/wordoftheday.htm*	alacrity
Words@Random: The Mavens' Word of the Day	*www.randomhouse.com/wotd*	tribulation
Wordsmith.Org (click on "A.Word.A.Day")	*www.wordsmith.org/*	adamantine
yourDictionary.com (click on "Word of the Day")	*www.yourdictionary.com*	abattoir

Using the Dictionary

Traditional (Print) Dictionaries

No electronic device, no matter how flashy, can surpass the convenience of and the abundance of information in a good print dictionary. You should have two: an abridged (or shortened) paperback edition for class and an unabridged (complete) edition to use at home. Both should be up-to-date. (Using your father's old, tattered dictionary from the 1960s is a foolish economy; it will not reflect the wealth of new words that have entered the language, most during the past decade.) There are several excellent dictionaries of both varieties on the market. Ask your instructor to recommend one, or choose one from this list:

- *The American Heritage Dictionary of the English Language* (also available in a less expensive college edition)
- *The Random House Webster's College Dictionary*
- *Webster's New World Dictionary*
- *Merriam-Webster's Collegiate Dictionary*

If you are unsure about how current your dictionary is, check to see if it contains these relatively new words and phrases:

brewsky	killer app	trophy wife
no-brainer	intifada	reverse mortgage
emoticon	wilding	terabyte
geek	wanna-be	luminaria
fatwa	bloviate	zine

Online Dictionaries

The computer revolution has extended to the world of dictionaries. As I proofread this list in the spring of 2002, these websites are the best available.[6]

Merriam-Webster OnLine: The Language Center	*www.m-w.com/*
yourDictionary.com	*www.yourdictionary.com*
AllWords.com	*www.allwords.com*
The American Heritage Dictionary of the English Language	*www.bartleby.com/61*
OneLook Dictionaries	*www.onelook.com/*
Dictionary.com	*www.dictionary.com/*

Each site works a little differently, and it is worth spending time with each one to see which best suits your needs. Having surveyed these dictionaries and after putting them through their paces with a few sample words and phrases, I see advantages and disadvantages to their use. These remarks also apply to electronic dictionaries, such as the various Franklin electronic spellers, which feature *Merriam-Webster's Collegiate Dictionary*.

Advantages of Online Dictionaries

- Entries are not cluttered with confusing symbols and multiple definitions.
- Most have good illustrative sentences using the word in context.
- AllWords.com provides translations of the entry into a few foreign languages.

---

[6]As with all other websites and URLs noted in this text, I cannot guarantee that these sites will remain available or that the URL will remain the same for the life of this edition. If you can't find a site mentioned here, perform a search with your favorite search engine.

- Some texts on websites have links with the *American Heritage* or *Merriam-Webster's* dictionaries so that you can click on a word and be taken immediately to the online dictionary entry.
- Many offer other amenities, such as word games, chat rooms, and other language-related information.
- The sites are free, though you should expect advertisements.

Disadvantages of Online Dictionaries

- Only the most common senses are listed; therefore, if the word you are looking up is used in an unusual way, you may not find the definition you need.
- Not all sites list obsolete and archaic forms.
- Only the *American Heritage* and *Merriam-Webster's* sites offer variant forms for spelling. (Are both *benefited* and *benefitted* correct?)
- Only the *American Heritage* site includes usage notes, which are helpful, for example, if you are preparing an essay for your literature class and you aren't sure whether you should write that the poet uses *sensual* imagery or *sensuous* imagery.
- The etymology (or language of origin) is not always provided. If it is, usually only the source language is provided but not the original meaning or an analysis of the word parts.
- Only *www.onelook.com* allows you to search for phrases, for example, *trophy wife, reverse mortgage,* and *catbird seat.*
- Access to websites can be slow, depending on your connection.
- Looking up a word on your laptop (assuming you have one) isn't convenient while you're riding on the subway or waiting at a doctor's office. A paperback dictionary, on the other hand, is inexpensive and portable.
- During a power blackout, you're out of luck!

It seems clear that online dictionaries have their uses, but to rely on one for all one's college work seems impractical.

Dictionary Features

The dictionary—the print variety—can provide the curious reader with a wealth of information beyond spellings and definitions. Because we can only scratch the surface in this introduction, it would be a good idea to read through your dictionary's introductory pages to become acquainted with its myriad features, particularly the way the dictionary arranges multiple definitions.

Order of Definitions

You may have been taught that the first definition is probably the one you want. This is bad advice, especially because some dictionaries organize their definitions historically rather than by frequency of meaning. The three leading dictionaries explain their arrangement of definitions as follows:

- *Random House Webster's College Dictionary* (2000 edition)
  The various definitions within an entry indicate how the word is used now and how it was used in the past. In searching for a particular sense of a word, keep in mind that within each part-of-speech group, the most common meanings generally come before those that are encountered less frequently. Specialized senses follow those that are part of the general vocabulary. Archaic or obsolete senses are listed last. This order may be modified slightly when it is desirable to group related meanings together.
- *The American Heritage Dictionary* (4th edition)
  Entries containing more than one sense are arranged for the convenience of contemporary dictionary users with the central and often the most commonly sought meanings first. Senses and subsenses are grouped to show their relationships with each other.
- *Merriam-Webster's Collegiate Dictionary* (10th edition)
  The order of senses within an entry is historical: the sense known to have been first used in English is entered first. This is not to be taken to mean, however, that each sense of a multisense word developed from the immediately preceding sense. It is altogether possible that sense 1 of a word has given rise to sense 2 and sense 2 to sense 3, but frequently sense 2 and sense 3 may have arisen independently of one another from sense 1.

Choosing the Right Definition

Students often complain—with good reason—that the dictionary lists so many definitions, it's hard to figure out which is the best one. Unfortunately, there is no easy remedy for this complaint, but here are a few suggestions:

- Become familiar with the way your dictionary organizes its definitions.
- Study the context of the sentence or paragraph you are reading to determine the word's part of speech and its likely meaning.
- Substitute the definition you chose in the sentence to see if it makes sense.

- If you are not sure which definition works best, ask your instructor for help.
- Realize that sometimes a word may straddle two definitions.

Here are the opening sentences of Albert Camus's essay, "Reflections on the Guillotine." (So influential was this essay when it was published in 1960 that the French government was persuaded to ban capital punishment.)

> Shortly before the war of 1914, an assassin whose crime was particularly repulsive (he had slaughtered a family of farmers, including the children) was condemned to death in Algiers. He was a farm worker who had killed in a sort of bloodthirsty frenzy but had *aggravated* his case by robbing his victims. The affair created a great stir. It was generally thought that decapitation was too mild a punishment for such a monster.[7]

Which of these two dictionary definitions best suits the way Camus uses *aggravated?*

1. to make worse or more troublesome.
2. to rouse to exasperation or anger.

Only the first definition works because one can substitute it for the original word: he had made his case worse, *not* roused his case to exasperation or anger.

Even seemingly easy words can cause difficulty, as this example from Rosalie Pedalino Porter's book *Forked Tongue: The Politics of Bilingual Education* illustrates:

> My family was poor, so the first necessity was for us to gain the economic means to survive. We children did not *enjoy* the middle-class luxury of a choice of schooling or careers.

Which of these two definitions for *enjoy* from *The American Heritage Dictionary* is right for this context?

1. to receive pleasure or satisfaction from.
2. to have the use or benefit of.

[7]From *Resistance, Rebellion, and Death,* Trans. Justin O'Brien (Knopf, 1960).

Number 2 is the better choice: Since her family was poor, they could not have the benefit of choices available to middle-class families.

Parts of Speech

A knowledge of grammar helps when you look up unfamiliar words, because many words in English fall into more than one grammatical category (part of speech). The dictionary labels parts of speech by means of abbreviations (n. = noun; v. = verb; adj. = adjective; adv. = adverb, and so on.) The word *temper* is one example of a word that crosses over grammatical lines. Here are a few definitions for the word *temper* from the *Random House Webster's College Dictionary:*

tem · per (tem′ pər). *n.* **1.** a particular state of mind or feelings. **2.** habit of mind, esp. with respect to irritability or patience; disposition: *an even temper . . . v.t.* **9.** to moderate: *to temper justice with mercy.* **10.** to soften or tone down. **11.** to make suitable by or as if by blending. **12.** to work into proper consistency, as clay or mortar. **13.** to impart strength or toughness to by heating and cooling. **14.** to tune (a keyboard instrument) so as to make the tones available in different keys or tonalities.

Write the definition number and part of speech for each use of *temper* in these four sentences.

1. _____ Senator Jackson *tempered* his remarks about his opponent after the polls showed that his attacks had cost him voters.

2. _____ Most county building inspectors require a homeowner to install *tempered* glass windows if they are low enough to the floor for someone to fall through them.

3. _____ Professor Wilson appears to be in a bad *temper* tonight; perhaps she is disappointed in our test scores.

4. _____ Our neighbor's *temper* is so predictably calm that even little Johnny's home run hit through his living room window didn't upset him.

Using Context Clues

Although a good dictionary is indispensable, it is unrealistic to think that you must look up every unfamiliar word you come across. If you are unable to figure out the meaning of the word by analyzing its word parts, the **context**—the way the word is used in its particular setting—may yield a reasonably accurate meaning. (The word *context* comes from Latin, "to weave together.")

Relying on context clues is not a substitute for looking up exact meanings in the dictionary, nor will every sentence with unfamiliar words necessarily provide you with a clue. But if one is there, a clue is a useful shortcut toward efficient reading, especially when the word is not absolutely crucial to your understanding of the text.

Types of Context Clues
- Synonyms
- Antonyms
- Examples and illustrations
- Opinion and tone

Synonyms

The most frequently used context clue is a **synonym,** a word or phrase similar in meaning to the unfamiliar word. Although the synonym may not have the exact meaning, it may be close enough to give you an approximate definition. For example:

> The candidate for student body president was having difficulty. When called upon to give a campaign speech, he was so *reticent* that his long silences made everyone uncomfortable.

The phrase "long silences" is the context clue, from which you could probably figure out that *reticent* means "unwilling to speak."

Consider this example:

> When Sarah Smith discovered that her husband had cheated on her, she filed for divorce, citing *infidelity* as the reason.

Infidelity most likely means

1. lack of respect.
2. addiction.
3. mental instability.
4. unfaithfulness.

Antonyms

When a sentence suggests a contrast or a contradiction, the context clue may be in the form of an **antonym,** a word or phrase that means the opposite of the word in question. If you know the meaning of the antonym, then you may be able to figure out the unfamiliar word. For example:

> Because Professor Rivera wants his writing students to develop a concise writing style, Melvin often receives low grades because his style is too *verbose.*

Since it is obviously being contrasted with *concise,* a word with which you are probably familiar, *verbose* means the opposite, "overly wordy."

Here is another example:

> A well-known writer was most upset when he learned that his publisher planned to release his new novel, which contained profanity and steamy sex scenes, in an *expurgated* version. Therefore, he canceled the contract and found a company that would publish the book without removing any of the objectionable parts.

Expurgated most likely means

1. thoroughly revised.
2. having offensive material removed.
3. simplified, made easier to understand.
4. made more concise.

Examples and Illustrations

The meaning of an unfamiliar word may be suggested by nearby examples and illustrations. In this case, no single word or phrase implies the definition, but taken together, the examples help us infer the meaning. Try this sentence:

> The *squalid* conditions of many American inner cities—with their burned-out buildings, high crime rates, crumbling schools, and high unemployment—pose a problem for parents trying to raise their children in such grim circumstances.

From the examples noted between the dashes, you can probably determine that *squalid* means "wretched and neglected."

Now try this one:

Professor Dyer applies *stringent* rules for his students' papers:
Margins have to be exactly one and a quarter inches on all sides (he
even measures them), and after the third sentence fragment or
spelling error he assigns a failing grade.

Stringent most likely means

1. unnecessary.
2. useful.
3. severe.
4. unusual.

Opinion and Tone

This last kind of context clue is less direct and consequently more difficult to rely on. The writer's **tone**—that is, his or her attitude toward the
subject or the **opinions** the writer expresses—may give you a clue for
an unfamiliar word. Study this example:

Some critics of mass media blame daytime television talk shows
for their *insidious* influence on the viewing public, because
these programs parade their guests' bizarre and deviant behaviors
and create an unhealthy appetite for ever more grotesque
revelations.

The obvious critical nature of this sentence suggests that *insidious* refers
to something bad, and indeed it does, because it means "progressing or
spreading in a harmful way."
Consider one last example:

Charley is an *ardent* champion of the poor. His dedication to
helping poverty-stricken people get jobs and qualify for low-cost
medical treatment is admirable.

Ardent most likely means

1. careful.
2. merely competent.
3. passionate.
4. consistent.

Now try your hand at using context clues to determine the meaning of words. Read each passage carefully, and choose the definition that best fits the way the italicized word is used. It would also be helpful to underline the word or phrase that provides the context clue.

1. Plutonium is the most *lethal* substance known to man—a spoonful of it could wipe out a city. (Bill Bryson)
   (a) destructive.
   (b) deadly.
   (c) evil.
   (d) difficult to dispose of.

2. Zebra mussels can wreak extraordinary damage in a brief period because they can attach to virtually any surface and are extraordinarily *prolific.* Each female mussel produces up to 1 million eggs per year and reproduces throughout the year. (Alex Barnum)
   (a) highly efficient.
   (b) highly fruitful.
   (c) highly energetic.
   (d) highly damaging.

3. (The writer is reporting on the 2001 earthquake in Bhuj, India, which killed more than 6,000 people.)
   The vast majority of deaths and damage were reported in the city of Bhuj, only 12 miles from the epicenter of Friday's 7.9-magnitude quake. The city remains without electricity, water or telecommunications. Dozens of high-rise buildings were *listing* at a steep angle and the main hospital had collapsed. (Pamela Constable)
   (a) falling down.
   (b) evacuated.
   (c) entered in official records.
   (d) leaning to one side.

4. The hot dry sand in India . . . A *corrosive* wind drives rivulets of sand across the land; *torpid* animals stand at the edge of dried-up water holes. The earth is cracked and in the rivers the sluggish, falling waters have exposed the sludge of the mud flats. (Peggy and Pierre Streit)

   corrosive
   (a) hot and dry.
   (b) mild and gentle.
   (c) destructive.
   (d) unpredictable.

   torpid
   (a) physically inactive.
   (b) domestic.
   (c) skittish, excitable.
   (d) malnourished, excessively thin.

5. No aspect of the civil rights movement has generated so much controversy and so little agreement as affirmative action. The idea is a simple one: To help *redress* the long history of racial and gender discrimination in this country, racial minorities and women should be given preference over white males in education, jobs training, hiring and promotion. (Daniel McLoughlin)
    (a) understand.
    (b) address, consider the problem of.
    (c) aggravate, make worse.
    (d) set right, remedy.

6. Try to imagine a star so big it would fill all the solar system within the orbit of Earth, which is 93 million miles from the sun. A star so *turbulent* its eruptions would spread a cloud of gases spanning four light-years, the distance from the sun to the nearest star. (John Noble Wilford)
    (a) disturbed, agitated.
    (b) enormous.
    (c) defying gravity.
    (d) hard to see, elusive.

Practice Exercise 2

For these excerpts, write your definition for the italicized word(s) in the first space. Then look up the word and write the dictionary definition in the second space. How close did you come to the correct meaning?

1. Termites make *percussive* sounds to each other by beating their heads against the floor in the dark, resonating corridors of their nests. . . . spectrographic analysis of sound records has recently revealed a high degree of organization in the drumming; the beats occur in regular, rhythmic phrases. (Lewis Thomas)

    percussive _____

    _____

2. Few people can remember now what the standard of living was half a century ago. . . . Years ago, only a couple of movie theaters and one drugstore had air conditioning to cope with the summer heat. You couldn't buy a pizza or a taco, but as a faded sign on the side of a building . . . reminds us, Coca-Cola was "sold everywhere, 5¢." And only a few lucky people could get television broadcasts beginning in 1948 by WBT in far away Charlotte, N.C. Today, of course, television sets are *ubiquitous.* (John M. Berry)

    ubiquitous _____

    _____

3. To know what to do about vocabulary, you need some basic information about the size of the task students face. If the average high school senior knows eight thousand words, as some people have claimed, then all you have to do is teach twenty words a week for twelve years, and you can cover all of them. But if the average high school senior knows forty thousand words, as other people maintain, you would have to teach twenty words a day to cover them, a much more *formidable* task. (Richard C. Anderson and William E. Nagy)

formidable _____

_____

4. American cuisine is an *oxymoron,* but so are Americans. Here we have National Pork Month, National Pizza Month, and Chocolate Awareness Month all at the same time. Here we eat too much and too little of just about everything. We consume more good food and more bad food than any other group of people in history. (Sallie Tisdale)

oxymoron _____

_____

5. In the current happy excitement about whether we may soon discover signs of primitive life on Mars, there is a weird and tragic *incongruity,* because we are losing dozens of more complex but unexamined species every day right here on Earth and doing little about it. And it isn't just beetles. (Edward Hoagland)

incongruity _____

_____

6. (The writer's husband suffered a serious brain injury, the result of a boating accident.)
It is not just about words. I am also *dyscalculic,* struggling with the math required to halve a recipe or to figure out how many more pages are left in a book I'm reading. (Cathy Crimmins)

dyscalculic _____

_____

■ PUNCTUATION

Punctuation is a relatively modern invention, and punctuation marks as we know them today were not codified until around the twelfth century. Before then, manuscripts were hand-copied laboriously by scribes; very early manuscripts contained no punctuation marks, paragraph divisions, or even word divisions! Given the lack of graphical clues, manuscripts could be read only by the most educated people—rabbis, other clergy, scholars, and nobles. People who were barely literate or semiliterate were unable to decipher complex ideas embedded in unpunctuated sentences whose words all ran together.[8]

The need for punctuation arose as a direct result of the rise of democratic governments, mass education, and literacy, and these little marks (along with word and paragraph divisions) significantly improved the ordinary reader's comprehension skills. With this background in mind, it seems sensible to look at modern punctuation marks to see their various uses in making written prose clear and readable.

Punctuation and Meaning

An extensive discussion of grammar and punctuation is beyond the scope of this text, but we can examine punctuation marks briefly, especially the more sophisticated ones, such as parentheses, dashes, semicolons, and colons. Punctuation marks do more than enclose and separate. Good writers choose punctuation marks carefully—to enclose and to separate, to be sure—but also to emphasize, or to slow us down, or to speed us up, or to clarify. Like transitional elements that you will study in Chapter 5, punctuation marks help you follow the writer's ideas. The writer's words are meant to be heard in your head, and punctuation allows you to recreate them as the author intended you to.

Commas

Let us begin with the **comma.** There are many uses of the comma, the rules for which you can find in any good grammar handbook. No matter how it is used, a comma always indicates that you should pause, however briefly. Commas affect the cadence of the prose. To demonstrate this, read this passage by Gretel Ehrlich aloud. Notice as you read how these little markers enhance the rhythm and flow of her description of a Wyoming winter.

> The name Wyoming comes from an Indian word meaning "at the great plains," but the plains are really valleys, great arid valleys, 1600 square miles, with the horizon bending up on all sides into mountain ranges. This gives the vastness a sheltering look.
>
> Winter lasts six months here. Prevailing winds spill snowdrifts to the east, and new storms from the northwest replenish them. This white bulk is sometimes dizzying, even nauseating, to look at. At twenty, thirty, and forty degrees below zero, not only does your car not work but neither do your mind and

[8]An examination of the origins and history of punctuation can be found in M. B. Parkes, *Pause and Effect: Punctuation in the West* (University of California Press, 1993).

body. The landscape hardens into a dungeon of space. During the winter, while I was riding to find a new calf, my legs froze to the saddle, and in the silence that such cold creates I felt like the first person on earth, or the last.

Gretel Ehrlich, *The Solace of Open Spaces*

Note that although the comma following "earth" in the last sentence is grammatically unnecessary, it contributes to the effect. Do you see how?

Semicolons

The **semicolon** is useful for connecting two independent clauses with a clear relationship to each other. Stronger than a comma but not quite as strong as a period, the semicolon shows that the writer wants you to consider the clauses together, as a unit, because there is some logical connection between them, for example, cause–effect, contrast, or general statement–supporting example. Sometimes a transitional word or phrase indicating the logical relationship is placed between the two clauses, as in the last two examples.

- Steeped in new moods and ideas, I bought a ream of paper and tried to write; but nothing would come, or what did come was flat beyond telling. (Richard Wright, *Black Boy*)
- The act of exploration alters the perspective of the explorer; Odysseus and Marco Polo and Columbus returned home as changed men. (Timothy Ferris, *Coming of Age in the Milky Way*)
- But however immature they are, these lovers are not dull characters; on the contrary, they are hauntingly and embarrassingly real. (Arthur Mizener, *The Far Side of Paradise*)
- . . . while there were occasional battles and raids, the Ohlones [a California Indian tribe] were in no way a war-ridden people. In fact they felt in their hearts that war was wrong and the way of peace was right; thus they were forever presenting themselves as victims—as a peaceful, proper people forced into warfare against their wills by the intolerable insolence of their enemies. (Malcolm Margolin, *The Ohlone Way*)

Colons

Besides introducing lists, the **colon** has a special function within independent clauses. A colon introduces something in the first clause that will be further explained in the second one. Study these examples:

- Indeed, the life of a sharecropper's wife, which often demanded twelve-hour days in the fields, normally allowed little time for food preparation at all. Typically, she would rise at 4 A.M. in a one- or two-room cabin to prepare breakfast: thinly sliced fat salt pork fried over an open fire and corn bread spread with fat and molasses. (Harvey Levenstein, *Revolution at the Table: The Transformation of the American Diet*)

- Because of Columbus's exaggerated report and promises, his second expedition was given seventeen ships and more than twelve hundred men. The aim was clear: slaves and gold. (Howard Zinn, *A People's History of the United States*)
- Besides the old charges of usury and fencing, Las Vegas pawnshops have another image they would like to disown: they are often seen as overpriced banks for gamblers. (Joe Heim, "Pawnshops," *The Real Las Vegas: Life beyond the Strip*)
- For all the complaints, Las Vegas still has one advantage over Fort Lauderdale, Palm Desert, or Phoenix: this is, after all, as civic boosters still remind us, the "Entertainment Capital of the World." (Michelle Ling, "Bingo!" *The Real Las Vegas: Life beyond the Strip*)

Parentheses

First, a word about **parenthetical remarks,** which refer to explanatory or qualifying material set off in varying ways from the main idea. The writer's choice of punctuation determines how strongly he or she intends the parenthetical information to be interpreted. Parenthetical information may be enclosed with three kinds of punctuation—parentheses, commas, or dashes. You can remember their differences with this little formula: Parentheses whisper; commas state; dashes shout. In other words, parentheses convey the least emphasis, commas are plain and factual, and dashes emphasize. Consider this sentence by Ivan Doig, from his autobiography, *This House of Sky,* which refers to his Montana hometown of White Sulphur, and note how the sentence changes depending on the punctuation. (The original sentence used commas to set off the parenthetical remark.)

- The plainest fact I found (so plain that it seemed to me then it could never change) was that White Sulphur totally lived on livestock.
- The plainest fact I found, so plain that it seemed to me then it could never change, was that White Sulphur totally lived on livestock.
- The plainest fact I found—so plain that it seemed to me then it could never change—was that White Sulphur totally lived on livestock.

Parentheses enclose additional or "extra" information within a sentence, and because they whisper, they suggest that the material enclosed could be dropped without any significant loss of meaning. Study these examples:

- Different peoples acquired food production at different times in prehistory. Some, such as Aboriginal Australians, never acquired it at all. Of those who did, some (for example, the ancient

Chinese) developed it independently by themselves, while others (including ancient Egyptians) acquired it from neighbors. (Jared Diamond, *Guns, Germs, and Steel*)

- Television's greatest minute-by-minute appeal is that it engages without demanding. One can rest while undergoing stimulation. Receive without giving. In this respect, television resembles certain other things one might call Special Treats (e.g., candy, liquor), treats that are basically fine and fun in small amounts but bad for us in large amounts and *really* bad for us if consumed in the massive regular amounts reserved for nutritive staples. (David Foster Wallace, *A Supposedly Fun Thing I'll Never Do Again*)

- A further reason for football's intensity is that the game is played like a war. The idea is to win by going through, around, or over the opposing team and the battle lines, quite literally, are drawn on every play. Violence is somewhere at the heart of the game, and the combat quality is reflected in football's army language ("blitz," "trap," "zone," "bomb," "trenches," etc.). (Murray Ross, "Football Red and Baseball Green")

Dashes

The **dash** is a dramatic mark of punctuation. One of its functions is to introduce an afterthought or a punch line at the end of a joke, as you can see in this example:

People who live in Maine say that they have two seasons—winter and July.

In prose, however, the dash is more commonly used to enclose parenthetical elements, where the writer wishes to convey emphasis or drama or both, or to signal an abrupt interruption in the middle of a sentence. Study these examples, all written by David Remnick, editor of *The New Yorker,* concerning the Americans' efforts to eliminate the Taliban's rule over Afghanistan in late 2001:

- When it came to Afghanistan, we readily summoned the memories of the British and Russian experience there—the cruelty and the snows, the slaughters and the chastening retreats.
- The images of liberation in Kabul—of singing in the streets, of beards being shorn, of kites flying—were unambiguously thrilling.
- There is no doubt that in the very short run the ruthless American-led pursuit of the leaders of Al Qaeda [Osama bin

Laden's terrorist network] and the Taliban is indispensable. But no Afghans—to say nothing of the volatile political constituencies in Pakistan and other Muslim countries— would tolerate a situation in which the United States imposes, or is seen to impose, a new political order on their country.

- Sited where the northern edge of the valley began to rumple into low hills—by an early-day entrepreneur who dreamed of getting rich from the puddles of mineral water bubbling there, and didn't—White Sulphur somehow had stretched itself awkwardly along the design of a very wide **T.** (Ivan Doig, *This House of Sky*)

Ellipses

An **ellipsis,** usually composed of three dots (. . .), indicates an omission of material in quotations. A writer quoting someone may intentionally omit a word, phrase, or sentence if it is unnecessary to the idea he or she is discussing. If the omission occurs at the end of a sentence, as it does in the following example, the ellipsis consists of four dots, the last one being the period. Notice also Rodriguez's use of dashes to indicate rhetorical questions his observations give rise to in his mind.

Without question, it would have pleased me to have heard my teachers address me in Spanish when I entered the classroom. . . . But I would have delayed—postponed for how long?—having to learn the language of public society. I would have evaded—and for how long?—learning the great lesson of school: that I had a public identity. (Richard Rodriguez, *Hunger of Memory*)

Quotation Marks

Quotation marks generally indicate quoted material. Double quotation marks (" ") are the standard form. Single quotation marks (' ') indicate quoted material *within* another quotation. Quotation marks can also be used to set off words or phrases used as illustrations. For example, in explaining doublespeak and levels of abstraction, William Lutz uses quotation marks to set off his examples. (In the same sentence, some writers would italicize these examples.)

Using a high level of abstraction we can call the new dump a "resource development park" and sewage sludge "biosolids" or "organic biomass."

But quotation marks have another use, one not so readily apparent. A writer may use quotation marks to convey irony, to cast doubt on the authenticity of the material quoted. The author is saying, in effect, "I don't accept the meaning of this use of the word." Study these two examples:

- Cuba Shows "Evidence" That Planes Violated Airspace (Newspaper headline for a story by Juanita Darling, *The Los Angeles Times*)
- The history of the word "creole" itself dates back to the slave trade. After slaves had been gathered from many parts of Africa, they were imprisoned in West African camps, euphemistically called "factories," for "processing" before being shipped out to "markets." (Peter Farb)

Of the four pairs of quotation marks used in the second example, only one pair does not indicate irony. Which pair is it?

Finally, read this passage describing the Vietnam Veterans Memorial in Washington, D.C., and study the writer's use of commas, the colon, and the dash. Perhaps you will now have a greater appreciation for these seemingly insignificant little marks.

The memorial, an angle of polished black stone subtly submerged in a gentle slope, is an artistic abstraction. Yet its simplicity dramatizes a grim reality. The names of the dead engraved on the granite record more than lives lost in battle: they represent a sacrifice to a failed crusade, however noble or illusory its motives. In a larger sense they symbolize a faded hope—or perhaps the birth of a new awareness. They bear witness to the end of America's absolute confidence in its moral exclusivity, its military invincibility, its manifest destiny. They are the price, paid in blood and sorrow, for America's awakening to maturity, to the recognition of its limitations. With the young men who died in Vietnam died the dream of an "American century."

Stanley Karnow, *Vietnam: A History*

🖱 ON THE WEB

An excellent site devoted to grammar, usage, and punctuation, with both instruction and practice quizzes, is available at this address: ccc.commnet.edu/grammar

Reading for Understanding: Practice in Basic Comprehension Skills

1

Reading for the Main Idea and Author's Purpose

CHAPTER OBJECTIVES

This first chapter introduces you to the following fundamental concepts to improve your reading comprehension:

- Main idea in paragraphs

- Placement of the main idea

- Implied main ideas

- Major and minor supporting details

- Author's purpose and modes of discourse

■ THE MAIN IDEA OF THE PARAGRAPH

In the first five chapters of this book, the focus of our study is on the individual paragraph. It might seem odd—and perhaps artificial—to devote so much time to paragraphs. After all, essays, articles, and textbook chapters contain multiple paragraphs; we seldom read an isolated paragraph.

Yet my students have found that focusing initially on shorter passages promotes careful reading and analysis. It is far easier and less intimidating to analyze a 100-word paragraph than a 10-page essay. For that reason, we begin with paragraphs and learn what to look for.

In nonfiction prose, the paragraph is the fundamental unit of written thought. Simply put, a paragraph is a group of related sentences that develop and support one idea. It may be any length as long as it keeps to that one idea. The main idea of a paragraph is a general statement telling the reader what the paragraph is about; the main idea may be explicitly stated in a sentence that *often* appears at or near the beginning of the paragraph. As you will see, however, many writers of adult prose do not adhere to this pattern.

Main Idea and Controlling Idea

In elementary grades, you were probably taught that the first sentence of a paragraph is the topic sentence. This rule is convenient but misleading; it suggests that each paragraph should contain such a sentence at the beginning. As we shall see, adult writers frequently violate this principle. For this reason, I prefer the term **main idea.**

If one is present, a main-idea sentence consists of two parts: the **topic** and the **controlling idea.** The topic is the general subject (though not necessarily the grammatical subject) of the paragraph. The controlling idea—often a descriptive word or phrase—limits, qualifies, or narrows the topic to make the larger subject manageable. Diagrammed, then, a typical main-idea sentence might look like this:

> Topic + Controlling idea = Main idea

Consider this sentence:

The World Wide Web has revolutionized the way we obtain and retrieve information.

In this example, the topic—"The World Wide Web"—is underlined once and the controlling idea—"has revolutionized the way we obtain and retrieve information"—twice. Stated another way, the controlling idea restricts the writer to only that information, and every subsequent sentence—assuming the paragraph is unified—is limited to that idea. But if the writer shifted direction and changed the controlling idea, the focus of the paragraph would change:

Spending hours a day surfing the World Wide Web, according to some social critics, may isolate users from reality and damage their social relationships.

And here is a third example, showing yet another controlling idea and thus a different direction:

The World Wide Web, where users move quickly from one link to another and view flashy graphics, may alter users' ability to concentrate on sustained reading of print.

Note that you do not need to label irrelevant information, as this example suggests:

Although some diehard writers like Danielle Steel still use a typewriter to write, the widespread availability of inexpensive personal computers has revolutionized and simplified the writing process.

The first part of the sentence (beginning with "Although") will probably not be discussed because the writer is not interested in the *disadvantages* of using a typewriter. The writer mentions this fact only to concede a truth and to avoid generalizing. The controlling idea points to only positive results of the computer revolution—"has revolutionized and simplified the writing process." Thus, the controlling idea serves as a sort of umbrella for the remainder of the paragraph. Identifying the topic and controlling idea keeps you on track as you read.

Although this pattern—**topic + controlling idea**—is the typical one, the elements may be reversed. Whether the topic precedes the controlling idea or follows it, the meaning is still the same.

The writing process has been revolutionized and simplified because of the widespread availability of inexpensive personal computers, although some diehard writers like Danielle Steel still use a typewriter to write.

Although the meaning is the same, the effect is not. Which version, the first or second, better emphasizes the controlling idea?

Practice Exercise 1	Label these main-idea sentences by underlining the topic once and the controlling idea twice. Start with these easier examples.

1. The bathroom is the most dangerous room in the house.
2. The most dangerous room in the house is the bathroom.
3. Crows are the most intelligent of all birds.
4. The most intelligent of all birds are crows.
5. The cow is considered a sacred animal in India for many reasons.

6. Giving children ridiculous names like Petunia or Tiddler can mar their lives in ways that the parents may not anticipate.

7. Psychologists agree that children who watch too much television may have difficulty becoming good readers.

8. The most useful book a college student can own is an unabridged dictionary.

9. Part of the appeal of popular music, from the emergence of rock' n' roll in the early 1950s to contemporary music such as punk rock, death metal, and gangsta rap, is its ability to irritate adults.

10. Copying music on the Internet has vast repercussions for musicians concerned with protecting their intellectual property.

Now try these more difficult main-idea statements, which are taken from paragraphs you will encounter later in this book.

11. Computer analysis of the English language as spoken today shows that the hundred most frequently used words are all of Anglo-Saxon origin. (Robert Lacey and Danny Danziger, *The Year 1000*)

12. Well into modern times, the act of writing was occasioned by much preparation and inconvenience. (Henry Petroski, *The Pencil: A History of Design and Circumstances*)

13. Some animals have senses humans do not possess. (Jeffrey Masson and Susan McCarthy, *When Elephants Weep*)

14. Such a simple invention, or discovery, the compass. (Jonathan Raban, *Passage to Juneau*)

15. The difference between spinning and fly casting lies mostly with the reel. (Bill Barich, *The Sporting Life*)

16. Protected from predation by the Arabian Desert, the wild camel was relatively docile. (William Langewiesche, *Sahara Unveiled*)

17. No technology [e-mail] has ever become so ubiquitous so fast. (Michael Specter, "Your Mail Has Vanished")

18. Desertion, like indiscipline and drunkenness, was a chronic problem during the Civil War—seriously so because it deprived the commanders of the manpower they so badly needed. (Simon Winchester, *The Professor and the Madman*)

19. In a sense, tabloids—that is, news in condensed form (the word "tabloid" was registered in 1884 as a trademark to describe condensed substances used in pharmacy)—have been with us in oral tradition ever since people began entertaining one another with ballads and popular stories. (Sue Hubbell, *Far-Flung Hubbell*)

20. Consider just how guilt-ridden our relationship with food has become. (Jeremy Iggers, "Innocence Lost")

Placement of the Main Idea

As a college reader, you must learn to cope with diverse writing styles and techniques, requiring you to rethink some of the rules you may have been taught in the past. Adult prose is not so neatly formulaic as students would like it to be, and the careful reader has to be alert for any variation. The main idea may be buried in the middle of the paragraph, it may be at the end, it may occur in bits and pieces throughout the paragraph, or to complicate matters, it may be implied. A glance at the paragraphs in the essays in Part 5 will confirm that the old rules are often violated. Let us examine a few paragraphs to determine the location of the main idea, beginning with a passage about the movie *Star Wars*. Study my annotations.

Star Wars— dominant feeling throughout is one of great speed

The first Star Wars movie is like a two-hour-long image of <u>raw speed</u>. If you saw it when you were young, this tends to be what you remember— the feeling of <u>going really fast</u>. Lucas is <u>a genius of speed</u>. His first ambition was to be a race-car driver, and it was only after he was nearly killed in a terrible accident, when he was eighteen—he lived because his seat belt unaccountably broke and he was hurled free of the car—that his interest shifted to film. (His first moving pictures were of race cars.) Perhaps the most memorable single image in "Star Wars" is the shot of the Millennium Falcon going into hyperspace for the first time, when the <u>stars blur past the cockpit.</u> Like all the effects in the movie, this works not because it is a cool effect (it's actually pretty low tech—merely "motion blur" photography) but because it's a powerful graphic distillation of the feeling the whole movie gives you: an image of <u>pure kinetic energy</u> which has become a permanent part of the world's visual imagination. (The other day, I was out running, and as a couple of rollerbladers went <u>whizzing by</u> I heard a jogger in front of me say to his friend, "It's like that scene in 'Star Wars' when they go into hyperspace.") Insofar as a <u>media-induced state of speed</u> has become a condition of modern life, Lucas was anticipating the Zeitgeist in "Star Wars."

Lucas anticipated that speed is part of modern life

John Seabrook, "Why Is the Force Still With Us?"
The New Yorker

The underlined words and phrases all reinforce the controlling idea, "raw speed." Rather than repeating the word *speed,* Seabrook uses several synonymous words and phrases. Everything works together to create "a network of interlocking ideas," as Richard Marius has described it.[1] Reading in this way makes it easier to follow the chain of ideas.

[1]Richard Marius, *A Writer's Companion,* 4th ed. (McGraw-Hill, 1999).

Another useful comprehension skill is to put a writer's main idea into your own words (in other words, to paraphrase it). Many exercises in the text will ask you to do this. Here is a suggested paraphrase of this paragraph's main idea:

Star Wars effectively conveys a feeling of raw speed and kinetic energy.

However, not all paragraphs are organized so simply, with the main idea stated at the beginning. In the following paragraph, which sentence represents the main idea? After you identify it, restate the main idea in your own words.

[1]Biology is destiny—or at least more and more people seem ready to believe that it is. [2]Perhaps this is because recent scientific advances—gene splicing, in vitro fertilization, DNA identification of criminals, mapping the human genome—have been repeatedly echoed and amplified by popular culture. [3]From science fact to science fiction (and back again), the gene has become a pervasive cultural symbol. [4]It crops up not just in staid scientific journals and PBS documentaries, but also with increasing regularity in political discourse, popular entertainment, and advertising.

Jeff Reid, "The DNA-ing of America," *Utne Reader*

Main-idea sentence: _____

Main idea paraphrased: _____

_____

And in this one? Again, restate the main idea in your own words after you make your choice.

[1]The Bear Paw Mountains, a low-slung range south of Chinook, Montana, get their name from an Indian tale of a hunter who ventures into a land of giant bears in order to feed his starving family. [2]When he kills a deer, an angry bear grabs him. [3]In a flash, the Creator severs the bear's paw. [4]Another version tells of an Indian girl who comes to bathe in a virginal lake. [5]A bear bewitched by her beauty reaches out, and the Creator saves her in the same way. [6]The naming of these mountains, like all Indian naming, is poetically exact. [7]From the High Plains, they appear magically inviting, and also remarkably like the just severed paw of a giant bear, its knuckles rippling across the horizon.

Mark Stevens, "Chief Joseph's Revenge,"
The New Yorker

Main-idea sentence: _____

Main idea restated: _____

_____

Another pattern that you will encounter occasionally is the straw man pattern, in which the writer sets up an idea or popular assumption to be refuted (or knocked down), as Tom Regan does in this passage. After you read it, write a sentence stating the main idea in your own words.

Someone might think that though what one person thinks or feels about moral issues does not settle matters, what all or most people think or feel does. A single individual is only one voice; what most or all people think or feel is a great deal more. There is strength in numbers. Thus, the correct method for answering questions about right and wrong is to find out what most or all people think or feel; opinion polls should be conducted, statistics compiled. That will reveal the truth.

This approach to moral questions is deficient. All that opinion polls can reveal is what all or most people think or feel about some moral question—for example, "Is capital punishment morally right or wrong?" What such polls cannot determine is whether what all or most people think about such an issue is true or that what all or most people feel is appropriate. There may be strength in numbers, but not truth, at least not necessarily. This does not mean that "what we all think (or feel)" is irrelevant to answering moral questions. Later on, in fact . . . , we will see how, given that certain conditions have been met, "what we all think" might provide us with a place from which to begin our search for what is right and wrong, and why. Nevertheless, *merely* to establish that all (or most) people think that, say, capital punishment is morally justified is not to establish that it *is* morally justified. In times past, most (possibly even all) people thought the world is flat. And possibly most (or all) people felt pleased or relieved to think of the world as having this shape. But what they thought and felt did not make it true that the world is flat. The question of its shape had to be answered without relying on what most people think or feel. There is no reason to believe moral questions differ in this respect. Questions of right and wrong cannot be answered just by counting heads.

Tom Regan, *Matters of Life and Death*

Main idea: _____

_____

Occasionally, the main idea of a passage is not contained in a single sentence; rather, it emerges in bits throughout. Read this short passage, look at the underlined words and phrases, and then write a main-idea sentence for it.

The <u>Ohlones</u>, like all other California Indians, were a "<u>Stone-Age</u> <u>people</u>. Their arrows were tipped with flint or obsidian, their mortars and pestles were of stone, and other tools were made of bone, shell, or wood. To fell a tree they hacked away at it with a chert blade, pausing now and then to burn out the chips before they renewed their hacking. They used no metal, had no agriculture (at least as we understand it), wove no cloth, and did not even make pottery. They lived entirely by <u>hunting and gathering</u>.

<u>But</u> while the <u>Ohlones were a Stone-Age people</u>, hunting was not just a matter of bludgeoning an animal to death with a club, as it is sometimes pictured. <u>Hunting</u>, especially deer hunting, was <u>among the most important things in a man's life</u>. The <u>hunter pursued and killed deer</u> without pity, but <u>never without reverence</u>. Deer were spiritually powerful animals in a world in which animals were still gods, and <u>deer hunting was an undertaking</u> surrounded at every step with <u>dignity, forethought, and ritual</u>.

Malcolm Margolin, *The Ohlone Way*

Main idea: _____

_____

_____

Implied Main Ideas

Sometimes, rather than stating the main point explicitly, the writer merely suggests it; thus the main idea is **implied,** or suggested. In the following paragraph, the key words—those suggesting the main idea—are underlined.

There are some 16,000 species of <u>lichens</u> in the world. All are <u>slow-growing</u>, but <u>those that encrust the rocks</u> of <u>mountain peaks</u> are <u>particularly so</u>. At high altitudes, there may be only a single day in a whole year when growth is possible and a lichen may take as long as 60 years to cover just one square centimeter. Lichens as big as plates, which are very common, are therefore likely to be hundreds if not thousands of years old.

David Attenborough, *The Living Planet*

After looking at the underlined words and phrases, choose the main-idea sentence that best represents the point of the paragraph.

1. There are 16,000 species of lichens in the world.
2. Lichens, especially those found in mountainous areas, are slow-growing.
3. Some lichens grow as large as plates.
4. Lichens are unusual plants that everyone should learn to identify.

Notice that answer 2 contains all the important elements; the others do not. Answers 1 and 3 are too narrow; answer 4 is not mentioned.

Read this paragraph and underline the key words.

> Sagebrush covers 58,000 square miles of Wyoming. The biggest city has a population of fifty thousand, and there are only five settlements that could be called cities in the whole state. The rest are towns, scattered across the expanse with as much as sixty miles between them, their populations two thousand, fifty, or ten. They are fugitive-looking, perched on a barren, windblown bench, or tagged onto a river or a railroad, or laid out straight in a farming valley with implement stores and a block-long Mormon church. In the eastern part of the state, which slides down into the Great Plains, the new mining settlements are boomtowns, trailer cities, metal knots on flat land.
>
> Gretel Ehrlich, *The Solace of Open Spaces*

Now decide which of these statements best represents Ehrlich's implied main idea.

1. Wyoming towns are forlorn-looking
2. There are only five cities in Wyoming.
3. Wyoming's sparse population lives in towns scattered across the state.
4. There is more sagebrush in Wyoming than there are people.

Answer 1 is too specific; answer 2 is a small detail; answer 4 focuses too much on the minor detail of sagebrush. Only answer 3 incorporates all the essential elements of the paragraph.

Practice Exercise 2

Read these paragraphs; then write a sentence stating the main idea *in your own words.*

> There is a revolution in the life cycle. In the space of one short generation the whole shape of the life cycle has been fundamentally altered. Puberty arrives earlier by several years than it did at the turn of the century. Adolescence is

now prolonged for the middle class until the end of the 20s, and for blue-collar men and women until the mid-20s, as more young adults live at home longer. True adulthood doesn't begin until 30. Most baby boomers, born after World War II, do not feel fully "grown up" until they are into their 40s, and even then they resist. Unlike members of the previous generation, who almost universally had their children launched by that stage of life, many late-baby couples or stepfamily parents will still be battling with rebellious children who are on the catastrophic brink of adolescence while they themselves wrestle with the pronounced hormonal and psychic changes that come with the passage into middle life.

Middle age has already been pushed far into the 50s—if it is acknowledged at all today. The territory of the 50s, 60s, and beyond is changing so radically that it now opens up whole new stages of life that are nothing like what our parents or grandparents experienced.

Fifty is now what 40 used to be.

Sixty is now what 50 used to be.

Gail Sheehy, "Am I an Adult Yet?" *Utne Reader*

Main idea: _____

_____

Boring vs. Interesting Instruction   Academic subject matters such as ancient history and science are to be withheld from children in the early grades on the grounds that true education proceeds from the child's interest rather than from an external imposition. Children learn best when new knowledge is built upon what they already know (true), and it is further claimed that the child's interest in a subject will derive from its connection with his or her immediate experiences and home surroundings. Early schooling should therefore teach subjects that have direct relevance to the child's life, such as "my neighborhood" and similar "relevant" topics. Yet every person with enough schooling to be reading these words knows that subject matters by themselves do not repel or attract interest, and that an effective teacher can make almost any subject interesting, and an ineffective one can make almost any subject dull. The presumption that the affairs of one's neighborhood are more interesting than those of faraway times and places is contradicted in every classroom that studies dinosaurs and fairy tales—that is, in just about every early classroom in the nation. The false polarity between "boring" and "interesting" or "relevant" and "irrelevant" really conceals an anti-intellectual, anti-academic bias.

E. D. Hirsch, Jr., *The Schools We Want and Why We Don't Have Them*

Main idea: _____

_____

_____

Unlike birds, bats don't lay eggs. Life might be easier for them if they did. Like all mammals, they bear their young alive. Difficult though it sounds, a pregnant bat must sometimes fly with her hefty fetus inside, and then, once the baby bat is born, maneuver with it clinging to her breast. Adult bats don't weigh much. They're mainly fur and appetite. So traveling with an attached, quickly growing baby would mean becoming a beast of burden. Therefore, most bats leave their babies home as soon as possible, to crawl around the cave walls and play with other babies, while the adults go out to dine. When the mother returns, she flies through the nursery, shouting to her baby, which shouts back. So individual are their voices and smells that even in the nursery's pandemonium of thousands of calling bats, mothers and babies find one another with ease. (In a place like Bracken Cave, that means being able to smell well enough to pick out one scent among 240 tons of individuals.) A mother will flutter to her baby, scoop it up with a wing, press it against her chest, and carry it to their usual perch, where the baby will nurse at her nipple. Bats can hang upside-down with their tummies pressed against the cave wall, because their feet turn sideways, a nifty trick. And where they hang isn't random.

Diane Ackerman, *The Moon by Whale Light*

Main idea: _____

_____

For my Cuba shopping I went to Wal-Mart. Now, Wal-Mart overwhelms me in normal circumstances. I am but a lost child when it comes to the immense variety of objects this cornucopia contains. I could live for years, unnoticed, inside Wal-Mart, eating out of cans and riding around in sleek lawn mowers. I could change clothes every day. I could create a new living space every few hours with new curtains, new furniture, and new plants. I could listen to music, though only the discounted variety, and read cheap but entertaining books. In the materially poor universe I grew up in, Wal-Mart would have been our utopia's fulfillment. What Karl Marx described as "communism" was Wal-Mart. What I wanted to do was tow the whole store to Cuba. Then I would set up shop at some intersection in Havana and distribute everything. I bet the throng would be bigger than the one for Fidel's biggest (and longest) speech. The irony of course, was that starved Cubans would find Wal-Mart heaven, while bored Americans are constantly in search of spiritual nourishment. The problem with communism is that it started at the wrong end: instead of promising people material fulfillment at the end of the journey, it should have stuffed them at the beginning.

Andrei Codrescu, Ay, Cuba! A Socio-Erotic Journey

Main idea: _____

_____

_____

Levels of Support

Now we can turn our attention to the paragraph's supporting sentences. Distinguishing between **major supporting statements** and **minor supporting statements** is an important thinking skill. Briefly, major statements directly relate to, and develop, the main idea, whereas minor ones further explain, illustrate, or otherwise develop the major ones. Analysis of levels of support trains you to think logically: You must weigh the relative importance of ideas in relation to the main idea.

In an ideally constructed paragraph, when diagrammed, the supporting sentences might look like this:

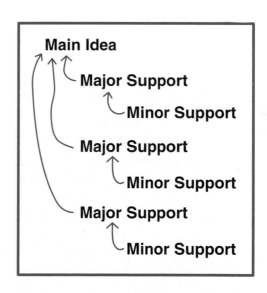

The following paragraph nicely exemplifies this model. Notice that the major supporting sentences identify each of the three types of book owners; the minor supporting sentences comment on each type, using parentheses. The main idea, stated in the first sentence, is reinforced by the paragraph's remaining six sentences.

[1]There are three kinds of book owners. [2]The first has all the standard sets and best-sellers—unread, untouched. [3](This deluded individual owns wood-pulp and ink, not books.) [4]The second has a great many books—a few of them read through, most of them dipped into, but all of them as clean and shiny as the day they were bought. [5](This person would probably like to make books his own, but is restrained by a false respect for their physical appearance.) [6]The third has a few books or many—every one of them dog-eared and dilapidated, shaken and loosened by continual use, marked and scribbled in front to back. [7](This man owns books.)

Mortimer Adler, "How to Mark a Book," *Saturday Review*

The following paragraph varies this pattern. (Notice that the first two sentences consist of introductory descriptive details; they are minor details of a sort, though not exactly supporting ones.)

[1]The entire body of a tarantula, especially its legs, is thickly clothed with hair. [2]Some of it is short and woolly, some long and stiff. [3]Touching this body hair produces one of two distinct reactions. [4]When the spider is hungry, it responds with an immediate and swift attack. [5]At the touch of a cricket's antennae the tarantula seizes the insect so swiftly that a motion picture taken at the rate of 64 frames per second shows only the result and not the process of capture. [6]But when the spider is not hungry, the stimulation of its hairs merely causes it to shake the touched limb. [7]An insect can walk under its hairy belly unharmed.

Alexander Petrunkevitch, "The Spider and the Wasp," *Scientific American*

Here is the paragraph printed again, this time in graphic form, showing the relative importance of the supporting details:

Introductory descriptive details:
The entire body of a tarantula, especially its legs, is thickly clothed with hair. Some of it is short and wooly, some long and stiff.
[sents. 1 and 2]

Main idea:
Touching this body hair produces one of two distinct reactions. [sent. 3]

Major support:
When the spider is hungry, it responds with an immediate and swift attack. [sent. 4]

Minor support:
At the touch of a cricket's antennae the tarantula seizes the insect so swiftly that a motion picture taken at the rate of 64 frames per second shows only the result and not the process of capture. [sent. 5]

Major support:
But when the spider is not hungry, the stimulation of its hairs merely causes it to shake the touched limb. [sent. 6]

Minor support:
An insect can walk under its hairy belly unharmed. [sent. 7]

If the minor details were omitted, we would not know how fast the spider's rate of capture is when hungry nor the spider's indifference when not hungry. As you can see, the supporting sentences operate on two different levels—some general, some more specific—suggesting two considerations: Ideas have relative significance, and the ideas may not be equally important. The ability to distinguish between the two helps you see the *texture* (for want of a better word) good writers try hard to achieve. Clearly then, the most important part of the paragraph is the main idea, and two types of supporting details are there to buttress and reinforce the general idea.

Unfortunately, not every paragraph is balanced as this one is, nor does every paragraph follow this alternating pattern. Try your hand at distinguishing between the two kinds of support in the following paragraph. In the space before each sentence, indicate whether the sentence represents the main idea (MAIN), major support (MA), or minor support (MI):

_____ (1) People feel safer behind some kind of physical barrier. _____ (2) If a social situation is in any way threatening, then there is an immediate urge to set up such a barricade. _____ (3) For a tiny child faced with a stranger, the problem is usually solved by hiding behind its mother's body and peeping out at the intruder to see what he or she will do next. _____ (4)

If the mother's body is not available, then a chair or some other piece of solid furniture will do. _____ (5) If the stranger insists on coming closer, then the peeping face must be hidden too. _____ (6) If the insensitive intruder continues to approach despite these obvious signals of fear, then there is nothing for it to do but to scream or flee.

Desmond Morris, *Manwatching: A Field Guide to Human Behavior*

Now check your answers: (1) MAIN, (2) MA, (3) MI, (4) MI, (5) MI, (6) MI.

■ THE AUTHOR'S PURPOSE AND MODES OF DISCOURSE

The last skill we will take up in this chapter is identifying the **mode of discourse,** which refers to the kind of writing in nonfiction prose. These modes are closely related to the **author's purpose**—why the writer is writing and what he or she wants to accomplish. There are four modes: **narration,** to tell a story; (2) **description,** to show what something looks or feels like; (3) **exposition,** to inform, explain, or set forth; (4) and **persuasion,** to convince the reader to adopt the writer's point of view. The following box shows author's purpose and mode of discourse.

Author's Purpose ⟶	**Mode of Discourse**
• To tell a story ⟶	Narration
• To show what something looks like or feels like ⟶	Description
• To inform, to set forth, to explain, to discuss ⟶	Exposition
• To convince the reader to adopt the writer's point of view ⟶	Persuasion

Narration

Narration is the most easily recognized mode of discourse; it means simply to tell a story. A writer uses narration to relate events, either real or imagined, in chronological order, not to entertain, but to provide evidence for some larger truth, as Lewis Thomas does in this passage:

We may be about to rediscover that dying is not such a bad thing to do after all. Sir William Osler took this view: he disapproved of people who spoke of the agony of death, maintaining there was no such thing.

In a nineteenth-century memoir on an expedition in Africa, there is a story by David Livingston about his own experience of near-death. He was caught by a lion, crushed across the chest in the animal's great jaws, and saved in the instant by a lucky shot from a friend. Later, he remembered the episode in clear detail. He was so amazed by the extraordinary sense of peace, calm, and total painlessness associated with being killed that he constructed a theory that all creatures are provided with a protective physiologic mechanism, switched on at the verge of death, carrying them through in a haze of tranquillity.

Lewis Thomas, "The Long Habit," Lives of a Cell

State the main idea that the preceding little narrative supports.

_____

_____

Description

The mode of discourse called **description** shows what someone or something looks like or what something feels like. The author's purpose is to show a visual picture of a *particular* scene, not a generalized one based on a composite of many such scenes. Descriptive writing typically relies on sensory details appealing to the five senses. It may also use figures of speech (imaginative comparisons such as metaphors and similes, which are covered in Chapter 6). Although a descriptive passage by itself usually does not have a sentence stating the main idea, there usually is a **dominant impression,** revealed little by little as the details accumulate. This illustrating paragraph by Susan Orlean describes Florida's Fakahatchee swamp. Underline the key details as you read it.

The levee was high and dry and we walked for a mile or two before we stepped off. The water we stepped into was as black as coffee. It was hard to tell how far down we would go, and when our feet touched the bottom it yielded like pudding. Duckweed floating on the water's surface wound around our calves. There is a deep stillness in the Fakahatchee, but there is not a moment of physical peace. Something is always brushing against you or lapping at you or snagging you or tangling in your legs, and the sun is always pummeling your skin, and the wetness in the air makes your hair coil like a phone cord. You never smell plain *air* in a swamp—you smell the tang of mud and the sourness of rotting leaves and the cool musk of new leaves and the perfumes of a million different flowers floating by, each distinct but transparent, like soap bubbles. The biggest number in the universe would not be big enough to count the things your eyes see. Every inch of land holds up a thatch of tall grass or a bush or a tree, and every bush or tree is girdled with another plant's roots, and every root is topped with a flower or a fern or a swollen bulb, and every one of those flowers and ferns is the pivot around which a world of bees and gnats and spiders and dragonflies revolve. The sounds you hear are twigs cracking underfoot and branches whistling past you and leaves murmuring and water slopping over the trunks of old dead trees and every imaginable and unimaginable insect noise and every kind of bird peep and screech and tootle, and then all those unclaimed sounds of something moving in a hurry, something low to the ground and heavy, maybe the size of a horse in the shape of a lizard, or maybe the size, shape, and essential character of a snake. In the swamp you feel as if someone had plugged all of your senses into a light socket. A swamp is logy and slow-moving but at the same time highly overstimulating. Even in the dim, sultry places deep within it, it is easy to stay awake.

Susan Orlean, The Orchid Thief

In your own words, state the dominant impression that the details

suggest. _____

_____

Exposition

Exposition, or expository writing, is the most common kind of reading you will encounter in your college courses. Expository readings very likely make up the bulk of the reading in your freshman English anthology and in your textbooks. Exposition is essentially objective writing with a straightforward purpose: to inform, to explain, to make clear, to discuss, or to set forth. It is usually *factual,* because its purpose is to provide information. By its very nature, then, exposition presents subject matter without the intent to influence opinions or emotions or to criticize or argue. In this first example, the unnamed writer presents information on play habits of octopuses.

Octopuses are the geniuses of the invertebrate world. They can navigate mazes, unscrew jars, and escape into neighboring tanks to feed. And now it seems that octopuses are even smart enough to have fun. Roland Anderson, a marine biologist at the Seattle Aquarium, and Jennifer Mather, an animal behaviorist at the University of Lethbridge in Alberta, Canada, were surprised to find that octopuses play. Birds and mammals engage in all sorts of play: cats bat at string; birds appear to soar for the sheer joy of it. Invertebrates, however, were thought to lack the sophistication to play, or as a scientist might define it, "to engage in repetitive behavior unrelated to food gathering or reproduction." Anderson had heard colleagues casually mention that octopuses seemed to like floating thermometers. "I happened to have a bottle of Tylenol that I was about done with, so we filled it with water and glued it shut," he says. When he put the pill bottle into a tank with an octopus, the octopus first brought the bottle to its mouth, in case it might be food. Then it gently pushed the bottle away with a squirt of water, directing it toward a current that brought it back toward the octopus. When the bottle returned, the octopus squirted it away again. One of the eight octopuses tested played with the bottle for nearly half an hour. Anderson says that octopuses will squirt water at objects that annoy them, "but then they blow quite hard." If that doesn't work, he says, the octopus might attack the object. That the octopuses repeatedly directed gentle squirts at the bottle, says Anderson, "is an indication that this might be play behavior."

"Octoplay," *Discover*

Write a sentence stating the main idea in your own words. _____

In this second expository paragraph, Genelle Moraine also presents information objectively, in keeping with her purpose—to inform.

Members of the same culture share a common body idiom—that is, they tend to read a given nonverbal signal in the same way. If two people read a signal in a different way, it is partial evidence that they belong to different cultures. In Colombia, an American Peace Corps worker relaxes with his feet up on the furniture; his shocked Colombian hostess perceives the gesture as disgusting. Back in the United States, a university president poses for a photograph with his feet up on the desk; newspaper readers react with affection for "good old President Jones." While Americans use the feet-on-furniture gesture to signal "I'm relaxed and at home here," or "See how casual and folksy I am," neither message is received by a Colombian, who reads the signal as "boor!" An understanding of the role gestures play within a culture is critical to sensitive communication.

Genelle G. Morain, "Kinesis and Cross-Cultural Understanding,"
Language in Education: Theory and Practice

Write a sentence stating the main idea. _____

_____

Persuasion

The terms *persuasion* and *argumentation* are sometimes used interchangeably, though technically, there is a difference. **Argumentation** traditionally refers to writing that is supported by logical evidence in defense of a specific issue. In contrast, **persuasion** is an attempt to change another person's feelings or opinions by using emotional or ethical appeals. For now, the distinction is not particularly important. A writer persuades when he or she wants to *convince* the reader that a particular idea or opinion is worth holding, to win the reader over to a certain viewpoint, or to get the reader to change his or her mind. By its very nature, persuasive writing deals with controversial issues and relies more on opinion than on fact. By definition, opinions are subjective, meaning that they exist in the mind—influenced as it is by experience and opinion—rather than in external, objective reality.

As you read this first example of persuasive writing, consider the underlined words or phrases.

> In an era when citizens are upset about needless government agencies, the Central Intelligence Agency may stand out as the ultimate example of a bureaucracy whose lifespan has been pointlessly prolonged. Long after its original mission ceased to matter, a combination of iniquity and inertia has kept the CIA intact.
>
> Unlike other controversial government agencies that merely squander taxpayers' money, the Central Intelligence Agency is a sinister enterprise with a long criminal record. Its sole rationale—engaging in shadowy combat with its equally nefarious communist counterparts—crumbled at about the same time the Berlin Wall did. Without a Cold War to wage, the CIA has become a dinosaur desperate to avoid extinction.
>
> Kevin J. Kelley, "R.I.P. for the CIA?" *Utne Reader*

What is the writer's main objection to the CIA? _____

_____

_____

In this second example, Lewis Lapham, editor-in-chief of *Harper's* magazine, criticizes the American school system.

> For the last twenty years the communiqués from the nation's classrooms have resembled the casualty reports from a lost war. Ever since the early hours of the Reagan Administration, anxious committees have been publishing statements about the dwindling supplies of verbal aptitude and mathematical comprehension, about the urgent need for more money and better teachers, about next semester's redesign of special programs for the poor, the foolish, the outnumbered, and the inept.
>
> The expressions of alarm I take to be a matter of pious ritual, like a murmuring of prayers or the beating of ornamental gongs. If as a nation we wished to improve the performance of the schools, I assume that we could

do so. Certainly we possess the necessary resources. We are an energetic people, rich in money and intelligence, capable of making high-performance automobiles and venture-capital funds, and if our intentions were anything other than ceremonial, I don't doubt that we could bring the schools to the standard of efficiency required of a well-run amusement park. Over the last twenty years we have added $10 trillion to the sum of the national wealth, cloned monkeys, reconfigured the weather, multiplied (by factors too large to calculate) the reach and value of the Internet.

Why, then, do the public schools continue to decay while at the same time the voices of the proctors poking through the wreckage continue to rise to the pitch of lamentations for the dead? Possibly because the condition of the public schools is neither an accident nor a mistake. The schools as presently constituted serve the interests of a society content to define education as a means of indoctrination and a way of teaching people to know their place. We have one set of schools for the children of the elite, another for children less fortunately born, and why disrupt the seating arrangement with a noisy shuffling of chairs? Serious reform of the public schools would beg too many questions about racial prejudice, the class system, the division of the nation's spoils. A too well-educated public might prove more trouble than it's worth, and so we mask our tacit approval of an intellectually inferior result with the declarations of a morally superior purpose. The sweet words come easy and cheap, and, if often enough repeated, they gain the weight of hard decision and accomplished fact.

Lewis Lapham, "School Bells," *Harper's*

According to Lapham, why have our public schools deteriorated to their alarming state? _____

_____

_____

_____

Mixed Modes of Discourse

Thus far, each passage you have read in this section represents one dominant mode. But prose writers often combine modes. In this excerpt from her classic memoir *Out of Africa,* the Danish writer Isak Dinesen relates the experience of shooting an iguana. Can you spot the shifts back and forth between the two modes of discourse represented in the passage?

In the Reserve I have sometimes come upon the Iguana, the big lizards, as they were sunning themselves upon a flat stone in a river-bed. They are not pretty in shape, but nothing can be imagined more beautiful than their colouring. They shine like a heap of precious stones or like a pane cut out of an old church window. When, as you approach, they swish away, there is a flash of azure, green and purple over the stones, the colour seems to be standing behind them in the air, like a comet's luminous trail.

Once I shot an Iguana. I thought that I should be able to make some pretty things from his skin. A strange thing happened then, that I have never afterwards forgotten. As I went up to him, where he was lying dead upon his stone, and actually while I was walking the few steps, he faded and grew pale, all colour died out of him as in one long sigh, and by the time that I touched him he was grey and dull like a lump of concrete. It was the live impetuous blood pulsating within the animal, which had radiated out all that glow and splendour. Now that the flame was put out, and the soul had flown, the Iguana was as dead as a sandbag.

Often since I have, in some sort, shot an Iguana, and I have remembered the one of the Reserve. Up at Meru I saw a young Native girl with a bracelet on, a leather strap two inches wide, and embroidered all over with very small turquoise-coloured beads which varied a little in colour and played in green, light blue and ultramarine. It was an extraordinarily live thing; it seemed to draw breath on her arm, so that I wanted it for myself, and made Farah buy it from her. No sooner had it come upon my own arm than it gave up the ghost. It was nothing now, a small, cheap, purchased article of finery. It had been the play of colours, the duet between the turquoise and the "nègre,"—that quick, sweet, brownish black, like peat and black pottery, of the Native's skin,—that had created the life of the bracelet.

Isak Dinesen, "The Iguana," Out of Africa

Write a sentence stating the main idea of the passage. _____

_____

_____

What modes of discourse are most evident? Be sure to consider her

primary purpose in writing. _____

_____

■ CHAPTER EXERCISES

Be sure to read the following explanation before undertaking the exercises.

Each chapter in Parts 1, 2, and 3 ends with a group of exercises. Specifically, you will be asked to read three short selections and a short practice essay. Each tests your understanding and mastery of the concepts taken up thus far. For example, the exercises in this chapter test for main idea, levels of support, modes of discourse, and vocabulary in context. For immediate feedback, the answers to Selection 1's questions are provided in the text. Your instructor will decide the best way to proceed for the remaining exercises.

In addition to questions on content and structure, each selection includes one of two types of vocabulary exercises. For the multiple-choice exercises, first try to determine the meaning from context. The sentence or paragraph number is always listed; you should return to the reading and refer to the paragraph for the context. Often you will be able to choose the appropriate definition in this way. If you are unsure of the proper answer, turn to the dictionary rather than taking a blind stab. It is not cheating to look up words you don't know, even while you are working through exercises. You should follow this procedure for all the multiple-choice vocabulary exercises in this book. The second type of exercise is open-ended: You are asked to look up the word and write an appropriate definition.

For both types of vocabulary exercises, I strongly recommend that you use an unabridged dictionary rather than an abridged paperback version. The introduction to the text recommends several good ones. A good dictionary is worth the money and is an indispensable aid to your becoming a better reader.

Selection 1

[1]It will not do to blame television for the state of our literacy. [2]Television watching does reduce reading and often encroaches on homework. [3]Much of it is admittedly the intellectual equivalent of junk food. [4]But in some respects, such as its use of standard written English, television watching is acculturative. [5]Moreover, as Herbert Walberg points out, the schools themselves must be held partly responsible for excessive television watching, because they have not firmly insisted that students complete significant amounts of homework, an obvious way to increase time spent on reading and writing. [6]Nor should our schools be excused by an appeal to the effects of the decline of the family or the vicious circle of poverty, important as these factors are. [7]Schools have, or should have, children for six or seven hours a day, five days a week, nine months a year, for thirteen years or more. [8]To assert that they are powerless to make a significant impact on what their students learn would be to make a claim about American education that few parents, teachers, or students would find it easy to accept.

E. D. Hirsch, Jr., *Cultural Literacy: What Every American Needs to Know*

A. Vocabulary

For each italicized word from the selection, choose the best definition according to the context in which it appears.

1. *encroaches on* [sentence 2]:
   (a) substitutes for.
   (b) makes irrelevant.
   (c) intrudes upon.
   (d) is more important than.

2. *acculturative* [4]: Describing the process of
    (a) acquiring new ideas.
    (b) accumulating material goods.
    (c) restructuring and reshaping the culture.
    (d) learning about and adopting cultural traits.
3. *assert* [8]:
    (a) complain about.
    (b) declare, claim.
    (c) accuse, blame.
    (d) debate both sides of an issue.

B. Content and Structure

Complete the following questions.

1. In your own words, write a main-idea sentence for the paragraph.

    _____

    _____

2. What is the state of our literacy, according to what the author suggests?

    _____

    _____

    What word or phrase helped you arrive at your answer? _____

    _____

3. The mode of discourse is
    (a) narration.
    (b) description.
    (c) exposition.
    (d) persuasion.
4. Look again at sentences 1 to 3. Then label the next three sentences according to whether they represent major support (MA) or minor support (MI):

    _____ sentence 4   _____ sentence 5   _____ sentence 6
5. Whom or what does Hirsch criticize *most* for the state of our literacy?
    (a) television itself, for its poor programming quality.
    (b) children, who watch television rather than doing homework or reading.
    (c) parents, who do not limit their children's television viewing.
    (d) schools, which do not demand enough work from children.

6. Which of the following best restates the idea expressed in sentence 6? The decline of the family and poverty are factors that
   (a) explain children's poor performance in school.
   (b) cannot be dismissed, although schools should not use them as an excuse to require little work from their students.
   (c) make it impossible for many teachers to teach effectively.
   (d) explain why affluent schools produce better-educated students than poor schools.

Answers for Selection 1

A. Vocabulary

1. (c)
2. (d)
3. (b)

B. Content and Structure

1. The schools, not excessive television viewing, must be held accountable for declining literacy.
2. The state of our literacy is poor, suggested by the word "blame" in sentence 1.
3. (d)
4. Sentence 4: MA; sentence 5: MI; sentence 6: MI
5. (d)
6. (b)

Selection 2

[1]Over the last three decades, fast food has infiltrated every nook and cranny of American society. [2]An industry that began with a handful of modest hot dog and hamburger stands in southern California has spread to every corner of the nation, selling a broad range of foods wherever paying customers may be found. [3]Fast food is now served at restaurants and drive-throughs, at stadiums, airports, zoos, high schools, elementary schools, and universities, on cruise ships, trains, and airplanes, at K-Marts, Wal-Marts, gas stations, and even at hospital cafeterias. [4]In 1970, Americans spent about $6 billion on fast food; in 2000, they spent more than $110 billion. [5]Americans now spend more money on fast food than on higher education, personal computers, computer software, or new cars. [6]They spend more on fast food than on movies, books, magazines, newspapers, videos, and recorded music—combined.

[7]Pull open the glass door, feel the rush of cool air, walk in, get in line, study the backlit color photographs above the counter, place your order, hand over a few dollars, watch teenagers in uniforms pushing various buttons, and moments later take hold of a plastic tray full of food wrapped in colored paper and cardboard.

8The whole experience of buying fast food has become so routine, so thoroughly unexceptional and mundane, that it is now taken for granted, like brushing your teeth or stopping for a red light. **9**It has become a social custom as American as a small, rectangular, hand-held, frozen, and reheated apple pie.

Eric Schlosser, *Fast Food Nation: The Dark Side of the All-American Meal*

A. Vocabulary

For each italicized word from the selection, write the dictionary definition most appropriate for the context.

1. fast food has *infiltrated* [sentence 1]: _____

2. every *nook and cranny* [1]: _____

3. so thoroughly *unexceptional* [8]: _____

4. *mundane* [8]: _____

B. Content and Structure

Complete the following questions.

1. Which two modes of discourse are represented in the passage?
   (a) narration.
   (b) description.
   (c) exposition.
   (d) persuasion.
2. The main idea of the passage is that
   (a) the fast-food industry got its start in Southern California.
   (b) fast food has become a pervasive social custom.
   (c) Americans spend more money on fast food than on education, computers, cars, books, and reading material.
   (d) fast food is as American as mom and apple pie.
3. Sentences 3 to 6, taken together, support the idea that
   (a) fast food has made inroads in every part of American life and accounts for a large amount of our yearly expenditures.
   (b) Americans spend more money at fast-food restaurants than at traditional restaurants.
   (c) the fast-food industry has set a bad precedent for Americans' dining habits.
   (d) the fast-food industry is the largest-growing segment in the American economy today.

4.   Read sentence 7 again, which suggests that
     (a) teenagers are exploited in the fast-food industry.
     (b) fast-food restaurants are clean and sanitary.
     (c) fast-food restaurants are uniform and generally operate in the
          same way.
     (d) fast-food restaurants offer inexpensive food served quickly.

5.   Label the following sentences from paragraph 1 as follows: MAIN
     (main idea); MA (major support); or MI (minor support).

_____ sentence 1   _____ sentence 2   ___ sentence 3

_____ sentence 4   _____ sentence 5   ___ sentence 6

6.   Read sentence 9 again. What does Schlosser mean when he compares
     the social custom of buying fast food to "a small, rectangular, hand-
     held, frozen, and reheated apple pie"?
     (a) Fast-food apple pies are cheap and nutritious.
     (b) We no longer know what real food tastes like.
     (c) The fast-food industry has perverted even the traditional American
          dessert of apple pie.
     (d) The fast-food industry has figured out ingenious ways to
          serve even a difficult-to-make dessert like apple pie in its
          restaurants.

Selection 3

In this excerpt from *Harper's,* Jacques Leslie examines the lavish use of water
in Las Vegas.

¹Las Vegas is America's city of fantasy, and water, not wealth, is its greatest fantasy
of all. ²The city that Hoover Dam made possible is the nation's fastest-growing
metropolis in the country's driest state, the perfect manifestation of the notion
that water will never run out. ³Las Vegas and the desert don't match: the city
looks as if it didn't so much emerge from its surroundings as get deposited on
them. ⁴In this desert of ostentation, water is displayed more lasciviously than sex.
⁵Among the city's hotel casinos, Caesars Palace laid down the archetype, festooning its property with fountains and aqueducts in 1966. ⁶Now the Mirage sports a
one-acre outcropping of terraced waterfalls, and a rain forest has been installed
beneath the glass canopy at the entrance. ⁷At Treasure Island the main feature is a
naval battle between British and pirate ships that employs live actors and a large
supply of fireworks; this event attracts a few hundred sidewalk onlookers five times
a night. ⁸The Mandalay Bay's grounds include a sandy beach with three- to four-
foot waves. ⁹In pursuit of an impressive water display, I recently chose to stay at
the Venetian, which features—can you guess?—canals, but unfortunately they resemble nothing so much as brightly lit, elongated bathtubs. ¹⁰The Venetian even

contains a Grand Canal and a Basilica di San Marco, whose dissimilarities from the originals include being miniature and plasterboard and on the second floor. [11]Bewildered tourists wait in line for the chance to pay money to stripe-shirted "gondoliers," who pole them down the hall, singing into the air-conditioning ducts.

Jacques Leslie, "Running Dry," *Harper's*

A. *Vocabulary*

For each italicized word from the selection, choose the best definition according to the context in which it appears.

1. the perfect *manifestation* [sentence 2]:
   (a) symbolic gesture.
   (b) inventive strategy.
   (c) realistic perception.
   (d) outward indication.

2. this desert of *ostentation* [4]:
   (a) pleasure seeking.
   (b) pretentious display.
   (c) ever-increasing growth.
   (d) environmental control.

3. more *lasciviously* than sex [4]: Describing something that
   (a) arouses sensual urges.
   (b) exploits natural resources.
   (c) is in poor taste.
   (d) is exorbitantly expensive.

4. laid down the *archetype* [5]:
   (a) rule to be adhered to strictly.
   (b) original pattern or model.
   (c) challenge to competitors.
   (d) management system.

5. *festooning* its property [5]:
   (a) adorning.
   (b) surrounding.
   (c) dominating.
   (d) brightening.

B. *Content and Structure*

Complete the following questions.

1. State the subject of the paragraph. _____

   State the controlling idea. _____

   _____

2. The mode of discourse is
    (a) narration.
    (b) description.
    (c) exposition.
    (d) persuasion.

3. What specifically does Leslie refer to in sentence 3 when he says, "Las Vegas and the desert don't match"? _____

    _____

4. Las Vegas would not be possible without
    (a) luxury hotels.
    (b) tourists.
    (c) Hoover Dam.
    (d) water imported from other states.

5. What is Leslie's opinion of the Venetian's Grand Canal, its Basilica di San Marco, and the gondoliers who ferry visitors around the canals? He thinks they are
    (a) impressive.
    (b) realistic.
    (c) educational.
    (d) fake.

6. A good title for this paragraph would be
    (a) "Visiting Las Vegas."
    (b) "Las Vegas Hotels."
    (c) "Las Vegas: The City Meets the Desert."
    (d) "Las Vegas: An Urban Fantasy."

■ *PRACTICE ESSAY*

Among the Thugs
Bill Buford

In Great Britain the word football *refers to the game Americans and Canadians call* soccer. *European soccer matches are notoriously rowdy, and British football fans have perhaps the worst reputations of all Europeans in this regard. Many British football club members follow their local teams as they compete all over Europe, drinking, picking fights, and engaging in violence and lawlessness. In* Among the Thugs, *Bill Buford takes a look at this phenomenon. He writes from a personal point of view: Although he is an American, at the time he wrote this essay he resided in England, where he spent several months traveling around with two or three football clubs, observing their fans' behavior and the crowd mentality that marks it. He notes that these fans tend to be working-class people who engage in these activities for weekend entertainment.*

Until recently, Buford was the editor of Granta, *a well-respected British magazine that publishes high-quality fiction and nonfiction. In 1996 he returned to the United States, where he is currently fiction editor at* The New Yorker *magazine.*

1   It is not uncommon, in any sport, to see spectators behaving in a way that would be uncharacteristic of them in any other context: embracing, shouting, swearing, kissing, dancing in jubilation. It is the thrill of the sport, and expressing the thrill is as important as witnessing it. But there is no sport in which the act of being a spectator is as *constantly* physical as watching a game of English football on the terraces. The physicalness is insistent; any observer not familiar with the game would say that it is outright brutal. In fact, those who do not find it brutal are those so familiar with the traditions of attending an English football match, so certain in the knowledge of what is expected of them, that they are incapable of seeing how deviant their behavior is—even in the most ordinary things. The first time I attended White Hart Lane on my own, everyone made for the exit within seconds of the match ending: I looked at the thing and couldn't imagine an exit more dangerous—an impossibly narrow passageway with very steep stairs on the other side. There was no waiting; there was also no choice, and this peculiar mad rush of people actually lifted me up off my feet and carried me forward. I had no control over where I was going. Stampede was the word that came to mind. I was forced up against the barrier, danger looming on the other side, was crushed against it, wriggled sideways to keep from bruising my ribs, and then, just as suddenly, was popped out, stumbling, as the others around me stumbled, to keep from falling down the remaining stairs. I looked up behind me: everyone was grimacing and swearing; someone, having been elbowed in the face, was threatening to throw a punch. What was this all about? This was not an important moment in the game: it was the act of leaving it. This, I thought, is the way animals behave, but the thought was not a metaphoric one. This was genuinely the way animals behave—herd animals. Sheep behave this way—cattle, horses.

2   At the heart of any discussion about crowds is the moment when many, many different people cease being many, many different people and become only one thing—a crowd. There is the phrase, becoming "one with the crowd." In part, it is a matter of language: when the actions of diverse individuals are similar and coherent enough that you must describe them as the actions of one body, with a singular subject and a singular verb. They are . . . It is . . . The many people are . . . The crowd is . . . The English football game expects the spectator to be-

come *one* with the crowd; in a good football game, a game with "atmosphere," the spectator assumes it: it is one of the things he has paid for. But, even here, it is more than an ordinary crowd experience.

3   It is an experience of constant physical contact and one that the terraces are designed to concentrate. The terraces look like animal pens and, like animal pens, provide only the most elementary accommodation: a gate that is locked shut after the spectators are admitted; a fence to keep them from leaving the area or spilling on to the pitch; a place for essential refreshment—to deal with elementary thirst and hunger; a place to pee and shit. I recall attending the Den at Millwall, the single toilet facility overflowing, and my feet slapping around in the urine that came pouring down the concrete steps of the terrace, the crush so great that I had to clinch my toes to keep my shoes from being pulled off, horrified by the prospect of my woollen socks soaking up this cascading pungent liquid still warm and steaming in the cold air. The conditions are appalling but essential: it is understood that anything more civilized would diffuse the experience. It seems fitting that, in some grounds, once all the supporters have left in their herdlike stampede, the terraces are cleaned by being hosed down: again, not just the images but the essential details are those of an animal pen. That is what the terraces offer, not just the crowd experience but the herd experience, with more intensity than any other sport, with more intensity than any other moment in a person's life—week after week.

4   Here, in Cambridge, on a Tuesday night, me a stranger among strangers: the physicalness was constant; it was inescapable—unless you literally escaped by leaving. You could feel, and you had no choice but to feel, every important moment of play—through the crowd. A shot on goal was a felt experience. With each effort, the crowd audibly drew in its breath, and then, after another athletic save, exhaled with equal exaggeration. And each time the people around me expanded, their rib cages noticeably inflating, and we were pressed more closely together. They had tensed up—their arm muscles flexed slightly and their bodies stiffened, or they might stretch their necks forward, trying to determine in the strange, shadowless electronic night-light if this shot was the shot that would result in a goal. You could feel the anticipation of the crowd on all sides of your body as a series of sensations.

5   Physical contact to this extent is unusual in any culture. In England, where touch is not a social custom and where even a handshake can be regarded as intrusive, contact of this kind is exceptional—unless you become a member of the crowd.

6   When I arrived at this match, coming straight from a day of working in an office, my head busy with office thoughts and concerns that were distinctly my own, I was not, and could not imagine becoming "one" with any crowd. It was windy and cold and that biting easterly weather was felt by *me* personally—in *my* bones. I was, in what I was

sensing and thinking, completely intact as an individual. And it was *me,* an individual, who was then crushed on all sides by strangers, noticing their features, their peculiarities, their smells—*except* that, once the match began, something changed.

7   As the match progressed, I found that I was developing a craving for a goal. As its promises and failures continued to be expressed through the bodies of the people pressed against me, I had a feeling akin to an appetite, increasingly more intense, of anticipation, waiting for, hoping for, wanting one of those shots to get past the Millwall goalkeeper. The business of watching the match had started to exclude other thoughts. It was involving so many aspects of my person—what I saw, smelled, said, sang, moaned, what I was feeling up and down my body—that I was becoming a different person from the one who had entered the ground: I was ceasing to be me. There wasn't one moment when I stopped noticing myself; there was only a realization that for a period of time I hadn't been. The match had succeeded in dominating my senses and had raised me, who had never given a serious thought to the fate of Cambridge United, to a state of very heightened feeling.

8   And then the game—having succeeded in apprehending me so—played with me as it played with everyone else. It teased and manipulated and encouraged and frustrated. It had engendered this heightened feeling and, equally, the expectation that it would be satisfied: that there would be gratification—or not. That the team would score—or be scored against. That there would be victory—or defeat. Climax—or disappointment. Release: But what happens when all that energy, concentrated so deep into the heart of the heart of the crowd, is not let go?

9   At ninety minutes, there was the whistle. There was no score. There would be extra time.

A. Comprehension

Choose the answer that best completes each statement. Do not refer to the selection while doing this exercise.

1. Buford was alarmed when he attended the White Hart Lane match because
    (a) the uniformed police officers prevented the fans from exiting.
    (b) the sponsors had run out of tickets for the large number of fans present.
    (c) the home team threatened revenge against the opposing team for an earlier defeat.
    (d) the exit was too narrow for the number of fans trying to use it to leave.

2. Buford compares the crowd of spectators at football matches to
    (a) a band of uncivilized men.
    (b) robbers and thieves.
    (c) herd animals.
    (d) political protesters and rioters.

3. Buford emphasizes that a football spectator experiences
    (a) constant and intense physical contact with the crowd.
    (b) the joys and sorrows of the home team's performance.
    (c) the thrill of impending or potential violence and danger.
    (d) the pleasures of watching expert players performing at their best.

4. Once the match began, Buford writes that
    (a) he became bored with the game's progress.
    (b) he felt like an uninvolved outside observer.
    (c) he felt himself changing, until the game completely dominated his existence.
    (d) the game's complex rules confused him.

5. With respect to his own reactions in the stadium and to his experience there, Buford strongly suggests that he was
    (a) indifferent.
    (b) surprised.
    (c) bewildered.
    (d) angry.

B. Vocabulary

For each italicized word from the selection, choose the best definition according to the context in which it appears. You may refer to the selection to answer the questions in this section and in all the remaining sections.

1. dancing in *jubilation* [paragraph 1]:
    (a) anticipation.
    (b) joy.
    (c) religious fervor.
    (d) a competitive spirit.

2. how *deviant* their behavior is [1]:
    (a) insulting.
    (b) threatening.
    (c) departing from accepted standards.
    (d) unpredictable.

3. *grimacing* and swearing [1]:
    (a) making an ugly, contorted face.
    (b) pushing and shoving.
    (c) engaging in fistfights.
    (d) yelling obscenities.

4. *coherent* enough [2]:
    (a) consistent, sticking together.
    (b) composed of differing elements.
    (c) chaotic, lacking order.
    (d) single-minded, obsessed.

5. *pungent* liquid [3]: Describing a smell that is
    (a) sweet.
    (b) sharp, offensive.
    (c) delicate.
    (d) hard to define.

6. *diffuse* the experience [3]:
    (a) spread out, dilute.
    (b) pour out.
    (c) soften, lessen.
    (d) change too radically.

7. *audibly* drew its breath [4]:
    (a) angrily.
    (b) loudly enough to be heard.
    (c) collectively, as a group.
    (d) excitedly.

8. in *apprehending* me so [8]: Here, a metaphorical use, meaning
    (a) taking fully, seizing.
    (b) understanding the true significance of.
    (c) perceiving with all the senses.
    (d) failing to involve or make an impact on.

C. Structure

Complete the following questions.

1. Which mode of discourse predominates in this essay?
    (a) narration.
    (b) description.
    (c) exposition.
    (d) persuasion.

2. Read paragraph 1 again. Write the sentence that expresses the main
    idea. _____

    _____

    _____

3. What seems to be Buford's central concern in paragraph 2?

_____

_____

4. Read paragraph 3 again. Explain in your own words the meaning of this sentence: "The conditions are appalling but essential: it is understood that anything more civilized would diffuse the experience."

_____

_____

5. The conclusion of the essay is meant to leave the reader with a feeling of
   (a) confusion.
   (b) anxiety.
   (c) suspense.
   (d) disappointment.

Questions for Discussion and Analysis

1. On balance, would you characterize Buford's description of English football matches as favorable or unfavorable? Explain, citing references to the essay.
2. As Buford has described it, how does a crowd behave? What are its characteristics?

ON THE WEB

A study of violence among British football fans and of football hooliganism in general was published in 1996 by a nonprofit institution, the Social Issues Research Centre, of Oxford, United Kingdom. The report examines the causes of hooliganism, its social implications, and the role of the media in sensationalizing football violence. It also provides a comparison of British football fan violence with that of fans in other European countries.

• The report can be accessed at this site:
www.sirc.org/publik/footballviolence.pdf
Click on "text version."

Reading between the Lines: Making Accurate Inferences

CHAPTER OBJECTIVES

Chapter 2 introduces you to the inference-making process and includes these topics:

• Facts and inferences

• Inferences defined

• Problems with inferences

• Explaining sample inferences

• Making open-ended inferences

■ FACTS AND INFERENCES

Before we discuss inferences, we must first distinguish them from facts. A fact is a verifiable piece of information; that is, it can be duplicated, measured, confirmed in other sources, demonstrated, or proved. If I say that our living room is 20 feet long, the matter can easily be proved or disproved with a tape measure. Here are three more facts:

- Eucalyptus trees are native to Australia.
- The gestation period for an elephant is 18 months.
- Watermelon contains more vitamin C than oranges.

An **inference**—whether in the real world or in our reading—is, as William Lutz defines the term later in this text, "a statement about the unknown based on the known." It is a conclusion from our observations or from facts that are presented to us. So facts and inferences are different: As these definitions suggest, inferences are *derived* from facts. Let's say we are planning a wedding reception. After measuring the reception area adjoining the church, we have these facts: The hall is 60 feet long and 40 feet wide. Another fact is that we are inviting only 25 people to the ceremony and reception. From these two sets of facts, we might draw these inferences:

- The reception hall is too large for that small a crowd.
- People will feel lost in such a large space.
- A smaller location would be more suitable for a small group.

Inferences, then, proceed from facts.

We also need to distinguish between two often confused verbs—*imply* and *infer*. To **imply** means to hint at or suggest an idea indirectly; to **infer** means to draw a conclusion from what the writer's words suggest. A writer or speaker *implies;* a reader or listener *infers.* As you read, you infer by drawing reasonable or probable conclusions from the author's words. In other words, you read between the lines. In this chapter, you will practice making inferences with several passages of varying levels of difficulty.

Practice Exercise 1	Carefully read the following report and the observations based on it. On the basis of the information presented, indicate whether you think the observations are true, false, or doubtful. Circle "T" if the observation is definitely true, circle "F" if the observation is definitely false, and circle "?" if the observation may be either true or false. Judge each observation in order.[1]

A well-liked college teacher had just completed making up the final examinations and had turned off the lights in the office. Just then a tall, broad figure

---

[1]This exercise is adapted from Joseph A. DeVito, *General Semantics: Guide and Workbook.* The test is based on one developed by William Honey, *Communication and Organizational Behavior.* 3rd ed. (Irwin, 1973).

with dark glasses appeared and demanded the examination. The professor opened the drawer. Everything in the drawer was picked up and the individual ran down the corridor. The dean was notified immediately.

1.	The thief was tall, broad, and wore dark glasses.	**T**	**F**	**?**
2.	The professor turned off the lights.	**T**	**F**	**?**
3.	A tall, broad figure demanded the examination.	**T**	**F**	**?**
4.	The examination was picked up by someone.	**T**	**F**	**?**
5.	The examination was picked up by the professor.	**T**	**F**	**?**
6.	A tall, broad figure appeared after the professor turned off the lights in the office.	**T**	**F**	**?**
7.	The man who opened the drawer was the professor.	**T**	**F**	**?**
8.	The professor ran down the corridor.	**T**	**F**	**?**
9.	The drawer was never actually opened.	**T**	**F**	**?**
10.	In this report three persons are referred to.	**T**	**F**	**?**

Answers

1. **?** There is no evidence that there was a thief.
2. **?** Are the college teacher and the professor the same person?
3. **T** There is an exact statement in the story that proves this to be true.
4. **?** There is no mention of the examination being or not being picked up by someone.
5. **?** We don't know if anyone picked up the examination.
6. **?** We don't know who turned off the lights.
7. **?** We don't know if the professor was a man or a woman.
8. **?** We don't know who ran down the corridor.
9. **F** The drawer was opened.
10. **?** There could have been three or four people: We don't know if the professor and the college teacher were the same person.

■ PROBLEMS WITH INFERENCES

The foregoing exercise reveals these difficulties with inferences:

- Our assumptions often get in the way of making accurate inferences.
- We may not read carefully enough or pay close enough attention to the language.
- We may indulge in stereotyping; this problem is particularly evident in question 7, if we incorrectly infer that a professor is more likely a man than a woman.

In the real world, inferences cause difficulty as well. Suppose you are driving down the freeway and you observe a car swerving in and out of lanes, moving erratically, and narrowly missing other cars. On the basis of your knowledge of the world, you might infer that the driver is drunk. But there may be other explanations. Perhaps the driver has suffered a heart attack or a stroke. Perhaps the steering mechanism failed. Or you could engage in more absurd flights of fancy and infer that the driver is a kid who has stolen the car and has no idea how to drive it, or that the driver is a stunt car driver who is practicing maneuvers on the freeway. These last two seem unlikely, since even the most intrepid yet inexperienced car thief would probably not venture out onto a highway, and stunt car drivers wouldn't use a busy freeway, where lives would be endangered, for practice. As you can see, the more we get carried away with our assumptions and make inferences on *facts we do not have,* the less probable it is that these inferences are correct.

This particular illustration suggests something about the nature of inferences: They have a high degree of *probability* rather than of absolute certainty. Our first inference was *probably* accurate because it was based on our prior experiences and our ability to reason from our observations and those experiences. However, because we don't have all the facts, our inference about this *particular* situation may be inaccurate. And our attempts to draw a conclusion are only speculative: We simply do not have enough facts here to make a valid inference.

It is the same in reading. We should not "read into" the author's words *beyond what they suggest or imply.* Further, bringing in our own experiences may lead us astray from the author's real intentions, resulting in misreading, misinterpretation, or inaccurate comprehension. To become adept at making inferences, study carefully the examples and explanations that follow.

■ EXPLAINING SAMPLE INFERENCES

In this chapter you will encounter three kinds of inferences, and you will be asked to mark them as follows:

- **Probably accurate (PA).** This kind of inference follows from the facts presented or is strongly implied by the author's words. We have enough information to say the inference is most likely accurate.
- **Probably inaccurate (PI).** An inaccurate inference either misstates or distorts the writer's words and observations.
- **Not in the passage (NP).** These are inferences that you can't reasonably make because they're not implied in the passage. Either there is insufficient evidence or there is no information in the passage that lets you determine probable accuracy or inaccuracy.

The first example is from Tobias Wolff's engaging autobiography, *This Boy's Life.* In it, Wolff describes the grades he received while attending the public high school in Concrete, a town in eastern Washington State.

> I brought home good grades at first. They were a fraud—I copied other kids' homework on the bus down from Chinook and studied for tests in the hallways as I walked from class to class. After the first marking period I didn't bother to do that much. I stopped studying altogether. Then I was given C's instead of A's, yet no one at home ever knew that my grades had fallen. The report cards were made out, incredibly enough, in pencil, and I owned some pencils myself.
>
> Tobias Wolff, *This Boy's Life*

On the basis of the evidence in the paragraph, mark these statements as follows: PA (probably accurate), PI (probably inaccurate), or NP (not in the passage). Then study the explanations that follow.

1. _____   Students at the high school in Concrete had to work hard to receive A's.
2. _____   The narrator continued to receive good grades only because he erased the teacher's marks and changed them to higher ones.
3. _____   The teachers were naive to record students' grades in pencil.

The first inference is *probably inaccurate.* If Wolff received A's for studying while walking to class, we can infer that the grading standards must have been pretty lax. We can infer that the second statement is *probably accurate* because, as Wolff so nicely puts it, "I owned some pencils myself." And the third inference is also *probably accurate* because of the phrase Wolff uses to characterize the teachers' use of pencils—"incredibly enough."

Next, read these two well-known fables, one relatively simple, the other more difficult.

A dispute once arose between the Wind and the Sun as to which was the stronger of the two. They agreed, therefore, to try their strength upon a traveler to see which should be able to take his cloak off first. The Wind began and blew with all his might and main, a cold and fierce blast; but the stronger he blew the closer the traveler wrapped his cloak about him and the tighter he grasped it with his hands. Then broke out the Sun and with his welcome beams he dispersed the vapor and the cold. The traveler felt the genial warmth and as the Sun shone brighter and brighter, he sat down, overcome with the heat, and cast his cloak on the ground. Thus the Sun was declared the conqueror.

"The Wind and the Sun," from *Aesop's Fables*

Which of these moral truths can you accurately infer from this fable?

1. The mighty rule the world.
2. The meek shall inherit the earth.
3. Force is more effective than persuasion.
4. Persuasion is more effective than force.
5. Competition breeds jealousy.

Did you mark answer choice 4? The gentle warmth of the Sun's rays—in other words, persuasion—was more effective than the harsh force of the Wind's blowing.

The second fable is slightly more difficult.

Death speaks:

1There was a merchant in Bagdad who sent his servant to market to buy provisions and in a little while the servant came back, white and trembling, and said, Master, just now when I was in the market-place I was jostled by a woman in the crowd and when I turned I saw it was Death that jostled me. **2**She looked at me and made a threatening gesture; now, lend me your horse and I will ride away from this city and avoid my fate. **3**I will go to Samarra and there Death will not find me. **4**The merchant lent him his horse, and the servant mounted it, and he dug his spurs in its flanks and as fast as the horse could gallop he went. **5**Then the merchant went down to the market-place and he saw me standing in the crowd and he came to me and said, Why did you make a threatening gesture to my servant when you saw him this morning? **6**That was not a threatening gesture, I said, it was only a start of surprise. **7**I was astonished to see him in Bagdad, for I had an appointment with him tonight in Samarra.

W. Somerset Maugham, "Death Speaks," *Sheppey*

On the basis of the evidence in the fable, label these inferences as follows: PA (probably accurate), PI (probably inaccurate), or NP (not in the passage).

1. _____   The servant misinterpreted Death's gesture in the market-place.
2. _____   The merchant thought his servant was foolish to go to Samarra.

3. _____   The time and place of our death are predetermined before we are born.

4. _____   The servant thought he could outwit Death.

5. _____   Ironically, in trying to escape Death, the servant sealed his own fate.

Here are the answers: (1) PA; (2) PI; (3) NP; (4) PA; (5) PA. Let us examine the reasoning behind them.

The first inference is clearly *accurate* based on the information in sentences 6 and 7; however, to make this inference, we must accept Death's explanation for her gesture and reject the servant's explanation. The second inference should be marked *probably inaccurate;* sentence 4 implies that the merchant willingly lent his horse, suggesting that he agreed with his servant's decision to flee Death's threatening gesture. Further evidence is that later the merchant scolded Death for frightening his servant. Also, a good master would not want his servant to die. Thus the original inference statement misinterprets the events of the story.

The third inference should be marked *not in the passage* for the following reasons: Death says that she already knew in advance that the servant would be in Samarra, implying that the servant's death was predetermined; however, the fable says nothing about our own death being predetermined, much less predetermined before our birth.

Last, inferences 4 and 5 should be labeled *probably accurate:* In attempting to outwit Death and escape his fate, the servant, instead, sealed his own fate. We and the narrator, Death, know what the servant does not. (This fable nicely illustrates the concept of dramatic irony.)

As should be plain by now, these inference questions make you think. Although some of these inferences may seem trivial or even nit picky, they do force you to look carefully at a passage and to exercise care in considering the evidence. Practicing with inferences will help you become both an active, questioning reader and a better thinker, seeing implications beyond the writer's literal words. Because these inference questions are quite challenging, be sure to look back at the text to find the phrase or sentence that pertains to each question. Try not to jump to conclusions or to intrude your own assumptions, stereotypes, or personal beliefs. Remember that in making inferences, you may encounter a gray area—that is, you may not be wholly certain that the inference is verifiably true, only that it is *probably* accurate or *probably* inaccurate. If you disagree with an answer, try to determine by yourself where you went wrong; if you are still unsure, ask your instructor for help.

■ USING EVIDENCE TO MAKE INFERENCES

Here are two excerpts for you to practice with. For each you must locate the evidence that leads to the inference. The first excerpt is a parable from the beginning of Donald Hall's short story "Argument and Persuasion." Read it carefully and then answer the inference questions that follow.

A husband and wife named Raoul and Marie lived in a house beside a river next to a forest. One afternoon Raoul told Marie that he had to travel to Paris overnight on business. As soon as he left, Marie paid the Ferryman one franc to row her across the river to the house of her lover Pierre. Marie and Pierre made love all night. Just before dawn, Marie dressed to go home, to be sure that she arrived before Raoul returned. When she reached the Ferryman, she discovered that she had neglected to bring a a second franc for her return journey. She asked the Ferryman to trust her; she would pay him back. He refused: A rule is a rule, he said.

If she walked north by the river she could cross it on a bridge, but between the bridge and her house a Murderer lived in the forest and killed anybody who entered. So Marie returned to Pierre's house to wake him and borrow a franc. She found the door locked; she banged on it; she shouted as loud as she could; she threw pebbles against Pierre's bedroom windows. Pierre awoke hearing her but he was tired and did not want to get out of bed. "Women!" he thought. "Once you give in, they take advantage of you. . . ." Pierre went back to sleep.

Marie returned to the Ferryman: She would give him *ten* francs by midmorning. He refused to break the rules of his job; they told him cash only; he did what they told him. . . . Marie returned to Pierre, with the same lack of result, as the sun started to rise.

Desperate, she ran north along the riverbank, crossed the bridge, and entered the Murderer's forest.

Donald Hall, "Argument and Persuasion,"
The Ideal Bakery

What specific evidence in the story suggests that Marie died? _____

_____

_____

Which character is morally directly responsible for Marie's death? _____

_____

_____

This next passage is reprinted from an article called "The End of the Book?" by D. T. Max. Again, identify the evidence necessary to make an accurate inference.

> Paper has limitations, but the computer may have more. As a physical object, it is hardly comforting. "Who'd want to go to bed with a Powerbook?" John Baker, a vice-president at Broderbund, asks. And even if the laptop goes on shrinking, its screen, whose components represent nearly all the machine's cost, remains at best a chore to read. At the Xerox Palo Alto Research Center (where the receptionist's cubicle still houses an IBM Selectric typewriter) is a display room with half a dozen prototype six-million-pixel AMLCD screens. The quiet hum of the room, the bright white lighting, the clean, flat antiseptic surfaces, give the impression of an aspirin commercial. "It was clear to us that no reader was going to read a book off any of the current screens for more than ten minutes," says Malcolm Thompson, the chief technologist. "We hoped to change that." A large annotated poster on the wall illustrates point for point the screen's superiority to paper, as in an old-fashioned magazine ad. This flat panel display is indeed better than commercial screens, but it is neither as flexible nor as mobile as a book, and it still depends on fickle battery power. A twentysomething software marketer who began as an editorial assistant in book publishing points out, "A book requires one good eye, one good light source, and one good finger."
>
> D.T. Max, "The End of the Book?"
> *The Atlantic Monthly*

If you paraphrase the article title to ask, Will books become obsolete in the future? what answer, according to Max's evidence, would you give?

_____

Now list at least three pieces of evidence in the paragraph that lead to

this inference. _____

_____

_____

What other evidence can you provide from your own knowledge to

support the idea that the demise of the book is not imminent? _____

_____

_____

Practice Exercise 2

In this section are four short passages arranged in order of progressive difficulty, each of which is followed by two or more inference questions. For the first passage, label each inference PA, PI, or NP. Be prepared to defend your answer choices.

> About 750,000 airplane components are manufactured, machined or assembled for Boeing Co., by workers from the Seattle Lighthouse for the Blind. A Boeing spokeswoman says that the parts have an "exceptionally low" rejection rate of one per one thousand. "Think about that the next time you hop on a 737," says Andrew Sims, a program manager for the National Industries for the Blind.
>
> "Work Week: Hardly Flying Blind," *The Wall Street Journal*, February 15, 2000

1. _____ Blind workers are more dependable and take fewer sick days than nonhandicapped employees.
2. _____ Other airplane manufacturers besides Boeing use blind workers to manufacture, machine, and assemble airplane components.
3. _____ Nonhandicapped (i.e., sighted workers) have higher rejection rates for airplane components than blind workers do.
4. _____ Rejected airplane parts are retooled so that they can be used rather than merely thrown away.
5. _____ Sight is an unimportant sense in machining and assembling airplane components.

This excerpt describes the writer's first experiences in elementary school.

> For four years I attended St. John's Catholic School where short nuns threw chalk at me, chased me with books cocked over their heads, squeezed me into cloak closets and, on slow days, asked me to pop erasers and to wipe the blackboard clean. Finally, in the fifth grade, my mother sent me to Jefferson Elementary. The Principal, Mr. Buckalew, kindly ushered me to the fifth grade teachers, Mr. Stendhal and Mrs. Sloan. We stood in the hallway with the principal's hand on my shoulder. Mr. Stendhal asked what book I had read in the fourth grade, to which, after a dark and squinting deliberation, I answered: *The Story of the United States Marines.* Mr. Stendhal and Mrs. Sloan looked at one another with a "you take him" look. Mr. Buckalew lifted his hand from my shoulder and walked slowly away.
>
> Gary Soto, *Living Up the Street*

1. Which of the following can you infer about the author?
    (a) He was a model student.
    (b) He had a reputation among teachers for being a troublemaker.
    (c) He had been asked to leave Catholic school.
    (d) He enjoyed public school more than Catholic school.

2. What inference can you make about the book Soto says he read in fourth grade, *The Story of the United States Marines?*
    (a) It was assigned reading at his former school.
    (b) He probably hadn't read it.
    (c) He probably had read it.
    (d) There is no way to tell whether he had read it or not.

3. What inference can you make about his new teachers, Mr. Stendhal and Mrs. Sloan?
    (a) They were impressed with Soto's answer.
    (b) Soto ended up in Mrs. Sloan's class.
    (c) Soto ended up in Mr. Stendhal's class.
    (d) They both thought Soto was something of a wise guy.

The author describes a job interview with William Shawn, the legendary editor of *The New Yorker* magazine.

When I was nineteen, William Shawn interviewed me for a summer job at *The New Yorker.* To grasp the full import of what follows, you should know that I considered *The New Yorker* a cathedral and Mr. Shawn a figure so godlike that I expected a faint nimbus to emanate from his ruddy head. During the course of our conversation, he asked me what other magazines I hoped to write for.

"Um, *Esquire,* the *Saturday Review,* and—"

I wanted to say *"Ms.,"* but my lips had already butted against the *M*—too late for a politic retreat—when I realized I had no idea how to pronounce it. Lest you conclude that I had been raised in Ulan Bator, I might remind you that in 1973, when I met Mr. Shawn, *Ms.* magazine had been published for scarcely a year, and most people, including me, had never heard the word *Ms.* used as a term of address. (Mr. Shawn had called me Miss Fadiman. *He* was so venerated by his writers that "Mister" had virtually become part of his name.) Its pronunciation, reflexive now, was not as obvious as you might think. After all, *Mr.* is not pronounced "Mir," and *Mrs.* is not pronounced "Mirz." Was it "Mzzzzz"? "Miz"? "Muz"?

In that apocalyptic split second, I somehow alighted on "Em Ess," which I knew to be the correct pronunciation of *ms.,* or manuscript.

Mr. Shawn didn't blink. He gave no indication that I had said anything untoward. In fact, he calmly proceeded to discuss the new feminist magazine—its history, its merits, its demerits, the opportunities it might offer a young writer like myself—for four or five minutes *without ever mentioning its name.*

Anne Fadiman, "The His'er Problem," *Ex Libris*

1. Which of the following can you accurately infer about Mr. Shawn?
   (a) He had never heard of *Ms.* magazine.
   (b) He didn't want to hire Fadiman for a job at *The New Yorker.*
   (c) He didn't know how to pronounce the title of *Ms.* magazine himself.
   (d) He didn't want to embarrass Fadiman by pronouncing *Ms.* correctly.
2. Which of the following can you accurately infer about Anne Fadiman?
   (a) She finally got a job at *The New Yorker.*
   (b) She was impressed with Mr. Shawn's good manners.
   (c) She was raised in Ulan Bator, the capital of Mongolia.
   (d) She did not really want to write for *Ms.* magazine.

In this passage from Bill Bryson's *Notes from a Small Island,* about his travels in England, he relates an experience that happened to him in Calais, France, the small city where one catches a ferry to cross the English Channel to England.

For reasons that I have never understood, the French have a particular genius when it comes to tacky religious keepsakes, and in a gloomy shop on a corner of the Place d'Armes, I found one I liked: a plastic model of the Virgin Mary standing with beckoning arms in a kind of grotto fashioned from seashells, miniature starfish, lacy sprigs of dried seaweed, and a polished lobster claw. Glued to the back of the Madonna's head was a halo made from a plastic curtain ring, and on the lobster claw the model's gifted creator had painted an oddly festive-looking *"Calais!"* in neat script. I hesitated because it cost a lot of money, but when the lady of the shop showed me that it also plugged in and lit up like a fun-fair ride at Blackpool, the only question in my mind was whether one would be enough. *"C'est très jolie,"*[2] she said in a kind of astonished hush when she realized that I was prepared to pay real money for it, and bustled off to get it wrapped and paid for before I came to my senses and cried, "Say, where am I? And what, pray, is *this* tacky piece of Franco-*merde*[3] I see before me?"

"C'est très jolie," she kept repeating soothingly, as if afraid of disturbing my wakeful slumber. I think it may have been some time since she had sold a Virgin Mary with Seashells Occasional Light. In any case, as the shop door shut behind me, I distinctly heard a whoop of joy.

Bill Bryson, *Notes from a Small Island*

---

[2] *C'est très jolie:* French for "It's very pretty."
[3] *merde:* French for "shit."

1. When Bryson refers to the maker of the religious keepsake as a "gifted creator," we can infer that he
   (a) truly admired the artist's talent.
   (b) is being sarcastic.
   (c) wanted to see more of his work.
   (d) recognized the artist's work.

2. We can accurately infer that the shopkeeper let out a "whoop of joy" after Bryson left because she
   (a) thought Bryson was a sucker for buying such a tacky object.
   (b) had made an expensive sale and was celebrating her luck.
   (c) knew Bryson would be back to buy more items the next day.
   (d) had never sold another copy of the model before.

3. Concerning Bryson, we can also infer that he
   (a) is a deeply religious person.
   (b) delights in buying tacky tourist souvenirs.
   (c) wanted to give the Virgin Mary to a religious friend at home.

■ MAKING OPEN-ENDED INFERENCES

In another kind of exercise in this text, you will practice making inferences by answering open-ended questions; you must draw your own inferences and state them in your own words. Following are three such exercises. In the first, John Hildebrand is describing a horse named Blue.

> Not much bigger than a pony, Blue stood fourteen hands high and weighed 950 pounds. His mother was a bucking horse bought from a rodeo, mean and ornery as they come, her history written in overlapping brands that covered her flanks.
>
> John Hildebrand, *Mapping the Farm*

Why did Blue's mother have so many brands? _____

_____

_____

(Making the correct inference here depends on your knowing the meaning of the word *brand* as it pertains to livestock. If you are unsure, check the dictionary.)

In *Over the Hills,* David Lamb describes a cross-country bicycle trip he made from Virginia to California. In this excerpt he contrasts the typical overweight American's concern with dieting and his own nutritional intake while on the road.

Between 1980 and 1991—when the diet business was in full bloom—the average adult American put on eight pounds. That, says the National Center for Health Statistics, is the equivalent of an extra one million tons of fat on the waistline of a nation where one in three persons is certifiably overweight. Ironically, the more we spend trying to get thin—$15 billion a year on diet soft drinks alone, another $4 billion on stuff like Lean Cuisine and pseudofood appetite suppressants—the plumper we become. Something is clearly out of whack. These contradictions were of no concern to me, however, because I had learned the secret of gluttony without guilt. Day after day I started the morning with French toast or pancakes, enjoyed apple pie with double scoops of ice cream during pre-noon coffee breaks, drank milk shakes, Hawaiian Punch and chocolate milk by the bucketful, snacked on three or four candy bars in the afternoon and often had room for a hot dog or two before I started thinking about dinner. Unlike the rest of America, the more I ate, the less I weighed. I could eat two pieces of coconut custard pie at 11 A.M. and within an hour on the road burn off the 450 calories and then some. By the time I reached western Arkansas, the love handles on my waist had disappeared and I had to tighten my belt an extra notch to keep my pants up.

David Lamb, *Over the Hills*

According to Lamb's experiences (and aside from overeating), why are so many Americans overweight? _____

_____

Probably all of us have heard the truism that no two snowflakes are identical. Cullen Murphy here explains where this idea originated.

For all the scientific awareness of the symmetrical character of snow crystals, the ubiquity of their popular image—the one we see in children's paper cutouts and on bags of ice and signs for motels that have air-conditioning—is a relatively recent phenomenon. What snowflakes actually looked like was not widely known until the middle of the nineteenth century, when the book *Cloud Crystals,* with sketches by "A Lady," was published in the United States. The lady had caught snowflakes on a black surface and then observed them with a magnifying glass. In 1885 Wilson Alwyn ("Snowflake") Bentley, of Jericho, Vermont, began taking photographs of snowflakes through a microscope. Thousands of Bentley's photomicrographs were eventually collected in his book *Snow Crystals* (1931). The fact that not one of the snowflakes photographed by Bentley was identical to another is probably the basis for the idea that no two snowflakes are ever exactly the same—an idea that is in fact unverifiable.

Cullen Murphy, "In Praise of Snow,"
The Atlantic Monthly

The author ends by saying "the idea that no two snowflakes are ever exactly the same" is "in fact unverifiable." Why is this statement

likely to be true? What evidence in the paragraph suggests it? _____

_____

_____

_____

_____

_____

Finally, here is a joke making the e-mail rounds, with two humorous but accurate inferences at its heart:

A man piloting a hot-air balloon discovers he has wandered far off course and is hopelessly lost. He descends to a lower altitude and locates a man down on the ground. He lowers the balloon to within hearing distance and shouts, "Excuse me, can you tell me where I am?"

The man below says, "Yes, you're in a hot-air balloon, about thirty feet above this field."

"You must work in information technology," says the balloonist.

"Yes, I do," replies the man. "And how did you know that?"

"Well," says the balloonist, "what you told me is technically correct, but of no use to anyone."

The man below says, "You must work in management."

"I do," replies the balloonist, "how did you know?"

"Well," says the man, "you don't know where you are, or where you're going, but you expect my immediate help. You're in the same position you were before we met, but now it's my fault!"

■ CHAPTER EXERCISES

Selection 1

¹Computer analysis of the English language as spoken today shows that the hundred most frequently used words are all of Anglo-Saxon origin: *the, is, you*—the basic building blocks. ²When Winston Churchill wanted to rally the nation in 1940, it was to Anglo-Saxon that he turned: "We shall fight on the beaches; we shall fight on the landing grounds; we shall fight in the fields and the streets; we shall fight in the hills; we shall never surrender." ³All these stirring words came from Old English as spoken in the year 1000, with the exception of the last one, *surrender,* a French import that came with the Normans in 1066—and when man set foot on the moon in 1969, the first human words spoken had similar echoes: "One small step for a man, one giant leap for mankind." ⁴Each of Neil Armstrong's famous words was part of Old English by the year 1000.

⁵Perhaps this is also the place to remark that many of the earthy epithets often described as "Anglo-Saxon" did not arrive until comparatively recent times: *fokkinge, cunte, crappe,* and *bugger* were all much later imports, probably coming from Holland as the later Middle Ages shaded into the great age of seafaring and exploration. ⁶There are absolutely no swear words or obscenities in Anglo-Saxon English, at least as the language has come down to us in the documents composed by its monkish scribes. ⁷The Anglo-Saxons could swear *to do* something, or could swear *by* something, but there is no record of them swearing *at* anything at all.

Robert Lacey and Danny Danziger, *The Year 1000*

A. Vocabulary

For each italicized word from the selection, write the dictionary definition most appropriate for the context.

1. wanted to *rally* the nation [sentence 2]: _____

2. all these *stirring* words [3]: _____

3. the *earthy* epithets [5]: _____

4. the earthy *epithets* [5]: _____

5. monkish *scribes* [6]: _____

B. Content and Structure

Complete the following questions.

1. Write a main-idea sentence in your own words for the *first*

    paragraph._____

    _____

2. Write a main-idea sentence in your own words for the *second*

    paragraph. _____

    _____

3. In relation to sentence 1, label the next three sentences MA (major
    support) or MI (minor support).

    _____ sentence 2   _____ sentence 3   _____ sentence 4

4. The first paragraph strongly implies that Anglo-Saxon–based
    words are
    (a) those we are most familiar with.
    (b) more suitable for expressing strong emotions on momentous
        occasions than borrowed words.
    (c) easier for the common listener to understand.
    (d) more appropriate for swearing than borrowed words.

5. Look through the passage and locate the two factors that allowed

    "earthy epithets" to be imported into English. _____

    _____

6. The writers' attitude toward the idea that swear words were absent in
    Anglo-Saxon is
    (a) one of astonishment.
    (b) skeptical.
    (c) critical.
    (d) not evident from the passage.

C. Inferences

On the basis of the evidence in the passage, mark these statements as follows:
PA (probably accurate), PI (probably inaccurate), or NP (not in the passage).

1. _____   The Normans who came to England in 1066 spoke French.
2. _____   The authors know how to read and write Anglo-Saxon.

3. _____ Anglo-Saxon has no word or words to express the idea of "surrender."

4. _____ The "monkish scribes" mentioned in sentence 6 most likely purged the manuscripts they worked on of Anglo-Saxon swear words.

5. _____ All languages except Anglo-Saxon contain swear words and obscenities.

Answers for Selection 1

A. Vocabulary

1. inspire
2. rousing
3. crude or indecent
4. curse words or obscenities
5. people who hand-copied manuscripts before the invention of the printing press

B. Content and Structure

1. The most commonly used words in English are of Anglo-Saxon origin.
2. Earthy epithets were imported into English, since Anglo-Saxon lacked these words.
3. sentence 2: MA; sentence 3: MA; sentence 4: MA
4. (b)
5. seafaring and exploration
6. (d)

C. Inferences

1. PA
2. NP
3. NP
4. PI
5. NP

Selection 2

The author, who lived in Belgium before World War II, had a childhood fascination with the Lowara band of Gypsies, who camped every year near his village and who earned their livelihood by horse trading. At the age of 12, in the 1930s, he asked his parents if he could leave home and live with the Gypsies, for at least part of each year, and incredibly, they agreed. This is the opening paragraph of his book recounting his experiences.

¹As I approached the Gypsy camp for the first time, yellow, wild-looking stiff-haired dogs howled and barked. ²Fifteen covered wagons were spread out in a wide half circle, partly hiding the Gypsies from the road. ³Around the campfires sat women draped in deep-colored dresses, their big, expressive eyes and strong, white teeth standing out against their beautiful dark matte skin. ⁴The many gold pieces they wore as earrings, necklaces and bracelets sharpened their color even more. ⁵Their shiny blue-black hair was long and braided, the skirts of their dresses were ankle-length, very full and worn in many layers, and their bodices loose and low-cut. ⁶My first impression of them was one of health and vitality. ⁷Hordes of small barefoot children ran all over the campsite, a few dressed in rags but most nearly naked, rollicking like young animals. ⁸At the far end of the encampment a number of horses, tethered to long chains, were grazing; and of course there were the ever-present half-wild growling dogs. ⁹Several men lay in the shade of an oak tree. ¹⁰Thin corkscrews of bluish smoke rose skyward and the pungent, penetrating smell of burning wood permeated the air. ¹¹Even from a distance the loud, clear voices of these Gypsies resounded with an intensity I was not accustomed to. ¹²Mingling with them, farther away, were the dull thuds of an ax, the snorting and neighing of horses, the occasional snapping of a whip and the high-pitched wail of an infant, contrasting with the whisper of the immediate surroundings of the camp itself.

Jan Yoors, *The Gypsies*

A. *Vocabulary*

For each italicized word from the selection, choose the best definition according to the context in which it appears.

1. *vitality* [sentence 6]:
   (a) laziness.
   (b) enthusiasm.
   (c) curiosity.
   (d) energy.
2. *rollicking* [7]:
   (a) rolling.
   (b) prancing.
   (c) behaving.
   (d) romping.
3. *pungent* [10]:
   (a) sweetish.
   (b) biting.
   (c) sickening.
   (d) familiar.

4. *permeated* [10]:
   (a) perfumed.
   (b) polluted.
   (c) wafted through.
   (d) spread throughout.

B. Content and Structure

Complete the following questions.

1. Find the two nouns that Yoors uses to state his dominant impression

   of these Gypsies. _____

2. Yoors uses many words that appeal to our senses. Which sense is *not* emphasized? Words pertaining to
   (a) sight.
   (b) smell.
   (c) sound.
   (d) touch.

3. Yoors most likely found these Gypsies to be
   (a) weird.
   (b) fascinating.
   (c) alien.
   (d) lazy.

4. A good title for this paragraph would be
   (a) "A Study of Gypsy Life."
   (b) "The Survival of the Gypsies."
   (c) "I Decide to Become a Gypsy."
   (d) "First Impressions of a Gypsy Camp."

C. Inferences

On the basis of the evidence in the paragraph, mark these statements as follows: PA (probably accurate), PI (probably inaccurate), or NP (not in the passage).

1. _____ The Gypsy camp the author came across was in America.

2. _____ The writer had been to the Gypsy camp many times before.

3. _____ Gypsies are persecuted in many European countries.

4. _____ Gypsy culture, at least the culture represented by this group, is essentially nomadic.

5. _____ In Gypsy culture, the women do all the work while the men lie around, enjoying themselves.

6. _____ Despite the children's ragged appearance, they appeared to be happy.

Selection 3

¹In Japan, specially licensed chefs prepare the rarest sashimi delicacy: the white flesh of the puffer fish, served raw and arranged in elaborate floral patterns on a platter. ²Diners pay large sums of money for the carefully prepared dish, which has a light, faintly sweet taste, like raw pompano. ³It had better be carefully prepared, because, unlike pompano, puffer fish is ferociously poisonous. ⁴You wouldn't think a puffer fish would need such chemical armor, since its main form of defense is to swallow great gulps of water and become so bloated it is too large for most predators to swallow. ⁵And yet its skin, ovaries, liver, and intestines contain tetrodotoxin, one of the most poisonous chemicals in the world, hundreds of times more lethal than strychnine or cyanide. ⁶A shred small enough to fit under one's fingernail could kill an entire family. ⁷Unless the poison is completely removed by a deft, experienced chef, the diner will die midmeal. ⁸That's the appeal of the dish; eating the possibility of death, a fright your lips spell out as you dine. ⁹Yet preparing it is a traditional art form in Japan, with widespread aficionados. ¹⁰The most highly respected *fugu* chefs are the ones who manage to leave in the barest touch of the poison, just enough for the diner's lips to tingle from his brush with mortality but not enough to actually kill him. ¹¹Of course, a certain number of diners do die every year from eating *fugu,* but that doesn't stop intrepid *fugu*-fanciers. ¹²The ultimate *fugu* connoisseur orders *chiri,* puffer flesh lightly cooked in a broth made of the poisonous livers and intestines. ¹³It's not that diners don't understand the bizarre danger of puffer-fish toxin. ¹⁴Ancient Egyptian, Chinese, Japanese, and other cultures all describe *fugu* poisoning in excruciating detail: It first produces dizziness, numbness of the mouth and lips, breathing trouble, cramps, blue lips, a desperate itchiness as of insects crawling all over one's body, vomiting, dilated pupils, and then a zombielike sleep, really a kind of neurological paralysis during which the victims are often aware of what's going on around them, and from which they die. ¹⁵But sometimes they wake. ¹⁶If a Japanese man or woman dies of *fugu* poison, the family waits a few days before burying them, just in case they wake up. ¹⁷Every now and then someone poisoned by *fugu* is nearly buried alive, coming to at the last moment to describe in horrifying detail their own funeral and burial, during which, although they desperately tried to cry out or signal that they were still alive, they simply couldn't move.

Diane Ackerman, *A Natural History of the Senses*

A. *Vocabulary*

For each italicized word from the selection, choose the best definition according to the context in which it appears.

1. *deft* [sentence 7]:
   (a) skillful.
   (b) efficient.

    (c) clever.
    (d) well-trained.
2. *aficionados* [9]:
    (a) customers.
    (b) trendsetters.
    (c) gourmets.
    (d) enthusiastic followers.
3. *intrepid* [11]:
    (a) serious.
    (b) courageous.
    (c) foolish.
    (d) stubborn.
4. ultimate [12]: Representing the
    (a) farthest extreme.
    (b) first in a sequence.
    (c) last in a sequence.
    (d) largest.
5. *connoisseur* [12]:
    (a) a newcomer, novice.
    (b) a daredevil.
    (c) a person who does not understand the consequences of his or her actions.
    (d) a person who has knowledge of food, wine, or other esthetic matters.
6. *excruciating* [14]:
    (a) intensely painful and exact.
    (b) overly simplified.
    (c) boring, monotonous.
    (d) nauseating, sickening.

B. Content and Structure

Complete the following questions.

1. With regard to puffer fish, Ackerman's purpose in writing is
    (a) to persuade and encourage the reader to sample it.
    (b) to warn the reader about the dangers of eating it.
    (c) to explain the fundamentals of preparing puffer fish and its appeal.
    (d) to describe its appearance.
2. The main idea of the paragraph is stated in
    (a) sentence 2.
    (b) sentence 5.
    (c) sentence 8.
    (d) sentence 13.

3. In sentence 4 what does Ackerman mean when she compares the puffer fish's poison to armor? _____

_____

4. What inference can we make from sentence 11 about why a certain number of diners die each year from eating *fugu*? _____

_____

_____

5. Why does Ackerman characterize a diner who eats *chiri* as the "ultimate *fugu* connoisseur"? _____

_____

6. Which of the following best describes the author's attitude toward puffer fish connoisseurs?
   (a) She thinks they are weird.
   (b) She thinks they are foolish.
   (c) She thinks they are admirable.
   (d) Her attitude is not evident from the passage.

C. Inferences

On the basis of the evidence in the paragraph, mark these statements as follows: PA (probably accurate), PI (probably inaccurate), or NP (not in the passage).

1. _____ *Fugu* is another word for puffer fish.
2. _____ The puffer fish is poisonous only when it is served raw as sashimi.
3. _____ The danger in eating puffer fish results from the possibility that the chef may leave too much of the poison in the diner's portion.
4. _____ People who eat puffer fish seek the thrill of the possibility of being poisoned.
5. _____ Eating puffer with a tiny amount of poison left in it makes one's entire body feel tingly.
6. _____ The author has sampled puffer fish.
7. _____ Puffer fish is served only in Japan.

■ *PRACTICE ESSAY*

"Making the Grade"
Kurt Wiesenfeld

Each week Newsweek *publishes a column titled "My Turn," in which people in various professions express personal viewpoints. "Making the Grade" is one such article. This particular column written by Kurt Wiesenfeld, a physicist who teaches at Georgia Institute of Technology in Atlanta, caused much discussion among college students and teachers after its publication in the June 17, 1996, issue.*

1   It was a rookie error. After 10 years I should have known better, but I went to my office the day after final grades were posted. There was a tentative knock on the door. "Professor Wiesenfeld? I took your Physics 2121 class? I flunked it? I wonder if there's anything I can do to improve my grade?" I thought: "Why are you asking me? Isn't it too late to worry about it? Do you dislike making declarative statements?"

2   After the student gave his tale of woe and left, the phone rang. "I got a D in your class. Is there any way you can change it to 'Incomplete'?" Then the e-mail assault began: "I'm shy about coming in to talk to you, but I'm not shy about asking for a better grade. Anyway, it's worth a try." The next day I had three phone messages from students asking *me* to call *them*. I didn't.

3   Time was, when you received a grade, that was it. You might groan and moan, but you accepted it as the outcome of your efforts or lack thereof (and, yes, sometimes a tough grader). In the last few years, however, some students have developed a disgruntled-consumer approach. If they don't like their grade, they go to the "return" counter to trade it in for something better.

4   What alarms me is their indifference toward grades as an indication of personal effort and performance. Many, when pressed about why they think they deserve a better grade, admit they don't deserve one but would like one anyway. Having been raised on gold stars for effort and smiley faces for self-esteem, they've learned that they can get by without hard work and real talent if they can talk the professor into giving them a break. This attitude is beyond cynicism. There's a weird innocence to the assumption that one expects (even deserves) a better grade simply by begging for it. With that outlook, I guess I shouldn't be as flabbergasted as I was that 12 students asked me to change their grades *after* final grades were posted.

5   That's 10 percent of my class who let three months of midterms, quizzes and lab reports slide until long past remedy. My graduate student calls it hyperrational thinking: if effort and intelligence don't matter, why should deadlines? What matters is getting a better grade through an unearned bonus, the academic equivalent of a freebie T-shirt or toaster giveaway. Rewards are disconnected from the quality of one's work. An act and its consequences are unrelated, random events.

6   Their arguments for wheedling better grades often ignore academic performance. Perhaps they feel it's not relevant. "If my grade isn't raised to a D I'll lose my scholarship." "If you don't give me a C, I'll flunk out." One sincerely overwrought student pleaded, "If I don't pass, my life is over." This is tough stuff to deal with. Apparently, I'm responsible for someone's losing a scholarship, flunking out or deciding whether life has meaning. Perhaps these students see me as a commodities broker with something they want—a grade. Though intrinsically worthless, grades, if properly manipulated, can be traded for what has value: a degree, which means a job, which means money. The one thing college actually offers—a chance to learn—is considered irrelevant, even less than worthless, because of the long hours and hard work required.

7   In a society saturated with surface values, love of knowledge for its own sake does sound eccentric. The benefits of fame and wealth are more obvious. So is it right to blame students for reflecting the superficial values saturating our society?

8   Yes, of course it's right. These guys had better take themselves seriously now, because our country will be forced to take them seriously later, when the stakes are much higher. They must recognize that their attitude is not only self-destructive, but socially destructive. The erosion of quality control—giving appropriate grades for actual accomplishments—is a major concern in my department. One colleague noted that a physics major could obtain a degree without ever answering a written exam question completely. How? By pulling in enough partial credit and extra credit. And by getting breaks on grades.

9   But what happens once she or he graduates and gets a job? That's when the misfortunes of eroding academic standards multiply. We lament that school children get "kicked upstairs" until they graduate from high school despite being illiterate and mathematically inept, but we seem unconcerned with college graduates whose less blatant deficiencies are far more harmful if their accreditation exceeds their qualifications.

10   Most of my students are science and engineering majors. If they're good at getting partial credit but not at getting the answer right, then the new bridge breaks or the new drug doesn't work. One finds examples here in Atlanta. Last year a light tower in the Olympic Stadium collapsed, killing a worker. It collapsed because an engineer miscalculated

how much weight it could hold. A new 12-story dormitory could develop dangerous cracks due to a foundation that's uneven by more than six inches. The error resulted from incorrect data being fed into a computer. I drive past that dorm daily on my way to work, wondering if a foundation crushed under kilotons of weight is repairable or if this structure will have to be demolished. Two 10,000-pound steel beams at the new natatorium collapsed in March, crashing into the student athletic complex. (Should we give partial credit since no one was hurt?) Those are real-world consequences of errors and lack of expertise.

11   But the lesson is lost on the grade-grousing 10 percent. Say that you won't (not can't, but won't) change the grade they deserve to what they want, and they're frequently bewildered or angry. They don't think it's fair that they're judged according to their performance, not their desires or "potential." They don't think it's fair that they should jeopardize their scholarships or be in danger of flunking out simply because they could not or did not do their work. But it's more than fair; it's necessary to help preserve a minimum standard of quality that our society needs to maintain safety and integrity. I don't know if the 13th-hour students will learn that lesson, but I've learned mine. From now on, after final grades are posted, I'll lie low until the next quarter starts.

A. Comprehension

Choose the answer that best completes each statement. Do not refer to the selection while doing this exercise.

1. Wiesenfeld states that some college students do not consider grades a measure of their
   (a) mastery of the subject.
   (b) personal performance and effort.
   (c) ability to organize their time wisely.
   (d) performance in relation to other students' performance in the class.

2. Some students try to get high grades by
   (a) cheating.
   (b) cramming at the last minute.
   (c) begging and pleading.
   (d) threatening the instructor.

3. The students described in the article receive low grades because they
   (a) attend class sporadically.
   (b) are unprepared academically for the course work.
   (c) work too many hours, which interferes with their studies.
   (d) let an entire semester's work slide without doing anything.

4. The idea that students deserve high grades without working for them reflects
   (a) parental pressure for them to succeed.
   (b) the superficial values of the larger society.
   (c) the importance of getting into a good graduate school.
   (d) grade inflation.

5. One particularly serious consequence of undeserved grades in science and engineering courses is that
   (a) educational standards in other disciplines are also weakened.
   (b) unsafely designed buildings and structures can result in loss of lives.
   (c) graduates expect similar undeserved rewards when they enter the working world.
   (d) professors feel as if they are under siege.

B. Vocabulary

For each italicized word from the selection, write the dictionary definition most appropriate for the context. You may refer to the selection to answer the questions in this section and in all the remaining sections.

1. the e-mail *assault* [paragraph 2]: _____

2. a *disgruntled*-consumer approach [3]: _____

3. *hyperrational* thinking [5]: The prefix *hyper-* means _____

4. *wheedling* better grades [6]: _____

5. sincerely *overwrought* student [6]: _____

6. *intrinsically* worthless [6]: _____

7. illiterate and mathematically *inept* [9]: _____

8. less *blatant* deficiencies [9]: _____

9. *eroding* academic standards [9]: _____

10. maintain safety and *integrity* [11]: _____

C. Inferences

On the basis of the evidence in the paragraph, mark these statements as follows: PA (probably accurate), PI (probably inaccurate), or NP (not in the passage).

1. _____ Many students equate good grades with high salaries rather than with knowledge acquired.

2. _____ It is not only science and engineering students who plead for higher grades; liberal arts students do as well.

3. _____ Parental pressure and the large financial investment college entails may account for some students' begging for grades they do not deserve.

4. _____ The designers of the faulty bridge and the Olympic Stadium light tower received higher grades than they should have in their college courses.

5. _____ Professors in engineering courses should give partial or extra credit on examinations or projects.

6. _____ Professors should understand that today's students are under tremendous pressure and grade more leniently.

D. Structure

Complete the following questions.

1. The mode of discourse represented in this article is
   (a) narration.
   (b) description.
   (c) exposition.
   (d) persuasion.

2. From the information in paragraph 1, explain the "rookie error" that

   Wiesenfeld made. _____

   _____

3. Write a main-idea sentence in your own words for paragraph 4.

   _____

   _____

   _____

4. With respect to the practices of giving partial credit for incomplete answers or giving easy grades, the purpose of paragraphs 7 to 10 is to
   (a) warn the reader about their long-term consequences.
   (b) explain their origins.
   (c) prove how widespread they are.
   (d) present the students' point of view.

5. According to paragraph 10, who was responsible for the uneven foundation in the new dormitory?
   (a) The engineers who designed the building and who had been given partial credit and undeservedly high grades while they were undergraduates.
   (b) Wiesenfeld's own engineering students, who designed the dormitory as a class project.
   (c) The construction firm that cut corners to save money.
   (d) Wiesenfeld does not blame anyone in particular for feeding the computer incorrect data.

Questions for Discussion and Analysis

1. Do you see any contradiction in Wiesenfeld's explanation of what grades mean to many students today and what they should mean? (See paragraphs 3 and 4, in particular, the writer's phrase "their indifference toward grades.")
2. Is Wiesenfeld accurate in his criticism of today's students and their attitude about grades? Do you detect any bias? Does he avoid generalizing about his students, and if so, how? From your experience and observation, comment on his most significant points.

ON THE WEB

The following sites offer two articles on the phenomenon of grade inflation in American colleges and are well worth reading in the light of Wiesenfeld's article.

• Bradford P. Wilson, PhD, "The Phenomenon of Grade Inflation in Higher Education," Meeting of the Governor's Blue Ribbon Commission on Higher Education, Longwood College, Farmville, VA, April 1999.
www.frontpagemag.com/archives/academia/wilson04-13-99.htm
Wilson is the executive director the National Association of Scholars.

• Harvey C. Mansfield, "Grade Inflation: It's Time to Face the Facts," *The Chronicle of Higher Education,* April 6, 2001.
chronicle.com/free/v47/i30/30b02401.htm
Mansfield is a professor of government at Harvard University.

Note that these two websites are the basis of a critical reading exercise in Chapter 10. See page 357.

P A R T

2

Discovering Meaning: The Importance of Form

CHAPTER 3

Four Methods of Paragraph Development

CHAPTER OBJECTIVES

Here is an overview of the methods of paragraph development discussed in this chapter:

- Facts and statistics

- Examples and illustration

- Process (directive and informative)

- Comparison and contrast

■ MODES OF DISCOURSE AND METHODS OF DEVELOPMENT COMPARED

In Chapter 1 you were introduced to the four modes of discourse—narration, description, exposition, and persuasion—that are the predominant forms of writing in nonfiction prose. In Chapters 3 and 4 you will study the methods of paragraph development. These methods refer to various kinds of *evidence*. A main idea cannot be left unexplored; it must be examined, supported, proved, explained, illustrated, or defined, as befits the subject.

How do modes of discourse and methods of development relate to each other? In reading longer pieces, as you have already done with the Practice Essays at the end of Chapters 1 and 2, you see that an essay typically has a predominant mode of discourse, though a secondary one may also be present. For example, the excerpt from Bill Buford's *Among the Thugs* is essentially a narrative, though two or three of the paragraphs contain strong descriptive elements.

On the other hand, the term **methods of development**[1] refers to evidence—ways of supporting an idea *within* a paragraph. In a typical essay, then, a writer might use several methods of development. One paragraph might be developed with facts and statistics; another, with the definition of an ambiguous word; a third, with contrasting information. The choice of method depends on the writer's assessment of how best to clarify and support the main assertion. As you will see, identifying these various methods in an essay will make you a more analytical reader and teach you blueprints for thinking logically. An equally important skill is the ability to *predict* what method of development a writer is likely to use.

■ METHODS OF PARAGRAPH DEVELOPMENT

This chapter introduces you to the four most easily recognizable methods of paragraph development; Chapter 4 takes up the remaining methods. As you study them, you will see that although the majority appear in expository writing, they may be evident in persuasive or argumentative writing as well.

Facts and Statistics

As you learned in Chapter 2, a **fact** is a piece of objective information. Facts are verifiable: One can prove their truth by scientific measurement, by personal observation, by duplication, and so on. **Statistics**

---

[1]Although some teachers of reading use the term *organizational patterns,* I have followed the terminology used in the majority of rhetorically arranged introductory-level composition anthologies. Since the terms *methods of development* and *expository rhetorical modes* are familiar to students in composition courses, I have adhered to this terminology to avoid confusion.

are data in the form of numbers, derived from research studies, polls, census figures, or other similar sources. The use of statistics is the simplest method of development to recognize.[2]

The evidence in this first paragraph, by William Langewiesche, consists of a series of facts regarding camels.

> Camels do not store water in their humps. They drink furiously, up to twenty-eight gallons in a ten-minute session, then distribute the water evenly throughout their bodies. Afterward, they use the water stingily. They have viscous urine and dry feces. They breathe through their noses, and keep their mouths shut. They do sweat, but only as a last resort, after first allowing their body temperatures to rise 10 degrees Fahrenheit. As they begin to dehydrate, the volume of their blood plasma does not at first diminish. They can survive a water loss of up to one-third of their body weight, then drink up and feel fine. Left alone, unhurried and unburdened, they can live two weeks between drinks.
>
> William Langewiesche, *Sahara Unveiled*

The next passage uses statistics pertaining to the numbers of troops who deserted during the Civil War; taken together, the numbers support the idea that such desertions weakened the ability of both the Union and the Confederate armies to fight effectively.

> Desertion, like indiscipline and drunkenness, was a chronic problem during the Civil War—seriously so because it deprived the commanders of the manpower they so badly needed. It was a problem that grew as the war itself endured—the enthusiasm of the two causes abating as the months and years went on and the numbers of casualties grew. The total strength of the Union army was probably 2,900,000, and that of the Confederacy 1,300,000 . . . they suffered staggering casualty totals of 360,000 and 258,000 respectively. The number of men who simply dropped their guns and fled into the forest is almost equally spectacular—287,000 from the Union side, 103,000 from the Southern states. Of course these figures are somewhat distorted: They represent men who fled, were captured, and set to fighting again, only to desert once more and maybe many times subsequently. But they are still gigantic numbers—one in ten in the Union army, one in twelve from the rebels.

---

[2]Ironically, however, statistics are capable of leading readers astray or of presenting false information. One can find numbers to fit any theory, and statistics cited often contradict each other, depending on their source and their purpose in being compiled. A recent book, *Lies! Damned Statistics,* by Joel Best, explains this problem.

By the middle of the war more than five thousand soldiers were deserting every month—some merely dropping behind during the interminable route marches, others fleeing in the face of gunfire. In May 1864—the month when General Grant began his southern progress, and the month of the Wilderness—no fewer than 5,371 Federal soldiers cut and ran. More than 170 left the field every day—they were both draftees and volunteers, and either heartsick or homesick, depressed, bored, disillusioned, unpaid, or just plain scared. William Minor had not merely stumbled from the calm of Connecticut into a scene of carnage and horror: He had also come across a demonstration of man at his least impressive—fearful, depleted in spirit, and cowardly.

Simon Winchester, *The Professor and the Madman*

In the passage, identify in the margin the sentence that states the main idea. Then underline the topic once and the controlling idea twice. Why are the numbers of men who deserted both armies "somewhat

distorted"? _____

_____

The final paragraph in this section uses both facts and statistics. In it, Tom Chaffin, a teacher of U.S. history at Emory University, traced the Oregon Trail from its beginning in St. Louis to the mouth of the Columbia River in Oregon. As he traveled, he stood in the same places that the explorer John C. Frémont had written about in his journal. This particular stopping point was in former Sioux Indian territory along the South Fork of Nebraska's Platte River. (Meta is Chaffin's wife; Zoie is their dog.)

Although the bloodiest chapters of the U.S. wars with the plains Indians were decades away, Frémont's maps and journals anticipated, and in some ways precipitated, the violence to come. "Good guard ought to be kept all the way," Frémont warns of this section of the trail. "Sioux Indians are not to be trusted." A decade after Frémont published his report, the U.S. Army began its thirty-year campaign against the tribes of the plains—a campaign that was, in the long run, horrendously successful. Perhaps nothing so distinguishes the West that Frémont explored from the wilderness preserves and impoverished ranch land through which Meta, Zoie, and I drove as this: In 1842, Native Americans still controlled nearly all of the territory west of the Mississippi and north of the Rio Grande; by 1895, the U.S. had obtained, by chicanery, massacre, diplomacy, and theft, some 90 million acres, or 95 percent, of these lands. Although elsewhere tribes have in recent years reclaimed lost territory and treaty rights, in Nebraska—one third of which

Congress had set aside for the Indians in the 1830s—tribes now control a mere 100 square miles, or one tenth of one percent of the entire state. The only sign of Sioux to be found along this stretch of the Platte today is the occasional billboard for the Rosebud Casino & Quality Inn, located on the Lakota reservation, 150 miles north of here on the South Dakota border.

Tom Chaffin, "How the West Was Lost:
A Road Trip in Search of the Oregon Trail," Harper's

What is the main point Chaffin wants to convey in this paragraph?

_____

_____

_____

Identify the piece of evidence that best supports this point. _____

_____

_____

Examples and Illustration

An **example** is a specific instance of a more general concept. Suppose you come across this sentence in a magazine article:

Miss Plum's Ice Cream Shop in Rockport, Maine, offers a wide variety of exotic flavors.

If the sentence stands alone, the writer is asking the reader to supply his or her own examples. A more careful writer would add three or four examples of "exotic flavors"—perhaps mango-mango, peanut butter toffee, mandarin orange–strawberry, and coconut-pineapple-rum.

A writer may support a general idea by citing two or three specific examples—specific instances—of the main idea or by using a single longer, extended example called an **illustration.** Both methods function in the same way: They point to typical and concrete instances of a more general idea. The only difference between them is that examples are short and are usually found in clusters, whereas an illustration typically involves a little narrative, in effect, an extended and more detailed discussion.

In the following passage, Marjorie Garber develops the main idea with three short examples. Study my annotations to see where each new example begins.

At a time when "universal" ideas and feelings are often compromised or undercut by group identities, the dog tale still has the power to move us. Paradoxically, the dog has become the repository of those model human

1—Lyric dialled 911

2—Sheba rescued puppies

properties which we have cynically ceased to find among human beings. On the evening news and in the morning paper, dog stories supply what used to be called "human interest." There was the story of <u>Lyric</u>, for instance—<u>the 911 dog</u>, who <u>dialled emergency services to save her mistress</u>, and wound up the toast of Disneyland. Or the saga of <u>Sheba</u>, the <u>mother dog in Florida who rescued her puppies</u> after they were buried alive by a cruel human owner. His crime and her heroic single-motherhood were reliable feature stories, edging out mass killings in Bosnia and political infighting at home. Here, after all, were the family values we'd been looking for as a society—right under our noses.

3—Balto brought medicine in diphtheria outbreak

Indeed, at a time of increasing human ambivalence about human heroes and the human capacity for "unconditional love," dog heroes—and dog stories—are with us today more than ever. Near the entrance to Central Park at Fifth Avenue and Sixty-seventh Street stands the statue of <u>Balto</u>, the <u>heroic sled dog</u> who led a team <u>bringing medicine to diphtheria-stricken Nome, Alaska</u>, in <u>the winter of 1925</u>. Balto's story recently became an animated feature film, joining such other big-screen fictional heroes as Lassie, Rin Tin Tin, Benji, and Fluke.

Marjorie Garber, "Dog Days," *The New Yorker*

Write a sentence stating the main idea of the passage. _____

_____

_____

In this next paragraph, Jeffrey Masson and Susan McCarthy use a single dramatic illustration in support of the main idea, which occurs in the first sentence.

Tenderness may also cross the species barrier, with some animals showing distinct pleasure in caretaking. When a young sparrow crash-landed in the chimpanzee cage at the Basel Zoo, one of the apes instantly snatched it in her hand. Expecting to see the bird gobbled up, the keeper was astonished to see the chimpanzee cradle the terrified fledgling tenderly in a cupped palm, gazing at it with what seemed like delight. The other chimpanzees gathered and the bird was delicately passed from hand to hand. The last to receive the bird took it to the bars and handed it to the astounded keeper.

Jeffrey Masson and Susan McCarthy,
When Elephants Weep

Process

Process is the next method of development. There are two kinds of process writing, and both use step-by-step or chronological (time) order. In the **directive** process method, the author explains the steps that *one must follow* to perform a task, such as how to make a pizza, how to develop a photograph, or how to lose ten pounds. Process writing is found most often in laboratory or technical manuals and in how-to and self-help books. In the following paragraph, Jonathan Raban lists the steps he followed to improvise a homemade compass for his young daughter, Julia. I have numbered the steps for easy identification. If you followed the steps, you could duplicate this process yourself.

Such a simple invention, or discovery, the compass. One wet Saturday afternoon, I made one for Julia: *¹*we rubbed the eye of a sewing needle against a magnet on the fridge door; *²*slipped the needle into a sawn-off drinking straw to make it float; and *³*launched it in a water-filled salad bowl. Breasting the resistance of the surface-tension, *⁴*the needle obediently swung slowly around to align itself with the earth's magnetic field, pointing 21½° east of True North. With the sofa to the south, TV to the north, bookshelves to the east, and dining table to the west, *⁵*I set Julia to walking the room on a succession of compass courses. Preschool Navigation: Lesson One.

Jonathan Raban, *Passage to Juneau*

In the **informative** process method, the author describes a phenomenon—how something works, how something developed, or how it came into existence. The informative process, like the directive process, uses chronological order, but the underlying purpose is different: The writer does not expect us to duplicate the process, perhaps because it would be impossible to do so. An especially good example of an informative process occurs in the next paragraph, in which Ruth Brandon describes the "Substitution Trunk," a trick performed by the famous magician and master of illusion, Harry Houdini. For this paragraph, number each step of the process.

The very first trick ever performed by Houdini on the professional stage was a simple but effective illusion known generally as the "Substitution Trunk," though he preferred to call it "Metamorphosis." Houdini and his partner would bring a large trunk onto the stage. It was opened and a sack or bag produced from inside it. Houdini, bound and handcuffed, would get into the sack, which was then sealed or tied around the neck. The trunk was closed over the bag and its occupant. It was locked, strapped and chained. Then a screen was drawn around it. The partner (after they married, this was always Mrs. Houdini) stepped behind the screen which, next moment, was thrown aside—by Houdini himself. The partner had meanwhile disappeared. A committee of the audience was called onstage to verify that the ties, straps, etc., around the trunk had not been tampered with. These were then laboriously loosened; the trunk was opened; and there, inside the securely fastened bag, was—Mrs. Houdini!

Ruth Brandon, The Life and Many Deaths of Harry Houdini

What phrase serves as the controlling idea for the paragraph? _____

_____

Comparison and Contrast

The method of **comparison and contrast** is used to explain similarities and differences between two subjects. **Comparison** discusses *similarities,* often between two apparently dissimilar things, for example, how building a house is like writing an essay. But comparison can also be used to examine two related things. If a writer in an automotive magazine, for example, were to compare two *cars,* two Japanese imported cars—say, Toyotas and Hondas—he or she would focus on insightful or significant similarities, rather than on obvious ones. That both types have steering wheels, engines, brakes, and other necessary equipment is hardly worth pointing out. In trying to recommend which make to buy, the writer would note the significant similarities in body styling, structural workmanship, and fuel efficiency. He or she might then assess the differences, the contrasting points.

A discussion of insightful similarities is undertaken by Peter Steinhart in this next excerpt. Note that he opens with a rather questionable assertion—that we are more similar to wolves than to any other animal. Then he continues to show that, although we are structurally closer to chimpanzees and gorillas, our behavior is more similar to that of wolves.

We are drawn to wolves because no other animal is so like us. Of all the rest of creation, wolves reflect our own images back to us most dramatically, most realistically, and most intensely. We recognize chimpanzees and gorillas, which are more like us in body structure and which show capacities for language and tool-making, as our closest evolutionary relatives. But long ago we diverged from chimpanzees and gorillas, and we have been shaped by different habits. As a result, though we are in many ways like chimpanzees, we are in some ways more like wolves. Like wolves, we evolved as hunters; we have long legs and considerable powers of endurance, adaptations to the chase rather than to hiding; we have minds that are capable of fine calculation, not just of spatial relationships, but of strategy and coordination. Like wolves, we band together to kill larger prey, and that has given us a different social system and a different personality from the chimpanzee; we have long childhoods, strong social bonds, complex social roles, and status differences; we tend to claim and defend territories; we have complex forms of communication; we are individuals; we have strong emotions. Humans and wolves are so much alike that they take an unusual interest in one another. Wild wolves have often followed humans with what the humans felt was friendly curiosity, perhaps even a desire for company. And humans have, for thousands of years, adopted wolves and felt with them a mutual sense of companionship.

Peter Steinhart, *The Company of Wolves*

Steinhart's writing is easy to follow because the key phrase "like wolves" is repeated at the beginning of two sentences. Write two other

phrases that suggest a comparison. _____

_____

    Contrast properly refers to a discussion of the *differences* between two related or similar things—for example, the presidential terms of George Bush and of his son, George W. Bush; *Star Wars* and its first sequel, *The Empire Strikes Back;* or the German import the VW Passat and the American-made Ford Taurus. Comparison and contrast may be used together or singly, depending on the subject and the author's purpose. Contrast is the dominant method of development in this next passage, also by Peter Steinhart, in which he shows the evolutionary differences between cats and dogs.

Cats split off the line that would lead to dogs about forty million years ago. The differences between dogs and cats tell much about the kinds of choices that were being made. Dogs are relatively long-limbed and slender-bodied. The lower part of the leg is generally longer than the upper part, for greater leverage. Dogs evolved in open country, where hunting requires pursuit. They are built for speed and endurance. Cats, on the other hand, are designed largely to lie in wait and take prey by stealth. Because they are built for speed, dogs walk on the very tips of their toes. Cats are slightly more flat-footed, a trait that allows them to maintain sharp claws, whereas dogs wear theirs down. Cats have wrists that turn, and with their extensible claws they can grab a prey and hold on to it while biting. . . .

Dog skulls tell yet more about evolution's choices. Cats are shorter-muzzled and have, for the size of their jaws, a more powerful bite than dogs. A lion, for instance, can bite through the neck of a buffalo. Cats tend to hunt alone, coming together solely to breed. Only lions and cheetahs hunt in groups. The solitary habit probably explains, too, why the largest cats are larger than the largest dogs. A single lion or tiger or leopard can bring down a large prey that even a pack of dogs might be unable to tackle.

Peter Steinhart, *The Company of Wolves*

List the four main differences between dogs and cats. _____

_____

A paragraph developed by comparison or contrast does not have to give equal treatment to the two subjects under discussion. Read this excerpt by Luis Alberto Urrea.

> One of the most beautiful views of San Diego is from the summit of a small hill in Tijuana's municipal garbage dump. People live on that hill, picking through the trash with long poles that end in hooks made of bent nails. They scavenge for bottles, tin, aluminum, cloth; for cast-out beds, wood, furniture. Sometimes they find meat that is not too rotten to be cooked.
>
> This view-spot is where the city drops off its dead animals—dogs, cats, sometimes goats, horses. They are piled in heaps six feet high and torched. In that stinking blue haze, amid nightmarish sculptures of charred ribs and carbonized tails, the garbage-pickers can watch the buildings of San Diego gleam gold on the blue coastline. The city looks cool in the summer when heat cracks the ground and flies drill into their noses. And in the winter, when windchill drops night temperatures into the low thirties, when the cold makes their lips bleed, and rain turns the hill into a gray pudding of ash and mud, and babies are wrapped in plastic trash bags for warmth, San Diego glows like a big electric dream. And every night on that burnt hill, these people watch.
>
> Luis Alberto Urrea, *Across the Wire: Life and Hard Times on the Mexican Border*

Why does Urrea focus more on the Tijuana side of the border than on

the American side? _____

_____

_____

Practice Exercise Read the following passages. First, decide which of the following methods of development predominates:

- Facts and statistics
- Examples and illustration
- Process (directive or informative)
- Comparison and contrast

Then write a sentence stating the main idea in your own words.

The difference between spinning and fly casting lies mostly with the reel. A spinning reel has a fixed spool. When you cast with it, the weight of the lure uncoils your line and pulls it out. By contrast, a fly is almost weightless. What you actually cast with a fly rod is your line. Fly line is heavy. The earliest types were made of braided horsehair, but now they are usually nylon coated with heat-cured plastic. The line used on spinning reels is called monofilament—a single strand of nylon, much like the leader material you tie to the end of a plastic-coated fly line. Spinning tackle, which originated in Europe, became popular in the United States in the nineteen-forties, and in many respects it represents a technological advance over fly tackle. Yet the best and most discriminating anglers always prefer to fish for trout with flies. This is something of an anomaly in sporting life. You don't find tennis players tossing out their jumbo graphite racquets and replacing them with old-fashioned wood.

Bill Barich, *The Sporting Life*

Method of development: _____

Main idea: _____

_____

. . . pasta is far easier to cook than to classify. Choose a good brand made exclusively from durum wheat. Boil water, add coarse salt, toss in the pasta, and stir to prevent sticking. Check regularly by biting a piece in two. Chew attentively, testing for firmness without a hint of granularity against the teeth—perfectly cooked pasta is al dente, literally "to the tooth." Then scan the remaining section for that faint white trace in the middle that some Italians call the anima, the soul, of perfectly cooked pasta. Don't add oil to the water or on any account throw a strand of pasta against the wall to see if it sticks. Italians have never heard of these bizarre practices, mutations probably born in the 19th-century United States that are about as Italian as canned elbow macaroni.

Tom Mueller, "Cultural Icon," *Hemispheres*

Method of development: _____

Main idea: _____

_____

Some animals have senses humans do not possess, capacities only recently discovered. Other animal senses may remain to be discovered. By extension, could there be feelings animals have that humans do not, and if so, how would we know? It will take scientific humility and philosophical creativity to provide even the beginning of an answer.

A mother lion observed by George Schaller had left her three small cubs under a fallen tree. While she was away, two lions from another pride killed the cubs. One male ate part of one of the cubs. The second carried a cub away, holding it as he would a food item, not as a cub. He stopped from time to time to lick it and later nestled it between his paws. Ten hours later, he still had not eaten it. When the mother returned and found what had happened, she sniffed the last dead cub, licked it, and then sat down and ate it, except for the head and front paws.

This mother lion was acting like a lion, not like a person. But in understanding what lions do, what she felt is part of the picture. Maybe she felt closer to her dead offspring when it was part of her body once again. Maybe she hates waste, or cleans up all messes her cubs make, as part of her love. Maybe this is a lion funeral rite. Or maybe it is something only a lion can feel.

Jeffrey Masson and Susan McCarthy, *When Elephants Weep*

Method of development: _____

Main idea: _____

_____

No technology has ever become so ubiquitous so fast. It took the telephone forty years to reach its first ten million customers; fax machines were adopted that widely in less than half the time. Personal computers made it to ten million American homes within five years after they were introduced, in 1981, but E-mail reached that many users in little more than a year. In fact, in 1995, the amount of electronic mail delivered in the United States surpassed the amount of "snail" mail printed on paper and handled by the United States Postal Service. Among those few people who noticed were worried postal officials; recent predictions suggest that the volume of first-class mail delivered in the United States will peak in 2002. After that, the trend lines all point seriously in the wrong direction. It is impossible to predict how many of America's 38,019 post offices will be around in a decade, but, unless the Postal Service manages to ship a large percentage of all future purchases made on the Internet, the number certainly isn't going to be anywhere near thirty-eight thousand. So E-mail matters.

Michael Specter, "Your Mail Has Vanished," *The New Yorker*

Method of development: _____

Main idea: _____

_____

In a sense, tabloids—that is, news in condensed form (the word "tabloid" was registered in 1884 as a trademark to describe condensed substances used in pharmacy)—have been with us in oral tradition ever since people began entertaining one another with ballads and popular stories. A seventeenth-century ballad told of a phantom drummer who threw children out of bed. The 10 November 1992 *Sun* features a story with pictures: YOUNG FAMILY FLED THEIR HOME IN HORROR AFTER A CHILD-HATING SPIRIT REPEATEDLY TERRORIZED THEIR LITTLE BOYS. Printing presses, once developed, were often used for single newssheets—broadsides— to satisfy a universal human desire to read about sensational events. An early broadside tells the story of one Mary Dudson, who swallowed a small snake that grew inside her and eventually killed her. In 1924, the *New York World* published a story about a girl who died and was found to be "harboring" a living snake that had hatched from an egg she had swallowed. *WWN* of 10 November 1992: X-RAY SHOWS LIVE SNAKE TRAPPED IN MAN'S STOMACH.

Sue Hubbell, "Space Aliens Take Over the U.S. Senate!!!" *Far-Flung Hubbell*

Method of development: _____

Main idea: _____

_____

Combination of Methods	Finally, you should recognize that, like many of life's challenges, the task of reading is a complex undertaking. Not all paragraphs can be as neatly categorized as those you have examined here. Although some writers use an easily recognizable method of development, many do not. In particular, within an essay or article, a writer may use several different methods from paragraph to paragraph or within the same passage. In the following passage, Michael Specter examines the new technology called GPS, which stands for "global positioning system," now available on some makes of automobiles. As you read the passage, try to identify the various expository methods of development it encompasses.

Twenty-four satellites, along with four spares, circle the planet twice each day. They move in six orbital planes, placing, in effect, a giant birdcage around the Earth, assuring that there will usually be eight satellites in range. The satellites send out a constant stream of radio signals that contain information about their orbit and speed, along with the exact time. That allows them to deliver precise location information to anyone who has a device that can receive the signals. The receiver works like a radio: to establish a location, one need only turn it on.

The satellites function as reference points—the way stars once did for mariners—and not since the twelfth century, when the compass came into use, has a navigational tool promised to more fundamentally alter the way we live. Within a few years, every cell phone, quartz watch, and laptop computer may come with a tiny G.P.S. receiver embedded in it. In fact, by December 31, 2002, federal law will require cellular carriers to be able to locate the position of every user making a 911 call. That should eventually make it possible for emergency personnel to find anyone in America who calls 911.

Though there are earthbound means of complying with the new "E911" mandate, many carriers will rely on G.P.S. technology. The National Park Service is already using G.P.S. to map trails, keep their snowplows on the road, and even track bears. Air routes routinely have a geographical tag and so do coastal waterways and shipping lanes. It is even possible to rig a driver's air bag so that, as it is deployed, it activates a G.P.S. device that reports the car's location to the nearest ambulance. Our children may never fully understand the word "lost"—just as few people under the age of ten have any idea what it means to "dial" a phone number.

Michael Specter, "No Place to Hide," *The New Yorker*

List the methods of development (I counted three.) _____

_____

■ CONCLUSION: METHODS OF DEVELOPMENT AND PATTERNS OF THOUGHT

The methods of development you have just studied parallel the ways we impose order on our thought processes. Consider these real-life situations, and decide which method of development underlies the mental process involved.

1. You want to build a new cabinet for your CD player, TV, and

   DVD player. _____
2. Are flat-panel computer screens really better than the

   conventional kind? _____
3. How are the other students in my section of Physics 1 performing

   in the class? _____

4. A friend from Arkansas decides she wants to move to Chicago, where you live. She writes, asking you about apartment rents in various parts of the city. _____

5. Your 10-year-old niece asks you how babies are born. _____

_____

■ CHAPTER EXERCISES

Selection 1   Jeremy Iggers writes on ethics and reviews restaurants for the *Minneapolis–St. Paul Star Tribune.*

[1]Consider just how guilt-ridden our relationship with food has become. [2]Today, there is hardly an element in the American diet that doesn't carry some moral stain.

[3]Bumper stickers remind us that meat is murder, and magazine ads confront us with gruesome pictures of anemic penned-up calves, brood sows chained to concrete slabs, hens stuffed in wire mesh cages, downed cattle in slaughterhouses. [4]We turn away but the images remain. [5]The pride we once felt in producing the cheapest food in the world has given way to guilt over how it is produced: over the exploitation of farmworkers; the profligate use of pesticides and synthetic fertilizers; the destruction of family farms, rural economies, and the natural environment.

[6]We feel guilty, too, about eating foods that contain too much fat and too much cholesterol. [7]This goes far beyond a prudent concern for our health and appearance; it takes on strong overtones of guilt and moral judgment as we wrestle with our own weakness, with our inability to keep our bodies under control. [8]And this isn't a moral judgment we impose exclusively on ourselves; it is also a judgment that we make on others, and they on us. [9]To paraphrase Will Rogers, it's no sin to be fat, but it might as well be.

Jeremy Iggers, "Innocence Lost," *Utne Reader*

A. *Vocabulary*

For each italicized word from the selection, choose the best definition according to the context in which it appears.

1. *gruesome* pictures [sentence 3]:
    (a) realistic, vivid.
    (b) exhaustive, thorough.
    (c) arousing sympathy.
    (d) repugnant, horrible.

2. the *profligate* use of pesticides [5]:
    (a) recklessly extravagant.
    (b) damaging to the environment.
    (c) morally depraved.
    (d) liberally generous.
3. a *prudent* concern [7]:
    (a) obsessive.
    (b) wise.
    (c) showing poor judgment.
    (d) uncontrollable.

B. Content and Structure

Complete the following questions.

1. Locate the sentence that states the main idea. Underline the topic once and the controlling idea twice.
2. With respect to our attitudes toward food, the writer's purpose is to
    (a) examine the reasons that account for these attitudes.
    (b) persuade us that these attitudes are damaging.
    (c) provide solutions to the problem these attitudes give rise to.
    (d) demonstrate how widespread these attitudes have become.
3. The method of paragraph development from sentences 3 to 6 is
    (a) facts and statistics.
    (b) informative process.
    (c) comparison.
    (d) examples.
4. Label these ideas from the first two paragraphs as follows: MAIN (main idea); MA (major support); or MI (minor support):
    (a) _____ Consider just how guilt-ridden our relationship with food has become.
    (b) _____ Today, there is hardly an element in the American diet that doesn't carry some moral stain.
    (c) _____ Bumper stickers remind us that meat is murder, and magazine ads confront us with gruesome pictures of anemic penned-up calves, brood sows chained to concrete slabs, hens stuffed in wire mesh cages, downed cattle in slaughterhouses.
    (d) _____ We turn away but the images remain.
    (e) _____ The pride we once felt in producing the cheapest food in the world has given way to guilt over how it is produced: over the exploitation of farmworkers; the profligate use of pesticides and synthetic fertilizers; the destruction of family farms, rural economies, and the natural environment.

5. The writer keeps us on track and establishes coherence by repeating the controlling idea and by using synonyms for it. Identify these

   words and phrases. _____

   _____

6. We can infer from the passage that guilt feelings about what we eat are
   (a) both excessive and unhealthy.
   (b) fostered entirely by the media.
   (c) both positive and long overdue, as too many Americans are seriously overweight.
   (d) shared by residents of other developed nations.

Answers for Selection 1

A. *Vocabulary*

1. (d)
2. (a)
3. (b)

B. *Content and Structure*

1. Consider just how <u>guilt-ridden</u> <u>our relationship with food</u> <u>has become</u>.
2. (d)
3. (d)
4. (a) MAIN; (b) MA; (c) MI; (d) MA; (e) MA.
5. "moral stain," "guilt," "goes far beyond a prudent concern," and "strong overtones of guilt and moral judgment"
6. (a)

Selection 2

[1]So many disturbing traits, once you look into them—with a somewhat morbid curiosity, I'd begun prowling around the University Science Library,[3] an airy new building with gestures toward native construction materials, a self-conscious sensitivity to the surrounding redwoods, and the rational and anti-septic calm of too many quantitative minds padding silently down well-carpeted corridors. [2]A few tidbits: sharks are the world's only known *intrauterine cannibals;* as eggs hatch within a uterus, the unborn young fight and devour each other until one well-adapted predator emerges. [3](If the womb is a battleground, what then the sea?) [4]Also, without the gas-filled bladders that float other fish, sharks, if they stop swimming, sink. [5]This explains their

[3]The library Duane refers to is at the University of California at Santa Cruz.

tendency to lurk along the bottom like twenty-one-foot, 4,600-pound benthic land mines with hundred-year life spans. **6**Hard skin bristling with tiny teeth sheathes their flexible cartilage skeletons—no bone at all. **7**Conical snouts, black eyes without visible pupils, black-tipped pectoral fins. **8**Tearing out and constantly being replaced, their serrated fangs have as many as twenty-eight stacked spares (a bite meter embedded in a slab of meat once measured a dusky shark's bite at eighteen tons per square inch). **9**And all of the following have been found in shark bellies: a goat, a tomcat, three birds, a raincoat, overcoats, a car license plate, grass, tin cans, a cow's head, shoes, leggings, buttons, belts, hens, roosters, a nearly whole reindeer, even a headless human in a full suit of armor. **10**Swimming with their mouths open, great whites are indiscriminate recyclers of the organic—my sensitive disposition, loving family and affection for life, my decent pickup, room full of books, preoccupation with chocolate in the afternoons, and tendency to take things too personally: all immaterial to my status as protein.

Daniel Duane, *Caught Inside: A Surfer's Year on the California Coast*

A. Vocabulary

For each italicized word from the selection, write the dictionary definition most appropriate for the context.

1. *morbid* [sentence 1]: _____

   _____

2. *lurk* [5]: _____

3. *serrated* [8]: _____

B. Content and Structure

Complete the following questions.

1. Locate the topic of the paragraph. _____

   Then write the controlling idea. _____

2. Consider again the phrase you wrote for the question above. Which of the following methods of development in the remainder of the paragraph is most evident as support for that phrase?
   (a) informative process.
   (b) comparison.
   (c) contrast.
   (d) example.
   (e) illustration.

3. Paraphrase Duane's parenthetical remark from sentence 3: "If the womb is a battleground, what then the sea?" _____

_____

_____

4. Why must sharks constantly swim? _____

_____

5. Look again at sentence 5, in which Duane imaginatively compares the shark to "a benthic land mine." (*Benthic* is an adjective referring to benthos, or organisms that live on ocean or lake bottoms.) What does Duane intend to suggest in this comparison?

_____

_____

6. From the information given in sentences 9 and 10, we can conclude that sharks
   (a) can and will eat anything, whether it is food or not.
   (b) prefer humans to any other food.
   (c) are basically carnivorous.
   (d) are able to digest inorganic objects.

7. Consider again the list of items found in sharks' stomachs. Now read sentence 10 again and locate the phrase that best describes

sharks' function in the ocean. _____

_____

Selection 3

Suketu Mehta, the writer of the following passage, was born in Calcutta and grew up in Bombay. Mumbai, the new official name of Bombay, is the biggest city in India, with a population of over 12 million people. Understanding the impact of this passage requires a little background about India's caste system. A caste is a social hierarchy. In traditional Indian society, Brahmins were at the top, followed by four different Hindu castes, then Muslims, and finally, the so-called untouchables, the lowest caste, who performed menial jobs such as sweeping streets and collecting garbage. The caste system has been officially illegal for many years, and discrimination based on one's caste is prohibited. Yet the system remains ingrained in behavior, and remnants persist.[4] Mehta's passage presents a rather different version of human behavior.

1The manager of Bombay's suburban railway system was recently asked when the system would improve to a point where it could carry its five million daily passengers in comfort. 'Not in my lifetime,' he answered. Certainly, if you commute into Bombay, you are made aware of the precise temperature of the human body as it curls around you on all sides, adjusting itself to every curve of your own. A lover's embrace was never so close.

2One morning I took the rush hour train to Jogeshwari. There was a crush of passengers, and I could only get halfway into the carriage. As the train gathered speed, I hung on to the top of the open door. I feared I would be pushed out, but someone reassured me: 'Don't worry, if they push you out they also pull you in.'

3Asad Bin Saif is a scholar of the slums, moving tirelessly among the sewers, cataloguing numberless communal flare-ups and riots, seeing first-hand the slow destruction of the social fabric of the city. He is from Bhagalpur, in Bihar, site not only of some of the worst rioting in the nation, but also of a famous incident in 1980, in which the police blinded a group of criminals with knitting needles and acid. Asad, of all people, has seen humanity at its worst. I asked him if he felt pessimistic about the human race.

4'Not at all,' he replied. 'Look at the hands from the trains.'

5If you are late for work in Bombay, and reach the station just as the train is leaving the platform, you can run up to the packed compartments and you will find many hands stretching out to grab you on board, unfolding outward from the train like petals. As you run alongside you will be picked up, and some tiny space will be made for your feet on the edge of the open doorway. The rest is up to you; you will probably have to hang on to the door frame with your fingertips, being careful not to lean out too far lest you get decapitated by a pole placed close to the tracks. But consider what has happened: your fellow passengers, already packed tighter than cattle are legally allowed to be, their shirts drenched with sweat in the badly ventilated compartment, having stood like this for hours, retain an empathy for you, know that your boss might yell at you or cut your pay if you miss this train and will make space where none exists to take one more person with them. And at the moment of contact, they do not

---

[4]A recent example occurred in the aftermath of the devastating earthquake that hit the state of Gujarat in the winter of 2001. Residents complained that when relief groups arrived to help, officials presented them with six lists of residents according to their caste. As reported in an Associated Press article, "those at the top of the pecking order use their connections and prestige to get the pick of the goods." Quoted in Joseph Coleman, "Caste System Complicates Relief Efforts after Indian Quake," February 2001.

know if the hand that is reaching for theirs belongs to a Hindu or Muslim or Christian or Brahmin or untouchable or whether you were born in this city or arrived only this morning or whether you live in Malabar Hill or Jogeshwari; whether you're from Bombay or Mumbai or New York. All they know is that you're trying to get to the city of gold, and that's enough. Come on board, they say. We'll adjust.

Suketu Mehta, "Mumbai: A Lover's Embrace," *Granta*

A. *Vocabulary*

For each italicized word from the selection, write the dictionary definition most appropriate for the context.

1. *cataloguing* numberless communal flare-ups [paragraph 3]:

   _____

2. numberless communal *flare-ups* [3] _____

3. retain an *empathy* for you [5]: _____

B. *Content and Structure*

Complete the following questions.

1. What central impression do paragraphs 1 and 2 convey about

   Bombay's railway system? _____

   _____

2. The behavior of the railway passengers on the trains leading to Bombay has led Asad Bin Saif, the "scholar of the slums" mentioned in paragraph 3, to be
   (a) optimistic about the human race.
   (b) pessimistic about the human race.
   (c) antisocial and isolated from the human race.
   (d) indifferent, callous toward the human race.

3. What method of development is represented in paragraph 5?
   (a) process.
   (b) comparison.
   (c) contrast.
   (d) illustration.
   (e) facts.

4. In paragraph 5, locate the verb phrase "retain an empathy for." Then, in the same sentence, locate the *subject* that goes with this verb

   phrase. _____

5. What emotion or motivation governs those already on the trains to

    pull latecomers on board? _____

    _____

6. What is the point, the larger lesson, of the story related in paragraph 5?

    _____

    _____

    _____

■ *PRACTICE ESSAY*

"Book of Dreams: The Sears Roebuck Catalog"
Rose Del Castillo Guilbault

*In 1993 Sears Roebuck & Company announced that it would stop publishing
its mail-order catalog, a venerable institution begun in 1886. For generations
Americans had shopped at home with the catalog, especially farm families,
who made infrequent trips to town.*

> *Rose Guilbault was born in Mexico and later immigrated with her
family to the United States, where they settled in the Salinas Valley, an
agricultural area in central California. She writes of her childhood that she
discovered books early on, but she never had enough books to read. The
local library allowed children to check out only two books at a time, and her
father could take her to town only twice a month. Guilbault has had a
varied career in journalism: She formerly wrote a column for the Sunday*
San Francisco Chronicle, *called "Hispanic, USA"; she worked in
community relations, public relations, and production for three Bay Area
television stations; currently, she is vice president of corporate
communications and public affairs for the California State Automobile
Association.*

1   The news that Sears is closing 113 stores and folding its 97-year-old
catalog sent me scurrying through the basement in search of one of my
favorite possessions, a 1941 Sears Roebuck & Company catalog. I was
relieved to find it, still inside a metal filing cabinet, underneath a jum-
ble of old Chronicles and a 1939 *Liberty* magazine.

2   I've always had an affinity for the 1940s. I love the Big Band music,
the movies and the fashions. As a child I sat mesmerized, listening to
my mother's stories about dances under the stars where local groups
played and my young mother and her sisters flirted the night away.

3   But that's not the only reason I've held onto this ragged catalog through college, marriage, children and numerous moves. It symbolizes the America my parents and I believed in when we arrived in this country from Mexico. An America where everything you could possibly want was in an emporium inside a book. A book that came to your home from which you could leisurely, conveniently choose items that would be delivered to your doorstep. The concept was amazing to us. This wasn't about accumulating goods but about obtaining a piece of the American pie.

4   Many of today's immigrants are easily caught in this country's web of materialism, easy credit and easy debt. But in the early '60s, the values in rural areas were different. These "wish books" were a metaphor for America's bounty and what could be had with hard work.

5   Every new catalog was savored. We all had our own dream sections. Papa, eyes sparkling, would ease himself into his chair after dinner and briskly examine the tools, hunting rifles and cameras. Then he'd pass the catalog to Mama, who—for what seemed to me to be hours—studied the pretty dresses, household appliances, dishes and plants.

6   By the time the catalog made its way into my hands, my palms itched with anxiety. At Easter time, I would lose myself in pages of frilly, pastel dresses with matching hats and purses. In the Christmas season, which brought my favorite edition of the year, I would sit for hours, staring glassy-eyed at the pages of toys, dolls and games.

7   But nothing frivolous was ever ordered. We lived on a farm in the Salinas Valley, miles and miles from a big city and miles from the nearest small town. To get there, you'd turn off the main paved road onto a bumpy dirt trail that led to two farmhouses—one big one where the boss and his family lived, and a small, four-room cottage where we lived. The inside was sparsely furnished, mostly with hand-me-down furniture from the boss, except for the spindly TV and a cheap, forest-green nylon sofa set my father bought my mother as a wedding gift.

8   Extravagances were unaffordable. Only the most practical and necessary items would be given consideration—my mother's first washing machine, a school coat for me, and thick, dark denim overalls to keep Papa warm in the frostiest of dawns.

9   The Sears catalog had other uses. I'd cut out the models and use them as paper dolls. My mother would match English words with pictures, *"Y estas ollas? Seran "pots" en ingles?"* And in my most desperate hours of boredom, when only sports programs dominated afternoon television, rain fell outdoors, and absolutely nothing interested me indoors, I'd pick up the thick catalog, sit in the bedroom with the faded cabbage-rose print linoleum and spin fantasies about living the good life I imagined the Americans in the catalogs lived.

10   In the front of my 1941 Sears catalog are two stories about typical Sears customers. One profiles the Browns of Washington state, who arrived there as homesteaders, lived in a tent with their children, until their farm produced enough for them to build a two-room shack, and eventually build a comfortable white clapboard farmhouse on their land. Photos show Mr. and Mrs. Brown with their new cream separator, daughter Evelyn with her new Elgin bicycle, and the whole family listening to their silver-tone radio-phonograph—all from Sears, of course.

11   The second article describes the Yeamens of Glendale, in Los Angeles County. Mr. Yeamen works at Lockheed Aviation, a mile and a half commute from their "modern, five-room bungalow . . . with a barbecue grill in the back yard and a view of the mountains from every window." Photographs show the various family members with their Sears products: Dad relaxing on a glider swing in the back yard, Mom putting avocado sandwiches in lunch boxes and the kids romping in their stylish clothes.

12   The Browns and Yeamens, the catalog summarizes, are what all of us want to be—good, solid, dependable Americans.

13   As corny and blatantly commercial as these stories are, I like reading them. It reminds me of the America of my youth, or perhaps of my imagination. Even though my family of Mexican immigrants probably didn't have a whole lot in common with the Browns and the Yeamens, we all shopped from that Sears Catalog—a book that made us believe everything was reachable, and ours to have.

14   My family prospered too. Not in great leaps and bounds like the Browns of Washington state, but little by little. Our progress was marked by the occasional splurge from the Sears catalog.

15   When I got to the point where I had to own my own clarinet or drop out of the school band—there was a limit to how long we could borrow from the music department—my family had to make a choice. I was not a great musician; we all knew that. But the band was a wholesome activity that integrated me into school life, into America. One evening after dinner, my parents called me into the living room. I searched their faces for a clue, but they remained mysteriously impassive until my father brought out a wrinkled brown package from behind his back.

16   My heart began pounding when I saw the Sears return address. Out came a compact gray and white case, and inside it, lying on an elegant bed of royal blue rayon velvet, were the pieces of a brand-new ebony clarinet. Never in my stolen afternoons with the Sears catalog had I imagined possessing something so fine!

17   Somehow I can't envision today's kids reminiscing about a Lands' End or Victoria's Secret catalog. Times have changed, and so have demographics. People in rural America no longer need a catalog. They now have Kmarts or Wal-Marts in their own mini-malls.

18   Newspaper articles reporting on the Sears closures have described the catalog as "the best record of American material culture." But to many of us, this catalog wasn't about materialism at all. It was about making dreams come true.

A. *Comprehension*

Choose the answer that best completes each statement. Do not refer to the selection while doing this exercise.

1. For Guilbault, the Sears Roebuck catalog primarily represented
   (a) an unobtainable vision of America for her and her family.
   (b) the possibility of obtaining a piece of the American pie.
   (c) a simpler, less stressful life.
   (d) a convenient way to shop for necessities at home.

2. For the author and her family, the most important American virtue was
   (a) a competitive spirit.
   (b) generosity.
   (c) hard work.
   (d) the desire for an education.

3. Guilbualt's mother looked at the catalog both to enjoy the pictures of clothing and household items and to
   (a) get ideas for gifts.
   (b) practice English.
   (c) covet the possessions of the wealthier families depicted.
   (d) help choose farm equipment with her husband.

4. The catalog's description of the model families—the Browns and the Yeamans—suggested that
   (a) her family was just like them.
   (b) America was not really the land of opportunity.
   (c) it was important to buy one's belongings from Sears.
   (d) everything in America was reachable.

5. Guilbualt remembers one especially memorable acquisition, a clarinet. Aside from marking her family's economic prosperity, this purchase also
   (a) meant that she could reach her dream of becoming a great musician.
   (b) improved her social status at school.
   (c) allowed her to be integrated into American life.
   (d) contributed to the family's love of music.

B. *Vocabulary*

For each italicized word from the selection, choose the best definition according to the context in which it appears. You may refer to the selection to answer the questions in this section and in all the remaining sections.

1. an *affinity* for the 1940s [paragraph 2]:
    (a) natural attraction.
    (b) obsession.
    (c) slight interest in.
    (d) reaction.
2. an *emporium* inside a book [3]:
    (a) playground.
    (b) educational center.
    (c) imaginary toyland.
    (d) large retail store.
3. a metaphor for America's *bounty* [4]:
    (a) high reputation.
    (b) amalgamation of goods and services.
    (c) generosity, liberality in giving.
    (d) treasure chest.
4. nothing *frivolous* was ever ordered [7]:
    (a) insignificant, trivial.
    (b) attractive, esthetically pleasing.
    (c) expensive, costly.
    (d) of good quality.
5. they remained mysteriously *impassive* [15]:
    (a) silent, withdrawn.
    (b) showing no emotion.
    (c) excited, jubilant.
    (d) embarrassed, uncomfortable.
6. [t]imes have changed, and so have *demographics* [17]: The study of
    (a) social values.
    (b) populations and their characteristics.
    (c) ethnic and minority groups.
    (d) social classes.

C. Structure

Complete the following questions.

1. This article has a clear beginning, middle, and end. Locate the major divisions in the essay and indicate the appropriate paragraph numbers.

    Introduction: _____

    Body: _____

    Conclusion: _____

2. With respect to her childhood and the role the Sears Roebuck catalog played in her family, what is the author's point of view?
    (a) nostalgic.
    (b) objective.
    (c) envious.
    (d) philosophical.
    (e) self-pitying.

3. What method of development is used in paragraph 4?
    (a) example.
    (b) process.
    (c) comparison.
    (d) contrast.

4. What primary method of development is used in paragraphs 5 to 9?
    (a) example.
    (b) comparison.
    (c) contrast.
    (d) process.

5. What is the relationship between paragraph 14 and paragraphs 15 and 16?
    (a) They all represent steps in an informative process.
    (b) Paragraph 14 includes a term to be defined, and the other two define it.
    (c) Paragraphs 15 and 16 offer a contrast to paragraph 14.
    (d) Paragraph 14 makes a general statement, and paragraphs 15 and 16 serve as a supporting illustration.

Questions for Analysis and Discussion

1. In paragraph 4, Guilbault implicitly criticizes today's culture for its emphasis on materialism, yet it is clear that the Sears catalog, too, promoted materialism. Guilbault suggests a difference, however. What is it?

2. In paragraph 17, Guilbault writes, "Somehow I can't envision today's kids reminiscing about a Lands' End or Victoria's Secret catalog." What does she mean? Do you agree with her?

AT THE MOVIES

My Family, Mi Familia (1995), directed by Gregory Nava and featuring Jimmy Smits and Edward James Olmos, is a drama about the hopes, failures, and dreams of three generations of Mexican Americans living in East Los Angeles from the 1930s to the 1960s.

Four More Methods of Paragraph Development

CHAPTER OBJECTIVES

Chapter 4 continues discussing the primary methods of paragraph development common to exposition and persuasion. In this chapter, you will practice reading and analyzing passages representing the following four remaining methods, which are somewhat more complicated than those you studied in Chapter 3:

- Cause and effect

- Classification and analysis

- Definition

- Analogy

■ METHODS OF PARAGRAPH DEVELOPMENT: THE SECOND GROUP

Cause and Effect   The **cause-and-effect method** of development is related to reasons and consequences, or results. A writer may provide *reasons (causes)* to explain events, problems, or issues, and the *consequences (effects)* of those events, problems, or issues. Like the comparison-and-contrast method, which can be used singly or in combination, a writer may discuss only causes or only effects or both, and the causes and effects can be used in any order.

The cause–effect pattern always involves the question *why,* whether stated or implied. If you read a paragraph that begins, "There are many reasons that college students are borrowing more money to pay for college than in previous years," it is obvious that the writer will examine the *causes* of increased borrowing. But even if this sentence said, "College students are borrowing more money to pay for college than in previous years," the cause–effect method is implied.

In the same way, if a paragraph opens with this sentence—"Increased government loan programs for college students are creating an enormous financial burden for graduates"—the writer is establishing a logical connection between the ideas: the economic *effects* of borrowing (the *cause*), even though such words as *effect, consequence,* or *result* are not present. Read the following passage; then identify the cause–effect connection.

When two friends meet and talk informally they usually adopt similar body postures. If they are particularly friendly and share identical attitudes to the subjects being discussed, then the positions in which they hold their bodies are liable to become even more alike, to the point where they virtually become carbon copies of each other. This is not a deliberate imitative process. The friends in question are automatically indulging in what has been called Postural Echo, and they do this unconsciously as part of a natural body display of companionship.

There is a good reason for this. A true bond of friendship is usually only possible between people of roughly equal status. This equality is demonstrated in many indirect ways, but it is reinforced in face-to-face encounters by a matching of the postures of relaxation or alertness. In this way the body transmits a silent message, saying: "See, I am just like you"; and this message is not only sent unconsciously but also understood in the same manner. The friends simply "feel right" when they are together.

Desmond Morris, *Manwatching: A Field Guide to Human Behaviour*

Cause: _____

Effect: _____

_____

A cause–effect relationship may be implied rather than stated explicitly, as in this sentence by Peter Steinhart from his book *The Company of Wolves:*

Cheetahs in Africa suffered a major population decline as human settlement expanded in the nineteenth and twentieth centuries.

Which part of the sentence suggests the cause, and which part suggests the effect?

Cause: _____

_____

Effect: _____

Here is the entire paragraph. Study the annotations showing the link between the immediate effects with more serious, long-term effects.

immediate effects of inbreeding

Cheetahs in Africa suffered a major population decline as human settlement expanded in the nineteenth and twentieth centuries. The reduced population is so inbred that it has less than a tenth of the genetic variety of humans or domestic cats; cheetah genetic resources have been compared to what one would find after ten to twenty generations of brother-sister matings. Immune systems within a species are normally diverse, but skin grafts from one cheetah to another are not rejected—an indication that they have identical, or nearly identical, immune systems. The consequences of such uniformity can be grim. In some zoos, 70 percent of cheetah cubs die without reaching maturity. When an epidemic of feline infectious peritonitis ran through a captive population in an Oregon wildlife park, it was hardly noticed in the lions, but it infected all the park's forty-two cheetahs and proved fatal to twenty-five of them. Inbreeding usually reduces a species' reproductive success, too. Abnormalities in sperm cells begin to proliferate. Studies have found *70 percent of cheetah sperm to be abnormally formed,* compared with only 29 percent of domestic-cat sperm.

long-term effects

Peter Steinhart, *The Company of Wolves*

Why does Steinhart emphasize the consequences of the population decline rather than the cause? _____

_____

_____

Occasionally, the cause–effect method of development forms a sort of chain, as you see in this paragraph on the decline of the Asian elephant population (the major effect) by Sallie Tisdale. Read the paragraph; then list the chain of causes and effects pertaining to this decline.

There are between twenty-five thousand and forty thousand Asian elephants left in the world. Their gradual elimination in the wild is the result of a number of changes, most of them recent and a few subtle. The invention of the chain saw, for instance, made forest-clearing much easier and quicker work. But basically there is just not enough room in Southeast Asia for both elephants and people. The elephant's jungle habitat is being replaced by cropland, and many of the crops are delectable to the now homeless elephant. The elephant raids the millet and sugarcane, and is killed for his efforts, and kills in turn; in India, nearly a hundred and fifty people are killed by elephants every year. Wild elephants are found from India to Indonesia; most inhabit shrinking parks and preserves, in shrinking populations, separated from each other by human settlements as uncrossable as an ocean. Bulls, being more aggressive, are killed far more often than cows. Not only does this deplete the gene pool but the cows' opportunities to breed grow fewer, and as the birth rate falls their mean age increases. Because elephants will feed on the youngest, tenderest trees available, finding them the most appetizing, herds quickly denude small parks beyond the point of natural recovery. Several countries, notably Thailand and India, are attempting to conserve these insular environments and to confront the problems of the diminished gene pool and male-to-female ratio, but quite a few people in elephant biology wonder whether the wild elephant is past saving. There are estimated to be a million elephants left in Africa; however, their numbers are also dropping. Certainly its future, one way or another, resides in zoos.

Sallie Tisdale, "The Only Harmless Great Thing," *The New Yorker*

The first effect is already provided for you.

Effect: <u>The gradual elimination of the Asian elephant population</u>

Locate and identify the three causes of the population decline.

Cause 1: _____

_____

Cause 2: _____

_____

Cause 3: _____

_____

_____

Now locate and identify the two effects that lead from these causes.

Effect 1: _____

_____

Effect 2: _____

Classification and Analysis

Classification and analysis are traditionally considered together. Although they are actually separate methods, their underlying purpose is the same. In each, the writer takes apart a larger subject and examines its separate parts to see how each relates to the whole. With the **classification** method, a writer puts *several* things (or ideas) into classes or categories, following a consistent system. **Analysis** is different, involving a *single* entity, the parts of which are examined one at a time.

Let us look at classification first. In the real world, we classify all the time. For example, if you decide to reorganize your CD collection, you would first determine a *system* for grouping the CDs; of course, the system would have to make sense. You might organize them by type of music (all the hard rock CDs in one group, all the jazz in another, all the blues in a third, and so on). Or if your music collection is international, you might classify them by country. If your collection consists solely of rock music, you might classify your CDs by artist or group, by subgenres of rock, or perhaps even by decade. The classification system must remain consistent to avoid confusion and to be useful.

If you read a paragraph that begins, "At the tourist trap where I work during the summers, I have observed three different kinds of customers," or "There are five subspecies of fish called darters," you can expect the classification method to follow. But with analysis, a writer examines the parts of *one* thing. He or she might use analysis to evaluate a political speech. Let's suppose a student has been assigned to analyze Richard Nixon's famous "Checkers" speech, one often studied by politicians and communications students. She would examine Nixon's purpose, the ideas he presented, his delivery, the logical fallacies, and the emotional appeals. Analysis allows a writer to examine the parts in terms of how they relate to the whole. The reader of an analysis passage must look at these elements one by one before putting them together to form a conclusion.

You can keep analysis and classification straight if you remember that analysis takes apart a *single* subject, while classification takes *several* items and groups them into categories. Let us now look at two examples of paragraphs using these methods.

Although the topic of the following classification paragraph is a bit grisly, it illustrates the method clearly. In a chapter describing the horrors inflicted on residents of the Central African Republic by its former leader Bokassa, Alex Shoumatoff classifies cannibalism into four types.

There are many kinds of cannibalism. Revenge cannibalism—the gloating, triumphant ingestion of a slain enemy's heart, liver, or other vital parts—is common at the warring-chiefdom stage of social evolution. Emergency cannibalism was resorted to by the Uruguayan soccer team whose plane crashed in the Andes.[1] Ritual endocannibalism is practiced by certain tribes like the Yanonamo of northern Amazonia, whose women drink the pulverized ashes of slain kin mixed with banana gruel before their men go off on a raiding party. In the Kindu region of Zaire there are to this day leopard men who wear leopard skins, smear their bodies with leopard grease (which protects them even from lions), chip their teeth to points, and attack and eat people. Among their victims were some Italian soldiers who were part of the U.N. peace-keeping force during the turbulence after independence in 1960. The rarest kind of cannibals are gustatory cannibals—people who are actually partial to the taste of human flesh.

Alex Shoumatoff, "The Emperor Who Ate His People," *African Madness*

List the four types of cannibalism. _____

_____

Now explain the basis for the author's classification system. _____

_____

_____

As stated earlier, analysis examines a single idea and looks at its separate parts. Consider this paragraph by Robert N. Bellah and his co-authors from their study of American values. Here they analyze the cowboy—his characteristics and his importance in American culture.

[1]The experiences of the Uruguayan soccer team have been recorded in a fine book by Piers Paul Read, *Alive!*, which was made into a 1993 film of the same name.

America is also the inventor of that most mythic individual hero, the cowboy, who again and again saves a society he can never completely fit into. The cowboy has a special talent—he can shoot straighter and faster than other men—and a special sense of justice. But these characteristics make him so unique that he can never fully belong to society. His destiny is to defend society without ever really joining it. He rides off alone into the sunset like Shane, or like the Lone Ranger moves on accompanied only by his Indian companion. But the cowboy's importance is not that he is isolated or antisocial. Rather, his significance lies in his unique, individual virtue and special skill and it is because of those qualities that society needs and welcomes him. Shane, after all, starts as a real outsider, but ends up with the gratitude of the community and the love of a woman and a boy. And while the Lone Ranger settles down and marries the local schoolteacher, he always leaves with the affection and gratitude of the people he has helped. It is as if the myth says you can be a truly good person, worthy of admiration and love, only if you resist fully joining the group. But sometimes the tension leads to an irreparable break. Will Kane, the hero of *High Noon,* abandoned by the cowardly townspeople, saves them from an unrestrained killer, but then throws his sheriff's badge in the dust and goes off into the desert with his bride. One is left wondering where they will go, for there is no longer any link with any town.

Robert N. Bellah, et al., *Habits of the Heart*

Definition

Unlike the other methods described, **definition** is often associated with other methods of development. As a method, it is nearly self-explanatory, but the purposes of the definition method may differ, as we shall see in this section. Definition is useful when a writer wants to clarify a term that may be open to varying interpretations (or to misinterpretation) or that he or she is using in a subjective or personal way. Definition is especially useful for abstract terms such as *machismo, feminism, honor, racism,* or *patriotism.* Even when we think *we* know what a word means, we must keep in mind that not everyone else may share that definition.

First, let us look at the way definitions are constructed. In traditional rhetoric, a **formal definition** follows this classic model:

Term to be defined = Class + Distinguishing characteristics

(The distinguishing characteristics show how the term is different from other members of the same class.)

For example, using the formal definition model, we might define the word *sofa* like this:

> Term: sofa
> Class: a piece of furniture
> Distinguishing characteristics: with an upholstered seat and back, intended to seat two or three people

Let us apply this method to a more difficult, more complex word—racism.

> Term: racism
> Class: a belief or doctrine
> Distinguishing characteristics: that one's abilities and character are determined by race and that one race is superior to another

Do you accept that definition? Here is another definition of the same word, but with the distinguishing characteristics changed:

> Term: racism
> Class: a belief or doctrine
> Distinguishing characteristics: involving the mistreatment and oppression of a member of one race by a member of another race

As you can see, it is the distinguishing characteristics of definitions that pose the problem. Definitions are important in argument, as you will see later in Part 4, "Reading Critically," because your acceptance of an argument may hinge on your acceptance of an underlying definition. For instance, in challenges to English-only rules in the workplace, some employees, forbidden by management to speak their native language on the job, have filed suit to make such a rule illegal, often citing racism as a factor. Do either of the definitions listed above fit this situation? If not, can you write a definition of *racism* that would?

Before we look at extended definition as a method of paragraph development, you should know that writers often define a term in just a single sentence, as Simon Winchester does in this short paragraph from *The Professor and the Madman.*

The "English Dictionary," in the sense that we commonly use the phrase today—as an alphabetically arranged list of English words, together with an explanation of their meanings—is a relatively new invention. Four hundred years ago there was no such convenience available on any English bookshelf.

Notice that Winchester's definition is enclosed inside dashes for easy identification.

The expository method of development used in paragraphs, and occasionally in entire essays, is called an **extended** definition. In the examples that follow, besides definition, each writer uses a secondary method; in fact, definition is commonly used with other expository methods, most typically examples or illustration, comparison and contrast, and analysis.

In the first example, a physician, Larry Dossey, defines the word *healing* as he intends to use it in the remainder of the article. This type of definition is called a **stipulated** definition, meaning that the writer stipulates, or specifies, the way he intends to use the word ("By 'healing' I mean . . .").

> Though healing is a universal phenomenon that has been recognized by every culture in history, the term has many meanings. By "healing" I mean the *distant,* positive influence of one individual (the healer) on another (the healee) in the absence of any obvious intervening physical influence. It goes by many names: nonlocal, mental, spiritual, psychic, and prayer-based healing. Healing has been linked to spectacular events, such as cancers vanishing without treatment, that cannot be explained by medical science.
>
> These radical healings cause immense intellectual indigestion. "This is the sort of thing I wouldn't believe, even if it really happened," trumpeted one skeptical scientist in an oft-quoted remark.
>
> Larry Dossey, "Healing Happens," *Utne Reader*

What does the writer mean by the word *healing?* _____

_____

A writer may use definition to **contrast** similar-sounding or easily confused words, as Jeffrey Masson and Susan McCarthy do in this example with the words *domestic* and *tame.*

> Evidence of emotion in captive animals and pets is often discounted as irrelevant. Captive animals, the argument goes, are in unnatural situations, and what domesticated animals do is irrelevant to what animals are *really* like, as if they are not really animals. While genuinely domesticated animals *are* different from wild animals, *domestic* and *tame* do not mean the same thing. Domestic animals are animals that have been bred to live with humans—they have been changed genetically. Dogs, cats, and cows are domestic animals. Captive animals like elephants are not, since through the generations that people have trained elephants, they have almost

invariably caught and tamed wild elephants, rather than *bred* elephants. Since the nature of elephants remains unchanged, observations on tame or captive elephants are in fact highly relevant to free-living elephants.

Jeffrey Masson and Susan McCarthy, *When Elephants Weep*

Besides definition and contrast, what other method of development is

evident? _____

Definitions can also be **personal,** as Joseph Epstein illustrates in this paragraph in which he first presents a dictionary definition, then follows it with his own definition.

Ambition is one of those Rorschach words: define it and you instantly reveal a great deal about yourself. I do not mind revealing a great deal about myself—and in the pages that follow, doubtless do—but I hesitate to lock myself into a definition that, though precise, is also needlessly confining. Even that most neutral of works, *Webster's,* in its Seventh New Collegiate Edition, gives itself away, defining ambition first and foremost as "an ardent desire for rank, fame, or power." *Ardent* immediately assumes a heat incommensurate with good sense and stability, and *rank, fame,* and *power* have come under fairly heavy attack for at least a century. One can, after all, be ambitious for the public good, for the alleviation of suffering, for the enlightenment of mankind, though there are some who say that these are precisely the ambitious people most to be distrusted. Yet, if a brief definition is needed, I should define ambition as the fuel of achievement.

Joseph Epstein, *Ambition*

Another kind of definition is the **historical** definition, in which the writer presents the historical interpretations of a word whose meaning has changed through the years. In spring 2000, when President Clinton was impeached, there was much discussion about the rather vague phrase "high crimes and misdemeanors." In the next passage, Jeffrey Toobin, a legal writer for *The New Yorker,* examines the original definition of the word *misdemeanors,* as it referred to presidential criminal actions, followed by the present-day meaning of the term.

The final wording of the provision for impeachment in the Constitution emerged from a brief debate among some of the greatest of the Framers, on September 8, 1787, in Philadelphia. The working draft of the document allowed Congress to remove the President only for bribery and for treason, but George Mason, fearing an unduly powerful chief executive, proposed that "maladministration" be added as another ground for impeachment. His fellow-Virginian James Madison objected, because "so vague a term will be equivalent to a tenure during pleasure of the Senate." Gouverneur Morris added a similar point, noting that "an election of every four years will prevent maladministration." As an alternative, Mason offered to add instead a phrase that had been used in English law as early as 1386—"high Crimes and Misdemeanors."

Today, the word "misdemeanor" suggests a minor or trivial offense, but the Framers had a very different understanding of it. In eighteenth-century England, high misdemeanors referred to offenses against the state, as opposed to those against property or other people. Thus, from the start, impeachment was meant to police those who abused the powers of their office. As Charles Cotesworth Pinckney said in the debate over ratification of the Constitution in South Carolina, impeachment was for "those who behave amiss, or betray their public trust."

Jeffrey Toobin, "Terms of Impeachment," *The New Yorker*

Analogy

The last method of development, **analogy,** is the most sophisticated and therefore the hardest to interpret. An analogy is an *extended metaphor,* in which the writer discusses the literal subject in terms of something else. In an imaginative yoking of two unlike things, shared characteristics are emphasized and a fresher insight ensues. A writer, for instance, might explain the functioning of a human heart in terms of the way a pump works—in other words, in terms of a more familiar object. The analogy starts with a metaphor, as this diagram shows:

```
                        A : B
         A (the subject) is compared to B (the metaphor)
                 the human heart : a pump
```

Unlike a simple metaphor, however, the analogy is *sustained,* typically over a few sentences or—less commonly—even throughout an essay.[2]

Consider the following paragraph, which is developed by analogy. It represents the opening sentences of a news article on the terrible fires during the summer of 1988 that destroyed 25 percent of Yellowstone National Park.

Visiting this fire-scarred but still magnificent park is like watching one of those Hollywood melodramas in which the gorgeous heroine suffers some horrible accident and wakes up in the next scene with her face covered in white bandages. The audience can only wait in suspense to know whether she will still be beautiful when the gauze is removed.

T. R. Reid, "New Yellowstone to Rise from Ashes," *The Washington Post*

[2]See the website for this book, *www.mhhe.com/spears,* for verbal analogy exercises.

Note that the literal subject, the park, is mentioned only once, and it is imaginatively compared to a once-beautiful heroine who has suffered a terrible accident. (The key word "like" introduces the analogy.) The "audience," in an extension of the analogy, is a metaphor referring to anyone interested in the park's future and its chances for recovery. The analogy allows the main idea to be stated with more drama and suspense. Will her beauty be restored, or will she be permanently and hideously disfigured? As is the case with Yellowstone, we don't know. Good analogies like this one are effective and compelling: They are more than a mere attention-getting device because they provide a new way of looking at things.

A writer may use an analogy to help us understand complex ideas. Science writer David Perlman employs a homely analogy to explain the concept of the Hubble Constant, which he characterizes as a "mysterious and controversial number." He begins the discussion by describing the movement of galaxies: "[E]very galaxy in the universe is now speeding away from every other galaxy at a rate that increases by 160,000 miles an hour for every 3.3 light-years that each galaxy finds itself away from Earth's own Milky Way." Then he continues:

> Considering that a single light-year is equal to about 6 trillion miles, such speeds are almost inconceivable. Even harder to grasp is the fact that the Milky Way itself is part of this vast explosion. What that means is that we're not at the center of the universe, after all; instead, we're like a single raisin in a vast lump of dough that is rising in an oven where all the other raisins are moving away from each other, faster and faster as the oven gets hotter and hotter.
>
> That rate of expansion for the universe, known as the Hubble Constant, is named after Edwin Hubble, who first found evidence for the expansion in 1929. Since then, other astronomers have used the Hubble Constant to estimate the age of the universe as anywhere from 10 billion to 20 billion years old.
>
> David Perlman, "At 12 Billion Years Old, Universe Still Growing Fast,"
> *San Francisco Chronicle,* May 26, 1999

Analogies can also be fanciful and whimsical, as is the case in this opening paragraph of an article about golf.

> I fell in love with golf when I was twenty-five. It would have been a healthier relationship had it been an adolescent romance or, better yet, a childhood crush. Though I'd like to think we've had a lot of laughs together, and even some lyrical moments, I have never felt quite adequate to her demands, and she has secrets she keeps from me. More secrets than I can keep

track of; when I've found out one, another one comes out, and then three more, and by this time I've forgotten what the first one was. They are sexy little secrets that flitter around my body—a twitch of the left hip, a pronation of the right wrist, a cock of the head one way, a turn of the shoulders the other—and they torment me like fire ants in my togs; I can't get them out of my mind, or quite wrap my mind around them. Sometimes I wish she and I had never met. She leads me on, but deep down I suspect—this is my secret—that I'm just not her type.

John Updike, "An Ode to Golf," *The New Yorker*

What, literally, do the "secrets" refer to? _____

_____

What does Updike mean when he writes in the last sentence that "I'm

just not her type"? _____

Here is a final analogy, which intends to amuse and to make a pointed statement about politics:

During Clinton's impeachment hearing, Democratic Representative Barney Frank of Massachusetts was quoted in *Newsweek*[3] as saying, "[Republicans] thought that impeachment represented a horse they could ride all the way home. It is now clear that horse is not going to make it. And they can't decide whether they should shoot it and sell it for dog food or paint stripes on it and call it a zebra."

Practice Exercise Read the following passages. First, decide which of the following methods of development predominates:

- Cause and effect
- Definition
- Classification and analysis
- Analogy

Then write a sentence stating the main idea in your own words.

The central United States is divided into two geographical zones: the Great Plains in the west and the prairie in the east. Though both are more or less flat, the Great Plains—extending south from eastern Montana and western North Dakota to eastern New Mexico and western Texas—are the drier of the two

[3]November 30, 1998, p. 23.

regions and are distinguished by short grasses, while the more populous prairie to the east (surrounding Omaha, St. Louis, and Fort Leavenworth) is tall-grass country. The Great Plains are the "West"; the prairie, the "Midwest."

Robert D. Kaplan, *An Empire Wilderness: Travels into America's Future*

Method of development: _____

Main idea: _____

_____

Those who learn that they have been lied to in an important matter—say, the identity of their parents, the affection of their spouse, or the integrity of their government—are resentful, disappointed, and suspicious. They feel wronged; they are wary of new overtures. And they look back on their past beliefs and actions in the new light of the discovered lies. They see that they were manipulated, that the deceit made them unable to make choices for themselves according to the most adequate information available, unable to act as they would have wanted to act had they known all along.

Sissela Bok, *Lying: Moral Choices in Public and Private Life*

Method of development: _____

Main idea: _____

_____

The first law of gossip is that you never know how many people are talking about you behind your back. The second law is thank God. The third—and most important—law is that as gossip spreads from friends to acquaintances to people you've never met, it grows more garbled, vivid, and definitive. Out of stray factoids and hesitant impressions emerges a hard mass of what everyone knows to be true. Imagination supplies the missing pieces, and repetition turns these pieces into facts; gossip achieves its shape and amplitude only in the continual retelling. The best stories about us are told by perfect strangers.

Tad Friend, "The Harriet-the-Spy Club," *The New Yorker*

Method of development: _____

Main idea: _____

The following passage is an excerpt from an article written during the 2000 presidential campaign. Its subject is John McCain, a Republican contender who subsequently dropped out of the primaries.

For many election observers, the coverage of McCain is neither a joke nor a conspiracy. It is a vivid case study of how political journalism operates in an age of all-news cable TV shows—a crucial lifeline for charismatic but initially underfunded candidates like McCain—and an illustration of perhaps the oldest law of media physics: Journalists will always be attracted to a tough scrap and a good story.

Earlier in the race, many were attracted to McCain and his gritty life-story for "symbolic" purposes, because it appeared his campaign wasn't going anywhere, says Jay Rosen, a New York University professor of media studies. "But when he won the New Hampshire primary, it produced a boom in the press, and he was suddenly all over these cable television talk shows."

Last week, when McCain attacked the Christian right in a much-heralded Virginia speech, Boston Globe columnist David Nyhan wrote that the candidate had "carved out a slot in our nation's political history," adding: "The old fighter pilot put the stick over, throttled to the redline, and screamed in low over the conservative heartland, firing off rockets, bullets, bombs, the works. He was never the kind of naval aviator to return to his carrier with unused ordinance."

Josh Getlin, "The McCain-Media Chemistry," *Los Angeles Times*

Method of development: _____

Main idea: _____

_____

_____

Flirting can be dangerous. The flirt does not necessarily have full control of her or his actions. A flirt with low self-esteem is a dangerous human indeed.

A flirt without a moral sense is also dangerous. Like the Shadow, a flirt has the power to cloud men's minds. Or women's minds—whatever minds the flirt is aiming for. The object of a full-on flirt can feel disoriented, toxic, hormonally imbalanced. A flirtee with an appreciation of the art form can feel exhilarated, as though taken on a roller coaster ride.

Like the rider on a roller coaster, a flirtee always ends up back at the same place. Flirting is not transportation; it is social excitement for its own sake. If everyone understands that, then all is well. If they do not, uh-oh.

A flirt, though, escapes before the authorities are alerted. A flirt is back home smoking a cigarette while the evidence is being collected. A flirt has deniability.

I should now give an example of flirting, but I cannot. I could repeat some sentences used by flirts: "I haven't seen you in ages" would be an example. Or: "Sit down here and tell me everything." Or: "Could you possibly get me another glass of that fizzy water?"

But those are unremarkable sentences. A thousand people could say them, and the sexual temperature in the room would remain precisely the same. Put them in mouths of a flirt, though, and the jungle tom-toms start.

Flirting is popularly supposed to consist of eyelash-batting, sentences ripe with double meaning and hands brushed discreetly across forearms. A true flirt requires nothing so obvious; the genius of flirting is that it's exactly like normal behavior, except that it isn't.

What a flirt does is sexual, although it is in no sense an invitation. It is a sort of art form using human emotions.

Jon Carroll, "Some Thoughts about Flirting," *San Francisco Chronicle*

Method of development: _____

Main idea: _____

_____

The viewers also know that no matter how grave any fragment of news may appear (for example, on the day I write a Marine Corps general has declared that nuclear war between the United States and Russia is inevitable), it will shortly be followed by a series of commercials that will, in an instant, defuse the import of the news, in fact render it largely banal. This is a key element in the structure of a news program and all by itself refutes any claim that television news is designed as a serious form of public discourse. Imagine what you would think of me, and this book, if I were to pause here, tell you that I will return to my discussion in a moment, and then proceed to write a few words in behalf of United Airlines or the Chase Manhattan Bank. You would rightly think that I had no respect for you and, certainly, no respect for the subject. And if I did this not once but several times in each chapter, you would think the whole enterprise unworthy of your attention. Why, then, do we not think a news show similarly unworthy? The reason, I believe, is that whereas we expect books and even other media (such as film) to maintain a consistency of tone and a continuity of content, we have no such expectation of television, and especially television news.

Neil Postman, *Amusing Ourselves to Death*

Method of development: _____

Main idea: _____

_____

_____

_____

Combination of Methods

As we discussed at the end of Chapter 3, a writer may use a mix of expository methods of development. In the following paragraph, Michael Krieger explains the daily lives of Kwaio women. The Kwaio are a mountain people who live on Malaita Island in the Solomon Islands of Oceania. Their lives are brutally hard; their villages are almost completely untouched by outside civilization. As you read the paragraph, locate the main idea and the controlling idea. Then identify the expository methods of development.

The existence of Kwaio women, never secure, was also one of continual drudgery. Even today, although a woman no longer has to fear for her life, she has little to smile about. She may walk only on certain trails and in specified areas of the village. She may not enter the men's house or even mingle with the men except under certain prescribed conditions. She must continually tend the gardens, which supply almost all the Kwaios' food, and daily she must carry on her back the heavy bamboo water containers, the yams, and all the firewood, often over miles of steep and narrow mountain trails. Because there is so little flat or terraced ground on which to plant a garden, and because the ravines down which the streams tumble are devastated by flash floods in the wet season, the village may be located an hour's strenuous hike away from the nearest stream or vegetable garden. Consequently, Kwaio women climb three or four hours a day, and their arms and legs are like bands of steel. Owing to their low status—just above the village pigs—and to generations of subservience, the women, for the most part, are like shy, overgrown children. Most have babies clinging to them. Besides rearing the children and all their other jobs, the women are also responsible for caring for the Kwaios' most prized possessions, their pigs. The pigs are either sold or sacrificed and eaten in male-only ceremonies, and so the women generally don't get to eat their charges. In spite of the sexual inequities to which the women are subjected, they seem to harbor no rancor or resentment.

Michael Krieger, *Conversations with the Cannibals*

Main idea: _____

Controlling idea: _____

List two expository methods of development: _____

_____

■ CONCLUSION: METHODS OF DEVELOPMENT AND PATTERNS OF THOUGHT

As I pointed out at the end of Chapter 3, it helps to think of methods of development as relating to patterns of thought in the real world. For example, which methods of development covered in this chapter would be appropriate for these situations?

1. You have just moved to a new apartment. In your kitchen are three drawers, one on top of the other. You have a couple of large boxes

    of kitchen utensils to store in these drawers. _____

2. Why did the founders of *www.google.com*—a popular and eminently useful World Wide Web search engine—choose that

    name? _____

    _____

    _____

3. Your English teacher said in class that the eyes are the window of

    the soul. What does that mean? _____

4. You are considering quitting school for a year and working full-time. What impact would that decision have on your life?

    _____

5. Your literature instructor has assigned you to write a paper on the unique characteristics of science fiction as a literary genre.

    _____

■ CHAPTER EXERCISES

Selection 1

[1]Those of us who have to spend a great deal of time in crowded conditions become gradually better able to adjust, but no one can ever become completely immune to invasions of Personal Space. [2]This is because they remain

forever associated with either powerful hostile or equally powerful loving feelings. [3]All through our childhood we will have been held to be loved and held to be hurt, and anyone who invades our Personal Space when we are adults is, in effect, threatening to extend his behaviour into one of these two highly charged areas of human interaction. [4]Even if his motives are clearly neither hostile nor sexual, we still find it hard to suppress our reactions to his close approach. [5]Unfortunately, different countries have different ideas about exactly how close is close. [6]It is easy enough to test your own "space reaction": when you are talking to someone in the street or in any open space, reach out with your arm and see where the nearest point on his body comes. [7]If you hail from western Europe, you will find that he is at roughly fingertip distance from you. [8]In other words, as you reach out, your fingertips will just about make contact with his shoulder. [9]If you come from eastern Europe you will find you are standing at "wrist distance." [10]If you come from the Mediterranean region you will find that you are much closer to your companion, a little more than "elbow distance."

[11]Trouble begins when a member of one of these cultures meets and talks to one from another. [12]Say a British diplomat meets an Italian or an Arab diplomat at an embassy function. [13]They start talking in a friendly way, but soon the fingertips man begins to feel uneasy. [14]Without knowing quite why, he starts to back away gently from his companion. [15]The companion edges forward again. [16]Each tries in this way to set up a Personal Space relationship that suits his own background. [17]But it is impossible to do. [18]Every time the Mediterranean diplomat advances to a distance that feels comfortable for him, the British diplomat feels threatened. [19]Every time the Briton moves back, the other feels rejected. [20]Attempts to adjust this situation often lead to a talking pair shifting slowly across a room, and many an embassy reception is dotted with western-European fingertip-distance men pinned against the walls by eager elbow-distance men. [21]Until such differences are fully understood, and allowances made, these minor differences in "body territories" will continue to act as an alienation factor which may interfere in a subtle way with diplomatic harmony and other forms of international transaction.

Desmond Morris, *Manwatching: A Field Guide to Human Behaviour*

A. Vocabulary

For each italicized word from the selection, write the dictionary definition most appropriate for the context.

1. *immune* to [sentence 1]: _____

2. *charged* [3]: _____

3. *suppress* [4]: _____

4. *alienation* [21]: _____

B. Content and Structure

Complete the following questions.

1. Write a sentence stating the main idea of the passage. _____

   _____

2. This passage represents a combination of methods of development. Write the method represented in each group of sentences. (Note: One answer is a method of development from Chapter 3.)

   Sentences 1 to 4: _____

   Sentences 6 to 10: _____

   Sentences 11 to 20: _____

3. What is the relationship between sentences 2 and 3?
   (a) They show steps in a process.
   (b) Sentence 2 shows a contrast from sentence 1.
   (c) Sentence 2 represents a cause, and sentence 3 shows the effect.
   (d) Sentence 2 presents a general idea, and sentence 3 gives examples.

4. From Morris's description of this hypothetical conversation between the diplomats in sentences 13 to 19, we can conclude that
   (a) the Briton and the Mediterranean felt equally offended.
   (b) the Briton was more offended than the Mediterranean.
   (c) the Mediterranean was more offended than the Briton.
   (d) both diplomats deliberately violated each other's Personal Space to establish dominance.

5. The author's point of view in sentence 20 is
   (a) sneering, ridiculing.
   (b) objective, impartial.
   (c) mildly humorous.
   (d) highly negative, critical.

Answers for Selection 1

A. Vocabulary

1. unconcerned
2. intensified
3. hold back
4. describing a state of isolation

B. Content and Structure

1. Our concept of Personal Space is linked to powerful feelings, which make it difficult for us to be immune when it is invaded.

2. Sentences 1 to 4: cause–effect
   Sentences 6 to 10: classification or example
   Sentences 11 to 20: illustration
3. (d)
4. (a)
5. (c)

Selection 2

[1]One cannot easily realize what a tremendous thing it is to know every trivial detail of twelve hundred miles of river and know it with absolute exactness. [2]If you will take the longest street in New York, and travel up and down it, conning[4] its features patiently until you know every house and window and door and lamppost and big and little sign by heart, and know them so accurately that you can instantly name the one you are abreast of when you are set down at random in that street in the middle of an inky black night, you will then have a tolerable notion of the amount and the exactness of a pilot's knowledge who carries the Mississippi River in his head. [3]And then if you will go on until you know every street crossing, the character, size, and position of the crossing-stones, and the varying depth of mud in each of those numberless places, you will have some idea of what the pilot must know in order to keep a Mississippi steamer out of trouble. [4]Next, if you will take half of the signs in that long street, and *change their places* once a month, and still manage to know their new positions accurately on dark nights, and keep up with these repeated changes without making any mistakes, you will understand what is required of a pilot's peerless memory by the fickle Mississippi.

Mark Twain, *Life on the Mississippi*

A. Vocabulary

For each italicized word from the selection, choose the best definition according to the context in which it appears.

1. *trivial* [sentence 1]:
   (a) silly.
   (b) ordinary.
   (c) of little significance.
   (d) unobserved.
2. *abreast of* [2]:
   (a) in the vicinity of.
   (b) near.
   (c) alongside.
   (d) behind.

[4]Studying, examining carefully so as to memorize.

3. *tolerable* [2]:
   (a) fair, adequate.
   (b) able to be endured.
   (c) permissible.
   (d) exact, accurate.
4. *peerless* [4]:
   (a) reliable.
   (b) well-trained.
   (c) hazy.
   (d) unmatched.
5. *fickle* [4]:
   (a) hard to get along with.
   (b) changeable.
   (c) hard to please.
   (d) complicated.

B. Content and Structure

1. The method of development in this passage is clearly analogy. First

   state what Twain is comparing to what. _____

   _____ is compared to _____

   _____

   Now explain in your own words what, in literal terms, the analogy
   means—that is, what is required of a Mississippi river pilot.

   _____

   _____

   _____

2. Twain most likely uses this analogy because
   (a) we can understand how hard it would be to learn all of a street's
       characteristics.
   (b) the familiar can be explained better in terms of the unfamiliar.
   (c) a river and a street have nearly identical characteristics.
   (d) everyone should learn the characteristics of a single street as well
       as Twain suggests.
3. It is apparent from sentence 2 that learning to be a Mississippi pilot
   (a) can be quickly and easily accomplished.
   (b) takes an enormous amount of patience.
   (c) requires a person who follows orders.
   (d) requires a person who can make quick life-and-death decisions.

4. We usually reserve the word *fickle* to describe human behavior. From what Twain suggests in sentence 4, what are some factors that would make a river fickle? _____

_____

_____

Selection 3

¹Coffee has never been just a drink, but has always been loaded with social and political consequence as well. ²The desire for it helped spur French, British, and Dutch colonial expansion. ³Its infusion into 18th-century life helped create a nightlife culture and provided a social context in which political dissidents gathered to discuss the issues of the day. ⁴Historians have ascribed to it at least partial responsibility for the Enlightenment—a period that valued alert and rational thought. ⁵"The powers of a man's mind are directly proportional to the quantity of coffee he drank" wrote the 18th-century Scottish philosopher Sir James MacKintosh in one of the many pamphlets that circulated through London's coffeehouses in a raging war of arguments for and against the new drink. ⁶It was celebrated as a substance that would lengthen the workday and provide stimulation to those engaged in the new sedentary occupations that accompanied the Industrial Revolution, according to Wolfgang Schivelbusch, a German social scientist and author of *Tastes of Paradise: A Social History of Spices, Stimulants and Intoxicants.* ⁷"Not to drink coffee," writes Schivelbusch, "[was] almost as great a sin for the puritanical bourgeoisie as wasting time itself."

⁸Most importantly, it was egalitarian in its easy accessibility to all social classes. ⁹In Britain, 17th-century coffeehouses were the first gathering places where ability to pay the bill was far more important than social class in gaining access; tradesmen joined with gentry in consuming the new brew.

¹⁰That tradition continued in the United States: American colonists heaved tea over the side of a British schooner in Boston Harbor, and coffee became a symbol of defiance against the British. ¹¹George Washington signed the British terms of surrender to American rebels in a still-operating coffeehouse/tavern in New York. ¹²Everywhere they opened, coffeehouses became the centers of political intrigue and philosophical discussion, fostering the concepts of individual liberty and freedom of opinion in the budding republic. ¹³Some analysts even claim that coffee has been key to the development of the urban work ethic. ¹⁴"Coffee," says Irene Fizer, a scholar who teaches a course called "Caffeine Culture" at New York's New School, "has been keyed to the construction of a rigidified work life. ¹⁵The urban workaday economy would be unthinkable without coffee."

Mark Schapiro, "Muddy Waters," *Utne Reader*

A. *Vocabulary*

For each italicized word from the selection, write the dictionary definition most appropriate for the context.

1. *infusion* [sentence 3]: _____

2. *dissidents* [3]: _____

   _____

3. *ascribed* [4]: _____

4. *sedentary* [6]: _____

5. *bourgeoisie* [7]: _____

6. *egalitarian* [8]: _____

7. *gentry* [9]: _____

8. *intrigue* [12]: _____

B. *Content and Structure*

Complete the following questions.

1. Which sentence expresses the main idea of the first paragraph?

   _____

   In the sentence you chose, locate the topic of the first paragraph.

   _____

   Write the controlling idea. _____

   _____

2. Which sentence expresses the main idea of the second paragraph?

   _____

   The topic is the same in this paragraph as for the first paragraph, but what is the controlling idea? _____

   _____

3. Which two methods of development are used in the paragraph?

   _____

4. The author evidently sees a strong connection between the increasing popularity of coffee and
    (a) the beginning of unions to protect laborers from exploitation.
    (b) the Industrial Revolution.
    (c) a rigid workday.
    (d) the increasing importance of democracy and social equality.

5. Look again at sentence 5. The author writes that pamphlets circulating in London coffeehouses offered "a raging war of arguments for and against the new drink." From the evidence, on which side of this argument—for or against coffee—does the writer appear to stand? _____ How can you tell? _____

    _____

6. In the last sentence, the author quotes Irene Fizer, who writes that the "urban workaday economy would be unthinkable without coffee." What seems to be the author's personal opinion about this statement?
    (a) His opinion is favorable.
    (b) His opinion is unfavorable.
    (c) His opinion is not evident.
    (d) His opinion is mixed or ambiguous.

■ *PRACTICE ESSAY*

"In Praise of the Humble Comma"

Pico Iyer

© Jerry Bauer.

Pico Iyer has built his reputation primarily as a travel writer. His best-known books are Video Night in Kathmandu: And Other Reports from the Not-So-Far East *(1989) and* Falling Off the Map: Some Lonely Places of the World *(1994). He has most recently served as editor of a collection of travel writing first published for Salon.com,* Salon.com Wanderlust: Real-Life Tales of Adventure and Travel *(2000). "In Praise of the Humble Comma," first published in* Time *magazine in 1988, examines the significance of punctuation in writing.*

1   The gods, they say, give breath, and they take it away. But the same could be said—could it not?—of the humble comma. Add it to the present clause, and, of a sudden, the mind is, quite literally, given pause to think; take it out if

you wish or forget it and the mind is deprived of a resting place. Yet still the comma gets no respect. It seems just a slip of a thing, a pedant's tick, a blip on the edge of our consciousness, a kind of printer's smudge almost. Small, we claim, is beautiful (especially in the age of the microchip). Yet what is so often used, and so rarely recalled, as the comma—unless it be breath itself?

2   Punctuation, one is taught, has a point: to keep up law and order. Punctuation marks are the road signs placed along the highway of our communication—to control speeds, provide directions and prevent head-on collisions. A period has the unblinking finality of a red light; the comma is a flashing yellow light that asks us only to slow down; and the semicolon is a stop sign that tells us to ease gradually to a halt, before gradually starting up again. By establishing the relations between words, punctuation establishes the relations between the people using words. That may be one reason why schoolteachers exalt it and lovers defy it ("We love each other and belong to each other let's don't ever hurt each other Nicole let's don't ever hurt each other," wrote Gary Gilmore[5] to his girlfriend). A comma, he must have known, "separates inseparables," in the clinching words of H.W. Fowler, King of English Usage.

3   Punctuation, then, is a civic prop, a pillar that holds society upright. (A run-on sentence, its phrases piling up without division, is as unsightly as a sink piled high with dirty dishes.) Small wonder, then, that punctuation was one of the first proprieties of the Victorian age, the age of the corset, that the modernists threw off: the sexual revolution might be said to have begun when Joyce's Molly Bloom[6] spilled out all her private thoughts in 36 pages of unbridled, almost unperioded and officially composed press; and another rebellion was surely marked when E.E. Cummings[7] first felt free to commit "God" to the lower case.

4   Punctuation thus becomes the signature of cultures. The hotblooded Spaniard seems to be revealed in the passion and urgency of his doubled exclamation points and question marks ("¡Caramba! ¿Quien sabe?"), while the impassive Chinese traditionally added to his so-called inscrutability by omitting directions from his ideograms. The anarchy and commotion of the '60s were given voice in the exploding exclama-

[5]Gary Gilmore committed a murder in Utah, for which he was subsequently executed. His story is superbly detailed in Norman Mailer's classic study of crime and punishment, *The Executioner's Song.*

[6] Molly Bloom is a character in the 1922 novel *Ulysses,* written by Irish writer James Joyce. Bloom is famous in literature for her frank soliloquy using the stream-of-consciousness technique.

[7] e. e. cummings (Edward Estlin Cummings) was a twentieth-century American poet known for unconventional punctuation and uncapitalized words, as you can see in his name.

tion marks, riotous capital letters and Day-Glo italics of Tom Wolfe's[8] spray-paint prose; and in Communist societies, where the State is absolute, the dignity—and divinity—of capital letters is reserved for Ministries, Sub-Committees and Secretariats.

5   Yet punctuation is something more than a culture's birthmark; it scores the music in our minds, gets our thoughts moving to the rhythm of our hearts. Punctuation is the notation in the sheet music of our words, telling us when to rest, or when to raise our voices; it acknowledges that the meaning of our discourse, as of any symphonic composition, lies not in the units but in the pauses, the pacing and the phrasing. Punctuation is the way one bats one's eyes, lowers one's voice or blushes demurely. Punctuation adjusts the tone and color and volume till the feeling comes into perfect focus: not disgust exactly, but distaste; not lust, or like, but love.

6   Punctuation, in short, given us the human voice, and all the meanings that lie between the words. "You aren't young, are you?" loses its innocence when it loses the question mark. Every child knows the menace of a dropped apostrophe (the parent's "Don't do that" shifting into the more slowly enunciated "Do not do that"), and every believer, the ignominy of having his faith reduced to "faith." Add an exclamation point to "To be or not to be . . ." and the gloomy Dane[9] has all the resolve he needs; add a comma, and the noble sobriety of "God save the Queen" becomes a cry of desperation bordering on double sacrilege.

7   Sometimes, of course, our markings may be simply a matter of aesthetics. Popping in a comma can be like slipping on the necklace that gives an outfit quiet elegance, or like catching the sound of running water that complements, as it completes, the silence of a Japanese landscape. When V.S. Naipaul,[10] in his latest novel, writes, "He was a middle-aged man, with glasses," the first comma can seem a little precious. Yet it gives the description a spin, as well as a subtlety, that it otherwise lacks, and it shows that the glasses are not part of the middle-agedness, but something else.

8   Thus all these tiny scratches give us breadth and heft and depth. A world that has only periods is a world without inflections. It is a world without shade. It has a music without sharps and flats. It is a martial music. It has a jackboot rhythm. Words cannot bend and curve. A comma, by comparison, catches the gentle drift of the mind

[8] In *The Electric Kool-Aid Acid Test,* a nonfiction work about Ken Kesey and the Merry Pranksters, Tom Wolfe indulged his penchant for the startling use of punctuation and for other typographical oddities.
[9] The "gloomy Dane" is a reference to Hamlet, Prince of Denmark, celebrated in Shakespeare's play of the same name.
[10] V. S. Naipaul is a British writer, born in Trinidad.

in thought, turning in on itself and back on itself, reversing, redoubling and returning along the course of its own sweet river music; while the semicolon brings clauses and thoughts together with all the silent discretion of a hostess arranging guests around her dinner table.

9   Punctuation, then, is a matter of care. Care for words, yes, but also, and more important, for what the words imply. Only a lover notices the small things: the way the afternoon light catches the nape of a neck, or how a strand of hair slips out from behind an ear, or the way a finger curls around a cup. And no one scans a letter so closely as a lover, searching for its small print, straining to hear its nuances, its gasps, its sighs and hesitations, poring over the secret messages that lie in every cadence. The difference between "Jane (whom I adore)" and "Jane, whom I adore," and the difference between them both and "Jane—whom I adore—" marks all the distance between ecstasy and heartache. "No iron can pierce the heart with such force as a period put at just the right place," in Isaac Babel's[11] lovely words; a comma can let us hear a voice break, or a heart. Punctuation, in fact, is a labor of love. Which bring us back, in a way, to gods.

A. *Comprehension*

Choose the answer that best completes each statement. Do not refer to the selection while doing this exercise.

1. Choose the sentence that best represents the main idea of the essay.
    (a) Punctuation rules must be consistently applied to make the reader's task easier.
    (b) Punctuation marks determine both the meanings and rhythms of a writer's words as well as our emotional responses to them.
    (c) Use of punctuation marks in the twentieth century has become more daring and unorthodox.
    (d) Each culture has a unique system of punctuating to determine meaning.
2. Iyer labels the comma a "humble" mark of punctuation because
    (a) its appearance is so insignificant.
    (b) there are too many rules governing its use.
    (c) it should be used only when the reader takes a breath or pauses.
    (d) it lacks the authority and finality of other marks of punctuation.

---

[11] Isaac Babel was a twentieth-century Russian short-story writer.

3. The writer compares punctuation marks to road signs to emphasize their
   (a) shape.
   (b) difficult rules.
   (c) use as controls over our reading.
   (d) ease of recognition.

4. Iyer states that by "establishing the relations between words," punctuation
   (a) establishes a relationship between the writer and the reader.
   (b) establishes a relationship between the writer and his or her publisher.
   (c) serves as an agreed-upon system for distinguishing between important and less important ideas.
   (d) establishes the relations between people using words.

5. Iyer characterizes a world with "only periods" as one without
   (a) love and affection.
   (b) inflections and shade.
   (c) music.
   (d) interest or enthusiasm.

B. *Vocabulary*

For each italicized word from the selection, choose the best definition according to the context in which it appears. You may refer to the selection to answer the questions in this section and in all the remaining sections.

1. a *pedant's* tick [paragraph 1]: Referring to a person who
   (a) pays excessive attention to learning and rules.
   (b) is uneducated about the rules of grammar.
   (c) writes well.
   (d) refuses to follow conventional rules.

2. schoolteachers *exalt* it [2]:
   (a) instruct.
   (b) identify.
   (c) clarify.
   (d) glorify.

3. the first *proprieties* [3]:
   (a) customs of polite society.
   (b) religious traditions.
   (c) qualities of ownership.
   (d) civic virtues.

4. his so-called *inscrutability* [4]:
   (a) difficulty of understanding.
   (b) lack of precision.
   (c) explanatory remarks.
   (d) reverence, devotion.

5. the *ignominy* of having his faith reduced [6]:
   (a) unfortunate event.
   (b) voluntary submission to a higher authority.
   (c) great personal dishonor.
   (d) nobility of spirit.

6. double *sacrilege* [6]:
   (a) punishable crime.
   (b) evil portent.
   (c) disrespect for something sacred.
   (d) matter of speculation.

7. the silent *discretion* [8]:
   (a) thought, rumination.
   (b) freedom to act on one's own.
   (c) scheme, plot.
   (d) devil-may-care attitude.

8. to hear its *nuances* [9]:
   (a) rhythmic melodies.
   (b) poetic images.
   (c) rising and falling tones.
   (d) subtle shades of meaning.

C. Inferences

On the basis of the evidence in the paragraph, mark these statements as follows: PA (probably accurate); PI (probably inaccurate); or NP (not in the passage).

1. _____ Good writers would be wise never to break the rules of punctuation.

2. _____ Punctuation marks are more important than the words on the page for determining meaning.

3. _____ The rules for punctuation and for music are identical.

4. _____ Without punctuation marks, words would be dead and lifeless and lacking rhythm and nuance.

5. _____ When parents say to their child, "Do not do that," it is much more frightening than "Don't do that."

6. _____ Iyer teaches grammar and punctuation at a university.

D. *Structure*

Complete the following questions.

1. Which of these sentences best states the main idea of the essay?
   (a) "Punctuation, one is taught, has a point: to keep up law and order."
   (b) "Punctuation, then, is a civic prop, a pillar that holds society upright."
   (c) "Punctuation thus becomes the signature of cultures."
   (d) "Punctuation, in short, gives us the human voice, and all the meanings that lie between the words."
2. The mode of discourse in the essay is
   (a) narration.
   (b) description.
   (c) exposition.
   (d) persuasion.
3. Which three methods of paragraph development are evident in the

   essay? _____

4. Read paragraph 3 again. Then write a sentence in your own words

   stating the main point Iyer makes in it. _____

   _____

   _____

5. If you are unsure of its meaning, look up the word *jackboot* (paragraph 8). Then explain why this word is appropriate for this

   context. _____

   _____

   _____

   _____

6. In calling punctuation marks "tiny scratches" (see paragraph 8), Iyer emphasizes their
   (a) apparent lack of purpose.
   (b) seeming insignificance.
   (c) odd appearance.
   (d) lack of grace and elegance.

Questions for Discussion and Analysis

1. Look through Iyer's essay and point to sentences whose use of punctuation reinforces his meaning, whose use "scores the music in our minds," as he writes in paragraph 5.
2. Identify all the analogies and figures of speech (imaginative comparisons) Iyer uses to explain his subject.
3. Why are marks of punctuation, aside from periods, so hard to master in writing? Which marks of punctuation are you uncomfortable or unsure about using? What might be some ways to remedy this problem—assuming that it is one—and expand your proficiency in this area?

ON THE WEB

Students have found the following website an invaluable aid in mastering grammar, usage, and punctuation rules:

ccc.commnet.edu/grammar

The site's "Guide to Grammar and Writing" provides instruction, quizzes, and answers.

5

Patterns of Paragraph Organization

CHAPTER OBJECTIVES

The last element in analyzing paragraphs is to study the ways
writers arrange ideas within paragraphs and the devices they
use to achieve coherence. Here is an overview of the topics
discussed in Chapter 5:

- Patterns of paragraph organization

- Coherence in paragraphs

- Transitions

■ PATTERNS OF ORGANIZATION DEFINED

The **patterns of organization** refer to the various ways that a paragraph's sentences can be arranged. As you have seen, the paragraph is remarkably flexible; nevertheless, we can identify four standard patterns:

- Chronological
- Spatial

- Deductive
- Inductive

The first and second patterns are found most often in narrative and descriptive writing; the other two are found more in expository or persuasive writing.

Chronological Order

Chronological (or time) order, the easiest pattern to recognize, refers to the order in which events happen. This pattern is used to tell a story, to relate an incident, to recount a historical event, or to describe the steps in a process. In the following excerpt, Susan Orlean traces the history of the so-called Florida Indians, starting with their forced evacuation from their original homes in Georgia and Alabama to their persecution by the U.S. government during the Seminole Wars. As you read it, study the underlined words and phrases that reveal the sequence of events.

"Florida Indians" are the descendants of the Yuchi, Creek, and Cherokee Indians who lived in Georgia and Alabama until the eighteenth century, when white settlers forced them off their fertile land. Once the Indians relocated to Florida they began calling themselves Seminole or Miccosukee, which means "wild wanderers" or "outlanders" or "run-aways." After the United States took possession of Florida from Spain in 1821, white settlers made their way south to Florida and soon coveted that Indian land, too, and the federal government responded by spending more than $40 million in three Seminole "subjugation and removal efforts." The last of the three Seminole Wars, the Billy Bowlegs War, ended in 1848; by then the U.S. Army had "subjugated and removed" more than 90 percent of the Seminoles to Oklahoma. The remaining 10 percent—about three hundred members—fled to the Everglades and the Big Cypress Swamp and set up chikee-hut camps on the edge of the wetlands. The government persisted in the removal efforts, at one point offering Chief Billy Bowlegs $215,000 to lead the remaining tribe members to Oklahoma. He refused. He was later persuaded to come to Washington for negotiations. Along with another Seminole chief and a team of government "removal specialists," Chief Billy Bowlegs traveled to the capital on horseback. The group stopped along the way in Tampa, Palatka, Orange City, and in Savannah, Georgia. At hotels Chief Billy registered as "Mr. William B. Legs." The summit was unsuccessful in persuading the Seminoles to leave, as was a law passed in 1853 that made it illegal for them to live in Florida, as were further incursions by government soldiers. In 1858 Secretary of War Jefferson Davis admitted that the Seminoles had "baffled the energetic efforts of our army to effect their subjugation and removal." Because they never surrendered, the Florida Seminoles came to refer to themselves as the Unconquered. To this day their descendants have never signed a peace treaty with the United States.

Susan Orlean, *The Orchid Thief*

Spatial Order

The term **spatial** is related to the word *space*. Spatial order refers to the arrangement of objects in an environment. Most often used in descriptive writing, spatial order helps a writer organize descriptive details and present them so that we can visualize the scene. Without spatial order, the details would be a helter-skelter assemblage of impressions, and the scene would be difficult to recreate in our minds.

Some typical ways writers arrange details spatially are from left to right or right to left, near to far or far to near, top to bottom or bottom to top. The transitions showing movement from one part of a scene to another—often in the form of prepositional phrases—allow us to visualize the whole. This passage by Sallie Tisdale describes a cabin her family owned in the Klamath National Forest of southern Oregon. Tisdale's process is almost photographic, as if she were holding a movie camera and filming the scene, beginning with outside of the cabin, then moving to the first floor, then to the staircase, and finally to the second floor.

> The cabin was a small, boxy two-story building with a deck, which we called the porch, perched on stilts outside the front door—a room-size platform with a rail on three sides and a dusty porch swing in constant shade. On the first floor was a long, narrow kitchen, which was lined—floor, walls, and ceiling—with a wood so old that it was black from years of lamp-oil and wood smoke. Across from it was a square open stairway, which led to a single room twice as large as the kitchen and extending up the stretch of a hill. To the right at the top of the stairs was the bathroom; the floor of the shower was always gritty with sand, and the shower head yielded no more than a drizzle of cold water. Over the kitchen, facing the river, was a sleeping porch—a narrow screened room with several iron beds, each one piled with musty, lumpy mattresses two or three deep. I slept on them in perfect peace.
>
> Sallie Tisdale, "The Pacific Northwest," *The New Yorker*

In the second example, Kenneth Boulding uses spatial order in an unusual way: to locate himself first in his narrow environment and then to locate Earth in the larger universe. By repeating the key preposition *beyond*, Boulding allows us to follow his mind's journey. (A knowledge of basic world geography also helps.)

> As I sit at my desk, I know where I am. I see before me a window; beyond that some trees; beyond that the red roofs of the campus of Stanford University; beyond them the trees and the roof tops which mark the town of Palo Alto; beyond them the bare golden hills of the Hamilton Range. I know, however, more than I see. Behind me, although I am not looking in that direction, I know there is a window, and beyond that the little campus of the Center for the Advanced Study in the Behavioral Sciences; beyond that the

Coast Range; beyond that the Pacific Ocean. Looking ahead of me again, I know that beyond the mountains that close my present horizon, there is a broad valley; beyond that a still higher range of mountains; beyond that other mountains, range upon range, until we come to the Rockies; beyond that the Great Plains and the Mississippi; beyond that the Alleghenies; beyond that the eastern seaboard; beyond that the Atlantic Ocean, beyond that is Europe; beyond that is Asia. I know, furthermore, that if I go far enough I will come back to where I am now. In other words, I have a picture of the earth as round. I visualize it as a globe. I am a little hazy on some of the details. I am not quite sure, for instance, whether Tanganyika is north or south of Nyasaland. I probably could not draw a very good map of Indonesia, but I have a fair idea where everything is located on the face of this globe. Looking further, I visualize the globe as a small speck circling around a bright star which is the sun, in the company of many other similar specks, the planets. Looking still further, I see our star the sun as a member of millions upon millions of others in the Galaxy. Looking still further, I visualize the Galaxy as one of millions upon millions of others in the universe.

Kenneth Boulding, *The Image*

Aside from his unusual geography tour, what is the central

philosophical point Boulding makes? _____

_____

_____

Deductive Order **Deductive** order is the most common pattern in the English paragraph. You may recall from Chapter 1 that paragraphs often begin with a main idea, which is then reinforced by specific supporting sentences. For this reason, deductive order is sometimes called **general-to-specific order.** This term actually refers to a pattern of thinking, which you will read about in more detail in Chapter 9. For now, it is enough to know that the deductive pattern is determined by the location of the main idea. You can better visualize deductive order if you imagine an inverted triangle, with the base at the top:

Typically, expository paragraphs use deductive order, as Lewis Thomas does in the first example. Notice that the main idea in sentence 1 is supported with a single effective illustration.

> Animals seem to have an instinct for performing death alone, hidden. Even the largest, most conspicuous ones find ways to conceal themselves in time. If an elephant missteps and dies in an open place, the herd will not leave him there; the others will pick him up and carry the body from place to place, finally putting it down in some inexplicably suitable location. When elephants encounter the skeleton of an elephant out in the open, they methodically take up each of the bones and distribute them, in a ponderous ceremony, over neighboring acres.
>
> Lewis Thomas, *Lives of a Cell*

In the second passage, Joan Acocella uses deductive order to examine the "wealth of imagination," the "sheer, shining fullness" of the Harry Potter books written by J. K. Rowling.

> The great beauty of the Potter books is their wealth of imagination, their sheer, shining fullness. Rowling has said that the idea for the series came to her on a train trip from Manchester to London in 1990, and that, even before she started writing the first volume, she spent years just working out the details of Harry's world. We reap the harvest: the inventory of magical treats (Ice Mice, Jelly Slugs, Fizzing Whizbees—levitating sherbet balls) in the wizard candy store; the wide range of offerings (Dungbombs, Hiccup Sweets, Nose-Biting Teacups) in the wizard joke store. Hogwarts is a grand, creepy castle, a thousand years old, with more dungeons and secret passages than you can shake a stick at. There are a hundred and forty-two staircases, some of which go to different places on different days of the week. There are suits of armor that sing carols at Christmas time, and get the words wrong. There are poltergeists—Peeves, for example, who busies himself jamming gum into keyholes. We also get ghosts, notably Nearly Headless Nick, whose executioner didn't quite finish the job, so that Nick's head hangs by an "inch or so of ghostly skin and muscle"—it keeps flopping over his ruff—thus, to his grief, excluding him from participation in the Headless Hunt, which is confined to the thoroughly decapitated.
>
> Joan Acocella, "Under the Spell," *The New Yorker*

Inductive Order   **Inductive** order, the opposite of deductive order, is sometimes called **specific-to-general order.** Inductive order derives from a kind of thinking called induction, which will be taken up later in Chapter 9. For now, it is enough to know that inductive order involves a series of specific observations leading to a generalization (the main idea) that the reader can validly infer from those statements.

A diagram of an inductively arranged paragraph looks like this:

In the following paragraph, Paul Gallico uses the inductive pattern to classify sports fans. (Note: The essay this paragraph comes from was published in 1931. How have sports fans changed in the intervening 70-plus years?)

> The fight crowd is a beast that lurks in the darkness behind the fringe of white light shed over the first six rows by the incandescents atop the ring, and is not to be trusted with pop bottles or other hardware. The tennis crowd is the pansy of all the great sports mobs and is always preening and shushing itself. The golf crowd is the most unwieldy and most sympathetic, and is the only horde given to mass production of that absurd noise written generally as "tsk tsk tsk tsk," and made between tongue and teeth with head-waggings to denote extreme commiseration. The baseball crowd is the most hysterical, the football crowd the best-natured and the polo crowd the most aristocratic. Racing crowds are the most restless, wrestling crowds are the most tolerant, and soccer crowds the most easily incitable to riot and disorder. Every sports crowd takes on the characteristics of the individuals who compose it. Each has its particular note of hysteria, its own little cruelties, mannerisms, and bad mannerisms, its own code of sportsmanship and its own method of expressing its emotions.
>
> Paul Gallico, "Fans"

Notice that Gallico first classifies sports crowds to distinguish among them; these statements lead to his main point, stated in the last two sentences of the paragraph. Gallico's paragraph is clearly expository, but inductive order can also be used, less commonly, in descriptive writing, as you can see in this excerpt from George Orwell's classic semiautobiographical book, *Down and Out in Paris and London.*

> It was a very narrow street—a ravine of tall, leprous houses, lurching toward one another in queer attitudes, as though they had all been frozen in the act of collapse. All the houses were hotels and packed to the tiles with lodgers, mostly Poles, Arabs, and Italians. At the foot of the hotels were tiny *bistros,* where you could be drunk for the equivalent of a shilling. On

Saturday nights about a third of the male population of the quarter was drunk. There was fighting over women, and the Arab navvies who lived in the cheapest hotels used to conduct mysterious feuds, and fight them out with chairs and occasionally revolvers. At night the policemen would only come through the street two together. It was a fairly rackety place. And yet amid the noise and dirt lived the usual respectable French shopkeepers, bakers and laundresses and the like, keeping themselves to themselves and quietly piling up small fortunes. It was quite a representative Paris slum.

George Orwell, *Down and Out in Paris and London*

Which sentence states the main idea? _____

Practice Exercise Read the following paragraphs. First, decide which of the following patterns of organization each represents:

- Chronological order
- Spatial order
- Deductive order
- Inductive order

Then write a sentence stating the main idea in your own words.

Pawn is one of the oldest and most basic of financial transactions. A customer presents an item to a pawnbroker as collateral on a loan. The customer then has a fixed period of time in which to repay the loan, plus interest, or forfeit the item. The amount of the loan is usually between 10 and 50 percent of what the broker believes he can sell the merchandise for, should the customer not return to claim it. In Nevada, the maximum interest rate a pawn broker can charge is 10 percent a month (or 120 percent a year). The customer has 120 days in which to repay the loan before the pawned item becomes the property of the broker.

Joe Heim, "Pawnshops," *The Real Las Vegas: Life beyond the Strip*

Pattern of organization: _____

Main idea: _____

The following paragraph concerns an Italian anthropologist named Giancarlo Scoditti, who has studied the peoples of Kitawa, a tiny island in the Trobriand Islands, 300 miles from Papua New Guinea.

Although the vast constellation of small islands that dot the South Pacific (generally called Melanesia, Micronesia, and Polynesia) has a population of only a few million people, it is home to about a sixth of the world's sixty-five hundred languages. Because of the number of islands that have existed for centuries in comparative isolation, the region is to linguistic and cultural diversity what Madagascar or the Galápagos Islands are to biodiversity. And yet it is estimated that approximately half of the world's languages will disappear over the next century, as the pressures of a global economy further homogenize culture. Each one of these languages represents a world—and if the language happens to be unwritten that world will die with little trace. Thus Scoditti has become the sole repository of an entire civilization—a small but rich, vital, and ancient culture in imminent danger of extinction. He has come to fulfill Towitara's early vision of him: he is, indeed, the one who remembers.

Alexander Stille, "The Man Who Remembers," *The New Yorker*

Pattern of organization: _____

Main idea: _____

_____

_____

Lyndon Baines Johnson, a consummate politician, was a kaleidoscopic personality, forever changing as he sought to dominate or persuade or placate or frighten his friends and foes. A gigantic figure whose extravagant moods matched his size, he could be cruel and kind, violent and gentle, petty, generous, cunning, naive, crude, candid, and frankly dishonest. He commanded the blind loyalty of his aides, some of whom worshiped him, and he sparked bitter derision or fierce hatred that he never quite fathomed. And he oscillated between peaks of confidence and depths of doubt, constantly accommodating his lofty ideals to the struggle for influence and authority. But his excesses reflected America's dramas during his lifetime, among them the dramas he himself created.

Stanley Karnow, *Vietnam: A History*

Pattern of organization: _____

Main idea: _____

_____

_____

Atlanta is a city of contradictions. It is home to the largest concentration of black universities in the United States, has a rich and educated black middle class, and has been run by black mayors for the last twenty-four years; it is referred to as Black Mecca. But the Confederate battle flag still flies over the Georgia statehouse. Between 1915 and 1945, the city was the official head-quarters of the Ku Klux Klan, and yet in the fifties and sixties it became the cradle of the civil-rights movement. Atlanta seems obsessed with its history: the heroes of the old Confederacy—Jefferson Davis, Robert E. Lee, and Stonewall Jackson—stand watch over the city from their perch on the side of Stone Mountain, Atlanta's version of Mt. Rushmore. When people in Atlanta speak about "the war," they are talking not about Vietnam or any of the wars of the last hundred years but about "the war of Northern aggression." Yet Atlanta is also an upstart city: it is much younger than Richmond, Charleston, or Savannah, and has a brash, openly commercial nature. While Savannah basks in its former glory, having chosen historic preservation over economic growth, Atlanta has become the boomtown of the fastest-growing region of the United States, going from one million to three and a half million people in about thirty years. Unfortunately, in its drive to become a major capital, it has lost much of its regional character, and looks remarkably like every other new American city: it could be Phoenix, Houston, Denver, or Seattle.

Alexander Stille, "Who Burned Atlanta?" *The New Yorker*

Pattern of organization: _____

Main idea: _____

_____

The following passage was written after the writer's visit to the world's largest pile of used tires, in Stanislaus County, between the California Central Valley towns of Modesto and Merced.

Aerial crop dusters use burning tires as wind socks. To attract fish, tires are piled in oceans as artificial reefs. Tires are amassed around harbors as porous breakwaters. In Guilford, Connecticut, Sally Richards grows mussels on tires. Tires are used on dairy farms to cover the tarps that cover silage. They stabilize the shoulders of highways, the slopes of drainage canals. They are set up as crash barriers, dock bumpers, fences, and playground tunnels and swings. At Churchill Downs, the paving blocks of the paddock are made of scrap tires. Used tires are used to fashion silent stairs. They weigh down ocean dragnets. They become airplane shock absorbers. They become sandals. Crumbled and granulated tires become mud flaps, hockey pucks, running tracks, carpet padding, and office-floor anti-fatigue mats. Australians make crumb rubber by freezing and then crushing tire chips. Japanese have laid railroad track on crumbled tires. Dirt racetracks seeded with crumbled tires are easier on horses. Crumbled tires added to soil will increase porosity and allow more oxygen to reach down to grass roots. Twelve thousand crumbled tires will treat one football field. In Colorado, corn was planted in soil that had been laced with crumbled tires. The corn developed large, strong roots. A mighty windstorm came and went, and the tire-treated field was the only corn left standing in that part of Colorado. All such uses, though, as imaginative and practical as they may be, draw down such a small fraction of the tires annually piled as scrap that while they address the problem they essentially do not affect it.

John McPhee, *Irons in the Fire*

Pattern of organization: _____

Main idea: _____

_____

_____

Monday, August 6, 1945, began like any other wartime day in Japan. By 8 A.M. most Hiroshima office workers were at their desks, children were at school, soldiers were doing physical exercises, high-school students and civilian work gangs were busy pulling down wooden houses to clear more fire-breaks. During the night, there had been two air-raid alerts—and then all-clears. At 7:09 A.M., there was another alert, as a B-29 on a last weather check approached the city, and, at 7:31 A.M., another all-clear as it turned away. Minutes after eight, watchers in the city saw two B-29s approaching from the northeast: these were an observation plane and the Enola Gay. (Colonel Paul Tibbets, the pilot, had only the day before named the bomber after his mother.) The Enola Gay, in the lead, held its course straight and level for ten miles; at eight-fifteen, it let fall its single bomb. Immediately, the other B-29 banked hard to the left, the Enola Gay to the right; both quit the scene. Released at thirty one thousand six hundred feet, or nearly six miles, the bomb fell for forty-three seconds and was triggered (by a barometric switch) by heavily symbolic chance nineteen hundred feet directly above a small hospital that was two hundred and sixty yards from the aiming point, the T-shaped Aoio Bridge.

Murray Sayle, "Letter from Hiroshima: Did the Bomb End the War?" *The New Yorker*

Pattern of organization: _____

Main idea: _____

_____

_____

■ COHERENCE IN PARAGRAPHS

With any of the above patterns how do writers help ensure that you stay on track? As you learned in Chapter 1, careful writers try to help the reader follow the main idea by ensuring that the paragraph has *unity,* or singleness of purpose. In good writing, there should be no irrelevant or extraneous sentences to lead you astray. But in addition to unity, well-constructed paragraphs also have **coherence,** the quality of "sticking together." Coherence means that each sentence leads logically and smoothly to the next, the sentences in effect forming a chain of interconnected thoughts. Writers achieve coherence through three primary techniques: by repeating key words, by using pronouns, and occasionally, by using transitions.

In the following paragraph, Olga Knopf analyzes the effects of aging on taste and smell; she achieves unity by sticking only to that idea, which is stated in the first sentence and restated in the last one. She achieves coherence by repeating key words and by using pronouns relating to key nouns to keep the reader focused. These repetitions and pronouns are italicized so that you can see their function more easily.

Taste and smell are also affected by *aging,* but *their* changes are less understood and appreciated. People who are in contact with *the elderly* will tell you *they* have two major *complaints—food* and their children. The *complaint about food* is easily explained when one considers how *the taste buds work.* Distributed over the tongue, *they* last no longer than a few days each and then are replaced. In keeping with the general slowing-down process, *they* are renewed more slowly than *they* are used up. This means that the total number of effective *taste buds* declines, and, therefore, *food tastes less savory.* Extensive dentures that cover a large portion of the oral cavity *diminish the perception of taste* even further. In addition, there is the close interrelationship between *smell and taste.* Anyone who has ever had a cold can testify to the fact while the cold lasts, not only is *the sense of smell reduced,* but *food loses its taste* as well. There is *a similar deterioration in the sense of smell* as a result of *the process of aging.*

Olga Knopf, *Successful Aging*

Although it may seem that studying the ways writers achieve coherence would be more appropriate for a composition course than for a reading course, becoming aware of these methods will improve your concentration and comprehension, and equally important, will help you see the logical connections between ideas. Sometimes an accurate understanding of a passage may depend on a seemingly unimportant little word such as *but* or *for* or *as.*

■ TRANSITIONS

Writers also establish coherence by using **transitions,** signposts or markers that indicate a logical relationship between ideas or a shift in direction. Transitions can be single words or phrases; occasionally, an entire paragraph can serve as a bridge between the major sections of an essay. Transitions usually appear at the beginning of sentences, but placing them there is not a hard-and-fast rule. As a demonstration of how crucial they are, this paragraph by George Orwell is printed with the transitions omitted:

> After getting into the water the toad concentrates on building up his strength by eating small insects. He has swollen to his normal size again. He goes through a phase of intense sexiness. All he knows, at least if he is a male toad, is that he wants to get his arms round something. If you offer him a stick, or even your finger, he will cling to it with surprising strength and take a long time to discover that it is not a female toad. One comes upon shapeless masses of ten or twenty toads rolling over and over in the water, one clinging to another without distinction of sex. They sort themselves out into couples, with the male duly sitting on the female's back. You can distinguish males from females. The male is smaller, darker, and sits on top, with his arms tightly clasped round the female's neck. The spawn is laid in long strings which wind themselves in and out of the reeds and soon become invisible. The water is alive with masses of tiny tadpoles which rapidly grow larger, sprout hind legs, then forelegs, then shed their tails. The new generation of toads, smaller than one's thumbnail but perfect in every particular, crawl out of the water to begin the game anew.

Obviously, something is wrong here. Reading this paragraph is like reading a novel with every tenth page missing, or like trying to put a bicycle together when the manufacturer has left out some of the necessary screws. It just does not hold together, and the sentences sound monotonous and choppy. Here is the actual version, this time printed with the transitions restored and italicized, making it much less tedious to read.

> *For a few days* after getting into the water the toad concentrates on building up his strength by eating small insects. *Presently* he has swollen to his normal size again, *and then* he goes through a phase of intense sexiness. All he knows, at least if he is male toad, is that he wants to get his arms round something, *and* if you offer him a stick, or even your finger, he will cling to it with surprising strength and take a long time to discover that it is not a female toad. *Frequently* one comes upon shapeless masses of ten or twenty toads rolling over and over in the water, one clinging to another without distinction of sex. *By degrees, however,* they sort themselves out

into couples, with the male duly sitting on the female's back. You can *now* distinguish males from females, *because* the male is smaller, darker and sits on top, with his arms tightly clasped round the female's neck. *After a day or two* the spawn is laid in long strings which wind themselves in and out of the reeds and soon become invisible. A *few more weeks, and* the water is alive with masses of tiny tadpoles which rapidly grow larger, sprout hind legs, then forelegs, then shed their tails; *and finally, about the middle of the summer,* the new generation of toads, smaller than one's thumbnail but perfect in every particular, crawl out of the water to begin the game anew.

George Orwell, "Some Thoughts on the Common Toad," *The Orwell Reader*

The boxes in this section of the chapter present various transitional words and phrases according to their function, that is, the logical relationship they bring to the sentences they join. An example is provided for each category of transition.

**Transitions Signaling an Additional Statement
(usually of equal importance)**
and, in addition (to), additionally, as well as, besides, furthermore, moreover

---

Example: The house was badly neglected: The windows were broken, *and* the paint was blistered. *Moreover,* what had once been a well-tended lawn was now only an overgrown weed patch.

Transitions Signaling a Contrast
but, yet, however, nevertheless, nonetheless, while, whereas, on the other hand, in contrast (to), contrary to

---

Example: Basset hounds and St. Bernards are known for their placid and friendly natures; *in contrast,* terriers are often high-strung and highly excitable.

Transitions Signaling an Example or Illustration
for example, as an example, to illustrate, as an illustration, for instance, namely, specifically, a case in point

---

Example: Many residents of urban neighborhoods believe that an influx of national franchise stores can ruin local businesses and destroy a neighborhood's unique quality, resulting in a homogenized, bland environment. *For instance,* neighbors of

Larchmont Boulevard, a two-block street in Los Angeles lined with trees and small independent businesses, fought, unsuccessfully, to preserve its local character from intrusion by Payless Drugs, Koo Koo Roo, a fast-food enterprise, and Starbucks.

Transitions Signaling Steps in a Process or Chronological Order

first, second, third, next, the next step, further, then, before, after that, finally, last, in July, last week, in a few days, in 2003, and so on

---

Example: To use the spellcheck function in Microsoft Word, *first* pull down under the "Tools" menu to "Spelling and Grammar." The computer will *then* scan through the document to identify any misspelled or questionable words. *After* each word is flagged, select the correct spelling. *Finally,* be sure to save the changes in your file.

Transitions Signaling a Conclusion

therefore, thus, then, to conclude, in conclusion, in summary, to summarize, consequently, hence

---

Example: Charley spent two hours a day working in the reading laboratory, and he looked up every unfamiliar word he encountered. *As a result,* there was a dramatic improvement in his reading comprehension by the end of the semester.

Transitions Signaling Emphasis

indeed, in fact, certainly, without a doubt, undoubtedly, admittedly, unquestionably, truly

---

Example: The level of violence and intimidation directed at abortion clinics and the physicians who perform abortions has seriously escalated in recent years. *In fact,* in the 1990s, two abortion providers were killed, and protestors have posted abortion providers' names and addresses on antiabortion websites.

Transitions Signaling a Concession (an admission of truth)

although, even though, in spite of, despite, after all

Example: Although chimpanzee society is characterized by power displays, especially among males, the social hierarchy is usually quite stable. (In this sentence, the first clause *concedes* a truth. Another way to think of a concession is to mentally substitute "regardless of the fact that" or to look for a situation that suggests that "even though that is true, this is also true.")

Transitions Signaling Spatial Order

above, below, to the right, to the left, nearby, from afar, beyond, farther on, up the road, on top, underneath

---

Example: "Where the mountains meet the sea" is the official motto of Camden, Maine, a New England village known for its splendid harbor. No wonder. *Behind the harbor, not far from* where schooners, sailboats, and cabin cruisers are anchored, Ragged Mountain rises precipitously. *Near the peak of the mountain* one can find Maiden Cliffs, where, according to legend, an Indian maiden leaped to her death because of an unhappy love affair. *At the base of the mountain* is Lake Megunticook, a local swimming hole for midcoast Maine residents.

■ CHAPTER EXERCISES

Selection 1   The writer grew up in White Sulphur in north-central Montana, where he lived with his father, an experienced ranch hand and sheepherder.

[1]White Sulphur was as unlovely but interesting as the sounds of its livelihood. [2]A teacher who had arrived just then to his first classroom job would remember to me: *The town didn't look too perky. It had been through the Depression and a world war, and obviously nobody had built anything or painted anything or cleaned anything for twenty years.*

[3]Sited where the northern edge of the valley began to rumple into low hills—by an early-day entrepreneur who dreamed of getting rich from the puddles of mineral water bubbling there, and didn't—White Sulphur somehow had stretched itself awkwardly along the design of a very wide T. [4]Main Street, the top of the T, ran east and west, with most of the town's houses banked up the low hills on either side of the business area at its eastern end. [5]To the west lay the sulphur slough, the railroad and shipping pens, and the creamery and grain elevator. [6]The highway, in its zipper-straight run up the valley, snapped in there like the leg of the T onto Main Street. [7]Much of the countryside traffic, then,

was aimed to this west end of town, while all the saloons and grocery stores and cafes—and the post office and the druggist and the doctor and the two lawyers, since it took two to fight out a court case—did business at the east end.

8This gave White Sulphur an odd, strung-out pattern of life, as if the parts of the community had been pinned along a clothesline. **9**But it also meant there was an openness to the town, plenty of space to see on to the next thing which might interest you. **10**Even the school helped with this sense of open curiosity, because it had been built down near the leg of the T where two of the town's main attractions for a boy also had ended up—the county jail, and the sulphur slough.

Ivan Doig, This House of Sky: Landscape of a Western Mind

A. *Vocabulary*

For each italicized word from the selection, write the dictionary definition most appropriate for the context.

1. an early-day *entrepreneur* [sentence 3]: _____

2. a sulphur *slough* [5 and 10]: _____

B. *Content and Structure*

Complete the following questions.

1. The main idea of the passage is that White Sulphur
   (a) was a good, safe place for a boy to grow up in.
   (b) was not pretty to look at but was nonetheless filled with interesting things to arouse a boy's curiosity.
   (c) attracted many types of businesses.
   (d) was designed in the shape of a T.
2. The main economic activity in White Sulphur revolved around
   (a) ranching and livestock.
   (b) mining sulfur and other minerals.
   (c) small stores and cafeterias serving the surrounding areas.
   (d) railroad lines.
3. The central impression Doig conveys of the town's main parts is one of
   (a) openness and spaciousness.
   (b) efficiency and orderliness.
   (c) prosperity and affluence.
   (d) oddness, a sense of being out of place.
4. The pattern of organization in paragraph 2, from sentences 3 to 7, is
   (a) chronological.
   (b) deductive.
   (c) inductive.
   (d) spatial.

5. The transitional word "then" in sentence 7 indicates
    (a) emphasis.
    (b) the next step in a process.
    (c) a conclusion.
    (d) a contrast.

6. Read sentence 8 again. In your own words, explain what the pronoun

    "this" refers to. _____

7. From the last paragraph we can infer that, as a young boy, Doig
    (a) was told to stay away from the jail and the slough.
    (b) knew he wanted to be a writer.
    (c) spent a lot of time near the school, the jail, and the slough.
    (d) was a curious child who excelled in school.

Answers for Selection 1

A. Vocabulary

1. a person who organizes a business venture
2. a muddy pond or inlet, often containing minerals

B. Content and Structure

1. (b)
2. (a)
3. (a)
4. (d)
5. (c)
6. "This" refers to the town's T-shaped design.
7. (c)

Selection 2

This selection, written by a corrections officer, describes an area of the Sing Sing Correctional Facility[1] in Ossining, New York, a maximum-security prison.

[1]A-block and B-block are the most impressive buildings in Sing Sing. [2]One wonders how a democratic society could commission such horrific structures, and how a debased enough architect could be found to draw up a plan. [3]They are stupefyingly vast, and you come upon them with no preamble. [4]There is no wide staircase or arched entryway leading to them, just the corridor and then a pair of solid metal doors, neither of them much bigger than the front door of the average house. [5]A-block, which is probably the largest freestanding cellblock in the world,

[1]The phrase "the big house," referring to a prison, derives from the immensity of the cellblocks at Sing Sing. In another part of the article, the writer also points out that the slang phrase "to be sent up the river," meaning to be sent to jail, refers to the early days when criminals, upon being convicted, were taken by boat up the river to Sing Sing, slang for the town of Ossining about 30 miles north of New York City.

is five hundred and eighty-eight feet long, twelve feet shy of two football fields. [6]There are some six hundred and eighty inmates in there, more than the entire population of many prisons. [7]You can hear them—an overwhelming cacophony of radios, of heavy gates slamming, of shouts and whistles and running footsteps—but, oddly at first, you can't see a single incarcerated soul. [8]All you see is the bars that form the narrow fronts of the cells, extending four stories up and so far into the distance on the left and right that they melt into an illusion of solidity. [9]Then, as you walk down the gallery, eighty-eight cells long, the human dimensions of the place become clear. [10]There might be a half-dozen small mirrors[2] thrust through the bars, and the arms holding them retract as you draw even. [11]Some of the inmates make eye contact and glare, others doze, some sit bored on the toilet.

[12]Both A-block and B-block were completed in 1929, and they're practically identical, except that B-block is twenty cells shorter (sixty-eight), and one story taller (five). [13]The design is typical of American prisons: tiny cells back-to-back on tiers, with stairways on either end and in the center. [14]Each cellblock consists of two practically separate components. [15]One is the all-metal interior, containing the tiers of cells; it's painted gray, and looks as though it could have been welded in a shipyard. [16]The other element is a huge brick-and-concrete shell that fits over the tiers like a dish over a stick of butter. [17]One does not touch the other. [18]A series of tall, barred windows runs down either side of the shell; they would let in twice as much light if they were washed. [19]As it is, they let pass a diffuse, smog-colored glow, which crosses about fifteen feet of open space on each side before it reaches the metal, which it does not warm. [20]The flat, leaky roof of the shell is maybe ten feet from the top of the metal cellblock. [21]If the whole structure were radically shrunk, the uninitiated might perceive a vaguely agricultural purpose: the cages could be thought to contain chickens, or mink. [22]The cellblocks are loud because they are hard. [23]There is nothing in them to absorb sound, except the inmates' thin mattresses and perhaps their own bodies. [24]Every other surface is metal or concrete or brick.

Ted Conover, "Guarding Sing Sing," *The New Yorker*

A. *Vocabulary*

For each italicized word from the selection, choose the best definition according to the context in which it appears.

1. a *debased* enough architect [sentence 2]:
    (a) clever.
    (b) alented.
    (c) morally corrupt.
    (d) malicious.

[2]The mirrors are thrust through the bars to allow prisoners to see who is walking down the gallery.

2. with no *preamble* [3]:
   (a) preconceived idea.
   (b) introductory warning.
   (c) hesitation.
   (d) recognition.
3. an overwhelming *cacophony* (pronounced kə-kŏf'-ə-nē) [7]:
   (a) mixture of pleasant sounds.
   (b) sounds that are difficult to distinguish between.
   (c) loud chattering.
   (d) jarring, discordant sounds.
4. the *uninitiated* [21]:
   (a) uninvited.
   (b) uninterested.
   (c) inattentive.
   (d) inexperienced.

B. Content and Structure

Complete the following questions.

1. The mode of discourse in the passage is
   (a) narration.
   (b) description.
   (c) exposition.
   (d) persuasion.
2. Which two central impressions does Conover's writing convey about Sing Sing's A-block and B-block? The blocks are
   (a) vast.
   (b) primitive.
   (c) inhumane.
   (d) orderly.
   (e) representative of all prisons.
3. Explain in your own words what Conover means in sentence 8 by the phrase "an illusion of solidity." _____

   _____

   _____
4. Choose the two patterns of organization evident in sentences 1 to 11.
   (a) chronological.
   (b) deductive.
   (c) inductive.
   (d) spatial.

5. Fundamental to our understanding of the passage is the contrast between
    (a) the behavior of the prisoners and that of the prison visitors.
    (b) the absence of any concern for human comfort in the prison's environment and the human beings housed there.
    (c) the coldness of the prison's temperature and the heated anger of the inmates.
    (d) the treatment of prisoners at Sing Sing and their treatment in other state prisons.

C. Inferences

On the basis of the evidence in the paragraph, mark these statements as follows: PA (probably accurate), PI (probably inaccurate), or NP (not in the passage).

1. _____   Sing Sing is run ruthlessly yet inefficiently.
2. _____   Sing Sing is not particularly well maintained.
3. _____   The writer was terrified as he walked past the inmates' bars.
4. _____   Inmates are allowed to decorate their cells with homey touches.
5. _____   The prisoners are wary of the footsteps they hear walking down the gallery.
6. _____   New York's most violent offenders are sent to Sing Sing.

Selection 3

The subject of this passage is the impact of invasive (nonnative) species of animals and plants on the environment.

¹What do fire ants, zebra mussels, Asian gypsy moths, tamarisk trees, maleleuca trees, kudzu, Mediterranean fruit flies, boll weevils, and water hyacinths have in common with crab-eating macaques or Nile perch? ²Answer: They're *weedy* species, in the sense that animals as well as plants can be weedy. ³What that implies is a constellation of characteristics: They reproduce quickly, disperse widely when given a chance, tolerate a fairly broad range of habitat conditions, take hold in strange places, succeed especially in disturbed ecosystems, and resist eradication once they're established. ⁴They are scrappers, generalists, opportunists. ⁵They tend to thrive in human-dominated terrain because in crucial ways they resemble *Homo sapiens:* aggressive, versatile, prolific, and ready to travel. ⁶The city pigeon, a cosmopolitan creature derived from wild ancestry as a Eurasian rock dove (*Columba livia*) by way of centuries of pigeon fanciers whose coop-bred birds occasionally went AWOL, is a weed. ⁷So are those species that, benefiting from human impacts upon landscape, have increased grossly in abundance or ex-

panded their geographical scope without having to cross an ocean by plane or by boat—for instance, the coyote in New York, the raccoon in Montana, the white-tailed deer in northern Wisconsin or western Connecticut. **8**The brown-headed cowbird, also weedy, has enlarged its range from the eastern United States into the agricultural Midwest at the expense of migratory songbirds. **9**In gardening usage the word "weed" may be utterly subjective, indicating any plant you don't happen to like, but in ecological usage it has these firmer meanings. **10**Biologists frequently talk of weedy species, meaning animals as well as plants.

David Quammers, "Planet of Weeds," *Harper's*

A. Vocabulary

For each italicized word from the selection, write the dictionary definition most appropriate for the context.

1. a *constellation* of characteristics [sentence 3]: _____

    _____

2. They are *scrappers* [4]: _____

3. *opportunists* [4]: _____

    _____

4. versatile, *prolific* [5]: _____

5. a *cosmopolitan* creature [6]: _____

6. occasionally went *AWOL* [6]: _____

    _____

B. Content and Structure

Complete the following questions.

1. Explain the logical relationship between sentences 1 and 2. _____

    _____

2. In relation to the main idea, what is the function of sentence 10?
    (a) It restates the main idea.
    (b) It draws a conclusion.
    (c) It states a warning for the future.
    (d) It presents an effect of several causes.

3. The pattern of organization in the paragraph is
    (a) chronological.
    (b) spatial.
    (c) deductive.
    (d) inductive.

4. What method of development is most evident in sentences 2 to 5?
    (a) analogy.
    (b) informative process.
    (c) example.
    (d) definition.

5. The author's main point is that
    (a) invasive plants and animals must be eradicated at all costs.
    (b) invasive animal species thrive in a wide variety of habitats.
    (c) weedy animals are amazingly similar to humans.
    (d) in ecological terms, animals as well as plants can be weedy.

6. We can accurately infer that weedy animal species
    (a) are a purely modern phenomenon.
    (b) probably would not have occurred to such a great extent without human interventions or human settlement.
    (c) are a problem only in developed nations like the United States.
    (d) are the target of government eradication programs.

■ PRACTICE ESSAY

"Surviving Deer Season: A Lesson in Ambiguity"
Castle Freeman, Jr.

A resident of Newfane, Vermont, Castle Freeman is an essayist and short-story writer. He is the author of The Bride of Ambrose and Other Stories *(1987) and* Spring Snow: The Seasons of New England from The Old Farmer's Almanac *(1995). This article was first published in* The Atlantic Monthly.

1   The foothills of southeastern Vermont were once dairy country, although by the time I arrived, twenty years ago, dairying was mostly finished. One farm in the neighborhood still kept a few milkers, though, and it was there that I became acquainted with a particular local custom that is, I find, rarely celebrated in articles on endearing rural ways through the seasons. Their authors will tell you how to tap a maple in March, mow hay in June, and make cider in October, but by failing to touch on the subject I refer to, they neglect a passage in the turning year that is as venerable as these but darker and more pointed.

2   One morning in November, looking into my neighbor's pasture, I observed an uncanny thing: on the nearest of his animals the word COW had been painted with whitewash in letters two feet high. A further look revealed that the entire herd had been painted the same way. What was this? Was the herd's owner perhaps expecting a visit from city people in need of rural education? Was his tractor painted TRACTOR, his barn BARN? I asked him.

3   "Well, you know what tomorrow is," my neighbor said.

4   "Saturday?" I said.

5   "You're new around here," he said. "You'll see."

6   I saw, all right. More precisely, I heard. The next morning Vermont's two-week deer-hunting season began. Just before dawn the slumbering woods erupted with the fell echo of small arms. Single gunshots, doubles, volleys of three or four, came from all points of the compass, some far off, others seemingly in the living room. By eleven the fire had mounted to a fusillade worthy of Antietam.[3] Across the road, however, my neighbor's cows survived. They hugged the earth fearfully, like Tommies[4] at the Somme,[5] but they were alive. After all, no deer hunter who could read would shoot a cow.

7   Since then I have become a close student of the lengths to which people go each year on the eve of deer season to provide a margin of safety for themselves, their loved ones, their livestock, their pets. This is the season when dogs wear brightly colored bandannas around their necks, like John Wayne and Montgomery Clift in *Red River*. Cats and smaller dogs, as far as I can tell, have to take their chances along with the deer, although I don't know why the kind of elegant dog vest to be seen on the Pekingeses of Park Avenue shouldn't be produced in hunter orange for the greater safety of their country cousins.

8   That same hunter orange, a hideous toxic color, suddenly appears everywhere in mid-November, like the untimely bloom of an evil flower. Hunters themselves, of course, wear hunter orange to make it less likely that they'll be shot by their peers. But civilians, too, turn up in hunter-orange caps, vests, sweaters, and jackets, as they go about their business outdoors during this uneasy fortnight in the year.

9   Uneasy indeed. Are you a hiker, a birder, an idle tramper through the woods? In deer season you think twice before setting out—think twice and then stay home. If you're a nonhunter, it's painful to avoid the woods and fields as though they were a deserted street in the South Bronx. There is also the trouble of preparing for deer season. It's not as though you don't have enough to do to get the place ready for

[3]Antietam was a major Civil War battle.
[4]British slang for "soldiers," short for Tommy Atkins, the name used in sample official British army forms.
[5]The site of the devastating Battle of the Somme during World War I (1916).

winter without having to find time to paint the cow, flag the dog, pray for the cat, and plan two weeks' worth of useful projects to do in the cellar.

10   The heaviest demand that deer season makes on the nonhunter, however, it makes not on his time but on his mind. You have to reflect. You have to collect your thoughts. You don't want to move into deer season without having examined your responses, your beliefs.

11   I don't object to deer hunting: let everyone have his sport, I say. I don't for a moment doubt the value, importance, and dignity of hunting for those who do it. Deer hunting teaches skill, discipline, and patience. More than that, it teaches the moral lesson of seriousness—that certain things must be entered into advisedly, done with care, and done right. That hunting provides an education I am very willing to believe. And yet deer season is for me a sad couple of weeks. Because with all its profound advantages for the hunter, the fact remains that deer season is a little tough on the deer.

12   Suddenly deer turn up in strange places: thrown down in the backs of pickup trucks; roped on top of cars; hanging in front of barns; flopped in blood across platform scales in front of country stores and gas stations. It's hard to recognize in those abject, inert cadavers the agile creatures you surprise along the roads at night or see sometimes in the woods picking their way on slender legs and then bounding off, the most graceful animals in North America. It's hard to see them so defeated, so dead.

13   It's particularly hard for children, those instinctive animal lovers, to see deer season's bloody harvest hauled out of the woods. It's especially hard to explain to them why it isn't wrong to kill deer—or, if it is wrong, why nobody can stop it, and how it is that the hunters themselves, who are also your friends and neighbors, are otherwise such familiar, decent, innocent people. It's a lesson in ambiguity, I guess—a lesson in tolerance.

14   I had a number of conversations along these lines with my children when they were young, inconclusive conversations with on their side conviction and passion, and on my own . . . nothing satisfactory. What do you tolerate, why, and how? How do you separate the act from the friend, and condemn the one but not the other? Not an easy matter at any age, in any season.

15   We don't have those talks anymore. The children are older now. They know that with some things all you can do is figure out how you will conduct your own life and let others do the same. Perhaps they have learned this in part from deer season. If so, I'm content. Let the gunners fire at will—and as for the nonhunters, good luck to them, too. It's not only hunters who can learn from hunting.

A. *Comprehension*

Choose the answer that best completes each statement. Do not refer to the selection while doing this exercise.

1. One farmer protected his cows at the beginning of deer season by
   (a) moving them into barns.
   (b) moving them into pastures away from the woods.
   (c) painting "COW" on each animal.
   (d) putting brightly colored bandannas around their necks.
2. During deer season, to prevent themselves from accidentally being shot, people wear clothing in
   (a) hunter green.
   (b) neon green.
   (c) neon yellow.
   (d) hunter orange.
3. For the author, deer season requires him to
   (a) examine his beliefs carefully.
   (b) join his friends in hunting.
   (c) write letters protesting the hunting season.
   (d) join antihunting organizations.
4. For Freeman, deer hunting, both for himself and for his children, represents
   (a) a chance to bond with the neighbors.
   (b) a lesson in ambiguity and tolerance.
   (c) a chance to learn new skills.
   (d) the loss of one's innocence.
5. Freeman is very much concerned with how to separate
   (a) the hunter's professed reason for killing deer and the actual reason.
   (b) the pros and cons of hunting as a sport.
   (c) the activity of hunting from the affection he feels for a friend who hunts.
   (d) the activity of hunting from the hostility he feels for a friend who hunts.

B. *Vocabulary*

For each italicized word from the selection, write the dictionary definition most appropriate for the context. You may refer to the selection to answer the questions in this section and in all the remaining sections.

1. as *venerable* as [paragraph 1: _____

2. an *uncanny* thing [2]: _____

3. those *abject,* inert cadavers [12]: _____

4. those abject, *inert* cadavers [12]: _____

5. a lesson in *ambiguity* [13]: _____

_____

C. Inferences

Complete the following questions.

1. At the end of paragraph 1, Freeman writes that Vermonters describe many annual rituals associated with rural living but that they neglect to write about hunting season. What can you infer is the reason for this neglect?
   (a) There is no need to write articles about hunting because the practice is so ingrained and accepted in the community.
   (b) Vermonters are ashamed of their fondness for hunting.
   (c) Vermonters do not want to call attention to the sport for fear of angering the antihunting and antigun lobbies.
   (d) One cannot accurately infer a reason.
2. We can infer from nonhunters' behavior during deer season, as described in paragraphs 7 to 9, that
   (a) innocent animals and people have been shot by accident.
   (b) nonhunters are too intimidated to speak out against hunting.
   (c) hunters are very careful about who or what they shoot.
   (d) nonhunters are so accustomed to the sport that they take no special precautions.
3. The subtitle of this essay is "A Lesson in Ambiguity." Another good subtitle would be
   (a) "Autumn Vermont Customs."
   (b) "Why I Am Opposed to Deer Hunting."
   (c) "A Lesson in Tolerance."
   (d) "How to Avoid Danger and Survive during Hunting Season."

D. Structure

Complete the following questions.

1. The author's purpose is to
   (a) criticize hunting as a sport.
   (b) analyze the advantages and disadvantages of hunting as a sport.
   (c) examine the ambiguities hunting presents to a nonhunter.
   (d) explain the benefits of hunting.

2. Read footnotes 3, 4, and 5 again. In the context of the discussion, how do these allusions, references to historical material, reinforce

   Freeman's main point? _____

   _____

   _____

3. The pattern of organization in paragraphs 2 to 6 is
   (a) chronological.
   (b) spatial.
   (c) deductive.
   (d) inductive.

4. What is the purpose of paragraph 10? It serves as
   (a) background information.
   (b) a transition from the background to the main point.
   (c) a conclusion from the earlier paragraphs.
   (d) a cause–effect connection.

5. With respect to the essay as a whole, what is the purpose of

   paragraph 11? _____

   _____

   _____

6. Locate the transitional phrase "and yet" in paragraph 11. What logical relationship does it signify?
   (a) steps in a process.
   (b) a contrast.
   (c) a conclusion.
   (d) emphasis.

7. The pattern of organization in paragraph 12 is
   (a) chronological.
   (b) spatial.
   (c) deductive.
   (d) inductive.

8. The emotional attitude of the writer in the essay can best be described as
   (a) contemplative, regretful, and sad.
   (b) sentimental, maudlin.
   (c) accepting, condoning.
   (d) unsure, hesitant, and indecisive.

Questions for Discussion and Analysis

1. Discuss your own experience with and/or thinking about hunting as a sport. Has this essay changed your thinking in any way?

2. It can be argued that in earlier stages of American history, hunting was a necessity if homesteaders and pioneers wanted to eat. But the practice seems less defensible today. Freeman writes of the skill and patience hunting requires. Does the sport have any other virtues?

3. Freeman writes this essay as much to show the importance of tolerance as he does to show his concerns about the sport of hunting. What is another practice that, fundamentally, you do not accept but that you have developed tolerance for? How did you achieve this tolerance?

⌖ ON THE WEB

Read about gun enthusiasts' and hunters' perspectives on a variety of issues relating to gun laws, hunting restrictions, and weapons culture at these two sites:

- www.gunsnet.net/forums/
The Guns Network Forums

- mynra.com
The National Rifle Association

Discovering Meaning:
The Importance of Language

Language and Its Effects on the Reader

CHAPTER OBJECTIVES

In this chapter, we will be concerned with language in prose writing—with words and the effect the writer intends them to have on you. Specifically, we will examine these elements of language:

- Denotation and connotation

- Figurative language (metaphors, similes, and personification)

- Language misused and abused

■ DENOTATION AND CONNOTATION

Good writers choose their words carefully. Most strive to recreate as precisely as is humanly possible the thoughts and emotions in their heads to words on the printed page. Gustave Flaubert, the nineteenth-

184

century French writer, to cite only one example, was a consummate craftsman. He agonized over his words, always searching for what he called "the right word" *(le mot juste)* and often spending an entire day working and reworking his sentences. On some days he would produce for his efforts only a single page. Much of our pleasure in reading derives from savoring the emotional associations such efforts afford us. An understanding of these associations will significantly improve your literal understanding and enhance your enjoyment of reading.

In the first section, we will study **word choice,** or **diction.** Some words are meant to arouse positive feelings, some are meant to be neutral or literal, while others are meant to convey a negative impression. The following chart shows the difference between **denotation** and **connotation,** the two elements in word choice:

Diction, or Word Choice

Denotation: The literal or explicit meaning of a word; often called the dictionary definition.

> Examples: *Home*—one's physical residence; the place where one lives.
>
> *Lemon*—a sour, yellow-skinned citrus fruit.

Neither of these words implies any particular judgment or suggests an emotional attitude.

Connotation: The cluster of suggestions, ideas, or emotional associations a word conjures up.

> Examples: *Home*—a place of safety, privacy, comfort, nurturing.
>
> *Lemon*—a piece of defective equipment, usually a car.

These two examples show that connotative values refer to an emotional response, in the first case, positive; in the second, negative.

Connotation extends the meaning beyond the denotative. As Richard Altick, author of *Preface to Critical Reading,* has written: "Nothing is more essential to intelligent, profitable reading than sensitivity to connotation." However, no one can teach you this sensitivity. It comes from a wide exposure to reading and a willingness to consult the dictionary definitions and the accompanying usage notes for help. This sensitivity may take years to develop. After all, the process of acquiring new words is a lifetime commitment, and learning the connotations of words is part of that commitment.

Connotation and Synonyms

The English language contains an irksome number of words that appear to be synonymous but that, upon closer examination, are not. (It is this feature of the English language that makes its study so difficult and yet so gratifying.) Consider the verb *walk*. It is simply neutral, denoting a forward movement by putting one foot in front of the other. But what of these related verbs: *stride, saunter, stroll, meander, glide, mince, lumber, plod, trudge, stagger, lurch, stomp,* and *march?* Study their associations and try to visualize the motion each suggests.

Stride: To walk purposely or resolutely.

Saunter, stroll: To walk in a leisurely, unhurried way.

Meander: To walk in no particular direction; to wander here and there with no fixed destination.

Glide: To walk in an elegant, graceful manner.

Mince: To walk in little steps, with exaggerated affectation or primness.

Lumber: To walk heavily and/or clumsily; often reserved for describing the movements of large, bulky animals such as bears.

Plod, trudge: To walk in a heavy or laborious way; may suggest discouragement or defeat.

Stagger, lurch: To walk in an unsteady manner, whether because of illness, drunkenness, or some other affliction; *stagger* is stronger than *lurch.*

Stomp: To walk with purposeful steps, often in anger.

March: To walk as in a regiment, in describing a military person; used in an ordinary way, it suggests walking purposefully or steadily.

Waddle: To walk in a slow, swaying, or side-to-side manner; often used to describe the way ducks or obese people walk.

Now consider these pairs of words. In each case, mark the item in the pair that carries a positive connotation with a plus sign; mark the item with the negative connotation with a minus sign. Consult a dictionary if necessary.

---

chubby	plump
assertive	aggressive
shopping binge	shopping spree

faux	fake
childish	childlike
loiter	wait
Frankenfoods	genetically altered foods
pedantic	learned (adj.)
modest	prudish

Connotative Restrictions

In addition to the positive or negative "charge" that words can convey, some words in English are restricted to describe a particular group. For example, the word *spry* usually applies to old people or animals. The *American Heritage Dictionary* usage note states that *spry* suggests "unexpected speed and energy of motion," traits that would be characteristic of an old person or an old dog more than they would be of, say, a six-year-old child. Similarly, the denotative meaning of the adjective *debonair* is "handsome, suave, and worldly." However, its connotation suggests that the word is better applied to a man than to a woman. Although neither of my two dictionaries suggests this connotation, from the many contexts where I have encountered this word, that is how the word is used and that is the image conjured up in my mind. A woman may be handsome, attractive, elegant, and so on, but not debonair.

Consider the word *demure:*

What is the word's denotative meaning? _____

_____

Is its connotation positive or negative? _____

Which gender does it seem more appropriate for? _____
Does it suggest any particular age? (Hint: Which person would you

describe as demure—a 50-year old man or a 13-year-old girl?) _____

_____

Words are powerful. Armed as they are with these associative values, words can arouse passions, dreams, hostility or any other strong emotion. What occurs to you, for example, when you think of the word *prairie*? Without consulting a dictionary, write the word's denotation and its connotation.

Denotation: _____

_____

Connotation: _____

_____

_____

In the United States and Canada, the word *prairie*—the endless expanse of rolling grassland in the central part of North America (the denotative meaning)—arouses strong feelings. We may see in our mind's eye tall, waving grass under an immense blue sky. Perhaps we visualize the Plains Indians living freely or buffalo grazing. Or perhaps not: To some extent we have a better sense of what words connote if we have some familiarity with them and with the thing they refer to. Experience helps.

Let's practice with a short passage. As you read it, pay particular attention to the circled words and phrases.

> The (persistent cloud cover,) the almost (constant patter of rain,) are (narcotic.) They seem to (seal) Seattle inside (a damp, cozy cocoon,) (muffling reality) and (beckoning) residents (to snuggle up) with a good book and a cup of coffee or a glass of wine. (Mary Bruno, "Seattle Under Siege," *Lear's*)

Taken together, do these words and phrases have a positive or a

negative connotation? _____
Once you establish that, does the writer intend the word *narcotic* to

have a positive or negative connotation? _____

Explain your thinking. How is she using the word here? _____

_____

To see how connotation works in longer prose passages, consider these two excerpts on the same topic, one by the American novelist John Steinbeck, the other by Ray Allen Billington, an American historian. Both are concerned with the westward migration following the 1849 gold rush, but you will immediately see that the authors' word choices are radically different, reflecting their radically different points of view. Pay attention to the underlined words.

> The railroads brought new <u>hordes</u> of <u>land-crazy people</u>, and the new Americans <u>moved like locusts</u> across the continent until the western sea put a boundary to their movements. Coal and copper and gold drew them on; <u>they savaged the land, gold-dredged the rivers</u> to <u>skeletons of pebbles and debris</u>. An <u>aroused and fearful government</u> made laws for the distribution of public lands—a quarter section, one hundred and sixty acres, per

person—and a claim had to be proved and improved; but there were ways of getting around this, and legally. My own grandfather proved out a quarter section for himself, one for his wife, one for each of his children, and, I suspect, acreage for children he hoped and expected to have. Marginal lands, of course, suitable only for grazing, went in larger pieces. One of the largest landholding families in California took its richest holdings by a trick: By law a man could take up all the swamp or water-covered land he wanted. The founder of this great holding mounted a scow on wheels and drove his horses over thousands of acres of the best bottom land, then reported that he had explored it in a boat, which was true, and confirmed his title. I need not mention his name: his descendants will remember.

John Steinbeck, *America and Americans*

Opportunity was the magnet that drew men westward during those three centuries, for nature's untapped riches promised pioneers the fortunes that fate had denied them in older societies. There, where a king's ransom in furs could be had for the taking, where lush grasslands beckoned the herdsman, where fortunes in gold and silver lay scarcely hidden, where virgin soils awaited only the magic touch of man to yield their wealth, men and women could begin life anew with only their brains and brawn and courage to sustain them. There they could realize the social equality that was the goal of every democratically inclined American. These were the lures that drew the frontiersmen ever westward toward the Pacific.

They moved in an orderly procession. The fur trappers came first, roaming far in advance of the settled areas as they gathered the bales of shiny beaver peltry that would gladden the hearts of Europe's elite. Then came the miners, who also left civilization far behind as they prospected mountain streams and desert wastes in their endless quest for gold or silver. Behind them were the cattlemen, seeking the grassy pastures where their herds could graze without the confinement of fences. Cowboys were a familiar sight on the frontiers of Virginia or Kentucky or Illinois long before they won their places in the sun and cinema on the High Plains of the Far West. These shock troops of civilization made little impression on the wilderness; instead they adapted themselves so completely to the forest environment that they altered the face of the country but slightly.

Ray Allen Billington, "The Frontier Disappears," *The American Story*

Write the central impression of the westward march Steinbeck conveys.

_____

_____

_____

Now do the same for the Billington passage. _____

_____

_____

Do you see how the two writers' diction makes all the difference?

Connotation in Fiction

In fiction, a writer may use descriptive details that are designed to evoke in the reader a particular emotional response to the characters. These details help you both visualize and assess the character. In this paragraph from *David Copperfield,* Charles Dickens introduces the reader to a character named Miss Murdstone. As you read the excerpt, identify and underline the descriptive words associated with metal and with unpleasantness.

> It was <u>Miss Murdstone</u> who was arrived, and a <u>gloomy-looking</u> lady she was: <u>dark</u>, like her brother, whom she greatly resembled in face and voice, and with <u>very heavy eyebrows</u>, nearly meeting over her <u>large nose</u>, as if, being disabled by the wrongs of her sex from wearing whiskers, she had carried them to that account. She brought with her <u>two uncompromising hard black boxes</u>, with her initials on the lids in <u>hard brass nails</u>. When she paid the coachman she took her money out of a <u>hard steel purse</u>, and she kept the purse in a <u>very jail of a bag</u> which hung upon her arm by <u>a heavy chain</u>, and <u>shut up like a bite</u>. I had never, at that time, seen such <u>a metallic lady</u> altogether as Miss Murdstone was.
>
> Charles Dickens, *David Copperfield.*

Consider the words and phrases you underlined; then write a sentence explaining what these connotative words and phrases

suggest about Miss Murdstone's character. _____

_____

■ FIGURATIVE LANGUAGE

Next, we come to the most difficult, but perhaps the most inventive and interesting, use of language. **Figurative language** or the use of a **figure of speech** refers to the use of language not in its literal sense, but in a metaphorical or imaginative way. Although you may associate figures of speech primarily with poetry, many prose writers also employ them to give immediacy or drama to their writing, to create a mental image, or to clarify a difficult concept. Here is a summary of the kinds of figurative language we will take up in this section of the chapter:

Figures of Speech

- **Metaphor:** A direct and imaginative comparison.
- **Simile:** An imaginative comparison using "like" or "as."
- **Personification:** A comparison in which something nonliving is described as if it were human.

Metaphors and Similes

Metaphors and **similes** are closely enough related that we can treat them together. Both represent imaginative comparisons between two *essentially unlike* things. This point is important. The sentence "My house looks like your house" is not figurative; because houses are in the same class, there is no imaginative comparison. A good definition of metaphor can be found in the charming and poignant film *Il Postino (The Postman)*. The main character, a semiliterate postman, wants to write a love poem to the barmaid Beatrice, the object of his affections. He asks the great Chilean poet, Pablo Neruda, who lives in his town, how to go about writing such a thing, and Neruda says that love poems must have lots of metaphors, which he defines as "a way of describing something by comparing it to something else."

A **metaphor** refers to a *direct* comparison, in which a particular quality or characteristic of one thing (the figurative) is transferred to another (the literal). Although literally, such transfer of meaning does not make sense, the reader knows to interpret it as imaginative. Consider this sentence:

The farmer's leathery, lined face revealed years of toil in the sun.

The writer is directly comparing the farmer's skin to leather (in other words, transferring directly the characteristics of leather to skin), suggesting that the man's skin is browned, thick, and tough.

A **simile,** in contrast, is an imaginative comparison stated *indirectly,* usually with the words "like," " as," "as though," "as if," and, occasionally, "seem." In the above example, a change in the wording would result in a simile:

The farmer's lined face looked like leather, revealing years of toil in the sun.

It is probably fair to say that metaphors are stronger than similes, if only because the two things—literal and metaphorical—are joined without the reader's being *told* that they are similar. Let us examine a few figures of speech in detail before you analyze some on your own. We will begin with similes, because they are easier to identify. In the first excerpt, from the novel *The Kitchen God's Wife* by Amy Tan, the narrator of the novel is describing her mother's house.

> The front of her place is Day-Glo pink, the unfortunate result of her being talked into a special deal by a longtime customer, a painting contractor. And because the outside is bumpy stucco, the whole effect looks like Pepto-Bismol poured over cottage cheese.

To analyze any figure of speech, you first must know what is being compared to what. In this case, the garish pink color of the narrator's house is being compared to the color of Pepto-Bismol, and the bumpy surface texture of the exterior stucco is compared to the texture of cottage cheese. This amusing simile presents a striking visual image.

Here is an excerpt from John Berendt's novel *Midnight in the Garden of Good and Evil*, describing the main character, Jim Williams.

> He was tall, about fifty, with darkly handsome, almost sinister features: a neatly trimmed mustache, hair turning silver at the temples, and eyes so black they were like the tinted windows of a sleek limousine—he could see out, but you couldn't see in.

The word "sinister" at the beginning of the passage is reinforced by the simile, comparing his black eyes to a limousine's tinted windows. The simile also suggests a certain coldness, a deliberate attempt to separate himself from other people, which is precisely why celebrities travel in limousines with tinted glass. In this case, Berendt uses the familiar to explain the unfamiliar.

Now let us examine two metaphors with the literal and figurative elements underlined. The first is from Gabriel García Marquez's novel *Love in the Time of Cholera.*

> The death of his mother left Florentino Ariza condemned once again to his maniacal pursuits: the office, his meetings in strict rotation with his regular mistresses, the domino games at the Commercial Club, the same books of love, the Sunday visits to the cemetery. It was the <u>rust</u> of <u>routine</u>, which he had despised and feared so much, but which had protected him from an awareness of age.

We see first the catalog of Ariza's humdrum weekly activities; then García Marquez ingeniously connects his routine to rust. The pairing is brilliant. Rust or corrosion usually results from disuse or neglect, but in this case, it results in Ariza's rusting away; he does the same thing week after week, and his life has become corroded by routine, just as disuse eventually rusts a metal object.

Here is an example from Lewis Lapham in an article titled "Hazards of the New Fortune," published in *Harper's*. The subject is modern American politics.

> Before Watergate the realm of politics was <u>a land of orchards and sweet-running streams</u>; after Watergate the realm of politics was a <u>swamp inhabited by foul and crawling things</u>.

"Watergate" refers to a break-in in 1972 of the Democratic headquarters at the Watergate complex near Washington, D.C., by people paid for by the Republican National Committee. President Nixon's repeated lying about his involvement in the scandal resulted in his eventual resignation in disgrace. In comparing politics before the Watergate scandal to politics since, Lapham uses language that sounds metaphorically as if it is referring to a paradise. The underlying meaning is that politicians and politics have become corrupt and treacherous.

Uses of Metaphors and Similes

Metaphors and similes have a wide range of uses. Study these purposes and the accompanying examples.

- *To provide a visual image.*
  Consuelo was easy to distinguish even from a distance, her long red hair like a whip of fire against the eternal green of that landscape. (Isabel Allende, *Eva Luna*)
- *To establish a mood.*
  I remember that the Gabilan Mountains to the east of the valley were light gray mountains full of sun and loveliness and a kind of invitation, so that you wanted to climb into their warm foothills almost as you want to climb into the lap of a beloved mother. (John Steinbeck, *East of Eden*)
- *To reinforce an observation.*
  Phoenix is among the five fastest-growing metropolises in the country, and few places are as relentlessly suburban in character. It has a downtown so exiguous that a pedestrian outside its biggest office building at 9 on a weekday morning is a phenomenon as singular as a cow in Times Square. (Jerry Adler, "Paved Paradise," *Newsweek*)

- *To clarify a difficult scientific concept.*
  Astronomers have followed the motion of stars circling a hugely massive black hole at the center of the Milky Way, shedding new light on one of our galaxy's greatest mysteries. For decades, astronomers have theorized that a black hole must lie at the center of the galaxy like some dark and deadly spider, its gravity so enormous that it sucks all nearby gas and stars into it until they disappear with a final flash of energy. (David Perlman, "New Clues to What Lies at Center of Earth's Galaxy," *San Francisco Chronicle*)

- *To persuade or convince.*
  We have waited for more than 340 years for our constitutional and God-given rights. The nations of Asia and Africa are moving with jetlike speed toward gaining political independence, but we still creep at horse-and-buggy pace toward gaining a cup of coffee at a lunch counter. (Martin Luther King, Jr., "Letter from Birmingham Jail," 1963)

Playful Aspects of Figurative Language

Not all figures of speech are used in service of such serious purposes. Some writers simply like to play with language, relishing the chance to show off or to dazzle the reader with ingenious comparisons. One writer who often indulges in daring and often bizarre figures of speech is T. Coraghessan Boyle. His story "Beat," included in a collection titled *Without a Hero,* tells of a teenager who embarks on a fictional journey to meet Jack Kerouac, writer of the 1960s cult novel *On the Road.* The narrator runs away from his home in California and travels to New York, locates Kerouac's house, and finally musters enough courage to knock on the front door. Here is his description of the woman, supposedly Kerouac's mother, who answers the door.

My first surprise was in store. It wasn't Jack who answered the door but a big blocky old lady with a face like the bottom of a hiking boot. She was wearing a dress the size of something you'd drape over a car to keep the dust off it. . . . She gave me the kind of look that could peal the tread off a recapped tire.

Taken together, what impression of Kerouac's fictional mother do these figures of speech suggest? _____

Personification

The last figure of speech we will consider in this chapter is **personification,** in which inanimate or nonhuman objects—for example, objects, animals, plants, or concepts—are given human attributes or feelings. Here are three examples:

Just then they heard a faraway rumble: Thunder dragging its furniture. (Joao Guimaraes Rosa, "The Aldacious Navigator," *The Third Bank of the River*)

Does the writer suggest here that the thunder is loud or soft? _____

> Few [residents of Nanking, China] could predict that within months war would march by their very doorsteps—leaving their homes in flames and their streets drenched in blood. (Iris Chang, *The Rape of Nanking*)

To what is war being compared? _____

> The building was hanging on grimly to the vestiges of respectability. A threadbare runner [a long, narrow rug] climbed the stairs wearily, and there were dusty plastic flowers in cheap vases on the window ledges. (Ken Follett, *The Third Twin*)

What image of this building does Follett convey? _____

_____

Practice Exercise 1

Here are several short passages containing figurative language to analyze. Write the answers on a separate sheet of paper. First, decide whether the excerpt represents a simile, a metaphor, or personification. Then, decide what the literal subject is and what that subject is metaphorically being compared to. Finally, briefly explain the meaning. Start with these easier examples.

1. It was a late hour on a cold wind-bitten autumn day when I climbed a great hill spined like a dinosaur's back. (Loren Eiseley, *The Immense Journey*)

2. . . . we watched some of the little brown forest skinks hunting among the roots of the trees around us. These little lizards always looked neat and shining, as though they had been cast in chocolate and had just that second stepped out of the mould, gleaming and immaculate. (Gerald Durrell, *A Zoo in My Luggage*)

3. America is a large, friendly dog in a very small room. Every time it wags its tail, it knocks over a chair. (Arnold Toynbee)

4. Regret grew only more insistent. She didn't just wait on his stoop any longer, she began to rap her icy knuckles against the door. (Andre Dubus III, *The House of Sand and Fog*)

5. Regret grew more intense with the passage of time. In the pale afternoon sunlight that filtered through the filthy upper window of Hong King's shack, Hong King looked more than old. He looked dead. His skin, stretched taut over fragile bones, was the color and texture of old wax. (Ruthanne Lum McCunn, *Thousand Pieces of Gold*)

6. (The writer is describing a small town in the Peruvian Andes.)
It had been a hostile town that lived in anger, infecting others with it. (José María Arguedes, *Deep Rivers*)

7. Second terms far too often have been marred by scandals, and few reelected presidents [had] more buzzards circling than Bill Clinton. (David S. Broder, *The Washington Post*)

8. Parker's wife was sitting on the front porch floor, snapping beans. Parker was sitting on the step, some distance away, watching her sullenly. She was plain, plain. The skin on her face was thin and drawn as tight as the skin on an onion and her eyes were grey and sharp like the points of two toothpicks. (Flannery O'Connor, "Parker's Back")

The next group is slightly more difficult. Some passages may contain more than one figure of speech.

9. Two flickering bugs were zigzagging their way toward each other, their attraction looking haphazard yet predestined. They flashed on and off like airplanes headed for the same runway, closer and closer, until they sparked for an instant as one, then extinguished themselves and flitted darkly away. (Amy Tan, *The Hundred Secret Senses*)

10. In the upper middle of the emptiness of eastern Oregon is a place known as the Painted Hills. The Painted Hills are weird mounds leaking the colors of mineral layers like paint—orange and yellow, black and dark green and rust. The soil here is a crumbly mix that looks from a distance like the texture of a sponge, and up close as though it had been milled to a uniform shape. . . There are signs posted telling people not to drive on the hills—on the hills as soft as the interior of an angel food cake. (Sallie Tisdale, *Stepping Westward*)

11. It seems that Father had learned some painful lessons about prejudice while searching for an apartment in Paterson [New Jersey]. Not until years later did I hear how much resistance he had encountered with landlords who were panicking at the influx [of] Latinos into a neighborhood that had been Jewish for a couple of generations. But it was the American phenomenon of ethnic turnover that was changing the urban core of Paterson, and the human flood could not be held back with an accusing finger. (Judith Ortiz Cofer, *Silent Dancing*)

12. (The writer is describing the weather in Wyoming.)
     Spring weather is capricious and mean. It snows, then blisters into heat. There have been tornadoes. They lay their elephant trunks out in the sage until they find houses, then slurp everything up and leave. (Gretel Ehrlich, "The Solace of Open Spaces")

13. The man who has not the habit of reading is imprisoned in his immediate world, in respect to time and place. His life falls into a set routine; he is limited to contact and conversation with a few friends and acquaintances, and he sees only what happens in his immediate neighborhood. From this prison there is no escape. (Lin Yu-T'ang, "The Art of Reading")

14.   My mother died at the moment I was born, and so for my whole life there was nothing standing between myself and eternity; at my back was always a bleak, black wind. I could not have known at the beginning of my life that this would be so; I only came to know this in the middle of my life, just at the time when I was no longer young and realized that I had less of some of the things I used to have in abundance and more of some of the things I had scarcely had at all. And this realization of loss and gain made me look backward and forward: at my beginning was this woman whose face I had never seen, but at my end was nothing, no one between me and the black room of the world. (Jamaica Kincaid, *The Autobiography of My Mother*)

15.   (The narrator is describing an early-morning reaction to her lover.) And then, abruptly, she woke up beside him in her own bed one early spring morning and knew she loathed him and couldn't wait to get him out of the house. She felt guilty, but guilty in the way one feels guilty when about to discommode some clinging slug that has managed to attach itself to one's arm or leg. (Gail Godwin, "Amanuensis," *Mr. Bedford and the Muses*)

Finally, see how well you can do with these more difficult figures of speech.

16.   As I looked about me I felt that the grass was the country, as the water is the sea. The red of the grass made all the great prairie the color of winestains, or of certain seaweeds when they are first washed up. And there was so much motion in it; the whole country seemed, somehow, to be running. (Willa Cather, *My Ántonia*)

17. (In the novel this passage comes from, the main character, Abel Grey, is in love with a woman who does not reciprocate his feelings.)
He had thought he could walk through life without any pain; he'd thought solitude would comfort him and keep him safe all the rest of his days, but he was wrong. His grandfather always told him that love never arrived politely, knocking on the front door like a kindhearted neighbor, asking to be let in. Instead, it ambushed a man when he least expected it, when his defenses were down, and even the most obstinate individual, no matter how bullheaded or faithless, had no choice but to surrender when love like this came to call. (Alice Hoffman, *The River King*)

18. The logic that pointed to the death of writing and reading was compelling. Each new medium was more visually and sensually rich than the last: movies gave way to talking movies, which gave way to round-the-clock talking color television. In that context, words just hung around looking glum, with hardly enough energy left to compose themselves into sentences. (Adam Gopnik, "The Return of the Word," *The New Yorker*)

19. (Martin Luther King, Jr., went to Birmingham, Alabama, in 1963, to organize a black boycott of white businesses. In so doing, King, the president of the Southern Christian Leadership Conference, had been accused of being an outsider coming in to cause trouble. Here is part of his defense.)
I am cognizant of the interrelatedness of all communities and states. I cannot sit idly by in Atlanta and not be concerned about what happens in Birmingham. Injustice anywhere is a threat to justice everywhere. We are caught in an inescapable network of mutuality, tied in a single garment of destiny. (Martin Luther King, Jr., "Letter from Birmingham Jail")

20. Time is but the stream I go a-fishing in. I drink at it; but while I drink I see the sandy bottom and detect how shallow it is. Its thin current slides away, but eternity remains. (Henry David Thoreau, "Where I Lived, and What I Lived For")

■ LANGUAGE MISUSED AND ABUSED

From one edition of this book to the next, deceptive and manipulative uses of the language have proliferated and become even more entrenched in the language. For easier reference, I have alphabetized these misuses and abuses in this section. The examples here come from writers, politicians, the new breed of political advisors called spin doctors, advertising copywriters, and others. Most writers, at least those who write for mainstream, legitimate publications, are ethical and honest. They adhere to the rules of good journalism, strive for integrity in their reporting, and resist the temptation to inject personal bias. But not all writers are so honest, and advertising and politicking have become so cutthroat that manipulative and deceptive uses of the language are commonly condoned or ignored. Such misuse or abuse of language is like elevator music; it's there, but we no longer hear how awful it is.

An unscrupulous writer may use language to exploit the reader, to incite or inflame passions, or to soften the impact of ideas that might otherwise be more realistically or harshly interpreted. As a critical reader, you should be particularly alert to language that seeks to influence you in this way through the clever misuse of words. In this section, we will examine several types of misused language:

Misuses and Abuses of Language

- **Clichés:** Tired, overused expressions.
- **Doublespeak:** Language used to deceive or to misrepresent the truth.
- **Euphemisms:** Inoffensive language used as a substitute for offensive terms.
- **Jargon:** Specialized language used by a particular group.

- **Politically correct language:** Language that attempts to avoid insensitivity related to diversity, historical injustices, racism, and the like.
- **Sneer words:** Words with strong negative connotations.

Do not worry if some of these terms appear to overlap because, in fact, they occasionally may. The point is to develop a sensitivity to words and to see through linguistic sleaze and sludge when you encounter it. Many examples of language abuses follow so that you can learn to identify them readily.

Clichés

Clichés—tired, overused expressions—tell the careful reader that a lazy writer is at work. Good writers avoid clichés because such fossilized expressions long ago lost their effectiveness; many no longer make sense, for example, "like grist to the mill," "get down to brass tacks," or "fight tooth and nail." Some clichés probably sounded clever the first time they were used, but now, at the beginning of the twenty-first century, many sound ridiculous. Yet we still hear them.

For fun, you might begin your own list of clichés to add to this one:

Common Clichés

as bright as a penny	as rich as Croesus
as fresh as a daisy	to be up in arms
to come to a grinding halt	as easy as pie
as healthy as a horse	as cool as a cucumber
leave no stone unturned	a labor of love
as clear as mud	slower than molasses in January
happy as a clam	a chip off the old block

Merle Rubin, a book reviewer, has compiled a list of contemporary clichés. She opens her article with this observation:[1]

There are certain words and phrases that creep into our daily lives, taking over our patterns of speech until it seems as if they are almost indispensable. They are often trite and misleading, and yet they will not go away. Indeed, they seem to grow stronger with repetition, making everyday conversation a special kind of ordeal.

[1]Merle Rubin, "A Nightmare of Cliché," *The Wall Street Journal,* June 8, 2001.

Here are a few examples from Rubin's list of new catchphrases: "closure," "getting on with my life," "I'll always be there for you," "support," "judgmental," "issues," and "deal with it."

Some writers, however, deliberately turn clichés upside down, and in so doing, renew them, either to be inventive or to be humorous. In one passage of Russell Baker's autobiography, *Growing Up,* he describes a conversation with his uncle, who has asked the eight-year-old boy what he wants to be when he grows up. Russell answers, "I want to be a garbage man." Baker writes, "My uncle smiled, but my mother had seen the first distressing evidence of a bump budding on a log." In this sentence, Baker takes the cliché "to be a bump on a log" (meaning to be dull or lazy), and twists it into something new and funny.

Doublespeak

The term **doublespeak** combines the words *doublethink* and *newspeak,* coined by George Orwell in his novel *1984.* In the novel, he describes a future in which the government twists words to manipulate its citizens' thoughts. William D. Lutz, a member of Rutgers University's English department, for many years edited the *Quarterly Review of Doublespeak,* a periodical dedicated to publishing especially egregious examples of doublespeak. He has compared doublespeak to "an infection that sickens the language through the pollution of words carefully chosen." In the introduction to his recent book, *The New Doublespeak: Why No One Knows What Anyone's Saying Anymore,* Lutz writes:

> Doublespeak is language that pretends to communicate but really doesn't. It is language that makes the bad seem good, the negative appear positive, the unpleasant appear attractive or at least tolerable. Doublespeak is language that avoids or shifts responsibility, language that is at variance with its real or purported meaning. It is language that conceals or prevents thought; rather than extending thought, doublespeak limits it.

Doublespeak is further described as language that is "grossly deceptive, evasive, euphemistic, confusing or self-contradictory" with the potential for "pernicious social or political consequences." Doublespeak may or may not involve euphemism (see next section).

Here is an excellent candidate for a future doublespeak award: In March 2001, Cisco Systems, the giant Internet equipment manufacturer, announced that 8,000 employees (one-sixth of its workforce) would be let go, subject to "involuntary normal attrition." Everyone was confused over this announcement. As Julian Boyd, a professor emeritus of English at the University of California–Berkeley, noted: "It's not good English, it's not good logic, it's not good reasoning. You can't have normal involuntary 'attrition.' If a thing happens—like attrition or digestion or growth—then you don't do it. You can't have an involuntary happening."[2] Here is list of recent examples of doublespeak:

Examples of Doublespeak

Retrievable storage site: A nuclear fuel dump

Uncontrolled contact with the ground: A safety expert's term for an airplane crash

Runway incursion: The FAA's term for a hazard or collision caused by planes or airport vehicles that stray off course

Water landing: United Airlines term for a crash in the ocean

Therapeutic misadventure: The medical profession's term for a doctor's incompetence that results in a patient's death

---

Corporate Doublespeak for "Employee Layoffs"

Census reduction

Negative employee retention

Career change opportunity

Vocational relocation

Workers who are uninstalled, excessed, or rightsized

Doublespeak in Politics

Receipts proposals and *users fees:* President George H. W. Bush's terms for new taxes after he had pledged, "Read my lips; no new taxes."

Reality augmentation: Lying

Contained depression: An economic recession

Doublespeak in the Military

Civilian irregular defense soldiers: Mercenaries paid for by the U.S. government during the Vietnam conflict

Predawn vertical insertion: White House term used in the first Bush administration to refer to the invasion of Grenada by parachutists

---

[2]Quoted in Steve Rubenstein, "Plain Speaking Also Falls Victim to Cisco's Ax," *San Francisco Chronicle,* March 10, 2001.

Suppression of assets: Bombing of both civilian and military targets during Operation Desert Storm

Ethnic cleansing: Genocide as practiced by Serbians against ethnic Albanians in Kosovo

Collateral damage: NATO term for bombs that killed refugees and Serbian civilians during the 1999 war in Kosovo; Timothy McVeigh, who was convicted and executed for the bombing of the Oklahoma City federal building, used this same term in reference to the 19 children killed among the 168 victims

Euphemisms

A **euphemism** is an inoffensive word or phrase substituted for an offensive one. Writers use euphemisms to soften our perception of unpleasant events, to change our beliefs, or perhaps even to cover up wrongdoing. Because euphemisms pervade our culture, you should learn to spot them readily and to recognize the intent behind them.

Here are some examples: A trendy restaurant in Los Angeles refers to toast as "grilled peasant bread." A "Jeopardy!" contestant, a bookie, called himself a "turf information specialist." The American Hair Loss Council prefers that toupees (men's hairpieces) be called "hair systems." The winner of the Miss America pageant no longer "reigns" (which sounds too royalist and elitist); now she "does a year of service." Real estate agents often use euphemisms in describing property for sale. For example, the adjective "cozy" is a euphemistic code word meaning "very small"; "fixer-upper" or "handyman's special" may refer to a house in a horrendous state of disrepair; and "close to transportation" might very well refer to a house next to the train tracks.

During the Vietnam era, euphemisms were widely used in government and military reports about the American presence in Southeast Asia. The Nixon administration euphemistically described the 1970 American invasion of Cambodia as an "incursion." Herbicides—used to kill the foliage so that North Vietnamese troop movements would be more visible from the air—were called "defoliants."

As noted earlier, doublespeak may involve euphemism (though not all euphemisms involve doublespeak), and sometimes the line between them is hard to see. The difference is that doublespeak, as defined earlier, is *deliberately* and grossly deceptive, whereas the motives for using euphemisms are less nefarious. One's interpretation of such phrases perhaps depends on one's worldview (see Chapter 8). Consider George W. Bush's use of the term "faith-based programs," an expression designed to deflect criticism by those who claim that religious groups should not receive federal funds for community work (because it violates the separation of church and state). Would you characterize this as a euphemism or as doublespeak?

Consider this example: In April 2001, a Summit of the Americas was held in Quebec City, Canada. Antiglobalization protestors denounced the negotiations because they would create the world's largest free trade zone, which would benefit corporations rather than workers. In response, the Canadian police set up a 10-foot-high chain-link fence to keep the protestors away from the center of the city. Quebec City's leaders referred to this fence as "the perimeter." This example demonstrates that perhaps we need to distinguish between harmless euphemisms and those intended to obscure the truth.

We should note, in concluding this section, that some euphemisms do serve a useful purpose: to blunt the impact of a terrible situation. This intent undoubtedly lay behind the phrase "preventive clearing," used to describe the mass slaughter of cattle and sheep in England, Wales, and Ireland in the spring of 2001. Healthy animals living within a 2-mile radius of animals infected with the highly contagious foot-and-mouth disease were destroyed. Perhaps the euphemism helped in some small way to soften the terrible financial and emotional blow to these countries' farmers.

Jargon

Jargon refers to the specialized language used by members of a particular trade, group, or profession. Like doublespeak and euphemisms, jargon can be used to deceive, but for the most part, its purpose is to make the writer or speaker sound more intelligent or learned than if he or she used ordinary discourse. In and of itself, jargon is not necessarily harmful, at least not in the way the other kinds of misused language are that we have examined. All specialists—whether they're plumbers, neurosurgeons, or college reading teachers—have their own special terminology that nonspecialists or the lay audience might not understand.

For example, stockbrokers often refer to the "dead-cat bounce," a phrase describing a trading session when the market makes a modest comeback after a day or two of serious price declines. (The phrase comes from the fact that even a dead cat bounces, though not very high.) Comic book artists use the term "ash can" to refer to a few sample pages of the first version of a comic book—sort of a partial prototype.

These are inoffensive uses of jargon that the reader might be able to figure out from the context, but even if he or she can't figure out the meaning, the intention is not to hoodwink. At its best, jargon is useful, providing a verbal shorthand between people who are fluent in the terminology and the subject. At its worst, however, jargon is pretentious, obscure, and impossible to read. For example, what is one to make of this sentence?

> The artist's employment of a radical visual idiom serves to decontextualize both conventional modes of representation and the patriarchal contexts on which such traditional hegemonic notions as representation, tradition, and even conventional contextualization have come to be seen as depending for their privileged status as aestheto-interpretative mechanisms. (Author unknown; quoted in David Foster Wallace, "Tense Present: Democracy, English, and the Wars over Usage," *Harper's,* April 2001.)

Even the most skilled reader would have trouble translating that statement.

Like doublespeak, jargon can sometimes be employed to mislead. In 2000, the giant online bookseller Amazon.com announced a new strategy called "dynamic pricing." This term sounded positive, as if consumers could compare deals on merchandise with a mouse click. But what consumers didn't know was that Amazon intended to use the information about their buying habits and their geographical location (determined by their zip code) to charge *different prices to different customers* on the basis of their likely financial status. Fortunately, the jargon was exposed for what it was, and Amazon dropped the plan.[3]

Politically Correct Language

During the 1980s, a movement called **political correctness** (PC) grew out of increased sensitivity to diversity in the country. Briefly, this movement was an attempt by liberals to purge the language of words and phrases that might be considered insensitive or racially charged or that called into question people's differences. The PC movement also sought to redress historical injustices in matters of race, gender, and ethnicity. Thus evolved a whole new vocabulary of **politically correct language.**[4] Some examples: An animal rights organization called In Defense of Animals lobbied the Berkeley City Council to go on record as opposing the term "pet owner" because it suggested that an animal was property. The new PC term approved by the council is "pet

[3]Quoted in David Streitfeld, "Amazon Flunks Its Pricing Test," *Washington Post,* September 28, 2000.
[4]For a comprehensive overview of the origins of politically correct speech, see *www.cyberpat.com/shirlsite/samples/polcor.html.*

guardian." Blind people are now referred to as "visually challenged," liars may be referred to (humorously) as "ethically challenged," and the overweight may be called "calorically challenged."[5]

Despite the sometimes humorous substitutions that PC language has created, many attempts to replace insensitive terms have validity. For example, in Maine, the state legislature was pressured by Native Americans to purge the word "squaw" from place-names in that state (Maine has a Squaw Pond, Squaw Bay, and Big and Little Squaw Townships). Donna Loring, a representative of the Penobscot Nation addressed the legislature: "I can say with 99% certainty, if you are a native woman and live on a reservation, you have heard the word and felt the sting and pain." Similarly, Native Americans have brought suits against several sports teams to force them to change their names; among these are the Cleveland Indians, the Atlanta Braves, and the Florida State Seminoles.[6]

Sneer Words

As we learned in the section on euphemisms, a writer can shape our perceptions of events, making things seem not as bad as they actually are. Similarly, a writer can intensify an already bad situation by using **sneer words,** words with strong negative connotations suggesting derision and scorn. When a foreign political leader is out of favor with the American government, he may be described by administration sources as a "strongman." This is the way Manuel Noriega, the now deposed leader of Panama, and Slobodan Milosevic, the former president of Serbia, were routinely characterized in the American media. Oddly, Saddam Hussein of Iraq is generally accorded more respect, being called "president" or "leader," even though his stronghold on Iraq is every bit as ruthless as Milosevic's was on Serbia.

The Wall Street Journal's editorial page often reflects a politically conservative point of view. In an article about the future of the Republican Party in California, Joel Kotkin, writing on the paper's editorial page, characterized John Burton, the president pro tempore of the U.S. Senate, as "an archetypal product of the People's Republic of San Francisco," a reference to the city's traditional liberal political climate.[7]

[5]The PC movement extends beyond language, however; on many American college and university campuses, especially those traditionally considered liberal, there are unspoken doctrines or sets of beliefs concerning certain political and social issues. Affirmative action is one such issue. Students are meant to hold the "correct" political view, and those who argue against the orthodoxy are denounced. Perhaps you can supply examples from your own campus.

[6]Quoted in "Maine to Decide If 'Squaw' Is Offensive," *San Francisco Examiner,* March 5, 2000.

[7]Joel Kotkin, "GOP Wiped Out in Land of Reagan," *The Wall Street Journal,* November 6, 1998.

("People's Republic" was the official name of many East European Communist nations, and in fact, China is still officially known as the People's Republic of China.) Environmentalists often refer to farmers, ranchers, and corporate executives who are opposed to environmental protections as "toad stabbers." Environmentalists are sometimes called "tree huggers" or "wolf worshipers." Here are some other sneer words:

Common Sneer Words

Lackey: A servant; also a fawning, servile follower who serves as a master's yes-man

Hack: A person, usually a writer, who produces mediocre work and whose only motivation is to make money

Self-styled or *self-proclaimed* (as in "self-styled expert"): Word labels suggesting that the person's status or reputation is undeserved or that a title has been self-conferred

---

Practice Exercise 2

Read the following passages; then decide which type of misuse or abuse of language is used—cliché, doublespeak, euphemism, PC language, or sneer words.

1. When Maryland beat Stanford in the 2001 NCAA basketball tournament in March 2001, one television sportswriter noted that

   Stanford had suffered an "agonizing defeat." _____

2. In 1998 President Clinton appeared before Kenneth Starr's committee and was asked questions about answers he had given earlier to the grand jury. That group had asked Clinton whether he had had sexual relations with Monica Lewinsky. Before Starr's committee, Clinton

   characterized his earlier answers as "legally accurate." _____

3. A brochure for a memorial park advertises its services with this message: "It must be wise to protect yourself and your family AGAINST THE ONE EVENT THAT MOST CERTAINLY WILL HAPPEN. AND WHAT is the event? It is the same day—it is never a question of IF, only a question of WHEN . . . you will have a break in your family circle and as a result have to make hurried decisions for final arrangements, and we sincerely hope that the need is a remote one." (Brochure for Skylawn Memorial Park, San Mateo, California)

   _____

4. Employees at Sea World in Orlando, Florida, are instructed to use a particular vocabulary, especially when answering park visitors' questions. Here are some examples: "enclosure" (not "cage"); "controlled environment" (not "captivity"); "natural environment" (not "wild"); and "acquired" (not "captured"). (Quoted in "Chickens

   of the Sea," *Harper's*) _____

5. During the Vietnam War, the Defense Department referred to refugees fleeing the war as "ambient noncombatant personnel."

   _____

6. O. J. Simpson, the famous football player and actor, was accused of killing his former wife, Nicole Brown Simpson, and her friend, Ronald Goldman. Simpson's attorneys tried to argue that the term "domestic discord" should replace "domestic violence" or "spousal abuse." Further, they requested that Judge Lance Ito disallow the terms "battered wife" and "stalker." The judge refused the request. (Quoted in Andrea Dworkin, "In Nicole Brown Simpson's Words," *Los Angeles*

   Times, January 29, 1995.) _____

7. In Jonathan Harr's *A Civil Action,* Harr quotes Judge Skinner, the presiding judge in a pesticide case, as saying, first to the prosecuting attorneys: "I'm putting this case on a tight leash." Later in the same case, the judge tells the lead prosecuting attorney, "I'm going to

   lower the boom on you." _____

8. During both the 1996 and 2000 political campaigns, Bob Dole and George W. Bush, the Republican presidential candidates, referred to Al Gore, the Democratic candidate as a "tree hugger" because he

   espoused environmental protections. _____

9. In New York, one cannot advertise a house as having "a beautiful ocean view, a spacious master bedroom, walk-in closets, maid's quarters, and a downstairs family room. This particular house is located in a private community with shopping and a beach within walking distance." According to R. Randy Lee, lawyer and president of a Staten Island real estate company, such an ad would make the builder or seller liable for lawsuits because the description discriminates against potential buyers in five different ways. Those who might be offended include blind people (the house has an "ocean view"); women ("master bedroom" sounds sexist); singles (there is a "family room"); the disabled (the house is within "walking" distance of desirable places); and minorities ("private" is sometimes used as a code word to keep minorities out of white

communities). (Quoted in R. Randy Lee, "Housing for the Non-Discriminating Buyer," *The Wall Street Journal,* November 3, 1994.)

_____

10. At the First International Conference of Love and Attraction, delegates came up with the following definition for "love": "The cognitive-affective state characterized by intrusive and obsessive fantasizing concerning reciprocity of amorant feeling by the object of amorance."

_____

■ CHAPTER EXERCISES

Selection 1   The writer of this passage grew up in Canada.

[1]Hockey has [been] and always will be there in my life, like a trusty family dog ever willing to uncurl from its bed over in the corner and be palpitating to go, cheerfully ready to lend itself again to my attentions. [2]Sometimes it has waited patiently for years. [3]Good dog, hockey! [4]Baseball was always more complicated. [5]For my first fourteen or so years on earth, it lay out there with Indian clubs and curling[8] on the periphery of my sports interest, largely unplayed, its big-league sagas churning through season after season without so much as a nod from me. [6]And then, wham! [7]Almost from one day to the next, baseball fever—better, baseball malaria: long sieges of delirium now and then cooling off and even receding until you think the bug has gone and then, wham! [8]Back again, more virulent than ever.

Bruce McCall, *Thin Ice: Coming of Age in Canada*

A. Content and Structure

Complete the following questions.

1. Identify the simile used in sentence 1. What is compared to what?

   _____ is compared to _____.

2. Identify the metaphors used in sentences 7 and 8.

   _____ is compared to _____

   and to _____.

[8]An Indian club is a large, bottle-shaped, wooden club that one swings as an arm exercise; curling, played on ice and originating in Scotland, is a popular team sport in Canada.

3. Explain why these figures of speech are appropriate for the content of the paragraph. _____

    _____

4. Locate the sentence that represents the central transition between the two major ideas in the paragraph. _____

5. We can accurately infer that McCall
    (a) played hockey better than he played baseball.
    (b) was required to play both hockey and baseball at school.
    (c) became nearly obsessed by baseball once he began to play it.
    (d) also enjoyed curling and working out with Indian clubs.

6. Which of these inferences is more likely?
    (a) McCall merely followed the sport of baseball rather than playing it himself.
    (b) McCall actively played baseball.

B. Language Analysis

Complete the following questions.

1. The word *palpitating,* in sentence 1, means "quivering" or "shaking." In light of the simile the author uses here, why is this adjective particularly appropriate in this context? _____

    _____

2. In comparing hockey to a "trusty family dog" and in addressing the sport with "Good dog, hockey!" what feature of the sport is he praising? _____

    _____

3. Explain the underlying meaning of this phrase in sentence 5: "its big-league sagas churning through season after season without so much as a nod from me." _____

    _____

4. The adjective *virulent,* in the last sentence, means "extremely infectious." What meaning does McCall intend here?
    (a) neutral, or denotative.
    (b) connotative with positive overtones.
    (c) connotative with negative overtones.

Answers for
Selection 1

A. Content and Structure

1. Hockey [is compared to] a faithful family dog.
2. Baseball [is compared to] a fever [and to] malaria.
3. They reveal the writer's sentiments with regard to these two sports: Hockey, like a dog waiting patiently for a walk, is always present, always available, and therefore lacks the excitement of more novel sports. The fever/malaria metaphor shows the hold baseball had over the young McCall's life.
4. Sentence 4: "Baseball was always more complicated."
5. (c)
6. (b)

B. Language Analysis

1. Dogs quiver or shake with excitement if they think a walk is in the works.
2. They suggest the sport's dependability, its unchanging nature.
3. McCall paid little attention to professional baseball.
4. (b)

Selection 2

The novel this passage is taken from is set during World War II.

[1]. . . It was so hot that I went down to the creek instead, to cool my feet in one of its stagnant sumps, a poor substitute for my Red Cross swims, which had just ended, but at least water.

[2]The heat was always more intense in the creek, more dusty and dry and piercing than anywhere else. [3]Crackling and powdery, it stung the nostrils and eyes, prickled in little hives all over the body. [4]Beds of gravel glared; dragonflies glittered in tall, chalky weeds; cicadas droned, broke off, droned again. [5]Sweat rolled down my ribs as I walked, patching my shirt and gathering damply in the band of my shorts. [6]When I saw a swarm of gnats, I plodded over to it and with the toe of my tennis shoe splashed aside the scum of a sunken pool. [7]Then, after pulling off my shoes, I stepped in and stood immersed to the ankles. [8]The water was sun-filled, warm, the clear golden brown of cider. [9]I scratched my prickling body, rubbed my stinging eyes until little stars revolved, then slowly took off my shorts and shirt, and then my undershirt, and stretched out full length in the shallow water, rolling with lazy greed until I was wet all over. [10]After getting up again, I stood looking down my glistening body for a while, then, picking up my clothes and shoes, walked on in my underpants. [11]I felt sun-dazed, reckless, like an African animal, sleepy, yet somehow intent and ready for anything, a hot, loose-limbed beast prowling.

Ella Leffland, *Rumors of Peace*

A. *Content and Structure*

Complete the following questions.

1. The dominant impression the passage suggests is that the creek was
   (a) open and spacious.
   (b) clear and cool.
   (c) hot and dusty.
   (d) lonely and isolated.
2. We can infer that the narrator of the passage is probably
   (a) a little girl of about 5 or 6.
   (b) a girl of about 11 or 12.
   (c) a young woman of 19 or 20.
   (d) a middle-aged woman.
3. What evidence in the passage helped you arrive at your answer for

   question 2 above? _____

B. *Language Analysis*

Complete the following questions.

1. Consider the words "sumps" in sentence 1 and "glared" in sentence 4.
   How would you characterize their use in the passage?
   (a) denotative.
   (b) connotative with positive overtones.
   (c) connotative with negative overtones.
   (d) figurative.
2. In sentence 3, which of the five senses is Leffland appealing to? _____
3. Identify the figure of speech in sentence 8. _____

   is compared to _____

   Is it a metaphor or a simile? _____
   What characteristic of the literal subject does this figure of speech

   emphasize? _____
   Finally, would you characterize the sensation described as pleasant or

   unpleasant? _____
4. In the context of sentence 11, the writer intends the adjective
   "reckless" to be
   (a) strictly denotative.
   (b) connotative with positive overtones.
   (c) connotative with negative overtones.
   (d) figurative.

5. In sentence 11, the adjective "hot" is used ambiguously, suggesting

    two different but complementary meanings. What are they? _____

    _____

    _____

6. Identify the figure of speech in sentence 11. _____

    is compared to _____

    Is it a metaphor or a simile? _____
    What attribute or characteristic does Leffland emphasize about the

    narrator in choosing this comparison? _____

    _____

Selection 3

[1]The noses of a great many Canadians resemble Porky Pig's. This comes from spending so much time pressing them against the longest undefended one-way mirror in the world. The Canadians looking through this mirror behave the way people on the hidden side of such mirrors usually do: They observe, analyze, ponder, snoop and wonder what all the activity on the other side means in decipherable human terms.

[2]The Americans, bless their innocent little hearts, are rarely aware that they are even being watched, much less by the Canadians. They just go on doing body language, playing in the sandbox of the world, bashing one another on the head and planning how to blow things up, same as always. If they think about Canada at all, it's only when things get a bit snowy, or the water goes off, or the Canadians start fussing over some piddly detail, such as fish. Then they regard them as unpatriotic; for Americans don't really see Canadians as foreigners, not like the Mexicans, unless they do something weird like speak French or beat the New York Yankees at baseball. Really, think the Americans, the Canadians are just like us, or would be if they could.

[3]Or we could switch metaphors and call the border the longest undefended backyard fence in the world. The Canadians are the folks in the neat little bungalow with the tidy little garden and the duck pond. The Americans are the other folks, the ones in the sprawly mansion with the bad-taste statues on the lawn. There's a perpetual party, or something, going on there—loud music, raucous laughter, smoke billowing from the barbecue. Beer bottles and Coke cans land among the peonies. The Canadians have their own beer bottles and barbecue smoke, but they tend to overlook it. Your own mess is always more forgivable than the mess someone else makes on your patio.

4The Canadians can't exactly call the police—they suspect that the Americans are the police—and part of their distress, which seems permanent, comes from their uncertainty as to whether or not they've been invited. Sometimes they do drop by next door, and find it exciting but scary. Sometimes the Americans drop by their house and find it clean. This worries the Canadians. They worry a lot. Maybe that Americans want to buy up their duck pond, with all the money they seem to have, and turn it into a cesspool or a water-skiing emporium.

Margaret Atwood, "The View from the Backyard,"
The Nation

A. *Content and Structure*

Complete the following questions.

1. In your own words, write a sentence stating Atwood's main idea.

_____

_____

2. When Atwood writes at the beginning of paragraph 2, in referring to Americans, "bless their innocent little hearts," she is being
   (a) honest.
   (b) scornful.
   (c) sarcastic.
   (d) religious.
   (e) admiring.

3. From what Atwood implies in paragraph 2, explain what Americans

   think about Canadians. _____

   _____

   _____

4. From the information in paragraph 4, why specifically do Canadians

   "worry a lot" about their southern neighbor? _____

   _____

5. What are the broader implications of Atwood's passage? What is the central inference you can make about the relationship between

   Canada and the United States? _____

   _____

B. *Language Analysis*

Complete the following questions.

1. Read paragraph 1 again. Why do Canadians' noses resemble Porky

    Pig's? _____

    _____

    _____

2. What does Atwood mean when she refers to the border between
    Canada and the United States as a "one-way mirror"? What does this

    metaphor say about Canadians? _____

    _____

    _____

    _____

3. How would you characterize the word "snoop" in the context it is
    used toward the end of paragraph 1? It suggests a
    (a) neutral, denotative meaning.
    (b) positive connotation.
    (c) negative connotation.
    (d) cliché.

4. Atwood says in paragraph 2 that Americans go on "playing in the
    sandbox of the world, bashing one another on the head and planning
    how to blow things up, same as always." What does the sandbox

    metaphor refer to? _____

    Explain what the metaphor means. _____

    _____

5. In paragraph 3, Atwood switches metaphors, comparing the border
    between Canada and the United States to "the longest undefended
    backyard fence in the world." In your own words, explain Atwood's
    thinking about how these neighboring nations get along. Specifically,
    try to determine what she means when she refers to the Canadians'
    "neat little bungalow," the Americans' "sprawly mansion," and the
    "perpetual party" with the "raucous laughter" and the beer bottles

    and Coke cans thrown in the peonies. _____

    _____

6. In paragraph 4, what is the literal meaning of these sentences? "Sometimes they do drop by next door, and find it exciting but scary. Sometimes the Americans drop by their house and find it clean."

_____

_____

_____

_____

■   *PRACTICE ESSAY*

"The Death of the Moth"

Virginia Woolf

Hulton/Archive by Getty Images.

The British writer Virginia Woolf (1882–1941) was one of the most important writers of the twentieth century. Known for her unconventional lifestyle and experimental novelistic methods, Woolf remains widely read in American universities today. Her best-known novels are Mrs. Dalloway *and* To the Lighthouse. *"The Death of a Moth" is one of Woolf's most famous essays; indeed, it is often reprinted in English anthologies as a model of descriptive writing.*

1   Moths that fly by day are not properly to be called moths; they do not excite that pleasant sense of dark autumn nights and ivy-blossom which the commonest yellow-underwing asleep in the shadow of the curtain never fails to rouse in us. They are hybrid creatures, neither gay like butterflies nor sombre like their own species. Nevertheless the present specimen, with his narrow hay-coloured wings, fringed with a tassel of the same colour, seemed to be content with life. It was a pleasant morning, mid-September, mild, benignant, yet with a keener breath than that of the summer months. The plough[9] was already scoring the field opposite the window, and where the share[10] had been, the earth was pressed flat and gleamed with moisture. Such vigour came rolling in from the fields and the

[9]British spelling for *plow.*
[10]Short for *plowshare,* or the cutting blade of a plow.

down[11] beyond that it was difficult to keep the eyes strictly turned upon the book. The rooks[12] too were keeping one of their annual festivities; soaring round the tree tops until it looked as if a vast net with thousands of black knots in it had been cast up into the air; which, after a few moments sank slowly down upon the trees until every twig seemed to have a knot at the end of it. Then, suddenly, the net would be thrown into the air again in a wider circle this time, with the utmost clamour and vociferation, as though to be thrown into the air and settle slowly down upon the tree tops were a tremendously exciting experience.

2   The same energy which inspired the rooks, the ploughmen, the horses, and even, it seemed, the lean bare-backed downs, sent the moth fluttering from side to side of his square of the window-pane. One could not help watching him. One was, indeed, conscious of a queer feeling of pity for him. The possibilities of pleasure seemed that morning so enormous and so various that to have only a moth's part in life, and a day moth's at that, appeared a hard fate, and his zest in enjoying his meagre opportunities to the full, pathetic. He flew vigorously to one corner of his compartment, and, after waiting there a second, flew across to the other. What remained for him but to fly to a third corner and then to a fourth? That was all he could do, in spite of the size of the downs, the width of the sky, the far-off smoke of houses, and the romantic voice, now and then, of a steamer out at sea. What he could do he did. Watching him, it seemed as if a fibre, very thin but pure, of the enormous energy of the world had been thrust into his frail and diminutive body. As often as he crossed the pane, I could fancy that a thread of vital light became visible. He was little or nothing but life.

3   Yet, because he was so small, and so simple a form of the energy that was rolling in at the open window and driving its way through so many narrow and intricate corridors in my own brain and in those of other human beings, there was something marvellous as well as pathetic about him. It was as if someone had taken a tiny bead of pure life and decking it as lightly as possible with down and feathers, had set it dancing and zigzagging to show us the true nature of life. Thus displayed one could not get over the strangeness of it. One is apt to forget all about life, seeing it humped and bossed and garnished and cumbered so that it has to move with the greatest circumspection and dignity. Again, the thought of all that life might have been had he been born in any other shape caused one to view his simple activities with a kind of pity.

[11]A down, sometimes used in the plural as in paragraph 2, is a grassy expanse where cattle graze.
[12]Rooks are crows.

4   After a time, tired by his dancing apparently, he settled on the window ledge in the sun, and, the queer spectacle being at an end, I forgot about him. Then, looking up, my eye was caught by him. He was trying to resume his dancing, but seemed either so stiff or so awkward that he could only flutter to the bottom of the window-pane; and when he tried to fly across it he failed. Being intent on other matters I watched these futile attempts for a time without thinking, unconsciously waiting for him to resume his flight, as one waits for a machine, that has stopped momentarily, to start again without considering the reason of its failure. After perhaps a seventh attempt he slipped from the wooden ledge and fell, fluttering his wings, on to his back on the window sill. The helplessness of his attitude roused me. It flashed upon me that he was in difficulties; he could no longer raise himself; his legs struggled vainly. But, as I stretched out a pencil, meaning to help him to right himself, it came over me that the failure and awkwardness were the approach of death. I laid the pencil down again.

5   The legs agitated themselves once more. I looked as if for the enemy against which he struggled. I looked out of doors. What had happened there? Presumably it was midday, and work in the fields had stopped. Stillness and quiet had replaced the previous animation. The birds had taken themselves off to feed in the brooks. The horses stood still. Yet the power was there all the same, massed outside indifferent, impersonal, not attending to anything in particular. Somehow it was opposed to the little hay-coloured moth. It was useless to try to do anything. One could only watch the extraordinary efforts made by those tiny legs against an oncoming doom which could, had it chosen, have submerged an entire city, not merely a city, but masses of human beings; nothing, I knew had any chance against death. Nevertheless after a pause of exhaustion the legs fluttered again. It was superb this last protest, and so frantic that he succeeded at last in righting himself. One's sympathies, of course, were all on the side of life. Also, when there was nobody to care or to know, this gigantic effort on the part of an insignificant little moth, against a power of such magnitude, to retain what no one else valued or desired to keep, moved one strangely. Again, somehow, one saw life, a pure bead. I lifted the pencil again, useless though I knew it to be. But even as I did so, the unmistakable tokens of death showed themselves. The body relaxed, and instantly grew stiff. The struggle was over. The insignificant little creature now knew death. As I looked at the dead moth, this minute wayside triumph of so great a force over so mean an antagonist filled me with wonder. Just as life had been strange a few minutes before, so death was now as strange. The moth having righted himself now lay most decently and uncomplainingly composed. O yes, he seemed to say, death is stronger than I am.

A. Comprehension

Choose the answer that best completes each statement. Do not refer to the selection while doing this exercise.

1. The main idea of the essay is that, for Woolf,
   (a) the death of the moth illustrated the cruelty of nature.
   (b) rural life is the scene of daily tragedies and triumphs.
   (c) observing death up close makes the observer more accepting and reflective of this inevitability.
   (d) the little moth embodied life itself, but it could not overcome death's power.

2. The sentence, "It was as if someone had taken a tiny bead of pure life and decking it as lightly as possible with down and feathers, had set it dancing and zigzagging," shows
   (a) what moths look like and how they fly.
   (b) the strangeness of insect life.
   (c) the true nature of life.
   (d) how pathetic and insignificant the moth was.

3. Woolf views the little moth with pity because
   (a) his shape so limited his activities.
   (b) he would not survive the heat of the day.
   (c) his death would be unnoticed by everyone but her.
   (d) he would live for only one day.

4. In the moth's death, Woolf sees
   (a) an admirable yet futile struggle to survive death's superior force.
   (b) a foreshadowing of her own death.
   (c) a rebellion against and a refusal to accept death's inevitability.
   (d) a triumph over a force greater than life itself.

5. In observing the little moth, Woolf concludes that
   (a) life and death are inextricably linked.
   (b) death's triumph over the forces of life was both strange and moving.
   (c) all organisms have an innate desire to triumph over death.
   (d) its death shows the impersonality and indifference of the universe.

B. Vocabulary

For each italicized word from the selection, choose the best definition according to the context in which it appears. You may refer to the selection to answer the questions in this section and in all the remaining sections.

1. a pleasant morning, . . . *benignant* [paragraph 1]:
   (a) mild, gentle.
   (b) promising good fortune.
   (c) hot, humid.
   (d) inactive, lazy.

2.   his zest in enjoying his *meagre* opportunities (British spelling of *meager*) [2]:
     (a) unusual, different.
     (b) limitless, abundant.
     (c) paltry, limited.
     (d) curious, strange.

3.   to move with the greatest *circumspection* [3]:
     (a) care, watchfulness.
     (b) frenzy, frantic activity.
     (c) grace, elegance.
     (d) curiosity, inquisitiveness.

4.   triumph . . . over so mean an *antagonist* [5]:
     (a) victor.
     (b) opponent.
     (c) instigator of trouble.
     (d) bearer of bad tidings.

C. *Language Analysis*

Complete the following questions.

1.   Read paragraph 1 again. In her description of the ploughman, the rooks, and the horses, the dominant mood and atmosphere she establishes are
     (a) sleepy and languid.
     (b) full of life, energy, and vigor.
     (c) mournful, somber.
     (d) exciting, adventurous.

2.   In paragraph 1, Woolf figuratively compares the rooks to _____

     _____

     _____

3.   This figure of speech is meant to illustrate
     (a) the birds' movement and energy.
     (b) the great clamor the birds were making.
     (c) the birds' mating habits.
     (d) the birds' disruption by the ploughman and his horses.

4.   Read paragraph 2 again, which emphasizes that, despite its insignificant size and simple activities, the moth
     (a) represented all the energy and life in the world.
     (b) longed to be more than merely insignificant.
     (c) reflected the same energy as the rooks and the horses.
     (d) had probably been injured somewhere before flying into the house.

5. What realization does Woolf come to when she considers trying to

    help the struggling moth with her pencil? _____

    _____

6. Consider this excerpt from paragraph 5: "One could only watch the
    extraordinary efforts made by those tiny legs against an oncoming
    doom which could, had it chosen, have submerged an entire city, not
    merely a city, but masses of human beings. . . ." Explain what Woolf

    means in your own words. _____

    _____

Questions for Discussion and Analysis

1. Explain in detail why Woolf feels such pity for the little moth.
2. Go through the essay and comment on the mood established in each
    paragraph. What devices contribute to it? How is it achieved?

IN THE BOOKSTORE

Virginia Woolf: A Biography (1974), by Quentin Bell, Woolf's nephew, is
a fine introduction to her extraordinary and tragic life and to the
Bloomsbury literary coterie, of which Woolf and her husband, Leonard,
were leading members.

Tone, Point of View, and Allusions

CHAPTER OBJECTIVES

In this second chapter dealing with the importance of language, we will examine some rather sophisticated elements that will enhance and deepen your understanding of what you read. Our central concern in Chapter 7 is putting together several elements you have studied thus far. Here is an overview of the chapter's topics:

- Point of view

- An overview of tone

- Allusions

- Special effects

■ POINT OF VIEW

The phrase **point of view** refers to the writer's attitude toward or position on a subject—his or her **stance.** A writer's point of view—especially with regard to controversial matters—can be favorable, unfavorable, neutral, or ambivalent. This point of view leads to the other important elements in writing: mode of discourse (a subject you studied in Chapter 1); diction, or word choice (the subject of in the preceding chapter); and **tone** (which we examine in more detail in this chapter).

Let us illustrate these connections with a passage about the Central Intelligence Agency that you read in Chapter 1. As you read it, pay attention to the circled words and phrases and refresh your understanding of any unfamiliar words, if necessary.

In an era when citizens are upset about (needless government agencies) the Central Intelligence Agency may stand out as the ultimate example of a (bureaucracy) whose lifespan has been (pointlessly prolonged.) Long after its original mission ceased to matter, a combination of (iniquity and inertia) has kept the CIA intact.

Unlike other controversial government agencies that merely (squander) taxpayers' money, the Central Intelligence Agency is (a sinister enterprise,) with (a long criminal record.) Its sole rationale—engaging (in shadowy combat) with its equally nefarious communist counterparts—crumbled at about the same time the Berlin Wall did. Without a Cold War to wage, the CIA has become (a dinosaur desperate to avoid extinction.)

Kevin J. Kelley, "R.I.P. for the CIA?" Utne Reader

Follow the arrows from element to element in the circle below to see how they all work together.

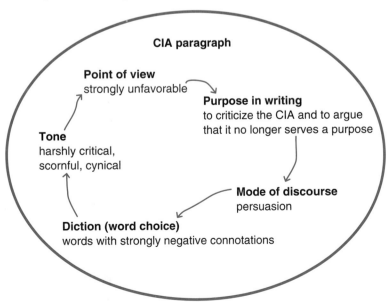

In summary, the writer's unfavorable **point of view** toward the CIA leads to his **purpose** in writing: to convince the reader that the agency has outlived its usefulness. Persuasion is the **mode of discourse** appropriate for both the point of view and the purpose, and Kelley's word choice—with the strong negative connotations—reflects all three elements. Taken together, these elements produce the harsh, scornful tone, and we come full circle—to point of view. As you practice with this chapter's exercises, analyze each reading in this way.

■ AN OVERVIEW OF TONE

Let us begin with a real-life workplace situation that nicely illustrates why ascertaining tone can be so tricky. These opening paragraphs are from an article titled "Misunderstandings @ the Office," written by Sarah Schafer, a staff writer for *The Washington Post*.[1]

> The e-mail seemed so innocent. "Betty, hi," he remembers cheerfully typing to his colleague. "I haven't been successful reaching you by phone, so I'll try e-mail instead." And so Bill Lampton—then an employee of a large hospital—dashed off the rest of his note on some trivial office matter and hit the send button.
>
> Betty never got past the greeting.
>
> "I have no idea what you mean about my not returning phone calls," Lampton recalls Betty firing back. "To have you accuse me of ignoring your calls is unthinkable and inexcusable. . . . As to the purpose of the e-mail that you sent me, I prefer not to respond, as I dislike dealing with anyone who assumes the worst of me."

A few paragraphs later, Schafer writes:

> In a recent survey of 1,000 workers, Vault [vault.com, a New York workplace research firm] found that 51 percent of respondents said that the tone of their e-mails is often perceived—as angry, or too casual or abrupt, for example. One survey respondent said, "I wrote a question to [my boss] one day; she thought I was being insubordinate by the tone. I almost lost my job!

---

[1]*The Washington Post National Weekly Edition*, November 13, 2000, p. 21.

Schafer's observation brings up an important consideration: **Tone**—the feeling, mood, or emotional quality of a piece of writing—is hard to perceive on paper, or more accurately, it is easy to *mis*perceive. When we read, visual and vocal cues are absent. In conversation, however, a speaker's tone is readily apparent from gestures, tone of voice, vocal pitch (the voice's rise and fall), and facial expression, in addition to the actual words spoken. In writing, all we have are the black words on the white page (or screen). The reader must infer the tone from the writer's words and their connotative values, from the details included, occasionally from the sentence structure, and from the writer's point of view toward the subject. It's a complicated business but one worth mastering.

Tone in Textbooks

The textbooks that you read in your social science and science courses reflect an objective and impartial tone: Textbooks are not forums for controversy or for arousing emotions. The tone corresponds to the writer's purpose—to convey factual information. A glance at a chapter in any of your current textbooks will confirm this observation.

Tone in Nonfiction Prose

In the nonfiction reading you do in this course and in your other English courses—as well as in the reading you do for pleasure—tone is an important component of the reading process; it can run the gamut of human feelings or moods, reflecting the complex beings we humans are. The following box presents some of the more common and easy-to-recognize tones. (A second group of more difficult ones is taken up later.) Check an unabridged dictionary if you are unsure of any of these words' meanings. Sometimes students have difficulty articulating the tone of a passage because they lack the vocabulary to express the emotion it embodies.

For ease of learning, the tones are grouped into clusters showing gradations in meaning, so that the first one is typically mild; the second one, stronger; and so on. For example, in the second cluster below, "approving" is more neutral than its more positive cousin "admiring," while "laudatory" is even more strongly admiring.

Common Varieties of Tone
Informative, impartial, instructive
Approving, admiring, laudatory
Sincere, honest, candid
Serious, somber, grave
Philosophical, reflective, pensive
Questioning, skeptical

> Amusing, funny, humorous
> Sorrowful, mournful, lamenting
> Nostalgic, wistful, melancholy
> Critical, fault-finding, disparaging
> Complaining, aggrieved, whining
> Harsh, mean-spirited, nasty
> Provocative, shrill, rabble-rousing, inflammatory
> Sentimental, gushy, maudlin, mawkish

Space limitations make it impossible for us to examine each of these tones; for now it is sufficient just to know that they exist and that you will encounter them in the course of your reading newspapers, magazines, and books. Identifying tone requires you to duplicate the "sound" of the sentences as the writer intended you to hear them. Because complete objectivity, even in expository prose, is nearly impossible for a writer to achieve (even assuming it were desirable), the careful reader must be alert to the nuances that contribute to a reading's tone.

Examples of Tone

We will start with relatively easy examples and work our way up to more difficult ones; answers are provided for the first two. The first excerpt is from a fine little book, *The Year 1000,* in which the authors recount a month-by-month appraisal of what life was like at the end of the first millennium.

Before leaving the month of February, let us spare a nod for Valentinus—the third-century priest who was martyred in Rome in the reign of the Emperor Claudius and whose feast day was celebrated on February 14, as it has been ever since. The details of St. Valentine's life are obscure, and ecclesiastical experts have been unable to discover any reason why he should have become the patron saint of lovers and romance. Historians note that mid-February was the occasion of the licentious Roman fertility festival of Lupercalia, when women sought cures for sterility, while folklorists trace the modern orgy of card-sending and candle-lit dinners back to the old country belief that birds commence coupling on February 14. Either or both of these explanations may be correct, and they would seem to illustrate the cleverness with which the early church appropriated heathen superstitions for its own purposes. But there is no Christian reason why St. Valentine should be the only saint in the calendar whose feast is celebrated with universal ardour today.

Robert Lacey and Danny Danziger, *The Year 1000*

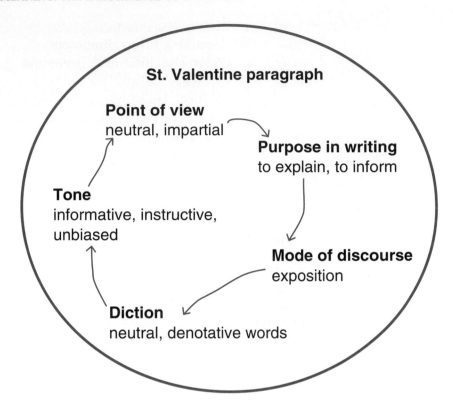

St. Valentine paragraph

Point of view
neutral, impartial

Purpose in writing
to explain, to inform

Tone
informative, instructive,
unbiased

Mode of discourse
exposition

Diction
neutral, denotative words

In the next example, Harvard biologist Edwin O. Wilson discusses indigenous people's contributions to the world's food supply. Circle the connotative words as you read it.

From the mostly unwritten archives of native peoples has come a wealth of information about wild and semicultivated crops. It is a remarkable fact that with a single exception, the macadamia nut of Australia, every one of the fruits and nuts used in western countries was grown first by indigenous peoples. The Incas were arguably the all-time champions in creating a reservoir of diverse crops. Without the benefit of wheels, money, iron, or written script, these Andean people evolved a sophisticated agriculture based on almost as many plant species as used by all the farmers of Europe and Asia combined. Their abounding crops, tilled on the cool upland slopes and plateaus, proved especially suited for temperate climates. From the Incas have come lima beans, peppers, potatoes, and tomatoes. But many other species and strains, including a hundred varieties of potatoes, are still confined to the Andes. The Spanish conquerors learned to use a few of the potatoes, but they missed many other representatives of a vast array of cultivated tuberous vegetables, including some that are more productive and savory than the favored crops. The names are likely to be unfamiliar: achira, ahipa, arracacha, maca, mashua, mauka, oca, ulloco, and yacon. One, maca, is on the verge of extinction, limited to 10 hectares in the highest plateau region of Peru and Bolivia. Its swollen roots, resembling brown radishes and rich in sugar and starch, have a sweet, tangy flavor and are considered a delicacy by the handful of people still privileged to consume them.

Edwin O. Wilson, *The Diversity of Life*

Now complete the following items:

Point of view: _____

Purpose in writing: _____

Mode of discourse: _____

Diction: _____

Tone: _____

Did you circle these positive connotative phrases—"a wealth of information," "a remarkable fact," "arguably the all-time champions," "a sophisticated agriculture," "abounding crops," and "vast array of cultivated tuberous vegetables"? Besides word choice, the content—especially the impressive list of foods he provides—also suggests both an informative and admiring tone, since these foods were grown "[w]ithout the benefit of wheels, money, iron, or written script," inventions that seem like essential prerequisites for agriculture.

Abraham Lincoln's "Farewell at Springfield" was delivered to a vast audience of his fellow citizens on February 11, 1861, as he was leaving for Washington to assume the duties of president. Keep in mind as you read it that Lincoln's primary goal was to preserve the Union.

My friends—No one not in my situation, can appreciate my feeling of sadness at this parting. To this place, and the kindness of these people, I owe everything. Here I have lived a quarter of a century, and have passed from a young to an old man. Here my children have been born, and one is buried. I now leave, not knowing when, or whether ever, I may return, with a task before me greater than that which rested upon Washington. Without assistance of that Divine Being, who ever attended him, I cannot succeed. With that assistance I cannot fail. Trusting in Him, who can go with me, and remain with you and be everywhere for good, let us confidently hope that all will yet be well. To His care commending you, as I hope in your prayers you will commend me, I bid you an affectionate farewell.

Apart from the obviously strong religious tone, Lincoln's tone can also be described as

1.   nostalgic, almost melancholy and dejected.
2.   eloquent, yet modest and unassuming.
3.   sorrowful, mournful, lamenting.
4.   irritable, complaining, aggrieved.

For a completely different type of writing, read these opening paragraphs from a newspaper article.

Evil lurks in many insidious forms. I am staring at one form right now, this TV-like machine with the soothing blue screen perched atop a box that looks like a mutant VCR.

Don't get me wrong. The computer is a boon to anyone's job, with its promise of efficiency, speed, and skills never before imagined and I'll slug anyone who tries to take it away from me.

But the computer also promised to relieve me of all my paper. It hasn't. Instead, I now have both paper files and digital files. The computer has presented me with gigabytes of new material to organize: interview notes, story drafts, half-cocked ideas, project lists, research downloaded from online services, and contact lists.

Then there's the time element. I spend hours every month backing up files to protect myself from accidental deletions, lethal viruses, hard-disk crashes, or faulty floppies. Hey, I never had to clone my filing cabinet.

Hal Lancaster, "Chaos in a Box: Messy Computer Files Can Strain Your Job," *The Wall Street Journal*

Lancaster's tone is

1.   sincere, earnest.
2.   instructive, informative.
3.   breezy and informal, mildly humorous.
4.   pessimistic, skeptical.

The following passage is an excerpt from Charlton Heston's keynote address at the Free Congress Foundation's twentieth-anniversary gala.[2] Charlton Heston, the president of the National Rifle Association, is speaking of the Second Amendment and the culture wars:

> What an honor it is to address the Free Congress Foundation. . . . Imagine being point man for the National Rifle Association, preserving the right to keep and bear arms. I ran for office, I was elected, and now I serve . . . as a moving target for pundits who've called me everything from "ridiculous" and "duped" to "brain-injured, senile and crazy old man."
>
> Maybe that comes with the territory. But as I have stood in the crosshairs of those who aim at Second Amendment freedom, I have realized that guns are not the only issue, and I am not the only target. It is much, much bigger than that—which is what I want to talk to you about today.
>
> I have come to realize that a cultural war is raging across our land . . . storming our values, assaulting our freedoms, killing our self-confidence in who we are and what we believe.
>
> How many of you own a gun? A show of hands maybe? How many own two or more guns?
>
> Thank you. I wonder—how many of you own guns but chose not to raise your hand? How many of you considered revealing your conviction about a constitutional right, but then thought better of it?
>
> Then you are a victim of the cultural war. You are a casualty of the cultural warfare being waged against traditional American freedom of beliefs and ideas. Now maybe you don't care one way or the other about owning a gun. But I could've asked for a show of hands of Pentecostal Christians, or pro-lifers, or right-to-workers, or Promise Keepers, or school voucher-ers, and the result would be the same. What if the same question were asked at your PTA meeting? Would you raise your hand if Dan Rather were in the back of the room with a film crew?
>
> See? You have been assaulted and robbed of the courage of your convictions. Your pride in who you are and what you believe has been ridiculed, ransacked and plundered. It may be a war without bullets or bloodshed, but with just as much liberty lost. You and your country are less free. . .
>
> Now, I am not really here to talk about the Second Amendment of the NRA, but the gun issue clearly brings into focus the warfare that's going on.

---

[2]This address was delivered on December 20, 1997. The entire address can be accessed at *www.vpc.org/nrainfo/heston.html*. Other Heston speeches are available at *www.mynra.com*, the website for the National Rifle Association.

Rank-and-file Americans wake up every morning, increasingly bewildered and confused at why their views make them lesser citizens. After enough breakfast-table TV hyping tattooed sex-slaves on the next Ricki Lake, enough gun-glutted movies and tabloid shows, enough revisionist history books and prime-time ridicule of religion, enough of the TV anchor who cocks her head, clucks her tongue and sighs about guns causing crime and finally the message gets through: heaven help the God-fearing, law-abiding, Caucasian, middle-class, Protestant, or—even worse—admitted heterosexual, gun-owning or even worse—NRA-card-carrying, average working stiff, or—even worse—male working stiff, because not only don't you count, you're a downright obstacle to social progress. . . . And frankly mister, you need to wake up, wise up and learn a little something about your new America . . . and until you do, would you mind shutting up?

That's why you didn't raise your hand. That's how cultural war works. And you are losing.

Heston's tone is

1. serious, somber, grave.
2. inflammatory, shrill, rabble-rousing.
3. sincere, honest, candid.
4. nostalgic, wistful, melancholy.

A Special Case: Sentimentality

In the earlier list of tones at the beginning of the chapter, the final item is "sentimental, gushy, maudlin, mawkish." Each merits a little discussion. *Sentimentality* is an umbrella word describing a tone that appeals to one's tender emotions. My dictionary defines *gushy* as "showing excessive displays of sentiment or enthusiasm." A maudlin tone is embarrassingly or tearfully sentimental, and mawkishness is even stronger—referring to sentimentality so overdone that it is objectionable, almost sickening.

Sentimentality can be genuine or fake, depending on the writer's motive and care in writing. And it can be both effective and affective. A writer may appeal to our tender and compassionate instincts and win us over. Many readers enjoy reading about those who have overcome serious obstacles, found true love, or conquered grave illnesses. Such reading ennobles us, gives us hope, and inspires us to muddle through our daily lives and to cope with our fears and our shortcomings.

What can go wrong with the sentimental point of view? If the writer deliberately plays to our heartstrings with fake emotions and clichés, the effect is offensive or ludicrous. We see through the fakery.

Richard D. Altick, in his excellent book *Preface to Critical Reading,* explains that writers may lapse into sentimentality because most of the important things in life—love, loss, the innocence of childhood, old age and death, for example—have already been written about, making it difficult to say anything new about them. Altick explains further:

> Sentimentality can be defined as shallow and exaggerated emotion. Taking an emotional symbol or situation—home, mother, death of a pauper, return of a wanderer—the sentimentalist, perhaps from the sincerest of motives, extorts more feeling from it than a reasonable person would find there, and dwells upon it longer and more insistently than he should. Furthermore, the sentimentalist, lacking fresh ideas, depends heavily upon the cliché in all its forms—upon the tried-and-true devices by which too many preceding writers have stirred their readers' feelings. But those images and phrases are now emotionally dehydrated; they have been used so often that they have lost their power to affect. And so the effect of sentimentality, to the reader who has a sense of proportion, is the opposite of what is intended.[3]

Anyone assigned to write about the death of a child has an enormously difficult task, one that requires sensitivity and understanding. I did not want to use a present-day piece on this topic to illustrate a maudlin tone, and while searching on the World Wide Web, I came across a series of old news articles on a site devoted to Mother's Day. One anonymously written article dated February 22, 1937, was published in a Kansas newspaper; it tries to justify the children's deaths, perhaps as a way of assuaging the parents' grief. Their ages and the manner of their deaths are not given; the title is simply "Two Outstanding Students Lost in Wreck." Here are the pertinent paragraphs (with intact punctuation):

> Life and its uncertainty is a mystery through which no man has ever seen. . . . Just why fate should choose two from our midst who were such perfect examples of young life in full bloom, as Frances and Floyd Ellsaesser, is beyond explanation. . . .
>
> Dwight L. Moody tells a story of a certain mother and father who lost their children, and were unable to ascertain why such a calamity should befall them. They turned to travel in the hopes of compensation for their grief, and traveled in all of Europe and Asia without finding solace. Eventually they arrived in Syria and were standing one evening watching a shepherd

---

[3]Richard D. Altick, *Preface to Critical Reading,* 5th ed. (Holt, Rinehart and Winston, 1969), p. 169.

bring his flock into their evening quarters. The sheep were reluctant about crossing the stream, and finally the shepherd took two little lambs and crossed with them and placed them on the opposite side of the stream, after which the entire flock willingly followed. This is a homely illustration which appeared in a Sunday School Quarterly, but it did bring home to that mother and father the fact that there might be a divine reason why their little ones had been taken. The shock of sorrow and grief has been almost too much for family and friends to bear, but let us hope that these two splendid lives have been lived and lain down in a beautiful example of sacrifice to point out and guide us in the way to a fuller, more kindly, life of devotion and brotherly love.

If it was necessary to sacrifice two; it would be hard to compensate for their loss, but if it were my opportunity to choose two lives to lead this school and community into a better existence; a better choice could not be made. Indeed those two have not died in vain, unless we in negligence disregard the road which the Master has shown to us.[4]

Though this unnamed writer tries to offer another perspective on this tragedy, the sentiments expressed ring false, and the clichés create an artificially sugary or cloying tone. Good writers avoid such sentimentality.

Liz Smith, the well-known gossip columnist, is widely printed in North American daily newspapers. Her columns are often breathless and gushy, as she reports on celebrities' comings and goings. Here is a sample. The subject is actress Reese Witherspoon.

'Blonde' role a dream for Reese

Hollywood had a real, old-fashioned premiere the other eve, the kind that hasn't been seen in a while. In true movie-star fashion, Reese Witherspoon arrived 20 minutes late for her "Legally Blonde" premiere. But the diminutive, perky actress didn't disappoint her screaming fans when she strolled the red carpet at the Mann Village Theater in Westwood. Reese was wearing a pink slip dress with black lace, holding hands with her handsome husband, actor Ryan Phillippe. They gave everybody a look at a new power couple.

This girl is so popular and engaging that she was surrounded by swarms of people all night. Everybody wants a piece of Reese.

"Legally Blonde" also offers us Luke Wilson, Selma Blair, Ali Larter, Jennifer Coolidge and Raquel Welch! The delicious Raquel wore vibrant orange bellbottoms, which glowed against her rich tan. She was on the arm of hubby

---

[4]"Two Outstanding Students Lost in Wreck," *The Kismet Gazelle,* vol. no. 1, Kismet, Kansas, Monday, February 22, 1937, no. 8. Available at *www.freepages.genealogy.rootsweb.com/~mgo1025/obituaries/obits/.*

Richie Palmer and wearing a shoulder-length fall. (Different colored falls were given out later as party favors, and guest David Hasselhoff carried off two boxes. "I'm promoting Raquel's wigs now!" he quipped.)

Reese says, "This movie is a dream come true for me. My heroine is Goldie Hawn. 'Private Benjamin' was my inspiration. I wanted one day to portray a stereotypical blonde who is perceived as ditsy but is actually smart. 'Legally Blonde' gave me the opportunity."

Reese seems firmly grounded. She juggles stardom, a husband and a toddler. "Ava is at home with her grandmother," the legal blonde says.

Liz Smith, "The Next Power Couple," *San Francisco Chronicle,* July 2, 2001

Practice Exercise 1

Here are some passages for you to practice with. As before, pay careful attention to word choice (especially to connotation) and to the sound of the prose. Underline key words and phrases. Determine how point of view, mode of discourse, and diction point to the writer's tone. Then decide which of the four choices best represents the writer's tone.

One of the greatest and most intrepid travelers of all time, Marco Polo, journeyed to the Far East from the Mediterranean in the thirteenth century and spent twenty years in the court of Kublai Khan in China. On his return to Venice he set down in his book entitled *Description of the World* his impressions of the peoples and places and customs he had seen. There are at least two extraordinary omissions in his account. He says nothing about the art of printing unknown as yet in Europe but in full flower in China. He either did not notice it at all or if he did, failed to see what use Europe could possibly have for it. Whatever reason, Europe had to wait another hundred years for Gutenberg. But even more spectacular was Marco Polo's omission of any reference to the Great Wall of China, nearly 4000 miles long and already more than 1000 years old at the time of his visit. Again, he may not have seen it; but the Great Wall of China is the only structure built by man which is visible from the moon!* Indeed, travelers can be blind.

Chinua Achebe, *Hopes and Impediments*

*About the omission of the Great Wall of China, I am indebted to *The Journey of Marco Polo* as re-created by artist Michael Foreman, published by *Pegasus* magazine, 1974.

Achebe's tone is

1. solemn, dignified.
2. amusing, humorous.
3. questioning, instructive.
4. critical, fault-finding.

People who order their meat well-done perform a valuable service for those of us in the business who are cost-conscious: they pay for the privilege of eating our garbage. In many kitchens, there's a time-honored practice called "save for well-done." When one of the cooks finds a particularly unlovely piece of steak—tough, riddled with nerve and connective tissue, off the hip end of the loin, and maybe a little stinky from age—he'll dangle it in the air and say, "Hey, Chef, whaddya want me to do with *this?*" Now, the chef has three options. He can tell the cook to throw the offending item into the trash, but that means a total loss, and in the restaurant business every item of cut, fabricated, or prepared food should earn at least three times the amount it originally cost if the chef is to make his correct food-cost percentage. Or he can decide to serve that steak to "the family"—that is, the floor staff—though that, economically, is the same as throwing it out. But no. What he's going to do is repeat the mantra of cost-conscious chefs everywhere: "Save for well-done." The way he figures it, the philistine who orders his food well-done is not likely to notice the difference between food and flotsam.

Anthony Bourdain, "Don't Eat before Reading This," *The New Yorker*

Bourdain's tone is

1. honest, candid, frank.
2. critical, fault-finding, disparaging.
3. philosophical, reflective.
4. approving, admiring, laudatory.

The following passage refers to a case of sexual harassment filed by a city worker in Menlo Park, California. The reference in the first sentence is to a facsimile of Menlo Park's complaint form that victims of sexual harassment are required to fill out.

[1]This is the complaint form used by the city of Menlo Park, California, for allegations of discrimination or harassment in the workplace. On March 1, 1993, Donna Vincent, a twenty-nine-year-old computer operator, charged that an exhibition in Menlo Park's City Hall of woodcuts by Brazilian artist Zoravia Bettiol constituted sexual harassment because it disrupted her work environment. "The new art display in city hall has several (3 or more) drawings of women who are nude from the waist up and one that is a full nude," she wrote. "I have to walk through the hallways each day as part of my work and would prefer not to have to see this type of 'Art.' " One day after the complaint was filed, city officials removed two woodcuts: portraits of Aphrodite . . . and "Luxuria." The issue raised by Vincent's complaint is being faced by universities and municipalities across the country: Can a work of art be sexually harassing? In more than a dozen recent cases, allegations of sexual harassment have been used to force the removal of artwork from classrooms, municipal buildings, and public art galleries.

2How can one be a "victim" of art? In 1558, when Pope Paul IV viewed the male genitalia painted by Michelangelo on the ceiling of the Sistine Chapel, he insisted that they be brushed over with flowing draperies (only recently removed after more than 400 years). When Donna Vincent, a Seventh-Day Adventist, first objected to the naked female torsos, the Menlo Park Arts Commission ordered that the offending parts be covered. Canary yellow Post-It notes fluttered from Aphrodite's breasts overnight before the woodcuts were removed from the exhibit altogether. The artist, who was an outspoken proponent of artistic freedom under Brazil's former military government, brought a legal complaint against the city for violating her First Amendment rights. The case is pending.

Mark Schapiro, "The Fine Art of Sexual Harassment," *Harper's*

Consider the two paragraphs in the article separately. The tone of the *first* paragraph is

1. amusing, humorous.
2. approving, admiring.
3. informative, impartial.
4. philosophical, reflective.

The tone of the *second* paragraph is

1. solemn, dignified.
2. modest, unassuming.
3. harsh, mean-spirited, nasty.
4. questioning, skeptical.

Lost in the cities of America, the immigrant Jews succumbed to waves of nostalgia for the old world. "I am overcome with longing," wrote an early immigrant, "not only for my Jewish world, which I have lost, but also for Russia." Both the handful of intellectuals and the unlettered masses were now inclined to re-create the life of the old country in their imaginations, so that with time, distance and suffering, the past they had fled took on an attractive glow, coming to seem a way of rightness and order. Not that they forgot the pogroms, not that they forgot the poverty, but that they remembered with growing fondness the inner decorums of *shtetl* life. Desperation induced homesickness, and homesickness coursed through their days like a ribbon of sadness. In Russia "there is more poetry, more music, more feeling, even if our people do suffer appalling persecution. . . . One enjoys life in Russia better than here. . .

"There is too much materialism here, too much hurry and too much prose—and yes, too much machinery." Even in the work of so sophisticated a Yiddish poet as Moshe Leib Halpern, who began to write after the turn of the century, dissatisfaction with the new world becomes so obsessive that he "forgets that his place of birth was very far indeed from being a paradise." "On strange earth I wander as a stranger," wrote Halpern about America, "while strangeness stares at me from every eye."

Irving Howe, *World of Our Fathers*

Howe's tone is

1. angry, hostile, bitter.
2. honest, candid.
3. informative, instructive.
4. nostalgic, melancholy.

These excerpts are taken from a review of the 2001 summer blockbuster movie *Pearl Harbor,* starring Ben Affleck and Kate Beckinsale.

"Pearl Harbor" is a blockheaded, hollow-hearted industrial enterprise that rises to its subject's solemn grandeur only once, as a single bomb falls. The camera spots the bomb, a sleek, shiny thing with red paint on its nose, at the moment it's released from a Japanese plane, and follows it down and down to the deck of the USS *Arizona,* then through the deck and deep into the battleship's volatile innards. A heartbeat later, the *Arizona* thrusts up from the water orgasmically, a fireball erupts, and the gray leviathan blasts itself asunder. That's the high point of a spectacular 40-minute segment given over, in the middle of the film, to the sneak attack. The other 133 minutes are littered with low points— lame comedy, dubious history, fumbling drama and a love story so inept as to make a pacifist long for war.

The review ends with this sentence:

"Pearl Harbor," for all its cutting-edge pyrotechnics, remains a movie without a soul, a would-be epic whose most stirring character is a battleship in mortal agony.

Joseph Morgenstern, "Snore-a! Snore-a! Snore-a! Shallow 'Pearl Harbor' Is a Comic-Book Bomb," *The Wall Street Journal,* May 25, 2001

Morgenstern's tone is

1. honest, candid.
2. critical, scornful.
3. questioning, skeptical.
4. nasty, abusive.

This poem was published on a website devoted to Mother's Day poems.

Happiness is like a sunny day:
All one's bitterness is drowned in light.
Praise be the light, though it must pass away,
Perhaps because compassion needs the night.
Yet when one feels like swallowing barbed wire,
More or less does nothing for the pain.
Old memories return as if on fire,
Tormenting one with unforgiving shame.
How can I, who love you, come inside,
Each wound to bind up with an ointment rare,
Restoring the once effervescent bride
  'Neath misery no happiness can spare?
So shall I sing to you of all life's beauty,
Doing through the night my daytime duty.
A song of love may not bring back your noon,
Yet in your darkness, let me be your moon.

Nicholas Gordon, "Happiness Is Like a Sunny Day"[5]

The tone of the poem is

1. philosophical, reflective, pensive.
2. sincere, honest, candid.
3. sentimental, maudlin.
4. nostalgic, melancholy.

■ TONE CONTINUED: MORE DIFFICULT VARIETIES

In this section, you will study a more difficult group of tones. Cultural, social, and political observers point to an increased cynicism in our culture, an increased skepticism about the American dream and about the country's role in world politics.[6] The reasons are too complex to delve into here; suffice it to say, however, that you will frequently encounter these tones in modern prose.

[5]Available at *www.members.aol.com/nickgo5/happi7.html,* Mothers Day Poems by Nicholas Gordon.
[6]As one example, Jedediah Purdy's *For Common Things: Irony, Trust and Commitment in America Today* (Knopf, 2000) examines the excessive and destructive uses of irony in modern life.

> ### More Difficult Varieties of Tone
> Witty, playful, droll
> Ironic, tongue-in-cheek
> Sarcastic, scornful, sardonic
> Cynical, pessimistic
> Satirical, mocking

In the following sections, we will examine and illustrate them one by one.

Wit

We say a person is quick-witted if she or he can come up with clever, pointed remarks. A **witty** tone reveals the writer's mental keenness and sense of playfulness and an ability to recognize the comic elements of a situation or condition. Unlike sarcasm, with its obvious mean streak, wit succeeds because it is humorous, brief, clever in its use of words, and pointedly perceptive in its awareness of human frailty and folly. Notice that these witticisms all share a clever turn of phrase or a play on words.

- Samuel Johnson, the eighteenth-century English man of letters, commented on a friend's rather hasty remarriage by saying: "A second marriage is the triumph of hope over experience."
- Mae West, a famous American actress of the 1930s and 1940s, a "blonde bombshell" type known for her risqué remarks: "I speak two languages: English and Body."
- Also from Mae West, "I was as pure as the driven snow—but I drifted."
- From Zsa Zsa Gabor, a Hungarian-American actress known for her many marriages to rich men: "No rich man is ugly," and another, "A man in love is incomplete until he is married. Then he is finished."
- From Oscar Wilde, Irish playwright: "Bigamy is having one wife too many. Monogamy is the same."

Irony

Irony serves many masters. An ironic tone occurs when a writer deliberately says the opposite of what he or she really means or points to the opposite of what one would typically expect to occur. This unexpected contrast results in a curious heightening of intensity about the real subject. Irony can be used to poke fun at human weaknesses and inconsistencies, or more seriously, to criticize, to encourage reform, or to cast doubt on someone's motives. The writer assumes that the reader will see through the pretense and recognize that the words mean something different from their literal meaning.

Consider these two real-life examples of irony. John Wayne was invited to play the role of Dodge City sheriff Matt Dillon in the long-running TV Western series "Gunsmoke." Wayne turned the offer down, however, because he didn't want to be typecast as a cowboy. Why is this ironic? Because Wayne was forever associated with cowboy roles during his long film career.

Another example: Toward the end of his lifetime, in the late 1930s, F. Scott Fitzgerald, author of *The Great Gatsby* and other notable works of fiction, had been nearly forgotten by the reading public. There is a story about Fitzgerald's taking his then-mistress Sheilah Graham to the legendary Pickwick Bookstore in Hollywood to show off his books, only to discover that not a single copy of any of his books was available. (In fact, most were out of print.) Ironically, *The Great Gatsby,* now regarded 60 years after his death as one of the best American novels ever written, sells more copies in a month than it sold in Fitzgerald's lifetime.[7]

Sometimes, one can predict an ironic tone just from a title. For example, before the 2000 presidential election, *Harper's* magazine published a decidedly unflattering story written by Joe Conason, a political columnist for the website *Salon.com.* The article dug into the background of George W. Bush, then governor of Texas, and his oil and baseball cronies. The title was "Notes on a Native Son: The George W. Bush Success Story"; the subtitle was "A Heartwarming Tale about Baseball, $1.7 Billion, and a Lot of Swell Friends."[8] The article was indeed an unflattering portrait of George W. Bush's financial bailouts by his rich Texas friends before he ran for president.

Here are two examples of short passages representing an ironic tone. The first is from a news article.

> It finally happened. The waiting is over. It's here now.
>
> The new off-ramp has opened at San Francisco International Airport.
>
> For years we drove into the airport from the Bayshore Freeway on the old off-ramp. The old off-ramp was a concrete cloverleaf that arched over the freeway and deposited the motorist just past the Airport Hilton Hotel.
>
> Ah, but the new off-ramp! The new off-ramp is a concrete cloverleaf that arches over the freeway and deposits the motorist just past the Airport Hilton Hotel.
>
> Steve Rubenstein, *San Francisco Chronicle*

Rubenstein uses irony to good advantage here. The short sentences at the beginning create an atmosphere of expectation and suspense. Further, he uses identical words to describe the old and new off-ramps. We would *expect* something as costly as a new off-ramp to be more efficient, more convenient, somehow different from the one it replaced. Rubenstein's use of irony allows him to leave his main point unsaid:

---

[7]Claudia Roth Pierpont, "For Love and Money," *The New Yorker.* July 3, 2000.
[8]*Harper's,* February 2000.

Spending millions of dollars on this project wasted taxpayers' money. The irony allows us to recognize the ridiculousness of the situation and reflects a critical point of view.

Irony is at the heart of many jokes. In the following example, Page Smith uses irony to illustrate memory failure in older people. A man and his wife are sitting on their front porch.

> Wife: "I certainly would appreciate a vanilla ice cream cone."
> Husband: "I'll hobble right down to the drugstore and get you one, dear."
>
> Wife: "Now, remember, I want vanilla. You always get chocolate. Write it down. Vanilla."
>
> Husband: "I can certainly remember vanilla. The store is only two blocks away."

Husband comes back with a hamburger and hands it to his wife. She looks at it disgustedly. "I knew you'd forget the mustard," she says.

> Page Smith, "Coming of Age: Jokes about Old Age,"
> *San Francisco Chronicle*

Not all irony is amusing or instructive. Irony can also give offense. As Sarah Ellison wrote in a *Wall Street Journal* article on the subject, irony and black humor are "the essence of British advertising." A British advertising agency came up with an ad campaign to promote the Imperial War Museum exhibit on the Holocaust of World War II. Ellison describes three of the agency's posters.

> "Come and see what man can achieve when he really puts his mind to it," reads one black-and-white poster of train tracks leading off into the distance. "If you want to see how man made his mark on the 20th century, now's your chance," says another poster, showing a child's arm tattooed with an inmate number. "Once in a while someone invents a product that changes people's lives," reads a third poster, which features rows of canisters of the killer gas Zyklon B.[9]

There were a lot of angry complaints about the "edgy messages" and their bad taste, but not everyone objected to the irony. Ellison goes on to quote Simon Golden, chief executive of the Agency for Jewish Education in London, who said that the posters were "perhaps right for this particular time and place and culture." Whether irony in a case like this is effective or not depends on the reader's perceptions.

---

[9]Sarah Ellison, "Ads for a Holocaust Exhibit in London Cause a Stir," *The Wall Street Journal*, November 2, 2000.

Sarcasm	**Sarcasm** derives from the Latin words for "flesh-cutting," and this etymology will help you remember its purpose. The *American Heritage Dictionary* defines *sarcasm* as "a form of wit intended to taunt, wound, or subject another to ridicule or contempt." Although it often involves irony, instead of merely saying the opposite of what one means, sarcasm intends to be cruel and sneering. A subcategory of sarcasm is the **put-down,** a form of dismissal or rejection. Sometimes the line between irony and sarcasm is hard to discern. Probably the best way to separate the two is to consider the writer's intent. If the intent is a personal insult, the tone is more likely sarcastic than ironic. Consider these examples:

- From a movie review: "Both 'Blast from the Past' and 'My Favorite Martian' define dumbness downward: the question is which one plummets lower with less style. I'd vote for 'Blast from the Past,' a primitive comedy—primitive, hell, it's Cro-Magnon." (Quoted in Joe Morgenstern, "Blast from the Past," *The Wall Street Journal,* February 12, 1999)
- From a television review of an NBC drama called "Titans," produced by Aaron Spelling; the subject is Yasmine Bleeth's acting performance: "Bleeth is first glimpsed—opening scene of the show—in a white bikini that you could stash in a bottle cap and still have extra space for character development. That space won't be used." (Quoted in John Carman, " 'Titans' Emerge as a Giant Race of Idiots," *San Francisco Chronicle,* October 4, 2000, p. E2)
- It was the habit of Winston Churchill, prime minister of England during World War II, to drink a quart of brandy every day. One evening a woman at a dinner party told Churchill that he was drunk. Churchill replied: "And you, madam, are ugly. But tomorrow I shall be sober."
- A final example, again from Churchill: The playwright George Bernard Shaw once sent Churchill two tickets for the opening night of one of his new plays, noting, "Bring a friend—if you have one." Churchill wrote back to say that he was otherwise engaged on opening night but that he would appreciate tickets for the second performance—"if there is one."[10]

Cynicism	The generation who came of age during the Vietnam War and the Watergate scandal often point to those two pivotal eras as the source of the **cynicism** that infects modern attitudes. The *Random House College Dictionary* definitions of *cynical* are helpful:

- Distrusting or disparaging the motives or sincerity of others.
- Sneeringly distrustful, contemptuous, or pessimistic.

---

[10]Quoted in Joseph Epstein, *A Line Out for a Walk* (W. W. Norton & Co., 1992).

A cynic detects falseness in others and recognizes impure motives. Politicians are sometimes described as cynical because they underestimate the intelligence of the voting public. The cynical tone is sneering, just as sarcasm is, but it is on a deeper level and arises from a different motive: Cynicism suggests a questioning and distrusting of people's stated motives or virtues. It may or may not involve irony. Here are three examples, all of which have in common the elements of distrust and exposure of foolishness:

- Mort Sahl, American comedian, was quoted as saying during the 1996 presidential campaign: "God bless Bob Dole and Bill Clinton. Long may they waver."
- Voltaire, the eighteenth-century French writer and philosopher said, "The first clergyman was the first rascal who met the first fool."
- L. Ron Hubbard, founder of the religion Scientology: "The best way to get rich in this country is to start a religion."

Satire

Satire is a type of writing that seeks to expose folly or wickedness, to hold human behavior up to ridicule, and to show the reader that certain actions or behavior would be more desirable. Satire typically relies on exaggeration and imitation of real literary forms. Here is one example. In his book *Dave Barry's Complete Guide to Guys,* humorist Dave Barry includes a chapter titled "Tips for Women: How to Have a Relationship with a Guy." One of Barry's rules is this: "Don't make the guy feel threatened," which he follows with this advice:

SITUATION	THREATENING RESPONSE	NONTHREATENING RESPONSE
You meet a guy for the first time.	"Hello."	"I am a nun."
You're on your first date. The guy asks you what your hopes for the future are.	Well, I'd like to pursue my career for a while, and then get married and maybe have children."	"A vodka Collins."
You have a great time on the date, and the guy asks you if you'd like to go out again.	"Yes."	"Okay, but bear in mind that I have only three months to live."
The clergyperson asks you if you take this man to be your lawful wedded husband, for richer and poorer, in sickness and in health, etc., 'til death do you part.	"I do."	"Well, sure, but not *literally*."

Source: Dave Barry, *Dave Barry's Complete Guide to Guys*

**Practice
Exercise 2**

Read the following passages. Then, keeping in mind the writer's purpose and intent, decide which of the following tones is most accurately reflected in each excerpt:

- Witty
- Ironic
- Sarcastic
- Cynical
- Satirical

> The Kim Basinger movie "I Dreamed of Africa" bombed at the box office last weekend. It wasn't supposed to be that way. It was originally expected to bomb way back in September.
>
> Tom King, "Waiting for Their Closeups,"
The Wall Street Journal, May 12, 2000, p. W12

The tone of this selection is _____.

The following passage is a letter to the editor:

> As a Brit, someone who lives in a country where handguns are banned, I was delighted to read in The Talk of the Town (Comment, June 12th) that the National Rifle Association has adopted Eddie Eagle as its gun-safety mascot. It may, however, wish to note that Eddie (the Eagle) Edwards is a British popular icon, the man responsible for reinvigorating the generally rather dull sport of ski jumping. His brilliantly innovative technique was to slide down the ramp and plummet vertically to near certain injury and possible death. It was compelling viewing. I wish the N.R.A. mascot every success in following the example of his illustrious namesake.
>
> Adrian Gregory
Oxford, U.K.
>
> "The Mail: A Dubious Mascot," *The New Yorker,* July 17, 2000

The tone of this letter is _____.

> As every parent knows, the makers of Beanie Babies recently announced that they will be "retiring" their mawkish menagerie of stuffed animals at the end of the year. This revelation has left America's young collectors in some degree of suspense over whether a brand-new horde will be created to replace the retirees. "Oh, mama," these children are asking—their anguish an echo of a Bob Dylan dirge—"can this really be the end?"

> The company's ploy is . . . designed to provoke a paroxysm of Beanie buying in the time before Christmas. But my wife and I, never ones to miss a civilizing trick where our kids are concerned, decided that all this talk of Beanie retirement gave us the perfect opportunity to introduce our seven-year-old, Alice, to a brand-new hobby. "Alice," we said, "would you like to start collecting stamps?"

> Tunku Varadarajan, "Stamping Out Beanies,"
> *The Wall Street Journal,* September 14, 1999

The tone of this excerpt is _____.

A ham is a smoked leg of pork, typically weighing between 10 and 12 pounds. It is customarily served at Easter dinner.

Oscar Wilde, the British writer, defined eternity like this: Two people and a ham.

The tone of this definition is _____.

The writer's subject is the Oglala Sioux Reservation in Pine Ridge, South Dakota.

> People in Pine Ridge also talk about places in town that disappeared long ago. They talk about the old golf course—not much in the Pine Ridge landscape of today immediately calls a golf course to mind—or about the Pejuta Tipi, the drugstore that was once downtown. They sometimes mention the bowling alley, the moccasin factory, Gerber's Hotel, the motel. All these establishments have closed down for good, with no successors taking their place. A remembered name that comes up often is the fishhook factory. In 1960, the Wright & McGill Company of Denver, manufacturers of fishing tackle, opened a factory to make snelled hooks in Pine Ridge. A snelled hook is one with a short section of monofilament tied to it; a loop at the monofilament's other end makes the hook easier to attach to a fishing line. No machine satisfactorily ties monofilament in knots that small, so the tying must be done by hand. In the early 1960s Wright & McGill was employing over five hundred people at factories in Pine Ridge and other towns on the reservation. Most of the employees were Oglala women who earned from about $45 to about $140 a week, a real addition to the Pine Ridge economy. In 1968, citing foreign competition and a rise in the minimum wage, the company shut down all of its Pine Ridge operations. Today the packages of most Wright & McGill fishhooks bear the words *Made in the U.S.A.* and a picture of the American flag. On the snelled-hook package, however, it says *Hand tied in Mexico.* Today the snelled hooks are made in the

Mexican city of Agua Prieta, just across the Arizona border, where the knots may be more cheaply tied than in Pine Ridge, year after year the poorest place per capita (says the Census Bureau) in the United States.

Ian Frazier, *On the Rez*

The tone of this paragraph is _____.

In the late spring of 1999, the Makah tribe of Indians, who live in the Pacific Northwest, were granted permission by the U.S. government to hunt an endangered species of whale. A *Wall Street Journal* editorial had praised the government's decision to exempt the tribe, on the grounds that they were simply engaging in an ancestral activity. This writer is responding to the newspaper's editorial.

At first, I was outraged by the bloody spectacle of the Makah tribe's whale hunt that I saw broadcast on TV news. I was concerned over the moral aspects of allowing a group of people to murder what we now know is an intelligent, highly sentient creature, merely to attempt to revive a primitive culture.

However, after reading your supportive May 25 editorial "A Whale of a Hunt" and giving the matter some thought, I've come to realize that the Makahs are right. It's important that each of us reassert our ties to our ancestors. Therefore, being of Scandinavian ancestry, I intend to go to the nearest Sons of Norway hall and recruit some warriors to recreate the glorious culture of my Viking ancestors by pillaging and burning a small town or two.

Knowing how strongly the Makahs feel about preserving cultural roots, I hope they won't mind volunteering one of their villages for my raiding party's first cultural awareness project. To the longboats!

Jeffrey Voss
Charlotte, N.C.

Letters to the Editor, "Pillaging Near You: Voss the Terrible,"
The Wall Street Journal, June 2, 1999

The tone of this letter is _____.

[Sean (Puff Daddy) Combs] was supposedly flashing wads of cash inside Manhattan's crowded Club New York—arrogantly tossing it about like confetti. . . . One annoyed man reportedly threw a stack of bills at Combs. . . . Combs brandished a gun, and one of his artists, a rapper known as Shyne, drew a 9mm Ruger and opened fire.—*Newsweek, January 10, 2000*

Dear Mr. Daddy,

I am writing to apply for a position with your posse. I am available to start hanging with you 24–7, effective immediately.

You're probably saying to yourself, "I already have a huge entourage—what do I need some other clown for?" Well, the next time some guy throws a stack of money at you, wouldn't it be great to have someone in your posse whose job it is to catch the money before it even gets to you, thereby avoiding an unpleasant—and unnecessary—dis?

Mr. Daddy, I am that clown.

While no one has ever thrown a stack of money at *me,* I feel that catching flying stacks of money is the sort of work I'm cut out for. I always bend down to pick up money on the street, for example, and I can't tell you how many coins I've fished out of couches. Catching a stack of money should be a snap for a sharp-eyed fellow like me.

And here's the beauty part: not only will I catch the stack of money—I'll dispose of it, permanently, allowing you to enjoy the rest of your evening dis-free.

What will I do with the stack of money? Maybe I'll go to Brooks Brothers and buy a new pair of cotton twill pants, or maybe I'll get that new Palm VII I've had my eye on. It really depends on how much money is in the stack of money.

I wouldn't expect you to hire me sight unseen. If you like, I could come by your offices, and you and the members of your posse could take turns throwing stacks of money at me.

In closing, I have only one request: if you decide to hire me, I'd prefer it if you could start throwing money around like confetti in the early part of the evening, say, seven-thirty to nine. I've never been much of a "night person."

Sincerely,
Andy (Stacky) Borowitz

"A Letter to Puff Daddy," *The New Yorker,* January 17, 2000

The tone of this "letter" is _____.

■ ALLUSIONS

An **allusion** is a pointed and meaningful reference to something outside the text; such references to past associations can illuminate today's ideas. The reference may be from any field, but these are the most common:

> ### Sources of Allusions
> - The Bible or other religious texts
> - History
> - Literature
> - Greek, Roman, or other mythology

Indeed, although allusions can come from any discipline, they generally come from works or events that educated readers are familiar with. The reader who misses the connections allusions provide misses out not only on the literal meaning but on the deeper connotative meaning as well. The ability to recognize allusions—without having to turn to reference books—takes years to develop, but it is attainable through wide reading and exposure to our cultural tradition. In the meantime, however, ask your instructor to explain unfamiliar allusions or use reference books or the World Wide Web. Any good unabridged dictionary will probably indicate most of the allusions you will encounter in your everyday reading.

Here is an allusion used to good effect in the introduction to a newspaper article on the Sacramento River in Glenn County, California.

> From a drift boat, this stretch of the Sacramento is remarkably bucolic, particularly at this time of year.
>
> The water is green and swift, and cottonwoods and willows crowd the shore. The sky is a piercing blue, and the air crisp as a winesap apple. Alarmed beavers slap their tails at the approach of the boat, and wood ducks and great blue herons rise from backside eddies.
>
> It's easy to imagine you're in another time, when the trees were a lush, almost impenetrable forest that extended for miles beyond this river's banks.
>
> But this is not the Sacramento River of 1870. Magnificent as they are, the trees are merely a thin buffer strip, a kind of Potemkin village, obscuring the huge agricultural complex that lies beyond. Just past the levees are thousands of acres of orchards and rice fields.
>
> Glen Martin, "Wetlands, Birds and Salmon Returning to the Sacramento,"
> *San Francisco Chronicle*

The allusion to a Potemkin village underscores Martin's main point. The original Potemkin village dates from Catherine the Great's reign over Russia in the eighteenth century. Upon learning of her wish to tour the countryside, Grigori Potemkin, her lover and an army officer, designed elaborate fake villages that the Czarina could observe from her carriage. These façades would hide the reality of the grinding poverty of Russia's peasant villages. The *American Heritage Dictionary* defines *Potemkin village* as "something that appears elaborate and impressive but in actual fact lacks substance." What is Martin saying, then, about the trees along today's Sacramento River? As splendid as they are, they are nowhere near as impressive as they used to be; today they merely obscure the realities of modern agriculture just behind them.

■ SPECIAL EFFECTS

In this final section of the chapter, we will briefly look at some **special effects** that contribute to tone.

Special Effects

- Understatement
- Hyperbole (deliberate exaggeration)
- Alliteration
- Repetition for effect
- Unusual sentence structure

Understatement   Actually a form of irony, **understatement** involves deliberate restraint, downplaying a situation to heighten its significance. Consider this excerpt from an article about increased attendance at megabudget movies from the summer of 1999.

> "Even those of us who thought it would be a big summer never thought it could be this big," says Tom Sherak, who chairs the motion picture group for 20th Century Fox. His studio had a little movie called "Star Wars: Episode 1—The Phantom Menace." It has taken in $420 million in the United States and about $300 million abroad. That makes it the second most successful movie in history, after "Titanic."
>
> Sharon Waxman, "Summer Films Broke Rules," *The Washington Post*

Locate the one word that creates the understatement. _____

Hyperbole   **Hyperbole** (pronounced hī pŭr′ bə lē) is a figure of speech using deliberate exaggeration for effect. Consider this passage on Donald Trump and the hyperbolic effect of the last sentence.

Cities often run on a fuel of power, money, and ego, but sometimes they can run on pure hype, as Atlantic City, New Jersey, did in the days before Mike Tyson fought Michael Spinks for the undisputed heavyweight championship of the world. The man responsible for the bout was Donald Trump, who owned two profitable casinos in town and was constructing a third, modestly called the Taj Mahal. Trump appears to be in love with certain slick catchwords, including *plaza, success,* and *celebrity,* and he'd probably stamp his name on clouds and mountains if anybody gave him a chance.

Bill Barich, *The Sporting Life*

Alliteration

Alliteration—the repetition of initial consonant sounds in words—is more often associated with poetry than with prose. A repetition of sibilant ("s") sounds, for example, can be used to create a sinister mood. One part of Martin Luther King, Jr.'s, classic essay "Letter from Birmingham Jail" discusses the burdens prejudice has placed on African Americans. King uses alliteration—a sequence of initial "d" and "b" consonants—to create a heavy, brooding mood. Here is one illustrative sentence, which should be read aloud for the full effect.

Like so many experiences of the past we were confronted with blasted hopes, and the dark shadow of a deep disappointment settled on us.

Repetition for Effect

Repeating key words, phrases, or clauses brings about a pleasing balance and calls attention to important ideas. Such is the effect of Elie Wiesel's repeating the key word "never" in this moving passage. (Wiesel is a survivor of the Holocaust, and this passage, incidentally, is displayed on a large plaque at the United States Holocaust Memorial Museum in Washington, D.C.)

Never shall I forget that night, the first night in camp, which has turned my life into one long night, seven times cursed and seven times sealed. Never shall I forget that smoke. Never shall I forget the little faces of the children, whose bodies I saw turned into wreaths of smoke beneath a silent blue sky.

Never shall I forget those flames which consumed my faith forever.

Never shall I forget that nocturnal silence which deprived me, for all eternity, of the desire to live. Never shall I forget those moments which murdered my God and my soul and turned my dreams to dust. Never shall I forget these things, even if I am condemned to live as long as God Himself. Never.

Elie Wiesel, *The Night Trilogy*

Unusual Sentence Structure

Writers not only choose words carefully, but also endeavor to create sentences that reinforce both the content and the mood of the piece. Here are three examples of distinctive sentence structure. In the first, television critic John Carman describes the acting debut of Vanna White, better known as the letter-turner on the television game show "Wheel of Fortune," who appeared in a made-for-television movie, *Goddess of Love*. Carman pokes fun at the movie by writing in overly simple sentences. (For full effect, read this excerpt aloud and exaggerate the simplistic style.)

> This is Vanna White. Vanna is the star of her own movie Sunday night on NBC. Vanna's movie is called "Goddess of Love."
>
> Vanna plays Venus in her movie. Venus is a goddess. Venus comes back to life after 3,000 years. General Electric owns NBC. General Electric brings good things to life.
>
> When General Electric brings Venus to life, Venus falls in love with a hair stylist.
>
> Acting is new for Vanna. Vanna says that "It was very hard. It's very hard to sit there for my first major role on television and say, 'Where dost thou slumber?' "
>
> NBC did not let critics see "Goddess of Love." NBC is very smart. The critics are very sad. They wanted very much to see Vanna act and say, "Where dost thou slumber?"
>
> But NBC says it has not seen the movie either. The man who is in charge of NBC movies has not seen "Goddess of Love," even though it will be on TV Sunday (Channel 4, 9 P.M.). Where can it be?
>
> John Carman, " 'G-dd-ss -f L-v' Must be Vanna,"
> *San Francisco Chronicle*

Short sentences have a quite different effect in this paragraph in which the author describes the preparations of Harry Houdini, the famous magician, for a bridge jump while manacled.

> Picture the scene as Houdini performs one of his bridge jumps, so often described with such unvarying excitement. The excited crowd, several thousand strong, jostles around. Houdini and his team arrive. A silence falls. Houdini strips to his bathing suit and climbs onto the parapet. The attention of all these thousands of people is focused upon him—a small man,

slightly bow-legged, very muscular. The local chief of police comes forward carrying handcuffs, often two sets; leg-irons. Houdini allows himself to be manacled. He stands there, waiting until he "hears the voice." Then he jumps. The crowd surges forward. It is waiting for—what? What it sees, in a minute or so, is Houdini, swimming strongly for the bank or the boat, brandishing the irons in one hand. It is slightly disappointed, but also satisfied. Death has been defeated once more.

Ruth Brandon, The Life and Many Deaths of Harry Houdini

Underline the short sentences to see how they heighten suspense and contribute to the dramatic effect.

This final example, by Sherman Alexie, a Coeur d'Alene Indian from Washington state, is the opening paragraph of his 1996 novel *Indian Killer.* In it he describes an Indian Health Service hospital. The sentence fragments, taken together, create a series of impressions, almost as if he were sketching the hospital scene with charcoal rather than with words. What dominant impression of the hospital does the reader come away with?

The sheets are dirty. An Indian Health Service hospital in the early sixties. On this reservation or that reservation. Any reservation, a particular reservation. Antiseptic, cinnamon and danker odors. Anonymous cries up and down the hallways. Linoleum floors swabbed with gray water. Mop smelling like old sex. Walls painted white a decade earlier. Now yellowed and peeling. Old Indian woman in a wheelchair singing traditional songs to herself, tapping a rhythm on her armrest, right index finger tapping; tapping. Pause. Tap, tap. A phone ringing loudly from behind a thin door marked PRIVATE. Twenty beds available, twenty beds occupied. Waiting room where a young Indian man sits on a couch and holds his head in his hands. Nurses' lounge, two doctors' offices and a scorched coffee pot. Old Indian man, his hair bright white and unbraided, pushing his IV bottle down the hallway. He is barefoot and confused, searching for a pair of moccasins he lost when he was twelve years old. Donated newspapers and magazines stacked in bundles, months and years out of date, missing pages. In one of the exam rooms, an Indian family of four, mother, father, son, daughter, all coughing blood quietly into handkerchiefs. The phone still ringing behind the PRIVATE door. A cinder-block building, thick windows that distort the view, pine trees, flagpole. A 1957 Chevy parked haphazardly, back door flung open, engine still running, back seat damp. Empty now.

Sherman Alexie, Indian Killer

Practice Exercise 3

Identify the allusion or special effect in the following selections. If an allusion is evident, explain its meaning.

This excerpt is from a movie review of *Titanic.*

The film has everything a blockbuster should—big history, big danger, big romance (with partial nudity), Leonardo DiCaprio, big special effects, Leonardo DiCaprio, the "event"-size running time, Leonardo DiCaprio, and a record 3,103 U.S. theaters in which to weave its considerable spell.

Peter Stack, " 'Titanic' to Swamp 'Star Wars,' " *San Francisco Chronicle*

Allusion (and meaning) or special effect: _____

_____

For a long time, I've been preoccupied with why some folks stay and some stray. I read about a scientific study of cats in the wild. It had been assumed that cats who established a territory, or home base, were the successful ones, while those who remained roamers were the losers. The study uncovered evidence that the transients, not the residents, might be the more resourceful cats, accepting greater risks and more varied opportunities for prey and mates. It was almost as though they were exercising imagination. It's an old question—the call of the hearth or the call of the wild? Should I stay or should I go? Who is better off, those who traipse around or those who spend decades in the same spot, growing roots?

The way I see it, a clever cat prowls but calls home occasionally. The answer is the mingling of sunlight and shadow; it's ambiguity, not either-or. The best journeys spiral up and around—the journey of Odysseus on the wine-dark sea. . . . In the Zen journey, when you return, you know for the first time where you came from. We're always yearning and wandering, whether we actually leave or not. In America, we all come from somewhere else, and we carry along some dream myth of home, a notion that something—our point of origin, our roots, the home country—is out there. It's a place where we belong, where we know who we are. Maybe it's in the past—we dream of our own clear springs—or maybe it's somewhere ahead. In its inception, the idea of America was heaven on earth. Now that dream is fractured and we're looking for the pieces. Maybe we'll never find what we're looking for, but we have to look.

Bobbie Ann Mason, *Clear Springs*

Allusion (and meaning) or special effect: _____

_____

During the past forty years, some three hundred million children have played with Lego, and it is estimated that in the course of a single year these children spend five billion hours amid the bricks. At last count, Lego had filled the world with a hundred and eighty-nine billion molded elements. Most of them, given the unbreakable longevity of the product, must still be in circulation. Half, as far as I can make out, are in my attic.

Anthony Lane, "The Joy of Bricks," The New Yorker

Allusion (and meaning) or special effect: _____

_____

Joseph Epstein, writing under the pseudonym "Aristides," is a writer and college English professor describing his trepidation at the annual ritual of instructor evaluations.

Socrates may have had to take the hemlock, but at least he was spared the indignity of that relatively recent addition to the teaching transaction known as "teacher evaluation." On these evaluations, generally made during the last minutes of the final session of the college term, students, in effect, grade their teachers. Hemlock may on occasion seem preferable, for turn-about here can sometimes be cruel play, especially when students, under the veil of anonymity, take the opportunity of evaluation to comment upon their teacher's dress, or idiosyncrasies, or moral character. For the most part I have not fared too badly on these evaluations, though my clothes have been the subject of faint comedy, my habit of jiggling the change in my pockets and my wretched handwriting have been noted.

"Aristides" (Joseph Epstein), "Student Evaluations," The American Scholar

Allusion (and meaning) or special effect: _____

_____

_____

The writer is describing the departure of tourists from Ft. Lauderdale's airport on their way to Caribbean cruise ships. Hint: This one has two elements you have studied.

Apparently Ft. Lauderdale Airport is always just your average sleepy midsize airport six days a week and then every Saturday resembles the Fall of Saigon.

David Foster Wallace, A Supposedly Fun Thing I'll Never Do Again

Allusion (and meaning) or special effect: _____

_____

_____

_____

■ CHAPTER EXERCISES

Selection 1   This passage comes from a chapter on the American government's mistreatment of various Indian tribes during the nineteenth century.

> The most famous removal of Indians, of course, was the removal of the Cherokee from Georgia westward to Indian Territory in 1838 and 1839. There are many accounts of the forced march that came to be known as the Trail of Tears—of the Cherokee's previous peaceableness and prosperity on their lands in Georgia; of the Georgia settlers' hatred of Indians and desire for those lands; of the mercilessness of President Andrew Jackson; of Supreme Court Justice John Marshall's ruling that the removal was illegal; of Jackson's response: "He has made his law. Now let him enforce it"; of the opposition of people as diverse as Ralph Waldo Emerson and Davy Crockett to the removal; of the U.S. soldiers' roundup of the Georgia Cherokee; of the Cherokee's suffering in the stockades and along the trail; of the death of more than four thousand Cherokee, about a third of the population of the tribe, before the removal was through. The Cherokee had their own written language, with an alphabet devised by the Cherokee leader Sequoyah during the 1820s. But their success at following the ways of the whites proved no defense. As would happen again elsewhere, building houses and farms only gave the Indians more to lose when government policy changed.
>
> Ian Frazier, *On the Rez*

A. Content and Structure

Complete the following questions.

1. A good title for this paragraph would be
    (a) "A Sad Day in American History."
    (b) "A History of the Cherokee Indians."
    (c) "Forced Removals in American History."
    (d) "The Cherokee and the Trail of Tears."

2. The author suggests that the Cherokee
    (a) were envied for their prosperity by the Georgia settlers.
    (b) had waged wars with the Georgia settlers.
    (c) had little public support for remaining in Georgia.
    (d) were removed because of past broken treaties with the government.

3. Concerning the Cherokees' experiences along the Trail of Tears, what

    seems to be Frazier's central concern? _____

    _____

4. Frazier also suggests that the Cherokee
    (a) were singled out for retribution for trying to emulate whites.
    (b) were somewhat unusual among Indian tribes for having a written
        language.
    (c) had brought much of their misfortune upon themselves.
    (d) only (a) and (b).
    (e) (a), (b), and (c).

B. Language and Tone

Complete the following questions.

1. Frazier's tone can be best described as
    (a) complaining, aggrieved.
    (b) informative, instructive.
    (c) sad, lamenting.
    (d) sympathetic, admiring.

2. When President Jackson responded to Supreme Court Justice
    Marshall's ruling, "He has made his law. Now let him enforce it," we
    can infer that Jackson's tone was
    (a) honest, candid.
    (b) defiant, insolent.
    (c) complaining, aggrieved.
    (d) appeasing, conciliatory.

3. A special effect evident in the paragraph is
    (a) hyperbole.
    (b) understatement.
    (c) alliteration.
    (d) repetition for effect.

_____

Answers for *A. Content and Structure*
Selection 1

1. (d)
2. (a)

3. The Cherokees' mistreatment and suffering at the hands of the U.S. government

4. (d)

B. Language and Tone

1. (c)
2. (b)
3. (d)

Selection 2

[1]Human beings find the most ingenious ways to protect their privacy, even under conditions of near-constant physical proximity to others. [2]In many cultures, even minimal control over physical access can be hard to come by in the midst of communal and family life. [3]Some villages have huts with walls so thin that sounds can easily be heard through them; others have no walls at all separating couples, or families. [4]Many ways are then devised to create privacy. [5]Villagers may set up private abodes outside the village to which they go for days or even months when they want to be alone or with just one or two others. [6]Many cultures have developed strict rules of etiquette, along with means of dissimulation and hypocrisy that allow certain private matters to remain unknown or go unobserved. [7]In such ways, it is possible to exercise some control over one's openness to others even in the midst of communal life or crowds.

[8]An arresting example of how such control can be maintained is provided by the Tuareg men of North Africa who wear blue veils and long robes of indigo cotton, so that little of them shows except their hands, their feet, and the area around their eyes. [9]The veil is worn at home as well as outside, even when eating or smoking. [10]Some wear it even when asleep. [11]It is raised to cover the face most completely in the presence of highly placed persons or family members granted special respect, such as in-laws. [12]One observer noted that the veil protects ceremonial reserve and allows a "symbolic withdrawal from a threatening situation."

[13]The veil, though providing neither isolation nor anonymity, bestows facelessness and the idiom of privacy upon its wearer and allows him to stand somewhat aloof from the perils of social interaction while remaining a part of it.

Sissela Bok, *Secrets: On the Ethics of Concealment and Revelation*

A. Vocabulary

For each italicized word from the selection, write the dictionary definition most appropriate for the context.

1. the most *ingenious* ways [sentence 1]: _____

2. near-constant physical *proximity* [1]: _____

3. means of *dissimulation* [6]: _____

4. the veil *bestows* facelessness [13]: _____

B. Content, Structure, and Tone

Complete the following questions.

1. The main idea of the paragraph is that
    (a) privacy is a universal concern.
    (b) loss of personal privacy may have serious emotional consequences.
    (c) clothing can sometimes establish one's privacy.
    (d) human beings have devised ingenious ways to protect their privacy.
2. The primary method of paragraph development is
    (a) example.
    (b) analysis.
    (c) definition.
    (d) cause–effect.
3. The reader can infer that maintaining privacy is
    (a) more difficult in economically developed nations.
    (b) impossible to achieve or maintain in communal societies or in large families.
    (c) more important to cultures in North Africa than it is to Americans or Europeans.
    (d) a special problem in cultures where people live in close proximity.
4. Sentences 12 and 13 suggest that the veil allows the wearer to
    (a) withdraw from society whenever he wants to escape annoyances.
    (b) protect himself from enemies.
    (c) escape threatening situations while still being a part of the group.
    (d) adopt a modest position in front of highly placed officials or other important persons.
5. The author's tone can best be described as
    (a) philosophical, reflective.
    (b) admiring, laudatory.
    (c) informative, instructive.
    (d) ironic, amusing.

Selection 3

The chimpanzee who is the subject of this passage, Cholmondeley—or Chumley as he was known to his friends—was being donated to the London Zoo. The author had promised the owner to take the chimp back to England on his way home from Africa.

[1]He arrived in the back of a small van, seated sedately in a huge crate. [2]When the doors of his crate were opened and Chumley stepped out with all the ease and self-confidence of a film star, I was considerably shaken; standing on his bow legs

in a normal slouching chimp position, he came up to my waist, and if he had straightened up his head would have been on a level with my chest. **3**He had huge arms and must have measured at least twice my size round his hairy chest. **4**Owing to bad tooth growth, both sides of his face were swollen out of all proportion, and this gave him a weird pugilistic look. **5**His eyes were small, deep-set, and intelligent; the top of his head was nearly bald, owing, I discovered later, to his habit of sitting and rubbing the palms of his hands backward across his head, an exercise which seemed to afford him much pleasure and which he persisted in until the top of his skull was quite devoid of hair. **6**This was no young chimp such as I had expected, but a veteran about eight or nine years old, fully mature, strong as a powerful man, and, to judge by his expression, with considerable experience of life. **7**Although he was not exactly a nice chimp to look at (I had seen handsomer), he certainly had a terrific personality; it hit you as soon as you set eyes on him. **8**His little eyes looked at you with great intelligence, and there seemed to be a glitter of ironic laughter in their depths that made one feel uncomfortable.

9He stood on the ground and surveyed his surroundings with a shrewd glance, and then he turned to me and held out one of his soft, pink-palmed hands to be shaken, with exactly that bored expression that one sees on the faces of professional hand-shakers. **10**Round his neck was a thick chain, and its length drooped over the tailboard of the lorry[11] and disappeared into the depths of his crate. **11**With an animal of less personality than Chumley, this would have been a sign of his subjugation, of his captivity. **12**But Chumley wore the chain with the superb air of a Lord Mayor; after shaking my hand so professionally, he turned and proceeded to pull the chain, which measured some fifteen feet, out of his crate. **13**He gathered it up carefully into loops, hung it over one hand, and proceeded to walk into the hut as if he owned it. **14**Thus, in the first few minutes of arrival, Chumley had made us feel inferior; he had moved in, not, we felt, because we wanted him to, but because he did. **15**I almost felt I ought to apologize for the mess on the table.

Gerald Durrell, "The Life and Death of Cholmondeley"

A. Vocabulary

For each italicized word from the selection, choose the best definition according to the context in which it appears.

1. *sedately* [sentence 1]:
   (a) calmly, in a dignified manner.
   (b) nervously, apprehensively.
   (c) arrogantly, haughtily.
   (d) uncomfortably, awkwardly.

---

[11]*Lorry* is the British word for truck.

2. *pugilistic* [4]: Having the appearance of a
    (a) military officer.
    (b) movie star.
    (c) fighter.
    (d) vicious animal.
3. *ironic* [8]: In this context,
    (a) cynical, distrustful.
    (b) satirical, ridiculing.
    (c) sarcastic, suggesting a superior attitude.
    (d) nasty, cruel.
4. subjugation [11]:
    (a) boredom, indifference.
    (b) defeat, enslavement.
    (c) cooperative spirit.
    (d) subjectivity, introspective nature.

B. Content, Structure, and Tone

Complete the following questions.

1. The dominant impression of Chumley that Durrell wants to convey is his
    (a) weird appearance.
    (b) large size.
    (c) maturity.
    (d) superior attitude.
2. The passage contains three figures of speech that describe Chumley's behavior. Identify each one and note the sentence in which it appears.

    Sentence _____: _____

    Sentence _____: _____

    _____

    Sentence _____: _____
3. These three figures of speech, taken together, suggest that Chumley

    was accustomed to _____

    _____
4. Which of the following is an accurate inference?
    (a) Durrell had never seen a chimp before.
    (b) Chumley was embarrassed by the chains used to tether him to his crate.
    (c) Chumley insisted on having his surroundings be clean and orderly.
    (d) Durrell had expected Chumley to be an ordinary chimp.

5. The tone of the passage can best be described as
    (a) ironic, wry, and amused.
    (b) sarcastic, ridiculing.
    (c) serious, earnest.
    (d) sentimental, maudlin.

■ ***PRACTICE ESSAY***

"On Leavened Bread"

Salman Rushdie

Chris Felver/Hulton/Archive.

Salman Rushdie is a contemporary writer who was born in India. He is best known for his controversial novel The Satanic Verses, *whose publication was attacked by Muslims because they believed that Rushdie committed blasphemy by modeling a character on the prophet Muhammad. Iran's Ayatollah Khomeini issued a death threat against Rushdie, forcing him to live in hiding for many years. The Iranian government eventually lifted the death threat. You can see Rushdie in a cameo role playing himself in the 2001 film* Bridget Jones's Diary.

Do not let the names of the breads mentioned in the essay intimidate you. Leavened bread, mentioned in the title, refers to bread that is made to rise by adding a leavening agent such as yeast, in contrast to Indian breads, which are flat. Chapati, phulka, tandoori nan, Peshawari nan, feshmi roti, shirmal, and paratha, mentioned in the first paragraph, are all traditional Indian flat breads, meaning that because they contain no yeast, they do not rise. The two breads mentioned in paragraph 5 are European: Ciabatta is a rough Italian bread; brioche is a sweet, light French bread.

1   There was leavened bread in Bombay, but it was sorry fare: dry, crumbling, tasteless—unleavened bread's paler, unluckier relative. It wasn't "real." Real bread was the chapati, or phulka, served piping hot; the tandoori nan, and its sweeter Frontier variant, the Peshawari nan; and, for luxury, the feshmi roti, the shirmal, the paratha. Compared with these aristocrats, the leavened white loaves of my childhood seemed to merit the description that Shaw's immortal dustman, Alfred Doolittle, dreamed up for people like himself: they were, in truth, "the undeserving poor."[12]

---

[12] The reference here is to the play *Pygmalion* by George Bernard Shaw, which was later made into the Broadway musical and the film *My Fair Lady*. It concerns Eliza Doolittle, a flower-stall clerk, and Henry Higgins's attempts to rid her of her cockney accent. Alfred Doolittle, mentioned here, is Eliza's father. A dustman in England is a garbage collector.

2   My first inkling that there might be more to leavened bread than I knew came while I was visiting Karachi, Pakistan, where I learned that a hidden order of nuns, in a place known as the Monastery of the Angels, baked a mean loaf. To buy it, you had to get up at dawn—that is, a servant had to get up at dawn—and stand in line outside a small hatch in the monastery's wall. The nuns' baking facilities were limited, the daily run was small, and this secret bakery's reputation was high. Only the early bird caught the loaf. The hatch would open, and a nun would hand the bread out to the waiting populace. Loaves were strictly rationed. No bulk buying was permitted. And the price, of course, was high. (All this I knew only by hearsay, for I never got up at such an unearthly hour to see for myself.)

3   The nuns' bread—white, crusty, full of flavor—was a small revelation, but it was also, on account of its unusual provenance, eccentric. It came from beyond the frontiers of the everyday, a mystery trailing an anecdote behind it. It was almost—well, fictional. (Later, it became fictional, when I put the monastery in my novel "Midnight's Children.") Now, in the matter of bread such extraordinariness is not good. You want bread to be a part of daily life. You want it to be ordinary. You want it to be there. You don't want to get up in the middle of the night and wait by a hatch in a wall. So, while the Angels' bread was tasty, it felt like an aberration, a break in the natural order. It didn't really change my mind.

4   Then, aged thirteen and a half, I flew to England. And, suddenly, there it was, in every shopwindow. The White Crusty, the Sliced and the Unsliced. The Small Tin, the Large Tin, the Bloomer. The abandoned, plentiful promiscuity of it. The soft, pillowy mattressiness of it. The well-sprung bounciness of it between your teeth. Hard crust and soft center: the sensuality of that perfect textural contrast. I was done for. In the whorehouses of the bakeries, I was serially, gluttonously, irredeemably unfaithful to all those chapatis next door, waiting for me back home. East was East, but yeast was West

5   This, remember was long before British bread counters were enlivened by the European invasion, long before ciabatta and brioche; this was 1961. But the love affair that began then has never lost its intensity; the new exotic breads have served only to renew the excitement.

6   I should add that there was a second discovery, almost as thrilling; that is, water. The water back home was dangerous and had to be thoroughly boiled. To be able to drink water from the tap was a privilege indeed. I have never forgotten that when I first arrived in these immeasurably wealthy and powerful lands I found the first proofs of my good fortune in loaf and glass. Since that time, a regime of bread and water has never sounded like a hardship to me.

A. *Comprehension*

Choose the answer that best completes each statement. Do not refer to the selection while doing this exercise.

1. The leavened bread from Rushdie's childhood in Bombay was
   (a) of excellent quality.
   (b) of very poor quality.
   (c) bought only by aristocrats.
   (d) nearly impossible to buy.

2. Rushdie found the bread baked at the Monastery of the Angels in Karachi "eccentric" because of its
   (a) unusual origin.
   (b) resemblance to the traditional Indian breads of his youth.
   (c) strange color and flavor.
   (d) weird shape and texture.

3. According to the author, bread should be
   (a) made only at home.
   (b) served with every meal.
   (c) ordinary and easily available.
   (d) difficult to obtain and therefore more desirable.

4. The author characterizes the white leavened bread he encountered in England as almost
   (a) miraculous.
   (b) seductive.
   (c) mysterious.
   (d) addictive.

5. The safe water in England was, to Rushdie, another indication of England's
   (a) immense influence in the colonial world.
   (b) immeasurable wealth and power.
   (c) concern with the environment.
   (d) advanced technology.

B. *Vocabulary*

For each italicized word from the selection, write the dictionary definition most appropriate for the context. You may refer to the selection to answer the questions in this section and in all the remaining sections.

1. it was *sorry* fare [paragraph 1]: _____

2. nuns . . . baked a *mean* loaf (the slang or informal meaning) [2]:

   _____

3. its unusual *provenance* [3]: _____

4. it felt like an *aberration* [3]: _____

5. the abandoned, plentiful *promiscuity* [4]: Here, used ironically and

    humorously to mean _____

6. *irredeemably* unfaithful [4]: describing one who is _____

    _____

C. Structure

Complete the following questions.

1. The author's literal purpose is to
    (a) explain the differences between Indian unleavened bread and
        Western leavened bread.
    (b) classify types of bread.
    (c) explore his pleasurable sensory discoveries of different kinds of
        bread.
    (d) convince us that leavened breads are superior to unleavened
        types.

2. This essay is about more than just bread. In your own words, explain

    Rushdie's deeper purpose in writing this essay. _____

    _____

    _____

3. Rushdie strongly implies in paragraph 2 that
    (a) the Monastery of the Angels' bread was a well-kept secret.
    (b) Rushdie's family was sufficiently rich that they could afford to send
        a servant to buy the monastery's bread.
    (c) the monastery's white bread was superior to the bread he later
        discovered in England.
    (d) the nuns were probably English.

D. Language

Complete the following questions.

1. In paragraph 1 Rushdie uses two metaphors to contrast the white
    unleavened bread of Bombay and the "real" Indian breads, such as
    chapati, tandoori nan, and paratha. White leavened breads are

    imaginatively compared to _____.

    Traditional Indian breads are imaginatively compared to _____.

2. In paragraph 1, Rushdie describes leavened bread from his childhood as "dry, crumbling, tasteless." In paragraph 3, he describes the monastery bread he ate in Karachi as "white, crusty, full of flavor." These phrases are
   (a) denotative.
   (b) connotative.
   (c) examples of bakers' jargon.
   (d) euphemisms.

3. Consider the words "eccentric" and "mystery" in paragraph 3. How would you characterize their use?
   (a) denotative.
   (b) connotative with positive overtones.
   (c) connotative with negative overtones.
   (d) clichés.

4. At the heart of the essay, in paragraph 4, Rushdie imaginatively

   compares the English variety of white bread to _____

   _____

   The word "mattressiness," also in paragraph 4, refers specifically to

   which quality of English bread? _____

5. The emotional atmosphere that this essay conveys is
   (a) playful, amusing.
   (b) nostalgic, melancholy.
   (c) earnest, serious.
   (d) philosophic, questioning.

Questions for Discussion and Analysis

1. Examine a food that, as bread does for Salman Rushdie, reveals something more profound about the culture that produces it.
2. Explore the concept of food as a trigger for memory. What foods serve this function for you?

🖱 ON THE WEB

The New York Times archives contain a compendium of articles titled "Featured Author: Salman Rushdie." The address is www.nytimes.com/books/99/04/18/specials/rushdie.html

Reading Critically

Elements of Critical Reading

CHAPTER OBJECTIVES

In this chapter, the first of three chapters dealing with reading critically, you will learn to analyze and evaluate claims and evidence in arguments, building on the analytical skills developed in Parts 1, 2, and 3. Critical reading goes beyond literal and inferential comprehension. It means judging the worth of what you read—its legitimacy as argument, accuracy, fairness, reliability, and significance. The readings in Part 4 represent the persuasive or argumentative mode of discourse—nonfiction prose that expresses a writer's subjective opinion, whether it's a newspaper or magazine editorial, a letter to the editor, a political speech, a position paper, or an article on a World Wide Web site. Chapter 8 covers these critical-reading topics:

- Critical reading defined
- The reader's responsibilities
- Developing a worldview
- The structure of arguments
- Taking arguments apart

■ CRITICAL READING DEFINED

In the term **critical reading,** *critical* does not mean tearing down or finding fault. Critical reading is the slowest and most thorough kind of reading. It goes beyond literal comprehension. It means judging, evaluating, weighing the writer's words carefully, and applying your reasoning powers. It requires keeping an open mind, not accepting unquestioningly what you read just because it is in print—but also not rejecting ideas simply because they are different from your beliefs. Critical reading may also require suspending a judgment until you get more information or read other points of view on an issue. This type of reading requires what might be called a healthy skepticism. Finally, critical reading involves recognizing fallacious arguments, whether from deliberate manipulation, deceptive appeals to emotion, logical fallacies (errors in reasoning), or other illegitimate forms of argumentation. With the wealth of information available to us from both traditional and electronic sources, the ability to read that material critically has become more necessary than ever before—to protect our wallets, to safeguard our ability to think for ourselves, and to allow us to make up our own minds about the day's important issues.

■ THE READER'S RESPONSIBILITIES

If the writer's task is to muster convincing and fair evidence in support of an argument and to adhere to the rules of logic, what should the reader be doing? Why do we sometimes misread and misinterpret? One reason is laziness. We may not take the trouble to comprehend accurately, being content to graze over the contents with no more concentration than if we were checking out the TV guide. Also, we may not feel like looking up the definitions of important words. Consider, for example, this sentence:

> The defense attorney used a *meretricious* argument to ensure his client's acquittal.

A lazy student who encounters this sentence might think, "*Meretricious* sounds sort of like *merit,* and I remember from high school French that *mère* is the French word for 'mother,' so *meretricious* probably means something good." Unfortunately, this conclusion is way off the mark; *meretricious* really means "attracting attention in a vulgar manner."

Another evasion of our responsibility occurs when we skim through an article (rather than reading it carefully) because we already agree with the author's point of view. However, the author's position may be flimsy, supported by weak or flawed evidence. The position may not really be worth holding or may not stand up to scrutiny. Haphazard reading never reveals these defects. Even worse, we may glance at an article and not read it because we think we know in advance that we *don't* agree with the author, thus missing an important part of the intellectual experience—examining opinions we do not share.

Still another obstacle to good reading is prejudice or bias, letting narrow personal experience or parochial values interfere with a clear-headed appraisal. Naturally, 18-year-olds cannot expect to have the same wealth of experience older adults do. Yet a willingness to see events from another perspective is an essential component of critical reading (and of the intellectual experience); all these skills are best developed during the college years when students are exposed to a wide assortment of political, social, and philosophical ideas. In the years following college, students can refine their thinking and call upon these skills in every aspect of their lives.

An incident that occurred in my advanced reading class illustrates how bias or prejudice can interfere with accurate reading. One student, a Polish immigrant in his mid-twenties, reacted vehemently to a newspaper article about Fidel Castro's playing host to Rajiv Gandhi, the prime minister of India. The article described how Castro wanted to give Gandhi a big send-off at the conclusion of his visit and so assembled thousands of Cubans, who lined the streets of Havana, cheering and clapping. Here are the pertinent sentences from the article:

> Rounding up a half-million people on short notice is no small task. But it took only a snap of Castro's fingers. By dawn, Havana was abuzz with activity in preparation for Gandhi's midmorning departure. Mass organizations were alerted and buses normally used to take commuters to their jobs were mobilized. Half a million cheering Cubans saw the Indian leader off that day in 1985.
>
> George Gedda, *San Francisco Examiner*

During discussion, the student stated that Castro had "forced" the population to stop their daily activities to attend the parade in Gandhi's honor. Gedda's discussion, however, is factual and implies no coercion. Nor does the tone convey anything sinister; if anything, the statement "Havana was abuzz with activity" suggests a positive connotation. In this case, the student's experience of growing up in a communist country colored his perception, and he inferred something that the writer never implied. Critical readers try—insofar as it is humanly possible—to suspend their biases and personal prejudices so that they do not interfere with accurate comprehension.

■ DEVELOPING A WORLDVIEW

Although it is impossible for human beings to be wholly free of bias and prejudice, identifying the source of our beliefs helps us both understand why we think as we do and interpret what we read. One obstacle is **ethnocentrism,** the belief that your own group is superior, that it is at the center of the universe, and that a different way of perceiving events is wrong or flawed, as if everyone else in the world should look at issues and problems the same way you do.

Sorting out the opinions your college experience exposes you to is difficult. As you grow intellectually and reflect on what you have read, learned, and experienced firsthand, you will develop a **worldview**—your perspective on the world, the way you see and interpret events and issues. Too often we are content to hang on to our opinions because evaluating other viewpoints is too much trouble; then, too, our opinions are so comfortable, providing us with a ready-made set of beliefs. These beliefs may be sufficient for day-to-day life experiences, but they may fall short when we are confronted with serious social, economic, or political issues.

Where does one's worldview come from? Obviously, from the many influences that you have come into contact with during your formative years: parents, siblings, teachers, friends, acquaintances, members of the clergy, co-workers, to name a few. To these we add personal experience, observation of the world around you, and the reading you have done. But your worldview is also formed by intangibles, such as the value system you were raised with; your family's economic status, level of education, racial or ethnic background, and expectations; and your religious and moral foundation. All these influences leave their imprint on you and shape the way you interpret the world around you.

Our worldviews undergo constant change as part of the educational process afforded by contact with the intellectual world and with the everyday world. Note that the verb *educate* derives from Latin and literally refers to "a leading out" (from the prefix *e,* meaning "from," and the root *ducare,* meaning "leading"). To characterize your worldview, begin by questioning why you think the way you do. Consider your upbringing and the people who influenced you most. To what extent does your thinking conform to the way you were raised? To your education? Becoming an independent thinker and reader involves developing one's *own* worldview, not adopting uncritically someone else's views. Worldviews are personal and unique, and they should be respected, provided that they derive from careful thought and conviction rather than from automatic, conditioned responses. A recent television advertisement for Fujitsu expresses the idea of a worldview well: "No two eyes see the same world."

What does all this have to do with reading? A good critical reader determines if a writer's claim is in accord with his or her worldview. As you read more and reflect on serious issues, your worldview may alter subtly over time.

To test your worldview, consider this issue as Doug Struck described it in a *Washington Post* article.[1] Despite an international outcry and criticism from the International Whaling Commission, the Japanese government approved the killing of 22,000 dolphins by Japanese fishermen. According to Struck, "Japan insists that the animals are abundant, and rejects as racism the pressure to end what it calls a long tradition of eating them. 'We're not going to stop just because you don't like what we eat,' said a Japan Fisheries Agency official, Joji Morishita. 'If you say don't eat these mammals, we say don't eat cattle, pigs or sheep.' " The people of Futo, one of the fishing communities mentioned in the article, eat large amounts of tuna, lobsters, squid, mackerel, yellowtail—and dolphin.

In 1999 the Futo fishermen were allotted a quota of 75 dolphins. According to Struck, the fishermen maneuvered their boats into a semicircle around the school, and banged on iron pipes lowered into the water. To the dolphins, who are sensitive to vibrations, the sound was like cymbals, and they ran from the cacophony for four hours. "It was exciting," Hiyoshi [one of the Futo fishermen] said. "It was hunting in the wild, and I thought this is how it must have felt when people hunted in Africa, or hunted buffalo on the American plains." Struck further quotes Hiyoshi: "This is a culture of eating seafood, just like the U.S. culture is to eat beef. I like the American culture, but their argument is too emotional and too unreasonable."

Here is a summary of the remaining pertinent facts from the article:

1. There is no international ban on the hunting of dolphins as there is for whales.
2. Although the International Whaling Commission routinely denounces the annual dolphin hunt, Japan insists that it is legal.
3. Japan rejects the International Whaling Commission's rulings on all other animals with the exception of whales.
4. A biologist at Mie University in Japan was dropped from the Japanese delegation to the International Whaling Commission after he criticized the annual dolphin hunt.
5. After the 1986 international moratorium on whaling, Japanese fishermen caught 46,000 dolphins; when the government

[1]"Japanese Still Defiant on Dolphin Kill," October 16, 2000. The entire article can be read in the Archives at the *Washington Post*'s website: *www.washingtonpost.com.* Go into "Archives" and type in the date listed above and the author's name.

became concerned that the species was threatened, the quota was lowered to 22,000, divided among the traditional fishing communities.

6. Not everyone in Japan favors the hunt. The Dolphin and Whale Action Network opposes it. Nanami Kurasawa, one of its representatives, says, "They are confused about the difference between wild animals and farm animals. We cannot manage wild animals like farm animals. We oppose dolphin fishing. We think it's not appropriate, not proper to capture and kill these large wild animals or to hunt them commercially. The general trend of the world is moving toward the protection of these wild animals."

7. Japan defends the practice by saying that "dozens of other countries" also hunt dolphins. Struck mentions that in China the Yangstze River dolphin has been hunted almost to extinction. Fishermen in Peru catch about 10,000 dolphins a year; the Innuit [Eskimos] in Alaska are allowed to catch a limited number each year.

Write your reaction to this story and the issues it raises. _____

_____

_____

_____

Now, examine the *source* of your reaction, in other words, your worldview. Here are some questions to consider:

1. Should dolphins be afforded the same protection as whales?
2. Is fishing for dolphins the same as or different from fishing for other types of fish, say, tuna or mackerel?
3. Are dolphins the same as farm animals, such as cattle and pigs? Why or why not?
4. Where do your images of dolphins come from? (It's all right to mention Flipper.)
5. Do you eat meat and seafood? To what extent do your eating habits influence your views on this matter?
6. Do America and other nations have the right to criticize Japan's annual dolphin catch? Or, as the Japanese contend, is such criticism merely disguised racism?
7. Do you approve of the way the Japanese fishermen catch dolphins?
8. If you are uncertain about your position, what other information would help clarify your thinking?

Compare your reactions with those of your classmates.

■ THE STRUCTURE OF ARGUMENTS

According to rules established by rhetoricians in ancient Greece, a sound argument had to conform to a rigid format. Through the centuries, these rules have been relaxed, with the result that the argumentative form today is as varied as any other kind of nonfiction writing. A conventional argument includes the elements listed below, although they may not appear in the order presented here.[2]

Elements of an Argument

- The claim (also called a thesis or proposition)—the writer's main idea or point.
- Evidence to support the claim.
- A refutation, sometimes called the concession—the writer's discussion of opposing viewpoints.
- A conclusion.

■ THE TEST OF A GOOD ARGUMENT

Some of what is published is very good, some is mediocre, and some is awful. How do you learn to tell the difference? What criteria should you use to determine whether a persuasive or argumentative piece of writing is good or bad, sound or unsound? Here are some simple standards for judging what you read:

- The writer should have some competence or expertise in the area; in other words, he or she should be considered an **authority.**
- The central **claim**—the **argument** or **proposition**—should be clearly stated, or at least clearly implied.
- **Key words** should be **defined,** especially abstract words open to subjective interpretation (such as *honor, responsibility, evil, censorship*). The language should be clear and unambiguous.
- The **supporting evidence** should be logically organized, relevant to the main idea, and sufficient to support the claim credibly. Moreover, the discussion should appeal to our intelligence and to our reason, not solely to our emotions.

[2]A more sophisticated method of analyzing arguments, called the Toulmin model, is discussed in Annette Rottenberg's two excellent books on the subject, *The Structure of Argument,* 2nd ed., 1997, and *Elements of Argument,* 6th ed., 2000. Both are published by Bedford Books.

- Ideally, the persuasive writer should include a **refutation,** in which he or she examines one or two of the opposition's strongest arguments and disproves or finds fault with them. No issue is black or white; disagreement is the essence of controversy. But the writer who ignores, disregards, or ridicules the opposing side runs the risk of not being taken seriously. A refutation can take several forms: The writer might concede that the opposition has merit but that her position is more productive; she might offer statistics disproving the opponent's claim; or she can dispel myths associated with the opposing side. Many editorial writers omit a refutation, requiring you to devise your own opposing arguments.

■ TAKING ARGUMENTS APART

The remainder of this chapter is concerned with how to break down an argument into its constituent elements. Since the process is complicated, we will take up these steps one at a time:

- Evaluating the writer as an authority.
- Identifying the type of claim.
- Stating the claim or argument in a sentence.
- Ascertaining any unstated assumptions.
- Evaluating the supporting evidence.

The Question of Authority

An **authority** is defined in the dictionary as "an accepted source of expert information or advice." The reader of persuasive prose should expect that the writer has firsthand knowledge of and/or experience with the problem. The writer may be a college or university professor, a scientific researcher, or a person with practical experience in the field. However, these are not hard-and-fast requirements, since ordinary citizens express their opinions in the letters-to-the-editor section of newspapers, in chat rooms, and in other venues. And although print journalists may not be experts in the strict sense of the word, good journalists are experienced at digging and delving into an issue and intelligently presenting their findings. When a writer establishes his or her credibility (or at least the reason for an interest in the subject), we can deem the information reliable. Knowing that the writer is an authority inspires our confidence. It does not mean, however, that we need to accept the argument, just that we may judge it worthy of consideration.

Practice Exercise 2

Read through this list of writers. If the person appears to be an authority on the subject, write "A" next to the name. If the person appears *not* to be an authority, write "N." If you are unsure, write a question mark.

1. _____ Haley Joel Osment, star of *The Sixth Sense* and *A.I.: Artificial Intelligence,* commenting on trying to be a "regular kid" while making movies.

2. _____ David Innes, senior minister of the Hamilton Square Baptist Church in San Francisco, writing an editorial about why Christians should oppose gay marriages.

3. _____ George Abraham Thampy, a 12-year-old boy who has been home-schooled all his life, writing on the virtues of home schooling.

4. _____ Robert Rector, senior policy analyst for welfare and poverty issues at the Heritage Foundation, a conservative think tank, explaining why recent Census Bureau poverty statistics are misleading.

5. _____ Ernie Goldthorpe, a community college English teacher, sounding off about the government's ban on cloning human beings.

6. _____ Louis Freeh, former director of the FBI, explaining the mechanical failures that caused the crash of a TWA jet off Long Island in 1997.

7. _____ Norman Borlaug, winner of the Nobel Peace Prize in 1970 for his accomplishments in agriculture and a professor at Texas A&M University, writing an editorial on why Third World countries would benefit from genetically engineered food.

8. _____ Cynthia Tucker, an African-American journalist and editor of the *Atlanta Journal-Constitution* opinion page, writing about race issues in America. (The paper is Atlanta's leading daily newspaper.)

9. _____ John R. Lott, Jr., a fellow at the University of Chicago Law School and author of *More Guns, Less Crime,* writing on common myths associated with gun-control laws.

10. _____ Bill Cosby, television entertainer and author, writing about the merits of Jello Pudding Pops.

11. _____ Ryszard Kapuściński, a foreign correspondent from Poland who has traveled throughout Africa for 40 years, writing on the current political situation in Ethiopia.

12. _____ The former Duchess of York, Sarah Ferguson ("Fergie"), advertising the Weight Watchers weight-loss program.

13. _____ Jo Laster, a Hewlett-Packard employee who commutes daily from Half Moon Bay to Palo Alto, California, writing a letter to the local newspaper to complain about traffic congestion caused by slow-moving dump trucks along Highway 92 during commuting hours.

14. _____ Kathy Snow Guillermo, author of a book on the animal-rights movement and a writer for PETA (People for the Ethical Treatment of Animals), arguing that circuses should ban animal acts.

Of the people listed, only Ernie Goldthorpe, Louis Freeh, and Bill Cosby seem to be nonauthorities. Goldthorpe is expressing his opinions on cloning as an interested citizen, but not as an authority. The FBI is not in the business of investigating airplane crashes, nor is Freeh an aviation engineer. Cosby is paid to advertise the Jello product; he is a comedian and an actor, not a nutritionist or dictician. One might argue that Fergie is not knowledgeable about nutrition either; however, her much publicized weight problems make her a credible spokesperson for Weight Watchers (assuming, that is, that she actually follows the Weight Watchers progam), even though she is paid for her testimony.

Identifying Claims

As stated before, the **claim** is the idea to be proved, the proposition. Claims can be divided into three types: **claims of fact, claims of value,** and **claims of policy.** Keep in mind that persuasive writing involves controversy, it is subject to speculation, and its essence is subjectivity. We begin with some simple examples:

Claims of fact: Broccoli contains high amounts of antioxidants that help prevent cancer.
The chemicals, preservatives, and additives in packaged foods may cause allergic reactions.
Long-term cigarette smoking is responsible for serious illnesses, including cancer and heart disease.
Cantaloupe contains more vitamin C than oranges.

These claims can be proved by citing factual evidence and the results of scientific research.

Claims of value: A college degree isn't worth as much as it used to be.
Compared with *Pearl Harbor, Titanic* had superior special effects.
Democracy is the best form of government.
Chocolate ice cream tastes better than vanilla.

These claims are harder to prove because they involve matters of taste, morality, opinion, and ideas about right and wrong. The support would be in the form of reasons, examples, and personal experience.

Claims of policy: American universities should reduce the emphasis on SAT scores for college admissions. The United States needs to recognize its role in the problem of global warming and establish stricter emission standards for automobiles. Public libraries ought not to censor Internet sites for their patrons. SUVs should be classified as automobiles rather than as light trucks.

These claims indicate a course of action, a proposal for change, or a problem that requires a remedy. Note that claims of policy frequently include verbs such as *should, ought, need,* and *must.*

Practice Exercise 3

Label each argument according to whether it represents a claim of fact, value, or policy.

1. _____ English 100 improved my writing skills.
2. _____ All college freshmen should be required to take English 100.
3. _____ English 100 is a more challenging and useful course than English 50.
4. _____ The countries of the world should unite in banning human cloning for the purpose of creating human beings.
5. _____ Juveniles who commit violent crimes should be tried as adults.
6. _____ Introducing sexual orientations other than heterosexuality to young schoolchildren is wrong.
7. _____ Distributing free condoms to high school students only encourages immoral behavior.
8. _____ College admissions officers should consider only an applicant's economic class rather than his or her racial or ethnic background.
9. _____ Decades of discrimination by the nation's colleges can be remedied only by race-based admissions.
10. _____ Nuclear power plants are safe and efficient.
11. _____ Jamoca almond fudge ice cream tastes better than chocolate chip cookie dough ice cream.
12. _____ Animal acts in circuses constitute a barbaric type of entertainment.

Identifying Claims in Editorials

The exercise you just completed consisted only of one-sentence claims. In reality, claims do not appear in isolation. As noted before, prose writers—no matter what mode of discourse they choose—may place the main idea wherever it best suits their purpose. With editorial or opinion pieces, it is the same. However, it is possible to isolate three *likely* positions:

- At the very beginning—the direct-announcement approach. This placement results in a **deductive argument,** because the claim or proposition (a general statement) leads to supporting evidence.
- In a sentence immediately after the introductory hook—a telling anecdote, a startling set of statistics, some relevant background. This placement is sometimes referred to as the funnel pattern. See the introduction to Part 5 for further explanation.
- At the very end, following all the supporting evidence. This placement is called an **inductive argument,** because the claim or proposition derives from the specific evidence.

Let us illustrate with an excerpt from an editorial on an issue that commanded world attention during 2001—the International Olympic Committee (IOC) meeting to choose a city to host the 2008 Summer Games. In the running were Beijing (the front-runner), Toronto, Paris, Osaka, and Istanbul. The controversy originated because of China's repressive government and its well-documented abuse of human rights and repression of political dissidents. Opponents feared that choosing Beijing would tarnish the reputation of the Olympics. Proponents believed that awarding the Summer Games to China would symbolically recognize its powerful role in world politics and its position as the world's most populous nation. With that background in mind, here are the first four paragraphs of an editorial, which I have annotated, arguing against China's being awarded the games. The writer is Hugo Restall, editorial page director of *The Asian Wall Street Journal.*

Opening ¶ gives background & states claim of policy (Olympics should not go to Beijing)— deductive argument

[1]HONG KONG—On June 23, the Chinese authorities staged a showpiece event, a "Three Tenors" concert in the Forbidden City, to show the world that they are ready to host the Olympic Games. It ended up having precisely the opposite effect, demonstrating why the games should not go to Beijing in 2008.

[2]As the guests arrived at the imperial palace dressed in their formal evening clothes, Stephen Shaver of Agence France-Presse was outside taking photographs of them. Suddenly the police detained a man who may have been a protester, and Mr. Shaver took a photo of the incident. The police pounced on the American photographer, telling him he had broken the law, and six

¶2-3—Relevant anecdote about journalist's bad treatment after taking a photo of a protester

Incident shows that China won't uphold its promises to allow journalists freedom to cover events in 2008. Argument restated w/two reasons to support (Olympics tarnished & tensions worsened btn China & other nations)

of them tried to put him in a van, punching and slapping him and ramming his head into the side of the car. A senior officer finally intervened, and Mr. Shaver was allowed to continue covering the concert.

Dragged Along

[3]But this was not the end of the matter. As Mr. Shaver left the area a few hours later, he ran into the same police who had earlier roughed him up. Apparently feeling that they had lost face because they had been over-ruled by a superior, they dragged him along the pavement. When a crowd of concert-goers gathered, the police told them that the foreigner had insulted China, which inspired the throng to yell anti-foreign slogans at the prostrate journalist. Only after he abjectly apologized to the Chinese people was Mr. Shaver allowed to go free.

[4]So much for China's promises to the International Olympic Committee that it will allow journalists to cover events freely in 2008. In eight days, the IOC members will make their decision on whether to believe that promise, and many others like it. They should consider the risk that the Olympics will end up tarnished by similar incidents, exacerbating conflict between an often brutal government and the rest of the world, rather than giving the Chinese people a triumphant debut on the international stage.

Hugo Restall, "China Doesn't Deserve the Olympics,"
The Asian Wall Street Journal, July 5, 2001

The annotations show that this editorial combines the first and second methods of placing an argument, since the claim of policy mentioned in paragraph 1 is restated at the end of paragraph 4, following the description of the American photographer's being roughed up by police for shooting a picture of a protester.[3]

Practice Exercise 4

In this exercise you are asked to locate the claim. Note that the claim may have to be inferred. Reprinted below are the beginning portions of eight representative opinion pieces one might encounter in newspapers or periodicals. I have included the writer's name, the source, and where possible, the writer's qualifications. The first two excerpts have been annotated and answers are provided.

First, identify the type of claim. You will see that some excerpts seem to straddle two types of claims, making it impossible to choose only one. If that situation occurs, write the secondary claim as well. Then, write a sentence stating the writer's claim or argument. Do not include evidence or support in your argument sentence.

---

[3]A few days after the editorial appeared, the IOC ignored the criticisms leveled here and in numerous other American and international publications and chose Beijing to host the 2008 Summer Games.

Reading more important than computer skills

Worried about how your kids are going to stack up in that Brave New e-World just over the horizon? First the good news: Don't worry if your children haven't mastered UNIX before puberty. <u>But if they haven't learned to read by fourth grade, the digital world isn't going to be their biggest problem</u>. They probably won't even make it through high school.

"If U Can Read This . . . ," *The Wall Street Journal*, October 27, 2000

Type of claim: fact
Argument: For long-term success, learning to read by the fourth grade is more important than mastering computer skills.

Street Sheet is a publication sponsored by San Francisco's Coalition on Homelessness. Homeless people write and produce the paper, which they then distribute on the streets of San Francisco in exchange for a donation of a dollar or two. The newspaper offers the homeless a legitimate way of earning money, rather than panhandling, as well as the opportunity to learn skills.

Background— problem is gentrification in SF. Effects on population are serious; 2nd claim—a "bleak situation"

The entire city is undergoing <u>gentrification</u>—from the destruction of 4,000 units of public housing in newly desirable neighborhoods, to the massive explosion of live–work space. San Francisco is the hip place to be for the financially comfortable. <u>As a result, rents have doubled</u>, we are <u>losing our diversity, families of color</u> are being <u>driven out</u>, and <u>thousands</u> are being <u>evicted</u>—which <u>leads us to homelessness</u>. A <u>bleak situation</u> indeed for all of us who love this city.

"The Gentrification of San Francisco's Homeless Shelters," *Street Sheet,* May 2000

Type of claim: fact; secondary claim: value
Argument: Gentrification has rapidly changed the character of San Francisco. Secondary argument: Gentrification has created a bleak situation for San Francisco residents.

Notice how the type of claim leads directly to the argument. For example, the first claim—one of fact—leads to a factual argument, whereas the second claim—one of value—leads to a value judgment.

"The idea that there is some pristine place—whether in the Pacific or the Caribbean or some other place in the Third World—where tourists can come and spend their money and have a fanstasy 14-day rest from the maniacal life of the First World is false," says activist and Hawaiian studies professor Haunani-Kay Trask in *The Progressive* (Dec. 2000). "My advice is, if you're thinking about Hawaii, don't come. Stay right where you are. If you do come, remember that you're contributing to the oppression of a native people in their home country."

While businesses in Hawaii benefit from tourism, not all its residents do. Foreign investment in the tourist economy has driven up inflation—and the cost of living. As a result, nearly one-fifth of Hawaii's resident population is classified as near homeless.

Karen Olson, "Please Stay Home," *Utne Reader,* July–August 2001

Type of claim: _____

Argument: _____

_____

_____

Jerry Della Femina is chairman of an advertising agency in New York.

It's a corny joke that goes back a million years. A man riding on the old Erie Railroad spots a bug crawling across his Pullman bed. Irate, he writes a letter complaining to the railroad.

He receives a letter from the president of the railroad apologizing and stating that this has never happened in the history of the railroad. Unfortunately, accidentally clipped to the letter is a note that the president had only intended for his secretary to see. It reads: "Send this guy the bug letter."

No one even gets the courtesy of "the bug letter" these days.

These days, what the consumer mostly gets is neglect. Firestone sells apparently defective tires but refuses to acknowledge responsibility. United Airlines cancels flights without notice; when weather grounds a flight, the airline holds you hostage on the runway with soft drinks and packets of peanuts to sustain you. Then, to make amends, it announces that it plans to cut down on the number of regular flights. Its new slogan, I guess, would be, "United Airlines . . . Fewer flights to fewer places, but it beats sitting on the runway for 12 hours."

Consumers feel as if they have no power . . . In the shadow of these behemoths, the consumer is reduced to a tiny figure crying in the wilderness. More often than not, his protests go unheard—literally.

Jerry Della Femina, "They've Got Us Where They Want Us,"
The Washington Post National Weekly Edition, October 9, 2000

Type of claim: _____

Argument: _____

_____

Mortimer B. Zuckerman is editor-in-chief of *U.S. News & World Report.*

For decades, cigarette smoking was cool. It suggested being grown up, sophisticated, macho, virile, sexy, sensuous, and even romantic. Cigarettes dangled from the lips of every movie star. Humphrey Bogart said in *Casablanca,* "Here's looking at you, kid," and millions played Bogey by lighting up.

We were had. The cigarette companies perverted or concealed the truth. Who can forget advertising slogans such as "Not a cough in a carload"? Even after 1964, when the surgeon general spelled out the risks, the cigarette companies kept pretending. Now hardly a month goes by without another study being released that conveys even worse news about smoking. Let the tobacco interests try to blow away these facts: Smoking is the most preventable cause of disease and death in the United States.

Mortimer B. Zuckerman, "Let's Stub Out Coffin Nails,"
U.S. News & World Report, October 19, 1998

Type of claim: _____

Argument: _____

_____

David Bergland is national chairman of the Libertarian Party. This editorial was written for the *San Francisco Chronicle's* "Open Forum," where nonjournalists express their opinions on a variety of topics.

The national nannies are at it again—and this time they literally want to take the food out of your mouth.

In recent months, the "fat tax"—a proposed new federal tax on high-calorie and high-fat foods—has been endorsed by several organizations as a solution to the national obesity "epidemic." And a fat tax might just be the beginning. If we don't stop them now, the grease Gestapo will do to fatty foods what they've done to cigarettes.

Using language strikingly similar to the anti-tobacco forces, the health zealots want the government to launch a war against fatty foods—and they're making progress. Even Agriculture Secretary Dan Glickman has weighed in: He's announced a National Nutritional Summit for May 30–31 in Washington, D.C., to explore governmental solutions to overeating, including a pilot program in Mississippi to "audit" what people eat and help them make "better choices."

David Bergland, "Ready for the Twinkie Tax?"
San Francisco Chronicle, April 23, 2000

Type of claim: _____

Argument: _____

_____

The Economist is a weekly newsmagazine published in Great Britain.

At the base of the Sierra Nevada mountain range in central California, on the south fork of the Kern river, a small green valley sits in marked contrast to the surrounding brown hills. This hidden vale, crowded with willow and cotton-wood trees, is home to one of the largest breeding populations of an endangered bird called the south-western willow flycatcher. And it exists only because the Lake Isabella Dam, completed in 1953, created floodplains that allowed this riverside (or "riparian") habitat to flourish.

To America's environmental activists, dams are wicked. Calling for them to be removed has become one of the movement's loudest and most popular demands. Dams affect water quality, reduce species diversity and impede the progress of salmon and other fish as they make their way upriver from the sea. They can also harm downstream ecosystems that evolved to take advantage of a river's sporadic flood pattern. But as the Lake Isabella Dam illustrates, when endangered species are involved there can be competing environmental interests on the other side of the dam-removal debate. Indeed, campaigners are coming to realise that in some instances, removing a dam can do more environmental harm than good.

"Eliminating Dams: Not So Fast," *The Economist,* March 3–9, 2001

Type of claim: _____

Argument: _____

_____

Unstated Assumptions

Another analytical skill is uncovering **unstated assumptions,** underlying arguments. In our daily lives, we operate from assumptions all the time, most of which we never bother to articulate. For example, if you tell your friend that you will meet him at Gino's Pizza at 6:00 P.M. right after your last final exam, your statement implies several assumptions so obvious there is no need to list them:

- You will both be alive tomorrow.
- The bus you rely on to get you to Gino's Pizza by 6:00 P.M. will arrive on time.
- Your final exam will end in time for you to get to Gino's by 6:00.
- Gino's will be open for business.

Unlike this situation where we can safely take for granted the unstated assumptions, argumentative writing demands that we separate the argument from the assumptions that underlie it. These assumptions are seemingly self-evident beliefs that the writer assumes we share. Separating them out is more difficult than it sounds. If you look through the seven excerpts in Practice Exercise 4, you will see that none of them explicitly states the assumption that lies beneath the argument.

But more typically, assumptions are absent, and it takes practice to ferret them out. For example, consider this sentence from a film review: "The unusual special effects in 'Pearl Harbor' make it an especially good movie." The writer implicitly connects the argument—*Pearl Harbor* is a good movie (a claim of value)—and the presence of unusual special effects as an essential component of good movies. Can we accept this assumption? If so, then we can accept the argument; if not, then we can reject it, or at least expect the reviewer to justify it.

One way to ascertain unstated claims is to consider the audience: For whom is the writer writing? Do you share the thinking of that group? Another way is to ask yourself what *allegiances* the writer seems to have. Does he or she appear to favor one group over another?

Finally, consider that unstated assumptions lead to the kind of evidence the writer chooses. For example, in arguing against a government policy, such as the immediate deportation of illegal aliens found guilty of a crime, a writer starts from the unstated assumption that the policy is flawed. His argument is that the policy should be abandoned. This unstated assumption leads to three possible types of evidence: (1) He might offer the opinions of legal experts who agree with his position. (2) He might cite the personal experiences of illegal immigrants who have been denied proper legal representation. (3) He might describe immigrants who were victimized by unscrupulous law enforcement officials or of immigrants whose limited English prevented them from defending themselves. This connection between argument and evidence is sometimes called a **warrant**[4]—a guarantee that the evidence cited supports the claim and leads to a conclusion.

Here is one last example: Most of us probably accept the validity of vaccinating infants and toddlers against diseases such as polio, diphtheria, and measles. But the antivaccine forces have been vocal in recent years, claiming that vaccines cause all kinds of ailments, "from asthma to autism."[5] A writer who wishes to overturn these critics enhances the credibility of the argument by citing scientific research in support of the criticism. She proceeds from the unstated assumption that the antivaccine forces are wrong. She then cites top-notch research, perhaps studies conducted at a leading university or other research center, such

---

[4]See either of Rottenberg's two books, cited earlier, for a more detailed explanation of warrants, which is part of the Toulmin method of examining arguments.
[5]Tinker Ready, "This Won't Hurt a Bit," *Utne Reader,* September–October 2000.

as the Centers for Disease Control or Johns Hopkins University Medical School. In other words, the unstated assumption leads to the claim, which in turn leads to the evidence, forming a sort of chain.

Unstated assumptions are not necessarily bad or manipulative. In fact, they are necessary if the argument is not to bog down into mind-numbing tedium, the certain result if a writer spelled out every idea underlying the discussion. In other words, they represent a kind of shorthand. However, if the assumptions are invalid or if they don't accord with your thinking (does a movie really have to have unusual special effects to be good?), then the reader does not have to accept the argument.[6]

Practice Exercise 5

Study these arguments. Then write at least one assumption that underlies the discussion. The first one has been done for you.

1. School districts should not spend precious funds on expensive computer equipment at the expense of programs such as art and music.

   Unstated assumptions: Money allotted to school districts is limited. It is more important that students learn to appreciate art and music than to develop computer expertise.

   Comment: You should recognize that there is no right or wrong way of looking at this claim, but ask yourself if you accept either of these assumptions. Why or why not? This either–or situation (i.e., either computers or enrichment programs) could be resolved if school districts were properly funded to permit both kinds of programs to flourish. Perhaps the district money is limited because it is being wasted on frivolous expenditures. (In Chapter 9, you will learn to recognize that this argument rests upon a logical fallacy called false dilemma.)

   Start with these easy arguments.

2. Many parents prefer to educate their children at home so that the children can enter college at an age younger than that of their peers who attend traditional schools.

   Unstated assumption(s): _____

   _____

3. Colleges should reduce the number of part-time faculty they hire.

   Unstated assumption(s): _____

   _____

[6]I am indebted to Don Meagher's discussion of unstated assumptions in *Handbook for Critical Reading* (Harcourt Brace College Publishers, 1997). Meagher's more detailed analysis of this concept is worth looking at.

4. Grades are essential for motivating students to study. Grades let students know where they stand in the class.

   Unstated assumption(s): _____

   _____

   _____

5. A college English teacher assigned her students to select a nonfiction book and to write a critique of it. One student chose Truman Capote's *In Cold Blood,* but the instructor rejected her choice, saying that a made-for-TV movie based on the book was going to be aired in the next few days. The teacher thought that the student would simply watch the movie and not read the book.

   Unstated assumption(s): _____

   _____

   _____

   Now move on to these more difficult arguments:

6. Admitting minority students to our nation's colleges and universities under affirmative action programs will result in a freshman class with lower test scores.

   Unstated assumption(s): _____

   _____

   _____

   _____

   _____

7. Eliminating racial preferences in college admissions, particularly for law and medical schools, will result in fewer doctors and lawyers serving minority communities.

   Unstated assumption(s): _____

   _____

   _____

   _____

   _____

   _____

8. From a letter to T. Berry Brazelton, pediatrician and authority on children's health issues and author of the syndicated column "Families Today": A single woman in her mid-thirties wrote to Dr. Brazelton saying that she wanted to adopt a baby from another country (which she did not identify). Her question was whether or not raising a child without a father would be unfair to the child. Dr. Brazelton responded: "Providing a baby from another country with a caring home is like giving him or her a major gift. You will profit from it as much as the baby." ("Single Woman Wants to Adopt a Baby," *San Francisco Chronicle,* March 18, 1996)

Unstated assumption(s): _____

_____

_____

_____

_____

The Importance of Definitions in Arguments

Earlier in the chapter, you learned that one characteristic of good argumentative prose is that the author takes care to define key words, especially abstract words open to subjective interpretation or words used in a personal or idiosyncratic way. For example, consider this argument, cited in the *Washington Post:*[7]

> This much is undisputed: Soybeans do not lactate. So soy producers should not be calling their beverages "milk," according to the National Milk Producers Federation, which filed a complaint with the Food and Drug Administration this month seeking to banish the terms "soy milk" and "soymilk" from grocery shelves and dairy cases.

The article goes on to cite the testimony of Rob Byrne, the milk federation's vice president of regulatory affairs: "We don't want them using milk's good name for their product."

The dairy federation is relying on a narrow definition of *milk* in support of its argument: Milk comes from "the lacteal secretion" of cows; soybeans come from the ground and don't lactate. Do you accept this definition of *milk?* If you look it up in an unabridged dictionary, you will find three definitions, one referring to the liquid produced by female mammals used to nourish their offspring, one referring to the

[7]Cindy Skrzycki, "Dairy Group Tells FDA Soy Milk Is Full of Beans," *Washington Post,* February 29, 2000.

milk of cows and goats used by humans as food, and the third, "a liquid, such as coconut milk, milkweed sap, plant latex, or various medical emulsions, that is similar to milk in appearance."

Why the controversy in the first place? Because health-conscious consumers have turned to soy products as a replacement for the high fat and cholesterol found in cow's milk, milk sales have declined. The milk producers may not like the inroads soy products are making in their profits, but the dictionary does not bear out their restrictive use of the word *milk*. There is a better way to argue this point. (Also, if soy milk can't be called milk, what then should we call the liquid inside coconuts?)

Evaluating Evidence

The final step in evaluating arguments is looking at the **evidence,** a term that refers to any information or support used to back up a claim. A type of evidence can be used by itself or in combination. Study the following:

Types of Evidence
- Facts, statistics, including survey or poll results
- Examples and illustrations from observation, personal experience, or reading
- Good reasons (part of the cause–effect pattern)
- Historical analysis or citation of precedents from history
- Testimony of experts and authorities in the field
- Analogy

In judging the worth of an argument, note the main supporting points; it is especially helpful to annotate them in the margin. Then ask if the evidence relates to the claim and if it is sufficient (not based on generalizations). If statistics are used, are they current?

Practice Exercise 6

Examine these excerpts from editorials and opinion pieces. First write a sentence stating the writer's argument. Then identify the type(s) of evidence being used.

This opening paragraph concerns the 1997 settlement mandated by the federal government, requiring tobacco companies to pay states $350 billion to cover health care costs associated with smoking.

America has already had one disastrous experiment in prohibition. The tobacco settlement announced last week puts us on the verge of another. Like the first prohibition in this century, this new one promises an explosive increase in black markets, smuggling, criminality, and general cynicism. What's more, every indication is that the measures proposed by the settlement will serve not to diminish but to *increase* smoking. The settlement calls for spending hundreds of millions of dollars on efforts to discourage and deglamorize tobacco use. But emphasizing that tobacco is dangerous and disapproved will enhance the glamour, prestige and attractiveness—particularly among the young.

Richard Klein, "Prohibition II . . . ,"
The Wall Street Journal, June 26, 1997

Argument: _____

Type(s) of evidence: _____

John H. McWhorter is an African-American professor of linguistics at the University of California–Berkeley. In this excerpt from his book, he argues against several myths concerning African Americans. This particular myth is entitled "Article of Faith Number Two: Black People Get Paid Less Than Whites for the Same Job."

In 1995, the median income for black families was $25,970, while the figure for whites was $42,646. The figures were quickly translated into the claim that "black people make 61 percent of what white people make" and taken to mean that black people are regularly paid less than whites for the same work, so that, for example, the black assistant manager takes home a salary about 40 percent smaller than the white one working in the office next door. This is naturally read as indicating a deep-seated racism in the American fabric far outweighing the significance of increased numbers of doctors or interracial couples or black characters on TV.

But the figure is extremely misleading. The black median income is dragged down, again, by the extenuating factor of the low income of unwed mothers living on welfare, a larger proportion of the black population than the white. The median income of black *two-parent families* is about $41,307, as opposed to about $47,000 for whites. Even here, the gap is extremely difficult to pin on racism. In 1995, 56 percent of black Americans lived in the South, and wages are lower there. Finally, as often as not today, black two-parent families earn *more* than whites—they did in about 130 cities and counties in 1994, and in the mid-90s, their median income was rising faster than whites' was.

Thus it simply is not true that black people are paid less than white people for doing the same work, on any level. The proportion of black poor unwed mothers is a problem, but no one would argue that they get less welfare than their white counterparts; they do, however, pull down the aggregate figure for black American earnings as a whole.

John H. McWhorter, *Losing the Race: Self-Sabotage in Black America*

Argument: _____

Type(s) of evidence: _____

The following paragraph comes from a speech by Abraham Lincoln, in which he responds to critics who were complaining that the government was allowing the Civil War to drag on too long.

> Gentlemen, I want you to suppose a case for a moment. Suppose that all the property you were worth was in gold, and you had put it in the hands of Blondin, the famous rope-walker, to carry across the Niagara Falls on a tight rope. Would you shake the rope while he was passing over it, or keep shouting to him, "Blondin, stop a little more! Go a little faster!"? No. I am sure you would not. You would hold your breath as well as your tongue, and keep your hand off until he was safely over. Now, the Government is in the same situation. It is carrying an immense weight across a stormy ocean. Untold treasures are in its hands. It is doing the best it can. Don't badger it! Just keep still, and it will get you safely over.

Argument: _____

_____

Type(s) of evidence: _____

George Abraham Thampy, the winner of the 2000 Scripps Howard National Spelling Bee, has been home-schooled for his entire education. He was 12 years old when he wrote this opinion piece.

> Last week I won the Scripps Howard National Spelling Bee, and my picture was in the papers all over the world. It was a really tough competition. One letter missed or out of place and I would have been out of the competition with no second chances. I know that well because I had lost at the two previous national spelling bees.
>
> A lot of people noticed something particular about the bee this year: I am home-schooled, as were the two other finalists. A home-schooled girl won in 1997, but this is the first time home-schoolers have had a clean sweep. As a result, a lot of people have been asking questions about home schooling. So I would like to explain a little about what exactly home schooling means for me, and to tell you what I do all day.
>
> I study most everything a child would at school—science, math, English, history, geography and social sciences. I don't study all subjects every day, but concentrate instead on two or three subjects. On most days I would also do in-depth research over the Internet on one of my favorite topics.

My parents structure my time. But I study in periods of variable lengths, not exactly like class periods in school. I have six siblings, and five of them are home-schooled, so some subjects, such as geography, history and current events, are taught to us as a group. My mom often asks us to finish a task on a certain subject before we get a break for lunch, or before we move on to a different subject.

Most of the time, however, we are taught individually, and the instruction is tailored to our specific needs. We all use different textbooks and download material from the Internet. Science supply stores sell kits for chemistry experiments. My dad happens to be a biochemistry professor, so visits to a laboratory are often possible.

We go on plenty of field trips, sometimes with other home-schoolers. I've been to farms, banks, fire stations and museums. Also, whenever my dad has to make presentations at work, I go with him and help him with the slides. Occasionally, I fix his software problems too.

A lot of people can picture home schooling when it comes to study that's based on books, like English or math. But the other aspects of education are also well-covered—such as sports, religious activities, personal hygiene, letter writing and public speaking. For sports we go to the gym and to playgrounds. I love to play softball and soccer. I enjoy bike riding and kite-flying, as well as walking about the neighborhood.

My schedule is flexible enough to accommodate specific projects. I have chosen to do household chores as well as help my younger brothers and sisters with their studies and special projects. In the evening we concentrate on outdoor activities. At night, we sit with our dad and go over math and science. Occasionally he brings home some interesting articles on health-related problems and we have a family discussion. One such article was on rabies and its dissemination in certain regions of the country by bats and skunks. Another time we read about food poisoning in the Northwest and how it spread from one source to the entire community.

Since most kids who go to school make friends there, people might wonder about the social lives of home-schooled kids. It's not that complicated, really. I have friends at the church youth group—we belong to the Evangelical Free Church. Also, I have befriended numerous former competitors in the National Geography Bee and the National Spelling Bee, with whom I keep in touch via e-mail.

In any case, just because I don't go to a big classroom full of other children my age doesn't mean I'm lonely. I have brothers and sisters and other home-schooled friends, not to mention Boy Scout friends, and friends around the neighborhood and church. I have no trouble relating to kids who go to conventional schools. They don't think I'm strange because I'm home-schooled, especially since we study the same subjects, only in a different way. Besides, even they usually seem to know other kids who are home-schooled.

Home schooling is not so hard to understand. My mom and dad are my teachers, and most of the time my mom is home while my dad is at work. Financially, however, it is rather expensive for my parents to get all the latest and best materials, to update computers and software every six to 12 months, and to keep ahead in this race. It costs them about $7,500 a year for books, supplies and computer needs, as well as another $1,000 for field trips and other outings.

But it's not just a question of money. Home schooling all of us takes a lot of time, effort and commitment on their part. As a consequence, my dad and mom do not have much time for themselves. I see them often working late at night in order to keep up with their own work. My mom has not gone to bed before 2 A.M. in a long time.

George Abraham Thampy, "Home Schooling Spells Success,"
The Wall Street Journal, June 7, 2000

Argument: _____

_____

Type(s) of evidence: _____

William Bennett was formerly secretary of education in the Reagan administration and the "Drug Czar" for the Bush administration. He is currently co-director of Empower America and chairman of K12.com, an Internet-based elementary and secondary school. He frequently writes on education issues.

Those who, like me, grew up in the 1940s and '50s, recall vividly the seemingly unstoppable polio epidemic that plagued our nation for so long. Over half a million Americans were stricken by this crippling disease, and many mothers (mine included) worried about allowing their children near public swimming pools for fear of infection. In 1954, however, Jonas Salk announced the first polio vaccine; in 1961, it was approved for general use. Almost overnight, the number of new cases plummeted. Thanks to good research and quick action, the disease had been beat.

Today, the nation faces another epidemic, one that does not affect children physically, but that is equally destructive of their futures. The disease is functional illiteracy, and, according to the most recent National Assessment of Educational Progress (NAEP), it has overtaken one-third of America's children by the fourth grade—including two-thirds of black students and almost half of all children in the inner cities. And perhaps the worst news is this: We already have a cure for it, but it has been administered to far too few.

In his groundbreaking 1955 exposé, "Why Johnny Can't Read," Rudolf Flesch uncovered a worrisome fad in education. Schools had begun to replace time-honored and proven methods of teaching reading with the "look-say" method, the precursor of today's "whole language." These new techniques, Flesch argued, had no scientific basis and did not help children learn to read.

Then, in 1961—the same year that the polio vaccine became available—Jeanne Chall was commissioned to write a definitive report that showed it was exactly those time honored methods—what we refer to as "phonics"—that beginning readers needed to "break the code" of language. Chall had discovered the "vaccine" for preventing reading difficulty; it was up to schools to administer it.

But unlike the medical community's enthusiastic embrace of Salk's research, the education community has consistently ignored Chall's findings, as well as subsequent research confirming her work. Instead of seeing the number of illiterate children plummet, 37% of our fourth-graders are unable to read on a basic level 40 years later, while only 8% can read on an advanced level.

The evidence is clear and has been articulated best by Louisa Moats, one of today's leading reading experts. Schools need to teach phoneme awareness, phonics, fluent word recognition, vocabulary and comprehension. Most state education agencies, schools of education, and school districts, however, continue to advocate reading strategies that don't work. Many of these institutions march under the banner of "balanced instruction" but, in fact, they continue to push the flawed "whole language" methods at the expense of phonics. This is the educational equivalent of treating polio with aspirin. We would never stand for such malpractice in medicine, and we should not tolerate it in education.

President George W. Bush's proposals for reading are certainly a step in the right direction, insofar as they promote research-based methods, annual testing of students, and real accountability for school failure. But none of these initiatives on the federal level will succeed without similar efforts in the states. If local school districts continue to ignore clear research and promote ideologically driven methods that don't work, the president's actions will not bring the results he seeks and we need. The action is local, and so must be the fight.

This is not to suggest that phonics-based instruction is as magic a potion as the Salk vaccine. Teaching children to read involves far more than just a proven method, and it depends largely on the efforts of the parents. Parents must introduce their children to great stories, inculcating a love for books. Children who read for fun every day score 10% higher on the NAEP test than students who never or hardly ever read. Parents need to turn off the television, computer and video games.

At K12, the online elementary and secondary school I lead, kindergarten and first-grade students will receive intense phonics instruction and will be exposed to the world's literary heritage through the Junior Great Books program and other children's stories.

But just as phonics alone is insufficient to help children learn to read, parental efforts will be futile if schools do not do their part. The parents in 1951 were justified in their concern that their children would contract polio from swimming pools. Parents, 50 years later, should not have to worry that their school will not protect their child from illiteracy.

William J. Bennett, "A Cure for the Illiteracy Epidemic,"
The Wall Street Journal, April 24, 2001

Argument: _____

_____

Type(s) of evidence: _____

The author of the following editorial is an obstetrician and gynecologist who practices at the Fayetteville Women's Clinic in Arkansas.

Most of us in medicine now accept that tobacco is associated with major health consequences and constitutes the No. 1 health problem in this country.

What smokers have not yet come to terms with is that if they continue smoking, the probability of developing one or more of the major complications of smoking is 100%. It absolutely will happen. They will develop chronic bronchitis, laryngitis, pharyngitis, sinusitis and some degree of emphysema. It is also highly probable that they will develop serious disease in the arteries of all vital organs, including the brain and heart, markedly increasing their risk of heart attack and stroke. If they continue, they increase the probability of developing cancer of the lips, gums, tongue, pharynx, larynx, trachea, bronchi and lungs, of the bladder, cervix, gallbladder and other organs. Smoking contributes to rapid aging of the skin and connective tissues—women and men who smoke usually have the skin age of a person 10 to 20 years older than one who doesn't smoke, given the same degree of exposure to the sun.

About 415,000 people die prematurely each year in the U.S. as a result of smoking—the equivalent of 18 747s crashing every week with no survivors. Many of these victims die after long and excruciating illnesses, burdens to themselves, their families and society. The cost of this misery is incalculable, but we do know that the tobacco industry grosses about $50 billion a year from the agonies it inflicts.

How does all this damage come about?

In normal lungs, the trachea and bronchi—the large and small tubes leading to the alveoli (the tiny sacs that do the actual work of the lungs)—are lined with a film of tissue that is one cell layer thick. The surface of these cells is covered with tiny, finger-like structures called cilia. These cilia beat constantly in a waving motion, which moves small particles and toxic substances out of the lung and into the back of the throat where they are swallowed. In a smoker or someone like a coal miner, who constantly breathes in large amounts of toxic substances, many of the cilia soon disappear. If exposure continues, some ciliated cells die and are replaced by squamous cells, the same type that form the skin. Without the cleansing function of the ciliated cells, toxic materials and particles are breathed further into the lungs, staying longer in contact with all the tissue. Each group of ciliated cells killed and replaced by squamous cells decreases by a certain fraction the lungs' ability to cleanse themselves. As this occurs, the amount of damage done by each cigarette increases to a greater and greater degree. By the time one has been a pack-a-day smoker for 10 years or so, extensive damage has already been done. By 20 years, much of the damage is irreversible and progresses more rapidly. After 10 years of smoking, each cigarette may do as much damage to the body as three or more packs did when a smoker first started.

The longer one smokes, the harder it gets to quit. Smoking is one of the most addictive of human habits, perhaps as addicting as crack cocaine or heroin. One has to quit every day, and there are no magic pills or crutches that make stopping easy. It is tough to do. Only those who keep trying ever quit. And even those who have smoked for only a short time or few cigarettes a day will probably find it difficult to stop. But the sooner a smoker makes this self-commitment, the more probable it is that he or she will quit before having done major damage to the body.

William F. Harrison, "Why Stop Smoking? Let's Get Clinical,"
Los Angeles Times, July 7, 1996

Argument: _____

_____

Type(s) of evidence: _____

■ EXERCISES: EVALUATING EDITORIALS

The following three newspaper editorials will give you practice in implementing your critical reading skills. These editorials, from the op-ed pages of major newspapers, discuss current, controversial issues. For each selection that your instructor assigns (or that you read on your own), consider these questions:

1. Who is the writer? Is he or she considered an authority? On what basis?
2. What type of claim does the argument make?

3. What is the writer's main argument or proposition? Be sure that you can state it in your own words.

4. If possible, list one or two unstated assumptions underlying the argument.

5. What kind of evidence does the writer provide in support of the argument? Does the evidence meet the criteria discussed in this chapter? Is it fair, accurate, sufficient, and relevant? List two or three of the main supporting points.

6. Is the argument, as the author presents it, convincing or at least worth considering?

7. Do you accept the argument? Why or why not? What other information do you need?

Selection 1   Arthur Levine is president of Teachers College at Columbia University.

The merits of reducing the college degree to three years from four are being broadly discussed in academic circles. The debate was started by Fred Starr, the president of Oberlin, and is being fueled by a Stanford University curriculum re-examination that considers whether the time it takes to earn a baccalaureate degree should be reduced to three years.

The idea is appealing on the surface. At a time when college tuitions are soaring, cutting a year from undergraduate study would appear to reduce costs 25%. But like many other academic exercises, it is out of touch with reality.

The idea is not new. Harvard had a three-year degree in the 1640s. Its second president got into a battle royal with his board of trustees when he turned it into a four-year degree. Periodically in the years since, both the debate and "new" three-year degree have reappeared. Most recently, in the early 1970s, the Carnegie Corporation supported the creation of three-year programs at colleges and universities across the country. Nearly all of those programs are now gone. There was too little student interest to justify their continuation.

If anything, three-year degree programs probably would be even less successful now than they were then. There are several reasons:

First, student academic skills have declined since the late 1960s. More than a third of undergraduates report that they are in need of remedial courses. In short, students appear to need more education today, not less.

Second, the average time required to earn a college degree is actually increasing. A growing proportion of students are taking five years of classes, particularly at large public universities, which the majority of students now attend.

Third, a majority of college students work today while attending college. Most work 20 hours or more a week to be able to pay their tuition. The promise of not paying a fourth year of tuition would not eliminate their need to work. As a consequence, the notion of extending the college year or even the college day is impractical.

Fourth, eliminating the final year of college would be a financial disaster for most institutions, which are heavily dependent on tuition or enrollments to fund their operations. Schools would lose a quarter of their student bodies. Outside the West and the South, the demographics of the nation are such that the loss of students simply could not be made up. Colleges might have to raise tuition substantially to compensate.

However, there is a much larger problem for the three-year degree than any mentioned so far: It does not make educational sense. The four-year degree is entirely arbitrary. And so is the three-year degree. Degree time measures how long students sit in class. It is not a measure of how much they learn.

Imagine taking your clothes to a laundry and having the proprietor ask, "How long do you want me to wash them: three hours or four?" The question would be absurd. We don't care how long the clothes are washed. We want them clean. We want the launderer to focus on the outcome of his washing, not the process.

Education should operate similarly. Colleges and universities should define the skills and knowledge a student needs to possess in order to earn a baccalaureate degree, rather than the number of hours of lectures and classes a student should attend to earn a degree.

Students enrolled in college now are more heterogeneous than ever before. More than half of all high-school graduates are going on to some form of post-secondary education, and the fastest-growing group attending college is older adults. As a result there is a greater range of knowledge, skills and experience among college students than in the past. Many will require more than four years of instruction to earn a degree. Others will come to college with such rich backgrounds that they will be able to complete a degree in less than four years and perhaps less than three. For these reasons, it is a mistake for colleges to tie in their degrees to time served.

Arthur Levine, "College—More Than Serving Time,"
The Wall Street Journal, December 21, 1993

Selection 2

Amitai Etzioni, a teacher at George Washington University in Washington, D.C., is the author of several books. His most recent book is *The Limits of Privacy.*

The good people of Loudon County, Va., thought they had found an effective way to protect their young children from pornography when they surf the Internet at the county library. The library installed X-Stop, one of a new category of software programs that block access either to a given list of Web sites or to messages that contain certain key words (say, *bestiality*). Other brand names include Cyber Patrol and Net Nanny.

But the Loudon County Library's board of trustees did not take into account the American Civil Liberties Union, which appears determined to ensure that kids have access to everything on the Internet, including hard-core porn. The ACLU is suing the library on behalf of eight plaintiffs who manage Web sites blocked by X-Stop. The case was to have gone to trial today, but federal Judge Leonie Brinkema—a Clinton appointee who in April sided with the ACLU against the government's motion to dismiss the case—has announced that she will soon decide the case summarily.

In January the ACLU celebrated a victory in Kern County, Calif., where the library agreed to give patrons—minors included—a choice between filtered and unfiltered computers. The ACLU gloats that "no parental consent will be required for minors to access unfiltered computers." The children involved are often quite young. One of the ACLU's plaintiffs in the Virginia case, who runs a Web site on "safer sex," reports that he responds to queries from children who are 13 and younger.

The ACLU predictably argues that Internet filters constrict the flow of ideas. The organization accuses the Loudon County Library of "removing books from the shelves of the Internet with value to both adults and minors in violation of the Constitution." Some ACLU representatives, including lawyer Marjorie Heins, even object to parents using filters in the privacy of their homes. "Rather than increasing opportunities for kids to learn and talk about sex, America seems poised to close them up," Ms. Heins laments.

The American Library Association also objects to Internet filters, stating with reference to the Internet that "the rights of minors shall in no way be abridged." This position is based on something called the Library Bill of Rights which commands that "a person's right to use a library should not be denied or abridged because of origin, age, background, or views."

The ALA goes even further. Its confidentiality rules prohibit disclosing any information about what patrons read to anybody, including parents. These rules have legal force in several states, including Wisconsin and Illinois. This can lead to some bizarre situations, as librarian Ron McCabe explains. Parents sign their child's application for a library card, promising to make the library whole if books are lost. The parents get a notice that a book is overdue. When they ask which book is missing, librarians reply that they can't disclose it—unless the parents bring a consenting note from their child!

On other fronts, too, the ACLU is fighting for what it sees as the First Amendment rights of children. It opposes limits on tobacco advertising aimed at children, even when the industry volunteered to do so while it was negotiating a deal with Congress. And when major corporations, including Disney and

Kellogg, offered to require parental permission before collecting information about children under 12 who visit their Web sites, they ran into fierce ACLU opposition.

The ACLU's determination to give minors the rights adults enjoy is a perversion of freedom. Underlying a free society is the assumption that individuals have a basic ability to render judgments. But we aren't born with that ability; children gradually develop it. For this reason we are not charged with violating children's right to free assembly when we prevent them from running into the street, or their privacy rights when we examine their homework.

Parents not only have a right but a duty to help shape the education of their children, help them choose which books they should read, which music they should listen to, which TV programs they should watch—and which to avoid. This seems indisputable when we're talking about preteens, and even the parents of teenagers need to be involved rather than shut out. If a classmate of my son has committed suicide, and my son seems rather depressed and is spending long hours alone in the library, it is my duty at a minimum to find out if he merely reads Dostoevsky or the Hemlock Society's how-to books. I also had better find out if one of my children is deep into "Mein Kampf," "The Anarchist's Cookbook" or the Unabomber's manifesto, so I can help him learn to deal properly with these poisonous works.

Helping children to develop the moral and intellectual faculties to make responsible choices when they grow up is what raising kids is all about. Anybody can provide room and board, and love comes naturally. But developing a child's character is a parent's highest duty—a duty no civil libertarian should interfere with.

Amitai Etzioni, "ACLU Favors Porn over Parents,"
The Wall Street Journal, October 14, 1998

Selection 3

Marjorie Hardy is an assistant professor of psychology at Muhlenberg College in Allentown, Pennsylvania. A related article, "Curiosity Kills," can be found at *www.sportshooter.com/features/curiosity_kills.htm.*

Would your child pick up a gun? Would he shoot a friend? Shoot himself?

Mine would, and so would dozens of other children at his day care center.

No, I'm not talking about toy guns. I'm not talking about children with emotional problems or violent tendencies. These were children 4 to 7 who are middle class. The .357 magnum, .22-caliber handgun and .38 with a four-inch barrel were disarmed, of course, but real. Had these children found the guns in a different situation, they might be dead.

This test took place in my son's day care center last month, but the results only reinforced the conclusions of previous studies. In 1995 and 1996, two of my students and I conducted two studies whose original purpose was to find a way to prevent children from playing with guns. We focused on young children, who are most at risk for accidental gun injuries. And we took the approach that most parents take: education. We expected that the children would listen to us and that we could make their lives safer. What actually happened was very different.

In the first study, we brought a police officer to a class of 60 children, and he told them: "Don't touch guns—they're dangerous. If you see a gun, leave the area. Go tell an adult." The children "learned" the lesson: they could tell you what they would do if they saw a gun. But when we left them alone with disarmed guns, they picked them up and shot everything in sight.

So in the second study, we taught a different group of children for five days how to make good choices, how to resist peer pressure, how to distinguish toys from dangerous objects.

But the results were similar: across the two studies, 65 percent of the children played with the guns. They even tried to use crayons as bullets.

We asked the children if they thought the guns were toys. Most of the 4-year-olds couldn't tell the difference between the real and the fake. About half of the 5-year-olds and most of the 6-year-olds could distinguish between the two. But they all played with the guns. What's scarier, a child not knowing what's safe and what's dangerous, or a child knowing the difference and playing anyway?

Not fair, the critics said; you put guns in a setting where children feel safe, in their own day care class. True, but aren't homes supposed to be safe, too? We childproof medicine bottles and swimming pools. But we put loaded handguns in bedroom drawers.

We asked the children and their parents about guns in their homes. We couldn't get a straight answer. Of the 109 parents interviewed, more than half reported that they owned guns, and four admitted to keeping a handgun loaded and readily accessible. Did their children know where the gun was? No, they said.

But the children told a different story. Seventeen children whose parents denied owning guns said their parents had them. Some told of one parent hiding a gun from another. "My daddy keeps it in the glove compartment of his truck, but my mom doesn't know," one child confided. Ten children said they not only knew where the gun was, but had touched it without permission.

Gun control laws are a start, but rules and warnings alone are not going to keep children safe. Parents have to monitor their children closely and rethink their decision to own a gun. They need to know if guns are in the homes of their children's friends.

Would your child touch a gun? Mine did. Then he lied about it when asked. Thank goodness it wasn't loaded.

Marjorie Hardy, "Very Young Guns," *New York Times,* May 14, 1999

Evaluating Arguments: Problems in Critical Reading

CHAPTER OBJECTIVES

Building on the primary skills from Chapter 8, the second chapter of Part 4 examines more complex elements of argumentation, specifically, how writers of argumentative prose intentionally or unintentionally go wrong. Learning to recognize these deceptive techniques will sharpen your critical reading skills and safeguard your ability to think independently. As in Chapter 8 the chapter ends with some editorials for further practice. Here are the specific topics addressed in Chapter 9:

• Inductive and deductive reasoning

• Problems with inductive and deductive reasoning

• Emotional appeals in arguments

• Common logical fallacies

• Bias and other deceptive techniques

■ INDUCTIVE AND DEDUCTIVE REASONING

Chapter 8 introduced you to the basic difference between inductive and deductive arguments. Without going into too much detail—since you are enrolled in a reading and not a logic course—Chapter 9 will discuss how problems in persuasive writing can result from faulty inductive or deductive reasoning.

Inductive Reasoning

We will start with induction because the conclusion of an inductive argument leads to the major premise of a deductive argument. As you recall from Chapter 5, inductive order moves from the specific to the general. An **inductive argument** is built on a set of factual statements derived from observation or experience that serve as evidence. The statements lead to a conclusion, which can take one of two forms: (1) a *generalization,* a statement asserting that something is true of a class, or (2) a *hypothesis*, a statement of conjecture of what will *probably* occur. Inductive arguments are sometimes called **probability arguments** because the conclusion is only probable, not certain. Consider this example:

Evidence:	The Krispy Kreme doughnut store in Torrance has been a phenomenal success.
Evidence:	The Krispy Kreme doughnut shop in Van Nuys is doing a booming business.
Evidence:	The Krispy Kreme outlet that recently opened in the Fremont location has been a big hit since the day it opened.
Conclusion:	If my family opens a Krispy Kreme shop in Daly City, it is sure to be a success.

Although it is based on three pieces of evidence, the conclusion—a **generalization**—is only probable, because other outcomes of the family's doughnut shop endeavor are possible. Not all franchise outlets succeed. However, the more instances of successful Krispy Kreme stores one provides, the stronger the probability that the conclusion derived from them is true.

Let us now look at an inductive argument with the other type of conclusion—a hypothesis:

Evidence:	Last week I saw my boss and his secretary having dinner together at an intimate French restaurant.
Evidence:	Yesterday I saw my boss and his secretary having lunch at the Mexican restaurant close to the office.

| Evidence: | This weekend my boss and his secretary are going away together on a business trip. |
| Conclusion: | My boss and his secretary are having an affair. |

Is this conclusion reasonable or probable, based on the evidence? Although three instances of possibly illicit meetings are cited, the conclusion represents only a **hypothesis**—a theory or conjecture. Perhaps they were planning the upcoming trip; perhaps they are just friends who enjoy each other's company; perhaps they *are* having an affair. In the absence of more compelling evidence, this conclusion is possible, even probable, but not necessarily true.

Deductive Reasoning

Unlike an inductive argument, a **deductive argument** moves from reason to conclusion or to specific application with certainty. For example, if you know that your textbook is in your backpack and you know that your backpack is in your car, then you can logically deduce that your textbook is in your car. This is a logical conclusion that necessarily proceeds from the two pieces of evidence, called **premises.** Taken together, the two premises and the conclusion derived from them constitute a **syllogism:**

Major premise:	My textbook is in my backpack.
Minor premise:	My backpack is in my car.
Conclusion:	Therefore, my textbook is in my car.

As long as the argument follows the prescribed form of the syllogism, it is *logically valid;* further, if the premises are true, then the argument is considered *sound* or reliable.

These two forms of reasoning are the foundation of persuasive writing. In an inductive argument, the reasons *suggest* that the conclusion is true, and as more evidence accumulates, the conclusion becomes stronger. Yet an inductive argument always involves a leap from the evidence to the conclusion—the matter of *probability*. But in a deductive argument, there is no leap or question of probability. Another way to keep the two forms of reasoning straight is this: Induction is more of an argument of *content,* whereas deduction is an argument of *form,* by virtue of the syllogism.

Here is another example of a deductive argument:

Major premise:	All men are mortal.
Minor premise:	John is a man.
Conclusion:	John is mortal.

This syllogism is valid because (a) the premises are true and (b) the premises already contain or imply the conclusion. By accepting the premises, we must also accept the conclusion, and it is therefore valid.

■ PROBLEMS WITH INDUCTIVE REASONING

With this background in mind, we can now turn to errors in reasoning that these two patterns of thinking sometimes lead to.

Hasty Generalizations and Stereotyping

The two most common types of errors in inductive thinking result from conclusions derived from insufficient or unrepresentative evidence. A **hasty generalization** is an all-inclusive statement made in haste, without allowing for exceptions and qualifiers. For example:

> If you're in the market to buy a dog, don't get a Shetland collie. All of them are too nervous and high-strung. My friend, Pamela Gentile, has a miniature collie, and that dog yaps at every little sound, even when the phone rings. He jumps all over people, too.

This generalization stems from the person's having observed only one Shetland collie and leaves no room for exceptions. Producing even one calm Shetland collie negates the argument. A careful writer might qualify this statement by saying, "some," "often," "the one Shetland I have observed," and so forth. Notice, too, that a characteristic such as nervousness is relative, calling for a subjective judgment. What some people might call nervous and high-strung, others might call spirited or playful.

Stereotyping is similar to the hasty generalization, except that it results in generalizations about people because of their gender, age, ethnic background, race, attire, or other characteristics.

> A narrow-minded father says to his daughter: "I don't want you dating a guy who wears an earring. Guys who wear earrings are undoubtedly punks, homosexuals, or gang members. No self-respecting man wears jewelry in his ear!"

This stereotype places all earring-wearing men into supposedly undesirable groups, and offers a blanket condemnation based only on personal appearance.

Incorrect Sampling

Inductive arguments often include a **sampling,** which, if done incorrectly, can produce a flawed argument. For example:

> Researchers interviewed 50 students at Lincoln Rock Community College. Sixty percent of those interviewed think that Internet sites such as Napster should allow users to download copyrighted music for their personal use.

From this statistic, the reader might infer that 60 percent of the population as a whole shares this opinion. Not only is the sample unrepresentative of the general population, but the number of students surveyed is too small. Later in this chapter we will briefly discuss how polls are conducted and some problems associated with them.

Here is another example of a sampling problem. In 2000 a team of scientists at the University of California–Berkeley published a study in the science journal *Nature* saying that differences in finger lengths might yield clues to sexual orientation. In brief, the researchers found that lesbians had more "masculine" hands than heterosexual women. Supposedly, the index fingers of lesbians—unlike those of heterosexual women—are significantly shorter than the ring fingers. The researchers concluded that "homosexual women were exposed to greater levels of fetal androgen than heterosexual women."[1] This article was picked up by the national media and had women all over the country measuring their index fingers.

However, the method of sampling was problematic: The scientists had set up booths at gay pride events in Berkeley and San Francisco. Then they offered willing participants a free $1 lottery ticket if they agreed to have their hands measured and to answer a detailed questionnaire. The team examined the hands of 720 adults. Why is this an example of faulty inductive reasoning? Wouldn't 720 pairs of hands be enough evidence to lead to a valid conclusion?

_____

_____

_____

■ PROBLEMS WITH DEDUCTIVE REASONING

A flawed deductive argument is termed *unsound* if one of the premises is untrue or if it is a generalization. It is interesting to note, however, that the argument can still be *valid* as long as the syllogism is properly constructed and follows the prescribed form. The following is a valid but unsound syllogism:

Major premise:	All Frenchmen are good lovers.
Minor premise:	Philippe is French.
Conclusion:	Therefore Philippe is a good lover.

Because Philippe has been placed in a class in which all the members are said to share the same characteristic, the statement is valid.

[1] Carl T. Hall, "Finger Length Points to Sexual Orientation," *San Francisco Chronicle,* March 30, 2000.

Therefore, we can deduce (arrive at the conclusion) that he shares that characteristic. Yet the argument is *unsound* because the major premise—that all Frenchmen are good lovers—is obviously untrue, representing a generalization that could be easily invalidated by only one unromantic Frenchman. Note that the major premise above is the *conclusion* of an unreliable *inductive* argument:

Evidence:	Claude is a romantic lover who has left behind a string of broken hearts.
Evidence:	André is such a good lover that he has all the women swooning.
Evidence:	Jules is a connoisseur of romance and is an excellent lover.
Conclusion:	Therefore, all Frenchmen are good lovers.

Faulty deductive reasoning can also proceed from an unsound or unacceptable assumption. For example, consider this argument:

People shouldn't be allowed to vote if they don't speak English.

What is the origin of this kind of thinking?

Major premise:	Only English speakers should be allowed to vote.
Minor premise:	This group of people cannot speak English.
Conclusion:	These people should not be allowed to vote.

Here, the major premise rests on a restrictive statement that not everyone would accept. Although there are several other types of syllogisms, they lie outside the scope of this text. Suffice it to say that the careful reader should be alert to arguments either proceeding from generalizations (faulty deductive arguments) or arising from generalizations (faulty inductive arguments).[2]

Practice Exercise 1	All the arguments in this exercise are faulty. First determine if the argument represents an inductive or a deductive argument. Then briefly explain the error in reasoning each argument represents.

1. The city of Seattle surveyed a thousand residents who regularly commute by bicycle to work. Nearly 75 percent of the bicyclists felt that the city should build no new freeways.

---

[2]A challenging exercise in deductive and inductive reasoning using simple arguments and observations from everyday life can be found at *www.sjsu.edu/depts/itl/graphics/induc/ind-ded.html.*

2. I take my VW Jetta to Heinrich for repairs. He's German, and Germans are the best car mechanics.

    _____

3. Sue Jensen is against abortion. She must be a member of the National Pro-Life Coalition.

    _____

    _____

4. The ballot proposition to build a new high school gym in Desert Hot Springs will undoubtedly fail. Last week *The Desert Sun* announced the results of a new poll, and 80 percent of the residents of Sunny Dunes Nursing Home were firmly opposed to the measure.

    _____

5. The Department of Agriculture ought to tighten up the food stamp program. Today I was behind a woman in line at my local IGA supermarket, and she paid for four T-bone steaks and a pound of shrimp with food stamps!

    _____

6. It's no wonder Linda Ng scored so high on the math part of the SAT. Everyone knows that Asians are good in math.

    _____

7. I don't see why people get so upset about small children seeing violent movies. Before the new codes went into effect, I took my seven-year-old nephew to see horror movies all the time, and he turned out all right. You don't see him engaging in violent acts!

    _____

8. A high school student says this, in reference to a new rule prohibiting students from wearing trench coats or dusters on campus: "The only reason the principal instituted the new rule is because of the Columbine massacre. The two guys who killed all those students dressed in black trench coats."

    _____

We can now examine manipulative techniques writers use to get readers to accept conclusions they might otherwise reject. To simplify matters, I have divided these persuasive techniques into two types: emotional appeals and logical fallacies.

■ EMOTIONAL APPEALS IN ARGUMENTS

Emotional appeals are acceptable, as long as other evidence is present that balances the discussion. We also need to distinguish between legitimate appeals to the emotions and illegitimate ones. The latter is an attempt to control our emotions by spurious means; the writer may play on emotions that are not relevant or appropriate to the argument, or the emotional appeal may disguise the argument.

When you examine a piece of writing or a promotional piece, ask yourself: How good is this argument or product *without the appeal?* Is there any evidence besides the appeal? Strip away the fluff from the argument and examine the claim *for itself,* unobscured by emotion or sentiment. Be aware that the more emotional the appeal, the weaker the argument. This section examines several types of emotional appeals, alphabetized for easy reference.

Appeal to Authority

A writer who uses the **appeal to authority** allows the claim to rest solely on the fact that a supposed authority is behind it. Further, the authority may not be identified; another possibility is that the authority is highly biased.

- I read in a recent journal that a scientific study showed no correlation between a high-fat diet and cancer. This is good news because now I can eat all the butter, sour cream, and Big Macs that I want. (Studies like this one come out all the time, offering conflicting evidence on nutrition. Before accepting such an argument, wait until more evidence is in.)
- Linus Pauling, a chemist from Stanford University who won both the Nobel Prize for Science and the Nobel Peace Prize, believed that massive doses of vitamin C could prevent cancer. (The fact that a famous scientist believes something doesn't make it so, nor in this case did the rest of the scientific and medical community accept his theory. Additionally, Pauling was a chemist, not a medical doctor or cancer specialist.)

Appeal to Fear

The **appeal to fear** makes us concerned about what will happen if we adopt a certain course, or what will happen if we don't adopt a certain course.

- Why would anyone ever move to California? That's earthquake country. Geologists predict that the "Big One" will hit sometime in the next 25 years.

- If the Oakland City Council doesn't stop medical marijuana from being distributed, pretty soon you'll have a whole bunch of drug addicts moving here and pretending they're sick just to get the drug.

   The following argument was heard during Bill Clinton's impeachment hearings in 1999:

- If President Clinton is impeached, we should all be afraid that our own civil liberties will be in jeopardy.

Appeal to Patriotism

The **appeal to patriotism** obviously relates to love of one's country, often implying an accusation that citizens who oppose a policy are not patriotic.

- If you really loved the United States, you wouldn't oppose its efforts to try to remove Saddam Hussein from power in Iraq.
- Common bumper sticker during the Vietnam War: "America: Love it or leave it."

Appeal to Pity or Sympathy

Should we adopt a policy simply because we feel sorry for someone? An **appeal to pity or sympathy** asks us to suspend our critical judgment because we pity a victim of sad circumstances or because we can identify with someone else's troubles.

- The fact that Emma Jones hasn't paid her rent for six months is no reason for her landlord to evict her. Her husband died, she recently found out that she suffers from high blood pressure, and she has three children to support on her salary as a Wal-Mart salesclerk.
- A recent television commercial for StainStick—a prewash product manufactured by DowBrands—showed a mother preparing the wash with her little girl, who clearly has Down's syndrome. The mother says, as the daughter applies StainStick to the spots, "We use StainStick because the last place we need a challenge is in the laundry room." (Critics of this ad charged that DowBrands was exploiting the child and preying on the viewing public's sympathy to buy the product. The criticism seems justified, since the purpose of the advertisement was to sell StainStick, not to make us feel sorry for a child with Down's syndrome.

Appeal to Prejudice

Like the appeal to fear, the **appeal to prejudice** inflames negative feelings, beliefs, or stereotypes about racial, ethnic, or religious groups; gender; or sexual orientation. Emotion replaces reasoned discourse.

- Letting so many immigrants into this country is a mistake. They take jobs away from Americans who are out of work, and they don't share our traditional values.
- Why would a man ever want to become a nurse? After all, women are the traditional caregivers in our culture.

Appeal to Tradition

An **appeal to tradition** asks us to accept a practice because it has always been done that way or because it represents some long-standing, venerable tradition.

- The Roman Catholic Church has forbidden women to become priests for nearly 2,000 years. Why should the church abandon this long-standing practice?
- The Republican Party has always been the party of Abraham Lincoln.

Bandwagon Appeal

The **bandwagon appeal** rests on the assumption that everyone likes to be on the winning side. The origin of this metaphorically named appeal comes from the fact that lots of people ride on the bandwagon during a parade. This emotional appeal tries to convince the reader that *everybody* is doing something and that he or she had better get on the bandwagon, too.

- Eighty percent of Mapleton residents support a petition asking the city council to build a new football stadium. That's why I'm voting yes on the measure in November.
- It's inconceivable that the United States still has the death penalty. All the nations of Western Europe abolished this barbaric practice years ago.

    Bandwagon appeals often use weasly phrases such as "everyone agrees" and "we all know that."

- Everyone knows that pornography is the main cause of rape.
- Of course, you can see the undeniable logic of requiring all residents to pay for garbage service, whether they use it or not.

    Look for evidence, not appeals to join the crowd. The crowd can be wrong. A related appeal tries to bully the reader into accepting an idea.

- Certainly no one sitting in this room is foolish enough to vote against allowing the annual rodeo to be held in Pescadero again this year.

Flattery

A writer who uses **flattery** tries to put us into a group of people that we admire and might hope to identify with, whether we share their convictions or not.

- Every well-educated person knows that James Joyce was one of the most important writers of the twentieth century.
- Women with good taste shop at Talbots.

We like to think of ourselves as being well educated or having good taste, and the writer hopes to arouse this emotion in us with this appeal.

Just Plain Folks

This appeal lies in the writer's desire to have himself or herself perceived as just an ordinary citizen, or **just plain folks.** It is the opposite of snob appeal.

- A candidate running for office tells his audience during a campaign speech: "I came from a little town just like this one; I went to school in a building just like the one across the street. I understand your values and what you stand for."
- When Bob Dole, Republican presidential candidate, was preparing to announce his candidacy in 1987, his media consultants chose Russell, Kansas, Dole's hometown for "the perfect backdrop." They chose Ol' Dawson's drugstore, where Dole had worked during his youth. (Journalists pointed out that this site had symbolic overtones. We know it as the "just plain folks" appeal.)

Ridicule

This appeal asks the reader to dismiss an idea by subjecting it to **ridicule** rather than by analyzing its inherent weaknesses. A related tactic allows humor to substitute for supporting evidence.

- The mayor's proposal to impose a license fee on all bicycles owned by city residents sounds like something an eight-year-old kid would come up with.
- Only irresponsible people would vote to oppose the Danbury City Council's proposed tree-trimming requirement.

Testimonial

Television and magazine advertisements abound with **testimonial** appeals whereby famous people—actors, athletes, celebrities, or other notable figures—are paid to endorse a particular product. Here are three examples: In 2000 Tiger Woods signed a five-year contract with Nike for $100 million, and Venus Williams signed a five-year $40 million contract with Reebok, the biggest ever for a female athlete. George Foreman's agreement with Salton, the company that manufactures the George Foreman Grill, pays him $137.5 million over five years.

While one could argue that all these athletes are credible spokespersons for the products they tout, not all endorsements are so reliable. A recent pharmaceutical company ad for Prinivil, a high blood pressure medication, featured baseball legend Cal Ripken, Jr., otherwise known as the "Iron Man." The ad's slogan is "Pressure under Control." The implication, of course, is that Ripken takes Prinivil to control his blood pressure. But the tiny print at the bottom of the ad states: "Cal Ripken, Jr., is not hypertensive and is not taking Prinivil." Here, the testimonial is not a personal endorsement, but an attempt to show that the medicine is strong and hard-working, just as Ripken was on the field. The ad is misleading, but only if the unwary reader ignores the fine print.

Transfer

This emotional appeal is most commonly associated with advertising. By using **transfer,** the writer (or advertiser) deliberately plants the idea that favorable impressions about one thing will transfer or carry over to something else. Ironically, the *association* of the image is almost more important than the product itself. Advertisers identify this phenomenon as "selling the sizzle, not the steak." A glance through *Cosmopolitan, GQ, Marie Claire, Self,* and similar glossy magazines will yield many examples of transfer. (Note that transfer also operates with the appeals of flattery and just plain folks.)

Sometimes attempts to use transfer are so clumsy or transparently deceptive that they backfire. Early in his presidency, critics accused George W. Bush of having a poor record on environmental issues (mainly because of his proposals to drill for oil off the Florida coast and in the Arctic National Wildlife Refuge in Alaska). To correct this supposed misapprehension among the American public, in spring 2001 Bush gave two speeches on environmental issues. Each speech lasted approximately three minutes, but more important than the substance of the speeches were the settings. In California, Bush stood before a magnificent giant sequoia in Sequoia National Park; in the Florida Everglades, the backdrop was a grove of sawgrass and mangrove. The choice of these sites was, of course, deliberate: The two backdrops, by means of transfer, would link Bush with the environment in the voters' minds.

Practice Exercise 2

Using the information in the preceding sections, study the following examples and identify the emotional appeal(s) each represents. For easy reference, the appeals are listed here:

- Appeal to authority
- Appeal to fear
- Bandwagon appeal
- Flattery

- Appeal to patriotism
- Appeal to pity or sympathy
- Appeal to prejudice
- Appeal to tradition

- Just plain folks
- Ridicule
- Testimonial
- Transfer

1. By the year 2030, if we continue to admit immigrants at the same level we do today, whites will constitute only 51 percent of the U.S. population. That will mean the death of American culture as we know it.

   Appeal(s): _____

2. The government should not have forced The Citadal, a military college in South Carolina, to admit women. The Citadel has always been a men's college, and it should just have been allowed to stay that way.

   Appeal(s): _____

3. In 1999, an American fisherman rescued five-year-old Elián Gonzales from a leaky boat off the coast of Florida. His mother and several other refugees had died trying to escape from Cuba. During the conflict over whether to return the boy to his father in Cuba, this argument was frequently heard: Elisabeth Gonzales gave her life to bring the little boy to our shores. To force him to return to Cuba, with its repressive Communist system, can't possibly be in the child's best interests.

   Appeal(s): _____

4. Bumper sticker: "When guns are outlawed, only outlaws will have guns."

   Appeal(s): _____

5. Professor Hornswoggle told us in our geology lecture today that there is enough oil in underground reserves to run automobiles until 2099. He's been teaching geology for 30 years, so he must be right.

   Appeal(s): _____

6. Teenage moms really have a tough time. After their boyfriends get them pregnant and abandon them, they have to care for their babies and juggle their schoolwork at the same time. That's why Garfield High School needs an on-campus day care center.

   Appeal(s): _____

7. I can't believe that the mayor is so foolish as to propose a living-wage law for Evansville workers. Nobody in his right mind would come up with a dumb idea like that!

   Appeal(s): _____

8. Try Aunt Bea's frozen pies in five delicious flavors. Fat-free, low-cholesterol, and microwaveable, too. Just like Grandma used to make!

    Appeal(s): _____

9. Clearly, the nation's new get-tough welfare laws are going to wreak havoc on recipients. For people who aren't equipped to deal with the real world and who have a limited education and no job experience, cutting off their benefits after two years will just increase the number of homeless on the streets.

    Appeal(s): _____

10. Let's face it. Sixty-five percent of the American people said in a recent poll that they didn't like the direction the country was headed. That shows that things need to change in this country!

    Appeal(s): _____

11. Paint store clerk to author: "Why did you choose Benjamin Moore paint to use on your bookcases?"
    Author: "I heard it's the best paint on the market."
    Clerk: "You made the right decision. Benjamin Moore paint is definitely the best paint available. You can't go wrong choosing it."

    Appeal(s): _____

12. Letter to the editor (paraphrased): Those so-called homeless people who hold up signs at intersections saying "Will Work for Food" are just a bunch of scam artists. What they really mean is "Will Gladly Take Your Money." Work is the last thing on their minds!

    Appeal(s): _____

13. The United States should not abandon its policy on immigration. This country has always been the refuge for people from all over the world seeking new opportunities. After all, doesn't the plaque at the base of the Statue of Liberty say, "Give me your tired, your poor, your huddled masses"?

    Appeal(s): _____

14. If God wanted homosexuals to marry, he would have created Adam and Steve instead of Adam and Eve.

    Appeal(s): _____

15. Letter to the editor (paraphrased): Why is your newspaper supporting the criminal border jumpers invading the United States from Mexico? The hard-working people of Arizona, Texas, and California have no interest in paying the bills of people who have no

legal right to be here. I don't care what color they are or where they come from. They should be sent home immediately, with just the clothes on their backs.

Appeal(s): _____

16. During the Clinton impeachment trial, Dale Bumpers, Democratic senator from Arkansas, urged his Senate colleagues to drop the impeachment hearings. He argued that his fellow senators should feel compassion for the Clintons, because they "have been about as decimated as a family can get." Bumpers continued: "The relationship between husband and wife, father and child, has been incredibly strained, if not destroyed. There's been nothing but sleepless nights, mental agony for this family for almost five years." (Quoted in "Ex-Senator Pleads with His Old Friends to Acquit," *San Francisco Chronicle,* January 22, 1999)

Appeal(s): _____

■ LOGICAL FALLACIES: PART 1

The second type of manipulative technique in arguments is the **logical fallacy,** an error in reasoning that also invalidates an argument. Because these fallacies are difficult, I have divided them into two sections arranged alphabetically; a practice exercise follows each section. It should be noted that, like emotional appeals, not all fallacies are purposely intended to dupe the unwary reader. Many writers lapse into them as a result of ignorance or sloppy thinking. If you want further instruction, check out these four websites devoted to critical thinking with a logical fallacies component.

Websites for Studying Logical Fallacies
- Argument: Links to Logical Fallacies and Writing the Argumentative Essay

  www.cdc.net/~stifler/en110/arg-res.html

  Note: Some links may no longer be available.
- The Nizkor Project: Fallacies

  www.nizkor.org/features/fallacies/

  This site is sponsored by a group dedicated to disseminating information about the Holocaust.

- Summit Ministries is a religious website with good explanations and examples with a Christian slant. From their home page at *www.summit.org,* type in "logical fallacies" in the search box.

  From the home page, click on "Critical Thinking."
- A site devoted to atheism issues sponsors a similar site from a nonreligious point of view: The Atheism Web: Logic and Fallacies.

  www.infidels.org/news/atheism/logic.html

Ad Hominem Argument

Ad hominem in Latin means "to the man." This fallacy can take two forms: (1) unfairly attacking the person rather than his or her position or (2) attacking the character and reputation of a position's supporters (guilt by association). In either case, the argument ignores the deeds or character of the person or group and relies instead on personal and abusive attack.

- Letter to the editor (paraphrased): George W. Bush has a lot of nerve taking a moral stand against cloning. What a hypocrite! His own past cocaine use and troubles with alcohol tell me that he has no business lecturing Americans on moral issues.
- During the Vietnam War, Vice President Spiro Agnew characterized intellectuals (who were generally opposed to President Nixon's war policies) with this famous alliterative phrase—"nattering nabobs of negativism"—thereby attacking their collective character rather than the principles they stood for.
- I'm certainly not going to vote for Proposition 16 in the next election. I just looked at the election pamphlet and discovered that the big oil companies are in favor of it. There must be something in it for them.

Begging the Question

When a writer **begs the question,** he or she treats an opinion yet to be proved and open to question as if it were a truth already proved. This unproved "truth" then becomes the basis of the discussion. A simpler way of understanding the begging-the-question fallacy is this: The writer assumes to be true that which it is his or her duty to prove. The classic example of this fallacy is this question: Have you stopped beating your wife? Either a yes or a no answer confirms that the person either has beaten his wife or still beats her, when in fact that charge needs to be established. Here are two more examples:

- Who is the best person to censor controversial articles in the Lincoln High School newspaper? (In phrasing the question like this, the writer begs the question, assuming without proof that censorship of the campus newspaper is desirable in the first place.)
- During a murder trial, the prosecuting attorney asks the jury, "Does it make sense to release this murderer so that he can commit the same atrocities again and again? We need to lock this person up for a very long time so that he can never kill someone again." (This argument begs the question, since the very purpose of a trial is to prove whether the defendant actually committed the murder.)

Cause–Effect Fallacies

Fallacies involving **cause–effect** relationships can be divided into two types.

False Cause

This first type results either from citing a false or a remote cause to explain a situation or from oversimplifying the cause of a complicated issue.

- In the 1950s researchers pointed to public swimming pools as a source of the polio virus, noting that children who contracted polio had swum in public pools. (Note: Since thousands of city children swam in public pools, there were bound to be outbreaks of polio among them.)
- It is obvious that Sam Anderson would grow up to be an axe murderer. According to an interview I read, he was subjected to a rigid toilet-training regimen when he was a toddler. (The remoteness of this "cause" makes the conclusion improbable or questionable.)
- Billboard ad for ABC Television: "Before TV, Two World Wars. After TV, Zero." (This ad makes it sound as if the ABC network was responsible for world peace.)

Post Hoc, Ergo Propter Hoc

In Latin, this second kind of cause–effect fallacy means "after this, therefore because of this." The fallacy suggests that because event B occurred after event A, event A caused event B; in other words, the writer makes a connection solely because of chronology. This fallacy accounts for many silly superstitions, for example, when someone breaks a mirror and then blames that action for seven years of bad luck.

- Yesterday I forgot to take my vitamins, and this morning I woke up with a cold. That proves that taking vitamins prevents colds.

Either–Or Fallacy

Sometimes called *false dilemma,* the **either–or fallacy** discusses an issue as if there are only two alternatives available, thereby ignoring other alternatives. Rejecting one choice requires one to accept the other.

- Police officers are either brutal or corrupt.
- A married woman should stay home and devote herself to raising her children. If she wants a career, she should forget about having children.

Neither of these fallacies offers a middle ground or other alternatives, such as working part-time and raising children.

Evasion

Evasion is a fallacy that occurs when a speaker or writer evades or ignores the question by talking around it.

- A reporter asks Mayor Sanchez how he proposes to solve the homeless problem. The mayor answers: "We must find a solution to the problem of homeless people on our streets. This is a complicated problem that I am taking very seriously."

  Here is another, lengthier example excerpted from a *Wall Street Journal* article ("Bill Gates under Questioning," June 8, 2000). During the federal trial of Microsoft, a prosecutor for the Justice Department asked Chairman Bill Gates a series of questions about his knowledge of Microsoft's work on Sun Microsystem's software program, Java, which internal documents had cited as a serious threat to his company's operations. Here is an excerpt from Gates's testimony:

  > Justice Department: I'm not now talking about what you do in competition with other products or other companies. What I'm talking about is whether or not you've had discussions with people within Microsoft in which you talked about the need to undermine Sun, using those words, if that will help you, within Microsoft.
  > Bill Gates: I don't remember using those words.
  > Justice: You don't?
  > Gates: No.
  > Justice: Do you think you did use those words or you just don't know one way or the other?

Gates: I don't know.

Justice: Would it be consistent with the way you felt about Java for you to have told people that you wanted to undermine Sun?

Gates: As I've said, anything about Java you've got to show me a context before I can answer because just the term *Java* itself can mean different things.

Practice Exercise 3

Study the following arguments carefully. Then decide which of these fallacies each argument represents:

- Ad hominem argument
- Begging the question
- Either–or fallacy (false dilemma)

- Evasion
- False cause
- Post hoc, ergo propter hoc

1. I knew I should have canceled my tennis match today. I'm a Sagittarius, and my astrological forecast warned Sagittarians not to engage in anything competitive. No wonder I lost!

   Fallacy: _____

2. Because children surely need a mother more than they need a father, women with children should not be allowed to engage in military combat where they could be killed and leave their children motherless.

   Fallacy: _____

3. The president of XYZ Widget Company reports: "The recent settlement between management and the labor union was a huge mistake. Giving in to the union's demands for a wage increase has resulted in low production figures."

   Fallacy: _____

4. Letter to the editor (paraphrased): Has anyone else noticed that all these schoolyard killings have occurred in suburban areas and that minorities are never responsible for such acts? This tells me that the suburbs breed violence more than inner cities.

   Fallacy: _____

5. Because having a common language is an essential requirement of any democratic government, I'm planning on voting for Proposition 227, which will eliminate bilingual education in my state's schools.

   Fallacy: _____

6. Spiro Agnew, among others, blamed Dr. Benjamin Spock's famous book *Baby and Child Care,* the bible for child rearing in the 1940s and 1950s, for being too permissive and causing the antiwar sentiments of students who protested the Vietnam War in the 1960s.

   Fallacy: _____

7. When George W. Bush, then governor of Texas, was the Republican candidate for President, he was asked many times if he had used cocaine in the past. Here is one of his responses: "Somebody floats a rumor and it causes you to ask a question, and that's the game in American politics, and I refuse to play it. That is a game. You just fell for the trap. I refuse to play. They're ridiculous and absurd, and the people of America are sick and tired of this kind of politics. And I'm not participating." (Quoted in Mike Downey, "Doing the Texas Sidestep," *Los Angeles Times,* August 22, 1999)

   Fallacy: _____

8. Growing industrial hemp is illegal in the United States. Hawaii Representative Cynthia Thielen has argued that planting hemp would help Hawaii's depressed economy. Her reasoning: "Sugar is dead. . . . Every day that passes, and we do not allow farmers to grow industrial hemp means agricultural workers are unemployed. And our land lies fallow." (Quoted in Leslie Guttman, "Hemp—It's Rope, Not Dope," San Francisco Chronicle, May 28, 1999)

   Fallacy: _____

9. The voters of the Red River Valley should vote against Congressman Lewis when he runs for reelection. He recently was accused of having an affair, and he is rumored to have smoked marijuana in college. He can't possibly represent our community's environmental concerns.

   Fallacy: _____

10. In August 1997 the Democratic National Committee (DNC) was under investigation for questionable fund-raising practices. When asked for his reaction to recent revelations about the alleged laundering of foreign money into the DNC coffers, President Clinton responded, "I was sick at heart" and "disappointed."

    Fallacy: _____

11. The violence that children observe on television influences their behavior for the worse. That's why the V-chip, which allows parents to control the amount of violence their children watch, is such an important technological breakthrough.

    Fallacy: _____

12. As I see it, residents of West Coast states can deal with the threats of rolling electrical blackouts either by conserving more or by allowing their governments to build more nuclear power plants.

    Fallacy: _____

13. After Evansville allowed pornographic movie theaters and bookstores to do business downtown, violent crime decreased by 25 percent. This proves that restrictions on pornography rather than pornography itself are a cause of such crimes.

Fallacy: _____

14. During one of the presidential debates in 2000, Democratic front-runner Al Gore turned to Bill Bradley, former Democratic senator from New Jersey and his challenger, and said, "You know, racial profiling practically began in New Jersey."

Fallacy: _____

15. In response to a reporter's question about Bill Clinton's sexual escapades, actor Alec Baldwin was quoted in the *New York Daily News* as saying: "Sexual promiscuity has always been the medicine of choice for the chief executive of the United States. What would you rather have him do: take drugs?" (March 16, 1998)

Fallacy: _____

16. These are the findings of a study conducted by Dr. Alan R. Hirsch, the neurologic director of the Smell and Taste Treatment and Research Foundation in Chicago, and funded by the Campbell Soup Company, which makes Pepperidge Farm products: "The odor and taste of Pepperidge Farm Garlic Bread was studied with regard to its effects on the interaction of family members. Fifty families were given two identical spaghetti dinners, though some were served Pepperidge Farm Garlic Bread and some were not. Researchers found that eating Pepperidge Farm Garlic Bread reduced the number of negative family interactions by 22.7 percent and increased the number of pleasant interactions by 7.4 percent. This suggests that, for a family of four, serving Pepperidge Farm Garlic Bread results in thirty-one fewer negative interactions and forty-five more positive interactions per dinner." (Quoted in "Garlic Therapy," *Harper's,* May 1999)

Fallacy: _____

■ LOGICAL FALLACIES: PART 2

False Analogy   Although it does not carry the same force as factual evidence or good reasons, arguing by analogy can be effective and persuasive in supporting an argument. As you will recall from Chapter 4 in Part 1, an analogy discusses one subject in terms of another, completely different subject. But a logical fallacy called **false analogy** results if there are fewer similarities than differences, if the resemblance is remote or ambiguous, or if there is no resemblance between the two at all.

For example, consider this argument:

- Every red-blooded American serviceman knows that gays should be banned from the military. In the military we're like one big family living in close quarters, and a homosexual just wouldn't fit in.

This argument rests on the dubious idea that people living in military quarters are comparable to a family. To see why the analogy is false, we have to see where it breaks down and if there are more dissimilarities than similarities. First, one chooses to enter the military, but one cannot choose which family to be born into. The analogy also implies that military personnel have no privacy whereas family members do. Further, the writer argues that gays should be excluded from the military because other members wouldn't be "comfortable" being around them, implying—contradictorily—that gays can't "fit in" with a family, either. In sum, when you examine these differences, the only real connection between the military and a family is that both are social institutions.

The tobacco industry has taken many hits in these critical reading chapters for fallacious thinking. Here is yet another example: In 1996 then-governor of Massachusetts William Weld signed a bill that, among other provisions, would force tobacco companies to reveal the additives in each cigarette brand, in particular "ammonia-based compounds that tobacco critics say boost nicotine delivery and make cigarettes more potent." Peggy Carter, a spokeswoman for RJR Nabisco, the parent corporation of its subsidiary, R.J. Reynolds Tobacco Co., responded, arguing: "They wouldn't ask Coke, Pepsi or the Colonel to divulge their soft-drink or chicken recipe, so why should we be deprived of trade-secret privileges?" (Quoted in Barbara Carton, "State Demands List of Contents for Cigarettes," *The Wall Street Journal,* August 2, 1996.) Why is this a

false analogy? Where does it break down? _____

_____

It is important to note that not all analogies used in persuasive writing are false, and in fact, as noted earlier, analogies can be both effective and cogent—as long as the similarities between the two things being compared are greater than the differences. To illustrate, in 1987 a group of parents from Minneapolis (a city with one of the highest Native-American populations in the country), called the Concerned American Indian Parents, designed a poster distributed to local high schools. They were protesting the practice in some high schools of calling their athletic teams the "Indians." The poster depicted the banner of the real Cleveland

Indians baseball team, along with three other hypothetical banners for the Pittsburgh Negroes, the Kansas City Jews, and the San Diego Caucasians. The slogan at the bottom of the poster read, "Maybe now you know how Native Americans feel." One of the schools that received the poster, Southwest Secondary School in Minneapolis, announced that it had changed the name of one of its teams from the Indians to the Lakers, demonstrating the compelling power of a good analogy.

Finally, consider this argument supported by an analogy. Education professor Richard Clark was quoted on *The CBS Evening News* as warning schools that trying to teach "by hooking students up to machines and technology" is like "trying to improve the nutrition of a neighborhood by bringing in more trucks to deliver groceries without having the money to buy groceries." Based on what you have learned about analogies, is it false

or not? What is being compared to what? _____

_____

Oversimplification

The fallacy of **oversimplification** can involve either reducing a complicated issue to overly simple terms or suppressing information that would strengthen the argument.

- Strikes should be illegal because they inconvenience innocent people.
- Human DNA has 23 chromosomes, whereas the DNA of dogs has 39. Therefore, dogs are more complex than humans. (This argument oversimplifies the differences between humans and dogs and rests on a simplistic meaning of the word *complex*.)

Non Sequitur

A **non sequitur,** from the Latin for "it does not follow," is a conclusion that does not logically follow from the evidence.

- We should hire Sam Hallstrom to be Mount St. Helens Community College's reading laboratory aide. He is a member of the local service employees union, you know. (Sam may be a union member in good standing, but drawing a conclusion about his ability to perform well as a lab aide does not follow from that evidence.)
- In 1994 a disk jockey at Dallas's country radio station KYNG–FM announced that he had hidden $5 and $10 bills in books in the fiction section of the Fort Worth public library. Predictably, hundreds of people stampeded through the library, pulling books off the shelves and dumping them on the floor in their frenzy to find the money. A spokesman for the station claimed that the disk jockey who thought up the stunt did so because he wanted to boost public interest in the library.

Rationalization

A **rationalization** is a self-serving but incorrect reason to justify one's position. It uses reasons that sound plausible but that are actually false.

- A student received a D in his college chemistry course. When asked by his parents why he received such a low grade, the student responded that he didn't like the instructor.
- It would be bad for my health if I stopped smoking. First, I would gain a lot of weight, and that would cause a strain on my heart, which might lead to high blood pressure. Anyway, science is surely bound to find a cure for cancer one of these days.

Red Herring

This colorfully named fallacy comes from the English tradition of fox hunts. Cheaters would drag a dead fish across the field in front of their opponents' dogs, thus throwing them off the scent of the fox. The fallacy works in a similar way: The writer who uses the **red herring** fallacy presents an argument that is unrelated to the real question, thus throwing the discussion off the track.

- It doesn't make sense for people to get so upset about violence on television. If they look around at the larger society, they'll see that violence is all around them. Why don't these critics worry about that issue? (The real issue that the writer should be concerned about is violence on television, not violence in the larger society.)

Slippery Slope

The metaphoric name of the **slippery slope** fallacy will help you remember it. It suggests that one step in the wrong direction will lead to increasingly dire occurrences. The image invoked is one of a person being unable to halt her or his descent of a muddy or icy incline once that first tentative step is taken.

- I'm opposed to censorship in any form. If we ban so-called hate speech or sexually explicit language, pretty soon the government will be telling us which books we can read and movies we can watch. And our hard-won freedoms will go down the drain!
- The New York law prohibiting drivers from talking on cell phones while driving provoked this typical response: Denying drivers in New York the right to talk on cell phones is a bad idea. The next thing you know, New York's legislature will be passing laws forbidding drivers to listen to the radio, change the radio station, eat a Big Mac, or talk to their passengers while driving.

Note, however, that not all references to a slippery slope suggest that the writer is arguing fallaciously. In a true slippery slope fallacy, the result has to be improbable and far removed from the first step. A case in point: American drug manufacturers have been accused of charging exorbitant prices for AIDS drugs. In South Africa, 40 drug manufacturers brought suit against the government in an attempt to overturn a law signed by former president Nelson Mandela allowing cheap versions of patented drugs to be imported to South Africa without permission from the patent owner.

The drug industry was caught in a bind on this issue: Although the drug manufacturers do not want to appear unsympathetic to the plight of AIDS sufferers in Africa, at the same time, they are aware that other countries might pursue legislation similar to that of South Africa, thereby cutting into their profits on patented drugs. As Mark Groombridge, a research fellow at the Cato Institute, a conservative think tank, was quoted as saying, "It is quite likely to be a slippery slope. If the question is AIDS today, why not heart disease and cancer drugs tomorrow?"[3] This situation does indeed suggest a true slippery slope in the form of financial losses. How does your worldview affect your stand on this issue?

Two Wrongs Make a Right

The **two wrongs make a right** fallacy is commonly used to defend wrongdoing and make it appear legitimate because others engage in the same practice. In other words, the writer accuses the opposition of holding the same views or behaving in the same way. During the campaign fund-raising investigations of 1997, President Clinton admitted that the Democratic National Committee had been guilty of certain abuses (money laundering, illegal contributions by foreigners, and so forth), but argued that the Republican National Committee had done exactly the same thing. (In fact, the Republicans were in a sticky position concerning the Senate hearings; they risked looking ridiculous if they came down too hard on the Democrats for practices that both parties had been guilty of using for years.)

Here is another example of the two wrongs fallacy.

- A driver has just received a speeding ticket.

  Policeman to driver: "Sir, did you know you were going 75 in a 65-mile-per-hour zone?"

  Driver: "I don't see why you pulled me over. Didn't you see that guy in the red Acura? He must have been doing 85!"

[3]Quoted in Helene Cooper et al., "AIDS Epidemic Traps Drug Firms in a Vise; Treatment vs. Profits," *The Wall Street Journal,* March 2, 2001.

Practice Exercise 4

Study the following arguments carefully. Then decide which of these fallacies each argument represents:

- False analogy
- Oversimplification
- Non sequitur
- Rationalization
- Red herring
- Slippery slope
- Two wrongs make a right

1. Bumper sticker spotted in Oregon, in response to the Forest Service's decision to stop logging in so-called old-growth forests to protect the endangered spotted owl: "Hungry and out of work? Eat an environmentalist."

    Fallacy: _____

2. If doctors are allowed to consult reference books, medical journals, and World Wide Web sites, why can't we medical students use our medical textbooks or websites during tests?

    Fallacy: _____

3. Letter to the editor (paraphrased): For all those bleeding-heart liberals who gripe about the death of the tobacco bill, I say that the idea that a tax increase will stop people from smoking is way out in left field. If the administration really wanted to protect kids, it would do something about all the illegal drugs available to our young people. Children don't die from smoking cigarettes, but plenty die from using illegal drugs.

    Fallacy: _____

4. When asked why she wanted to win the 2000 Miss USA Beauty Pageant, one contestant answered that she entered the contest to get scholarship money for college, adding, "I don't want people to say it's about beauty. I need the money for a college scholarship."

    Fallacy: _____

5. I don't see anything wrong with using the office copy machine to make copies of my personal income tax forms. Just yesterday I saw Joan Wilson downstairs in the duplicating room making copies of that mystery novel she's been writing on the side.

    Fallacy: _____

6. The way to stop drug abuse in this country is to increase dramatically the number of drug enforcement agents and to punish severely anyone caught possessing illegal drugs.

    Fallacy: _____

7.   The controversy over cloning human beings and using stem cells for medical research is misguided. People really ought to be concerned about the disregard for human life that proabortion types represent.

     Fallacy: _____

8.   A dog breeder refused to reimburse the author, who had purchased a pedigreed German shepherd that later was found to have a serious defect requiring corrective surgery. The breeder refused to pay even half of the surgery's cost, arguing, "You wouldn't expect your doctor to reimburse you if your child needed surgery, would you?"

     Fallacy: _____

9.   I'm opposed to those supermarket discount club cards. I don't trust the supermarket chains to keep my purchases private. What if health insurance companies got data on shoppers' buying habits? The next thing you know, we'll have the food police poking through our garbage cans looking for sour cream containers, candy bar and Twinkie wrappers, and empty liquor bottles. Then insurance companies might deny us health benefits just because we have unhealthy diets!

     Fallacy: _____

10. A university fund-raiser routinely sent her personal mail, including bills and gifts, using the university's postage, arguing that the university didn't pay her enough; thus the free postage helped compensate her for the salary she thought she deserved.

     Fallacy: _____

11. No wonder those guys at Columbine High killed all their classmates. They were known to play computer games like Doom and Quake. Violent video games are a leading cause of violence in our society.

     Fallacy: _____

12. A single woman decided to have her baby without marrying the father (who wanted nothing to do with the child). Her parents objected to her decision, arguing that the child would be damaged by not being raised by a father. In response, the young woman argued that lots of children are abandoned by their fathers.

     Fallacy: _____

13. French scientists inserted jellyfish genes into a rabbit embryo to create a bunny that emitted a green glow in the dark. Supporters of this sort of tinkering with nature by manipulating an organism's genes

defended it, saying that dog breeders manipulate mating all the time to produce dogs with desirable qualities, so why can't biotech breeders create glowing bunnies?

Fallacy: _____

14. All this talk about conserving electricity and buying more fuel-efficient cars is beside the point. What we really should be concerned with is becoming independent in our energy needs so that we don't have to go begging for oil from OPEC nations.

    Fallacy: _____

15. It was revealed that contestants on 1950s quiz shows such as "Twenty-One" and the "The $64,000 Question" had been fed answers before the programs were aired. The resulting quiz show scandals prompted a national debate over truth and honesty in broadcasting. (This deception was nicely depicted in Robert Redford's film *Quiz Show.*) One quiz show producer was quoted as saying, in defense of the rigged answers, "If we rig the contest and supply [the contestants] with answers, we'll make intellectualism and learning look glamorous."

    Fallacy: _____

16. In 1998, a member of the San Francisco Board of Supervisors, Amos Brown, proposed that public drinking should be outlawed in Golden Gate Park and in other public parks to solve the problem of homeless people drinking and causing disturbances. Benny Joyner, a member of the Coalition on Homelessness, testified before the board as follows: "These places [the parks] are homes to the homeless. Where are these people going to drink? In your back lawn?" ("The 'Right' to Drink," *San Francisco Chronicle,* December 4, 1998)

    Fallacy: _____

■ SUMMARY OF EMOTIONAL APPEALS AND LOGICAL FALLACIES

By now you may be wondering if legitimate forms of persuasion exist. Of course they do, and they have been outlined in Chapter 8, which you might want to review. The fallacies and appeals discussed here, in Chapter 9, are tricks used to obscure the issue, but their success is ensured only if the reader is unwary and accepts an argument without knowing the basis for accepting it. The best defense against fallacious reasoning and deceptive, manipulative techniques is critical awareness. Also keep in mind that not all writers who engage in these techniques have evil motives. Many writers are either sloppy or lazy, or they are such fervent crusaders for their beliefs that they stray from the rules. Others, of course, are simply ignorant of legitimate forms of argumentation.

■ BIAS AND OTHER DECEPTIVE TECHNIQUES

In this final part of Chapter 9, we will look briefly at other deceptive techniques used in persuasion. The topics discussed in this section are bias, misuse of authority, slanting, and distortion. We will also take a look at polls—how they are constructed and how poll questions can be slanted.

Bias

Bias occurs when a writer favors one side over the other, writing from a subjective viewpoint colored by—and possibly distorted by—his or her political, economic, social, ethnic or racial, or religious views. Knowing the background of a writer—not merely his or her qualifications for serving as an authority—can alert readers to subtle or not-so-subtle attempts to manipulate their thinking.

Although total objectivity is not humanly possible, in a factual news article we should expect that a writer will attempt to be fair and to exercise careful judgment about what material to select and what material to omit. In persuasive writing, however, the writer has more leeway. Because the writer's purpose is to argue from a subjective point of view, we cannot expect objectivity (associated more with exposition). To some extent, then, bias is a necessary consequence of persuasive writing because by definition, the starting position is one's point of view, in other words, one's bias. Thus, the critical reader must not suppose that bias always assumes a sinister motive, and we must distinguish between *acceptable* (or fair) and *unacceptable* (or unfair) *bias.* Unacceptable bias is based on racial, ethnic, religious, or political intolerance or prejudice; on one's own economic self-interest; or on the desire to hide or distort the truth.

Further, if bias is there, we must decide whether or not the writer is **credible,** or believable. Does the writer have expertise in the subject? What is the basis of the writer's ideas? Has the writer revealed any personal experience that lends credibility to the point of view? Assuming that the writer does a decent job of presenting evidence (as discussed in the previous chapter), then one can entertain the argument, perhaps even accept it. In contrast, unfair bias may be accompanied by one or more of the manipulative techniques you have studied—slanted language (euphemisms or sneer words), specious arguments, emotional appeals, logical fallacies, and the like.

Let us illustrate with a simple example: Suppose your English teacher tells you in a conference that your last essay received a D because it was weak. She recommends more specific development in the form of examples, analysis, or explanation, and more careful proofreading. This evaluation would be an example of fair bias, because your instructor's credibility is backed up by her expertise (by virtue of her academic background and teaching experience). Your teacher's preference for clear, well-developed, adequately supported, and grammatically correct prose is consistent with criteria endorsed by other college English teachers. On the other hand, if your instructor gave your essay a D because you wrote about professional football, which she knows or cares nothing about, that would be *unfair* bias, based on a personal prejudice, one not necessarily shared by other teachers.

In some rare instances, a writer may actually announce his or her subjective point of view, in which case you have at least been alerted up front. Consider these two opening paragraphs by British writer James Fenton from his essay "The Fall of Saigon." Upon being given a chance to go to Vietnam in 1973, he unequivocally states his motivation for going there and the anti-American sentiments that he and his comrades shared.

I was glad to be going off on a journey. I had been awarded a bursary for the purpose of travelling and writing poetry; I intended to stay out of England a long time. Looking at what the world had to offer, I thought either Africa or Indochina would be the place to go. I chose Indochina partly on a whim, and partly because, after the Paris Peace Agreement in February of that same year, it looked as if it was in for some very big changes. The essence of the agreement was that it removed American military personnel from Indochina and stopped the B-52 bombing raids. The question was how long could the American-backed regime last without that accustomed support. I wanted to see Vietnam for myself. I wanted to see a war, and I wanted to see a communist victory, which I presumed to be inevitable. I wanted to see the fall of a city.

I wanted to see a communist victory because, in common with many people, I believed that the Americans had not the slightest justification for their interference in Indochina. I admired the Vietcong and, by extension, the Khmer Rouge, but I subscribed to a philosophy that prided itself on taking a cool, critical look at the liberation movements of the Third World. I, and many others like me, supported these movements against the ambitions of American foreign policy. We supported them as nationalist movements. We did not support their political character, which we perceived as Stalinist in the case of the Vietnamese, and in the case of the Cambodians . . . I don't know. The theory was, and is, that when a genuine movement of national liberation was fighting against imperialism it received our unconditional support. When such a movement had won, then it might well take its place among the governments we execrated—those who ruled by sophisticated tyranny in the name of socialism.

James Fenton, "The Fall of Saigon," *The Best of Granta Reportage*

Few writers, however, are so explicit. And discovering a writer's hidden agenda is one of the most difficult tasks in critical reading. One solution is to read widely. When you become familiar with editorial writers' beliefs by reading their columns over time, you will have a better grasp of their politics. Also pay attention to biographical headnotes, for they may tell you something about the writer's beliefs. Last, when reading persuasive prose, ask this question: What does the writer stand to gain (or lose) by my accepting (or rejecting) this argument?

Since it is difficult for the ordinary citizen, who has precious little time, as well as limited energy and financial resources, to uncover the truth, he or she has little choice but to rely on the national media and electronic information sources, such as World Wide Web sites, to expose discrepancies, tainted findings, and other instances of corruption. Recently, there have been a rather large number of supposedly impartial research studies published that, upon inspection and exposure to the world at large, have been tarnished with conflict-of-interest charges. Fortunately, skeptical researchers often alert the media to such deception, and the media in turn publicize their doubts.

Following are just two cases of many from the past few years: *The New England Journal of Medicine,* the nation's most highly regarded medical journal, was forced to admit that "nearly half of the drug reviews published since 1997 were written by researchers with undisclosed financial support from companies marketing the drugs." In short, the journal found that 19 out of 40 drug therapy reviews "violated its famously tough conflict-of-interest policy. The policy bars researchers with ties to pharmaceutical companies from writing reviews or editorials about company products." (Quoted in "Prestigious Medical Journal Admits Conflict of Interest," *Los Angeles Times,* February 24, 2000.)

Another publication, *The Journal of the American Medical Association* (JAMA), published a study discrediting the use of St. John's Wort (SJW), a popular herbal substance, which has gained a following as an alternative to pharmaceutical antidepressants. However, Richard A. Friedman, director of the psychopharmacology clinic at New York's Weill Medical College of Cornell University, pointed out that the results were "premature and scientifically suspect." The details aren't important here, but it was revealed that the study had been funded by Pfizer, maker of the antidepressant Zoloft. In other words, researchers may have been predisposed to find SJW ineffective because Pfizer was paying their salaries. The virtues of SJW are still being debated in the scientific community; to date no study has proved, or disproved, its effectiveness in treating depression. (Quoted in Tara Parker-Pope, "Study Debunking Use of St. John's Wort Is Criticized for Flaws," *The Wall Street Journal,* April 27, 2001.)[4] Fortunately, ordinary citizens can now perform their own investigations via the World Wide Web. See in particular the section in Chapter 10 on the most useful health-related websites available.

Following is an article by Kathy Snow Guillermo, the author of *Monkey Business: The Disturbing Case That Launched the Animal Rights Movement* and a writer for PETA, People for the Ethical Treatment of Animals, a well-known animal-rights organization. After you read it, answer the questions that follow.

A recent article ("Circus Performs Well on Animal Care," Open Forum, March 12) took People for the Ethical Treatment of Animals (PETA) to task for claiming that circuses abuse elephants. In his account of life with the Carson & Barnes Circus, Mike Echols sounds as ingenuous and naive as Disney circus tyke Toby Tyler. He waxes lyrical about the enormous Big Top and the convoys that carry animals and people on an annual tour of 18,000 miles. He praises Carson & Barnes for building exercise yards for the elephants at their winter quarters.

But Echols' article raises more questions than it answers. Why, for instance, did Carson & Barnes wait more than 50 years to build a fence around a field so that the elephants could stretch their legs for a few weeks each winter? What about the months of endless travel these animals endure, chained in the backs of tractor-trailers, unable to escape their own waste?

Through freezing desert nights and broiling days, the elephants toil. They must "perform" acts unnatural to them before screaming crowds—always under threat of a jab with a sharp bull hook. The rest of the time they stand, chained at the ankles, waiting for the next assignment. What else can this be called but abuse? Even more troubling, the U.S. Department of Agriculture, which oversees the treatment of animals in circuses, has cited Carson & Barnes with numerous violations of the Animal Welfare Act. In 1994 and 1995, the most recent years for which inspection reports are available, the USDA found at least 20 violations, including elephant trucks with inadequate ventilation; sharp, jagged edges that could injure elephants inside the trucks; and inadequate exercise for one elephant, Paula.

In the summer of 1995, the same year Echols began traveling with Carson & Barnes, I visited the circus at one of its stops in Northern California. I arrived just after sunrise, video camera in hand, to document a typical day. I

---

[4]In February 2001, representatives from the top medical schools adopted recommendations that researchers be required to disclose any financial interest they have that might conflict with studies involving their patients. Whether these guidelines will stop such biased reports remains to be seen.

saw elephants lined up like a 1930s chain gang, legs shackled, unable to step more than a foot or two in any direction. After years of such boredom, elephants begin to act like human inmates in mental hospitals, rocking from side to side in an endless rhythmic motion. This is called stereotypic behavior, and whether exhibited by people or animals, it's a sign of mental disturbance. Every one of the Carson & Barnes elephants swayed back and forth, swinging their trunks, their eyes glazed.

Who wouldn't be driven mad by such deprivation? The people who run this circus may be fond of their elephants, but these magnificent beings, with the largest brains of any land animal, are deprived of nearly everything that makes their lives worth living. Every year brings more stories of circus elephants driven to rebellion. They wield their enormous strength to crush their "trainers" or run crazily through the streets. Such incidents have prompted some cities, such as Vancouver, to ban circuses with animal acts.

Though it's unlikely that any circus trainer can persuade an elephant to stand on a tiny platform or spin in a circle without some form of coercion, a decent life means more than not being beaten. It's difficult to imagine that an elephant would rather live shackled to a truck than roam with her family in her own environment.

Like elephants, other species suffer under the Big Top. For this reason, PETA believes circuses should retire all animal acts, place the animals in sanctuaries and follow the example of the wildly popular, human-only Cirque du Soleil. And yes, as a mother of three young children, I understand that children love to see animals. But they are too young to understand that the animals are exploited. When we expose kids to twirling elephants, tigers jumping through hoops, and bears on bicycles, we teach them nothing about the natural magnificence of these creatures. We owe our children—and the animals—much better.

Kathy Snow Guillermo, "Circuses—Cruel Shows Can't Go On,"
San Francisco Chronicle, April 11, 1997

What is the writer's tone? _____

What is the author's particular bias? _____

How is the bias conveyed? _____

Is the bias fair or unfair? _____

Is the writer credible? _____

Note that Guillermo relies on impassioned yet reasoned discourse, raising questions about the treatment of circus animals, disputing circus owners' claims about their treatment, and stating PETA's claim of policy ("PETA believes circuses should retire all animal acts") clearly.

Misuse of Authority

In Chapter 8, you learned that one criterion of a good argument is a reliable authority. But authority can also be misused, for example, when the high-sounding names of "research organizations" are used to hoodwink the unwary reader or consumer. A particularly blatant instance of **misuse of authority** occurred in 1992 when the *New York Times* published an article reporting that chocolate contains cavity-fighting properties. This startling announcement made headlines across the country. A few days later, however, it was revealed that the announcement had come from a newsletter published by the Princeton Dental Resource Center and distributed to dentists' offices. This organization, of course, is meant to sound as if it is affiliated with Princeton University; it is not. As it turns out, the Princeton Dental Resource Center is actually a front for the M&M/Mars Candy Company.

Slanting

From the discussion of connotation and denotation in Chapter 6, you may recall that a writer's word choice has significant power to influence the reader's perceptions. **Slanting** is a way of presenting information in such a way that it will appeal to the audience. It may be subtle, or it may involve more obvious misrepresentation to create either a positive or a negative impression in the reader's mind. We will examine two types of slanting.

Slanting by Means of Word Choice

First, slanting can be achieved simply by a writer's employing a carefully chosen word. For example, in a favorable editorial published in *The Wall Street Journal,* the unnamed writer praised a proposal by former secretary of education Lamar Alexander to give $1,000 scholarships to low- and moderate-income parents, which would allow them to send their children to a school of their own choice. The plan was called a "G.I. Bill for Kids." The *Journal* editorial homed in on the inevitable opposition from teachers' unions. (Some background: A voucher refers to a sum of money that parents can use to send their child to any school of their choice, private or religious or public. Voucher systems exist in only a handful of districts [Milwaukee is one such district], and voters have turned down school-choice initiatives in several state elections over the past few years.) The editorial writer states (italics are mine):

> The administration program is further evidence that empowering parents with choice is an idea whose time has come. Support for choice cuts across income, political and racial lines. Its major opponent is the *entrenched education bureaucracy that benefits from the status quo.*

The writer goes on to discuss a ballot initiative on vouchers, which the teachers' unions had opposed: *"Educrats did everything they could to block the initiative."* (Quoted in "The Education Revolution," *The Wall Street Journal,* June 25, 1992.)

The italicized words are slanted and as a result misrepresent the position of teachers who have two primary arguments against voucher plans: They fear (1) that public funds will be siphoned away from already troubled public schools and leave them in even worse shape than they are in now, and (2) that only middle-class parents will be financially able to take advantage of vouchers, leaving only poor children in public school districts and leading to a loss of diversity.

These two words are the culprits: "bureaucracy," with its implications of endless red tape and unbending rules and regulations, and "educrat," a sneer word you won't find in the dictionary, which combines the first syllables of *educator* and the last syllable of *bureaucrat.* Thus the editorial writer creates a negative impression in the reader's mind and depicts teachers and their unions as being more concerned with serving their narrow self-interests than with supporting a quality education for all children.

Slanting in Public Opinion Polls

In an informative article on political polls, "How to Tell If Political Polls Are about Truth, or Consequences" (*Los Angeles Times,* January 30, 2000), Janet Wilson first explains how polls are conducted.

> If polled properly, statisticians say, as few as 1,000 people can accurately reflect opinions of 185 million Americans. The most widely accepted method of sampling people is through random-digit dialing, which means everyone has an equal chance of being interviewed.
>
> Using area codes and exchanges in geographically stratified areas, computers generate more than 3,000 phone numbers to make up for hang-ups, refusals, those who aren't home, non-residences, and other dead-ends. Computer-generated dialing is vital, especially in California, which leads the nation in unlisted telephone numbers.
>
> Weighted formulas are used to make sure men and women, minorities and age groups are represented in the same proportion in which they appear in the general population. For political surveys, pollsters ask questions regarding voting history and intention to vote to identify likely or highly probable voters.

Next, the article looks at how the wording of a poll's questions can yield different results. Study these three sample questions on the issue of affirmative action.

1. Do you favor or oppose affirmative action programs to help women and minorities get better jobs and education?

2. Do you favor or oppose affirmative action programs that use quotas to help women and minorities get jobs or education?

3. Do you favor or oppose programs to rectify discrimination in jobs and education against women and minorities?

Did your answer change with each question?

Which question is designed to elicit the most favorable response?

_____

Which question is designed to elicit a slightly less favorable response?

_____

Which question is designed to elicit the most negative response?

_____

Finally, the article lists other types of polls (unlike the above-described reliable polls) to show that not all polls are created equally or are equally trustworthy.

Push Polls
Used by partisan political pollsters for their clients who are running for office. They are intended to push voters away from one candidate and toward another.

Dial-in Polls
Unscientific and not true polling. The sample is distorted because the respondents have to call in.

"Frugging"
The practice by special-interest groups or political parties of sending out questionnaires on a particular topic, often coupled with a plea for money. The results, also unscientific, are sometimes presented as poll findings.

"Sugging"
The practice of companies' sending out questionnaires and then trying to sell something to the respondents. Again, this is not a real poll.

Internet Polls

Though sometimes amusing to read and increasingly popular, these are not true polls because the respondents are not selected randomly. Some Internet polls are labeled "for entertainment only" which, at a minimum, indicates they are unscientific.

Distortion

Distortion means twisting facts or misrepresenting one's position or one's opponent's position. Here are two brief examples. The first is a paraphrased version of a letter by a pro-life activist.

> Editor—I have just read your article about women in China aborting their female fetuses after their sonogram reveals the sex of their unborn child. What's the big deal? I wish someone who is in favor of abortion would tell me why selectively aborting female babies is wrong. Isn't it simply the mother's choosing not to have a female child? And isn't this what the pro-abortion movement is all about?

Some women in China do indeed abort their female fetuses (and commit infanticide), a result of China's stringent one-child-per-family policy. However, in connecting abortion as it is practiced in North America and in Europe with abortion as it is practiced in China, this writer unfairly distorts the position of abortion supporters.

Here is a second example. During the 2000 presidential campaign, both candidates made education—specifically, improving public education in the United States—a top priority. When the National Assessment of Educational Progress (NAEP) released statistics on reading scores in February 1999, Al Gore called a press conference to announce that scores had improved and that this "great progress" was a direct result of the Clinton–Gore education program. In fact, eighth-grade reading scores did improve a little between 1992 and 1998 (during Clinton and Gore's tenure), but according to Diane Ravitch, an education specialist and author of several books on the subject, there was "no net gain" for fourth- or twelfth-graders. Ravitch continues:

> Far from the "amazing" progress that political appointees were describing, improvements in reading were slight at best. The vice-president had used the event to generate headlines about successes that didn't happen; worse, he attempted to claim credit for what little progress the nation was making; worse still, he left the impression that NAEP scores can be used to promote the political program of whoever happens to be in office, this despite the fact that Congress (at the behest of the Reagan administration) took considerable pains to try to insulate NAEP from political manipulation of every sort.

> Quoted in Diane Ravitch, "Education: See All the Spin," *The Washington Post National Weekly Edition*, March 29, 1999

■ EXERCISES: EVALUATING EDITORIALS

The following five newspaper editorials will give you practice in implementing your critical reading skills. These editorials, from the op-ed pages of major newspapers and periodicals, discuss current, controversial issues. For each selection that your instructor assigns (or that you read on your own), consider these questions:

1. Who is the writer? Does he or she represent an authority? On what basis?
2. What type of claim does the argument represent?
3. What is the writer's main argument or proposition?
4. What kind of evidence does the writer provide in support of the argument? Does the evidence meet the criteria discussed in Chapter 8? Is it fair, accurate, sufficient, and relevant? List two or three of the main supporting points.
5. Are there any instances of manipulation, whether in the form of emotional appeals or logical fallacies?
6. Is the argument, as the author presents it, convincing or at least worth considering? Do you accept the argument? Why or why not? What other information do you need?

Selection 1

Bob Herbert writes a syndicated column in several daily newspapers. This was written at the height of the bull stock market.

During the daylight hours the interior of Nellie Perez's home is nearly as dark as night. She lives with her disabled husband and five others in a dangerously rickety shack in Guadalupe, a tiny poverty-racked town tucked in the midst of one of the most affluent areas in America.

Guadalupe is part of Maricopa County, one of the fastest-growing counties in the country. Its neighbors, which include Phoenix, Tempe, Paradise Valley and Scottsdale, are feasting on the nation's unprecedented economic boom. Million-dollar homes and splendidly manicured golf courses abound. Some of the malls are glittering jewels.

But as Andrew Cuomo, the U.S. Secretary of Housing and Urban Development, said during a visit on Tuesday, Guadalupe is different. It was not invited to the economic feast. "That wealth," said Mr. Cuomo, "is not their wealth."

When night falls, Guadalupe, populated mostly by Yaqui Indians and Mexican-Americans, goes to bed hungry.

Mrs. Perez's home was built from scraps—old doors, tarpaper, chicken wire, rotted wooden planks. It is like something from the third world in the 19th century, not the United States on the verge of the 21st. There is no bathroom, no running water, no electricity and no heat. The air is so close it is difficult to breathe. When I asked where the bathroom was, Mrs. Perez, an affable woman in her 50's, pointed across the street to a reeking outhouse.

Mr. Cuomo stopped by the Perez dwelling during his daylong tour. Mrs. Perez led him through the four dark and cluttered rooms. There was no floor, only planks, or the bare ground. "I'm sorry it's a little bit dirty," Mrs. Perez said.

Mr. Cuomo has been trying to spread the word that even with the economy booming, and the Dow hurdling the 10,000 barrier, and millionaires being created at an astonishing rate, there are still many Americans struggling with the equivalent of an economic Depression.

"Real people are suffering," said Mr. Cuomo. "And now is the time to do something about that. Now is the time to invest in the things we know how to do that would make their lives better, that would bring housing and jobs to their communities—now, when the economy is strong and we have the largest surplus in history. If not now, when?"

Guadalupe is not an aberration. There are many pockets of extreme poverty across the country. Mr. Cuomo mentioned the Indian reservations, citing specifically the Pine Ridge Reservation in South Dakota, home of the Oglala Sioux. He spoke of the continuing poverty among African-Americans in the inner cities, and among whites in parts of Appalachia and other rural areas. He spoke of the struggles faced by poor Hispanic families in Arizona and in Texas, especially those near the Mexican border.

"The Dow at 10,000 almost makes the irony crueler," Mr. Cuomo said. "This phenomenon of terrific economic growth and yet so many people just left out. There is no reason why in 1999 Americans should be living in shacks, literally. This should be a nightmare from the past."

Mr. Cuomo said his department was attempting to bring affordable housing and economic opportunity to struggling Americans, but the need is immense and he acknowledged that the resources available from HUD were not nearly enough. He said he was trying to bring more public attention to the plight of the poor.

"This is not something you hear much about," he said. "By definition the people affected are voiceless, because they are poor. They are not on television. They are not in the newspapers. For most Americans a place like Guadalupe does not exist."

Mr. Cuomo seems to speak with more passion now than he did a few years ago, and he seems more comfortable as he travels the country, meeting with the powerful and listening to the powerless. His message is one that has not been particularly popular for many years now—that the country as a whole has an obligation to do what it can to assist those who are in danger of being left behind economically.

Before saying goodbye to Mrs. Perez on Tuesday, Mr. Cuomo asked if she had ever heard of the Dow Jones. "The Dow Jones?" she said "What does that mean?"

Bob Herbert, "The Other America," *The New York Times,* April 8, 1999

Selection 2

Andrew Bernstein is a senior writer for the Ayn Rand Institute (*www.aynrand.org*) in Marina del Rey, California. The institute promotes the philosophy of Ayn Rand, who espoused objectivism and political libertarianism. The philosophy is given novelistic treatment in her classic works *Atlas Shrugged* and *The Fountainhead.*

The Bush administration's proposals on energy come amidst cries from religious and political leaders that Americans have a moral obligation to conserve—to wash our clothes less often, to replace our comfortable SUVs with "econoboxes," to turn off our air conditioners and rot in the heat.

What motivates these pleas for conservation? Do these leaders fear that without their help we cannot balance our checkbooks? Would they like us to save our money for more important expenditures? Of course not.

Americans are being asked to conserve as a form of sacrifice: "We as humans are morally responsible to share the Earth's bounty with the poor and rich, the human and nonhuman. Every little bit we waste is a bit we can't share," states Lee Wallach, executive director of the Coalition on the Environment and Jewish Life in Los Angeles.

These advocates do not push conservation as a way of bettering our lives or as a way of lowering the cost of energy (for which increased production is the solution). Rather, they urge Americans to do with less, to lower their living standards, to live in a self-denying manner. Conservation is essentially the moral code of self-sacrifice applied to current energy problems.

President Bush seems to agree with this approach, ordering energy conservation at federal offices in California, offering assorted tax breaks for "alternative energy" proposals and endorsing a range of energy saving tips for homes, work sites and industrial plants.

In fact, Bush and Vice President Cheney—and California Gov. Gray Davis—should repudiate conservation as a policy because it is both impractical and immoral.

It is impractical because it does not address the real cause of the problem—government regulations and environmentalist restrictions that stifle energy producers. It is immoral because conservation repudiates the American Dream.

The United States became great because it embodied a moral code of national self-interest, the principle that men should be free to create abundance in pursuit of their own happiness.

The country grew to immense prosperity because it rejected the Dark Ages code of self-sacrifice and deprivation. Americans properly prize success, wealth and happiness, not self-denial, poverty and suffering.

We have become the most affluent country in history because we know that great producers of wealth like Andrew Carnegie, John D. Rockefeller and Bill Gates—not apostles of suffering like Mother Teresa—are mankind's real heroes.

The American Dream—of abundance and the unqualified moral right to enjoy it—resulted in the full flowering of the Industrial Revolution. Before our American Revolution, prior to the development of capitalism, few could have predicted the electric light, the telephone, radio and television, the airplane, organ transplant surgery—or the myriad other (energy-dependent) modern devices and methods that enrich our lives.

If, however, political leaders at the dawn of industrialization had promoted conservation and self-denial, rather than the freedom to produce, then the coal, oil, steel and other industries would not have been created and the United States would not enjoy the wealth it does today.

Given the same freedom to innovate and profit, energy producers today would construct nuclear and hydroelectric power plants, develop oil in both the Arctic National Wildlife Refuge and the Outer Continental Shelf, and exploit the country's huge natural gas supplies, such as the 39 trillion cubic feet of gas in Wyoming's Powder River Basin.

What Bush, Congress and the state of California should do is lift all socialist and environmentalist regulations shackling producers and establish a genuinely free market in the energy industry. Such a policy would result in a virtually unlimited supply of U.S. energy, thus greatly reducing cost to consumers.

Even in the short term, the free market is the only practical way to deal with the current energy supply/demand crisis. When supply of a good is scarce (in this case because of government regulations restricting energy production), its price must be allowed to rise, which will lead people to consume less of it. They will do so out of self-interest: in order to save money.

Further, the higher price motivates entrepreneurs to produce more of it and/or it leads innovators to develop alternatives, for example, the substitution of oil for coal beginning in the late 19th century and nuclear power for fossil fuels in the 20th century.

When individuals are free to pursue their self-interest, they are constantly motivated to produce more, continually raising man's standard of living.

Creating an unregulated free market will result in new technologies and inventions that could make such historic American advances as automobiles, jet travel, the personal computer and the Internet pale in comparison.

Conservation demands that Americans make do with less. In fact, they could have more. As such, conservation represents an unconscionable rejection of the moral code that made America great.

In our response to the current energy crisis we face a choice—the medieval code of self-denial and suffering or—the true meaning of the American Dream—freedom and prosperity.

Andrew Bernstein, "Conservation Is Retrograde, Immoral, and Un-American,"
San Francisco Chronicle, May 20, 2001

The following three editorials were published within a few days of September 11, 2001, when terrorists attacked New York's World Trade Center and the Pentagon. Each presents a different point of view about what changes the disaster will bring and what lies ahead in the years to come.

Selection 3

Tony Judt is a contributing editor at *The New Republic* magazine. He is also professor of European studies at New York University.

On Tuesday morning, September 11, from my window in lower Manhattan, I watched the twenty-first century begin. Of that I am certain. What I don't know is how to convey what I saw: two commercial aircraft slam into the World Trade Center, followed by the conflagration and collapse of the buildings. Where there was once something—elegant, soaring, confident—there is now nothing. The twin towers, symbol of the world's capital, are a void, filled as I write with smoke billowing from the rubble. We have been offered a glimpse into a possible future.

In the twentieth century, war was made *on* civilians. In the twenty-first century, war will be made *by* civilians. It will be the definitive "faith-based initiative," requiring neither guns, tanks, ships, planes, nor missiles. Like other faith-based initiatives it will bypass the conventional state. All it will need is planning skills and a willingness to die for your beliefs. Everything else—machinery, technology, targets—will be furnished by civil society, its victim. The point of such warfare will not be to achieve an objective, much less to win a final victory. It will be—it already is—simply to make a point.

In his televised speech on Tuesday night, President Bush misunderstood this completely. "They cannot dent the steel of American resolve," he asserted. But "they" were not trying to dent the steel of American resolve. They wanted to knock down the World Trade Center and blow up the Pentagon, and they succeeded. Their point was very well-made: The United States is vulnerable. When Mao Zedong first called the United States a "paper tiger," he knew he was whistling in the dark. But today is different. The contrast between American military bombast and the country's real exposure is palpable; until Tuesday morning, however, it was not understood by Americans themselves.

In recent years Americans have watched a spate of movie epics in which the United States wins World War II single-handedly and with valiant aplomb; in an earlier cycle, muscle-bound, bare-chested American heroes, wrapped (often literally) in the Stars and Stripes, refought the Vietnam War and other wars to U.S. advantage. I have watched some of these films in cinemas and on television—in Europe, in countries and among people well-disposed toward Americans. The commentaries have not been flattering. Elsewhere the temptation has been growing for years: to see in the bubble of American preening and pride an irresistible invitation to prick.

This urge to humiliate the United States has been made still more attractive by contemporary American reluctance to contemplate death in war. For all committed terrorists, now and in times past, death is an acceptable fee for a successful mission. For today's faith-based terrorists, it is the preferred price—the reward. Western European states, which accept military casualties as the price of resolve and have grown accustomed to a limited risk of civilian death, understand this mentality and partly for that reason make unsatisfactory symbolic targets. But Americans have made a virtue—some might say a fetish—of risk-free war. The special delight taken in causing large numbers of American deaths should thus not be underestimated.

The American domestic response is of anxious disorientation. Europeans, faced with a terrorist campaign, typically ask, "Why *does* this happen?" Every American I have spoken to or heard on television in the immediate aftermath of the catastrophe has demanded, "How *could* this happen?"—i.e., who *let* this happen?—as though the default position in modern life were 100 percent personal and collective security. Will this now change? Are we, after Pearl Harbor and the assassination of JFK, watching the end of American innocence—so often announced, so long postponed?

It is too soon to say. But something at least will be gained if three lessons are learned in Washington. The first is that the obsession with "missile defense" is a monstrous dereliction of duty. To be sure, there may be criminal states and obsessed individuals who dream even now of firing off an intercontinental missile. But that is their least likely weapon of choice, precisely because it so clearly advertises its point of origin and its owner. If I am right and the threat in coming decades is from men and organizations that want to make a point and mock and humble their adversary, then missile defense expenditure is a criminal waste.

The second lesson concerns the Middle East, the most likely source of such attacks now and in coming years. Like it or not, Israel is seen from Morocco to Pakistan as a surrogate for the United States. What Israel does, America will be blamed for. Israel will be the excuse and the catalyst for attacks on America. This will not change. The United States is thus not an optional presence in the Israel-Arab conflict, a great power that can choose, as the Bush administration has chosen, to fold its arms and step back from the front. When Israel applies tactics of which Washington disapproves—as it has done on recent occasions—it is

America, as much as Israel, that becomes a target. That is no reason to abandon Israel to its fate. It is time to make a virtue of necessity—since this is America's conflict willy-nilly, it is in our interest to get in there and find a way to peace.

The third lesson is the most important one. On Tuesday evening, Republican Senator John Warner, of the Senate Armed Services Committee, stood in the Pentagon and declared: "We call upon the entire world to step up and help." And so it will—as most of the rest of the world well knows, we are all in this to-gether. But American officials have spent the last few months denouncing treaties, promising a U.S. retreat from crisis zones, and explaining that the ad-ministration plans to put "U.S. national interests" first. It is good to hear conser-vative American politicians acknowledge that American national interests and those of the rest of the civilized world are utterly intertwined. But it would have been better if they had reached this conclusion a little sooner.

We live in a globalized political era. It is not just the financial markets that know no frontiers (and it was not without significance that terrorists targeted the World Trade Center, whose very name they took as a standing challenge and reproof). American national interests have no meaning in isolation. Alliances, treaties, international laws, courts, and agencies are not an alternative to na-tional security—they are its only hope. The rest is showy hardware and vain boasting. Will the present administration grasp this uncomfortable truth? I don't know, but I fear that it won't. It may be left to a future American leader, even to a new generation, to seize the full measure of this national disaster. There is a frightening, rubble-strewn emptiness where those proud towers stood just yesterday. A new era has begun.

Tony Judt, "New York Diarist: Burst," *The New Republic,* September 24, 2001

Selection 4   Lance Morrow is a columnist for *Time* covering national affairs.

For once, let's have no "grief counselors" standing by with banal consolations, as if the purpose, in the midst of all this, were merely to make everyone feel better as quickly as possible. We shouldn't feel better.

For once, let's have no fatuous rhetoric about "healing." Healing is inappropri-ate now, and dangerous. There will be time later for the tears of sorrow.

A day cannot live in infamy without the nourishment of rage. Let's have rage.

What's needed is a unified, unifying, Pearl Harbor sort of purple American fury—a ruthless indignation that doesn't leak away in a week or two, wander-ing off into Prozac-induced forgetfulness or into the next media sensation (O. J. . . . Elián . . . Chandra . . .) or into a corruptly thoughtful relativism (as has happened in the recent past, when, for example, you might hear some-one say, "Terrible what he did, of course, but, you know, the Unabomber does have a point, doesn't he, about modern technology?").

Let America explore the rich reciprocal possibilities of the *fatwa*. A policy of focused brutality does not come easily to a self-conscious, self-indulgent, contradictory, diverse, humane nation with a short attention span. America needs to relearn a lost discipline, self-confident relentlessness–and to relearn why human nature has equipped us all with a weapon (abhorred in decent peacetime societies) called hatred.

As the bodies are counted, into the thousands and thousands, hatred will not, I think, be a difficult emotion to summon. Is the medicine too strong? Call it, rather, a wholesome and intelligent enmity—the sort that impels even such a prosperous, messily tolerant organism as America to act. Anyone who does not loathe the people who did these things, and the people who cheer them on, is too philosophical for decent company.

It's a practical matter, anyway. In war, enemies are enemies. You find them and put them out of business, on the sound principle that that's what they are trying to do to you. If what happened on Tuesday does not give Americans the political will needed to exterminate men like Osama bin Laden and those who conspire with them in evil mischief, then nothing ever will and we are in for a procession of black Tuesdays.

This was terrorism brought to near perfection as a dramatic form. Never has the evil business had such production values. Normally, the audience sees only the smoking aftermath—the blown-up embassy, the ruined barracks, the ship with a blackened hole at the waterline. This time the first plane striking the first tower acted as a shill. It alerted the media, brought cameras to the scene so that they might be set up to record the vivid surreal bloom of the second strike ("Am I seeing this?") and then—could they be such engineering geniuses, so deft at demolition?—the catastrophic collapse of the two towers, one after the other, and a sequence of panic in the streets that might have been shot for a remake of *The War of the Worlds* or for *Independence Day.* Evil possesses an instinct for theater, which is why, in an era of gaudy and gifted media, evil may vastly magnify its damage by the power of horrific images.

It is important not to be transfixed. The police screamed to the people running from the towers, "Don't look back!"—a biblical warning against the power of the image. Terrorism is sometimes described (in a frustrated, oh-the-burdens-of-great-power tone of voice) as "asymmetrical warfare." So what? Most of history is a pageant of asymmetries. It is mostly the asymmetries that cause history to happen—an obscure Schickelgruber nearly destroys Europe; a mere atom, artfully diddled, incinerates a city. Elegant perplexity puts too much emphasis on the "asymmetrical" side of the phrase and not enough on the fact that it is, indeed, real warfare. Asymmetry is a concept. War is, as we see, blood and death.

It is not a bad idea to repeat a line from the 19th century French anarchist thinker Pierre-Joseph Proudhon: "The fecundity of the unexpected far exceeds the prudence of statesmen." America, in the spasms of a few hours, became a changed country. It turned the corner, at last, out of the 1990s. The menu of American priorities was rearranged. The presidency of George W. Bush begins now. What seemed important a few days ago (in the media, at least) became instantly trivial. If Gary Condit is mentioned once in the six months on cable television, I will be astonished.

During World War II, John Kennedy wrote home to his parents from the Pacific. He remarked that Americans are at their best during very good times or very bad times; the in-between periods, he thought, cause them trouble. I'm not sure that is true. Good times sometimes have a tendency to make Americans squalid.

The worst times, as we see, separate the civilized of the world from the uncivilized. This is the moment of clarity. Let the civilized toughen up, and let the uncivilized take their chances in the game they started.

Lance Morrow, "The Case for Rage and Retribution," *Time,* September 11, 2001

Selection 5 Based in the newspaper's Paris bureau, Frank Viviano is a staff writer on foreign affairs for the *San Francisco Chronicle.*

PARIS—At 8:45 a.m. on a brilliantly clear Tuesday morning in New York, a fatal combination of history, ignorance and power caught up with America. Thousands have probably died as a result. What remains to be seen is whether the same combination will now prove fatal to thousands more.

Unprecedented power has brought the United States into the daily lives of nearly everyone on Earth—and into their nations' often tortured histories. Yet as we have grown ever more powerful since the collapse of the Soviet Union, economically and militarily, we have also grown ever more ignorant of the world beyond our borders.

We are ignorant, especially, of the awful weight of that world's unresolved history, and our inevitable enmeshment in it. That is the starting point for understanding why so much of the Islamic world appears to detest the United States, to the point of cold, inhumanly calculated suicide assaults on countless innocent victims. Nothing can excuse such assaults. But neither can our blindness be excused.

The weight of history is oppressively evident in the tortured relationship between Israelis, the principal recipients of U.S. military aid, and the Palestinians with whom they are now at war. In the small corner of the planet they must share, the unresolved memory of the Jewish Holocaust meets the unresolved crisis of the Palestinian diaspora. The explosions in New York and Washington were ignited in that moral standoff.

Whoever planned and carried them out, the Israeli-Palestinian struggle is at their core. Americans, however, haven't begun to grapple with that history and its larger implications.

There is no shortage of culprits for our collective ignorance. "When I began teaching 20 years ago, our seniors were taken through an entire course of world history up to the year in which they graduated," says Mariann Nogrady, a faculty member at the prestigious Newton Highlands High School in suburban Boston.

Now, after funding cutbacks and a reordering of priorities, she says, "we're lucky if we get through U.S. history, let alone to the Civil War."

Our president, who professes pride in his lack of worldliness, has determinedly avoided serious engagement in foreign affairs, at the very moment when Washington's hand in the Mideast is critical.

American newspapers and television stations have all but abandoned any commitment to international coverage. The most powerful nation in modern history has become an ostrich with its head in the sand.

In the last days of the Bosnian war, a young couple, both of them U.S. Air Force officers, were traveling by train to Paris. She was a ground analyst with a graduate degree from Duke University. He was an F-16 pilot, educated at the Air Force Academy, participating in the NATO assault on the Bosnian Serb Republic. "Now this place Sarajevo," he asked another American passenger, "is it a country? Or is it just a city?"

America has a fondness for oversimplification. Most Israelis, in dress and lifestyle, resemble us. Most Muslims do not. The Arab-Israeli conflict, in mainstream American perception, pits a civilized, democratic state—born of the Holocaust, the 20th century's most heinous crime and the moral bulwark of Israel's existence—against barbaric tribes under the leadership of satanic monsters. Osama bin Laden today, following on the heels of Saddam Hussein of Iraq, Moammar Khadafy of Libya, Hafez Assad of Syria and the Ayatollah Khomeini in Iran.

Each of these leaders has deserved our informed contempt and level-headed hostility. But the reality of their societies is infinitely more complex. It is partially to be found in the images that galvanize ordinary Arabs and help keep them under the sway of despots: children confronting tanks and missile-equipped Israeli helicopters with stones, Jewish "settlers" consuming hundreds of square miles of Arab land in the Occupied Territories—with the consent of no authority apart from that of the Israeli government and the acquiescence of Washington.

In 1996, during a spate of suicide bombings in Israel, a Palestinian official living in the West Bank hills between Jerusalem and Ramallah asked, "Do you know what it means that four consecutive generations have lived here?" His squalid refugee camp was within walking distance of Israeli settlers' walled ranch-home subdivisions.

Two generations held onto the hope that they would once again see the land where they were raised," he said. The next was raised in the camp and lost hope." He paused, then went on: "As for the fourth generation, even I am afraid of them."

At that time, almost all of the bombers had come from the area around Ramallah. Five years and many "targeted assassinations" later, a far more lethal generation of martyrs has emerged, across the Islamic crescent from Algeria to Afghanistan, with New York City and Washington, as its latest targets.

The enveloping despair, the erosion of human values, are neither a sudden development nor a permanent feature of Arab life. This is a disaster that has been evolving, building, for four generations.

Now we appear ready to unleash our vast power on some part of the Muslim world. A world that recalls the past much more vividly, and remembers the fact that radical Muslims like Osama bin Laden and his followers were trained and armed by the United States to fight the Russians in Afghanistan. That such retaliation may set in motion an endless exchange of atrocities haunts many people around the world today.

"My God, I hope that America will not allow this horrible event to drive the world into war," wrote Zhou Qiu-xiang, a Chinese travel agent, in an e-mail to *The Chronicle* from Southeast Asia.

"What will become of America if it takes revenge on other innocent civilians to make up for these deaths?" Danielle Morand, a French educator, asked in a phone call.

As if in reply, President Bush said: "We will make no distinction between those who carried out the attacks and those who harbor them."

Frank Viviano, "The High Price of Disengagement,"
San Francisco Chronicle, September 13, 2001

Critical Reading and the World Wide Web

CHAPTER OBJECTIVES

This final chapter of Part 4 examines the effects of the information revolution on critical reading skills. It ends with five exercises requiring you to practice these skills by doing an in-depth appraisal of some World Wide Web sites. Specifically, we look at these topics:

- Reading online versus reading print

- Search engines

- Websites for critical reading skills

- Websites for online reading

First, a warning: Some of the information you read in this chapter by, say, 2003, may sound as antiquated as doilies on tables or telephones with rotary dials. The Internet is changing so rapidly that even the most inventive technology can quickly become obsolete. A decade ago, in the early 1990s, no one had ever heard of 'zines, blogs, cable wireless modems, megabytes, gigabytes, terabytes, or pedabytes. I have tried to include in this chapter websites that are likely to remain accessible for the life of this edition. But the warning holds: URLs listed here may have moved, may have expired, or may contain the message "This URL cannot be found." In fact, the whole system of World Wide Web addresses may have changed by the time you read this.

■ READING ONLINE VERSUS READING PRINT

There is no question that the World Wide Web has truly revolutionized the way information is disseminated and retrieved; ironically, that advantage is also its main drawback. The Web has exacerbated the problem of information overload, and we may feel overwhelmed by the glut of information available to us. In addition, turning to the Web first, as many people now do, rather than to traditional research tools in the library as a source of information, requires new warnings. Despite the convenience of having information available with a single mouse click at any time of the day or night, there are crucial differences between reading material on the printed page and reading material on a computer screen. Here is a summary of these differences as I see them:

- *Reading print on the Web is more difficult than reading a printed text.* Researchers at Ohio State University found that college students who read essays on a computer screen "found the text harder to understand, less interesting and less persuasive than students who read the same essay on paper." These results were the same no matter how much computer experience students had. More information from this study can be read at this address: *www.ncpa.org/pi/edu/pd090700e.html,* "Reading Comprehension: Cellulose over Silicon," sponsored by the National Center for Policy Analysis.

- *Concentrating is more difficult.* There are two reasons for this problem: The colorful waving, blinking, flashing, or pulsating banner ads or other elements are distracting to the reader, just as they are meant to be. More important, the use of hyperlinks, the technique that allows the Web surfer to move from one link to another to another, and so on, is *antithetical to sustained reading* and, by extension, to concentration. The Web surfer zips from one site to the next, skimming and scanning, sampling here, clicking there. This is a different sort of reading! Only the most dedicated, focused reader can withstand the temptation not to move quickly from link to link.

- *Technology is seductive.* The novelty of finding what we are looking for on a website with blazing speed may cause us to suspend our critical judgment. That, coupled with the sheer quantity of material available on a subject, makes sorting out the good from the bad even more difficult. It takes concentration to ignore the dazzle and the glitz and to work through a series of sites until you find exactly what you want.

- *Editorial scrutiny is not a given.* Undoubtedly, the Internet has democratized information and expanded access to that information. However, the typical magazine or newspaper article, for example, is pored over by editors and copyeditors before it arrives in your mailbox or on the newsstand. But with the Web (except for those sites sponsored by media outlets, news organizations, and nonprofit or research organizations), editorial scrutiny and fact checking are not requirements. The reader has to perform his or her own scrutiny and check facts for accuracy.

- *The Web is a paradox, at once egalitarian and anarchistic.* Anyone can create a website; indeed, thousands of new sites are added each week. If you are experienced in navigating websites, you are aware that anyone with an opinion or interest—no matter how trustworthy, no matter how crackpot—can create a site, resulting in an overabundance of terrifically useful material—and an overabundance of junk. In essence, the Web represents an anarchic nation, with no rules or strictures as to what can be published. (The instances of sites that have been shut down are infinitesimal compared with the millions of sites available.) These twin characteristics—egalitarianism and anarchy—are at once the Web's greatest virtue (no censorship) and its greatest handicap (no external, objective analysis for fairness, bias, evidence, and the like).

All these factors demand that the critical reader be even more vigilant while reading and gathering information on the Web than while reading traditional print sources. Trying to sort out the fair from the unfair, the true from the false, takes time, skill, and a healthy skepticism. Unbiased information can be found on sites maintained by nonprofit public interest groups (for example, the League of Women Voters), and most organizations involved in political and social issues now maintain websites. The important point is this: The critical reading skills you studied in Chapters 8 and 9 with conventional reading material will also help you appraise Web material.

■ SEARCH ENGINES

When using search engines to locate material, take a few minutes to learn proper search techniques. Each one offers tips and suggestions for refining and narrowing searches. If you want to get information on the subject of speed reading, for example, most search engines suggest that you type the phrase in quotation marks to keep the two words together ("speed reading"); otherwise, you'll get a zillion sites on "speed" and another zillion on "reading." The following list of search engines is not meant to be comprehensive, but they are all highly regarded, and they all work a little differently. Spend some time with a few of them until you find the two or three that work best for you.

> **Popular Search Engines**
> *www.yahoo.com*
> *www.google.com*
> *www.altavista.com*
> *www.askjeeves.com*
> *www.northernlight.com*
> *www.lycos.com*
> *www.infoseek.go.com*
> *www.wired.com*

Another useful tool is the so-called meta search engine, which queries several search engines for information and presents a compilation of websites. This feature allows you to obtain information from a variety of regular search engines by visiting only one site. Following is a list of the most widely known meta search engines. Use them, evaluate them, and then decide which ones best fit your needs.

> **Meta Search Engines**
> *www.metacrawler.com/index.html*
> *www.dogpile.com*
> *www.vivisimo.com*
> *www.ixquick.com*
> *www.copernic.com/index.html*
> *www.teoma.com*

A more complete list of meta search engines along with helpful suggestions for using them is available at *www.lib.berkeley.edu/TeachingLib/ Guides/Internet/MetaSearch.html*.

■ WEBSITES FOR CRITICAL READING SKILLS

Three excellent sites sponsored by UCLA, St. Louis University, and Cornell University offer guidance for students doing Web research, whether for their own edification and amusement or for compiling research for other courses. Although the sites offer similar suggestions, each is worth looking at.

> *www.library.ucla.edu/libraries/college/help/critical/index.htm*
> *www.slu.edu/departments/english/research,* and
> *www.library.cornell.edu/okuref/research/skill26.htm* (In addition, go to the link on evaluating websites.)

When you are evaluating websites, all the skills you have already studied—establishing the authority of the writer, identifying claims, evaluating evidence, and recognizing instances of manipulative appeal, logical fallacies, and bias—come into play. But as noted earlier, using the Internet requires special scrutiny. Here are three questions to ask when appraising websites:

- *Who sponsors the site?*[1] Is the sponsor identified clearly? What does the organization stand for? For example, in Chapter 9, I recommended a website for learning logical fallacies—*www.nizkor.org,* the Nizkor Project. Clicking on the home page button reveals that the organization is dedicated to "the millions of Holocaust victims." (In Hebrew, *Nizkor* means "we will remember.") The home page is a good starting point for determining who sponsors a site if you are unsure.

- *Is the information current?* How frequently is the site updated? Is a date provided? Sometimes you scroll down to the very bottom of a site only to find out that what you assumed is current is really several years old.

- *Is the sponsor of the site trying to sell you something?* You may use a Web address looking for factual information only to discover that the site is touting a product. Health care sites are particularly prone to

---

[1]Familiarize yourself with the suffixes in Web addresses that designate the source: **.com** (commercial); **.edu** (college or university); **.org** (nonprofit organization); **.gov** (government). Additional suffixes have been approved to go into effect sometime in the future: **.aero** (airlines, airports, reservation systems); **.biz** (businesses); **.coop** (business cooperatives such as credit unions); **.info** (general use); **.museum** (accredited worldwide museums); **.name** (individuals); **.pro** (professionals such as doctors and attorneys).

disguises for what turns out to be pure marketing hype. The site may appear to provide unbiased information until you look further and discover that you are meant to send money for a newsletter or for a product. For example, when I used the search engine *www.metacrawler.com* to get information on insomnia (a common complaint of college students), the first 20 sites yielded only commercial outfits selling these products: self-help tapes, aromatherapy oils, magnetic devices, kava herbal sleep aids, dream capsules, and something called the Mediflow Water-Based Cervical Pillow—and not one site for unbiased information!

A recent study by the American Medical Association confirms this experience. The researchers found that the best medical advice online is available from government sites (specifically, from *www.nih.gov*). Other good medical sites are *www.intelihealth.com, www.medscapehealth.com,* and *www.mayoclinic.com.* Using standard research engines for health information results in "mountains of useless information, much of it advertising." (Quoted in Ulysses Torassa, "Federal Health Web Sites Best, Study Says," *San Francisco Chronicle,* May 23, 2001.)

Your campus library's reference desk is another good resource for information on evaluating websites.

■ WEBSITES FOR ONLINE READING

There is something wonderfully liberating about sitting at one's desk in Memphis or in the campus library in Des Moines and being able to find out what is going on in Seattle or Alaska or Bahrain. The Web offers everyone the opportunity to read information online for free.[2] In 1999 the *Columbia Journalism Review,* the publication of Columbia University's prestigious School of Journalism, published a list of the 26 best American newspapers. The complete list can be found at *www.cjr.org/year/99/6/bestchart.asp.* Here are the top 15 from the CJR list, along with their ranking, location, and ownership. I have included Internet addresses.

---

[2]Note: Most newspapers offer that day's content for free. However, the trend among some newspapers is to charge for reading archived material. *The New York Times* and the *Los Angeles Times* charge a small fee for reading articles; *The Wall Street Journal* interactive edition has some free material, but a subscription is required for complete online access.

RANK	NEWSPAPER	LOCATION	OWNERSHIP
1	*The New York Times* www.nytimes.com	New York, NY	New York Times
2	*The Washington Post* www.washingtonpost.com	Washington, DC	Washington Post
3	*The Wall Street Journal* public.wsj.com/home.html	New York, NY	Dow Jones
4	*Los Angeles Times* www.latimes.com	Los Angeles, CA	Times Mirror
5	*The Dallas Morning News* www.dallasnews.com	Dallas, TX	A. H. Belo
6 (tie)	*Chicago Tribune* www.chicagotribune.com	Chicago, IL	Tribune
6 (tie)	*The Boston Globe* www.boston.com/globe/	Boston, MA	New York Times
8	*San Jose Mercury News* www.bayarea.com	San Jose, CA	Knight Ridder
9	*St. Petersburg Times* www.stpetersburgtimes.com	St. Petersburg, FL	Independent
10	*The Sun* www.baltimoresun.com	Baltimore, MD	Times Mirror
11	*The Philadelphia Inquirer* www.inq.philly.com/mld/philly/	Philadelphia, PA	Knight Ridder
12 (tie)	*The Oregonian* www.oregonian.com	Portland, OR	Newhouse
12 (tie)	*USA Today* usatoday.com	Arlington, VA	Gannett
14	*The Seattle Times* seattletimes.com	Seattle, WA	Independent
15	*Newsday* www.newsday.com	Melville, NY (Long Island)	Times Mirror

Many major North American magazines and periodicals also have websites, which you can easily access by typing the name in the search box of your favorite search engine. Other publications, however, are strictly Web-based. Here are some of the popular ones:

- *www.salon.com*   Salon.com publishes essays, articles, commentary, book and movie reviews, and so forth.
- *www.slate.com*   Slate.com publishes a variety of articles on political and social issues.
- *www.wired.com*   Wired.com is another resource for current technological information.
- *www.cnn.com*   Cable News Network sponsors one of the best online sites for current events and news from around the nation and the world.
- *www.inside.com*   Inside.com received a Webby award (an award for websites) for its coverage of news.
- *www.theonion.com*   The Onion.com is an irreverent humor site, which has also won several Webby awards.
- *www.nationalgeographic.com*   This website, sponsored by the venerable National Geographic organization, is an excellent education resource.
- *www.aldaily.com*   Arts and Letters Daily is a comprehensive site devoted to the arts, cultural events, essays, commentary, reviews, and much more.

Do not be limited by this list. Come up with your own list of favorite periodical sites and 'zines.

■ EXERCISE 1: EVALUATING TWO ONLINE ARTICLES

At the end of Chapter 2, two Web-based studies were listed, which examined the problem of grade inflation:

- Bradford P. Wilson, PhD, "The Phenomenon of Grade Inflation in Higher Education," Meeting of the Governor's Blue Ribbon Commission on Higher Education, Longwood College, Farmville, VA, April 1999. *www.frontpagemag.com/archives/academia/wilson04-13-99.htm*
- Harvey C. Mansfield, "Grade Inflation: It's Time to Face the Facts," *The Chronicle of Higher Education,* April 6, 2001. *chronicle.com/free/v47/i30/30b02401.htm*

Type these two URLs into your browser, print the articles, annotate them if you wish, and then, on a separate sheet of paper, answer the following questions:

1. Who are the authors? Is their affiliation clearly indicated? Do they appear to be authorities on the subject?
2. State in your own words the argument each writer puts forth.
3. What type of evidence does each article rely on to support the claim? Does the evidence meet the criteria discussed in Chapter 8? Is it fair, accurate, sufficient, and relevant?
4. List two or three supporting points the authors use.
5. Does either writer present a refutation, an examination of opposing views?
6. Is the argument, as the author presents it, convincing or at least worth considering?
7. Do you accept each argument? Why or why not? What other information do you need? How do these writers' observations accord with your own experience with grading standards in college?
8. Which writer does a better job of presenting his case?

■ **EXERCISE 2:** EVALUATING THREE POLITICAL PARTIES' WEBSITES

This exercise gives you an opportunity to evaluate official party sites for the Democratic, Republican, and Libertarian political parties. Access the three sites whose addresses are listed below. Then analyze each site by taking brief notes on the following features:

- Layout of page and ease of navigation
- An explanation of the party's mission
- Positions on major issues of the day
- Appeals to join and to give money
- News of the day's events
- Daily updates
- Appeals to patriotic sentiment
- Promotional visual images

www.democrats.org (Democratic National Committee)
www.rnc.org (Republican National Committee)
www.lp.org (Libertarian Party)

■ **EXERCISE 3:** APPRAISING WEBSITES ON A HEALTH OR AN ENVIRONMENTAL ISSUE

Using two or three search engines (or a meta search engine), gather information on one of these current issues (or come up with your own). However, for purposes of this exercise, it would be better to avoid issues involving morality or one's belief system, for example, abortion, the death penalty, or gay marriage.

- The effects of global warming in Antarctica
- The environmental effects of drilling for oil in Alaska's Arctic National Wildlife Refuge
- The medicinal uses of marijuana for treating the side effects of cancer and glaucoma
- Mercury poisoning in tooth fillings: fact or urban legend?
- The scientific benefits of performing research on stem cells derived from human embryos
- St. John's Wort as a medicinal aid to combat depression
- Mad cow disease and its threat to North American livestock

Look through a number of sites. Then list three or four that appear to present impartial information (and that aren't selling something). In addition, list the sponsor, the sponsor's authority to convey the information, and the date the site was last updated. Next, list three or four sites that you would *not* use. Briefly explain why.

■ **EXERCISE 4:** RESEARCHING A CONTROVERSIAL ISSUE

Should athletic teams use the names of Indian tribes as their mascots? The New York State Education Department recently issued a statement asking public schools to drop the use of American Indian mascots. Several years ago Stanford University changed the name of its football team from the Indians to the Cardinals, and the University of Illinois continues to debate retiring its mascot, Chief Illiniwek. In response to complaints by Native American groups, high school teams have dropped names such as Cherokee, Sequoia, and Apache as their mascots. Your task in this exercise is to assemble arguments for and against using Indian names for team mascots. A good place to start is these two websites *earnestman.tripod.com* (the American Indian Sports Team Mascots website) and *www.tolerance.org/images_action/08_intro.html.* Then click on "Dig Deeper." This site is sponsored by Tolerance.org, an organization dedicated to promoting tolerance and stopping hate crimes.

■ EXERCISE 5: ANALYZING RICHARD NIXON'S "CHECKERS" SPEECH

On September 23, 1952, Republican senator Richard Nixon delivered what has come to be known as the "Checkers" speech. Dwight D. Eisenhower, Republican presidential candidate, had chosen the young Nixon, then a senator from California, to be his vice-presidential running mate. Shortly after he was chosen, the *New York Post* ran an article titled, "Secret Rich Men's Trust Fund Keeps Nixon in Style Far beyond His Salary." Nixon was accused of receiving money from a secret slush fund sponsored by some of his rich California backers. Republicans demanded that Nixon be removed from the ticket; in response, Nixon took his case to the American people, using what was then the new medium of television. In a nationally televised speech, Nixon defended his actions and attacked the opposition.

"Checkers" refers to a black-and-white cocker spaniel that a supporter had given Nixon's two young daughters, which Nixon said the family intended to keep. This speech has long been a case study for college students enrolled in communications and critical thinking courses. It is a masterpiece of slanting, innuendo, manipulative appeals, and errors in reasoning. Access the "Checkers" speech from either of these two websites:

- *www.pbs.org/wgbh/amex/presidents/nf/resource/eisen/primdocs/ checkers.html*
- *www.watergate.info/nixon/checkers-speech.shtml*

In your evaluation, look for generalizations, appeals to the emotions, false cause–effect thinking, false analogy, begging the question, and non sequiturs.

Reading Essays and Articles

OUTLINE

■ INTRODUCTION TO READING ESSAYS

Why Read Essays in the First Place?

The essay is the staple of college courses where the assigned textbook is an anthology. The essay form has several advantages: It is short, it can be read in one sitting, and it can be discussed in one or two class meetings. Students acquire analytical tools more easily by studying short pieces of nonfiction prose, which they can then transfer to book-length works.

In my experience teaching both reading and composition, many students are unsure of their instructors' expectations with essay assignments. Part 5 will give you ample practice in various essay-reading skills. You will learn a great deal from your reading assignments if you allow sufficient time to complete each assignment. The truism that practice makes perfect surely applies here. The more experience you get reading your assignments attentively, the more competent you will become and the more you will enjoy preparing your assignments. An added bonus might be higher grades. There is no advantage in *not* reading. Students who seldom read on their own, who speed through their assignments, or who sit in the back of the classroom or look down, pretending to be engrossed in the text and hoping to avoid being called on, miss a significant part of the college experience.

The Characteristics of an Essay

If the paragraph is an essay in miniature, as it has often been described, then the essay exemplifies the techniques and characteristics that you studied in Chapters 1 through 5 in Parts 1 and 2. The essay form derives from the seventeenth-century French writer Michel de Montaigne. His short pieces were an *attempt* to explain his observations of human behavior and customs. (In French, the verb *essayer* means "to attempt," and an essay—*un essai*—pertains to the work itself.) Today an **essay** describes a sustained piece of nonfiction prose with a myriad of purposes and characteristics. Like the paragraph, an essay contains or suggests a main idea, which is called the **thesis**; the essay has a direction; and it has development, unity, and coherence. Unlike the paragraph, however, whose short length limits its scope, the essay is more varied in length, organization, and methods of development. Typically, essays published by professional writers run between 500 and 5,000 words, but length is not an important criterion for defining the form.

Essays may be personal narrative, a description of a scene or an emotion, a presentation of scientific information, a personal confession, an emotional plea to resolve a controversy, a satire on a practice or custom that the writer wants to mock, an explanation of a social or political issue, or an examination of a problem and its repercussions. In short, the essay is infinitely adaptable. It may represent any of the four modes of discourse—narration, description, exposition, or persuasion—singly or in combination, although one mode usually predominates. If you recall the practice essays you read in Parts 1, 2, and 3, you can see that the form is a diverse instrument for communicating ideas.

The remarks of two professional writers shed further light on the essay form. In *A Writer's Companion,* Richard Marius says that the essay "inevitably has about it the scent of argument," by which he means that even in narrative and descriptive essays, there is an underlying persuasive intent. In the introduction to *Best American Essays 1993,* Joseph Epstein wrote this perceptive comment about essays:

> I prefer it when the essay takes a small, very particular subject and, through the force of the essayist's artistically controlled maunderings, touches on unpredictably large general matters, makes hitherto unexpected connections, tells me things I hadn't hitherto known, or reminds me of other things I have always known but never thought to formulate so well as has the essayist I am reading at the moment.

The Parts of an Essay

An essay can be divided into three parts: the beginning (the introduction); the middle (the body or supporting paragraphs); and the end (the conclusion). We will look at these structural parts one by one. Try to separate each essay you read into these parts by asking at what point the introduction ends and the body paragraphs begin and at what point the body paragraphs give way to the conclusion. The importance of this skill cannot be emphasized enough. Rather than drowning in a sea of words, seeing the logical progression of ideas will help you distinguish the main points from the support. Often, making a brief outline of the component parts will help you see the overall structure, just as an aerial view of a city reveals its layout better than a ground-level view does. And annotating while you read, demonstrated later in this section, allows you to master the content.

The Introduction

All writing teachers tell their students that the opening paragraph of their essays should grab the reader's attention, that they should use some sort of hook to entice the reader to continue reading. Beginning college *readers* should be aware of these devices as well. There are no particular rules governing the hook—only the writer's estimation of how best to get into the subject. The introduction may directly state the essay's **thesis**—the main idea—or it may merely be suggested, in which case the thesis is **implied.** Few professional writers use the obvious direct-announcement approach to a thesis.

Given the diverse form of the essay, finding the thesis poses some difficulty because writers are under no obligation to adhere to a formula. Where should you look for the thesis? A writer may provide a thesis somewhere near the beginning of the essay, often following an opening paragraph or two (which provides the hook), introducing the general subject, setting the scene, establishing a problem to be solved—in other words, orienting us to the topic. These paragraphs may include a personal anecdote or a short narrative, they may provide historical background, or they may present a thorny issue or problem. The techniques at the writer's disposal are many and varied. After this section, the writer *may* state a thesis. (Some textbooks call this the funnel pattern.) But don't expect a bell to sound when you reach the thesis. Few writers announce that a particular sentence is meant to represent the main idea.

Practice Exercises To test your reading acumen, I selected six introductions from three essay anthologies in my bookshelves: *The Best American Essays 1993, The Best American Essays 1996,* and a widely used college anthology, *The Best American Essays.*[1] Read each excerpt carefully. Then do the following: First, write the mode of discourse (narration, description, exposition, or persuasion) that you predict will occur in the essay as a whole. If you are unsure, write a question mark. Second, write the thesis statement or main idea, if one is represented. If there is no thesis stated or implied, write a question mark.

The deserts of southern California, the high, relatively cooler and wetter Mojave and the hotter, dryer Sonoran to the south of it, carry the signatures of many cultures. Prehistoric rock drawings in the Mojave's Coso Range, probably the greatest concentration of petroglyphs in North America, are at least three thousand years old. Big-game-hunting cultures that flourished six or seven thousand years before that are known from broken spear tips, choppers, and burins left scattered along the shores of great Pleistocene lakes, long since evaporated. Weapons and tools discovered at China Lake may be thirty thousand years old; and worked stone from a quarry in the Calico Mountains is, some argue, evidence that human beings were here more than 200,000 years ago.

Because of the long-term stability of such arid environments, much of this prehistoric stone evidence still lies exposed on the ground, accessible to anyone who passes by—the studious, the acquisitive, the indifferent, the merely curious. Archaeologists do not agree on the sequence of cultural history beyond about twelve thousand years ago, but it is clear that these broken bits of chal-

---

[1] All are published by Houghton Mifflin. Each year this firm publishes a new volume in the *Best American Essays* series, compiled by a different guest editor. These anthologies are an excellent way to practice reading high-quality nonfiction prose.

cedony, chert, and obsidian, like the animal drawings and geometric designs etched on walls of basalt throughout the desert, anchor the earliest threads of human history, the first record of human endeavor here.

Barry Lopez, "The Stone Horse," *Antaeus*

Mode of discourse: _____

Thesis statement: _____

_____

I am not a scholar of English or literature. I cannot give you much more than personal opinions on the English language and its variations in this country or others.

I am a writer. And by that definition, I am someone who has always loved language. I am fascinated by language in daily life. I spend a great deal of my time thinking about the power of language—the way it can evoke an emotion, a visual image, a complex idea, or a simple truth. Language is the tool of my trade. And I use them all—all the Englishes I grew up with.

Amy Tan, "Mother Tongue," *The Threepenny Review*

Mode of discourse: _____

Thesis statement: _____

_____

I was thirty years old when I had my right nostril pierced, and back-home friends fell speechless at the news, lapsing into long telephone pauses of the sort that June Cleaver would employ if the Beave had ever called to report, "Mom, I'm married. His name's Eddie." Not that I resemble a Cleaver or have friends who wear pearls in the shower, but people who have known me the longest would say that for me to *draw* attention to my body rather than to work all out to *repel* it is at least as out of character as the Beave's abrupt urge for his-and-his golf ensembles. A nose ring, they might tell you, would be my last choice for a fashion accessory, way down on the list with a sag-enhancing specialty bra or a sign on my butt reading "Wide Load."

The fact is, I grew up ugly—no, worse than that, I grew up *unusual,* that unforgivable sin among youth. We lived in Alaska, where, despite what you might have heard about the Rugged Individualist, teenagers still adhere to the universal rules of conformity: If Popular Patty wears contact lenses, then you will by gum get contacts too, or else pocket those glasses and pray you can distinguish the girls' bathroom door from the boys'. The bad news was that I had only one eye, having lost the other in a dog attack at age seven; so although contacts, at half the two-eyed price, were easy to talk my parents into, I was still left with an eye patch and many facial scars, signs as gaudy as neon, telling everyone, "Here is a girl who is Not Like You." And Not Like Them, remember, was equivalent to Not from This Dimension, only half (maybe one third) as interesting.

Natalie Kusz, "Ring Leader," *Allure*

Mode of discourse: _____

Thesis statement: _____

_____

The time has come to rethink wilderness.

This will seem a heretical claim to many environmentalists, since the idea of wilderness has for decades been a fundamental tenet—indeed, a passion—of the environmental movement, especially in the United States. For many Americans wilderness stands as the last remaining place where civilization, that all too human disease, has not fully infected the earth. It is an island in the polluted sea of urban-industrial modernity, the one place we can turn for escape from our own too-muchness. Seen in this way, wilderness presents itself as the best antidote to our human selves, a refuge we must somehow recover if we hope to save the planet. As Henry David Thoreau once famously declared, "In Wildness is the preservation of the World."

William Cronon, "The Trouble with Wilderness," *Environmental History*

Mode of discourse: _____

Thesis statement: _____

_____

When my mother began using the electronic pump that fed her liquids and medication, we moved her to the family room. The bedroom she shared with my father was upstairs, and it was impossible to carry the machine up and down all day and night. The pump itself was attached to a metal stand on casters, and she pulled it along wherever she went. From anywhere in the house, you could hear the sound of the wheels clicking out a steady time over the grout lines of the slate-tiled foyer, her main thoroughfare to the bathroom and the kitchen. Sometimes you would hear her halt after only a few steps, to catch her breath or steady her balance, and whatever you were doing was instantly suspended by a pall of silence.

I was usually in the kitchen, preparing lunch or dinner, poised over the butcher block with her favorite chef's knife in my hand and her old yellow apron slung around my neck. I'd be breathless in the sudden quiet, and, having ceased my mincing and chopping, would stare blankly at the brushed sheen of the blade. Eventually, she would clear her throat or call out to say she was fine, then begin to move again, starting her rhythmic *ka-jug;* and only then could I go on with my cooking, the world of our house turning once more, wheeling through the black.

Chang-Rae Lee, "Coming Home Again," The New Yorker

Mode of discourse: _____

Thesis statement: _____

_____

A personality disorder is one of the more troubling diagnoses a mental health clinician can give to someone seeking relief from suffering, because unlike a neurosis, viewed as a set of curable symptoms, or a psychosis, increasingly believed to be the result of a trigger-happy brain in need of mere medication, the personality disordered individual is seen as close to hopeless, beyond the reach of either drugs or healing dialogue. The man or woman with such a diagnosis is thought of as a kind of blighted being, the udder of a cow on the belly of a gazelle, flippers on the side of a skunk. What can you do with this mishmash except try to soothe its confused cries?

George came to our clinic in early autumn and was diagnosed by the intake worker with an antisocial personality disorder—in short, a sociopath, a deviant—whom I, a newcomer to the field of psychology, was now assigned to work with in therapy for an undefined period of time. He looked almost ridiculously tough, sitting in a sleeveless leather vest in the clinic's lobby, hair scrunched back in a ponytail, a cigarette dangling from his mouth. Tattoos coiled over his arms, bloomed on his bare chest.

Lauren Slater, "Striptease," New Letters

Mode of discourse: _____

Thesis statement: _____

_____

The Body Paragraphs

The supporting paragraphs constitute the bulk of the essay, developing and exploring the thesis and its implications by whatever methods the writer considers appropriate. You might want to review the methods of development and organizational patterns in Chapters 3, 4, and 5, because body paragraphs very likely will employ many of these elements. As each paragraph moves the ideas forward, writers use these devices to ensure coherence: *transitions,* both within as well as between paragraphs; *parallel phrases, clauses, or sentences;* and *repetition of key words or phrases.* The careful writer also organizes the body paragraphs logically, typically arranging them in a least-important to most-important order, especially in persuasive writing.

The Conclusion

An essay's conclusion is usually short—perhaps only a paragraph or two. To find the conclusion, look for the spot where the supporting ideas give way to a summary, a restatement of the main idea, a logical deduction to be drawn from the evidence, a solution or recommendation, a warning for the future, or a challenge. The conclusion's form and length depend on the purpose, subject, and audience.

How to Read an Essay	Armed with this overview of the essay's characteristics and form, you can now tackle your assigned readings. The following suggestions constitute what your English teachers ideally hope their students will do to prepare for class discussion. For each assignment, set aside a minimum of an hour to prepare, perhaps two hours if the essay is long or difficult. First, read the essay through without stopping. Be sure to read with a pencil in your hand, and annotate the text like this: Note the main points with a symbol like asterisks or stars; write a question mark for material that you do not understand, that needs clarification, or that you disagree with; and underline or circle new words to look up during the second reading.

Then read the piece again, more slowly the second time, to put the pieces together. Of course, during this reading you should look up any troublesome words and allusions. While you are reading, consider the questions listed below. When you are done, review these questions to see if you can answer them in your own words. If something eludes your understanding, make a note of it so that you can raise the point in class discussion. This process allows you to be responsible for your own learning and to master a most worthwhile skill—the ability to analyze difficult prose, which will serve you well in all your academic courses.

■ ANALYZING ESSAYS: QUESTIONS TO ASK

Although your other English texts may provide discussion or critical thinking questions after each selection, the questions below are extensive and versatile enough for any reading in any course. They constitute the sorts of things your instructors want you to look for when you read. Eventually, the process will become automatic and you will not have to refer to them before each assignment.

1. Who is the author? In most anthologies, as in this text, the writer is identified by a brief biographical source note or headnote. This information helps you determine the writer's authority to write, intended audience, purpose in writing, and point of view or possible bias.

2. This question follows from the first: Who is the audience? Are the writer's ideas aimed toward the general reading public, or does the vocabulary suggest that the writer is appealing to a narrower group with specialized knowledge? What clues does the author provide that identify for whom he or she is writing? If the piece comes from a magazine or periodical, is it a mainstream vehicle, such as *Time, Newsweek, The New Yorker,* or *Vanity Fair,* or is it a source apt to appeal to a more specialized audience, for example, *Scientific American, Mother Jones, Yankee Magazine,* or *Foreign Affairs?*

3. What is the writer's purpose? Remember that purpose is closely related to mode of discourse. Is there a secondary purpose as well?

4. What is the thesis? Where is it located? Is its placement appropriate for the writer's purpose and subject? Can you restate the thesis in your own words?

5. What are the main parts of the essay? Note the divisions between introduction, body, and conclusion. How do these parts fit together?

6. Because we read to learn new information, what did you learn? What are the essay's main ideas? What are the major supporting points for the thesis?

7. What inferences did you draw? What conclusions? What has the essay done to educate you about the world? How do the essay's ideas accord with what you already know? What further information do you need?

8. Aside from unfamiliar words—which you should add to your vocabulary notebook, as suggested in Part 1—are any words used in unusual ways? Are there any metaphors or similes? Any strongly connotative words? Is the writer's word choice appropriate for the purpose, audience, and content?

To demonstrate a practical application of these remarks, we will now analyze a classic essay, which has been reprinted in countless English anthologies.

■ *PRACTICE ESSAY*

Sex, Drugs, Disasters, and the Extinction of the Dinosaurs

Stephen Jay Gould

© Wally McNamee/Corbis.

Stephen Jay Gould was the consummate scientific writer on the topic of evolution. After receiving his PhD from Columbia University in 1967, he taught geology and zoology at Harvard University. In addition, he served as curator of invertebrate paleontology for Harvard's Museum of Comparative Zoology. His most recent book is The Structure of Evolutionary Theory. *His 1989 essay "The Creation Myths of Cooperstown" was selected for inclusion in* The Best American Essays of the Century. *The essay reprinted here, however, is perhaps his most famous. It is reprinted from* The Flamingo's Smile *(1985). His ostensible subject is the extinction of the dinosaurs, but as you will see, his primary purpose is to distinguish between good science and bad. The essay has been annotated for you.*

Science: a mode of inquiry, not a list of enticing conclusions

1   Science, in its most fundamental definition, is a fruitful mode of inquiry, not a list of enticing conclusions. The conclusions are the consequence, not the essence.

Conclusions: the consequence of science, not its essence

2   My greatest unhappiness with most popular presentations of science concerns their failure to separate fascinating claims from the methods that scientists use to establish the facts of nature. Journalists, and the public, thrive on controversial and stunning statements. But science is, basically, a way of knowing—in P. B. Medawar's apt words, "the art of the soluble." If the growing corps of popular science writers would focus on *how* scientists develop and defend those fascinating claims, they would make their greatest possible contribution to public understanding.

Scientific writing should focus on how scientists develop claims, not on the claims themselves

Science is a way of knowing

3   Consider three ideas, proposed in perfect seriousness to explain that greatest of all titillating puzzles—the extinction of dinosaurs. Since these three notions invoke the primally fascinating themes of

A case in point: of 3 popular theories on extinction of dinosaurs, 2 are silly & only 1 is useful

our culture—sex, drugs, and violence—they surely reside in the category of fascinating claims. I want to show why two of them rank as silly speculation, while the other represents science at its grandest and most useful.

4   Science works with testable proposals. If, after much compilation and scrutiny of data, new information continues to affirm a hypothesis, we may accept it provisionally and gain confidence as further evidence mounts. We can never be completely sure that a hypothesis is right, though we may be able to show with confidence that it is wrong. The best scientific hypotheses are also generous and expansive: they suggest extensions and implications that enlighten related, and even far distant, subjects. Simply consider how the idea of evolution has influenced virtually every intellectual field.

Scientific proposals must be "testable"

Good scientific hypothesis—capable of expansion: suggest extensions & implications: evolution is good ex.

5   Useless speculation, on the other hand, is restrictive. It generates no testable hypothesis, and offers no way to obtain potentially refuting evidence. Please note that I am not speaking of truth or falsity. The speculation may well be true; still, if it provides, in principle, no material for affirmation or rejection, we can make nothing of it. It must simply stand forever as an intriguing idea. Useless speculation turns in on itself and leads nowhere; good science, containing both seeds for its potential refutation and implications for more and different testable knowledge, reaches out. But, enough preaching. Let's move on to dinosaurs, and the three proposals for their extinction.

Opposite is useless speculation: goes nowhere & can't be tested

3 theories for demise of dinosaurs

1. Sex: Testes function only in a narrow range of temperature (those of mammals hang externally in a scrotal sac because internal body temperatures are too high for their

1. sex (testes stopped working)

proper function). A worldwide rise in temperature at the close of the Cretaceous period caused the testes of dinosaurs to stop functioning and led to their extinction by sterilization of males.

2. Drugs: (Angiosperms)(flowering plants) first evolved toward the end of the dinosaurs' reign. Many of these plants contain psychoactive agents, avoided by mammals today as a result of their bitter taste. Dinosaurs had neither means to taste the bitterness nor livers effective enough to detoxify the substances. They died of massive overdoses.

3. Disasters: A large comet or asteroid struck the earth some 65 million years ago, lofting a cloud of dust into the sky and blocking sunlight, thereby suppressing photosynthesis and so drastically lowering world temperatures that dinosaurs and hosts of other creatures became extinct.

6   Before analyzing these three tantalizing statements, we must establish a basic ground rule often violated in proposals for the dinosaurs' demise. *There is no separate problem of the extinction of dinosaurs.* Too often we divorce specific events from their wider contexts and systems of cause and effect. The fundamental fact of dinosaur extinction is its synchrony with the demise of so many other groups across a wide range of habitats, from terrestrial to marine.

7   The history of life has been punctuated by brief episodes of mass extinction. A recent analysis by University of Chicago paleontologists Jack Sepkoski and Dave Raup, based on the best and most exhaustive tabulation of data ever assembled, shows clearly that five episodes of mass dying stand well above

5 periods of mass extinctions; Cretaceous era is important b/c plankton died suddenly, also ammonites (like squid); dinosaurs disappeared after 100 m. years of "unchallenged domination"

the "background" extinctions of normal times (when we consider all mass extinctions, large and small, they seem to fall in a regular 26-million-year cycle). . . . The Cretaceous debacle, occurring 65 million years ago and separating the Mesozoic and Cenozoic eras of our geological time scale, ranks prominently among the five. Nearly all the marine plankton (single-celled floating creatures) died with geological suddenness; among marine invertebrates, nearly 15 percent of all families perished, including many previously dominant groups, especially the ammonites (relatives of squids in coiled shells). On land, the dinosaurs disappeared after more than 100 million years of unchallenged domination.

Wrong to limit speculation to dinosaurs alone; need "coordinated explanation for a system of events"

8   In this context, speculations limited to dinosaurs alone ignore the larger phenomenon. We need a coordinated explanation for a system of events that includes the extinction of dinosaurs as one component. Thus it makes little sense, though it may fuel our desire to view mammals as inevitable inheritors of the earth, to guess that dinosaurs died because small mammals ate their eggs (a perennial favorite among untestable speculations). It seems most likely that some disaster peculiar to dinosaurs befell these massive beasts—and that the debacle happened to strike just when one of history's five great dyings had enveloped the earth for completely different reasons.

Testicular theory from '40s

Theory based on study of alligators & effects of high temps. on animal's ability to keep warm

9   The testicular theory, an old favorite from the 1940s, had its root in an interesting and thoroughly respectable study of temperature tolerances in the American alligator, published in the staid *Bulletin of the American Museum of Natural History* in 1946 by three experts on living and fossil reptiles—E.H. Colbert, my own first teacher in paleontology; R. B. Cowles; and C. M. Bogert.

10   The first sentence of their summary reveals a purpose beyond alligators: "This report describes an attempt to infer the reactions of extinct reptiles, especially the dinosaurs, to high temperatures as based upon reactions observed in the modern alligator." They studied, by rectal thermometry, the body temperatures of alligators under changing conditions of heating and cooling. (Well, let's face it, you wouldn't want to try sticking a thermometer under a 'gator's tongue.) The predictions under test go way back to an old theory first stated by Galileo in the 1630s—the unequal scaling of surfaces and volumes. As an animal, or any object, grows (provided its shape doesn't change), surface areas must increase more slowly than volumes—since surfaces get larger as length squared, while volumes increase much more rapidly, as length cubed. Therefore, small animals have high ratios of surface to volume, while large animals cover themselves with relatively little surface.

Large animals stay warm more easily than small animals b/c of relation btn surface area and volume

11   Among cold-blooded animals lacking any physiological mechanism for keeping their temperatures constant, small creatures have a hell of a time keeping warm—because they lose so much heat through their relatively large surfaces. On the other hand, large animals, with their relatively small surfaces, may lose heat so slowly that, once warm, they may maintain effectively constant temperatures against ordinary fluctuations of climate. (In fact, the resolution of the "hot-blooded dinosaur" controversy that burned so brightly a few years back may simply be that, while large dinosaurs possessed no physiological mechanism for constant temperature, and were not therefore warm-blooded in the technical sense, their large size and relatively small surface area kept them warm.)

Dinosaurs kept warm b/c of large size and low surface: temp. remained fairly constant: therefore, aren't like smaller alligators (basis of 1st theory)

12   Colbert, Cowles, and Bogert compared the warming rates of small and large alligators. As predicted, the small fellows heated up (and cooled down) more quickly. When exposed to a warm sun, a tiny 50-gram (1.76-ounce) alligator heated up one degree Celsius every minute and a half, while a large alligator, 260 times bigger at 13,000 grams (28.7 pounds), took seven and a half minutes to gain a degree. Extrapolating up to an adult 10-ton dinosaur, they concluded that a one-degree rise in body temperature would take eighty-six hours. If large animals absorb heat so slowly (through their relatively small surfaces), they will also be unable to shed any excess heat gained when temperatures rise above a favorable level.

13   The authors then guessed that large dinosaurs lived at or near their optimum temperatures; Cowles suggested that a rise in global temperatures just before the Cretaceous extinction caused the dinosaurs to heat up beyond their optimal tolerance—and, being so large, they couldn't shed the unwanted heat. (In a most unusual statement within a scientific paper, Colbert and Bogert then explicitly disavowed this speculative extension of their empirical work on alligators.) Cowles conceded that this excess heat probably wasn't enough to kill or even to enervate the great beasts, but since testes often function only within a narrow range of temperature, he proposed that this global rise might have sterilized all the males, causing extinction by natural contraception.

14   The overdose theory has recently been supported by UCLA psychiatrist Ronald K. Siegel. Siegel has gathered, he claims, more than 2,000 records of animals who, when given access, administer various drugs to themselves—from a mere swig of alcohol to massive doses of the big H. Elephants will swill the equivalent of

Study tried to prove temp. rise before Cretaceous extinction caused testicles to stop functioning; result was sterility

2nd theory: based on study of animals that deliberately use drug agents

What is the big H?

twenty beers at a time, but do not like alcohol in concentrations greater than 7 percent. In a silly bit of anthropocentric speculation, Siegel states that "elephants drink, perhaps, to forget . . . the anxiety produced by shrinking rangeland and the competition for food."

Dinosaurs ate flowering plants containing alkaloids (psychoactive agents)

15   Since fertile imaginations can apply almost any hot idea to the extinction of dinosaurs, Siegel found a way. Flowering plants did not evolve until late in the dinosaurs' reign. These plants also produced an array of aromatic, amino-acid-based alkaloids—the major group of psychoactive agents. Most mammals are "smart" enough to avoid these potential poisons. The alkaloids simply don't taste good (they are bitter); in any case, we mammals have livers happily supplied with the capacity to detoxify them. But, Siegel speculates, perhaps dinosaurs could neither taste the bitterness nor detoxify the substances once ingested. He recently told members of the American Psychological Association: "I'm not suggesting that all dinosaurs OD'd on plant drugs, but it certainly was a factor." He also argued that death by overdose may help explain why so many dinosaur fossils are found in contorted positions. (Do not go gentle into that good night.)

Though most animals avoid bitter foods, dinosaurs couldn't taste bitterness & their livers failed to detoxify bodies

What is this sentence in parentheses for? Maybe an allusion?

16   Extraterrestrial catastrophes have long pedigrees in the popular literature of extinction, but the subject exploded again in 1979, after a long lull, when the father-son, physicist-geologist team of Luis and Walter Alvarez proposed that an asteroid, some 10 km in diameter, struck the earth 65 million years ago (comets, rather than asteroids, have since gained favor. Good science is self-corrective).

3rd theory: Alvarezes proposed theory that giant asteroid or comet struck earth: caused huge dust cloud. Photosynthesis stopped, temps. dropped; result was deaths of marine & land animals

17   The force of such a collision would be immense, greater by far than the megatonnage of all the world's nuclear weapons. In trying to reconstruct a sce-

nario that would explain the simultaneous dying of dinosaurs on land and so many creatures in the sea, the Alvarezes proposed that a gigantic dust cloud, generated by particles blown aloft in the impact, would so darken the earth that photosynthesis would cease and temperatures drop precipitously. (Rage, rage against the dying of the light.) The single-celled photosynthetic oceanic plankton, with life cycles measured in weeks, would perish outright, but land plants might survive through the dormancy of their seeds (land plants were not much affected by the Cretaceous extinction, and any adequate theory must account for the curious pattern of differential survival). Dinosaurs would die by starvation and freezing; small, warm-blooded mammals, with more modest requirements for food and better regulation of body temperature, would squeak through. "Let the bastards freeze in the dark," as bumper stickers of our chauvinistic neighbors in sunbelt states proclaimed several years ago during the Northeast's winter oil crisis.

Land plants could survive b/c of seeds & also small animals; but not dinosaurs, who either starved or froze

18   All three theories, testicular malfunction, psychoactive overdosing, and asteroidal zapping, grab our attention mightily. As pure phenomenology, they rank about equally high on any hit parade of primal fascination. Yet one represents expansive science, the others restrictive and untestable speculation. The proper criterion lies in evidence and methodology; we must probe behind the superficial fascination of particular claims.

***All 3 theories are fascinating (see ¶1), but only Alvarez theory fits criteria of being testable and capable of expansion ***

19   How could we possibly decide whether the hypothesis of testicular frying is right or wrong? We would have to know things that the fossil record cannot provide. What temperatures were optimal for dinosaurs? Could they avoid the absorption of excess heat by staying in the shade, or in caves? At what temperatures

did their testicles cease to function? Were late Cretaceous climates ever warm enough to drive the internal temperatures of dinosaurs close to this ceiling? Testicles simply don't fossilize, and how could we infer their temperature tolerances even if they did? In short, Cowles's hypothesis is only an intriguing speculation leading nowhere. The most damning statement against it appeared right in the conclusion of Colbert, Cowles, and Bogert's paper, when they admitted: "It is difficult to advance any definite arguments against this hypothesis." My statement may seem paradoxical—isn't a hypothesis really good if you can't devise any arguments against it? Quite the contrary. It is simply untestable and unusable.

Testes theory raises too many unanswerable questions: leads nowhere & can't be refuted

20   Siegel's overdosing has even less going for it. At least Cowles extrapolated his conclusion from some good data on alligators. And he didn't completely violate the primary guideline of siting dinosaur extinction in the context of a general mass dying—for rise in temperature could be the root cause of a general catastrophe, zapping dinosaurs by testicular malfunction and different groups for other reasons. But Siegel's speculation cannot touch the extinction of ammonities or oceanic plankton (diatoms make their own food with good sweet sunlight; they don't OD on the chemicals of terrestrial plants). It is simply a gratuitous, attention-grabbing guess. It cannot be tested, for how can we know what dinosaurs tasted and what their livers could do? Livers don't fossilize any better than testicles.

Overdose theory ignores death of marine organisms who didn't eat alkaloids!

21   The hypothesis doesn't even make any sense in its own context. Angiosperms were in full flower ten million years before dinosaurs went the way of all flesh. Why did it take so long? As for the pains of a chemical death recorded in contortions of fossils, I regret to say (or rather I'm pleased

2nd theory ignores fact that angiosperms were available 10 m. years before dinosaurs died

to note for the dinosaurs' sake) that Siegel's knowledge of geology must be a bit deficient: muscles contract after death and geological strata rise and fall with motions of the earth's crust after burial—more than enough reason to distort a fossil's pristine appearance.

Alvarezes' theory can be supported by evidence: can be tested, extended, refined, and disproved

22   The impact story, on the other hand, has a sound basis in evidence. It can be tested, extended, refined and, if wrong, disproved. The Alvarezes did not just construct an arresting guess for public consumption. They proposed their hypothesis after laborious geochemical studies with Frank Asaro and Helen Michael had revealed a massive increase of iridium in rocks deposited right at the time of extinction. Iridium, a rare metal of the platinum group, is virtually absent from indigenous rocks of the earth's crust; most of our iridium arrives on extraterrestrial objects that strike the earth.

Evidence: rocks from Cretaceous era contain high amts. of iridium, rare metal found only in extraterrestrial objects

23   The Alvarez hypothesis bore immediate fruit. Based originally on evidence from two European localities, it led geochemists throughout the world to examine other sediments of the same age. They found abnormally high amounts of iridium everywhere—from continental rocks of the western United States to deep sea cores from the South Atlantic.

24   Cowles proposed his testicular hypothesis in the mid-1940s. Where has it gone since then? Absolutely nowhere, because scientists can do nothing with it. The hypothesis must stand as a curious appendage to a solid study of alligators. Siegel's overdose scenario will also win a few press notices and fade into oblivion. The Alvarezes' asteroid falls into a different category altogether, and much of the popular commentary has missed this essential distinction by focusing on the impact and its attendant results, and forgetting what really matters to a scientist—the

Asteroid theory produced more geological research, but other 2 theories are dead

iridium. If you talk just about asteroids, dust, and darkness, you tell stories no better and no more entertaining than fried testicles or terminal trips. It is the iridium—the source of testable evidence—that counts and forges the crucial distinction between speculation and science.

Iridium: the crucial piece of evidence that makes Alvarez theory science & the others mere speculation

25　The proof, to twist a phrase, lies in the doing. Cowles's hypothesis has generated nothing in thirty-five years. Since its proposal in 1979, the Alvarez hypothesis has spawned hundreds of studies, a major conference, and attendant publications. Geologists are fired up. They are looking for iridium at all other extinction boundaries. Every week exposes a new wrinkle in the scientific press. Further evidence that the Cretaceous iridium represents extraterrestrial impact and not indigenous volcanism continues to accumulate. As I revise this essay in November 1984 (this paragraph will be out of date when the book is published), new data include chemical "signatures" of other isotopes indicating unearthly provenance, glass spherules of a size and sort produced by impact and not by volcanic eruptions, and high-pressure varieties of silica formed (so far as we know) only under the tremendous shock of impact.

Criterion of good science: research is ongoing & hypothesis can be extended

26　My point is simply this: Whatever the eventual outcome (I suspect it will be positive), the Alvarez hypothesis is exciting, fruitful science because it generates tests, provides us with things to do, and expands outward. We are having fun, battling back and forth, moving toward a resolution, and extending the hypothesis beyond its original scope.

Hypothesis is being extended beyond original scope

27　As just one example of the unexpected, distant cross-fertilization that good science engenders, the Alvarez hypothesis made a major contribution to a theme that has riveted public attention in the past few months—so-called nuclear

Asteroid hypothesis extended to nuclear winter: consequences would be the same

winter. In a speech delivered in April 1982, Luis Alvarez calculated the energy that a ten-kilometer asteroid would release on impact. He compared such an explosion with a full nuclear exchange and implied that all-out atomic war might unleash similar consequences.

Effects: dust clouds & falling temps would be consequences of nuclear holocaust: same model as asteroid's impact

28   This theme of impact leading to massive dust clouds and falling temperatures formed an important input to the decision of Carl Sagan and a group of colleagues to model the climatic consequences of nuclear holocaust. Full nuclear exchange would probably generate the same kind of dust cloud and darkening that may have wiped out the dinosaurs. Temperatures would drop precipitously and agriculture might become impossible. Avoidance of nuclear war is fundamentally an ethical and political imperative, but we must know the factual consequences to make firm judgments. I am heartened by a final link across disciplines and deep concerns—another criterion, by the way, of science at its best: A recognition of the very phenomenon that made our evolution possible by exterminating the previously dominant dinosaurs and clearing a way for the evolution of large mammals, including us, might actually help to save us from joining those magnificent beasts in contorted poses among the strata of the earth.

Though nuclear weapons require moral judgment, scientific facts must precede that judgment—scientific knowledge at its best

Science helps us understand factors that made human evolution possible

Same knowledge might save us from same fate as dinosaurs

■ ANALYSIS OF PRACTICE ESSAY

Here are some suggested responses to the eight questions for analyzing essays (see page 369).

1. *Who is the author?* The headnote clearly identifies Gould as an expert in paleontology, geology, and zoology. He teaches at one of the best universities in the United States, and he is widely published. Therefore, he can likely be considered an authority whose observations are credible.

2. *Who is the audience?* The audience is the general reader, who is educated but not necessarily trained in science. Gould's style is clear and readable; terms apt to be unfamiliar to the reader are immediately defined. For example, Gould defines angiosperms as "flowering plants," plankton as "single-celled floating creatures," and ammonites as "relatives of squids in coiled shells." He does not assume that the reader knows these words. Another clue that Gould writes for a popular audience is this sentence from paragraph 3: ". . . these three notions invoke the primally fascinating themes of our culture—sex, drugs, and violence."

3. *What is the writer's purpose?* Gould's primary purpose is to show the difference between two types of scientific theories—those that are useful and enlightened, and those that are fascinating but worthless. The secondary purpose is to illustrate good and bad scientific hypotheses by examining a single issue: how the dinosaurs became extinct during the Cretaceous era. Both purposes are suggested in paragraph 3.

4. *What is the thesis?* The structure of this essay lends itself well to an inductively organized essay, leading up to a thesis implied at the beginning but stated explicitly in paragraph 26: "My point is simply this: Whatever the eventual outcome . . . the Alvarez hypothesis is exciting, fruitful science because it generates tests, provides us with things to do, and expands outward. We are having fun, battling back and forth, moving toward a resolution, and extending the hypothesis beyond its original scope."

5. *What are the main parts of the essay?* The essay can be outlined like this:

Introduction: Paragraphs 1 through 5
     Contrast between sound and silly scientific hypotheses; a list of the three hypotheses concerning the extinction of the dinosaurs.
Body: Paragraphs 6 through 26
     Explanation of the three hypotheses and their origins; refutation of the testicular and flowering plants theories; validation of the Alvarez theory.
Conclusion: Paragraphs 27 and 28
     A discussion of the implications of the Alvarez theory and a warning for the future.

Transitions between the essay's parts are clear. Notice, for example, this transition in paragraph 5: "But, enough preaching. Let's move on to dinosaurs, and the three proposals for their extinction."

6. *What did you learn from the essay?* The answer to this question depends on the individual, but the key points are these: Science operates best with the spirit of inquiry, not merely by pointing to

clever effects or intriguing claims. Scientists too often indulge in fanciful or outlandish claims, which garner public attention, but which really have nothing to do with the way true scientists work. Also scientists look at the interdependence between causes and effects. The two scientific theories that Gould labels "silly speculation" both ignored the fact that marine life as well as land animals died off during the Cretaceous era. The scientific method involves a hypothesis that can be tested, proved with solid evidence, and expanded on in related or distant fields. Gould is more interested in how scientists work than in the conclusions they draw.

7. *What inferences and conclusions can you draw?* Gould seems to have little affection for the flashier sides of science. You can see this best in paragraph 2, where he chides popular science writers for misleading the public. He states that they would do the public a greater service if they stayed away from "controversial and stunning statements" and instead would "focus on *how* scientists develop and defend those fascinating claims." Another solid inference is the use to which good scientific theory can be put, namely, that the Alvarez theory contains within it an admonition and an irony: The dinosaurs became extinct from the impact of an extraterrestrial object; ironically, humans, who flourished later in evolutionary history, could be wiped out by exactly the same physical phenomenon, only this disaster would be of our own making.

8. *Is the language unusual?* Gould occasionally indulges in a little humor to keep the discussion from getting too ponderous. He also introduces an allusion in the form of lines from a famous but uncredited poem by Dylan Thomas, "Do Not Go Gentle into That Good Night," about the individual's struggle against death. See the end of paragraph 15 and the middle of paragraph 17:
   "Do not go gentle into that good night."
   "Rage, rage against the dying of the light."
Otherwise, the language is straightforward, though Gould also relishes some lighthearted intrusions. Here is one from paragraph 10: "Well, let's face it, you wouldn't want to try sticking a thermometer under a 'gator's tongue."

◼ WRITING SUMMARIES

Why Write Summaries?

A colleague has described a summary as a distillation of ideas. As she put it, "We can reduce a large number of grapes into a very small, but potent glass of wine. The grapes are still there, but in a different, more condensed and concentrated form." In other words, a summary is a condensed version of an essay, an article, or a book, which presents only the essential information of the original. Writing a summary provides many intellectual benefits: It is a good measure of your reading and writing skills. It requires that you understand a piece accurately and can weigh the relative worth of ideas, deciding what is essential and what is nonessential, what to retain and what to omit. It forces you to discern the arrangement of ideas and to restate these ideas concisely, accurately, and fairly, without intruding your own opinion or judgment or distorting the thinking. Finally, it helps avoid plagiarism (copying). Your ability to restate the main points of a passage in your own words is a true indicator of how well you understand it.

How long should a summary be? If your instructor does not require you to conform to a particular length, you can use this formula as a guide: A summary of an essay or article should be roughly between 5 and 15 percent of the length of the original. Some instructors ask that a summary be no more than a single page, double-spaced, or roughly 250 words. The Stephen Jay Gould essay is 3,200 words long, and the sample summary I wrote—after much pruning, tinkering, and revising—is 415 words long, or around 12 percent of the original.

How to Write a Summary

The annotated essay and the sample summary below demonstrate the following suggestions:

- Read through the passage at least twice so that you have a good understanding of the content. Look up any unfamiliar words.
- Underline important words, phrases, and sentences. You may also make marginal notations—in other words, annotate the piece, noting main ideas and key supporting statements, as I have done for the Gould piece.
- Copy the underlined or annotated material onto a sheet of paper, using double or triple spacing to leave yourself plenty of room for changes or additions.
- Study this material. You may have to add information from the original or delete what you don't have room for or what you later decide is not important enough to include.
- Next, rewrite this material by paraphrasing it, using *your own words* as much as possible. Do not, however, change key terms. For example, in a summary of "Sex, Drugs, Disasters, and the Extinction of Dinosaurs," it would not be plagiarizing to use words from the essay, such as "angiosperms," "psychoactive agents," or "extraterrestrial objects." In other words, do not strain for synonyms for words that form the basis of the essay.

- Insert transitional words or phrases as necessary to show the relationships between ideas.

- Prepare a final draft by rewriting your sentences. Check to see that your summary is accurate and free of your own ideas and opinions. (Note, however, that many instructors assign summary-response papers, in which you would be asked both to summarize an essay and then to evaluate it by explaining your objections, criticisms, or other observations. In that case, your instructor is asking for your point of view. If you are unsure about an assignment, ask for clarification.)

- Your summary's first sentence should include the author's name and the essay title as well as the main idea. Use the present tense throughout. You may use quotations, but do so sparingly.

- Do a word count, making sure that your summary is the appropriate length. If it is too long, cut unnecessary verbiage or supporting examples.

◼ SAMPLE SUMMARY

In "Sex, Drugs, Disasters, and the Extinction of the Dinosaurs," Stephen Jay Gould examines the scientific method. He states that the aim of science is to investigate, and that consequences, no matter how enticing, are the result, not the essence, of the scientific method. He distinguishes between two kinds of hypotheses: Good hypotheses can be proved and tested; they are capable of extension into other areas, and if they don't work, they can be discarded. Useless speculations, however, are the result of intriguing theories that go nowhere. To illustrate, Gould examines three theories set forth to explain the massive die-off of dinosaurs that occurred during the Cretaceous era. He dismisses the first two as intriguing but useless because they both ignore one crucial fact: The dinosaurs' extinction was not an isolated incident.

The first theory points to the warming of the earth's atmosphere, resulting in dinosaurs' sterilization, since their testes could function only within a certain range of temperatures. The evidence for this theory comes from an earlier study of alligators, whose heating and cooling properties are dissimilar from those of dinosaurs. The second theory proposes that dinosaurs ate angiosperms containing alkaloids (psychoactive agents), whose toxins their livers could not process; they therefore starved to death. This hypothesis is intriguing but foolish: It can't be confirmed by fossil evidence, nor does it account for the fact that dinosaurs had flowering plants at their disposal for 10 million years before their demise, which they never ate. Further, both theories ignore the die-off of other organisms that occurred at the same time.

The Alvarez theory—that a massive asteroid hit the earth, sending up huge dust clouds and preventing photosynthesis—explains the simultaneous extinction of marine and terrestrial organisms from freezing or starvation. But the most important corroborating evidence comes from rocks containing iridium, a rare metal found only in extraterrestrial rocks dating from the Cretaceous era.

Gould concludes that the Alvarez theory exhibits an important criterion of good science: It is capable of extension, allowing scientists to use the asteroid model—with its darkened skies, precipitous drop in temperature, and lack of photosynthesis—to predict similar devastating consequences of a "nuclear winter." Good science gives us facts allowing us to judge other situations. Gould warns that the very phenomenon that made human evolution possible—the extinction of the dinosaurs—could occur again, but this disaster—a nuclear holocaust—would be of our own making. Our awareness of this possibility might save us from a similar fate.

(415 words)

■ FOURTEEN ESSAYS AND ARTICLES FOR FURTHER PRACTICE

Selection 1

An Ethnic Trump
Gish Jen

© Jerry Bauer.

This article, first published in Essence, *and reprinted in* The New York Times, *looks at cultural identity and the hard work that parents of biracial children face. Gish Jen is known primarily as a fiction writer; she is the author of* Typical American, Mona in the Promised Land, *and most recently,* Who's Irish?

1   That my son, Luke, age 4, goes to Chinese-culture school seems inevitable to most people, even though his father is of Irish descent. In America, certain ethnicities are seen as more ethnic than others: Chinese, for example, trumps Irish. This has something to do with the relative distance of certain cultures from mainstream America, but it also has to do with race. As we all know, it is not only certain ethnicities that trump others but certain colors: Black trumps White, for example, always and forever; a mulatto is not a kind of White person, but a kind of Black person.

2   And so it is, too, that my son is considered a kind of Asian person, whose destiny is to embrace Asian things: the Chinese language, Chinese food, Chinese New Year. No one cares whether he speaks

Gaelic or wears green on St. Patrick's Day, for though Luke's skin is fair and his features mixed, people see his straight black hair and *know* who he is.

3   But is this how we should define ourselves, by other people's perceptions? My husband, Dave, and I had originally hoped for Luke to grow up embracing his whole complex heritage. We had hoped to pass on to him values and habits of mind that had survived in both of us.

4   Then one day Luke combed his black hair and said he was turning it yellow. Another day, a mother I knew said her son had invited all blond-haired children like himself to his birthday party. And yet another day, Luke was happily scooting around the Cambridge Common playground when a pair of older boys, apparently brothers, blocked his way. "You're Chinese!" they shouted, leaning on the hood of Luke's scooter car. "You are! You're Chinese!" Even when I intervened, they kept shouting. Luke answered, "No, I'm not!" to no avail; the boys didn't seem to hear him. Then the boys' mother called to them from some distance away, and though her voice was no louder than Luke's, they left obediently.

5   Behind them opened a great, rippling quiet, like the wash of a battleship.

6   Luke and I immediately went over things he could say if anything like that happened again. I told him he was 100-percent American, even though I knew from my own childhood in Yonkers, New York, that these words would be met only with derision. It was a sorry chore. Since then I have not asked him about the incident, hoping, that he has forgotten about it, and wishing I could, too. I wish I could forget the sight of those kids' fingers on the hood of Luke's little car. I wish I could forget their loud attack, but also Luke's soft defense: "No, I'm not!"

7   Chinese school. After dozens of phone calls, I was elated to discover the Greater Boston Chinese Cultural Association in nearby West Newton, Massachusetts. The school takes children at 3, has a wonderful sense of community and is housed in a center paid for, in part, by karaoke fund-raising events. (Never mind what the Japanese meant to the Chinese in the old world. In this world, people donate $200 apiece for a chance at the mike, and the singing goes on all night.) At the school, there are even vendors who bring home-style Chinese food to sell after class, stuff you can't get in a restaurant. Dave and I couldn't wait for Luke's second class and a chance to buy more *bao* for our freezer.

8   But in the car on the way to the class, Luke announced that he didn't want to go to Chinese school anymore. He said the teacher talked mostly about ducks and bears, and he wasn't interested in ducks and bears. I knew this was true. Luke was interested only in whales and

ships. What's more, I knew we wouldn't push him to take swimming lessons if he didn't want to, or music. Chinese school was a wonderful thing, but weren't we making it somehow nonoptional? Was that right? Hadn't we always said that we didn't want our son to see himself as more Chinese than Irish?

9   Yet we didn't want to deny his Chinese heritage, either. And if there were going to be incidents on the playground, we wanted him to at least know what Chinese meant. So when Luke said again that he didn't want to go to Chinese school, I said, "Oh, really?" Later on we could try to teach him to define himself irrespective of race. For now, he was going to Chinese school. I exchanged glances with Dave. And then together, in a most casual manner, we squinted at the road and kept going.

A. Comprehension

Choose the answer that best completes each statement. Do not refer to the selection while doing this exercise.

1. Jen writes that not only do certain ethnicities "trump" others but also certain
    (a) neighborhoods.
    (b) skin colors.
    (c) cultural values.
    (d) hair colors.

2. Jen states that she and her husband wanted their son, Luke, to
    (a) learn what being Chinese meant.
    (b) consider himself American.
    (c) accept both sides of his cultural heritage.
    (d) learn to stand up for himself against bigotry.

3. When a pair of older boys on a playground taunted Luke about being Chinese, he responded by
    (a) retaliating against them.
    (b) getting beaten up.
    (c) running home.
    (d) denying their accusations.

4. Telling Luke that he was 100 percent American was, according to Jen,
    (a) wishful thinking on her part.
    (b) a deliberate lie.
    (c) a useful way to help Luke understand his heritage.
    (d) the way she dealt with her own youthful problems concerning race.

5. With regard to Chinese school, Jen and her husband decided to
    (a) allow Luke to leave.
    (b) make Luke continue attending.
    (c) allow Luke to attend less frequently.
    (d) let Luke make up his own mind about whether to continue or not.

B. *Vocabulary*

For each italicized word from the selection, write the best definition according to the context in which it appears. You may refer to the selection to answer the questions in this section and in all the remaining sections.

1. Chinese . . . *trumps* Irish [paragraph 1]: _____

    _____

2. *to no avail* [4]: _____

3. these words would be met only with *derision* [6]: _____

4. *irrespective* of race [9]: _____

C. *Inferences*

Complete the following questions.

1. From paragraphs 6 and 7, we can infer that Luke's parents sent him to Chinese school so that he could learn
    (a) to speak Chinese.
    (b) about the Chinese side of his heritage.
    (c) to defend himself against future playground attacks.
    (d) a martial art.
2. The fundamental conflict that Jen examines in this article is between
    (a) the labels placed on us by the larger society and the cultural heritage our parents hope to instill in us.
    (b) the heritage we hope to identify with and the heritage we actually do identify with.
    (c) Chinese and American cultural values.
    (d) the wish to remain identified with one's cultural background and the wish to assimilate into the larger culture.
3. When Jen writes in paragraph 2 that her son's "destiny is to embrace

    Asian things," what is the origin of this destiny? _____

    _____

4. Why does Luke say in paragraph 4 that he was turning his hair yellow?

_____

_____

5. In the last two sentences of the article, Jen suggests that she and her husband
   (a) disagreed about the best way to teach him.
   (b) had nothing more to say about the subject.
   (c) did not want to argue in front of their child.
   (d) were only feigning casualness and were, in fact, concerned.

D. Structure

Complete the following questions.

1. When Jen says that "Chinese trumps Irish" and "Black trumps White . . . always and forever," she means that
   (a) Whites and Blacks must learn to get along.
   (b) race is the most important element in the way people perceive others.
   (c) being Black or being Chinese allows one to outrank Whites.
   (d) one's race is more important than one's cultural or ethnic heritage.
2. At the beginning of paragraph 3, Jen asks a rhetorical question (one asked only for effect)—"But is this how we should define ourselves, by other people's perceptions?" If she did answer it, would she say yes or

   no? _____

Questions for Discussion and Analysis

1. What instance of prejudice have you observed and/or experienced firsthand? To what extent was your experience the result of race?
2. What should parents of biracial children do to educate and protect their children?

ON THE WEB

These two websites offer information about biracial children and multiracial families:

- ERIC, Educational Resources Information: "The Identity Development of Multiracial Youth." ERIC/CUE Digest, Number 137. www.ed.gov/databases/ERIC_Digests/ed425248.html

- Kelley Kenney, "Multiracial Families," ACA (American Counseling Association).
  www.counseling.org/conference/advocacy6.htm

Selection 2   # The Truck: Hitching through Hell
Ryszard Kapuściński

Associated Press.

Poland's most respected foreign correspondent, Ryszard Kapuściński has traveled throughout Africa, as well as through other Third World countries, for over 40 years. This essay, which was first published in The New Yorker, *appears in Kapuściński's most recent book,* The Shadow of the Sun, *a collection of accounts from his Africa travels. (In that book, the selection appears as "Salim.") Kapuściński lives in Warsaw, Poland. Mauritania, where the events described take place, lies on the Atlantic Ocean in northwest Africa. This essay was translated from the Polish by Klara Glowczewska.*

1   In the darkness, I suddenly spotted two glaring lights. They were far away and moved about violently, as if they were the eyes of a wild animal thrashing about in its cage. I was sitting on a stone at the edge of the Ouadane oasis, in the Sahara, northeast of Nouakchott, the Mauritanian capital. For an entire week now I had been trying to leave this place—to no avail. It is difficult to get to Ouadane, but even more difficult to depart. No marked or paved road leads to it, and there is no scheduled transport. Every few days—sometimes weeks—a truck will pass, and if the driver agrees to take you with him, you go; if not, you simply stay, waiting who knows how long for the next opportunity.

2   The Mauritanians who were sitting beside me stirred. The night chill had set in, a chill that descends abruptly and, after the burning hell of the sun-filled days, can be almost piercingly painful. It is a cold from which no sheepskin or quilt can adequately protect you. And these people had nothing but old, frayed blankets, in which they sat tightly wrapped, motionless, like statues.

3   A black pipe poked out from the ground nearby, a rusty and salt-encrusted compressor-pump mechanism at its tip. This was the region's sole gas station, and passing vehicles always stopped here. There is no other attraction in the oasis. Ordinarily, days pass uneventfully and unchangeably, resembling in this the monotony of the desert climate: the same sun always shines, hot and solitary, in the same empty, cloudless sky.

4   At the sight of the still-distant headlights, the Mauritanians began talking among themselves. I didn't understand a word of their language. It's quite possible they were saying: "At last! It's finally coming! We have lived to see it!"

5   It was recompense for the long days spent waiting, gazing patiently at the inert, unvarying horizon, on which no moving object, no living thing that might rouse you from the numbness of hopeless anticipation, had appeared in a long time. The arrival of a truck—cars are too fragile for this terrain—didn't fundamentally alter the lives of the people. The vehicle usually stopped for a moment and then quickly drove on. Yet even this brief sojourn was vital and important to them: it injected variety into their lives, provided a subject for later conversation, and, above all, was both material proof of the existence of another world and a bracing confirmation that that world, since it had sent them a mechanical envoy, must know that they existed.

6   Perhaps they were also engaged in a routine debate: will it—or won't it—get here? For traveling in these corners of the Sahara is a risky adventure, an unending lottery, perpetual uncertainty. Along these roadless expanses full of crevices, depressions, sinkholes, protruding boulders, sand dunes and rocky mounds, loose stones and fields of slippery gravel, a vehicle advances at a snail's pace—several kilometers an hour. Each wheel has its own drive, and each one, meter by meter, turning here, stopping there, going up, down, or around, searches for something to grip. Most of the time, these persistent efforts and exertions, which are accompanied by the roar of the straining and overheated engine and by the bone-bruising lunges of the swaying platform, finally result in the truck's moving forward.

7   But the Mauritanians also knew that sometimes a truck could get hopelessly stuck just a step away from the oasis, on its very threshhold. This can happen when a storm moves mountains of sand onto the track. In such an event, either the truck's occupants manage to dig out the road, or the driver finds a detour—or he simply turns around and goes back where he came from. Another storm will eventually move the dunes farther and clear the way.

8   This time, however, the electric lights were drawing nearer and nearer. At a certain moment, their glow started to pick out the crowns of date palms that had been hidden under the cover of darkness, and the shabby walls of mud huts, and the goats and cows asleep by the side of the road, until, finally, trailing clouds of dust behind it, an enormous Berliet truck drew to a halt in front of us, with a clang and thud of metal. Berliets are French-made trucks adapted for roadless desert terrain. They have large wheels with wide tires, and grilles mounted atop their hoods. Because of their great size and prominent shape of the grille, from a distance they resemble the fronts of old steam engines.

9   The driver—a dark-skinned, barefoot Mauritanian in an ankle-length indigo djellabah—climbed down from the cab using a ladder. He was, like the majority of his countrymen, tall and powerfully built. People and animals with substantial body weight endure tropical heat better, which is why the inhabitants of the Sahara usually have a magnifi-

cently statuesque appearance. The law of natural selection is also at work here: in these extremely harsh desert conditions, only the strongest survive to maturity.

10   The Mauritanians from the oasis immediately surrounded the driver. A cacaphony of greetings, questions, and well-wishings erupted. This went on and on. Everybody was shouting and gesticulating, as if haggling in a noisy marketplace. After a while they began to point at me. I was a pitiful sight—dirty, unshaven, and, above all, wasted by the nightmarish heat of the Sahara summer. An experienced Frenchman had warned me earlier: it will feel as if someone were sticking a knife into you. Into your back, into your head. At noon, the rays of the sun beat down with the force of a knife.

11   The driver looked at me and at first said nothing. Then he motioned toward the truck with his hand and called out to me: *Yalla!* (Let's go! We're off!)" I climbed into the cab and slammed the door shut. We set off immediately.

12   I had no sense of where we were going. Sand flashed by in the glow of the headlights, shimmering with different shades, laced with strips of gravel and shards of rock. The wheels reared up on granite ledges or sank down into hollows and stony fissures. In the deep, black night one could see only two spots of light—two bright, clearly outlined orbs sliding over the surface of the desert. Nothing else was visible.

13   Before long, I began to suspect that we were driving blind, on a shortcut to somewhere, because there were no demarcation points, no signs, posts, or any other traces of a roadway. I tried to question the driver. I gestured at the darkness around us and asked: "Nouakchott?"

14   He looked at me and laughed. "Nouakchott?" He repeated this dreamily, as if it were the Hanging Gardens of Semiramis that I was asking him about—so beautiful but, for us lowly ones, too high to reach. I concluded from this that we were not headed in the direction I desired, but I did not know how to ask him where, in that case, we were going. I desperately wanted to establish some contact with him, to get to know him even a little. "Ryszard," I said, pointing at myself. Then I pointed at him. He understood. "Salim," he said, and laughed again. Silence fell. We must have come upon a smooth stretch of desert, for the Berliet began to roll along more gently and quickly (exactly how fast, I don't know, since all the instruments were broken). We drove on for a time without speaking, until finally I fell asleep.

15   A sudden silence awoke me. The engine had stopped, the truck stood still. Salim was pressing on the gas pedal and turning the key in the ignition. The battery was working—the starter too—but the engine emitted no sound. It was morning, and already light outside. He began searching around the cab for the lever that opens the hood. This struck me as at once odd and suspicious: a driver who doesn't know how to open the hood? Eventually, he figured out that the latches that need to

be released were on the outside. He then stood on a fender and began to inspect the engine, but he peered at its intricate construction as if he were seeing it for the first time. He would touch something, try to move something, but his gestures were those of an amateur. Every now and then he would climb into the cab and turn the key in the ignition, but the engine remained dead silent. He located the toolbox, but there wasn't much in it. He pulled out a hammer, several wrenches, and screwdrivers. Then he started to take the engine apart.

16   I stepped down from the cab. All around us, as far as the eye could see, was desert. Sand, with dark stones scattered about. Nearby, a large black oval rock. (In the hours following noon, after being warmed by the sun, it would radiate heat like a steel-mill oven.) A moonscape, delineated by a level horizon line: the earth ends, and then there's nothing but sky and more sky. No hills. No sand dunes. Not a single leaf. And, of course, no water. Water! It's what instantly comes to mind under such circumstances. In the desert, the first thing man sees when he opens his eyes in the morning is the face of his enemy—the flaming visage of the sun. The sight elicits in him a reflexive gesture of self-preservation: he reaches for water. Drink! Drink! Only by doing so can he ever so slightly improve his odds in the desert's eternal struggle—the desperate duel with the sun.

17   I resolved to look around for water, for I had none with me. I found nothing in the cab. But I did discover some: attached with ropes to the bed of the truck, near the rear, underneath, were four goatskins, two on the left side and two on the right. The hides had been rather poorly cured, then sewn together in such a way that they retained the animal's shape. One of the goat's legs served as a drinking spout.

18   I sighed with relief, but only momentarily. I began to calculate. Without water, you can survive in the desert for twenty-four hours; with great difficulty, forty-eight or so. The match is simple. Under these conditions, you secrete in one day approximately ten liters of sweat, and to survive you must drink a similar amount of water. Deprived of it, you will immediately start to feel thirsty. Genuine, prolonged thirst in a hot and dry climate is an exhausting, ravaging sensation, harder to control than hunger. After a few hours of it you become lethargic and limp, weak and disoriented. Instead of speaking, you babble, ever less cogently. That same evening, or the next day, you get a high fever and quickly die.

19   If Salim doesn't share his water with me, I thought, I will die today. Even if he does, we will have only enough left for one more day—which means we will both die tomorrow, the day after at the latest.

20   Trying to stop these thoughts, I decided to observe him closely. Covered with grease and sweating, Salim was still taking the engine apart, unscrewing screws and removing cables, but with no rhyme or

reason, like a child furiously destroying a toy that won't work. On the fenders, on the bumper, lay countless springs, valves, compression rings, and wires; some had already fallen to the ground. I left him and went around to the other side of the truck, where there was still some shade. I sat down on the ground and leaned my back against the wheel.

21   Salim.

22   I knew nothing about the man who held my life in his hands. Or, at least, who held it for this one day. I thought, if Salim chases me away from the truck and the water—after all, he had a hammer in his hand and probably a knife in his pocket, and, on top of that, enjoyed a significant physical advantage—if he orders me to leave and march off into the desert, I won't last even until nightfall. And it seemed to me that was precisely what he might choose to do. He would thereby extend his life, after all—or, if help arrives in time, he might even save it.

23   Clearly Salim was not a professional driver, or at any rate, not a driver of a Berliet truck. He also didn't know the area well. (On the other hand, can one really know the desert, where successive storms and tempests constantly alter the landscape, moving mountains of sand to ever different sites and transposing features of the landscape with impunity?) It is common practice in these parts for someone with even a small financial windfall to immediately hire another with less money to carry out his tasks for him. Maybe the rightful driver of this truck had hired Salim to take it in his stead to one of the oases. And hereabouts no one will ever admit to not knowing or not being capable of something. If you approach a taxi driver in a city, show him an address, and ask him if he knows where it is, he will say yes without a second's hesitation. And it is only later, when you are driving all over the city, round and round, that you fully realize he has no idea where to go.

24   The sun was climbing higher and higher. The desert, that motionless, petrified ocean, absorbed its rays, grew hotter, and began to burn. The hour was approaching when everything would become a hell—the earth, the sky, us. The Yoruba are said to believe that if a man's shadow abandons him, he will die. All the shadows were beginning to shrink, dwindle, fade. The dread afternoon hours were almost upon us, the time of day when people and objects have no shade, exist and yet do not exist, reduced to a glowing, incandescent whiteness.

25   I thought that this moment had arrived, but suddenly I noticed before me an utterly different sight. The lifeless, still horizon—so crushed by the heat that it seemed nothing could ever issue forth from it—all at once sprang to life and became green. As far as the eye could see stood tall, magnificent palm trees, entire groves of them along the horizon, growing thickly, without interruption. I also saw lakes—yes, enormous blue lakes, with animated, undulating surfaces. Gorgeous shrubs also grew there, with wide-spreading branches of a fresh,

intense, succulent, deep green. All this shimmered continuously, sparkled, pulsated, as if it were wreathed in a light mist, soft-edged and elusive. And everywhere—here, around us, and there, on the horizon—a profound, absolute silence reigned: the wind did not blow, and the palm groves had no birds.

26   "Salim!" I called. "Salim!"

27   A head emerged from under the hood. He looked at me.

28   "Salim!" I repeated once more, and pointed.

29   Salim glanced where I had shown him, unimpressed. In my dirty, sweaty face he must have read wonder, bewilderment, and rapture—but also something else besides, which clearly alarmed him, for he walked up to the side of the truck, untied one of the goatskins, took a few sips, and wordlessly handed me the rest. I grabbed the rough leather sack and began to drink. Suddenly dizzy, I leaned my shoulder against the truck bed so as not to fall. I drank and drank, sucking fiercely on the goat's leg and still staring at the horizon. But as I felt my thirst subsiding, and the madness within me dying down, the green vista began to vanish. Its colors faded and paled, it contours shrank and blurred. By the time I had emptied the goatskin, the horizon was once again flat, empty, and lifeless. The water, disgusting Saharan water—warm, dirty, thick with sand and sludge—extended my life but took away my vision of paradise. The crucial thing, though, was the fact that Salim himself had given me the water to drink. I stopped being afraid of him. I felt I was safe—at least, until the moment when we would be down to our last sip.

30   We spent the second half of the day lying underneath the truck, in its faint, bleached shade. In this world circled all about with flaming horizons, Salim and I were the only life. I inspected the ground within my arm's reach, the nearest stones, searching for some living thing, anything that might twitch, move, slither. I remembered that somewhere on the Sahara there lives a small beetle which the Tuareg call Ngubi. When it is very hot, according to legend, Ngubi is tormented by thirst, desperate to drink. Unfortunately, there is no water anywhere, and only burning sand all around. So the small beetle chooses an incline—this can be a sloping fold of sand—and with determination begins to climb to its summit. It is an enormous effort, a Sisyphean task, because the hot and loose sand constantly gives way, carrying the beetle down with it, right back to where he began his toils. Which is why, before too long, the beetle starts to sweat. A drop of moisture collects at the end of his abdomen and swells. Then Ngubi stops climbing, curls up, and plunges his mouth into that very bead.

31   He drinks.

32   Salim has several biscuits in a paper bag. We drink the second goatskin of water. Two remain. I consider writing something. (It occurs to me that this is often done at such moments.) But I don't have the strength. I'm not really in pain. It's just that everything is becoming empty. And within this emptiness another one is growing.

33   Then, in the darkness, two glaring lights. They are far away and move about violently. Then the sound of a motor draws near, and I see the truck, hear voices in a language I do not understand. "Salim!" I say. Several dark faces, resembling his, lean over me.

A. Comprehension

Choose the answer that best completes each statement. Do not refer to the selection while doing this exercise.

1. Travel in Mauritania is particularly difficult because
    (a) the roads are badly maintained and fuel is expensive.
    (b) there are no paved roads and no scheduled transportation.
    (c) there are few skilled mechanics to repair the nation's public transit vehicles.
    (d) there is not enough demand for public transit to maintain a regular fleet.

2. Besides giving the Mauritanians something to talk about, the arrival of the truck near the Ouadane oasis also signified that
    (a) someone in authority had taken their request for transportation seriously.
    (b) they could finally leave for the city to find jobs.
    (c) the sand from a recent storm had been cleared from the tracks.
    (d) the outside world recognized their existence.

3. Which of these was *not* mentioned as a reason that travel in the Sahara is risky?
    (a) The roads are unsafe and filled with dangerous rocks and other obstacles.
    (b) There is always the threat of highway robbers stealing one's possessions.
    (c) A truck can easily get stuck in the sand and wait days for rescue.
    (d) The heat is punishing, so being stranded might result in death.

4. Kapuściński's first suspicions of Salim's status as a driver occurred when he discovered that Salim
    (a) had brought no map.
    (b) spoke no English or Polish.
    (c) had forgotten to bring food or water.
    (d) did not know how to open the truck's hood.

5. Kapuściński writes that a person can survive in the Sahara without water for 24 hours and, with great difficulty, for only
    (a) 36 hours.
    (b) 48 hours.
    (c) four days.
    (d) five days.

B. Vocabulary

For each italicized word from the selection, write the best definition according to the context in which it appears. You may refer to the selection to answer the questions in this section and in all the remaining sections.

1. it was *recompense* [paragraph 5]: _____

2. the *inert,* unvarying horizon [5]: _____

3. a *cacophony* of greetings [10]: _____

4. there were no *demarcation* points [13]: _____

    _____

5. a moonscape, *delineated* by a level horizon [16]: _____

6. soft-edged and *elusive* [25]: _____

C. Inferences

On the basis of the evidence in the essay, mark these statements as follows: PA (probably accurate), PI (probably inaccurate), or NP (not in the passage).

1. _____   Kapuściński was concerned that his family did not know his whereabouts.

2. _____   The writer had not realized that finding a ride to Nouakchott would be so difficult.

3. _____   Kapuściński's health had suffered during his stay in Mauritania.

4. _____   Salim's lack of mechanical experience is representative of drivers in the Sahara.

5. _____   Salim did not assume that the disabled truck would be rescued and shared his goatskin bags of water only out of pity for Kapuściński.

6. _____   If the truck had not arrived when it did, Kapuściński probably would not have lived very long.

D. *Language*

Complete the following questions.

1. In describing the truck in paragraph 5 as a "mechanical envoy," Kapuściński uses
   (a) irony.
   (b) personification.
   (c) a metaphor.
   (d) a simile.

2. When he describes the movements of the truck in paragraph 6 as "bone-bruising lunges," is the writer being literal or figurative?

   _____

3. Look again at paragraphs 10, 16, and 24, and locate a figure of speech in each. State what is compared to what.

   Paragraph 10: _____   _____   _____

   are compared to _____

   Paragraph 16: _____

   is compared to _____

   Paragraph 24: _____

   is compared to _____

4. Here are two allusions from the essay. Look them up and explain what they mean.

   Paragraph 14: The Hanging Gardens of Semiramis are famous gardens built in Babylon by its founder, Queen Semiramis; they are one of the

   Seven Wonders of the Ancient World. _____

   _____

   _____

   Paragraph 30: A little beetle called Ngubi continuously climbs a sand dune, a Sisyphean task, to achieve one drop of sweat, which it drinks

   to save itself. _____

   _____

   _____

   _____

Questions for Discussion and Analysis

1. What are some techniques and devices Kapuściński uses to make the reader feel as if he or she is present in the Saharan landscape?
2. What are the primary human emotions embodied in Kapuściński's experience?

ON THE WEB

Around the World in 80 Clicks:
www.traveladventures.org

IN THE BOOKSTORE

Things Fall Apart (1958), by Nigerian writer Chinua Achebe, is undoubtedly the most widely read novel from Africa. By focusing on one Ibo village in Nigeria, Achebe details the cultural upheaval that occurred after the arrival of European colonialists and Christian missionaries. The title, an allusion to a poem by William Butler Yeats, in the novel refers to the fracturing of African society ("things fall apart") if the villagers adopt European ways.

Selection 3 — **Faux Chicken & Phony Furniture: Notes of an Alien Son**

Andrei Codrescu

Reuters/Hulton/Archive by Getty Images.

Andrei Codrescu, a Romanian-born poet and nonfiction writer, is a professor of English at Louisiana State University in Baton Rouge. However, he is probably best known as a commentator on National Public Radio's "All Things Considered." First published in The Nation, *this article explores some of the paradoxes associated with the immigrant experience, using his mother's initial infatuation with American products as his starting point. (The word* Faux *in the title means "fake" and usually has a positive connotation. Codrescu is referring to supermarket chickens, which are shot full of hormones and raised in cages and which have less flavor than the free-range chicken his mother bought in Romania.) Codrescu's latest book is titled* Ay, Cuba! A Socio-Erotic *Journey.*

1   My mother, ever a practical woman, started investing in furniture when she came to America from Romania. Not just any furniture. Sears furniture. Furniture that she kept the plastic on for 15 years before she had to conclude, sadly, that Sears wasn't such a great investment. In Romania, she would have been the richest woman on the block.

2   Which brings us to at least one paradox of immigration. Most people come here because they are sick of being poor. They want to eat and they want something to show for their industry. But soon enough it becomes evident to them that these things aren't enough. They have eaten and they are full, but they have eaten alone and there was no one with whom to make toasts and sing songs. They have new furniture with plastic on it, but the neighbors aren't coming over to ooh and aah. If American neighbors or less recent immigrants do come over, they smile condescendingly at the poor taste and the pathetic greed. And so the greenhorns find themselves poor once more: This time they are lacking something more elusive than salami and furniture. They are bereft of a social and cultural milieu.

3   My mother, who was middle class by Romanian standards, found herself immensely impoverished after her first flush of material well-being. It wasn't just the disappearance of her milieu—that was obvious—but the feeling that she had, somehow, been had. The American supermarket tomatoes didn't taste at all like the rare genuine item back in Romania. American chicken was tasteless. Mass-produced furniture was built to fall apart. Her car, the crowning glory of her achievements in the eyes of folks back home, was only three years old and already beginning to wheeze and groan. It began to dawn on my mother that she had perhaps made a bad deal: She had traded in her friends and relatives for ersatz tomatoes, fake chicken, phony furniture.

4   Leaving behind your kin, your friends, your language, your smells, your childhood, is traumatic. It is a kind of death. You're dead for the home folk and they are dead to you. When you first arrive on these shores you are in mourning. The only consolations are these products, which were imbued with religious significance back at home. But when these things turn out not to be the real things, you begin to experience a second death, brought about by betrayal. You begin to suspect that the religious significance you attached to them was only possible back home, where these things did not exist. Here, where they are plentiful, they have no significance whatsoever. They are inanimate fetishes, somebody else's fetishes, no help to you at all. When this realization dawned on my mother, she began to rage against her new country. She deplored its rudeness, its insensitivity, its outright meanness, its indifference, the chase after the almighty buck, the social isolation of most Americans, their inability to partake of warm, genuine fellowship, and, above all, their deplorable lack of awe before what they had made.

5   This was the second stage of grief for her old self. The first, leaving her country, was sharp and immediate, almost tonic in its violence. The second was more prolonged, more damaging, because no hope was attached to it. Certainly not the hope of return.

6   And here, thinking of return, she began to reflect that perhaps there had been more to this deal than she'd first thought. True, she had left behind a lot that was good, but she had also left behind a vast range of daily humiliations. If she was ordered to move out of town she had to comply. If a party member took a dislike to her she had to go to extraordinary lengths to placate him because she was considered petit bourgeois and could easily have lost her small photo shop. She lived in fear of being denounced for something she had said. And worst of all, she was a Jew, which meant that she was structurally incapable of obtaining any justice in her native land. She had lived by the grace of an immensely complicated web of human relations, which was kept in place by a thousand small concessions, betrayals, indignities, bribes, little and big lies.

7   At this point, the ersatz tomatoes and the faux chicken did not appear all that important. An imponderable had made its appearance, a bracing, heady feeling of liberty. If she took that ersatz tomato and flung it at the head of the agriculture secretary of the United States, she would be making a statement about the disastrous effects of pesticides and mechanized farming. Flinging that faux chicken at Barbara Mandrell would be equally dramatic and perhaps even media-worthy. And she'd probably serve only a suspended sentence. What's more, she didn't have to eat those things, because she could buy organic tomatoes and free-range chicken. Of course, it would cost more, but that was one of the paradoxes of America: To eat as well as people in a Third World country eat (when they eat) costs more.

8   My mother was beginning to learn two things: one, that she had gotten a good deal after all, because in addition to food and furniture they had thrown in freedom; and two, America is a place of paradoxes— one proceeds from paradox to paradox like a chicken from the pot into the fire.

A. Comprehension

Choose the answer that best completes each statement. Do not refer to the selection while doing this exercise.

1.   According to Codrescu, most immigrants come to the United States to escape
      (a) political persecution.
      (b) religious persecution.
      (c) poverty and lack of opportunity.
      (d) the dislocation that results from years of civil wars.

2. Because immigrating is so traumatic, newcomers often console themselves by
    (a) acquiring American products.
    (b) making plans to return home.
    (c) preserving their language and culture.
    (d) becoming politically active in their adopted homeland.

3. Codrescu compares the immigrant experience of leaving their homelands to
    (a) a release.
    (b) a second chance at life.
    (c) an intermediate stage.
    (d) a kind of death.

4. One paradox about living in America concerns food, specifically, that
    (a) one can eat better in America than in Romania.
    (b) the ordinary food that one can buy cheaply in Romania is expensive in America.
    (c) American food is more nutritious than food available in Third World countries.
    (d) ordinary Americans do not eat as well as ordinary Romanians.

5. Eventually, Codrescu's mother realized that in this country she could escape religious and political persecution and enjoy
    (a) her family's economic success.
    (b) acceptance by her neighbors.
    (c) better-quality food.
    (d) her liberty.

B. Vocabulary

For each italicized word from the selection, choose the best definition according to the context in which it appears. You may refer to the selection to answer the questions in this section and in all the remaining sections.

1. one *paradox* of immigration [paragraph 2]:
    (a) result.
    (b) seeming contradiction.
    (c) fault.
    (d) unexplained event.

2. they smile *condescendingly* [2]: Describing an attitude that is
    (a) guilt-producing.
    (b) greedy and selfish.
    (c) patronizingly superior.
    (d) punishing, reproachful.

3. lacking something more *elusive* [2]:
   (a) difficult to describe.
   (b) harmful.
   (c) corrupting.
   (d) confirming one's status.

4. they are *bereft* [2]:
   (a) bewildered by.
   (b) in mourning for.
   (c) enslaved by.
   (d) lacking something necessary.

5. *ersatz* tomatoes (pronounced er´ - zäts) [3]: Describing something that
   (a) lacks nutritional value.
   (b) is an inferior imitation.
   (c) is juicy and succulent.
   (d) is of excellent quality.

6. she was considered *petit bourgeois* [6]: A member of
   (a) the ruling class.
   (b) the proletariat, or working class.
   (c) the lower middle class, including tradespeople and shop owners.
   (d) the professional class, including physicians and lawyers.

C. Inferences

On the basis of the evidence in the essay, mark these statements as follows: PA (probably accurate), PI (probably inaccurate), or NP (not in the passage).

1. _____ For Codrescu's mother, being able to purchase furniture from Sears Roebuck represented the pinnacle of success.

2. _____ Native-born Americans do not experience the same paradoxes as do the immigrants that the author describes.

3. _____ The author's mother eventually grew fond of hormone-filled supermarket chicken.

4. _____ Codrescu's mother eventually realized that life in Romania was more stable and more enjoyable than life in the United States.

D. Structure

Complete the following questions.

1. The author's purpose is to
   (a) examine the paradox of immigration and the emotional stages immigrants experience.
   (b) criticize Americans for not being more welcoming to recent immigrants.
   (c) explain his mother's decision to emigrate from Romania.
   (d) explain how recent arrivals can avoid trauma after immigrating.

2. Look again at paragraph 2. Although Codrescu is seemingly interested in his mother's Sears Roebuck furniture, what more significant

    concept did her furniture represent to her? _____

    _____

3. Near the end of paragraph 2, Codrescu writes, "And so the greenhorns find themselves poor once more." What does he mean by

    "poor"? _____

4. Look again at paragraph 7, where Codrescu describes the possibility of throwing ersatz tomatoes at the agricultural secretary or faux

    chicken at Barbara Mandrell. What is he referring to? _____

    _____

    Are these examples literal or metaphoric? _____

5. The tone of this article can be best described as
    (a) arrogant, snobbish.
    (b) unsympathetic, callous.
    (c) sympathetic, compassionate.
    (d) impartial, objective.

Questions for Discussion and Analysis

1. If possible, interview a recent immigrant to see if that person's experience confirms or refutes that of Codrescu's mother.
2. Explain in your own words the stages that immigrants experience, focusing in particular on the paradoxes Codrescu's mother encountered with American culture.
3. On the basis of the information the author includes in paragraph 4, do you think that Codrescu's mother was justified or not in her rage against Americans? Explain.

ON THE WEB

- Further information about Andrei Codrescu is available at his home page:
literati.net/Codrescu/

- The names of immigrants who came to America between 1892 and 1924 and went through the inspection stations at New York's Ellis Island are now available at a government-sponsored website. The site offers information on 22 million passenger records extracted from microfilms of the original paper manifests during the peak years of immigration.
www.ellisislandrecords.org

Selection 4   ## It's Just Too Late
                     Calvin Trillin

*Born in 1935 in Kansas City, Missouri, Calvin Trillin was educated at Yale,
after which he became a reporter for* Time. *He has written extensively for
several American magazines, in particular for* The New Yorker *and* The
Nation. *His most recent book is a novel,* Tepper Isn't Going Out *(2002).
"It's Just Too Late" is often reprinted in college anthologies, and in fact, was
included in the third edition of this text. It is from a collection of essays called*
Killings, *Trillin's attempt at understanding American culture by exploring
several cases involving the deaths of ordinary people. In "It's Just Too Late,"
Trillin reveals the circumstances of 16-year-old FaNee Cooper's death.*

Knoxville, Tennessee
March 1979

1   Until she was sixteen, FaNee Cooper was what her parents sometimes called an ideal child. "You'd never have to correct her," FaNee's
mother has said. In sixth grade, FaNee won a spelling contest. She
played the piano and the flute. She seemed to believe what she heard
every Sunday at the Beaver Dam Baptist Church about good and evil
and the hereafter. FaNee was not an outgoing child. Even as a baby, she
was uncomfortable when she was held and cuddled. She found it easy to
tell her parents that she loved them but difficult to confide in them. Particularly compared to her sister, Kristy, a cheerful, open little girl two
and a half years younger, she was reserved and introspective. The
thoughts she kept to herself, though, were apparently happy thoughts.
Her eighth-grade essay on Christmas—written in a remarkably neat
hand—talked of the joys of helping put together toys for her little
brother, Leo, Jr., and the importance of her parents' reminder that
Christmas is the birthday of Jesus. Her parents were the sort of people
who might have been expected to have an ideal child. As a boy, Leo
Cooper had been called "one of the greatest high-school basketball players ever developed in Knox County." He went on to play basketball at
East Tennessee State, and he married the homecoming queen, JoAnn
Henson. After college, Cooper became a high-school basketball coach
and teacher and, eventually, an administrator. By the time FaNee turned
thirteen, in 1973, he was in his third year as the principal of Gresham
Junior High School, in Fountain City—a small Knox County town that
had been swallowed up by Knoxville when the suburbs began to move
north. A tall man, with curly black hair going on gray, Leo Cooper has
an elaborate way of talking ("Unless I'm very badly mistaken, he has
never related to me totally the content of his conversation") and a manner that may come from years of trying to leave errant junior-high-

school students with the impression that a responsible adult is magnanimous, even humble, about invariably being in the right. His wife, a high-school art teacher, paints and does batik, and created the name FaNee because she liked the way it looked and sounded—it sounds like "Fawn-*ee*" when the Coopers say it—but the impression she gives is not of artiness but of soft-spoken small-town gentility. When she found, in the course of cleaning up FaNee's room, that her ideal thirteen-year-old had been smoking cigarettes, she was, in her words, crushed. "FaNee was such a perfect child before that," JoAnn Cooper said some time later. "She was angry that we found out. She knew we knew that she had done something we didn't approve of, and then the rebellion started. I was hurt. I was very hurt. I guess it came through as disappointment."

2   Several months later, FaNee's grandmother died. FaNee had been devoted to her grandmother. She wrote a poem in her memory—an almost joyous poem, filled with Christian faith in the afterlife ("Please don't grieve over my happiness/Rejoice with me in the presence of the Angels of Heaven"). She also took some keepsakes from her grandmother's house, and was apparently mortified when her parents found them and explained that they would have to be returned. By then, the Coopers were aware that FaNee was going to have a difficult time as a teenager. They thought she might be self-conscious about the double affliction of glasses and braces. They thought she might be uncomfortable in the role of the principal's daughter at Gresham. In ninth grade, she entered Halls High School, where JoAnn Cooper was teaching art. FaNee was a loner at first. Then she fell in with what could only be considered a bad crowd.

3   Halls, a few miles to the north of Fountain City, used to be known as Halls Crossroads. It is what Knoxville people call "over the ridge"— on the side of Black Oak Ridge that has always been thought of as rural. When FaNee entered Halls High, the Coopers were already in the process of building a house on several acres of land they had bought in Halls, in a sparsely settled area along Brown Gap Road. Like two or three other houses along the road, it was to be constructed basically of huge logs taken from old buildings—a house that Leo Cooper describes as being like the name FaNee, "just a little bit different." Ten years ago, Halls Crossroads was literally a crossroads. Then some of the Knoxville expansion that had swollen Fountain City spilled over the ridge, planting subdivisions here and there on roads that still went for long stretches with nothing but an occasional house with a cow or two next to it. The increase in population did not create a town. Halls has no center. Its commercial area is a series of two or three shopping centers strung together on the Maynardville Highway, the four-lane that leads north into Union County—a place almost synonymous in east Tennessee with mountain poverty. Its restaurant is the Halls Freezo Drive-In. The gathering place for the group FaNee Cooper eventually found herself in was the Maynardville Highway Exxon station.

4   At Halls High School, the social poles were represented by the Jocks and the Freaks. FaNee found her friends among the Freaks. "I am truly enlighted upon irregular trains of thought aimed at strange depots of mental wards," she wrote when she was fifteen. "Yes! Crazed farms for the mental off—Oh! I walked through the halls scream & loud laughter fill my ears—Orderlys try to reason with me—but I am unreasonable! The joys of being a FREAK in a circus of imagination." The little crowd of eight or ten young people that FaNee joined has been referred to by her mother as "the Union County group." A couple of the girls were from backgrounds similar to FaNee's, but all the boys had the characteristics, if not the precise addresses, that Knoxville people associate with the poor whites of Union County. They were the sort of boys who didn't bother to finish high school, or finished it in a special program for slow learners, or got ejected from it for taking a swing at the principal.

5   "I guess you can say they more or less dragged us down to their level with the drugs," a girl who was in the group—a girl who can be called Marcia—said recently. "And somehow we settled for it. It seems like we had to get ourselves in the pit before we could look out." People in the group used marijuana and Valium and LSD. They sneered at the Jocks and the "prim and proper little ladies" who went with the Jocks. "We set ourselves aside," Marcia now says. "We put ourselves above everyone. How we did that I don't know." In a Knox County high school, teenagers who want to get themselves in the pit need not mainline heroin. The Jocks they mean to be compared to do not merely show up regularly for classes and practice football and wear clean clothes; they watch their language and preach temperance and go to prayer meetings on Wednesday nights and talk about having a real good Christian witness. Around Knoxville, people who speak of well-behaved high-school kids often seem to use words like "perfect," or even "angels." For FaNee's group, the opposite was not difficult to figure out. "We were into wicked things, strange things," Marcia says. "It was like we were on some kind of devil trip." FaNee wrote about demons and vultures and rats. "Slithering serpents eat my sanity and bite my ass," she wrote in an essay called "The Lovely Road of Life," just after she turned sixteen, "while tornadoes derail and ever so swiftly destroy every car in my train of thought." She wrote a lot about death.

6   FaNee's girl friends spoke of her as "super-intelligent." Her English teacher found some of her writing profound—and disturbing. She was thought to be not just super-intelligent but super-mysterious, and even, at times, super-weird—an introverted girl who stared straight ahead with deep-brown, nearly black eyes and seemed to have thoughts she couldn't share. Nobody really knew why she had chosen to run with the Freaks—whether it was loneliness or rebellion or simple boredom. Marcia thought it might have had something to do with a feeling that

her parents had settled on Kristy as their perfect child. "I guess she figured she couldn't be the best," Marcia said recently. "So she decided she might as well be the worst."

7   Toward the spring of FaNee's junior year at Halls, her problems seemed to deepen. Despite her intelligence, her grades were sliding. She was what her mother called "a mental dropout." Leo Cooper had to visit Halls twice because of minor suspensions. Once, FaNee had been caught smoking. Once, having ducked out of a required assembly, she was spotted by a favorite teacher, who turned her in. At home, she exchanged little more than short, strained formalities with Kristy, who shared their parents' opinion of FaNee's choice of friends. The Coopers had finished their house—a large house, its size accentuated by the huge old logs and a great stone fireplace and outside "Paul Bunyan"- style furniture—but FaNee spent most of her time there in her own room, sleeping or listening to rock music through earphones. One night, there was a terrible scene when FaNee returned from a concert in a condition that Leo Cooper knew had to be the result of marijuana. JoAnn Cooper, who ordinarily strikes people as too gentle to raise her voice, found herself losing her temper regularly. Finally, Leo Cooper asked a counsellor he knew, Jim Griffin, to stop in at Halls High School and have a talk with FaNee—unofficially.

8   Griffin—a young man with a warm, informal manner—worked for the Juvenile Court of Knox County. He had a reputation for being able to reach teenagers who wouldn't talk to their parents or to school administrators. One Friday in March of 1977, he spent an hour and a half talking to FaNee Cooper. As Griffin recalls the interview, FaNee didn't seem alarmed by his presence. She seemed to him calm and controlled—Griffin thought it was something like talking to another adult—and, unlike most of the teenagers he dealt with, she looked him in the eye the entire time. Griffin, like some of FaNee's friends, found her eyes unsettling—"the coldest, most distant, but, at the same time, the most knowing eyes I'd ever seen." She expressed affection for her parents, but she didn't seem interested in exploring ways of getting along better with them. The impression she gave Griffin was that they were who they were, and she was who she was, and there didn't happen to be any connection. Several times, she made the same response to Griffin's suggestions: "It's too late."

9   That weekend, neither FaNee nor her parents brought up the subject of Griffin's visit. Leo Cooper has spoken of the weekend as being particularly happy; a friend of FaNee's who stayed over remembers it as particularly strained. FaNee stayed home from school on Monday because of a bad headache—she often had bad headaches—but felt well enough on Monday evening to drive to the library. She was to be home at nine. When she wasn't, Mrs. Cooper began to phone her friends. Finally, around ten, Leo Cooper got into his other car and took a swing

around Halls—past the teenager hangouts like the Exxon station and the Pizza Hut and the Smoky Mountain Market. Then he took a second swing. At eleven, FaNee was still not home.

10   She hadn't gone to the library. She had picked up two girl friends and driven to the home of a third, where everyone took five Valium tablets. Then the four girls drove over to the Exxon station, where they met four boys from their crowd. After a while, the group bought some beer and some marijuana and reassembled at Charlie Stevens's trailer. Charlie Stevens was five or six years older than everyone else in the group—a skinny, slow-thinking young man with long black hair and a sparse beard. He was married and had a child, but he and his wife had separated; she was back in Union County with the baby. Stevens had remained in their trailer—parked in the yard near his mother's house, in a back-road area of Knox County dominated by decrepit, unpainted sheds and run-down trailers and rusted-out automobiles. Stevens had picked up FaNee at home once or twice—apparently, more as a driver for the group than as a date—and the Coopers, having learned that his unsuitability extended to being married, had asked her not to see him.

11   In Charlie's trailer, which had no heat or electricity, the group drank beer and passed around joints, keeping warm with blankets. By eleven or so, FaNee was what one of her friends has called "super-messed-up." Her speech was slurred. She was having trouble keeping her balance. She had decided not to go home. She had apparently persuaded herself that her parents intended to send her away to some sort of home for incorrigibles. "It's too late," she said to one of her friends. "It's just too late." It was decided that one of the boys, David Munsey, who was more or less the leader of the group, would drive the Coopers' car to FaNee's house, where FaNee and Charlie Stevens would pick him up in Stevens's car—a worn Pinto with four bald tires, one light, and a dragging muffler. FaNee wrote a note to her parents, and then, perhaps because her handwriting was suffering the effects of beer and marijuana and Valium, asked Stevens to rewrite it on a large piece of paper, which would be left on the seat of the Coopers' car. The Stevens version was just about the same as FaNee's, except that Stevens left out a couple of sentences about trying to work things out ("I'm willing to try") and, not having won any spelling championships himself, he misspelled a few words, like "tomorrow." The note said, "Dear Mom and Dad. Sorry I'm late. Very late. I left your car because I thought you might need it tomorrow. I love you all, but this is something I just had to do. The man talked to me privately for one and a half hours and I was really scared, so this is something I just had to do, but don't worry, I'm with a very good friend. Love you all. FaNee. P.S. Please try to understand I love you all very much, really I do. Love me if you have a chance."

12   At eleven-thirty or so, Leo Cooper was sitting in his living room, looking out the window at his driveway—a long gravel road that runs almost four hundred feet from the house to Brown Gap Road. He saw the car that FaNee had been driving pull into the driveway. "She's home," he called to his wife, who had just left the room. Cooper walked out on the deck over the garage. The car had stopped at the end of the driveway, and the lights had gone out. He got into his other car and drove to the end of the driveway. David Munsey had already joined Charlie Stevens and FaNee, and the Pinto was just leaving, travelling at a normal rate of speed. Leo Cooper pulled out on the road behind them.

13   Stevens turned left on Crippen Road, a road that has a field on one side and two or three small houses on the other, and there Cooper pulled his car in front of the Pinto and stopped, blocking the way. He got out and walked toward the Pinto. Suddenly, Stevens put the car in reverse, backed into a driveway a hundred yards behind him, and sped off. Cooper jumped in his car and gave chase. Stevens raced back to Brown Gap Road, ran a stop sign there, ran another stop sign at Maynardville Highway, turned north, veered off onto the old Andersonville Pike, a nearly abandoned road that runs parallel to the highway, and then crossed back over the highway to the narrow, dark country roads on the other side. Stevens sometimes drove with his lights out. He took some of the corners by suddenly applying his hand brake to make the car swerve around in a ninety-degree turn. He was in familiar territory—he actually passed his trailer—and Cooper had difficulty keeping up. Past the trailer, Stevens swept down a hill into a sharp left turn that took him onto Foust Hollow Road, a winding hilly road not much wider than one car.

14   At a fork, Cooper thought he had lost the Pinto. He started to go right, and then saw what seemed to be a spark from Stevens's dragging muffler off to the left, in the darkness. Cooper took the left fork, down Salem Church Road. He went down a hill, and then up a long, curving hill to a crest, where he saw the Stevens car ahead. "I saw the car airborne. Up in the air," he later testified. "It was up in the air. And then it completely rolled over one more time. It started to make another flip forward, and just as it started to flip to the other side it flipped back this way, and my daughter's body came out."

15   Cooper slammed on his brakes and skidded to a stop up against the Pinto. "Book!" Stevens shouted—the group's equivalent of "Scram!" Stevens and Munsey disappeared into the darkness. "It was dark, no one around, and so I started yelling for FaNee," Cooper has testified. "I thought it was an eternity before I could find her body, wedged under the back end of that car. . . . I tried everything I could, and saw that I couldn't get her loose. So I ran to a trailer back up to the top of the hill back up there to try to get that lady to call to get me some help, and

then apparently she didn't think that I was serious. . . . I took the jack out of my car and got under, and it was dark, still couldn't see too much what was going on . . . and started prying and got her loose, and I don't know how. And then I dragged her over to the side, and, of course, at the time I felt reasonably assured that she was gone, because her head was completely—on one side just as if you had taken a sledge-hammer and just hit it and bashed it in. And I did have the pleasure of one thing. I had the pleasure of listening to her breathe about the last three times she ever breathed in her life."

16   David Munsey did not return to the wreck that night, but Charlie Stevens did. Leo Cooper was kneeling next to his daughter's body. Cooper insisted that Stevens come close enough to see FaNee. "He was kneeling down next to her," Stevens later testified. "And he said, 'Do you know what you've done? Do you really know what you've done?' Like that. And I just looked at her, and I said, 'Yes,' and just stood there. Because I couldn't say nothing." There was, of course, a legal decision to be made about who was responsible for FaNee Cooper's death. In a deposition, Stevens said he had been fleeing for his life. He testified that when Leo Cooper blocked Crippen Road, FaNee had said that her father had a gun and intended to hurt them. Stevens was bound over and eventually indicted for involuntary manslaughter. Leo Cooper testified that when he approached the Pinto on Crippen Road, FaNee had a strange expression that he had never seen before. "It wasn't like FaNee, and I knew something was wrong," he said. "My concern was to get FaNee out of the car." The district attorney's office asked that Cooper be bound over for reckless driving, but the judge declined to do so. "Any father would have done what he did," the judge said. "I can see no criminal act on the part of Mr. Cooper."

17   Almost two years passed before Charlie Stevens was brought to trial. Part of the problem was assuring the presence of David Munsey, who had joined the Navy but seemed inclined to assign his own leaves. In the meantime, the Coopers went to court with a civil suit—they had "uninsured-motorist coverage," which requires their insurance company to cover any defendant who has no insurance of his own—and they won a judgment. There were ways of assigning responsibility, of course, which had nothing to do with the law, civil or criminal. A lot of people in Knoxville thought that Leo Cooper had, in the words of his lawyer, "done what any daddy worth his salt would have done." There were others who believed that FaNee Cooper had lost her life because Leo Cooper had lost his temper. Leo Cooper was not among those who expressed any doubts about his actions. Unlike his wife, whose eyes filled with tears at almost any mention of FaNee, Cooper seemed able, even eager to go over the details of the accident again and again. With the help of a school-board security man, he conducted his own investigation. He drove over the route dozens of times. "I've thought about it

every day, and I guess I will the rest of my life," he said as he and his lawyer and the prosecuting attorney went over the route again the day before Charlie Stevens's trial finally began. "But I can't tell any alternative for a father. I simply wanted her out of that car. I'd have done the same thing again, even at the risk of losing her."

18   Tennessee law permits the family of a victim to hire a special prosecutor to assist the district attorney. The lawyer who acted for the Coopers in the civil case helped prosecute Charlie Stevens. Both he and the district attorney assured the jurors that the presence of a special prosecutor was not to be construed to mean that the Coopers were vindictive. Outside the courtroom, Leo Cooper said that the verdict was of no importance to him—that he felt sorry, in a way, for Charlie Stevens. But there were people in Knoxville who thought Cooper had a lot riding on the prosecution of Charlie Stevens. If Stevens was not guilty of FaNee Cooper's death—found so by twelve of his peers—who was?

19   At the trial, Cooper testified emotionally and remarkably graphically about pulling FaNee out from under the car and watching her die in his arms. Charlie Stevens had shaved his beard and cut his hair, but the effort did not transform him into an impressive witness. His lawyer—trying to argue that it would have been impossible for Stevens to concoct the story about FaNee's having mentioned a gun, as the prosecution strongly implied—said, "His mind is such that if you ask him a question you can hear his mind go around, like an old mill creaking." Stevens did not deny the recklessness of his driving or the sorry condition of his car. It happened to be the only car he had available to flee in, and he had fled in fear for his life.

20   The prosecution said that Stevens could have let FaNee out of the car when her father stopped them, or could have gone to the commercial strip on the Maynardville Highway for protection. The prosecution said that Leo Cooper had done what he might have been expected to do under the circumstances—alone, late at night, his daughter in danger. The defense said precisely the same about Stevens: he had done what he might have been expected to do when being pursued by a man he had reason to be afraid of. "I don't fault Mr. Cooper for what he did but I'm sorry he did it," the defense attorney said. "I'm sorry the girl said what she said." The jury deliberated for eighteen minutes. Charlie Stevens was found guilty. The jury recommended a sentence of from two to five years in the state penitentiary. At the announcement, Leo Cooper broke down and cried. JoAnn Cooper's eyes filled with tears; she blinked them back and continued to stare straight ahead.

21   In a way, the Coopers might still strike a casual visitor as an ideal family—handsome parents, a bright and bubbly teenage daughter, a little boy learning the hook shot from his father, a warm house with some land around it. FaNee's presence is there, of course. A picture of her, with a small bouquet of flowers over it, hangs in the living room.

One of her poems is displayed in a frame on a table. Even if Leo Cooper continues to think about that night for the rest of his life, there are questions he can never answer. Was there a way that Leo and JoAnn Cooper could have prevented FaNee from choosing the path she chose? Would she still be alive if Leo Cooper had not jumped into his car and driven to the end of the driveway to investigate? Did she in fact tell Charlie Stevens that her father would hurt them—or even that her father had a gun? Did she want to get away from her family even at the risk of tearing around dark country roads in Charlie Stevens's dismal Pinto? Or did she welcome the risk? The poem of FaNee's that the Coopers have displayed is one she wrote a week before her death:

> I think I'm going to die
> And I really don't know why.
> But look in my eye
> When I tell you good-bye.
> I think I'm going to die.

A. Comprehension

Choose the answer that best completes each statement. Do not refer to the selection while doing this exercise.

1. Even as a young child, FaNee Cooper was
   (a) outgoing and happy.
   (b) moody and sullen.
   (c) reserved and introspective.
   (d) alienated and withdrawn.

2. The two social extremes at Halls High School were represented by
   (a) the Jocks and the Freaks.
   (b) the college-bound and the dropouts.
   (c) the drug users and the abstainers.
   (d) the Christians and the nonbelievers.

3. Jim Griffin, the counselor who tried to talk to FaNee about her problems, was unsettled by her
   (a) incoherent speech.
   (b) distrust of her parents' motives.
   (c) cold, yet knowing eyes.
   (d) inability to distinguish between fantasy and reality.

4. Aside from the fact that he was older than FaNee and her friends, her parents also found Charlie Stevens unsuitable because he
   (a) had been in prison.
   (b) had dropped out of high school.
   (c) was continually stoned on drugs.
   (d) was married.

5. Concerning the death of FaNee Cooper, the jury
    (a) could not reach a verdict.
    (b) acquitted Charlie Stevens.
    (c) found Charlie Stevens guilty.
    (d) found FaNee's father guilty of contributory negligence.

B. Vocabulary

For each italicized word from the selection, choose the best definition according to the context in which it appears. You may refer to the selection to answer the questions in this section and in all the remaining sections.

1. *errant* junior-high-school students [paragraph 1]:
    (a) roving, especially in search of adventure.
    (b) straying from the proper course or standards.
    (c) describing those who commit serious offenses.
    (d) inconsistent and irresponsible.
2. a responsible adult is *magnanimous* [1]:
    (a) serious, solemn.
    (b) arrogant, egotistical.
    (c) noble of heart and mind.
    (d) greatly concerned, caring.
3. soft-spoken small-town *gentility* [1]: The characteristic of being
    (a) narrow-minded, having parochial values.
    (b) politically and socially conservative.
    (c) intolerant, bigoted.
    (d) refined, well-bred.
4. they . . . preach *temperance* [5]:
    (a) forgiveness.
    (b) repentance.
    (c) salvation.
    (d) moderation.
5. the Coopers were *vindictive* [18]:
    (a) cleared of suspicion or blame.
    (b) revengeful, unforgiving.
    (c) soft-hearted, lenient.
    (d) justified, excused.

C. Inferences

On the basis of the evidence in the selection, answer the following questions.

1. From paragraph 1, what can you infer about FaNee Cooper's religious

    upbringing? _____

2. What do FaNee's writings, described in paragraph 5, suggest about

her? _____

_____

3. What do you think FaNee meant by her response to Jim Griffin (see

paragraph 8): "It's too late"? _____

_____

_____

4. According to paragraph 19, why did his lawyer say that it would have
been impossible for Stevens to invent the story about FaNee's

reference to a gun? _____

_____

D. Structure

Complete the following questions.

1. Trillin's specific purpose in writing is to
   (a) warn young people about the dangers of drugs and of getting
       involved with the wrong crowd.
   (b) warn parents about the temptations teenagers are faced with
       today.
   (c) assign the blame for FaNee's death.
   (d) examine the circumstances surrounding FaNee's death.
2. In paragraph 1, Trillin describes Leo Cooper as "trying to
   leave . . . the impression "that a responsible adult is magnanimous,
   even humble, about invariably being in the right." First, paraphrase

   this description. _____

   _____

   Does this characterization confirm or contradict his subsequent

   actions regarding FaNee and the night she died? _____
3. Which statement from the selection best explains the reason for

   FaNee's rebellion? _____

   _____

4. Trillin suggests that FaNee's death was probably caused by
   (a) her own mistakes and the harmful influence of the Freaks she associated with.
   (b) Charlie Stevens's reckless driving.
   (c) Leo Cooper's pursuit of Stevens's car.
   (d) a tragic combination of circumstances and mistakes on the part of everyone involved.
5. The overall tone of the selection can be described as
   (a) hostile, judgmental.
   (b) impartial, objective.
   (c) skeptical, cynical.
   (d) accusatory, vindictive.

Questions for Discussion and Analysis

1. In what way is Trillin's description of Leo Cooper's character central to understanding the tragedy of FaNee's death?
2. Who do you think is most culpable in FaNee's death? What evidence can you point to in the essay? Does Trillin maintain his objectivity throughout the essay, or are there glimmerings of accusations against Leo Cooper?

IN THE BOOKSTORE

In *The Other Side of the River* (1998), American journalist Alex Kotlowitz, much in the manner of Trillin in this essay, investigates the suspicious drowning of a black teenager in the St. Joseph River in southwest Michigan. The twin cities of Benton Harbor and St. Joseph are divided geographically by the St. Joseph River and culturally by race. Kotlowitz interviewed dozens of people and, against the larger backdrop of race and geography, tries to understand how the tragedy occurred.

Selection 5

Colors

Diane Ackerman

The author of five books of poetry and the recipient of numerous literary prizes, Diane Ackerman is a poet and a writer of nonfiction. She has taught at many universities, among them Washington University, New York

Photo © Toshi Otsuki.

University, Columbia University, and Cornell University, where she is currently teaching English. The book that this essay is taken from, A Natural History of the Senses, *is part anthropology, part biology, part cultural history; it is an engaging look at the wonders to be found as we explore the world with our senses.*

1   Polar bears are not white, they're clear. Their transparent fur doesn't contain a white pigment, but the hair shafts house many tiny air bubbles, which scatter the sun's white light, and we register the spectacle as white fur. The same thing happens with a swan's white feathers, and the white wings of some butterflies. We tend to think of everything on earth as having its own deep-down rich color, but even razzmatazz colors that hit one's eyes like carefully aimed fireworks are just a thin rind on things, the merest layer of pigment. And many objects have no pigment at all, but seem richly colored nonetheless because of tricks played by our eyes. Just as the oceans and sky are blue because of the scattering of light rays, so are a blue jay's feathers, which contain no blue pigment. The same is true of the blue on a turkey's neck, the blue on the tail of the blue-tailed skink, the blue on a baboon's rump. Grass and leaves, on the other hand, are inherently green because of the green pigment chlorophyll. The tropical rain forests and the northern woods both sing a green anthem. Against a backdrop of chlorophyll green, earth brown, and sky-and-water blue, animals have evolved kaleidoscopic colors to attract mates, disguise themselves, warn off would-be predators, scare rivals away from their territory, signal a parent that it's time to be fed. Woodland birds are often drably colored and lightly speckled, to blend in with the branches and sifting sunlight. There are lots of "LBJs," or "little brown jobs," as birders sometimes call them.

2   Abbott Thayer, an early-twentieth-century artist and naturalist, noticed what he called *countershading,* a natural camouflaging that makes animals most brightly colored on the parts of their body that are least exposed to sunlight, and darker on those areas that are most exposed. A good example is the penguin, which is white on the breast so that it will look like pale sky when viewed from underneath in the ocean, and black on its back, so that it will blend in with the dark depths of the ocean when viewed from on top. Since penguins are not in much danger from land predators, their obvious two-tone linoleum-floor look doesn't matter when they're waddling on shore. Camouflage and display is the name of the game in the animal kingdom. Insects are especially good at disguise; one famous example is the British peppered moth, which took only fifty years to change from a lackluster salt-and-pepper gray to nearly black so that it could blend in with tree bark that had become stained by industrial pollution. Pale moths were easier for

a bird to spot as the tree trunks grew darker, and so darker moths survived to produce even darker moths which in turn survived. Animals will do most anything to disguise themselves: Many fish have what look like eyes on their tails so that a predator will aim its attack on a less vital part of the body; some grasshoppers look so much like quartz they become invisible on South African hills; clever butterflies sport large, dark eyespots on their wings, so that a songbird predator will think it's facing an owl; the insects called walking sticks appear dark and gnarly as twigs; Kenyan bush crickets blend in with the lichens on a tree trunk; katydids green up like leaves—some species even develop brown fungusy-looking sections; a Peruvian grasshopper mimics the crinkled dead leaves on the forest floor; the Malaysian tussock moth has wings that resemble decaying leaves: brown, torn, or perforated. Various insects costume themselves as snakes, others as bird droppings; lizards, shrimp, frogs, fish, and a few spiders tint their body color to blend in with their surroundings. Camouflage to a fish means scintillating like the water that surrounds it, breaking up the apparent outline of its body, and vanishing among the corridors of down-welling light. As Sandra Sinclair explains it in *How Animals See:* "Each scale reflects one-third of the spectrum; where three scales overlap, all colors are canceled out, leaving a mirrorlike effect." All a predator may see is a twisting flash of light. Luminescent squids maneuver at depths where there is little light; swimming through the gloom, they mimic the natural light from above, and can even disguise themselves as clouds floating over the surface of the water in order to become invisible to their prey. They are "stealth" squids. All sorts of animals can change color quickly by shrinking or enlarging their store of melanin; they either spread the color around so much that they look darker, or tug the color into a smaller space so that some underlying pigment becomes visible. In *Speak, Memory,* Vladimir Nabokov writes joyously of his fascination with the mimicry of moths and butterflies:

> Consider the imitation of oozing poison by bubblelike macules on a wing . . . or by glossy yellow knobs on a chrysalis ("Don't eat me—I have already been squashed, sampled and rejected"). Consider the tricks of an acrobatic caterpillar (of the Lobster Moth) which in infancy looks like bird's dung. . . . When a certain moth resembles a certain wasp in shape and color, it also walks and moves its antennae in a waspish, unmothlike manner. When a butterfly has to look like a leaf, not only are all the details of a leaf beautifully rendered but markings mimicking grub-bored holes are generously thrown in. "Natural selection," in the Darwinian sense, could not explain the miraculous coincidence of imitative aspect and imitative behavior, nor could one appeal to the theory of the "struggle for life" when a protective device was carried to a point of mimetic subtlety, exuberance,

and luxury far in excess of a predator's power of appreciation. I discovered in nature the nonutilitarian delights that I sought in art. Both were a form of magic, both were a game of intricate enchantment and deception.

3   Animals indulge in such lavish and luscious forms of display that it would take a whole book just to list their color-mad graces. The peacock's scintillating, many-eyed tail is so famous an example it's become eponymous. "What a peacock he is!" we say of a gentleman dandied up beyond belief. Color as a silent language works so well that nearly every animal speaks it. Octopuses change color as they change mood. A scared freshwater perch automatically turns pale. A king penguin chick knows to peck at the apricot comet on its parent's bill if it wants to be fed. A baboon flashes its blue rump in sexual or submissive situations. Confront a male robin with a handful of red feathers and it will attack it. A deer pops its white tail as a warning to its kin and then springs out of the yard. We lift our eyebrows to signal our disbelief. But many animals wear their gaudy colors as warnings, as well. The arrowpoison frog, which dwells in the Amazon rain forest, glistens with vibrant aqua blue and scarlet. *Don't mess with me!* its color shrieks at would-be predators. I was with a group of people who came upon such a frog squatting on a log, and the temptation to touch its cloisonné-like back was so strong one man automatically began to reach out for it when his neighbor grabbed his wrist, just in time. That frog didn't need to flee; it was coated with a slime so poisonous that if the man had touched it, and then touched his eye or mouth, he would have been poisoned on the spot.

A. *Comprehension*

Choose the answer that best completes each statement. Do not refer to the selection while doing this exercise.

   1.   The main idea of the selection is that
        (a) the colors we see in the world around us are not all that they seem.
        (b) animals have evolved an amazing variety of colors to disguise, protect, and display.
        (c) bright colors in nature add interest to the backdrop of greens, blues, and browns.
        (d) camouflage and countershading are forms of protective coloration used by birds and insects.
   2.   Polar bears look white because
        (a) their hair shafts contain a white pigment.
        (b) they are usually seen against a backdrop of ice or snow.
        (c) their hair reflects and scatters the sun's white light.
        (d) their hair appears lighter as the sun ascends to its zenith in the sky.

3. The term *countershading* refers to a form of natural camouflage whereby the
   (a) brightly colored parts of an animal's body are least exposed to sunlight and the darker areas are most exposed.
   (b) darker-colored parts of an animal's body are least exposed and the lighter colors are most exposed.
   (c) lighter and darker parts of an animal's body shift according to the play of the sun's light rays throughout the day.
   (d) black and white shadings are cleverly distributed to fool an animal's predators.

4. The color of the British peppered moth evolved from salt-and-pepper gray to nearly black in only 50 years because
   (a) the darker color would help the moth evade its predators.
   (b) the darker color could not be seen as easily against a brown and green landscape.
   (c) the darker color blended in better with tree bark darkened by industrial pollution.
   (d) the moths instinctively realized that a darker color would attract more mates.

5. The animal that best represents the use of color and display to attract attention is
   (a) the freshwater perch.
   (b) the arrowpoison frog.
   (c) the baboon.
   (d) the peacock.

B. Vocabulary

For each italicized word from the selection, choose the best definition according to the context in which it appears. You may refer to the selection to answer the questions in this section and in all the remaining sections.

1. even *razzmatazz* colors [paragraph 1]:
   (a) flashy—so as to confuse or deceive.
   (b) subtle, not obvious.
   (c) variegated, streaked.
   (d) overly bright and hurtful to the eyes.

2. grass and leaves . . . are *inherently* green [1]: Describing something that is
   (a) inherited, inborn.
   (b) essential, characteristic of.
   (c) restrained, inhibited.
   (d) vivid, vibrant.

3. animals have evolved *kaleidoscopic* colors [1]:
    (a) constantly changing.
    (b) unearthly, unworldly.
    (c) reflected, mirrored.
    (d) primary—red, blue, and yellow.
4. *scintillating* like the water [2]:
    (a) undulating, waving.
    (b) rising and falling, like the tides.
    (c) shining, sparkling.
    (d) swiftly flowing.
5. tail . . . [has become] *eponymous* [3]: Describing a word that
    (a) means the opposite of what most people think it means.
    (b) is identified with and derives from the source of the word.
    (c) is a slang term for a more formal word.
    (d) is used figuratively.
6. a gentleman *dandied* up [3]: From *dandy,* a man who
    (a) is careless about his dress and appearance.
    (b) affects great style and elegance in his dress, is a fashion plate.
    (c) spends great sums of money on clothing.
    (d) dresses too formally, even for casual occasions.

C. Inferences

Complete the following questions.

1. From paragraph 1, we can accurately infer that the colors we perceive on certain animals derive from
    (a) the play of the sun's rays.
    (b) the degree of pigment in the object.
    (c) the background environment against which we see them.
    (d) the tricks our eyes play on us.
2. From paragraph 2, we can accurately infer that nature's mimicry is designed to
    (a) allow the species to survive in hostile environments.
    (b) fool predators by allowing the prey to blend into the background.
    (c) successfully attract mates.
    (d) scare potential rivals away from their territories.
3. The quotation by Vladimir Nabokov in paragraph 2 suggests that, at least for him, mimicry in butterflies and moths
    (a) confirms Darwin's theory of natural selection.
    (b) reflects all organisms' struggle for life.
    (c) cannot be explained rationally.
    (d) parallels the magic and delight Nabokov found in art.

D. Structure

Complete the following questions.

1. This selection represents mixed modes of discourse, specifically,
   (a) narration and description.
   (b) description and exposition.
   (c) exposition and persuasion.
   (d) narration and exposition.

2. Read paragraph 1 again. Locate and write the sentence that expresses

   the thesis of the selection. _____

   _____

   _____

   _____

   _____

3. The predominant method of development throughout the selection is
   (a) informative steps in a process.
   (b) comparison and contrast.
   (c) definition.
   (d) example and illustration.

4. Concerning the subject of animal coloration, Ackerman's informative
   tone is also one of
   (a) amazement and wonder.
   (b) curiosity and questioning.
   (c) admiration and praise.
   (d) sentimentality and mawkishness.

Questions for Discussion and Analysis

1. Ackerman's paragraphs are quite dense. What are some devices she uses to keep the reader focused and to provide coherence within her discussion?
2. Point to some words, phrases, and sentences where Ackerman reveals her obvious enchantment with her subject.

ON THE WEB

An interview with Diane Ackerman is available at this URL:
www.januarymagazine.com/profiles/ackerman.html

Selection 6   # Abstracting Our Way into Doublespeak
William Lutz

You may recall the discussion of doublespeak and its pernicious influence from Chapter 6. William Lutz, a professor of English at Rutgers University in Camden, New Jersey, for several years has been a zealous crusader warning the public about the dangers of doublespeak, both as head of the Committee on Public Doublespeak for the National Council of Teachers of English and as editor of The Quarterly Review of Doublespeak. Doublespeak *is defined in the dictionary as "deliberately ambiguous or evasive language." Lutz defines it as "language that makes the bad seem good, the negative appear positive, the unpleasant appear attractive or at least tolerable."*

This excerpt is from his latest book, The New Doublespeak. *In it, he examines the origins of doublespeak and the importance of separating facts from inferences.*

1   Heraclitus of Ephesus, writing around 500 B.C., gave us what philosophers call the doctrine of perpetual change. Everything is in a constant state of flux, said Heraclitus, like a flowing river. We cannot step into the "same" river twice because the water we step into the second time is not the same water we stepped into the first time. So it is with the world.

2   The world isn't the stable place we think it is. Like Heraclitus's river, everything is in a constant state of flux, of change. We give stability to this constantly changing world through our ability to re-create it by focusing on similarities and ignoring differences. This process is called abstracting. When we abstract, we select the information we will pay attention to while ignoring the rest, focusing on a limited amount of information that we then arrange into recognizable patterns. Abstracting is a continuous process that allows us to give stability to a very unstable world.

3   All our senses are constantly selecting, organizing, and generalizing the information they receive. When we abstract, we create a kind of summary of what the world is like. We may not be able to step into the same river twice, but by abstracting we act as if we can.

4   [a]Watching television is a simple example of how we constantly abstract without being aware of the process. [b]We see a "picture" on the television screen when there isn't any picture there at all. [c]A television picture is composed of hundreds of thousands of tiny dots. [d]As some dots are lit and some aren't, our brains collect the sensations and organize them into patterns that we see as moving pictures. [e]Those tiny dots on the screen are lit about thirty times per second while our brains organize the dots they see into patterns about ten times per second. [f]Yet even after we understand this process, most of us think the picture is on the screen and not in our heads.

5   Consider this example of the abstraction process involved in seeing a chair. As any physicist will tell you, a chair isn't a "thing" at all; it's an event. A chair is composed of billions of atomic and subatomic particles in constant motion, and even those particles aren't solid matter but are made up of bundles of energy. We can't see these particles, but it's important to remind ourselves that our chair is made up of all these moving particles because then we will remember that the world is not the way we see it. What we see when we look at our chair, and at the rest of world, is a summary, an abstraction, of all the motion of all those particles.

6   Even then we don't see the chair because no one has ever seen a chair in its entirety, all at once. You can see parts of the chair, but not the whole chair—top, bottom, sides—all at once. But we can see enough of the chair that we can construct the entire chair and act as if we know the whole chair. But sometimes our construction can lead us astray, as when we don't see the crack in the leg and find ourselves on the floor when our chair collapses. Still, our assumption about our chair will serve us well enough most of the time so that we never question the abstracting process. Indeed, we continue our abstracting when we use language to name the events that make up our world.

Words and Things

7   Naming things—using language—is a very high level abstraction, and when we name something we "freeze" it by placing it in a category and making a "thing" out of it. But now we encounter a curious but most important aspect of this abstracting process. When through the process of abstraction we label an event a "chair," we have created a word for something that does not exist in the world. The word "chair" is an abstraction, a generalization and summary of all those things in the world that look and work in a similar way. The word "furniture" is a still higher abstraction that includes our chair and all those other things that don't look anything like a chair but share some similar features and functions. And we could abstract even further and include our chair in "home decoration" and "personal assets."

8   Here's another example, starting with a specific object and moving through increasingly higher levels of abstraction. Notice how each new level of abstraction ignores more and more differences while focusing on fewer and fewer similarities:

> 1996 red Toyota Camry → Toyota → new car → automobile → motor vehicle → vehicle → private transportation → transportation

9   By the time we get to "transportation" we've moved quite a distance from our 1996 red Toyota Camry. The higher the level of abstraction, the more detail we leave out, the more we ignore differences, and the more we concentrate on similarities, no matter how few or how

tenuous those similarities might be. When I talk about transportation, I am including only those aspects of the 1996 Toyota that place it in a category that includes bicycles, airplanes, and trucks.

10   Let's look at a cat named Phil.

Phil → Maine Coon → male cat → cat → mammal → vertebrate → animal → living thing → thing

11   Phil is a breed of cat known as a Maine Coon. He is also a male cat, and he is a mammal and a vertebrate. But by the time we get to "thing," we're a long way from the collection of atomic and subatomic particles that make up Phil.

12   There is usually less ambiguity at the lower levels of abstraction. If I refer to my 1996 red Toyota Camry, you have a better idea of what I'm talking about than if I refer to my "vehicle" or "private transportation." The words we use reveal the level of abstraction at which we are operating. The word "thing" excludes a lot of detail and can be used to refer to both my Camry and my house, and a whole lot of other objects in the universe. It is a word at the highest levels of abstraction.

13   The less abstract our language, the more concrete and specific we are because we are using language that includes a lot of detail and refers to a very low level of abstraction. I can say, "I like to play sports," or I can say, "I like to play baseball and basketball." Language that is more concrete and specific creates pictures in the mind of the listener, pictures that should come as close as possible to the pictures in your mind.

14   Highly abstract language is a common form of doublespeak, especially among politicians. "Revenue enhancement" is a good example of using a very abstract term to hide what is meant. The government has many forms of revenue besides taxes. And the government can increase its revenues in many ways, with a tax increase being just one of those ways. Indeed, even the term "tax increase" is fairly abstract. Which tax will be increased, and by how much? Are we talking about increasing the tax on corporations by 1 percent, or are we talking about increasing the income tax for anyone making $25,000 a year or less? Those are two very different tax increases, and we might want to talk about them.

15   However, some people would say that they don't care; any tax increase is bad. Of course, we might want to ask them what they mean by "bad," and "bad" for whom? It's bad for the economy, they reply. To which we might say, what do you mean by the "economy"? That's a very abstract term, probably as abstract as calling my 1996 Toyota Camry "transportation" and my cat Phil a "thing." Maybe we would like them to be a little less abstract and a little more specific.

16   Using a high level of abstraction we can call the new dump a "resource development park" and sewage sludge "biosolids" or "organic biomass." Such terms do not call to mind any specific picture because they are so far removed from the concrete reality they are supposed to symbol-

ize. In fact, the terms do exactly what their creators want them to do: They create no picture at all in our minds since we're not sure what they mean. When confronted with such abstractions we have to ask those who use them to give us some specific examples, to move down from their high levels of abstraction to specific examples that clearly illustrate what they are referring to. By using the doublespeak of abstraction, some officials were able to get approval to build a new dump in a residential neighborhood, while other officials won approval for a new sewage plant.

Reports, Inferences, and Judgments

17 At the lowest levels of abstraction we can use language that reports. Reports are based on what we have directly seen, heard, felt, or experienced. Reports are pretty straightforward: "It is raining." "I have a temperature of 101." "I paid $4.99 for that book." We can verify reports and confirm that they are accurate. We can look out the window and see the rain. We can use a thermometer to check a person's temperature. And we can see the sales receipt to verify the price paid for a book. Report language is concrete and specific.

18 In our everyday lives we accept reports of reports all the time. Did General Motors really make a profit last quarter? The newspapers said so, and even though we can't verify that report, we accept it. Without giving it much thought, we accept reports of reports all the time. We follow road maps and our doctor's advice. We read books on science, mathematics, and history, and assume that the authors are giving us reliable information.

Inferences

19 Much as we might like all language to be in the form of reports, we wouldn't get much done if it were. Instead, we use inferences to conduct our daily affairs. An inference is a statement about the unknown based on the known. It is a guess, sometimes an educated guess, and sometimes a wild leap of logic.

20 An inference starts with what is known or observed. You notice the newspapers piling up on your neighbors' porch. Then you notice the mail overflowing the mailbox. Since their car is gone and you haven't seen anyone around the house for a few days, you infer that they have gone on vacation. Your inference is based on your observations, observations that we could call reports because they are all verifiable. However, the statement that the Bergers have gone on vacation is an inference, a conclusion drawn from your observations.

21 It is possible, of course, that you are wrong in your inference. There are other possible inferences that you could draw. Perhaps the entire family has been murdered and the killer fled in their car. Or perhaps

Mrs. Berger took the children to her mother's in Florida for a visit while Mr. Berger is out of town on business. Or perhaps the Bergers haven't gone anywhere while their car is being repaired and they have forgotten to collect their mail and newspapers.

22   We make hundreds of inferences every day, and for the most part our inferences work. Since it is a weekday, we infer that stores will be open for business. We go to the bus stop because we infer that the bus will stop there again today to pick up passengers. We can test these inferences because either the stores are open or they aren't, and the bus will stop or it won't.

23   We also make other inferences that aren't so easily or quickly verifiable. We infer a person's economic and social status from the quality of her clothes, jewelry, and car. We infer the geopolitical strategy of Iran from its actions; we infer a person's feelings about us from his words and the way he treats us; we infer the existence of certain creatures based on fossils we collect; we infer the nature of Egyptian civilization from the ruins, written records, and artifacts we examine. Without inferences, we couldn't function in our everyday lives, and without inferences our knowledge of the world would be greatly reduced. However, we have to be aware of our inferences because we can easily draw false inferences without knowing it.

24   A segment on the television evening news shows us a home for unmarried, pregnant teenage girls. The reporter mentions that the home is overcrowded, that there are more pregnant teenagers than there is room at the home. This report is followed by an interview with a politician who says that we have to do something about teenagers having babies, which has become a crisis that demands action. Moreover, our politician adds somberly, teenagers having babies is more evidence of our moral decline. The next day, we mention in conversation that there's a serious problem with all those teenagers having babies.

25   From the television report we have drawn the inference that there are a large number of teenage girls having babies, a number that is growing. We might even infer that there is an "epidemic" of teenage pregnancies. But our inference would be wrong. Teenage pregnancies are not increasing. In fact, the birth rate among teenage girls is lower today than it was forty years ago. In 1955, approximately 90 out of every 1,000 women between the ages of fifteen and nineteen gave birth, while in 1993 the birth rate for that age group was down to 59 out of 1,000. And most of those babies are born to mothers who are eighteen or nineteen years old. So perhaps our inference that there is an epidemic of teenagers having babies is false. And if that inference is false, what about the inference that we are in a moral decline, assuming that we can all agree what we mean by such an abstract term? Drawing false inferences is sometimes called leaping to conclusions.

Judgments

26   Often we move from inference to a higher level of abstraction known as judgments. Instead of saying, "It is raining," "I have a temperature of 101," and "I paid $4.99 for that book," we might say, "The weather is terrible," "I look terrible," and "I paid too much for that book." These last three statements are judgments. A judgment is an expression of our approval or disapproval of what we are describing. In other words, judgments are nothing more than our personal opinions. We get into trouble when we confuse judgments with reports.

27   Consider these sentences:

1. The man lying in the street is unconscious.
2. The man lying in the street is drunk.
3. The man lying in the street is a bum.

28   The first sentence is a report, a description of fact. The second sentence is an inference, and the third sentence is a judgment. The first sentence is verifiable, while the second sentence is an interpretation of an observation, a statement about the unknown based on the known. We don't know that the man is drunk. We only see him, his physical condition, and his appearance. Based on those observations we may infer that he is drunk. That the man is a bum is a judgment, our evaluation of the man based on our inferences.

29   We often confuse reports and judgments. How often do we accept as a report statements such as: "Hemingway is a great writer." "The Toyota Camry is the best car you can buy," "Allen is stupid," "Socialized medicine is terrible," "Socialism and freedom are incompatible," "Conservatives are fascists," and "America is the greatest country in the world." Yet each of these statements is a judgment, an expression of the speaker's evaluation of the person or thing being discussed. These statements say nothing about the people and things being discussed but do reveal something of the speaker's values. Even if others agree with our judgments we do not have a report, just a similarity of values. Unfortunately, we too often treat judgments as if they were reports.

30   Here's a little story illustrating how we can use the abstraction process to make inferences and judgments that do not coincide with a description of the facts.

A Tale of Faulty Inferences

31   The train rushes across the Hungarian countryside. In a compartment sit a mother and her attractive daughter, a Nazi officer, and a Hungarian official. When the train passes through a tunnel, the compartment is engulfed in darkness. Suddenly there is the sound of a loud kiss followed by a shattering slap. When the train emerges from the tunnel, no one says a word, but the Nazi officer's face bears the unmistakable signs

of having been slapped. The mother looks at her daughter and thinks, "What a good daughter I have. She certainly showed that Nazi he can't fool with her." The daughter looks at her mother and thinks, "Mother sure is brave to take on a Nazi officer over one stolen kiss." The Nazi officer stares at the Hungarian official and thinks, "That Hungarian is clever. He steals a kiss and gets me slapped, and there's nothing I can do about it." The Hungarian official stares blankly as he thinks, "Not bad. I kiss my hand and get away with slapping a Nazi."

32   The facts of the story are simple: In the darkness there was a noise that sounded like a kiss, followed by a noise that sounded like a slap.

33   Based on these facts, each person in the compartment drew a different inference and arrived at a different judgment. The mother inferred that the Nazi had kissed her daughter and that her daughter had slapped the Nazi. The daughter inferred that the Nazi had kissed her mother and that her mother had retaliated with a slap. The Nazi inferred that the Hungarian had kissed the girl, prompting her to slap him in error.

34   Each of these people then made a judgment based on the inference. The mother thinks her daughter is "good" because she slapped the Nazi. The daughter thinks her mother is "brave" because she slapped the Nazi. The Nazi thinks the Hungarian is "clever" because he kissed the girl but got the Nazi slapped. The Hungarian, of course, knows what happened. While all the other people think they know the "facts" of the incident, they know only what they have inferred and the judgments they have made.

35   Abstracting is a fundamental and necessary process for dealing with the world. With it we can construct a coherent world with which we can interact. But we must remember that we are constantly engaged in a highly selective process, that we are choosing to ignore large chunks of our world. While abstraction can help us in dealing with our environment, it can also get us into trouble if we forget that we are abstracting and start to treat our inferences and judgments as if they are descriptive statements of the world.

A. Comprehension

Choose the answer that best completes each statement. Do not refer to the selection while doing this exercise.

1. According to Lutz, we give stability to the constantly changing world around us by abstracting, which he defines as
    (a) learning both written and spoken language.
    (b) focusing on similarities and ignoring differences.
    (c) learning to distinguish the abstract from the concrete.
    (d) paying attention only to the important things that happen around us.

2. When we look at a chair, we do not really see a chair because
    (a) we can't see every part of the chair, composed of constantly moving particles, at the same time.
    (b) the word *chair* is an abstract concept that doesn't mean the same thing to everyone.
    (c) we don't observe things around us, even simple objects like chairs, very well.
    (d) the word *chair* only stands for the object and doesn't represent the thing itself.

3. As we move up the ladder of abstraction, for example, from "1996 red Toyota Camry" to "transportation," we are really
    (a) showing that we do not think very clearly.
    (b) ignoring more differences and focusing on fewer similarities.
    (c) moving from the general to the specific.
    (d) demonstrating that these two terms are more alike than we think.

4. Lutz characterizes doublespeak, especially the language used by politicians, as
    (a) highly abstract and therefore unclear.
    (b) clear and concise.
    (c) unclear to everyone except the politicians who use it.
    (d) the result of lazy thinking and inattentiveness to the meanings of words.

5. An inference is a guess based on things we observe, and a judgment is
    (a) simply another word for *inference.*
    (b) similar to a report but with added subjective observations.
    (c) a kind of abstraction.
    (d) our evaluation based on our observation.

B. Vocabulary

For each italicized word from the selection, choose the best definition according to the context in which it appears. You may refer to the selection to answer the questions in this section and in all the remaining sections.

1. a constant state of *flux* [paragraph 1]:
    (a) chaos, confusion.
    (b) change, movement.
    (c) serenity, peace.
    (d) discomfort, uneasiness.

2. no matter how . . . *tenuous* [9]:
    (a) commonplace.
    (b) confusing.
    (c) having a strong connection.
    (d) lacking a sound basis.

3. usually less *ambiguity* [12]:
   (a) clarity, understanding.
   (b) difference of opinion.
   (c) uncertainty regarding interpretation.
   (d) dislocation.
4. the more *concrete* and specific [13]:
   (a) real, perceptible.
   (b) general, vague.
   (c) comprehensible.
   (d) limited in scope.
5. *engulfed* in darkness [31]:
   (a) made invisible.
   (b) hindered by.
   (c) interrupted by.
   (d) swallowed up.

C. Inferences

Complete the following questions.

1. Which would be more likely to result in doublespeak—general, more abstract words and phrases at the upper levels of abstraction or specific, more concrete words and phrases at the lower level of abstraction? _____

2. Why does Lutz object to the term "revenue enhancement"? (See paragraph 14.) _____

   _____

3. Look again at paragraph 16. Why do government officials use the doublespeak of abstraction? _____

   _____

D. Structure

Complete the following questions.

1. What is the meaning of the sentence "We cannot step into the 'same' river twice"? (See paragraph 1.) _____

   _____

2. Look again at the sentences in paragraph 4, which are identified by lowercase letters. Label each as MAIN (main idea), MA (major), or MI (minor).

_____ sentence a   _____ sentence b   _____ sentence c

_____ sentence d   _____ sentence e   _____ sentence f

3. The purpose of paragraphs 5 and 6 is, specifically, to
   (a) show that not all things that we call chairs are really chairs.
   (b) demonstrate the way we abstract to make sense of the world.
   (c) show the dangers of abstracting.
   (d) show the relationship between abstracting and making incorrect inferences.

4. Consider these three sentences in relation to the discussion in paragraphs 26 through 28. Then label each according to whether it is a report, an inference, or a judgment.

   _____ Henry must not have studied for his physics test.

   _____ Henry received a D on his physics test.

   _____ Henry is a poor student.

5. The "Tale of Faulty Inferences" in paragraphs 31 through 35 illustrates
   (a) how our cultural background can interfere with our good judgment.
   (b) how people make judgments based on incomplete facts.
   (c) why we should never make inferences or judgments.
   (d) how easy it is to blame the wrong person for a wrongdoing.

6. Which character in the story was the only one who knew the facts?

_____

Questions for Discussion and Analysis

1. For a class project, look through the daily newspaper and write down as many examples of doublespeak as you can find over a period of a few weeks. How many of the examples of doublespeak result from very high levels of abstraction, as Lutz explains it?
2. Create your own ladder of abstraction using, for example, a kind of fruit or a type of transportation.

ON THE WEB

Further examples of doublespeak can be found at these two websites. The second is a discussion list.

landru.i-link-2.net/monques/dblspk.html
www.ncte.org/lists/doublespeak/

Selection 7   # The Law of the Few
Malcolm Gladwell

© Jerry Bauer.

As a young child, Malcolm Gladwell emigrated with his family from the West Indies to Ontario, Canada. After graduating from the University of Toronto, he became a staff writer at The Washington Post, *covering business and science. Since 1996, he has been a staff writer at* The New Yorker. *This selection is reprinted from his book* The Tipping Point, *which examines the idea that ideas, behavior, and messages can spread just the way infectious diseases do. This particular excerpt examines "a select group of people—Salesmen [who have] the skills to persuade us when we are unconvinced of what we are hearing."*

1   The question of what makes someone—or something—persuasive is a lot less straightforward than it seems. We know it when we see it. But just what "it" is is not always obvious. Consider the following two examples, both drawn from the psychological literature. The first is an experiment that took place during the 1984 presidential campaign between Ronald Reagan and Walter Mondale. For eight days before the election, a group of psychologists led by Brian Mullen of Syracuse University videotaped the three national nightly news programs, which then, as now, were anchored by Peter Jennings at ABC, Tom Brokaw at NBC, and Dan Rather at CBS. Mullen examined the tapes and excerpted all references to the candidates, until he had 37 separate segments, each roughly two and a half seconds long. Those segments were then shown, with the sound turned off, to a group of randomly chosen people, who were asked to rate the facial expressions of each newscaster in each segment. The subjects had no idea what kind of experiment they were involved with, or what the newscasters were talking about. They were simply asked to score the emotional content of the expressions of these three men on a 21-point scale, with the lowest being "extremely negative" and the highest point on the scale "extremely positive."

2   The results were fascinating. Dan Rather scored 10.46—which translates to an almost perfectly neutral expression—when he talked about Mondale, and 10.37 when he talked about Reagan. He looked the same when he talked about the Republican as he did when he talked about the Democrat. The same was true for Brokaw, who scored 11.21 for Mondale and 11.50 for Reagan. But Peter Jennings of ABC was much different. For Mondale, he scored 13.38. But when he talked about Reagan, his face lit up so much he scored 17.44. Mullen and his colleagues went out of their way to try to come up with an innocent explanation for this. Could it be, for example, that Jennings is just more expressive in general than his colleagues? The answer seemed to be no. The sub-

jects were also shown control segments of the three newscasters, as they talked about unequivocally happy or sad subjects (the funeral of Indira Gandhi; a breakthrough in treating a congenital disease). But Jennings didn't score any higher on the happy subjects or lower on the sad subjects than his counterparts. In fact, if anything, he seemed to be the least expressive of the three. It also isn't the case that Jennings is simply someone who has a happy expression on his face all the time. Again, the opposite seemed to be true. On the "happy" segments inserted for comparison purposes, he scored 14.13, which was substantially lower than both Rather and Brokaw. The only possible conclusions, according to the study, is that Jennings exhibited a "significant and noticeable bias in facial expression" toward Reagan.

3   Now here is where the study gets interesting. Mullen and his colleagues then called up people in a number of cities around the country who regularly watch the evening network news and asked them who they voted for. In every case, those who watched ABC voted for Reagan in far greater numbers than those who watched CBS or NBC. In Cleveland, for example, 75 percent of ABC watchers voted Republican, versus 61.9 percent of CBS or NBC viewers. In Williamstown, Massachusetts, ABC viewers were 71.4 percent for Reagan versus 50 percent for the other two networks; in Erie, Pennsylvania, the difference was 73.7 percent to 50 percent. The subtle pro-Reagan bias in Jennings's face seems to have influenced the voting behavior of ABC viewers.

4   As you can imagine, ABC News disputes this study vigorously. ("It's my understanding that I'm the only social scientist to have the dubious distinction of being called a 'jackass' by Peter Jennings," says Mullen.) It is hard to believe. Instinctively, I think, most of us would probably assume that the causation runs in the opposite direction, that Reagan supporters are drawn to ABC because of Jennings's bias, not the other way around. But Mullen argues fairly convincingly that this isn't plausible. For example, on other, more obvious levels—like, for example, story selection—ABC was shown to be the network most hostile to Reagan, so it's just as easy to imagine hard-core Republicans deserting ABC news for the rival networks. And to answer the question of whether his results were simply a fluke, four years later, in the Michael Dukakis–George Bush campaign, Mullen repeated his experiment, with the exact same results. "Jennings showed more smiles when referring to the Republican candidate than the Democrat," Mullen said, "and again in a phone survey, viewers who watch ABC were more likely to have voted for Bush."

5   Here is another example of the subtleties of persuasion. A large group of students were recruited for what they were told was a market research study by a company making high-tech headphones. They were each given a headset and told that the company wanted to test to see how well they worked when the listener was in motion—dancing up and down, say, or moving his or her head. All of the students listened to

songs by Linda Ronstadt and the Eagles, and then heard a radio editorial arguing that tuition at their university should be raised from its present level of $587 to $750. A third were told that while they listened to the taped radio editorial they should nod their heads vigorously up and down. The next third were told to shake their heads from side to side. The final third were the control group. They were told to keep their heads still. When they were finished, all the students were given a short questionnaire, asking them questions about the quality of the songs and the effect of the shaking. Slipped in at the end was the question the experimenters really wanted an answer to: "What do you feel would be an appropriate dollar amount for undergraduate tuition per year?"

6   The answers to that question are just as difficult to believe as the answers to the newscasters poll. The students who kept their heads still were unmoved by the editorial. The tuition amount that they guessed was appropriate was $582—or just about where tuition was already. Those who shook their heads from side to side as they listened to the editorial—even though they thought they were simply testing headset quality—disagreed strongly with the proposed increase. They wanted tuition to fall on average to $467 a year. Those who were told to nod their heads up and down, meanwhile, found the editorial very persuasive. They wanted tuition to rise, on average, to $646. The simple act of moving their heads up and down—ostensibly for another reason entirely— was sufficient to cause them to recommend a policy that would take money out of their own pockets. Somehow nodding, in the end, mattered as much as Peter Jennings's smiles did in the 1984 election.

7   There are in these two studies, I think, very important clues as to what makes someone like Tom Gau[1]—or, for that matter, any of the Salesmen in our lives—so effective. The first is that little things can, apparently, make as much of a difference as big things. In the headphone study, the editorial had no impact on those whose heads were still. It wasn't particularly persuasive. But as soon as listeners started nodding, it became very persuasive. In the case of Jennings, Mullen says that someone's subtle signals in favor of one politician or another usually don't matter at all. But in the particular, unguarded way that people watch the news, a little bias can suddenly go a long way. "When people watch the news, they don't intentionally filter biases out, or feel they have to argue against the expression of the newscaster," Mullen explains. "It's not like someone saying: this is a very good candidate who deserves your vote. This isn't an obvious verbal message that we automatically dig in our heels against. It's much more subtle and for that reason much more insidious, and that much harder to insulate ourselves against."

[1]Tom Gau is a Southern California financial planner and, according to Gladwell's discussion in the passage preceding this one, is a "mesmerizing" salesman who could sell "absolutely anything."

8   The second implication of these studies is that nonverbal cues are as or more important than verbal cues. The subtle circumstances surrounding how we say things may matter more than what we say. Jennings, after all, wasn't injecting all kinds of pro-Reagan comments in his newscasts. In fact, as I mentioned, ABC was independently observed to have been the most hostile to Reagan. One of the conclusions of the authors of the headphones study—Gary Wells of the University of Alberta and Richard Petty of the University of Missouri—was that "television advertisements would be most effective if the visual display created repetitive vertical movement of the television viewers' heads (e.g., bouncing ball)." Simple physical movements and observations can have a profound effect on how we feel and think.

9   The third—and perhaps most important—implication of these studies is that persuasion often works in ways that we do not appreciate. It's not that smiles and nods are subliminal messages. They are straightforward and on the surface. It's just that they are incredibly subtle. If you asked the head nodders why they wanted tuition to increase so dramatically—tuition that would come out of their own pockets—none of them would say, because I was nodding my head while I listened to that editorial. They'd probably say that it was because they found the editorial particularly insightful or intelligent. They would attribute their attitudes to some more obvious, logical cause. Similarly the ABC viewers who voted for Reagan would never, in a thousand years, tell you that they voted that way because Peter Jennings smiled every time he mentioned the President. They'd say that it was because they liked Reagan's policies, or they thought he was doing a good job. It would never have occurred to them that they could be persuaded to reach a conclusion by something so arbitrary and seemingly insignificant as a smile or a nod from a newscaster. If we want to understand what makes someone like Tom Gau so persuasive, in other words, we have to look at much more than his obvious eloquence. We need to look at the subtle, the hidden, and the unspoken.

A. Comprehension

Choose the answer that best completes each statement. Do not refer to the selection while doing this exercise.

1. The participants in Brian Mullen's study at Syracuse University were asked to examine tapes of television newscasters, specifically, to score
   (a) their mannerisms as they delivered the news.
   (b) their dress and hairstyles.
   (c) bias in their spoken words.
   (d) their facial expressions.

2. People who voted for Reagan in larger numbers watched the evening news on
   (a) CNN.
   (b) NBC.
   (c) ABC.
   (d) CBS.

3. Another study asked students to nod or shake their heads while being asked a question concerning
   (a) the presidential candidate they planned to vote for.
   (b) an appropriate amount for college tuition.
   (c) ways to improve food in campus dining facilities.
   (d) an amount for a proposed increase in student financial aid.

4. Gladwell states that, in the student study, what made the difference in students' responses was the
   (a) wording of the question they were asked to respond to.
   (b) persuasive quality of the editorial.
   (c) shaking or nodding of their heads.
   (d) attitude and bias of the researchers conducting the study.

5. Gladwell concludes that, in determining how we feel, think, and react,
   (a) nonverbal clues are more important than verbal clues.
   (b) verbal clues are more important than nonverbal clues.
   (c) verbal and nonverbal clues are equally important.
   (d) more research needs to be done before one can decide whether nonverbal or verbal clues are more persuasive.

B. *Vocabulary*

For each italicized word from the selection, choose the best definition according to the context in which it appears. You may refer to the selection to answer the questions in this section and in all the remaining sections.

1. *unequivocally* happy or sad subjects [paragraph 2]:
   (a) clearly and unambiguously.
   (b) observably.
   (c) relatively.
   (d) unpredictably.

2. the *dubious* distinction [4]:
   (a) praiseworthy.
   (b) honorable.
   (c) doubtful.
   (d) untrustworthy.

3. simply a *fluke* [4]:
   (a) miracle.
   (b) chance occurrence.
   (c) predictable event.
   (d) difference of opinion.

4. *ostensibly* for another reason [6]:
    (a) predictably.
    (b) unintentionally.
    (c) clearly.
    (d) supposedly.
5. much more *insidious* [7]:
    (a) persuasive, convincing.
    (b) treacherous, intending to trap.
    (c) causing worry or concern.
    (d) subtle, difficult to detect.
6. harder to *insulate* ourselves [7]:
    (a) shield, isolate.
    (b) educate, receive instruction.
    (c) persuade, encourage.
    (d) defend, guard.

C. Inferences

On the basis of the evidence in the essay, mark these statements as follows: PA (probably accurate), PI (probably inaccurate), or NP (not in the passage).

1. _____   If the Syracuse psychologists had studied the newscasters' voices rather than their facial expressions, the results would have been quite different.
2. _____   Peter Jennings of ABC News was probably unaware that his facial expressions demonstrated pro-Reagan bias.
3. _____   The proof or evidence that Peter Jennings's bias toward Reagan swayed voters' sympathies is not well documented and therefore doesn't represent a firm conclusion.
4. _____   ABC warned Jennings after Mullen's results were published to act more neutral when he reported on Republican candidates.
5. _____   Although he was surprised at the results, Jennings agreed with Mullen's conclusions.
6. _____   The beginning of paragraph 6 suggests that the researchers were surprised at the results of the student research study.

D. Structure

Complete the following questions.

1. The mode of discourse in the essay is
    (a) narration.
    (b) description.
    (c) exposition.
    (d) persuasion.

2. Gladwell's purpose in writing, specifically, is to
    (a) instruct readers in ways to resist salespeople's attempt to persuade them.
    (b) illustrate how little things can influence our responses.
    (c) demonstrate how two separate research studies were conducted.
    (d) warn readers to be alert to bias when watching the evening news.

3. Look again at the second half of paragraph 2. What is its purpose?

    _____

4. With respect to paragraph 2, which *two* of these functions does paragraph 3 serve?
    (a) It confirms that researchers were right about Jennings's bias toward Reagan.
    (b) It confirms that Jennings's bias influenced voter behavior.
    (c) It underscores the importance of the study.
    (d) It explains why Ronald Reagan won the 1984 election.

5. Gladwell suggests in paragraphs 7 and 8 that the persuasive nonverbal clues he describes in the essay
    (a) threaten our rights to free expression and thought.
    (b) will change the way advertisers display their wares on television.
    (c) are a little frightening because they are so subtle.
    (d) are immediately obvious to those who bother to look for them.

Questions for Discussion and Analysis

1. If you have the time, videotape the three national networks' evening news programs for two or three days. Then watch the segments dealing with Republican and Democrat politicians. Do you detect any of the subtle biases Gladwell reports on?

2. What implications for advertising do the research studies described here have?

ON THE WEB

_____

Malcolm Gladwell's other *New Yorker* articles can be accessed at:
www.gladwell.com
Click on the *New Yorker* archives.

Selection 8   # SuAnne Big Crow
                   ## Ian Frazier

Photo © Sigrid Estrada.

Ian Frazier is a renowned nonfiction writer of essays and books whose subjects range from humor to New York life to the American Southwest. Among his most celebrated books are Great Plains *(1989) and* Coyote v. Acme *(1996). This selection comes from* On the Rez *(2000), a portrayal of the Oglala Sioux Pine Ridge Reservation in South Dakota (rez is slang for "reservation"). Pine Ridge is the site of the famous 1973 battle of Wounded Knee, between members of the American Indian Movement (AIM) and U.S. federal agents. Frazier is well acquainted with the Sioux, having spent a great deal of time among the Sioux people. One of Frazier's aims in* On the Rez *was to find a hero who could counteract the divisions and defeatism of reservation life. Among others, he found such a person in SuAnne Big Crow. This is her story.*

1   SuAnne Marie Big Crow was born on March 15, 1974, at Pine Ridge Hospital—the brick building, now no longer a hospital, just uphill from the four-way intersection in town. Her mother, Leatrice Big Crow, known as Chick, was twenty-five years old. Chick had two other daughters: Cecelia, called Cee Cee, who was three, and Frances, called Pigeon, who was five. Chick had been born a Big Crow, and grew up in her grandmother Big Crow's house in Wolf Creek, a little community about seven miles east of Pine Ridge. Chick had a round, pretty face, dark eyes, a determined chin, and wiry reddish-brown hair. Her figure was big-shouldered and trim; she had been a good athlete as a girl. Now she worked as an administrative assistant for the tribal planning office, and she was raising her daughters alone with the help of her sisters and other kin. People knew that Everett "Gabby" Brewer was the father of the two older girls, but Chick would never say who SuAnne's father was. If asked, Chick always said she didn't want to talk about it. When SuAnne got old enough to wonder, people sometimes told her that her father was Elvis. And sometimes, when SuAnne wore her hair a certain way with a curl in front, you would have to admit that a resemblance was there.

2   SuAnne's birth came at a dark time on the reservation. The on-going battle between supporters and opponents of Dick Wilson's tribal government showed no signs of letup, with violence so pervasive and unpredictable that many people were afraid to leave their homes. Just the month before, a nine-year-old boy named Harold Weasel Bear had been shot and seriously wounded as he sat in his father's pickup in

White Clay; his father was a Wilson man. Russell Means had campaigned against Wilson for the tribal chairmanship that winter and got more votes than Wilson in the primary. In the runoff election, however, Wilson won, by about two hundred votes out of the more than three thousand votes cast. Means had promised to "destroy" the present system of tribal government if he won, and many people were glad he wouldn't get a chance. He accused Wilson of stealing the election, and the federal Civil Rights Commission later agreed, saying that almost a third of the votes cast seemed to be improper and that the election was "permeated with fraud."

3   The beatings and stompings and shootings and bombings on the reservation would continue until the killing of the FBI agents the following year, after which a general exhaustion plus the presence of hundreds of FBI investigators brought the violence level down. In those days, if you were on the Pine Ridge Reservation you picked a side, and Chick Big Crow was for Dick Wilson all the way. She still calls Dick Wilson one of the greatest leaders the tribe ever had. Distinctions between those with anti- and pro-Dick Wilson loyalties, between AIM and goon, mean less today than they did then. Before SuAnne's sixteenth birthday, she would have a lot to do with causing those divisions to heal.

4   As a Big Crow, SuAnne belonged to one of the largest clans—the Lakota word for the extended family group is the *tiospaye*—on Pine Ridge. In the Pine Ridge telephone directory, Big Crow is the fourth-most-common name, behind Brewer, Pourier, and Ecoffey. (This method of figuring is not definitive, of course, since most people on the reservation don't have phones.) Chick Big Crow's mother, Alvina Big Crow, was one of nine children, and Chick had many Big Crow first cousins, as well as many with other last names. Her mother's sister Grace married a Mills; Olympic champion Billy Mills is a first cousin of Chick's. Chick's uncle Jimmy Big Crow married a woman named Marcella who bore him twenty-four children, including nine sets of twins. TV shows sometimes featured Jimmy and Marcella Big Crow and their family, and for a while they were listed in the *Guinness Book of World Records*. Basketball teams at Pine Ridge High School have occasionally been all or mostly Big Crow brothers or sisters and their first cousins.

5   The name Big Crow comes up rather often in the history of the Sioux. Big Crows are mentioned as headmen, though not as leaders of the first rank like Spotted Tail or Red Cloud. They seem to have been solidly upper-middle-class, if such a description can apply to nineteenth-century Sioux. When Francis Parkman arrived fresh out of Harvard to visit the Oglala in 1846, he stayed in the well-appointed tipi of a man called the Big Crow (Kongra Tonga), who was known for his friendliness to the whites. Parkman described in his book *The Oregon Trail* how the Big Crow sat in his tipi at night telling stories in a darkness suddenly made light by the flaring of a piece of buffalo fat on the

fire, and how the Big Crow returned from a buffalo hunt with his arms and moccasins all bloody, and how he particularly vexed his lodger by getting up every midnight to sing a long prayer the spirits had told him to sing. In 1859, this Big Crow or another was killed by Crow Indians on a raiding expedition; the event appears in a Sioux winter count which marks 1859 with a pictograph that translates as "Big Crow was killed." In 1871, a Big Crow is listed among the chiefs who accompanied Red Cloud to a council at Fort Laramie. In 1877, when Crazy Horse fled the Red Cloud Agency to seek refuge at the Spotted Tail Agency, a Brule Sioux named Big Crow confronted him and lectured him, saying that Crazy Horse never listened but that now he must listen and must go with Big Crow to the commanding officer.

6   Leatrice "Chick" Big Crow does not know for sure whether any of these Big Crows is an ancestor of hers, but she thinks not. She says that her branch of the family descends from Big Crows of the Sans Arc Lakota, a tribe much smaller than the Oglala, who lived on the plains to the north and west. A medicine man has told her that among the Sans Arc long ago lived a chief named Big Crow who was greater than any chief we know of. This chief was also so wise that he never put himself forward and never identified himself to the whites so they could single him out as chief; he knew the jealousy and division this would cause. For years the chief led the Sans Arc in war and peace, carefully avoiding all notoriety as the tribe prospered and grew strong. After he died, the tribe began to quarrel among themselves and dwindled away. The memory of this chief vanished except among a few, according to the medicine man. After SuAnne died, the medicine man told Chick that she had been the spirit of this great leader come back to reunite the people.

7   SuAnne grew up with her sisters in her mother's three-bedroom house in Pine Ridge. She was an active child; she sat up on her own while still an infant, and walked at nine months old. From when she was a baby, she wanted to do everything the bigger girls could do. When she was two, she told her mother that she wanted to go to school. She walked with Pigeon and Cee Cee to the school-bus stop in the mornings and often had to be restrained from getting on. Pigeon's memory of SuAnne is of her looking up at her from under the bill of her baseball cap. She was always looking up at her sisters and following them. When they went places around town, she went with them, telling Pigeon, "I'll walk in your footsteps." She played easily with kids much older than she. Chick came home from work one afternoon and found that SuAnne, then only four, had escaped from the babysitter and gotten on a big kid's ten-speed bicycle. Chick saw SuAnne coming down the hill, standing on the crossbar between the pedals and reaching up with her arms at full length to hold the handlebars.

8   Even today people talk about what a strict mother Chick Big Crow was. Her daughters always had to be in the house or the yard by the time the streetlights came on. The only after-school activities she let them take part in were the structured and chaperoned kind; unsupervised wanderings and (later) cruising around in cars were out. In an interview when she was a teenager, SuAnne said that she and her sisters had to come up with their own fun, because their mother wouldn't let them socialize outside of school. Pigeon remembers Monopoly games they played that went on for days, and Scrabble marathons, and many games of Clue. In summer they could take picnics to White Clay Creek and spend the day there in the shallows, lying back and seeing different shapes in the clouds. One summer when Pigeon was in summer school the girls had their own school in their basement when she came home in the afternoons, with a full schedule of math and geography and English and so on. They played badminton in their yard and did Tae Kwon Do, and they made up a version of kickball played under the sprinkler on their lawn's wet grass where they could slide for miles. On evenings when their mother bowled at a league in Rushville they held road races with shopping carts on a track they made in the basement; they later said that the shopping carts taught them how to drive. At night, though they were sent to bed early, the three girls would read by flashlight under the covers or by the light from the hall—they liked the Nancy Drew mystery books and the Little House on the Prairie series, and the stories of the Babysitters' Club, and books by Beverly Cleary and Lois Duncan and Judy Blume. They had a little radio they kept under the bed, and when a local station signed off at ten o'clock with the national anthem, they would unharmoniously sing along.

9   Chick Big Crow was (and is) strongly anti-drug and -alcohol. On the reservation, Chick has belonged for many years to the small but adamant minority who take that stance. When SuAnne was nine years old, she was staying with her godmother on New Year's Eve when the woman's teenaged son came home drunk and shot himself in the chest. The woman was too distraught to do anything, so SuAnne called the ambulance and the police and cared for her until the grown-ups arrived. Perhaps because of this incident, SuAnne became as opposed to drugs and alcohol as her mother was. She gave talks on the subject to school and youth groups, made a video urging her message in a stern and wooden tone, and as a high-schooler traveled to distant cities for conventions of like-minded teens. I once asked Rol Bradford, a Pine Ridge teacher and coach who is also a friend of her family, whether SuAnne's public advocacy on this issue wasn't risky given the prominence of alcohol in the life of the reservation. "You have to understand," Rol Bradford said, "SuAnne didn't *respond* to peer pressure, SuAnne *was* peer pressure. She was the backbone of any group she was in, and she was way wiser than her years. By coming

out against drinking, I know, she flat-out saved a lot of kids' lives. In fact, she even had an effect on me. It dawned on me that if a sixteen-year-old girl could have the guts to say these things, then maybe us adults should pay attention, too. I haven't had a drink since the day she died." . . .

10   As strongly as Chick forbade certain activities, she encouraged the girls in sports. At one time or another, they did them all—cross-country running and track, volleyball, cheerleading, basketball, softball. Some of the teams were at school and others were sponsored by organizations in town. Chick's sister, Yvonne "Tiny" De Cory, had a cheerleading drill team called the Tiny Tots, a group of girls eight years old and under who performed at local sporting events and gatherings. SuAnne became a featured star for the Tiny Tots when she was three; many in Pine Ridge remember first seeing her or hearing about her then. She began to play on her big sisters' league softball team at about the same time, when the bat was still taller than she was. Coaches would send SuAnne in to pinch-hit, hoping for a walk, and telling her not to swing. Often she swung anyway; once, in a tie game, she swung at the third strike, the catcher dropped it, and several errors later she had rounded the bases for the winning run.

11   Pine Ridge had a winter basketball league for girls aged seven to eleven, and SuAnne later recalled that she played her first organized game in the league when she was in kindergarten. She had gone with her sisters to a tournament in Rushville when a sudden snowstorm kept some of the players away. The coach, finding himself short-handed, put SuAnne in the game. "It was funny," SuAnne told a basketball magazine, "because all I really knew how to do was play defense, so that's all I did. I not only took the ball away from our opponents, but also from my own teammates!" A coach who watched her play then said, "If you ever saw the movie *Star Wars*—well, you remember the Ewoks? Well, SuAnne was so much smaller than the other kids, she looked like one of those little Ewoks out there runnin' around."

12   In the West, girls' basketball is a bigger deal than it is elsewhere. High school girls' basketball games in states like South Dakota and Montana draw full-house crowds, and newspapers and college recruiters give nearly the same attention to star players who are girls as they do to stars who are boys. There were many good players on the girls' teams at Pine Ridge High School and at the Red Cloud School when SuAnne was little. SuAnne idolized a star for the Pine Ridge Lady Thorpes named Lolly Steele, who set many records at the school. On a national level, SuAnne's hero was Earvin "Magic" Johnson, of the Los Angeles Lakers pro team. Women's professional basketball did not exist in those years, but men's pro games were reaching a level of popularity to challenge baseball and football. SuAnne had big posters of Magic Johnson on her bedroom walls.

13   She spent endless hours practicing basketball. When she was in the fifth grade she heard somewhere that to improve your dribbling you should bounce a basketball a thousand times a day with each hand. She followed this daily exercise faithfully on the cement floor of the patio; her mother and sisters got tired of the sound. For variety, she would shoot layups against the gutter and the drainpipe, until they came loose from the house and had to be repaired. She knew that no girl in an official game had ever dunked a basketball—that is, had leaped as high as the rim and stuffed the ball through the hoop from above—and she wanted to be the first in history to do it. To get the feel, she persuaded a younger boy cousin to kneel on all fours under the basket. With a running start, and a leap using the boy's back as a springboard, she could dunk the ball.

14   Charles Zimiga, who would coach SuAnne in basketball during her high school years, remembered the first time he saw her. He was on the cross-country track on the old golf course coaching the high school boys' cross-country team—a team that later won the state championship—when SuAnne came running by. She was in seventh grade at the time. She practiced cross-country every fall, and ran in amateur meets, and sometimes placed high enough to be invited to tournaments in Boston and California. "The fluidness of her running amazed me, and the strength she had," Zimiga said. "I stood watching her go by and she stopped right in front of me—I'm a high school coach, remember, and she's just a young little girl—and she said, 'What're you lookin' at?' I said, 'A runner.' She would've been a top cross-country runner, but in high school it never did work out, because the season conflicted with basketball. I had heard about her before, but that day on the golf course was the first time I really noticed her."

15   SuAnne went to elementary school in Wolf Creek, because of her family's connections there. Zimiga and others wanted her to come to Pine Ridge High School so she could play on the basketball team, and finally they persuaded Chick to let her transfer when she was in junior high. By the time SuAnne was in eighth grade, she had grown to five feet, five inches tall ("but she played six foot," Zimiga said); she was long-limbed, well-muscled, and quick. She had high cheekbones, a prominent, arched upper lip that lined up with the basket when she aimed the ball, and short hair that she wore in no particular style. She could have played every game for the varsity when she was in eighth grade, but Coach Zimiga, who took over girls' varsity basketball that year, wanted to keep peace among older players who had waited for their chance to be on the team. He kept SuAnne on the junior varsity during the regular season. The varsity team had a good year, and when it advanced to the district playoffs, Zimiga brought SuAnne up from the JVs for the play-off games. Several times she got into foul trouble; the referees rule strictly in tournament games, and SuAnne was used to a more headlong style of play. She

and her cousin Doni De Cory, a 5'10" junior, combined for many long-break baskets, with Doni throwing downcourt passes to SuAnne on the scoring end. In the district play-off against the team from Red Cloud, SuAnne scored thirty-one points. In the regional play-off game, Pine Ridge beat a good Todd County team, but in the state tournament they lost all three games and finished eighth.

16   Some people who live in the cities and towns near reservations treat their Indian neighbors decently; some don't. In cities like Denver and Minneapolis and Rapid City, police have been known to harass Indian teenagers and rough up Indian drunks and needlessly stop and search Indian cars. Local banks whose deposits include millions in tribal funds sometimes charge Indians higher loan interest rates than they charge whites. Gift shops near reservations sell junky caricature Indian pictures and dolls, and until not long ago, beer coolers had signs on them that said, INDIAN POWER. In a big discount store in a reservation border town, a white clerk observes a lot of Indians waiting at the checkout and remarks, "Oh, they're Indians—they're used to standing in line." Some people in South Dakota hate Indians, unapologetically, and will tell you why; in their voices you can hear a particular American meanness that is centuries old.

17   When teams from Pine Ridge play non-Indian teams, the question of race is always there. When Pine Ridge is the visiting team, usually their hosts are courteous, and the players and fans have a good time. But Pine Ridge coaches know that occasionally at away games their kids will be insulted, their fans will not feel welcome, the host gym will be dense with hostility, and the referees will call fouls on Indian players every chance they get. Sometimes in a game between Indian and non-Indian teams, the difference in race becomes an important and distracting part of the event.

18   One place where Pine Ridge teams used to get harassed regularly was in the high school gymnasium in Lead, South Dakota. Lead is a town of about 3,200 northwest of the reservation, in the Black Hills. It is laid out among the mines that are its main industry, and low, wooded mountains hedge it round. The brick high school building is set into a hillside. The school's only gym in those days was small, with tiers of gray-painted concrete on which the spectator benches descended from just below the steel-beamed roof to the very edge of the basketball court—an arrangement that greatly magnified the interior noise.

19   In the fall of 1988, the Pine Ridge Lady Thorpes went to Lead to play a basketball game. SuAnne was a full member of the team by then. She was a freshman, fourteen years old. Getting ready in the locker room, the Pine Ridge girls could hear the din from the fans. They were yelling fake-Indian war cries, a "woo-woo-woo" sound. The usual plan for the pre-game warm-up was for the visiting team to run onto the

court in a line, take a lap or two around the floor, shoot some baskets, and then go to their bench at courtside. After that, the home team would come out and do the same, and then the game would begin. Usually the Thorpes lined up for their entry more or less according to height, which meant that senior Doni De Cory, one of the tallest, went first. As the team waited in the hallway leading from the locker room, the heckling got louder. The Lead fans were yelling epithets like "squaw" and "gut-eater." Some were waving food stamps, a reference to the reservation's receiving federal aid. Others yelled, "Where's the cheese?"—the joke being that if Indians were lining up, it must be to get commodity cheese. The Lead high school band had joined in, with fake-Indian drumming and a fake-Indian tune. Doni De Cory looked out the door and told her teammates, "I can't handle this." SuAnne quickly offered to go first in her place. She was so eager that Doni became suspicious. "Don't embarrass us," Doni told her. SuAnne said, "I won't. I won't embarrass you." Doni gave her the ball, and SuAnne stood first in line.

20   She came running onto the court dribbling the basketball, with her teammates running behind. On the court, the noise was deafeningly loud. SuAnne went right down the middle; but instead of running a full lap, she suddenly stopped when she got to center court. Her teammates were taken by surprise, and some bumped into one another. Coach Zimiga at the rear of the line did not know why they had stopped. SuAnne turned to Doni De Cory and tossed her the ball. Then she stepped into the jump-ball circle at center court, in front of the Lead fans. She unbuttoned her warm-up jacket, took it off, draped it over her shoulders, and began to do the Lakota shawl dance. SuAnne knew all the traditional dances—she had competed in many powwows as a little girl—and the dance she chose is a young woman's dance, graceful and modest and show-offy all at the same time. "I couldn't believe it—she was powwowin', like, 'get down!'" Doni De Cory recalled. "And then she started to sing." SuAnne began to sing in Lakota, swaying back and forth in the jump-ball circle, doing the shawl dance, using her warm-up jacket for a shawl. The crowd went completely silent. "All that stuff the Lead fans were yelling—it was like she *reversed* it somehow," a teammate said. In the sudden quiet, all you could hear was her Lakota song. SuAnne stood up, dropped her jacket, took the ball from Doni De Cory, and ran a lap around the court dribbling expertly and fast. The fans began to cheer and applaud. She sprinted to the basket, went up in the air, and laid the ball through the hoop, with the fans cheering loudly now. Of course, Pine Ridge went on to win the game.

21   Because this is one of the coolest and bravest deeds I ever heard of, I want to stop and consider it from a larger perspective that includes the town of Lead, all the Black Hills, and 125 years of history:

22   Lead, the town, does not get its name from the metal. The lead the name refers to is a mining term for a gold-bearing deposit, or vein, running through surrounding rock. The word, pronounced with a long *e,* is related to the word "lode." During the Black Hills gold rush of the 1870s, prospectors found a rich lead in what would become the town of Lead. In April 1876, Fred and Moses Manuel staked a claim to a mine they called the Homestake. Their lead led eventually to gold and more gold—a small mountain of gold—whose value may be guessed by the size of the hole its extraction has left in the middle of present-day Lead.

23   In 1877, a mining engineer from San Francisco named George Hearst came to the Hills, investigated the Manuels' mine, and advised his big-city partners to buy it. The price was $70,000. At the time of Hearst's negotiations, the illegal act of Congress which would take this land from the Sioux had only recently passed. The partners followed Hearst's advice, and the Homestake Mine paid off its purchase price four times over in dividends alone within three years. When George Hearst's only son, William Randolph, was kicked out of Harvard for giving his instructors chamber pots with their names inscribed on the inside, George Hearst suggested that he come West and take over his (George's) share in the Homestake Mine. William Randolph Hearst chose to run the San Francisco *Examiner* instead. His father gave him a blank check to keep it going for two years; gold from Lead helped start the Hearst newspaper empire. Since the Homestake Mine was discovered, it has produced at least $10 billion in gold. It is one of the richest gold mines in the world.

24   Almost from the moment of the Custer expedition's entry into the Black Hills in 1874, there was no way the Sioux were going to be allowed to keep this land. By 1875, the Dakota Territorial Legislature had already divided the Black Hills land into counties; Custer Country, in the southern Hills, was named in that general's honor while he was still alive, and while the land still clearly belonged to the Sioux. Many people in government and elsewhere knew at the time that taking this land was wrong. At first, the Army even made halfhearted attempts to keep the prospectors out. A high-ranking treaty negotiator told President Grant that the Custer expedition was "a violation of the national honor." One of the commissioners who worked on the "agreement" that gave paper legitimacy to the theft said that Custer should not have gone into the Hills in the first place; he and the other commissioners reminded the government that it was making the Sioux homeless and that it owed them protection and care. The taking of the Black Hills proceeded inexorably all the same.

25   Sioux leaders of Crazy Horse's generation began working to receive fair compensation for the Hills in the early 1900s. The Black Hills claim which the Sioux filed with the U.S. Court of Claims in the 1920s got nowhere. In 1946, the government established the Indian Claims

Commission specifically to provide payment for wrongly taken Indian lands, and in 1950 the Sioux filed a claim for the Black Hills with the ICC. After almost twenty-five years of historical research and esoteric legal back-and-forth, the ICC finally ruled that the Sioux were entitled to a payment of $17.5 million plus interest for the taking of the Hills. Further legal maneuvering ensued. In 1980 the Supreme Court affirmed the ruling and awarded the Sioux a total of $106 million. Justice Harry Blackmun, for the majority, wrote: "A more ripe and rank case of dishonorable dealings will never, in all probability, be found in our history"—which was to say officially, and finally, that the Black Hills had been stolen.

26   By the time of the Supreme Court ruling, however, the Sioux had come to see their identity as linked to the Hills themselves, and the eight tribes involved decided unanimously not to accept the money. They said, "The Black Hills are not for sale." The Sioux now wanted the land back— some or all of it—and trespass damages as well. They especially wanted the Black Hills lands still owned by the federal government. These amount to about 1.3 million acres, a small proportion of what was stolen. At the moment, the chances of the Sioux getting these or any lands in the Black Hills appear remote. The untouched compensation money remains in a federal escrow account, where it, plus other compensation moneys, plus accumulated interest, is now over half a billion dollars.

27   Inescapably, this history is present when an Oglala team goes to Lead to play a basketball game. It may even explain why the fans in Lead were so mean: fear that you might perhaps be in the wrong can make you ornerier sometimes. In all the accounts of this land grab and its aftermath, and among the many greedy and driven men who had a part, I cannot find evidence of a single act as elegant, as generous, or as transcendent as SuAnne's dance at center court in the gym at Lead.

28   For the Oglala, what SuAnne did that day almost immediately took on the stature of myth. People from Pine Ridge who witnessed it still describe it in terms of awe and disbelief. Amazement swept through the younger kids when they heard. "I was, like, '*What* did she just do?' " recalled her cousin Angie Big Crow, an eighth-grader at the time. All over the reservation, people told and retold the story of SuAnne at Lead. Any time the subject of SuAnne came up when I was talking to people on Pine Ridge, I would always ask if they had heard about what she did at Lead, and always the answer was a smile and a nod—"Yeah, I was there," or "Yeah, I heard about that." To the unnumbered big and small slights of local racism which the Oglala have known all their lives, SuAnne's exploit made an emphatic reply.

29   Back in the days when Lakota war parties still fought battles against other tribes and the Army, no deed of war was more honored than the act of counting coup. To count coup means to touch an armed enemy in full possession of his powers with a special stick called a coup stick, or with the hand. The touch is not a blow, and only serves to indicate

how close to the enemy you came. As an act of bravery, counting coup was regarded as greater than killing an enemy in single combat, greater than taking a scalp or horses or any prize. Counting coup was an act of almost abstract courage, of pure playfulness taken to the most daring extreme. Very likely, to do it and survive brought an exhilaration to which nothing could compare. In an ancient sense which her Oglala kin could recognize, SuAnne counted coup on the fans of Lead.

30   And yet this coup was an act not of war but of peace. SuAnne's coup strike was an offering, an invitation. It took the hecklers at the best interpretation, as if their silly mocking chants were meant only in goodwill. It showed that their fake Indian songs were just that—fake—and that the real thing was better, as real things usually are. We Lakota have been dancing like this for centuries, the dance said; we've been doing the shawl dance since long before you came, before you had gotten on the boat in Glasgow or Bremerhaven, before you stole this land, and we're still doing it today; and isn't it pretty, when you see how it's supposed to be done? Because finally what SuAnne proposed was to invite us—us onlookers in the stands, which is the non-Lakota rest of this country—to dance, too. She was in the Lead gym to play, and she invited us all to play. The symbol she used to include us was the warm-up jacket. Everyone in America has a warm-up jacket. I've got one, probably so do you, so did (no doubt) many of the fans at Lead. By using the warm-up jacket as a shawl in her impromptu shawl dance, she made Lakota relatives of us all.

31   "It was funny," Doni De Cory said, "but after that game the relationship between Lead and us was tremendous. When we played Lead again, the games were really good, and we got to know some of the girls on the team. Later, when we went to a tournament and Lead was there, we were hanging out with the Lead girls and eating pizza with them. We got to know some of their parents, too. What SuAnne did made a lasting impression and changed the whole situation with us and Lead. We found out there are some really good people in Lead."

32   America is a leap of the imagination. From its beginning, people had only a persistent idea of what a good country should be. The idea involved freedom, equality, justice, and the pursuit of happiness; nowadays most of us probably could not describe it a lot more clearly than that. The truth is, it always has been a bit of a guess. No one has ever known for sure whether a country based on such an idea is really possible, but again and again, we have leaped toward the idea and hoped. What SuAnne Big Crow demonstrated in the Lead high school gym is that making the leap is the whole point. The idea does not truly live unless it is expressed by an act; the country does not live unless we make the leap from our tribe or focus group or gated community or demographic, and land on the shaky platform of that idea of a good country which all kinds of different people share.

33   This leap is made in public, and it's made for free. It's not a product or a service that anyone will pay you for. You do it for reasons unexplainable by economics—for ambition, out of conviction, for the heck of it, in playfulness, for love. It's done in public spaces, face-to-face, where anyone is free to go. It's not done on television, on the Internet, or over the telephone; our electronic systems can only tell us if the leap made elsewhere has succeeded or failed. The places you'll see it are high school gyms, city sidewalks, the subway, bus stations, public parks, parking lots, and wherever people gather during natural disasters. In those places and others like them, the leaps that continue to invent and knit the country continue to be made. When the leap fails, it looks like the L.A. riots, or Sherman's March through Georgia. When it succeeds, it looks like the New York City Bicentennial Celebration in July 1976, or the Civil Rights March on Washington in 1963. On that scale, whether it succeeds or fails, it's always something to see. The leap requires physical presence and physical risk. But the payoff—in terms of dreams realized, of understanding, of people getting along—can be so glorious as to make the risk seem minuscule.

34   I find all this hopefulness, and more, in SuAnne's dance at center court in the gym in Lead. My high school football coach used to show us films of our previous game every Monday after practice, and whenever he liked a particular play, he would run it over and over again. If I had a film of SuAnne at Lead (as far as I know, no such film or video exists), I would study it in slow motion frame by frame. There's a magic in what she did, along with the promise that public acts of courage are still alive out there somewhere. Mostly, I would run the film of SuAnne again and again for my own braveheart song. I refer to her, as I do to Crazy Horse, for proof that it's a public service to be brave.

Postscript: *SuAnne Big Crow died in a car accident in 1992. While driving with her mother to Huron, South Dakota, for the Miss Basketball in South Dakota awards banquet, she fell asleep at the wheel, and the car went over an embankment. Her mother survived. SuAnne was 17 years old.*

A. Comprehension

Choose the answer that best completes each statement. Do not refer to the selection while doing this exercise.

1. At the time of SuAnne Big Crow's birth, the reservation was experiencing
   (a) high unemployment and alcoholism.
   (b) persistent violence over tribal politics.
   (c) an unusual period of peace and prosperity.
   (d) an ongoing dispute with federal agents over ownership of tribal land.

2. Frazier writes that when the Indian girls' basketball teams from Pine Ridge play non-Indian teams,
    (a) the home team town is the site of protests and violence.
    (b) the question of race is always present.
    (c) both sides put their differences aside and play as well as they can.
    (d) the Indian teams almost always win.
3. When the Pine Ridge girls' team played at the nearby town of Lead, the Lead fans
    (a) threatened violence and roughed up some team members.
    (b) taunted the Indian team members with racial epithets and fake Indian calls.
    (c) performed a caricature of an Indian dance mocking the visitors.
    (d) swallowed their resentment and treated the visitors courteously.
4. After the Supreme Court ruling that awarded the Sioux over $100 million for their stolen lands, the Sioux tribes
    (a) demanded even more money as compensation.
    (b) spent the money on hospitals and schools for their reservations.
    (c) rejected the money and demanded the return of their lands.
    (d) began to fight among themselves about what to do with the money.
5. Frazier connects SuAnne's shawl dance at the Lead gymnasium with the ancient Lakota Sioux custom of "counting coup," which refers to
    (a) a brave act in which a warrior touches his armed enemy with a special stick.
    (b) playfully toying with the enemy until he concedes defeat.
    (c) engaging in hand-to-hand combat to see who is the stronger opponent.
    (d) counting the number of enemy troops defeated during an engagement.

B. Vocabulary

For each italicized word from the selection, write the best definition according to the context in which it appears. You may refer to the selection to answer the questions in this section and in all the remaining sections.

1. with violence so *pervasive* [paragraph 2]: _____

    _____

2. carefully avoiding all *notoriety* [6]: _____

    _____

3. small but *adamant* minority [9]: _____

4.   the woman was too *distraught* [9]: _____

5.   sell junky *caricature* Indian pictures [16]: Describing pictures that

_____

6.   fans were yelling *epithets* [19]: _____

7.   the taking of the Black Hills proceeded *inexorably* [24]: _____

_____

8.   *esoteric* legal back-and-forth [25]: _____

_____

9.   a single act as elegant . . . or as *transcendent* [27]: _____

_____

10.   make the risk seem *minuscule* [33]: _____

C. Inferences

Complete the following questions.

1.   From the information presented in paragraph 2, what was the source

of the violence on the Pine Ridge reservation? _____

_____

2.   From paragraph 6, what was Big Crow Chief's reputation among his

people? _____

_____

3.   Read paragraphs 7 to 9 again. How would you characterize SuAnne

Big Crow's personality and character? _____

_____

4.   From paragraph 16, what can we infer about Indian–white relations?

_____

_____

5.   From Frazier's description of SuAnne's shawl dance in paragraph 20,

what was her reason for giving such a performance? _____

_____

6. When Frazier writes in paragraphs 32 and 33 that SuAnne made a "leap," what exactly is he referring to? _____

_____

_____

D. Structure

Complete the following questions.

1. Frazier's purpose in writing this selection is to
    (a) trace the history of the Pine Ridge Oglala Sioux Indians.
    (b) expose the strained relations between whites and Indians in South Dakota.
    (c) show how one young girl's actions transcended race and hatred.
    (d) write the biography of one Indian girl from South Dakota.
2. With respect to the essay as a whole, paragraphs 2 and 3 serve to
    (a) establish a historical perspective for the events he later describes.
    (b) show the specific reasons behind the intertribal conflicts.
    (c) argue for more federal intervention in tribal politics and elections.
    (d) show the animosity between Indians and federal agents.
3. Read paragraph 16 again. The method of paragraph development is
    (a) classification.
    (b) comparison and contrast.
    (c) cause and effect.
    (d) example.
4. Paragraph 21 serves as a
    (a) transition from the narrative to its significance.
    (b) conclusion.
    (c) concession.
    (d) restatement of the main idea using different words.
5. In paragraphs 22 through 26, Frazier explains the federal government's land grab of the ancestral Sioux lands. Why does he go into so much detail about this history?
    (a) to add texture and depth to his discussion.
    (b) to explain the Indians' reactions to the Lead fans.
    (c) to offer one explanation of why the residents of Lead were so rude to the Indian visitors.
    (d) to show the role of the U.S. government in taking away Indian lands and breaking treaties throughout American history.

Questions for Discussion and Analysis

1. What stereotypes about Indians does Frazier's essay overturn?
2. What are some essential characteristics of the Pine Ridge Oglala Sioux that you can isolate and describe from Frazier's discussion?
3. How does Frazier communicate the magic that he, along with the observers who were present to witness it, finds in SuAnne's shawl dance with the warm-up jacket?

ON THE WEB

Two excellent websites with several links for learning more about Native American culture, concerns, and history in general and about the Oglala Sioux in particular can be found at:

www.travels.com/history/sioux/oglala.htm
www.geocities.com/Athens/Acropolis/3976/Hawk.html

Selection 9

In the Laboratory with Agassiz

Samuel H. Scudder

Samuel H. Scudder (1837–1911) graduated from Williams College in 1857 and entered the Lawrence Scientific School at Harvard University to study under the famous naturalist Jean Louis R. Agassiz. (A naturalist is now called a biologist.) Scudder's chosen field was entomology (the study of insects), and in fact, he later became one of his era's most important American experts in that field. But Professor Agassiz had other ideas for his young scholar as he began his graduate study of natural science. As Scudder relates in this classic essay, Agassiz set him to work describing a specimen of a disgusting fish, with surprising results.

1   It was more than fifteen years ago that I entered the laboratory of Professor Agassiz, and told him I had enrolled my name in the scientific school as a student of natural history. He asked me a few questions about my object in coming, my antecedents generally, the mode in which I afterwards proposed to use the knowledge I might acquire, and finally, whether I wished to study any special branch. To the latter I replied that while I wished to be well grounded in all departments of zoölogy, I purposed to devote myself specially to insects.

2   "When do you wish to begin?" he asked.

3   "Now," I replied.

4   This seemed to please him, and with an energetic "Very well," he reached from a shelf a huge jar of specimens in yellow alcohol.

5   "Take this *fish*," said he, "and look at it; we call it a Hæmulon; by and by I will ask what you have seen."

6   With that he left me, but in a moment returned with explicit instructions as to the care of the object entrusted to me.

7   "No man is fit to be a naturalist," said he, "who does not know how to take care of specimens."

8   I was to keep the fish before me in a tin tray, and occasionally moisten the surface with alcohol from the jar, always taking care to replace the stopper tightly. Those were not the days of ground glass stoppers, and elegantly shaped exhibition jars; all the old students will recall the huge, neckless glass bottles with their leaky, wax-besmeared corks, half eaten by insects and begrimed with cellar dust. Entomology was a cleaner science than ichthyology,[1] but the example of the professor, who had unhesitatingly plunged to the bottom of the jar to produce the fish, was infectious; and though his alcohol had "a very ancient and fish-like smell," I really dared not show any aversion within these sacred precincts, and treated the alcohol as though it were pure water. Still I was conscious of a passing feeling of disappointment, for gazing at a fish did not commend itself to an ardent entomologist. My friends at home, too, were annoyed, when they discovered that no amount of eau de cologne would drown the perfume which haunted me like a shadow.

9   In ten minutes I had seen all that could be seen in that fish, and started in search of the professor, who had however left the museum; and when I returned, after lingering over some of the odd animals stored in the upper apartment, my specimen was dry all over. I dashed the fluid over the fish as if to resuscitate the beast from a fainting-fit, and looked with anxiety for a return of the normal, sloppy appearance. This little excitement over, nothing was to be done but return to a steadfast gaze at my mute companion. Half an hour passed,—an hour,—another hour; the fish began to look loathsome. I turned it over and around; looked it in the face,—ghastly; from behind, beneath, above, sideways, at a three quarters view,—just as ghastly. I was in despair; at an early hour I concluded that lunch was necessary; so, with infinite relief, the fish was carefully replaced in the jar, and for an hour I was free.

10   On my return, I learned that Professor Agassiz had been at the museum, but had gone and would not return for several hours. My fellow-students were too busy to be disturbed by continued conversation. Slowly I drew forth that hideous fish, and with a feeling of desperation

[1]Entomology is the study of insects; ichthyology is the study of fish.

again looked at it. I might not use a magnifying glass; instruments of all kinds were interdicted. My two hands, my two eyes, and the fish; it seemed a most limited field. I pushed my finger down its throat to feel how sharp the teeth were. I began to count the scales in the different rows until I was convinced that that was nonsense. At last a happy thought struck me—I would draw the fish; and now with surprise I began to discover new features in the creature. Just then the professor returned.

11   "That is right," said he; "a pencil is one of the best of eyes. I am glad to notice, too, that you keep your specimen wet and your bottle corked."

12   With these encouraging words, he added,—

13   "Well, what is it like?"

14   He listened attentively to my brief rehearsal of the structure of parts whose names were still unknown to me; the fringed gill-arches and movable operculum; the pores of the head, fleshy lips, and lidless eyes; the lateral line, the spinous fins, and forked tail; the compressed and arched body. When I had finished, he waited as if expecting more, and then, with an air of disappointment,—

15   "You have not looked very carefully; why," he continued, more earnestly, "you haven't even seen one of the most conspicuous features of the animal, which is as plainly before your eyes as the fish itself; look again, look again!" and he left me to my misery.

16   I was piqued; I was mortified. Still more of that wretched fish! But now I set myself to my task with a will, and discovered one new thing after another, until I saw how just the professor's criticism had been. The afternoon passed quickly, and when, toward its close, the professor inquired,—

17   "Do you see it yet?"

18   "No," I replied, "I am certain I do not, but I see how little I saw before."

19   "That is next best," said he, earnestly, "but I won't hear you now; put away your fish and go home; perhaps you will be ready with a better answer in the morning. I will examine you before you look at the fish."

20   This was disconcerting; not only must I think of my fish all night, studying, without the object before me, what this unknown but most visible feature might be; but also, without reviewing my new discoveries, I must give an exact account of them the next day. I had a bad memory; so I walked home by Charles River in a distracted state, with my two perplexities.

21   The cordial greeting from the professor the next morning was reassuring; here was a man who seemed to be quite as anxious as I, that I should see for myself what he saw.

22   "Do you perhaps mean," I asked, "that the fish has symmetrical sides with paired organs?"

23   His thoroughly pleased, "Of course, of course!" repaid the wakeful hours of the previous night. After he had discoursed most happily and enthusiastically—as he always did—upon the importance of this point, I ventured to ask what I should do next.

24   "Oh, look at your fish!" he said, and left me again to my own devices. In a little more than an hour he returned and heard my new catalogue.

25   "That is good, that is good!" he repeated; "but that is not all; go on;" and so for three long days he placed that fish before my eyes, forbidding me to look at anything else, or to use any artificial aid. "Look, look, look," was his repeated injunction.

26   This was the best entomological lesson I ever had,—a lesson, whose influence has extended to the details of every subsequent study; a legacy the professor has left to me, as he has left it to many others, of inestimable value, which we could not buy, with which we cannot part.

27   A year afterward, some of us were amusing ourselves with chalking outlandish beasts upon the museum blackboard. We drew prancing starfishes; frogs in mortal combat; hydra-headed worms; stately crawfishes, standing on their tails, bearing aloft umbrellas; and grotesque fishes with gaping mouths and staring eyes. The professor came in shortly after, and was as amused as any, at our experiments. He looked at the fishes.

28   "Hæmulons, every one of them," he said; "Mr.—— drew them."

29   True; and to this day, if I attempt a fish, I can draw nothing but Hæmulons.

30   The fourth day, a second fish of the same group was placed beside the first, and I was bidden to point out the resemblances and differences between the two; another and another followed, until the entire family lay before me, and a whole legion of jars covered the table and surrounding shelves; the odor had become a pleasant perfume; and even now, the sight of an old, six-inch, worm-eaten cork brings fragrant memories!

31   The whole group of Hæmulons was thus brought in review; and, whether engaged upon the dissection of the internal organs, the preparation and examination of the bony frame-work, or the description of the various parts, Agassiz' training in the method of observing facts and their orderly arrangement was ever accompanied by the urgent exhortation not to be content with them.

32   "Facts are stupid things," he would say, "until brought into connection with some general law."

33   At the end of eight months, it was almost with reluctance that I left these friends and turned to insects; but what I had gained by this outside experience has been of greater value than years of later investigation in my favorite groups.

A. *Comprehension*

Choose the answer that best completes each statement. Do not refer to the selection while doing this exercise.

1. At Agassiz's initial interview, Scudder announced his intention to specialize in the study of
   (a) butterflies.
   (b) fish.
   (c) insects.
   (d) all branches of zoology.
2. Professor Agassiz was particularly strict about the way his students
   (a) prepared their laboratory notes.
   (b) handled and stored their specimens.
   (c) handled and organized their instruments.
   (d) arranged the specimens in their trays.
3. Agassiz directed Scudder to examine the fish
   (a) through a microscope.
   (b) with a set of instruments.
   (c) by dissecting it.
   (d) only with his hands and his eyes.
4. The conspicuous feature that Scudder finally observed in his specimen fish was its
   (a) unusual pattern and number of scales.
   (b) lidless eyes.
   (c) fringed gill-arches.
   (d) symmetrical structure.
5. Observing facts and their orderly arrangement was only part of Agassiz's lesson to Scudder. More important was the lesson of
   (a) developing a lifelong interest in ichthyology.
   (b) learning how to record the facts accurately.
   (c) connecting the facts and observations to a general law.
   (d) studying the structure of every living organism.

B. *Vocabulary*

For each italicized word from the selection, choose the best definition according to the context in which it appears. You may refer to the selection to answer the questions in this section and in all the remaining sections.

1. he asked me . . . about my *antecedents* [paragraph 1]: In this context,
   (a) academic interests.
   (b) ancestors.
   (c) research studies.
   (d) childhood and adolescent experiences.

2. with *explicit* instructions [6]:
    (a) clearly expressed.
    (b) vague, overly general.
    (c) difficult to understand.
    (d) uncomplicated.

3. dared not show any *aversion* [8]:
    (a) hesitation.
    (b) lack of understanding.
    (c) repugnance.
    (d) enthusiasm.

4. instruments . . . were *interdicted* [10]:
    (a) readily available.
    (b) rationed.
    (c) in good repair.
    (d) prohibited.

5. I was *piqued* [16]:
    (a) irritated, full of resentment.
    (b) intrigued, captivated.
    (c) discouraged, disheartened.
    (d) enraged, seriously angered.

6. this was *disconcerting* [20]:
    (a) challenging, demanding.
    (b) upsetting, frustrating.
    (c) noteworthy, of great significance.
    (d) disorienting, confusing.

7. "Look, look, look" was his repeated *injunction* [25]:
    (a) command, order.
    (b) question, request.
    (c) warning, admonition.
    (d) favorite word.

8. a *legacy* the professor has left to me [26]:
    (a) final set of instructions.
    (b) cherished memory.
    (c) something handed down.
    (d) scholarly study.

9. of *inestimable* value [26]:
    (a) invaluable, impossible to determine.
    (b) uncertain, dubious.
    (c) unappreciated until later.
    (d) easy to calculate or determine.

10. urgent *exhortation* [31]
    (a) demand, ultimatum.
    (b) wish, desire.
    (c) strong argument or advice.
    (d) complaint, criticism.

C. Inferences

On the basis of the evidence in the essay, mark these statements as follows: PA (probably accurate), PI (probably inaccurate), or NP (not in the passage).

1. _____ Scudder's interest in natural science was the result of his father's influence.

2. _____ Professor Agassiz chose a fish for Scudder to study, knowing that he was probably not familiar with it.

3. _____ Scudder was impressed with Agassiz's fetching of the fish from the bottom of the jar.

4. _____ Scudder was delighted with Agassiz's assignment and pursued his study of the fish with great enthusiasm.

5. _____ Agassiz left Scudder alone to observe his fish because he was too busy with his other commitments to be of much help.

6. _____ The conspicuous feature that Scudder had initially missed pertained to the structure of the fish.

D. Structure

Complete the following questions.

1. Scudder's purpose in writing is, specifically, to
   (a) explain the origin of his love of science.
   (b) show how a scientist must learn to observe.
   (c) argue for a change in the way science is taught in college.
   (d) tell an amusing and entertaining story.

2. Scudder's attitude toward Professor Agassiz can be best described as
   (a) respectful and serious.
   (b) hostile, angry.
   (c) indifferent, neutral.
   (d) resentful, irritated.

3. Look again at paragraph 8. The phrase "sacred precincts" refers literally to
   (a) the campus of Harvard University.
   (b) Agassiz's office.
   (c) Agassiz's laboratory.
   (d) the field of natural science.

4. Read paragraphs 14 and 15 again, which emphasize the idea that
   (a) most scientific observation is boring and dry.
   (b) observing an organism such as a fish is a good way to learn the scientific method.
   (c) observing the individual parts of the fish was less important than observing the whole.
   (d) Agassiz treated Scudder, as a new student, with scorn.

5. Read paragraphs 30 and 31, which list a few of the kinds of observations Scudder had to make with the Hæmulons. Choose as many of the methods of development you studied in Chapters 3 and 4 that these observations suggest.
    (a) analogy.
    (b) comparison and contrast.
    (c) analysis.
    (d) classification.
    (e) cause and effect.
    (f) steps in a process.
6. When Agassiz told his students, "Facts are stupid things," what

    exactly did he mean? _____

    _____

Questions for Discussion and Analysis

1. Consider your chosen field of study. How might Agassiz's "repeated injunction" to "look, look, look" be of some benefit for your academic work?
2. What kind of student did Scudder appear to be? What are his primary characteristics?
3. What are the important characteristics of a good teacher? How did Professor Agassiz embody these characteristics?

⌐ ON THE WEB

One of the best websites available on science is this one sponsored by San Francisco's Exploratorium:

www.exploratorium.edu

The site offers tours, exhibits, scientific experiments, games, and a wealth of information for laypersons and specialists alike.

Selection 10

The Insufficiency of Honesty

Stephen L. Carter

Stephen L. Carter is the William Nelson Cromwell Professor of Law at Yale University. He is also the author of three books: Reflections of an Affirmative Action Baby *(1991);* The Culture of Disbelief: How American Law and Politics Trivialize Religious Devotion *(1994); and* Integrity *(1996), from which "The Insufficiency of Honesty" is adapted. This version first appeared in the February 1996 issue of* The Atlantic Monthly.

Photo by Gail Zucker.

1   A couple of years ago I began a university commencement address by telling the audience that I was going to talk about integrity. The crowd broke into applause. Applause! Just because they had heard the word "integrity": that's how starved for it they were. They had no idea how I was using the word, or what I was going to say about integrity, or, indeed, whether I was for it or against it. But they knew they liked the idea of talking about it.

2   Very well, let us consider this word "integrity." Integrity is like the weather: everybody talks about it but nobody knows what to do about it. Integrity is that stuff that we always want more of. Some say that we need to return to the good old days when we had a lot more of it. Others say that we as a nation have never really had enough of it. Hardly anybody stops to explain exactly what we mean by it, or how we know it is a good thing, or why everybody needs to have the same amount of it. Indeed, the only trouble with integrity is that everybody who uses the word seems to mean something slightly different.

3   For instance, when I refer to integrity, do I mean simply "honestly?" The answer is no; although honesty is a virtue of importance, it is a different virtue from integrity. Let us, for simplicity, think of honesty as not lying; and let us further accept Sissela Bok's definition of a lie: "any intentionally deceptive message which is *stated*." Plainly, one cannot have integrity without being honest (although, as we shall see, the matter gets complicated), but one can certainly be honest and yet have little integrity.

4   When I refer to integrity, I have something very specific in mind. Integrity, as I will use the term, requires three steps: discerning what is right and what is wrong; acting on what you have discerned, even at personal cost; and saying openly that you are acting on your understanding of right and wrong. The first criterion captures the idea that integrity requires a degree of moral reflectiveness. The second brings in the ideal of a person of integrity as steadfast, a quality that includes keeping one's commitments. The third reminds us that a person of integrity can be trusted.

5   The first point to understand about the difference between honesty and integrity is that a person may be entirely honest without ever engaging in the hard work of discernment that integrity requires: she may tell us quite truthfully what she believes without ever taking the time to figure out whether what she believes is good and right and true. The problem may be as simple as someone's foolishly saying something that hurts a friend's feelings; a few moments of thought would have revealed the likelihood of the hurt and the lack of necessity for the comment. Or the problem may be more complex, as when a man who was raised from birth in a society that preaches racism states his belief in one race's infe-

riority as a fact, without ever really considering that perhaps this deeply held view is wrong. Certainly the racist is being honest—he is telling us what he actually thinks—but his honesty does not add up to integrity.

Telling Everything You Know

6 A wonderful epigram sometimes attributed to the filmmaker Sam Goldwyn goes like this: "The most important thing in acting is honesty; once you learn to fake that, you're in." The point is that honesty can be something one *seems* to have. Without integrity, what passes for honesty often is nothing of the kind; it is fake honesty—or it is honest but irrelevant and perhaps even immoral.

7 Consider an example. A man who has been married for fifty years confesses to his wife on his deathbed that he was unfaithful thirty-five years earlier. The dishonesty was killing his spirit, he says. Now he has cleared his conscience and is able to die in peace.

8 The husband has been honest—sort of. He has certainly unburdened himself. And he has probably made his wife (soon to be his widow) quite miserable in the process, because even if she forgives him, she will not be able to remember him with quite the vivid image of love and loyalty that she had hoped for. Arranging his own emotional affairs to ease his transition to death, he has shifted to his wife the burden of confusion and pain, perhaps for the rest of her life. Moreover, he has attempted his honesty at the one time in his life when it carries no risk; acting in accordance with what you think is right and risking no loss in the process is a rather thin and unadmirable form of honesty.

9 Besides, even though the husband has been honest in a sense, he has now twice been unfaithful to his wife: once thirty-five years ago, when he had his affair, and again when, nearing death, he decided that his own peace of mind was more important than hers. In trying to be honest he has violated his marriage vow by acting toward his wife not with love but with naked and perhaps even cruel self-interest.

10 As my mother used to say, you don't have to tell people everything you know. Lying and nondisclosure, as the law often recognizes, are not the same thing. Sometimes it is actually illegal to tell what you know, as, for example, in the disclosure of certain financial information by market insiders. Or it may be unethical, as when a lawyer reveals a confidence entrusted to her by a client. It may be simple bad manners, as in the case of a gratuitous comment to a colleague on his or her attire. And it may be subject to religious punishment, as when a Roman Catholic priest breaks the seal of the confessional—an offense that carries automatic excommunication.

11 In all the cases just mentioned, the problem with telling everything you know is that somebody else is harmed. Harm may not be the intention, but it is certainly the effect. Honesty is most laudable when we

risk harm to ourselves; it becomes a good deal less so if we instead risk harm to others when there is no gain to anyone other than ourselves. Integrity may counsel keeping our secrets in order to spare the feelings of others. Sometimes, as in the example of the wayward husband, the reason we want to tell what we know is precisely to shift our pain onto somebody else—a course of action dictated less by integrity than by self-interest. Fortunately, integrity and self-interest often coincide, as when a politician of integrity is rewarded with our votes. But often they do not, and it is at those moments that our integrity is truly tested.

Error

12   Another reason that honesty alone is no substitute for integrity is that if forthrightness is not preceded by discernment, it may result in the expression of an incorrect moral judgment. In other words, I may be honest about what I believe, but if I have never tested my beliefs, I may be wrong. And here I mean "wrong" in a particular sense: the proposition in question is wrong if I would change my mind about it after hard moral reflection.

13   Consider this example. Having been taught all his life that women are not as smart as men, a manager gives the women on his staff less-challenging assignments than he gives the men. He does this, he believes, for their own benefit: he does not want them to fail, and he believes that they will if he gives them tougher assignments. Moreover, when one of the women on his staff does poor work, he does not berate her as harshly as he would a man, because he expects nothing more. And he claims to be acting with integrity because he is acting according to his own deepest beliefs.

14   The manager fails the most basic test of integrity. The question is not whether his actions are consistent with what he most deeply believes but whether he has done the hard work of discerning whether what he most deeply believes is right. The manager has not taken this harder step.

15   Moreover, even within the universe that the manager has constructed for himself, he is not acting with integrity. Although he is obviously wrong to think that the women on his staff are not as good as the men, even were he right, that would not justify applying different standards to their work. By so doing he betrays both his obligation to the institution that employs him and his duty as a manager to evaluate his employees.

16   The problem that the manager faces is an enormous one in our practical politics, where having the dialogue that makes democracy work can seem impossible because of our tendency to cling to our views even when we have not examined them. As Jean Bethke Elshtain has said, borrowing from John Courtney Murray, our politics are so fractured and contentious that we often cannot even reach *disagreement.*

Our refusal to look closely at our own most cherished principles is surely a large part of the reason. Socrates thought the unexamined life not worth living. But the unhappy truth is that few of us actually have the time for constant reflection on our views—on public or private morality. Examine them we must, however, or we will never know whether we might be wrong.

17 None of this should be taken to mean that integrity as I have described it presupposes a single correct truth. If, for example, your integrity-guided search tells you that affirmative action is wrong, and my integrity-guided search tells me that affirmative action is right, we need not conclude that one of us lacks integrity. As it happens, I believe—both as a Christian and as a secular citizen who struggles toward moral understanding—that we *can* find true and sound answers to our moral questions. But I do not pretend to have found very many of them, nor is an exposition of them my purpose here.

18 It is the case not that there aren't any right answers but that, given human fallibility, we need to be careful in assuming that we have found them. However, today's political talk about how it is wrong for the government to impose one person's morality on somebody else is just mindless chatter. *Every* law imposes one person's morality on somebody else, because law has only two functions: to tell people to do what they would rather not or to forbid them to do what they would.

19 And if the surveys can be believed, there is far more moral agreement in America than we sometimes allow ourselves to think. One of the reasons that character education for young people makes so much sense to so many people is precisely that there seems to be a core set of moral understandings—we might call them the American Core—that most of us accept. Some of the virtues in this American Core are, one hopes, relatively noncontroversial. About 500 American communities have signed on to Michael Josephson's program to emphasize the "six pillars" of good character: trustworthiness, respect, responsibility, caring, fairness, and citizenship. These virtues might lead to a similarly noncontroversial set of political values: having an honest regard for ourselves and others, protecting freedom of thought and religious belief, and refusing to steal or murder.

Honesty and Competing Responsibilities

20 A further problem with too great an exaltation of honesty is that it may allow us to escape responsibilities that morality bids us bear. If honesty is substituted for integrity, one might think that if I say I am not planning to fulfill a duty, I need not fulfill it. But it would be a peculiar morality indeed that granted us the right to avoid our moral responsibilities simply by stating our intention to ignore them. Integrity does not permit such an easy escape.

21   Consider an example. Before engaging in sex with a woman, her lover tells her that if she gets pregnant, it is her problem, not his. She says that she understands. In due course she does wind up pregnant. If we believe, as I hope we do, that the man would ordinarily have a moral responsibility toward both the child he will have helped to bring into the world and the child's mother, then his honest statement of what he intends does not spare him that responsibility.

22   This vision of responsibility assumes that not all moral obligations stem from consent or from a stated intention. The linking of obligations to promises is a rather modern and perhaps uniquely Western way of looking at life, and perhaps a luxury that only the well-to-do can afford. As Fred and Shulamit Korn (a philosopher and an anthropologist) have pointed out, "If one looks at ethnographic accounts of other societies, one finds that, while obligations everywhere play a crucial role in social life, promising is not preeminent among the sources of obligation and is not even mentioned by most anthropologists." The Korns have made a study of Tonga, where promises are virtually unknown but the social order is remarkably stable. If life without any promises seems extreme, we Americans sometimes go too far the other way, parsing not only our contracts but even our marriage vows in order to discover the absolute minimum obligation that we have to others as a result of our promises.

23   That some societies in the world have worked out evidently functional structures of obligation without the need for promise or consent does not tell us what *we* should do. But it serves as a reminder of the basic proposition that our existence in civil society creates a set of mutual responsibilities that philosophers used to capture in the fiction of the social contract. Nowadays, here in America, people seem to spend their time thinking of even cleverer ways to avoid their obligations, instead of doing what integrity commands and fulfilling them. And all too often honesty is their excuse.

A. Comprehension

Choose the answer that best completes each statement. Do not refer to the selection while doing this exercise.

1. According to Carter, which of the following statements best explains the relationship between honesty and integrity?
   (a) Honesty is part of integrity, but integrity requires discernment, while honesty does not.
   (b) Honesty and integrity are so similar in meaning that it is pointless to try to distinguish between them.
   (c) Integrity is honesty with a social and moral conscience.
   (d) Integrity is similar to honesty but requires a stronger commitment to telling the truth.

2. Carter writes that integrity requires three steps. Which of the following is *not* included among them?
    (a) Distinguishing between what is right and what is wrong.
    (b) Acting upon this distinction, even if it costs you personally.
    (c) Always saying what is right and what is wrong even if it hurts another.
    (d) Stating openly that you are acting on your distinction between what is right and what is wrong.

3. According to Carter, honesty is the right course of action only when
    (a) we save our own good reputations despite the harm it may do to others.
    (b) it serves our self-interest.
    (c) it causes harm to ourselves and spares others from being harmed.
    (d) we are forced to disclose everything we know, for example, in a court of law.

4. A manager gives his female employees easier tasks because he is certain they will fail if he gives them harder tasks. Carter says that the manager lacks integrity because he has
    (a) not examined his beliefs to be sure they were right in the first place.
    (b) been dishonest with his employees.
    (c) remained true to his own beliefs, even if others do not agree with him.
    (d) made a generalization based on insufficient evidence.

5. A society functions best when its citizens believe in the importance of
    (a) making legal contracts to govern every aspect of human relationships.
    (b) being honest, even if it means abdicating one's responsibilities.
    (c) keeping promises.
    (d) recognizing the importance of responsibility rather than mere promises.

B. Vocabulary

For each italicized word from the selection, write the best definition according to the context in which it appears. You may refer to the selection to answer the questions in this section and in all the remaining sections.

1. *discerning* what is right and what is wrong [paragraph 4]: _____

    _____

2. the first *criterion* [4]: _____

3. a person of integrity as *steadfast* [4]: _____

4. a *gratuitous* comment [10]: _____

5. honesty is most *laudable* [11]: _____

6. he does not *berate* her [13]: _____

7. our politics are so . . . *contentious* [16]: _____

8. given human *fallibility* [18]: _____

9. an *exaltation* of honesty [20]: _____

10. *parsing* . . . our contracts [22]: _____

   _____

C. *Inferences*

Complete the following questions.

1. Carter suggests that, when discussing honesty and integrity, what is most important is
   (a) to avoid unnecessarily harming another person.
   (b) to recognize that not everyone knows what these terms mean.
   (c) to be true to one's beliefs no matter what the consequences.
   (d) not to disclose everything unless one is forced to.

2. Look again at the end of paragraph 5, from which the reader can infer that
   (a) racists usually act honestly based on their beliefs.
   (b) racists have not examined the validity of their beliefs, no matter how honest they think they are being.
   (c) racists are born, not made.
   (d) everyone is racist to some degree or other.

3. The hypothetical story of the dying man who confesses his past infidelity to his wife confirms Carter's observation that
   (a) his honesty derived from self-interest, not from integrity.
   (b) it was important for him to confess to wrongdoings before dying.
   (c) deathbed confessions are seldom a good idea.
   (d) he was probably punishing his wife for a miserable marriage.

4. A man who tells a woman that any resulting pregnancy from their relationship is her problem, not his,
   (a) is not absolved of responsibility just because he has been honest about his feelings.
   (b) is not responsible morally either for her or for the child.
   (c) has shown integrity by being forthright from the beginning.
   (d) is guilty of the worst sort of sexual exploitation.

D. Structure

Complete the following questions.

1. Carter never explicitly defines the word *integrity,* perhaps because
    (a) he does not clearly understand the word's meaning himself.
    (b) the examples he uses throughout the essay suggest and clarify the word's meaning.
    (c) everyone knows what *integrity* and *honesty* mean.
    (d) the word is impossible to define accurately.
2. Why does Carter include paragraphs 17 and 18? What do they add to

    his discussion? _____

    _____

3. The tone of this essay can be best described as
    (a) reflective, thoughtful.
    (b) impartial, objective.
    (c) scholarly, pedantic.
    (d) uncertain, ambivalent.

Questions for Discussion and Analysis

1. What is your personal definition of integrity?
2. Is Carter condoning lying? Concerning the hypothetical husband who confesses to an adulterous affair on his deathbed, what would have been the right course of action if his wife had asked him if he had ever been unfaithful to her?
3. Examine an incident in your life when your behavior showed honesty but not integrity.

AT THE MOVIES

The 1999 British movie *The Winslow Boy,* directed by playwright David Mamet, is an excellent film that embodies Carter's concept of integrity. When a 14-year-old boy is accused of stealing a small amount of money at his school, his family sacrifices a great deal to prove his accusers wrong and to restore his honor. The film stars Rebecca Pidgeon, Gemma Jones, and Guy Edwards II as Ronnie Winslow, the accused boy.

Selection 11   # Shiny Happy People Working at the Rat
Jane Kuenz

Inside the Mouse: Work and Play at Disney World, described as "an outsider's view of Disney World," is the collaborative effort of four people. Jane Kuenz, the author of this excerpt, received a PhD in English from Duke University. She currently teaches American literature and cultural studies at the University of Southern Maine. Her specialty is black women of the Harlem Renaissance. This selection focuses on working conditions at Disney World for the workers who portray Mickey Mouse, Minnie Mouse, Goofy, and other assorted characters in the Disney menagerie. (The little interview at the beginning was conducted by Kuenz, here abbreviated "JK.")

1   TED: *Let's say you were like Pluto, and you were the person in the costume. See, I would never say that to anybody that would write that in the paper, that there was somebody inside the costume. These kids come up and hug you and you sign the autographs and plus, you know, it's just something you have to experience, because you* are *the cartoon. You become Pluto. You have to experience it to understand.*
JK: *Is the "experience" the becoming Pluto or the interaction with the kids?*
TED: *The interaction with the kids.*
JK: *I see.*
TED: *As Pluto.*

2   At one end of the hole under Disney's Magic Kingdom, under the "Carousel," backstage, lies the "zoo." Here, mice and bears, the whole Disney menagerie, gather between their public appearances to kill time without being seen. They must arrive early for their shift to pick up and put on the heavy costumes they negotiate above ground for $5.60 an hour. Inside the huge heads, the heat of a Florida afternoon builds. Some say it gets as high as 130 degrees. All peripheral vision is cut off. Some of the heads are so unwieldy or the body of its wearer so small that a metal brace is worn on the shoulders with a post extending down the back and up into the head to keep it aloft. Without this, a child's overzealous hug might throw the characters off balance and send them, like grotesque babies, following the head to the ground. The working conditions are so bad that the characters are supposed to go above ground for only 20 to 25 minutes at a time, though in peak seasons they may stay longer. Even then, it is not unusual for the characters to pass out on stage. If you know what to look for you can see them around the park as they wait for a lead to scurry them back to the "zoo," where they can finally remove the head. Leaning against replicas of eighteenth-century lampposts or propped against a float's lit back-

board, their inhuman heads flashing a permanent smile, they wait, half conscious, hand raised from the elbow, waving absently to no one in particular.

3   Apparently the costumes alone can make wearers sick or, in conjunction with drugs and the Florida heat, can be so painful that wearers are more susceptible to heat exhaustion. Disney has an elaborate roster of height requirements for each kind of costume character: the costumes are built to the specifications of a particular body height and type, although not—as is the case for some performers in MGM Studios—to specific bodies. The bears, for example, require not just height, but strength because of the brace supporting the head. Problems arise when, in the crunch of the summer season, people (usually women, teenagers, and some younger kids) are put into costumes they are not equipped physically to handle:

> When you put a head on, it's supposed to fit on your shoulders. That's why there are height requirements for each individual costume. I have found kids that were 5′ given costumes that should have been given to someone who was 5′4″. So to hold that costume on, they strap the brace on you to make the shoulders stick out. This is how they're walking around for anywhere from 25–45 minutes. I've seen children being hurt by it. They are tired; they're fatigued; their backs, their necks are hurting. And if you were to say "I can't wear this costume," then you can be sure you won't be working there for very long. Your hours would be cut, or you're just not one of the favorites.

> It sounds crazy. The gummy bears costumes do not fit somebody that was 4′10″ and they were putting 4′10″ people in them. It was still too large and too heavy for the shoulders of someone with that frame. I played Sunny Gummy and Scruffy—that's the little mean gummy. The heads dig into your collar bones. When you're dancing or even if you're on the moving float, you are in pain. That's metal. There's no way out of it, and there's no relief when you're in it.

4   It's unclear how many of the Disney characters pass out on a given summer day, though everyone is sure that they do. One man reports that during the summer a goodly part of his job is devoted to driving around retrieving characters where they fall. One day he picked up three at one stop—Donald, Mickey, and Goofy: "All of them had passed out within five minutes of each other. They were just lined up on the sidewalk." This is in EPCOT which, unlike the Magic Kingdom with its system of underground tunnels, has a backstage behind the facades of the park's various attractions to which the characters can escape if they have to. If they are in the Magic Kingdom, however, or on a parade float, they must simply ride it out or wait until they've recovered

enough to walk to a tunnel entrace in costume and under their own steam. This can get a bit dicey. Passing out is sometimes prefaced by (and probably directly caused by) throwing up inside the head, which cannot be removed until out of public view:

> You're never to be seen in a costume without your head, *ever*. It was automatic dismissal. It's frightening because you can die on your own regurgitation when you can't keep out of it. I'll never forget Dumbo—it was coming out of the mouth during the parade. You have a little screen over the mouth. It was horrible. And I made $4.55 an hour.
>
> During the parades, I've seen many characters in 90° heat vomit in their costumes and faint on the floats and were never taken off the float. There's so much going on during a parade that people are not going to notice if Dopey is doing this [slumps] and he's not waving. . . . I've never seen them take a character off a float.

In one instance described to me, Chip of Chip 'n Dale fame passed out where he stood at the very top of a float, mounted to it by a post that ran up one leg of the costume and into the head. While this was a precaution to keep him from possibly falling off when the float jerked or hit a bump, the visual effect was crucifixion: Chip held up by a post for public exhibition, head hanging to one side, out cold.

5   The cardinal rule among Disney costume characters is never to be seen out of character and specifically out of the head or, alternately, never to let the costume be seen as a costume. Costumes must be black bagged when the characters travel to do work in town or out of the park: "Everything is black bagged. . . . God forbid if that black bag has a tear in it that you didn't know about, and a nose is sticking out of there. You're in trouble." The characters must follow rules about how to and not to move. They can't back up, for example, for the obvious reason that they can see only whatever is straight in front of them and even then only at eye level. They also cannot feel anything around them because the costumes stick out from their body and distort their sense of space. Sometimes these conditions provide the occasion for delight, as when Minnie Mouse came undone on stage: "I'm walking by the railroad and my pantaloons were around my ankles. You don't feel it because you have so much on you. People were hysterical. Finally, a lead came out, 'Minnie, Minnie, your panties have fallen.' " The fate of Winnie the Pooh, however, is also instructive:

> One time somebody dressed up as Winnie the Pooh backed up. When she backed up she hit a bush and the head popped off. The head popped off Winnie the Pooh, and all the kids see this girl walking around in a Winnie

the Pooh costume. And she's fired on the spot because her job is to be the character. And she didn't follow the rules. She should have turned around and walked out. Instead she backed up.

6   Her job is to be the character, and it is on this injunction to "be" a Disney character that the rule not to lose one's head is grounded. Apparently losing her panties is in character for Minnie; Winnie, however, is fired immediately for losing her head, the same way Dumbo would be fired immediately for taking off the one he had just thrown up in because both actions destroy the park's magic, the illusion that the characters are real. One person I spoke with refused for an hour to acknowledge even that there were actual human people inside the Disney character costumes: "That's one of the things I really can't talk about. Not because I work there, but because it keeps it kind of sacred." "Snow White *is* Snow White," another explains. Thus, when she goes to receive an award at a local hospital, Disney officials will not allow her to publicly accept it out of costume. Instead, she must appear as Snow White so those either assembled for the occasion or made privy to it later will not be disillusioned by her transformation into a regular person. In an attempt to impress upon newly-hired employees the significance of the rule not to break character, one management type recounted in a training session the story of taking his visiting niece into the tunnels to find that same Snow White. When they met her, she turned on them, cigarette and Diet Coke in hand, and told them "Get the hell out of here. I'm on break." The child was crushed, the spell broken, and a future shopper permanently lost. It's not a true story, of course—no one can smoke in the tunnels—but it's used apparently to great effect to confirm for new employees the importance of their work and what's at stake—a child's "dream"—in maintaining the company's high standards: "I was very much an idealist about it, about the job, and the whole Disney magic thing that they try to project to the public. I felt that all that magic and happiness was embodied in the character."

7   The extent to which Disney workers seem actually to become their roles and thus embody magic and happiness—and this includes everyone, not just those in head costumes—is one of the most remarked and generally praised aspects of the park and is said to be the thing that distinguishes Walt Disney World from its neighbor down the street, Universal Studios: "Why is Disney a happier place? Because it's Disney." For those not in character costumes but nevertheless cast and in costume, the transformation to "Disney" via "embodiment" amounts to a kind of leveling out of difference wherever possible. "They deliberately hire blondes," confides one brunette apparently not concerned with reconciling this contradiction. The perception is

that they do hire blondes or recreate them as blondes either with wigs or, in one case, enforcing a rule not to have two-toned hair: one woman wanted to stop coloring her hair and let it go gray, but was prevented from doing so by a rule designed to weed out those tending toward fashion experiments. It was okay to be gray; she just couldn't let it go gray. She was left with no choice but to continue coloring it the same honey blonde she had when she came in. Generally, however, it doesn't matter who or what you are when you come in since, once in, you will become whatever you were cast to be: "They have your personality waiting for you. That's literally true: Check it at the door."

8   It's uncanny, in fact, the way Disney's workers once through that door seem not to stop being their roles. One woman explains how it's hard for her to step out of character when she's in the park on her own time:

> I sometimes find myself smiling at people. They're like, "What are you smiling at me for?" I know they're thinking that, but it's because I still feel like I'm constantly this character. I have to say, "Oh, no one notices me, no one recognizes me. It's okay." It's strange sometimes. I'll smile at people or if a child falls down, I go to pick him up, and people probably don't understand that, but I forgot.

During our interviews, many Disney employees would break in and out of character as they spoke, beginning first in a descriptive or narrative mode and switching at some point to direct address as though I were a park guest they encountered in the course of the day. Moreover, their training at Disney University has left permanent marks on their memory. They and the half of Orlando that has worked in the park at some time or another can spout off Disney fun facts at will. How many spots were used in *101 Dalmatians?* 6,469,154. How do you remember the names of the Seven Dwarfs? Two s's, two d's, and three emotions. What kind of popcorn is used in the park? Orville Redenbacher. There's a Disney library and a Disney trivia line for emergencies, but many still have this stuff down years after leaving their jobs. They are information machines, walking advertisements for the park.

9   Apparently this transformation to Disney product is what many of them want when they apply to the park in the first place. These are frequently people who have migrated to Orlando specifically to work at Disney, often with exceedingly high, perhaps naive, expectations about the park. While these expectations are sometimes only vague notions that Disney must be "the epitome of the fun place to work," at other times they reflect a high level of personal investment with the

park and with its power to raise the innocuous or mundane lives of average people into the fantastical and magical existence of the Disney cast member:

> I came down in the summer. I told my parents I was going to work for Disney World, and they said, "Sure you are." I said, "No, really I am. I'm going to go down and work for Disney." They said, "No you're not." And I said, "Yes, I am." So, me and two friends of mine came down—I was just turning 21—in March or April. As soon as you walk in, you are so excited just to be there. Especially me. I'm from Dalton, Georgia. I was a little guy who'd never known anything or been anywhere, and I just decided to come down and do what I wanted to do.

> I had six kids in my family. We didn't have a lot of money. But I saw that the park was the one place I saw my parents be relaxed, be kids again. So the park was basically wonderful. What was amazing for me to see would be my dad. He's a truck driver, but he would wear this Goofy hat when he was there. He wouldn't wear it after he left the park, but he would wear it there. And I would see them smile and relax, unlike their usual lives. I saw the behavior change. That is what said to me, "There's something special here."

> I was going through a divorce after seventeen years of marriage. I was a dancer many years ago, and I never got the opportunity to do the craft again because I was raising children. I was out of New York. Never knowing what I was going to do and still in the process of raising children, I decided I was going to go to Disney. Why, I don't know; it was a fluke. When you fail at sixteen, it's okay. When you fail at thirty-six, it's kind of rough. It took me seventeen years to get out of my house and get on I-4 and have the courage to go down and apply for something. Well, I go, still never telling anybody, especially my ex-husband who'd said, "What are you going to do? Who's going to want you with three kids? You never worked a day in your life except in the family business, blah, blah, blah." But I thought to myself, I have to do this at least for something just for me.

> I was always kind of sentimental about it. I had never been to the park before I worked there. I had just moved down here to Florida from northwest Indiana, the Chicago area, in August 1988, and I got hired in September. It was a very quick thing. It was my senior year in a new school. I didn't know anybody. There was this great opportunity to do something. I picked the character department because it seemed like a lot of fun—the whole concept of "Hey, I'm Pluto."

This is who they are: a twenty-one-year-old homeboy from small town southern Georgia for whom the park represents escape from his parents—their arguments and negative dismissals—so that he can "do what [he wants] to do"; a young woman from a working-class background led back to the park by memories of her parents living one day that is "unlike their [and her] usual lives"; a woman for whom Disney represents a new life and opportunity and the chance to prove she can make it on her own; a seventeen-year-old who finds a place for himself in a new environment at a difficult point in his life by adopting the identity of Pluto. What these stories have in common is the hope that Disney World will provide people with a clean slate and something to write on it; here they can become part of the magic—a Disney item, familiar and reproducible. The park is the site for this transformation, a place where the past—and particularly past identities—is erased, where all bets are off because here a divorced mother of three can and does audition with sixteen-year-olds decked out in their "matching socks and headbands" and get selected over them because, as her director explains, "when she danced, she danced all over."

10   These narratives should be read alongside the various legends and myths that are told and retold in the park and Orlando about miscellaneous millionaires and former executives said to be ladling lemonade at Aunt Polly's Landing. I encountered many tales of these people— though no one who fit the description—who are supposed to have abandoned their former lives either permanently or on a twice-weekly basis to work at Walt Disney World: a former journalist for the *New York Times,* stock analysts in flight from Wall Street, semiretired doctors of various specialties, including a former emergency room doctor from "a New York hospital" (she "couldn't handle the trauma"), bank presidents, disillusioned heirs, and leisured women who jet in from the islands (which they own) for some quality time with the general public. Some of these are the $1-a-year-salary types: "Nothing for me, please. I'm just doing it for the children." Others are said to have walked out of their earlier lives (read: the money, the status, and their attendant problems) to refashion themselves in this new Disney environment. While some of these stories may be true, the veracity of individual cases is less important than the Disney truth produced by the circulation of them: Walt Disney World is the place where truck drivers' daughters work alongside corporate executives in their common mission of producing magic. Furthermore, it's important to see that both the firsthand accounts and the Disney myths trace the same narrative movement. Whether seen from outside as a rise or fall in status or morality, inside the world of Disney they are all the same story, Disney's story, in which everyone moves not up or down—since these implied inequities don't matter or exist in the park—but toward and within the place where each is remade in such a way that anyone can and would want to say "Hey, I'm Pluto. . . ."

11   If reciting the same scripted spiel every fifteen minutes to a new, yet somehow ever more familiar audience is difficult, it is at least made bearable by Disney's rotation system. Ostensibly—and this is its advertised benefit—rotation exposes each employee to the work of those around him or her; this is, in fact, what it does, but only to the extent that the employee is kept going through the shift. Without rotation, says one, "you'd be just sick to death. They tap into a good thing there by moving you around. It does get monotonous as all get-out even then." At a typical Disney attraction, rotation consists of a series of fifteen-minute or half-hour minishifts in which a worker is bumped from monitoring a line outside, to ushering crowds into a theater ("Walk all the way to the end of the row please"), to spieling itself, and back again to the line. In other words, they're not really learning other aspects of the park or of the company's business, but how the particular machinery of their attraction works and how they can function interchangeably as cogs at various points in it. Guests don't register this, of course. What they sense is functionality in its pure and purely invisible form. . . .

12   Those who literally do "put on a face" by putting on a character head routinely claim that park guests seem by their actions not to realize that there are people inside the costumes; guests seem not to see *them*. I find this frankly incredible, but their stories are consistent. A character lead says that "adults and children really believe what they're seeing. . . . Even adults, they believe that's Mickey. The kids go right on with it. That's Mickey that they see." One result of guests temporarily forgetting that Mickey is filled out by a living person is the threat of immediate physical danger. The little kids "pretty much consider you to be a large stuffed animal and treat you the way they treat their stuffed animals at home."

13   You can imagine the possibilities: either they "spot you from twenty yards away and come rushing toward you saying, 'I love you Donald' " or they "hit you, punch you, kick you, bite you." "They think it's fun," he continues. The kids think, "I've seen it in *Home Alone* where the guy gets kicked in the groin and everyone laughs, so, hey, I'll try it with Goofy." Apparently "adults are pretty much like the kids":

> You get the ones that are happy to see you even though you assume that they know better, that I'm not Goofy, that I'm a man wearing a costume that looks like Goofy. You get some that are just really happy to see you just like the kids. They want to get their picture taken. They want to get your autograph. Then you get the adults that are assholes. It's like "Yeah, you're Goofy. I'm going to mess with you." They punch you. I've gotten punched a few times. Punch punched.

14   Other than picking on Goofy for whatever thrill that provides, the more common response to the Disney characters is simple overexcitement, the kind that encourages guests not to think about the people inside the costume and what they're doing to them. Overexcitement is a bit of a euphemism; as Susan Willis[1] argues, a top priority of Disney guests is to get the right pictures that will document the success of the trip and thus the coherence and happiness of the family so captured in them. Most of the workers understand and are sympathetic to these feelings:

> When people come to Disney and they leave, they don't say, "Oh yeah, we rode Space Mountain, and there was a really nice guy who helped us in line" [in fact, people do say this]. No, it's "We went to Disney" and before they get to anything else they say, "We saw Mickey. We got our picture taken with Mickey."

> Visitors are hyped up by their travel agents, and they show them everything they'll get—Mickey and Minnie. These people forget. I really don't believe that they think there's something under the heads. They've got to take that picture home. They need that touch with the characters.

15   This last was told to me by a young woman who, appearing as Minnie, encountered a crowd that apparently needed her touch so badly that it knocked her down and eventually quite unconscious:

> I was taken down by two gentlemen, pulled off the conga line, knocked down to the ground—those heads are very heavy. I lost my balance. The bodice on the costume is wire, and if somebody were to push on that, it will go directly into me. Well, they bent down to help me up. Now there's a crowd of probably fifty people standing around looking at Minnie laying on the floor on Main Street. I was dragged about ten feet. At this point I don't know what's happening. I just think, get me up, get me out of here. That's a mob scene. It's very very frightening. All I know is that this gentleman must have bent down to help me up and his knee hits the body which hits my ribs. At this point I was locked into his head and could not breathe. I thought I was stabbed because there was pain in my side. It's black. There's no way for me to see if there's something sticking out of me. It is horrendous. They left me on Main Street for about fifteen minutes while they were trying to get security. I had passed out. Never to take off my head on Main Street, they took me underground on a stretcher, costume, head and all, and then took it off. I had contusions in two ribs and was out of work for quite a while.

[1]Susan Willis is the primary author of *Inside the Mouse.*

A. Comprehension

Choose the answer that best completes each statement. Do not refer to the selection while doing this exercise.

1. Ted, a Disney World worker who portrays Pluto, is quoted at the beginning of the essay as saying, "You *are* the cartoon. You become Pluto," meaning that
   (a) the costume makes him look like a cartoon character.
   (b) the Pluto costume is very realistic.
   (c) portraying Pluto is like acting in an animated movie.
   (d) playing a cartoon character means repressing one's own identity.

2. Those employees who portray Mickey Mouse, Goofy, Pluto, and others
   (a) often suffer from heat exhaustion and pass out.
   (b) receive the highest pay of all park employees.
   (c) are the least experienced workers.
   (d) rotate roles and play several different characters on each day's shift.

3. One cardinal rule at Disney World is that employees must
   (a) not divulge company secrets to the park's visitors.
   (b) never be seen out of the character they play or carrying a costume.
   (c) submit to random drug tests.
   (d) not tell park visitors their real identities or any other personal data.

4. When the woman who portrayed Snow White won an award at a local hospital, she accepted it wearing her costume because
   (a) Disney World wanted her to entertain the hospital patients.
   (b) Disney World wanted to preserve the illusion that she was Snow White.
   (c) her award had been for portraying Snow White in the first place.
   (d) she wanted to keep her identity a secret.

5. Those who move to Orlando to work at Disney World are attracted by the
   (a) park's reputation for being a good employer.
   (b) park's generous fringe benefits.
   (c) chance to work at a variety of jobs and learn new skills.
   (d) hope that Disney World will work its magic and erase their past lives.

B. Vocabulary

For each italicized word from the selection, write the best definition according to the context in which it appears. You may refer to the selection to answer the questions in this section and in all the remaining sections.

1. some of the heads are so *unwieldy* [paragraph 2]: _____

2. a child's *overzealous* hug [2]: *Zealous* means _____

3. made *privy* to it [6]: _____

4. the transformation to . . . *"embodiment"* [7]: _____

5. to raise the *innocuous* . . . lives [9]: _____

6. *mundane* lives [9]: _____

7. the *veracity* of individual cases [10]: _____

8. these implied *inequities* [10]: _____

C. Inferences

Complete the following questions.

1. From the selection as a whole, what can you infer about the working

    conditions at Disney World? _____

    _____

    _____

2. Reread paragraphs 2 and 3. How meticulous is Disney World about
    observing time limits and height and weight specifications for those

    employees who portray Disney characters? _____

    _____

3. From paragraph 7, what can you infer about Disney's method of

    training new employees? _____

    _____

4. Reread the information provided in paragraph 9. What attracts many

    people to seek work at Disney World? _____

    _____

5. Concerning the reference in paragraph 10 to the millionaires and
    business executives who dropped out and came to Disney World to
    work, why are these "legends and myths . . . told and retold"?

    _____

    _____

D. *Structure*

Complete the following questions.

1. The main idea of the selection is that
    (a) working at Disney World fulfills the dreams of many people who migrate to Orlando.
    (b) working at Disney World is demanding and difficult but quite lucrative.
    (c) Disney World goes to great, almost extreme, lengths to protect the image of the park's magic and the illusion that its characters are real.
    (d) Disney World is a gigantic, monolithic entertainment corporation, which, despite employee dissatisfaction, is the enterprise's most profitable element.

2. Write the two key ideas examined in paragraph 8. _____

    _____

    _____

3. Write a main-idea sentence for paragraph 14. _____

    _____

    _____

4. Look again at the last paragraph, which describes an incident when an employee was knocked unconscious and wheeled away by security.

    What main idea does this anecdote reinforce? _____

    _____

    _____

5. From the examples the author includes and her observations about the "shiny happy people" at Disneyland, how would you describe the

    author's tone? _____

    _____

Questions for Discussion and Analysis

1. Do you find any evidence of the author's bias?
2. What is the fundamental contradiction suggested in this essay? Does the author resolve it, and if so, how?

3. At the end of the essay, Kuenz describes the various attitudes and behaviors park visitors exhibit toward the Disney characters. Comment on these behaviors, especially the tendency of some children to punch Goofy. Does this behavior reveal a collective mean streak, or something else?

ON THE WEB

- "Media Circus" by Bruce Shapiro, a contributing editor at *The Nation,* is an article on working conditions within the media empire of the Disney Corporation. It is available online at: www.salon.com/may97/media/media970529.html

- Ted Friedman's article, "The World of *The World of Coca-Cola*" (originally published in a 1992 issue of *Communication Research*), is a fascinating description of Coca-Cola's museum in Atlanta, Georgia, the corporate headquarters. The museum is devoted to extolling the virtues of the corporation, and Friedman's article exposes the false sentiments and rosy-hued corporate history. The article is available at: eserver.org/theory/world-of-coca-cola.html

---

Selection 12   # History in Black and White
Michael Wilbon

© Greg Schaler.

In April 1997 two significant events in sports history took place. The country celebrated both the fiftieth anniversary of Jackie Robinson's entry into the previously all-white sport of baseball and Tiger Woods's first win at the Masters golf tournament in Augusta, Georgia. Tiger Woods has since won four major golf tournaments in a row, and in 2002, he won the Masters Tournament for the third time. Michael Wilbon is a sports columnist at The Washington Post, *where "History in Black and White" was first published. In it, Wilbon finds more significance in these accomplishments of Robinson and Woods than mere baseball and golf statistics.*

1   The image that I cannot shake, even days later, doesn't include Tiger Woods. He wasn't in the frame that's going to stay with me forever. He and his father Earl, not long past bypass surgery, had just concluded a long and loving embrace, which, given the state of fatherhood in black America, was emotional enough. Tiger had walked in one direction, toward Butler Cabin, to be

awarded his green jacket for winning The Masters. But the camera for some reason stayed on Earl Woods, who walked off in another direction.

2   And in the picture, pretty much all you could see was Earl Woods being royally escorted off Augusta National by a legion of what appeared to be Georgia state troopers. At that point, nothing else mattered. A brown-skinned father of a brown-skinned golfer was being guarded by Southern state troopers at a country club where some members only 10 years ago would rather have died and gone to hell than see that man even walk the course, much less play it.

3   Words cannot adequately describe the emotions felt at that moment by millions of people in the country, most of them people of color. The Southern state trooper, second only to the Klan, is the real face of the violent white South, of club-swinging, water-spraying days of the 1960s. Part of me wanted to sit there dispassionately and watch life as it ought to be and should have been. Part of me wanted to go to church and shout.

4   I was fortunate enough to be watching the final moments of The Masters on television with a passionate golfer, my father-in-law-to-be, an accomplished professional black man in his sixties and a Southerner who undoubtedly felt emotions that someone 30 years younger can't feel. After six people in the room had fallen totally silent, he said, "Can you believe all of this?"

5   It is a bit much to take in all at once. Tiger Woods winning The Masters on a Sunday and, 48 hours later, the 50th anniversary of Jackie Robinson breaking baseball's color line being celebrated at Shea Stadium.

6   Nothing like this just happens willy-nilly, this bridge from Robinson to Woods, from Brooklyn to Augusta, Ga., from one ballplayer who endured unspeakable hatred in the name of progress to this young golfer who now has to negotiate unimaginable adulation. It certainly seems the baton has been passed once again, from Jesse Owens to Joe Louis to Jackie Robinson to Muhammad Ali to Arthur Ashe and now to Tiger Woods.

7   Those of us looking for a sign that young Tiger can handle this, that he indeed understands his burden and is willing to carry it, got a clear one even before he received his green jacket. Talking to CBS's Jim Nantz, who asked him about being the first African American and Asian American to win golf's most prestigious tournament, Woods demonstrated a sense of history, of indebtedness and common sense beyond his years when he said, "I may be the first, but I'm not a pioneer." And then he went on to thank, by name, Charlie Sifford, Lee Elder and Ted Rhodes, black golfers—all pioneers—who had not a prayer until recently of walking through the front door at Augusta National.

8   Sifford, Elder and Rhodes are to Woods as Cool Papa Bell, Satchel Paige and Josh Gibson were to Jackie Robinson, the men who took all the earliest hits, who had doors slammed in their faces and roads blocked. It is only through Woods's light that people now will begin to learn more of Sifford, Elder and Rhodes. It's not difficult to find the similarities between them. Both became educated men, Robinson at UCLA and Woods at Stanford. I'm not talking about college degrees, I mean educated, learned, scholarly.

9   It was easy to see in both a great deal of dignity and humility. And it was easy to see in both a sincere sense of family, Woods with his parents and Robinson with his beautiful and tough-minded wife Rachel, who was with him in the trenches and responsible for her husband's endurance in ways most of us will never know. Just as Robinson once did, Woods speaks the King's English, not some mush-mouthed, excuse-making quasi-language that can't do our people any good outside of our own environs, but clear and to the point without hemming and hawing and certainly without struggle. My mother and mother-in-law-to-be, two former schoolteachers, were happier with the way Woods spoke and carried himself that they were with any drive he hit off the tee.

10   I should say at this point that I am not a golfer. I've had two lessons and have only recently started watching televised golf, but it seems clear that Woods and the golf explosion will in short time dramatically change the order of sports in America. This isn't just about sports, however; the venue is sports, and, as is often the case, sports is the earliest setting for significant social change. Jesse Owens and Hitler had their silent confrontation in Berlin three years before the start of World War II. Robinson, remember, came along eight years before Rosa Parks, and before *Brown v. Board of Education.* Title IX preceded by years and years certain mainstream battles for gender equity.

11   This isn't about more black youngsters playing golf, though that will happen automatically and happily. It's about people, particularly people who have been stereotyped and pigeonholed and systematically eliminated from some pursuit or another, to feel free to explore whatever passions are stirring within. It's about letting people explore those passions without restrictions, without having to face bigotry and ignorance.

12   That, not his baseball exploits, is why I think we should honor Jackie Robinson now and forever. Those too young or too far removed to identify with Robinson's struggle can now see the identifiable bridge that has been built across the past 50 years, one that has carried us to a time when a kid of African and Asian descent can be mobbed adoringly by a predominantly white audience in Georgia on land that used to be a slave plantation, and when the uniformed sons of the Confederacy are offering a handshake instead of a billy club.

13   Shut your eyes real tight and imagine Jackie Robinson on one side
of that bridge, young Tiger Woods on the other, and all the goodwill in
between that can be so wonderful to explore.

A. Comprehension

Choose the answer that best completes each statement. Do not refer to the
selection while doing this exercise.

1.   For the author, the central image from the Masters Tournament is
     that of
     (a) Tiger Woods's final victory stroke.
     (b) the clapping and cheering crowd.
     (c) the white Georgia state troopers' respectful treatment of Woods's
         father, Earl.
     (d) the lavish attention given to Tiger Woods by the television
         networks.
2.   Wilbon suggests that Tiger Woods's victory at Augusta National was
     emotionally most affecting for
     (a) young African Americans.
     (b) 1960s civil rights activists.
     (c) the Ku Klux Klan.
     (d) older African Americans who remember the struggles of the
         1960s.
3.   The affection shown Tiger Woods is as much the result of changed
     Southern attitudes regarding race as it is of
     (a) the accomplishments of earlier black athletes who fought for
         acceptance.
     (b) the influence of television networks.
     (c) increased opportunities for blacks to attend college.
     (d) federal civil rights legislation.
4.   According to Wilbon, the venue for "significant social change" in race
     relations is often
     (a) sports in general.
     (b) golf.
     (c) tennis.
     (d) the Olympics.
5.   Woods's victory represents a chance for African Americans and other
     previously excluded groups to
     (a) identify with Woods as a true cultural hero.
     (b) explore their interests without confronting bigotry and ignorance.
     (c) join formerly all-white country clubs.
     (d) remember and honor Jackie Robinson's accomplishments.

B. Vocabulary

For each italicized word from the selection, choose the best definition according to the context in which it appears. You may refer to the selection to answer the questions in this section and in all the remaining sections.

1. to sit there *dispassionately* [paragraph 3]:
    (a) pathetically.
    (b) disparagingly.
    (c) calmly.
    (d) cheerfully.
2. Nothing like this just happens *willy-nilly* [6]:
    (a) in an unplanned manner.
    (b) for better or for worse.
    (c) as part of a tradition.
    (d) for no reason.
3. to negotiate . . . *adulation* [6]:
    (a) complicated contracts.
    (b) economic barriers.
    (c) excessive admiration.
    (d) racially motivated hostility.
4. excuse-making, *quasi*-language [9]: A prefix meaning
    (a) false.
    (b) genuine.
    (c) incomplete.
    (d) resembling.

C. Inferences

On the basis of the evidence in the article, mark these statements as follows: PA (probably accurate), PI (probably inaccurate), or NP (not in the passage).

1. _____ Earl Woods, Tiger Woods's father, is also a professional golfer.
2. _____ The author worries that Tiger Woods will be unable to carry the burden that accompanies his Masters victory.
3. _____ Charlie Sifford, Lee Elder, and Ted Rhodes—former black golfers—were not permitted to play in previous Masters tournaments.
4. _____ Tiger Woods's first victory at the Masters Tournament had a special emotional significance for African Americans.
5. _____ Jackie Robinson endured the racial hostility directed at him with good grace and strength.

D. Structure

Complete the following questions.

1. Explain in your own words the central metaphor that runs through this article. _____

_____

_____

2. Read paragraph 6 again. Then summarize the change the past 50 years have brought with regard to race relations. _____

_____

_____

3. Read the last three sentences of paragraph 8 again. Then explain

Wilbon's comment about college degrees. _____

_____

_____

4. What quality of Woods is revealed in his quotation (in paragraph 7),

"I may be the first, but I'm not a pioneer"? _____

_____

5. The author's tone can be best described as
   (a) objective, impartial, neutral.
   (b) informative, instructive, didactic.
   (c) sincere, candid, forthright.
   (d) joyful, exuberant, optimistic.

Questions for Discussion and Analysis

1. In paragraph 10, Wilbon alludes to Rosa Parks and *Brown v. Board of Education.* What do these allusions refer to? What contributions did each event make to the civil rights movement?
2. Consider paragraph 9 again. What are the implications of Wilbon's remarks about language? And what characteristic or quality does it reveal about the author with respect to race and identification with it?
3. What are some reasons that athletes—of whatever race—represent role models for so many young people rather than, say, scientists, engineers, business leaders, or teachers?

🖱 ON THE WEB

- Michael Wilbon's sports columns can be read online at:
www.washingtonpost.com
Click on "Today's Columnists" and scroll down to his name.
- The following are two well-regarded sites specializing in African-American culture:
www.BET.com
www.netnoir.com

Selection 13

Talk Show Telling versus Authentic Telling: The Effects of the Popular Media on Secrecy and Openness

Evan Imber-Black

Evan Imber-Black is a practicing family therapist in New York. Currently, she is also director of program development of the Ackerman Institute for the Family and professor of psychiatry at the Albert Einstein College of Medicine. The following selection is reprinted from The Secret Life of Families: Truth-Telling, Privacy, and Reconciliation in a Tell-All Society *(1998). Its subject is the television talk show, especially those programs that air people's secrets for the titillation of the home viewer.*

> *Well, my guests today say that they can't bear to keep their secrets locked inside of them any longer. And they've invited their spouse or lover to come on national television to let them hear the secrets for the first time.*
>
> —Montel Williams

1   The young woman entered my therapy room slowly, with the usual hesitation of a new client. I settled her in a chair, expecting to begin the low-key question-and-answer conversation that usually takes the entire first session. Almost before she could pronounce my name, she began telling me a deeply personal and shameful secret. In an effort to slow her down and start to build a relationship that might be strong enough to hold her enormous pain, I gently asked her what made her think it was all right to tell me things so quickly. "I see people doing it on *Oprah* all the time," she replied.

2   Throughout history human beings have been fascinated by other people's secrets. In great literature, theater, and films we view how people create and inhabit secrets and cope with the consequences of

planned or unplanned revelation. Life-changing secrets are central to such ancient dramas such as *Oedipus* or Shakespeare's *Macbeth,* as well as to twentieth-century classics such as Ibsen's *A Doll's House,* Eugene O'Neill's *Long Day's Journey into Night,* Arthur Miller's *Death of a Salesman* and *All My Sons,* or Lorraine Hansberry's *A Raisin in the Sun.* Like me, you may remember the poignancy of the sweet secrets in the O. Henry tale "Gifts of the Magi," where a wife secretly cuts and sells her hair to buy her husband a watch chain for Christmas, while he, unbeknownst to her, sells his watch in order to buy silver combs for her hair. Contemporary popular films, such as *Ordinary People, The Prince of Tides,* or *The Wedding Banquet,* also illustrate the complexity of secrets and their impact on every member of a family. Literary and dramatic portrayals of perplexing secrets and their often complicated and messy resolutions help us to remember that keeping and opening secrets is not simple. Perhaps most important, they help us appreciate our own deep human connection to the dilemmas of others.

3   Since the advent of television, however, we have begun to learn about other people's secrets and, by implication, how to think about our own secrets in a very different way. Exploiting our hunger for missing community, both afternoon talk shows and evening magazine shows have challenged all of our previously held notions about secrecy, privacy, and openness. While such shows have been around for nearly thirty years, in the 1980s something new began to appear: Celebrities began to open the secrets in their lives on national television. As we heard about Jane Fonda's bulimia, Elizabeth Taylor's drug addiction, or Dick Van Dyke's alcoholism—formerly shameful secrets spoken about with aplomb—centuries of stigma seemed to be lifting. Other revelations enabled us to see the pervasiveness of wife battering and incest. The unquestioned shame and secrecy formerly attached to cancer, adoption, homosexuality, mental illness, or out-of-wedlock birth began to fall away.

4   This atmosphere of greater openness brought with it many benefits. In my therapy practice I experienced an important shift as the people I worked with displayed a greater ease in raising what might never have been spoken about a decade earlier. Frightening secrets lost some of their power to perpetuate intimidation. Those who had been silenced began to find their voices and stake their claim as authorities on their own lives.

5   But as the arena of the unmentionable became smaller and smaller, a more dangerous cultural shift was also taking place: the growth of the simplistic belief that telling a secret, regardless of context, is automatically beneficial. This belief, promulgated by television talk shows and media exposés, has ripped secrecy and openness away from their necessary moorings in connected and empathic relationships. Painful personal revelations have become public entertainment, used to sell dish soap and to manufacture celebrity.

6   If cultural norms once made shameful secrets out of too many happenings in human life, we are now struggling with the reverse assumption: that opening secrets—no matter how, when, or to whom—is morally superior and automatically healing. The daily spectacle of strangers opening secrets in our living rooms teaches us that no distinctions need be drawn, no care need be taken, no thought given to consequences.

Talk Show Telling

From a *Sally Jessy Raphael* show in 1994, we hear and see the following conversation:

SALLY: *Let's meet David and Kelly. They're newlyweds. They got married in December. . . . As newlyweds, what would happen if he cheated on you? What would you do?*
KELLY: *I don't know.*
   [Before David begins to speak, the print at the bottom of the screen reads, "Telling Kelly for the first time that he's cheating on her," thus informing the audience of the content of the secret before Kelly is told.]
DAVID: *I called Sally and told the producer of the show that I was living a double life. . . . I had a few affairs on her.*
SALLY *(TO KELLY): Did you know about that?*
   [Camera zooms in on Kelly's shocked and pained expression; she is speechless and in tears, and she shakes her head while members of the audience chuckle.]
SALLY: *Kelly, how do you feel? On the one hand, listen to how awful and bad this is. On the other hand, he could have just not ever told you. He loves you so much that he wanted to come and get this out. . . .*

8   In the late 1960s the *Phil Donahue Show* began a new media format for sharing interesting information and airing issues. This shifted in the late 1970s and 1980s to celebrity confessions and the destruction of taboos. In the 1990s talk TV brings us the deliberate opening of secrets that one person in a couple or a family has never heard before. In a cynical grab for ratings and profits, the format of such shows has changed rapidly from one where guests were told ahead of time that they were going to hear a secret "for the first time on national television" to one where guests are invited to the show under some other ruse. These programs are referred to as "ambush" shows.

9   According to former talk show host Jane Whitney, "Practically anyone willing to 'confront' someone—her husband's mistress, his wife's lover, their promiscuous best friend—in a televised emotional ambush could snare a free ticket to national notoriety. *Those who promised to reveal some intimate secret to an unsuspecting loved one got star treatment"*

(italics added). Presently there are over thirty talk shows on every weekday. Forty million Americans watch these shows, and they are syndicated in many other countries. Even if you have never watched a talk show, you live in an environment where assumptions about secrets have been affected by talk show telling.

10   Opening painful secrets on talk TV shows promotes a distorted sense of values and beliefs about secrecy and openness. While viewers are drawn into the sensational content of whatever secret is being revealed, the impact on relationships after the talk show is over is ignored. Indeed, when there has been severe relationship fallout, or even tragedy following the opening of a secret, talk show hosts and producers claim they have no responsibility, intensifying the belief that secrets can be recklessly opened.

11   The audience encourages further revelations through applause. As viewers, we get the message over and over that opening a secret, regardless of consequences, gains attention and approval. Loudly applauded, cheered, jeered, and fought over, secrets are in fact trivialized. On talk shows, a secret of sexual abuse equals a secret about family finances equals a secret about being a Nazi equals a secret of paternity.

12   Once a secret is revealed, both the teller and the recipient are immediately vulnerable to the judgmental advice and criticism of strangers. Blaming and taking sides abound. Not a moment elapses for reflection on the magnitude and gravity of what has occurred. Every secret is instantly reduced to a one-dimensional problem that will yield to simplistic solutions.

13   Soon after a secret is opened, the host goes into high gear with some variation of the message that opening the secret can have only good results. Sally Jessy Raphael tells the young wife who has just discovered the secret of her husband's affairs in front of millions of unasked-for snoopers, "He loves you so much that he wanted to come and get this out." The message to all is that telling a secret, in and of itself, is curative. There is no place for ambivalence or confusion. Indeed, guests are often scolded for expressing doubt or hesitation about the wisdom of national disclosure of the intimate aspects of their lives.

14   The host's position as a celebrity can frame the content of a given secret and the process of telling as either normal or abnormal, good or bad. When Oprah Winfrey joins guests who are exposing secrets of sexual abuse or cocaine addiction with revelations of her own, the telling becomes hallowed. No distinctions are drawn between what a famous person with a lot of money and power might be able to speak about without consequences and what an ordinary person who is returning to their family, job, and community after the talk show might be able to express. Conversely, some hosts display initial shock, dismay, and negativity toward a particular secret, its teller, or its recipient. When a guest on the *Jerry Springer Show* who has just discovered that a woman he had

a relationship with is a transsexual hides in embarrassment and asks the host what he would do, Springer responds, "Well, I certainly wouldn't be talking about it on national TV!" A context of disgrace is created, only to be transformed at the next commercial break into a context of understanding and forgiveness.

15   Toward the end of any talk show on which secrets have been revealed, a mental health therapist enters. A pseudo-therapeutic context is created. The real and difficult work that is required after a secret opens disappears in the smoke and mirrors of a fleeting and unaccountable relationship with an "expert" who adopts a position of superiority and assumed knowledge about the lives of people he or she has just met. While we are asked to believe that there are no loose ends when the talk show is over, the duplicitousness of this claim is evident in the fact that many shows now offer "aftercare," or real therapy, to deal with the impact of disclosing a secret on television.

16   The time needed even to begin to deal adequately with any secret is powerfully misrepresented on talk television. In just under forty minutes on a single *Montel Williams* show, a man told his wife he was in a homosexual relationship; a woman told her husband she was having an affair with his boss; another woman told her boyfriend that she was a transsexual; a wife revealed to her husband that they were $20,000 in debt; and a woman told her boyfriend that she had just aborted their pregnancy. An ethos of "just blurt it out" underpins these shows.

17   Talk show telling also erases age-appropriate boundaries between parents and children. Children are often in the audience hearing their parents' secrets for the first time. On one show an eight-year-old boy heard his aunt reveal that he had been abandoned by his mother because she "didn't want" him. Children may also be onstage revealing a secret to one parent about the other parent, without a thought given to the guilt children experience when they are disloyal to a parent. The impact on these children, their sense of shame and embarrassment, and what they might encounter when they return to school the next day is never considered.

18   Ultimately, talk show telling transforms our most private and intimate truths into a commodity. Shows conclude with announcements: "Do you have a secret that you've never told anyone? Call and tell us"; "Have you videotaped someone doing something they shouldn't do? Send us the tape." A juicy secret may get you a free airplane trip, a limousine ride, an overnight stay in a fancy hotel. While no one forces anyone to go on a talk show, the fact that most guests are working-class people who lack the means for such travel makes talk show telling a deal with the devil.

A. *Comprehension*

Choose the answer that best completes each statement. Do not refer to the selection while doing this exercise.

1. Television talk shows have changed the way we regard
   (a) the concepts of secrecy, privacy, and openness.
   (b) what we consider appropriate behavior in front of millions of viewers.
   (c) the benefits of confessing our sins and mistakes in public.
   (d) talk show hosts as therapists and psychiatrists.

2. Imber-Black lists several facts regarding talk shows that began to change in the 1980s. Which was *not* mentioned?
   (a) Celebrities began airing their own secrets on national television.
   (b) Secrets, such as homosexuality, alcoholism, mental illness, or cancer, which used to be considered shameful, were no longer stigmatized.
   (c) Talk show guests considered an appearance on a program as cheap psychological therapy.
   (d) Social problems were revealed to be more pervasive than we had known.

3. Imber-Black is particularly concerned that a cultural shift has occurred, one which suggests that telling secrets in public is
   (a) a way to improve television ratings.
   (b) automatically beneficial and results in automatic healing.
   (c) a form of therapy superior to traditional means, such as psychoanalysis or psychological counseling.
   (d) a good way to sell products and to boost ratings.

4. Programs on which a secret about a guest is revealed for the first time before a television audience are called
   (a) assault shows.
   (b) instant therapy shows.
   (c) entrapment shows.
   (d) ambush shows.

5. Imber-Black concludes that revealing secrets in the talk show format allows no room for
   (a) ambivalence, confusion, reflection, or true understanding of a secret's impact.
   (b) equal time so that the "victim" can tell his or her side of the story.
   (c) audience discussion of the secrets revealed.
   (d) learning the final impact on the people involved in revealing and hearing the secret.

B. Vocabulary

For each italicized word from the selection, write the best definition according to the context in which it appears. You may refer to the selection to answer the questions in this section and in all the remaining sections.

1. the *poignancy* of the sweet secrets [paragraph 2]: _____

   _____

2. secrets spoken about with *aplomb* [3]: _____

3. centuries of *stigma* [3]: _____

4. to *perpetuate* intimidation [4]: _____

5. *promulgated* by television talk shows [5]: _____

6. their necessary *moorings* [5]: _____

   _____

7. some other *ruse* [8]: _____

8. not a moment *elapses* for reflection [12]: _____

9. the telling becomes *hallowed* [14]: _____

10. the *duplicitousness* of this claim [15]: _____

C. Inferences

Complete the following questions.

1. Read paragraph 2 again. In the light of Imber-Black's comments about the practice of revealing secrets on national television, list three elements regarding secrets—mentioned in paragraph 2—that are

   missing from today's media format. _____

   _____

   _____

   _____

2. From paragraph 3, write the phrase that Imber-Black uses to explain

   today's penchant for baring secrets on television. _____

   _____

3. Reread the excerpt from a Sally Jessy Raphael program in paragraph 7. What is your reaction to the way Raphael interprets the motive for the young husband's confession of adultery—that "he loves you so much

   that he wanted to come and get this out"? _____

   _____

4. What does the discussion in the section comprising paragraphs 11 through 15 suggest about the format of most television talk shows?

   _____

5. At the end of paragraph 18, Imber-Black writes, "most guests are working-class people who lack the means for such travel." What

   inference can you draw from this remark? _____

   _____

   _____

   _____

   _____

D. Structure

Complete the following questions.

1. The purpose of paragraph 2 is, specifically, to
   (a) show how talk shows' treatment of secrets is different from their treatment in literature.
   (b) list several works with the keeping and telling of secrets as their theme.
   (c) show that the subject of secrets is legitimate and beneficial in literature.
   (d) prove that the author is well read on the subject of secrecy.
2. In relation to the essay as a whole, paragraph 4 serves as a
   (a) conclusion to what has gone before.
   (b) statement of the main idea.
   (c) concession, an admission of some positive qualities.
   (d) discussion of changes in the way therapy is practiced today.
3. To support her discussion of today's talk shows, Imber-Black relies on
   (a) examples from actual talk shows and analysis of consequences.
   (b) her own biases and preconceived notions.
   (c) the testimony of victims of ambush programs.
   (d) summaries of research studies.

4. Read paragraph 5 again. Then list two of Imber-Black's objections to

revealing secrets on national television. _____

_____

_____

_____

5. Which of the following quotations from the essay best states its thesis?
    (a) "Every secret is instantly reduced to a one-dimensional problem
        that will yield to simplistic solutions."
    (b) "Painful personal revelations have become public entertainment,
        used to sell dish soap and to manufacture celebrity."
    (c) "Opening painful secrets on talk TV shows promotes a distorted
        sense of values and beliefs about secrecy and openness."
    (d) "Ultimately, talk show telling transforms our most private and
        intimate truths into a commodity."
6. We can logically conclude from the essay as a whole that
    (a) the government should remove television talk shows from the air.
    (b) readers should boycott these talk shows and manufacturers'
        products that sponsor them.
    (c) talk shows have had damaging consequences for viewers and
        participants alike.
    (d) talk shows are just a fad that will soon disappear without
        intervention from watchers or government agencies.

Questions for Discussion and Analysis

1. What is the role of television in a tell-all society? In other words, was
    the advent of television talk shows the cause of our need to reveal or
    merely a reflection of a larger social trend?
2. As Imber-Black suggests in paragraph 2, if the problem of maintaining
    and disclosing secrets has been so important in literature throughout
    the ages, why couldn't one argue that the talk show format is simply
    an updated, twenty-first-century version of the same phenomenon?
    What is so reprehensible about the talk shows described in the essay?

☝ ON THE WEB

Evan Imber-Black further discusses the special problems secrets pose on
a website sponsored by Planet Tolerance. Titled "Concealing and Revealing a Secret," the information is available at:
www.planet-therapy.com/features/black.html

Selection 14   # The Brown Wasps
Loren Eiseley

A native of Lincoln, Nebraska, Loren Eiseley (1907–1977) had a long and distinguished career as an anthropologist and scientific historian. After finishing his degree at the University of Nebraska, he completed graduate work in anthropology at the University of Pennsylvania. During his career, he taught at many colleges, among them Oberlin College in Ohio, Harvard and Columbia universities, and the universities of California and Pennsylvania. For many years he was active in the search for early postglacial man in the western United States. His best known works are The Immense Journey *(1957) and* The Night Country *(1971), in which "The Brown Wasps" was first published.*

1   There is a corner in the waiting room of one of the great Eastern stations where women never sit. It is always in the shadow and overhung by rows of lockers. It is, however, always frequented—not so much by genuine travelers as by the dying. It is here that a certain element of the abandoned poor seeks a refuge out of the weather, clinging for a few hours longer to the city that has fathered them. In a precisely similar manner I have seen, on a sunny day in midwinter, a few old brown wasps creep slowly over an abandoned wasp nest in a thicket. Numbed and forgetful and frost-blackened, the hum of the spring hive still resounded faintly in their sodden tissues. Then the temperature would fall and they would drop away into the white oblivion of the snow. Here in the station it is in no way different save that the city is busy in its snows. But the old ones cling to their seats as though these were symbolic and could not be given up. Now and then they sleep, their gray old heads resting with painful awkwardness on the backs of the benches.

2   Also they are not at rest. For an hour they may sleep in the gasping exhaustion of the ill-nourished and aged who have to walk in the night. Then a policeman comes by on his round and nudges them upright.

3   "You can't sleep here," he growls.

4   A strange ritual then begins. An old man is difficult to waken. After a muttered conversation the policeman presses a coin into his hand and passes fiercely along the benches prodding and gesturing toward the door. In his wake, like birds rising and settling behind the passage of a farmer through a cornfield, the men totter up, move a few paces, and subside once more upon the benches.

5   One man, after a slight, apologetic lurch, does not move at all. Tubercularly thin, he sleeps on steadily. The policeman does not look back. To him, too, this has become a ritual. He will not have to notice it again officially for another hour.

6   Once in a while one of the sleepers will not awake. Like the brown wasps, he will have had his wish to die in the great droning center of the hive rather than in some lonely room. It is not so bad here with the shuffle of footsteps and the knowledge that there are others who share the bad luck of the world. There are also the whistles and the sounds of everyone, everyone in the world, starting on journeys. Amidst so many journeys somebody is bound to come out all right. Somebody.

7   Maybe it was on a like thought that the brown wasps fell away from the old paper nest in the thicket. You hold till the last, even if it is only to a public seat in a railroad station. You want your place in the hive more than you want a room or a place where the aged can be eased gently out of the way. It is the place that matters, the place at the heart of things. It is life that you want, that bruises your gray old head with the hard chairs; a man has a right to his place.

8   But sometimes the place is lost in the years behind us. Or sometimes it is a thing of air, a kind of vaporous distortion above a heap of rubble. We cling to a time and a place because without them man is lost, not only man but life. This is why the voices, real or unreal, which speak from the floating trumpets at spiritualist seances are so unnerving. They are voices out of nowhere whose only reality lies in their ability to stir the memory of a living person with some fragment of the past. Before the medium's cabinet both the dead and the living revolve endlessly about an episode, a place, an event that has already been engulfed by time.

9   This feeling runs deep in life; it brings stray cats running over endless miles, and birds homing from the ends of the earth. It is as though all living creatures, and particularly the more intelligent, can survive only by fixing or transforming a bit of time into space or by securing a bit of space with its objects immortalized and made permanent in time. For example, I once saw, on a flower pot in my own living room, the efforts of a field mouse to build a remembered field. I have lived to see this episode repeated in a thousand guises, and since I have spent a large portion of my life in the shade of a nonexistent tree I think I am entitled to speak for the field mouse.

10   One day as I cut across the field which at that time extended on one side of our suburban shopping center, I found a giant slug feeding from a runnel of pink ice cream in an abandoned Dixie cup. I could see his eyes telescope and protrude in a kind of dim uncertain ecstasy as his dark body bunched and elongated in the curve of the cup. Then, as I stood there at the edge of the concrete, contemplating the slug, I began to realize it was like standing on a shore where a different type of life creeps up and fumbles tentatively among the rocks and sea wrack. It knows its place and will only creep so far until something changes. Little by little as I stood there I began to see more of this shore that surrounds the place of man. I looked with sudden care and attention at

things I had been running over thoughtlessly for years. I even waded out a short way into the grass and the wild-rose thickets to see more. A huge black-belted bee went droning by and there were some indistinct scurryings in the underbrush.

11   Then I came to a sign which informed me that this field was to be the site of a new Wanamaker suburban store. Thousands of obscure lives were about to perish, the spores of puffballs would go smoking off to new fields, and the bodies of little white-footed mice would be crunched under the inexorable wheels of the bulldozers. Life disappears or modifies its appearances so fast that everything takes on an aspect of illusion—a momentary fizzing and boiling with smoke rings, like pouring dissident chemicals into a retort. Here man was advancing, but in a few years his plaster and bricks would be disappearing once more into the insatiable maw[1] of the clover. Being of an archaeological cast of mind, I thought of this fact with an obscure sense of satisfaction and waded back through the rose thickets to the concrete parking lot. As I did so, a mouse scurried ahead of me, frightened of my steps if not of that ominous Wanamaker sign. I saw him vanish in the general direction of my apartment house, his little body quivering with fear in the great open sun on the blazing concrete. Blinded and confused, he was running straight away from his field. In another week scores would follow him.

12   I forgot the episode then and went home to the quiet of my living room. It was not until a week later, letting myself into the apartment, that I realized I had a visitor. I am fond of plants and had several ferns standing on the floor in pots to avoid the noon glare by the south window.

13   As I snapped on the light and glanced carelessly around the room, I saw a little heap of earth on the carpet and a scrabble of pebbles that had been kicked merrily over the edge of one of the flower pots. To my astonishment I discovered a full-fledged burrow delving downward among the fern roots. I waited silently. The creature who had made the burrow did not appear. I remembered the wild field then, and the flight of the mice. No house mouse, no *Mus domesticus,* had kicked up this little heap of earth or sought refuge under a fern root in a flower pot. I thought of the desperate little creature I had seen fleeing from the wild-rose thicket. Through intricacies of pipes and attics, he, or one of his fellows, had climbed to this high green solitary room. I could visualize what had occurred. He had an image in his head, a world of seed pods and quiet, of green sheltering leaves in the dim light among the weed stems. It was the only world he knew and it was gone.

14   Somehow in his flight he had found his way to this room with drawn shades where no one would come till nightfall. And here he had smelled green leaves and run quickly up the flower pot to dabble his

---

[1]An opening that appears to have a voracious appetite.

paws in common earth. He had even struggled half the afternoon to carry his burrow deeper and had failed. I examined the hole, but no whiskered twitching face appeared. He was gone. I gathered up the earth and refilled the burrow. I did not expect to find traces of him again.

15   Yet for three nights thereafter I came home to the darkened room and my ferns to find the dirt kicked gaily about the rug and the burrow reopened, though I was never able to catch the field mouse within it. I dropped a little food about the mouth of the burrow, but it was never touched. I looked under beds or sat reading with one ear cocked for rustlings in the ferns. It was all in vain. I never saw him. Probably he ended in a trap in some other tenant's room.

16   But before he disappeared I had come to look hopefully for his evening burrow. About my ferns there had begun to linger the insubstantial vapor of an autumn field, the distilled essense, as it were, of a mouse brain in exile from its home. It was a small dream, like our dreams, carried a long and weary journey along pipes and through spider webs, past holes over which loomed the shadows of waiting cats, and finally, desperately, into this room where he had played in the shuttered daylight for an hour among the green ferns on the floor. Every day these invisible dreams pass us on the street, or rise from beneath our feet, or look out upon us from beneath a bush.

17   Some years ago the old elevated railway in Philadelphia was torn down and replaced by a subway system. This ancient El with its barnlike stations containing nut-vending machines and scattered food scraps had, for generations, been the favorite feeding ground of flocks of pigeons, generally one flock to a station along the route of the El. Hundreds of pigeons were dependent upon the system. They flapped in and out of its stanchions and steel work or gathered in watchful little audiences about the feet of anyone who rattled the peanut-vending machines. They even watched people who jingled change in their hands, and prospected for food under the feet of the crowds who gathered between trains. Probably very few among the waiting people who tossed a crumb to an eager pigeon realized that this El was like a food-bearing river, and that the life which haunted its banks was dependent upon the running of the trains with their human freight.

18   I saw the river stop.

19   The time came when the underground tubes were ready; the traffic was transferred to a realm unreachable by pigeons. It was like a great river subsiding suddenly into desert sands. For a day, for two days, pigeons continued to circle over the El or stand close to the red vending machines. They were patient birds, and surely this great river which had flowed through the lives of unnumbered generations was merely suffering from some momentary drought.

20   They listened for the familiar vibrations that had always heralded an approaching train; they flapped hopefully about the head of an occasional workman walking along the steel runways. They passed from one empty station to another, all the while growing hungrier. Finally they flew away.

21   I thought I had seen the last of them about the El, but there was a revival and it provided a curious instance of the memory of living things for a way of life or a locality that has long been cherished. Some weeks after the El was abandoned workmen began to tear it down. I went to work every morning by one particular station, and the time came when the demolition crews reached this spot. Acetylene torches showered passers-by with sparks, pneumatic drills hammered at the base of the structure, and a blind man who, like the pigeons, had clung with his cup to a stairway leading to the change booth, was forced to give up his place.

22   It was then, strangely, momentarily, one morning that I witnessed the return of a little band of the familiar pigeons. I even recognized one or two members of the flock that had lived around this particular station before they were dispersed into the streets. They flew bravely in and out among the sparks and the hammers and the shouting workmen. They had returned—and they had returned because the hubbub of the wreckers had convinced them that the river was about to flow once more. For several hours they flapped in and out through the empty windows, nodding their heads and watching the fall of girders with attentive little eyes. By the following morning the station was reduced to some burned-off stanchions in the street. My bird friends had gone. It was plain, however, that they retained a memory for an insubstantial structure now compounded of air and time. Even the blind man clung to it. Someone had provided him with a chair, and he sat at the same corner staring sightlessly at an invisible stairway where, so far as he was concerned, the crowds were still ascending to the trains.

23   I have said my life has been passed in the shade of a nonexistent tree, so that such sights do not offend me. Prematurely I am one of the brown wasps and I often sit with them in the great droning hive of the station, dreaming sometimes of a certain tree. It was planted sixty years ago by a boy with a bucket and a toy spade in a little Nebraska town. That boy was myself. It was a cottonwood sapling and the boy remembered it because of some words spoken by his father and because everyone died or moved away who was supposed to wait and grow old under its shade. The boy was passed from hand to hand, but the tree for some intangible reason had taken root in his mind. It was under its branches that he sheltered; it was from this tree that his memories, which are my memories, led away into the world.

24   After sixty years the mood of the brown wasps grows heavier upon one. During a long inward struggle I thought it would do me good to go and look upon that actual tree. I found a rational excuse in which to clothe this madness. I purchased a ticket and at the end of two thousand miles I walked another mile to an address that was still the same. The house had not been altered.

25   I came close to the white picket fence and relunctantly, with great effort, looked down the long vista of the yard. There was nothing there to see. For sixty years that cottonwood had been growing in my mind. Season by season its seeds had been floating farther on the hot prairie winds. We had planted it lovingly there, my father and I, because he had a great hunger for soil and live things growing, and because none of these things had long been ours to protect. We had planted the little sapling and watered it faithfully, and I remembered that I had run out with my small bucket to drench its roots the day we moved away. And all the years since it had been growing in my mind, a huge tree that somehow stood for my father and the love I bore him. I took a grasp on the picket fence and forced myself to look again.

26   A boy with the hard bird eye of youth pedaled a tricycle slowly up beside me.

27   "What'cha lookin' at?" he asked curiously.

28   "A tree," I said.

29   "What for?" he said.

30   "It isn't there," I said, to myself mostly, and began to walk away at a pace just slow enough not to seem to be running.

31   "What isn't there?" the boy asked. I didn't answer. It was obvious I was attached by a thread to a thing that had never been there, or certainly not for long. Something that had to be held in the air, or sustained in the mind, because it was part of my orientation in the universe and I could not survive without it. There was more than an animal's attachment to a place. There was something else, the attachment of the spirit to a grouping of events in time; it was part of our mortality.

32   So I had come home at last, driven by a memory in the brain as surely as the field mouse who had delved long ago into my flower pot or the pigeons flying forever amidst the rattle of nut-vending machines. These, the burrow under the greenery in my living room and the red-bellied bowls of peanuts now hovering in midair in the minds of pigeons, were all part of an elusive world that existed nowhere and yet everywhere. I looked once at the real world about me while the persistent boy pedaled at my heels.

33   It was without meaning, though my feet took a remembered path. In sixty years the house and street had rotted out of my mind. But the tree, the tree that no longer was, that had perished in its first season, bloomed on in my individual mind, unblemished as my father's words.

"We'll plant a tree here, son, and we're not going to move any more. And when you're an old, old man you can sit under it and think how we planted it here, you and me, together."

34   I began to outpace the boy on the tricycle.

35   "Do you live here, Mister?" he shouted after me suspiciously. I took a firm grasp on airy nothing—to be precise, on the bole of a great tree. "I do," I said. I spoke for myself, one field mouse, and several pigeons. We were all out of touch but somehow permanent. It was the world that had changed.

A. Comprehension

Choose the answer that best completes each statement. Do not refer to the selection while doing this exercise.

1. For the brown wasps who return to it, the abandoned hive represents
   (a) a refuge from the harsh winter weather.
   (b) the spring hive of earlier days.
   (c) a place of shelter.
   (d) a sad memory.

2. According to Eiseley, the people who frequent the waiting room of the great Eastern station are
   (a) arriving and departing travelers.
   (b) the dying and the abandoned poor.
   (c) homeless derelicts and panhandlers.
   (d) former mental patients.

3. From Eiseley's observations throughout the essay, we learn that humans and animals share a central feeling, that of
   (a) exile and alienation.
   (b) autonomy and independence.
   (c) self-consciousness and awareness.
   (d) nostalgia and melancholy.

4. For the pigeons that gathered there, the Philadelphia El served as
   (a) shelter.
   (b) a nesting site.
   (c) a place of refuge from the city's pollution.
   (d) a place to prospect for food.

5. The cottonwood tree had been growing in Eiseley's mind since he and his father planted it sixty years earlier. When he returned to Nebraska to see the tree, he found that
   (a) the house no longer existed.
   (b) the tree was large and healthy, just as he had imagined it to be.
   (c) the tree had been cut down by a later owner.
   (d) the tree had apparently died soon after it was planted.

B Vocabulary

For each italicized word from the selection, choose the best definition according to the context in which it appears. You may refer to the selection to answer the questions in this section and in all the remaining sections.

1. The hum still *resounded* faintly [paragraph 1]:
   (a) resembled.
   (b) reverberated.
   (c) returned.
   (d) was remembered.

2. the white *oblivion* of the snow [1]:
   (a) obsolescence.
   (b) confusion.
   (c) purity, freshness.
   (d) forgetfulness.

3. a kind of *vaporous* distortion [8]:
   (a) fanciful, imaginary.
   (b) vague, ephemeral.
   (c) crazy, bizarre.
   (d) imperceptible.

4. repeated in a thousand *guises* [9]:
   (a) scenes.
   (b) ways.
   (c) images.
   (d) appearances.

5. Thousands of *obscure* lives . . . an *obscure* sense of satisfaction. This word, used twice in paragraph 11, has two different meanings. Be sure to choose *two* definitions and to indicate which definition fits which word.
   (a) dark, gloomy.
   (b) dingy, dull.
   (c) inconspicuous, unnoticed. (first usage)
   (d) vague, not clearly understood. (second usage)
   (e) undistinguished, of humble origin.

6. the *inexorable* wheels of the bulldozer [11]:
   (a) unyielding.
   (b) injurious.
   (c) detestable.
   (d) inexcusable.

7. into the *insatiable* maw of clover [11]:
    (a) inedible.
    (b) invisible.
    (c) not able to be satisfied.
    (d) undetectable by smell.

8. that *ominous* Wanamaker sign [11]:
    (a) offensive.
    (b) menacing.
    (c) distorted.
    (d) intrusive.

9. for some *intangible* reason [23]:
    (a) irrational.
    (b) precisely defined.
    (c) unclear, vague.
    (d) immediately obvious.

10. part of an *elusive* world [32]:
    (a) carefree.
    (b) difficult to appreciate.
    (c) unnatural.
    (d) evading grasp or perception.

C. Inferences

Complete the following questions.

1. Look again at paragraphs 4 and 5. What can we infer about the way the policeman's order for the men to move is heeded? _____

    _____

    _____

2. According to paragraph 6, why exactly do these old people congregate in the waiting room? _____

    _____

3. From what Eiseley writes in paragraph 11, what is his opinion of the new Wanamaker store? _____

4. What are the two reasons Eiseley implies in paragraph 11 to explain
    the return of the pigeons to the old elevated railway site? _____

    _____

    _____

    _____

5. From paragraphs 30 to 35, what can you infer about what Eiseley felt
    when he realized that the cottonwood tree no longer existed? _____

    _____

D. Structure

Complete the following questions.

1. The main idea of the selection is that
    (a) life is not only impermanent but also incomprehensible.
    (b) there is a nearly universal tendency among all living things to cling
        to a time and a place.
    (c) as we grow older, we become more observant of both human and
        animal behavior.
    (d) part of our mortality is the way the spirit is attached to events in
        time.

2. Paragraph 1 metaphorically compares the corner of the waiting room
    and the old men who frequent it to an abandoned wasp nest and to
    the brown wasps who return to it each year. Explain the meaning of

    this dual metaphor. _____

    _____

    _____

3. Paraphrase this phrase from paragraph 1: "save that the city is busy in

    its snows" _____

    _____

4. In paragraph 6, Eiseley writes, "There are also the whistles and sounds
    of everyone, everyone in the world, starting on journeys. Amidst so
    many journeys somebody is bound to come out all right. Somebody."
    These sentences emphasize that the corner's occupants are
    (a) about to take a train trip.
    (b) optimistic about their health and future welfare.
    (c) desperate, possibly even suicidal.
    (d) alienated from society, but still determined to be part of it.

5. Consider the description of the field and the little field mouse in paragraph 11. What emotion does Eiseley intend for us to feel?

_____

6. Throughout the essay Eiseley's tone can best be described as
    (a) sorrowful, mournful.
    (b) nostalgic, lamenting.
    (c) uncertain, bewildered.
    (d) philosophical, ruminative.
    (e) sentimental, maudlin.

Questions for Discussion and Analysis

1. What are the principles that unify all of the elements in this essay?
2. Why does Eiseley return to his childhood home in Nebraska? What image of the tree has he held in his mind for sixty years, and why is it so important to him?

IN THE BOOKSTORE

The Immense Journey (1957) confirmed Eiseley's reputation as one of the United States' foremost naturalists who combined an extensive knowledge of science with original thought and imagination. In this book, Eiseley tells the story of mankind and of evolution. Among the essays are the often-reprinted "How Flowers Changed the World" and "The Judgment of the Birds." Eiseley's style is lucidly eloquent, even for the nonscientific audience.

6

Reading Short Stories

Literature, Aristotle wrote, serves to delight and to instruct. The four short stories in Part 6 will round out your reading experience and will enhance your understanding of the human condition. Each story is followed by some general questions for discussion and analysis, which are by no means meant to exhaust the possibilities. Here are some general questions about plot, characters, and theme that you can ask yourself after you read each story, or any story, for that matter.

■ QUESTIONS ABOUT PLOT

1. How are the incidents that make up the plot related to each other? Is there a cause–effect relationship implied?
2. What is the conflict in the story? Who or what is responsible for it?
3. Is the conflict resolved, and if it is, is it resolved satisfactorily?
4. Do the events in the story suggest an additional interpretation, one that perhaps the reader can see but that the characters cannot?

■ QUESTIONS ABOUT CHARACTERS

1. Define each character in terms of his or her essence, behavior, and motivation.
2. How are the characters revealed to us (through direct comment, through contact with others, through their own words, or through their behavior)?
3. Why do the characters act as they do? Are their actions consistent with what has been revealed about them?
4. What is your response to each character?
5. Does any character stand for something greater than the individual?

■ QUESTIONS ABOUT THEME

1. What is the theme, and how is it embodied in the story?
2. What do we learn about human existence, human behavior, and human nature from the story?

Selection 1

How Much Land Does a Man Need?
Leo Tolstoy

Hulton/Archive by Getty Images.

Count Leo Tolstoy (1828–1910) remains one of the most important figures in literature. He wrote two of the greatest novels in Western literature, War and Peace *(1869) and* Anna Karenina *(1877). Although he was a member of the Russian landowning class, he was always troubled by his position as a landowner; in his later years, he renounced all physical comforts and embarked on a new philosophy based on a simplified form of Christianity. (The reference on the first page to Pahóm's lying on top of the stove is puzzling to a non-Russian. Russian stoves, which resembled beehives, were the center of the main living area, and several people could sit or lie on them to enjoy their warmth.)*

1

An elder sister came to visit her younger sister in the country. The elder was married to a tradesman in town, the younger to a peasant in the village. As the sisters sat over their tea talking, the elder began to boast of the advantages of town life: saying how comfortably they lived there, how well they dressed, what fine clothes her children wore, what good things they ate and drank, and how she went to the theatre, promenades, and entertainments.

The younger sister was piqued, and in turn disparaged the life of a tradesman, and stood up for that of a peasant.

"I would not change my way of life for yours," said she. "We may live roughly, but at least we are free from anxiety. You live in better style than we do, but though you often earn more than you need, you are very likely to lose all you have. You know the proverb, 'Loss and gain are brothers twain.' It often happens that people who are wealthy one day are begging their bread the next. Our way is safer. Though a peasant's life is not a fat one, it is a long one. We shall never grow rich, but we shall always have enough to eat."

The elder sister said sneeringly:

"Enough? Yes, if you like to share with the pigs and the calves! What do you know of elegance or manners! However much your goodman may slave, you will die as you are living—on a dung heap—and your children the same."

"Well, what of that?" replied the younger. "Of course our work is rough and coarse. But, on the other hand, it is sure, and we need not bow down to anyone. But you, in your towns, are surrounded by temptations; to-day all may be right, but to-morrow the Evil One may tempt your husband with cards, wine, or women, and all will go to ruin. Don't such things happen often enough?"

Pahóm, the master of the house, was lying on the top of the stove and he listened to the women's chatter.

"It is perfectly true," thought he. "Busy as we are from childhood tilling mother earth, we peasants have no time to let any nonsense settle in our heads. Our only trouble is that we haven't land enough. If I had plenty of land, I shouldn't fear the Devil himself!"

The women finished their tea, chatted a while about dress, and then cleared away the tea-things and lay down to sleep.

But the Devil had been sitting behind the stove, and had heard all that was said. He was pleased that the peasant's wife had led her husband into boasting, and that he had said that if he had plenty of land he would not fear the Devil himself.

"All right," thought the Devil. "We will have a tussle. I'll give you land enough; and by means of that land I will get you into my power."

2

Close to the village there lived a lady, small landowner who had an estate of about three hundred acres.[1] She had always lived on good terms with the peasants until she engaged as her steward an old soldier, who took to burdening the people with fines. However careful Pahóm tried to be, it happened again and again that now a horse of his got among the lady's oats, now a cow strayed into her garden, now his calves found their way into her meadows—and he always had to pay a fine.

Pahóm paid up, but grumbled and, going home in a temper, was rough with his family. All through that summer, Pahóm had much trouble because of this steward, and he was even glad when winter came and the cattle had to be stabled. Though he grudged the fodder when they could no longer graze on the pasture-land, at least he was free from anxiety about them.

In the winter the news got about that the lady was going to sell her land and that the keeper of the inn on the high road was bargaining for it. When the peasants heard this they were very much alarmed.

"Well," thought they, "if the innkeeper gets the land, he will worry us with fines worse than the lady's steward. We all depend on that estate."

So the peasants went on behalf of their Commune, and asked the lady not to sell the land to the innkeeper, offering her a better price for it themselves. The lady agreed to let them have it. Then the peasants tried to arrange for the Commune to buy the whole estate, so that it

---

[1]120 desyatíns. The desyatína is properly 2.7 acres; but in this story round numbers are used.

might be held by them all in common. They met twice to discuss it, but could not settle the matter; the Evil One sowed discord among them and they could not agree. So they decided to buy the land individually, each according to his means; and the lady agreed to this plan as she had to the other.

Presently Pahóm heard that a neighbor of his was buying fifty acres, and that the lady had consented to accept one half in cash and to wait a year for the other half. Pahóm felt envious.

"Look at that," thought he, "the land is all being sold, and I shall get none of it." So he spoke to his wife.

"Other people are buying," said he, "and we must also buy twenty acres or so. Life is becoming impossible. That steward is simply crushing us with his fines."

So they put their heads together and considered how they could manage to buy it. They had one hundred rúbles laid by. They sold a colt and one half of their bees, hired out one of their sons as a laborer and took his wages in advance; borrowed the rest from a brother-in-law, and so scraped together half the purchase money.

Having done this, Pahóm chose out a farm of forty acres, some of it wooded, and went to the lady to bargain for it. They came to an agreement, and he shook hands with her upon it and paid her a deposit in advance. Then they went to town and signed the deeds; he paying half the price down, and undertaking to pay the remainder within two years.

So now Pahóm had land of his own. He borrowed seed, and sowed it on the land he had bought. The harvest was a good one, and within a year he had managed to pay off his debts both to the lady and to his brother-in-law. So he became a landowner, ploughing and sowing his own land, making hay on his own land, cutting his own trees, and feeding his cattle on his own pasture. When he went out to plough his fields, or to look at his growing corn, or at his grass-meadows, his heart would fill with joy. The grass that grew and the flowers that bloomed there seemed to him unlike any that grew elsewhere. Formerly, when he had passed by that land, it had appeared the same as any other land, but now it seemed quite different.

3

So Pahóm was well-contented, and everything would have been right if the neighboring peasants would only not have trespassed on his corn-fields and meadows. He appealed to them most civilly, but they still went on: now the Communal herdsmen would let the village cows stray into his meadows, then horses from the night pasture would get among his corn. Pahóm turned them out again and again, and forgave their owners, and for a long time he forbore to prosecute any one. But at last he lost patience and complained to the District Court. He knew it was the peasants' want of land, and no evil intent on their part, that caused the trouble, but he thought:

"I cannot go on overlooking it or they will destroy all I have. They must be taught a lesson."

So he had them up, gave them one lesson, and then another: and two or three of the peasants were fined. After a time Pahóm's neighbors began to bear him a grudge for this, and would now and then let their cattle on to his land on purpose. One peasant even got into Pahóm's wood at night and cut down five young lime trees for their bark. Pahóm passing through the wood one day noticed something white. He came nearer and saw the stripped trunks lying on the ground, and close by stood the stumps where the trees had been. Pahóm was furious.

"If he had only cut one here and there it would have been bad enough," thought Pahóm, "but the rascal has actually cut down a whole clump. If I could only find out who did this, I would pay him out."

He racked his brain as to who it could be. Finally he decided: "It must be Simon—no one else could have done it." So he went to Simon's homestead to have a look round, but he found nothing, and only had an angry scene. However, he now felt more certain than ever that Simon had done it, and he lodged a complaint. Simon was summoned. The case was tried, and retried, and at the end of it all Simon was acquitted, there being no evidence against him. Pahóm felt still more aggrieved, and let his anger loose upon the Elder and the Judges.

"You let thieves grease your palms," said he. "If you were honest folk yourselves you would not let a thief go free."

So Pahóm quarrelled with the Judges and with his neighbors. Threats to burn his building began to be uttered. So though Pahóm had more land, his place in the Commune was much worse than before.

About this time a rumor got about that many people were moving to new parts.

"There's no need for me to leave my land," thought Pahóm. "But some of the others might leave our village and then there would be more room for us. I would take over their land myself and make my estate a bit bigger. I could then live more at ease. As it is, I am still too cramped to be comfortable."

One day Pahóm was sitting at home when a peasant, passing through the village, happened to call in. He was allowed to stay the night, and supper was given him. Pahóm had a talk with this peasant and asked him where he came from. The stranger answered that he came from beyond the Vólga, where he had been working. One word led to another, and the man went on to say that many people were settling in those parts. He told how some people from his village had settled there. They had joined the Commune, and had had twenty-five acres per man granted them. The land was so good, he said, that the rye sown on it grew as high as a horse, and so thick that five cuts of a sickle made a sheaf. One peasant, he said, had brought nothing with him but his bare hands, and now he had six horses and two cows of his own.

Pahóm's heart kindled with desire. He thought:

"Why should I suffer in this narrow hole, if one can live so well elsewhere? I will sell my land and my homestead here, and with the money I will start afresh over there and get everything new. In this crowded place one is always having trouble. But I must first go and find out all about it myself."

Towards summer he got ready and started. He went down the Vólga on a steamer to Samára, then walked another three hundred miles on foot, and at last reached the place. It was just as the stranger had said. The peasants had plenty of land: every man had twenty-five acres of Communal land given him for his use, and any one who had money could buy, besides, at a rúble an acre as much good freehold land as he wanted.

Having found out all he wished to know, Pahóm returned home as autumn came on, and began selling off his belongings. He sold his land at a profit, sold his homestead and all his cattle, and withdrew from membership in the Commune. He only waited till the spring, and then started with his family for the new settlement.

4

As soon as Pahóm and his family reached their new abode, he applied for admission into the Commune of a large village. He stood treat to the Elders and obtained the necessary documents. Five shares of Communal land were given him for his own and his sons' use: that is to say 125 acres (not all together, but in different fields) besides the use of the Communal pasture. Pahóm put up the buildings he needed, and bought cattle. Of the Communal land alone he had three times as much as at his former home, and the land was good corn-land. He was ten times better off than he had been. He had plenty of arable land and pasturage, and could keep as many head of cattle as he liked.

At first, in the bustle of building and settling down, Pahóm was pleased with it all, but when he got used to it he began to think that even here he had not enough land. The first year, he sowed wheat on his share of the Communal land and had a good crop. He wanted to go on sowing wheat, but had not enough Communal land for the purpose, and what he had already used was not available; for in those parts wheat is only sown on virgin soil or on fallow land. It is sown for one or two years, and then the land lies fallow till it is again overgrown with prairie grass. There were many who wanted such land and there was not enough for all; so that people quarreled about it. Those who were better off wanted it for growing wheat, and those who were poor wanted it to let to dealers, so that they might raise money to pay their taxes. Pahóm wanted to sow more wheat, so he rented land from a dealer for a year. He sowed much wheat and had a fine crop, but the land was too far from the village—the wheat had to be carted more than ten miles. After a time Pahóm noticed that some peasant-dealers were living on separate farms and were growing wealthy; and he thought:

"If I were to buy some freehold land and have a homestead on it, it would be a different thing altogether. Then it would all be nice and compact."

The question of buying freehold land recurred to him again and again.

He went on in the same way for three years, renting land and sowing wheat. The seasons turned out well and the crops were good, so that he began to lay money by. He might have gone on living contentedly, but he grew tired of having to rent other people's land every year, and having to scramble for it. Wherever there was good land to be had, the peasants would rush for it and it was taken up at once, so that unless you were sharp about it you got none. It happened in the third year that he and a dealer together rented a piece of pasture-land from some peasants; and they had already ploughed it up, when there was some dispute and the peasants went to law about it, and things fell out so that the labor was all lost.

"If it were my own land," thought Pahóm, "I should be independent, and there would not be all this unpleasantness."

So Pahóm began looking out for land which he could buy; and he came across a peasant who had bought thirteen hundred acres, but having got into difficulties was willing to sell again cheap. Pahóm bargained and haggled with him, and at last they settled the price at 1,500 rúbles, part in cash and part to be paid later. They had all but clinched the matter when a passing dealer happened to stop at Pahóm's one day to get a feed for his horses. He drank tea with Pahóm and they had a talk. The dealer said that he was just returning from the land of the Bashkírs, far away, where he had bought thirteen thousand acres of land, all for 1,000 rúbles. Pahóm questioned him further, and the tradesman said:

"All one needs do is to make friends with the chiefs. I gave away about one hundred rúbles' worth of silk robes and carpets, besides a case of tea, and I gave wine to those who would drink it; and I got the land for less than a penny an acre."[2] And he showed Pahóm the title-deeds, saying:

---

[2]Five kopéks for a desyatína.

"The land lies near a river, and the whole prairie is virgin soil."

Pahóm plied him with questions, and the tradesman said:

"There is more land there than you could cover if you walked a year, and it all belongs to the Bashkírs. They are as simple as sheep, and land can be got almost for nothing."

"There now," thought Pahóm, "with my one thousand rúbles, why should I get only thirteen hundred acres, and saddle myself with a debt besides? If I take it out there, I can get more than ten times as much for the money."

5

Pahóm inquired how to get to the place, and as soon as the tradesman had left him, he prepared to go there himself. He left his wife to look after the homestead, and started on his journey taking his man with him. They stopped at a town on their way and bought a case of tea, some wine, and other presents, as the tradesman had advised. On and on they went until they had gone more than three hundred miles, and on the seventh day they came to a place where the Bashkírs had pitched their tents. It was all just as the tradesman had said. The people lived on the steppes, by a river, in felt-covered tents.[3] They neither tilled the ground, nor ate bread. Their cattle and horses grazed in herds on the steppe. The colts were tethered behind the tents, and the mares were driven to them twice a day. The mares were milked, and from the milk kumiss[4] was made. It was the women who prepared kumiss, and they also made cheese. As far as the men were concerned, drinking kumiss and tea, eating mutton, and playing on their pipes, was all they cared about. They were all stout and merry, and all the summer long they never thought of doing any work. They were quite ignorant, and knew no Russian, but were good-natured enough.

As soon as they saw Pahóm, they came out of their tents and gathered round their visitor. An interpreter was found, and Pahóm told them he had come about some land. The Bashkírs seemed very glad; they took Pahóm and led him into one of the best tents, where they made him sit on some down cushions placed on a carpet, while they sat round him. They gave him some tea and kumiss, and had a sheep killed, and gave him mutton to eat. Pahóm took presents out of his cart and distributed them among the Bashkírs, and divided the tea amongst them. The Bashkírs were delighted. They talked a great deal among themselves, and then told the interpreter to translate.

---

[3]A kibítka is a movable dwelling, made up of detachable wooden frames, forming a round, and covered over with felt.

[4]Fermented mare's milk.

"They wish to tell you," said the interpreter, "that they like you, and that it is our custom to do all we can to please a guest and to repay him for his gifts. You have given us presents, now tell us which of the things we possess please you best, that we may present them to you."

"What pleases me best here," answered Pahóm, "is your land. Our land is crowded and the soil is exhausted; but you have plenty of land and it is good land. I never saw the like of it."

The interpreter translated. The Bashkírs talked among themselves for a while. Pahóm could not understand what they were saying, but saw that they were much amused and that they shouted and laughed. Then they were silent and looked at Pahóm while the interpreter said:

"They wish me to tell you that in return for your presents they will gladly give you as much land as you want. You have only to point it out with your hand and it is yours."

The Bashkírs talked again for a while and began to dispute. Pahóm asked what they were disputing about, and the interpreter told him that some of them thought they ought to ask their Chief about the land and not act in his absence, while others thought there was no need to wait for his return.

6

While the Bashkírs were disputing, a man in a large fox-fur cap appeared on the scene. They all became silent and rose to their feet. The interpreter said, "This is our Chief himself."

Pahóm immediately fetched the best dressing-gown and five pounds of tea, and offered these to the Chief. The Chief accepted them, and seated himself in the place of honor. The Bashkírs at once began telling him something. The Chief listened for a while, then made a sign with his head for them to be silent, and addressing himself to Pahóm, said in Russian:

"Well, let it be so. Choose whatever piece of land you like; we have plenty of it."

"How can I take as much as I like?" thought Pahóm. "I must get a deed to make it secure, or else they may say, 'It is yours,' and afterwards may take it away again."

"Thank you for your kind words," he said aloud. "You have much land, and I only want a little. But I should like to be sure which bit is mine. Could it not be measured and made over to me? Life and death are in God's hands. You good people give it to me, but your children might wish to take it away again."

"You are quite right," said the Chief. "We will make it over to you."

"I heard that a dealer had been here," continued Pahóm, "and that you gave him a little land, too, and signed title-deeds to that effect. I should like to have it done in the same way."

The Chief understood.

"Yes," replied he, "that can be done quite easily. We have a scribe, and we will go to town with you and have the deed properly sealed."

"And what will be the price?" asked Pahóm.

"Our price is always the same: one thousand rúbles a day."

Pahóm did not understand.

"A day? What measure is that? How many acres would that be?"

"We do not know how to reckon it out," said the Chief. "We sell it by the day. As much as you can go round on your feet in a day is yours, and the price is one thousand rúbles a day."

Pahóm was surprised.

"But in a day you can get round a large tract of land," he said.

The Chief laughed.

"It will all be yours!" said he. "But there is one condition: If you don't return on the same day to the spot whence you started, your money is lost."

"But how am I to mark the way that I have gone?"

"Why, we shall go to any spot you like, and stay there. You must start from that spot and make your round, taking a spade with you. Wherever you think necessary, make a mark. At every turning, dig a hole and pile up the turf; then afterwards we will go around with a plough from hole to hole. You may make as large a circuit as you please, but before the sun sets you must return to the place you started from. All the land you cover will be yours."

Pahóm was delighted. It was decided to start early next morning. They talked a while, and after drinking some more kumiss and eating some more mutton, they had tea again, and then the night came on. They gave Pahóm a feather-bed to sleep on, and the Bashkírs dispersed for the night, promising to assemble the next morning at daybreak and ride out before sunrise to the appointed spot.

7

Pahóm lay on the feather-bed, but could not sleep. He kept thinking about the land.

"What a large tract I will mark off!" thought he. "I can easily do thirty-five miles in a day. The days are long now, and within a circuit of thirty-five miles what a lot of land there will be! I will sell the poorer land, or let it to peasants, but I'll pick out the best and farm it. I will buy two oxteams, and hire two more laborers. About a hundred and fifty acres shall be ploughland, and I will pasture cattle on the rest."

Pahóm lay awake all night, and dozed off only just before dawn. Hardly were his eyes closed when he had a dream. He thought he was lying in that same tent and heard somebody chuckling outside. He wondered who it could be, and rose and went out, and he saw the Bashkír Chief sitting in front of the tent holding his sides and rolling about with laughter. Going nearer to the Chief, Pahóm asked: "What are you laughing at?" But he saw that it was no longer the Chief, but the dealer who had recently stopped at his house and had told him about the land. Just as Pahóm was going to ask, "Have you been here long?" he saw that it was not the dealer, but the peasant who had come up from the Vólga, long ago, to Pahóm's old home. Then he saw that it was not the peasant either, but the Devil himself with hoofs and horns, sitting there and chuckling, and before him lay a man barefoot, prostrate on the ground, with only trousers and a shirt on. And Pahóm dreamt that he looked more attentively to see what sort of a man it was that was lying there, and he saw that the man was dead, and that it was himself! He awoke horror-struck.

"What things one does dream," thought he.

Looking round he saw through the open door that the dawn was breaking.

"It's time to wake them up," thought he. "We ought to be starting."

He got up, roused his man (who was sleeping in his cart), bade him harness; and went to call the Bashkírs.

"It's time to go to the steppe to measure the land," he said.

The Bashkírs rose and assembled, and the Chief came too. Then they began drinking kumiss again, and offered Pahóm some tea, but he would not wait.

"If we are to go, let us go. It is high time," said he.

8

The Bashkírs got ready and they all started: some mounted on horses, and some in carts. Pahóm drove in his own small cart with his servant and took a spade with him. When they reached the steppe, the morning red was beginning to kindle. They ascended a hillock (called by the Bashkírs a *shikhan*) and dismounting from their carts and their horses, gathered in one spot. The Chief came up to Pahóm and stretching out his arm towards the plain:

"See," said he, "all this, as far as your eye can reach is ours. You may have any part of it you like."

Pahóm's eyes glistened: it was all virgin soil, as flat as the palm of your hand, as black as the seed of a poppy, and in the hollows different kinds of grasses grew breast high.

The Chief took off his fox-fur cap, placed it on the ground and said:

"This will be the mark. Start from here, and return here again. All the land you go round shall be yours."

Pahóm took out his money and put it on the cap. Then he took off his outer coat, remaining in his sleeveless under-coat. He unfastened his girdle and tied it tight below his stomach, put a little bag of bread into the breast of his coat, and tying a flask of water to his girdle, he drew up the tops of his boots, took the spade from his man, and stood ready to start. He considered for some moments which way he had better go—it was tempting everywhere.

"No matter," he concluded, "I will go towards the rising sun."

He turned his face to the east, stretched himself, and waited for the sun to appear above the rim.

"I must lose no time," he thought, "and it is easier walking while it is still cool."

The sun's rays had hardly flashed above the horizon, before Pahóm, carrying the spade over his shoulder, went down into the steppe.

Pahóm started walking neither slowly nor quickly. After having gone a thousand yards he stopped, dug a hole, and placed pieces of turf one on another to make it more visible. Then he went on; and now that he had walked off his stiffness he quickened his pace. After a while he dug another hole.

Pahóm looked back. The hillock could be distinctly seen in the sunlight, with the people on it, and the glittering tires of the cart-wheels. At a rough guess Pahóm concluded that he had walked three miles. It was growing warmer; he took off his under-coat, flung it across his shoulder, and went on again. It had grown quite warm now; he looked at the sun, it was time to think of breakfast.

"The first shift is done, but there are four in a day, and it is too soon yet to turn. But I will just take off my boots," said he to himself.

He sat down, took off his boots, stuck them into his girdle, and went on. It was easy walking now.

"I will go on for another three miles," thought he, "and then turn to the left. This spot is so fine, that it would be a pity to lose it. The further one goes, the better the land seems."

He went straight on for a while, and when he looked round, the hillock was scarcely visible and the people on it looked like black ants, and he could just see something glistening there in the sun.

"Ah," thought Pahóm, "I have gone far enough in this direction, it is time to turn. Besides I am in a regular sweat, and very thirsty."

He stopped, dug a large hole, and heaped up pieces of turf. Next he untied his flask, had a drink, and then turned sharply to the left. He went on and on; the grass was high, and it was very hot.

Pahóm began to grow tired: he looked at the sun and saw that it was noon.

"Well," he thought, "I must have a rest."

He sat down, and ate some bread and drank some water; but he did not lie down, thinking that if he did he might fall asleep. After sitting a little while, he went on again. At first he walked easily: the food had strengthened him; but it had become terribly hot and he felt sleepy, still he went on, thinking: "An hour to suffer, a life-time to live."

He went a long way in this direction also, and was about to turn to the left again, when he perceived a damp hollow: "It would be a pity to leave that out," he thought. "Flax would do well there." So he went on past the hollow, and dug a hole on the other side of it before he turned the corner. Pahóm looked towards the hillock. The heat made the air hazy: it seemed to be quivering, and through the haze the people on the hillock could scarcely be seen.

"Ah!" thought Pahóm, "I have made the sides too long; I must make this one shorter." And he went along the third side, stepping faster. He looked at the sun: it was nearly half-way to the horizon, and he had not yet done two miles of the third side of the square. He was still ten miles from the goal.

"No," he thought, "though it will make my land lop-sided, I must hurry back in a straight line now. I might go too far, and as it is I have a great deal of land."

So Pahóm hurriedly dug a hole, and turned straight towards the hillock.

9

Pahóm went straight towards the hillock, but he now walked with difficulty. He was done up with the heat, his bare feet were cut and bruised, and his legs began to fail. He longed to rest, but it was impossible if he meant to get back before sunset. The sun waits for no man, and it was sinking lower and lower.

"Oh dear," he thought, "if only I have not blundered trying for too much! What if I am too late?"

He looked towards the hillock and at the sun. He was still far from his goal, and the sun was already near the rim.

Pahóm walked on and on; it was very hard walking but he went quicker and quicker. He pressed on, but was still far from the place. He began running, threw away his coat, his boots, his flask, and his cap, and kept only the spade which he used as a support.

"What shall I do," he thought again. "I have grasped too much and ruined the whole affair. I can't get there before the sun sets."

And this fear made him still more breathless. Pahóm went on running, his soaking shirt and trousers stuck to him and his mouth was parched. His breast was working like a blacksmith's bellows, his heart was beating like a hammer, and his legs were giving way as if they did not belong to him. Pahóm was seized with terror lest he should die of the strain.

Though afraid of death, he could not stop. "After having run all that way they will call me a fool if I stop now," thought he. And he ran on and on, and drew near and heard the Bashkírs yelling and shouting to him, and their cries inflamed his heart still more. He gathered his last strength and ran on.

The sun was close to the rim, and cloaked in mist looked large, and red as blood. Now, yes now, it was about to set! The sun was quite low, but he was also quite near his aim. Pahóm could already see the people on the hillock waving their arms to hurry him up. He could see the fox-fur cap on the ground and the money on it, and the Chief sitting on the ground holding his sides. And Pahóm remembered his dream.

"There is plenty of land," thought he, "but will God let me live on it? I have lost my life, I have lost my life! I shall never reach that spot!"

Pahóm looked at the sun, which had reached the earth: one side of it had already disappeared. With all his remaining strength he rushed on, bending his body forward so that his legs could hardly follow fast enough to keep him from falling. Just as he reached the hillock it suddenly grew dark. He looked up—the sun had already set! He gave a cry: "All my labor has been in vain," thought he, and was about to stop, but he heard the Bashkírs still shouting, and remembered that though to him, from below, the sun seemed to have set, they on the hillock could still see it. He took a long breath and ran up the hillock. It was still light there. He reached the top and saw the cap. Before it sat the Chief laughing and holding his sides. Again Pahóm remembered his dream, and he uttered a cry: his legs gave way beneath him, he fell forward and reached the cap with his hands.

"Ah, that's a fine fellow!" exclaimed the Chief. "He has gained much land!"

Pahóm's servant came running up and tried to raise him, but he saw that blood was flowing from his mouth. Pahóm was dead!

The Bashkírs clicked their tongues to show their pity.

His servant picked up the spade and dug a grave long enough for Pahóm to lie in, and buried him in it. Six feet from his head to his heels was all he needed.

Questions for Discussion and Analysis

1. How important is the presence of the Devil, or the Evil One, in the story? Does Pahóm have free will, or are his actions and his downfall predetermined by the Devil's intervention? Is there any evidence that Pahóm's destruction is inevitable?
2. What disguises does the Devil assume throughout the story?
3. How do you interpret the behavior of the Bashkírs? How does their presence in the story influence our attitude toward Pahóm?
4. Is there any evidence of foreshadowing?
5. "How Much Land Does a Man Need?" is a parable, a story that imparts a moral truth. How would you state that moral truth?

Selection 2	# The Knife Thrower

Steven Millhauser

*Steven Millhauser, an American writer, received the Pulitzer Prize for his
1996 novel* Martin Dressler: The Tale of an American Dreamer. *He has
also been honored by the Academy of Arts and Letters. Millhauser, who
teaches at Skidmore College, lives in New York State. "The Knife Thrower" is
part of a collection of short stories of the same name.*

When we learned that Hensch, the knife thrower, was stopping at our
town for a single performance at eight o'clock on Saturday night, we
hesitated, wondering what we felt. Hensch, the knife thrower! Did we
feel like clapping our hands for joy, like leaping to our feet and bursting
into smiles of anticipation? Or did we, after all, want to tighten our lips
and look away in stern disapproval? That was Hensh for you. For if
Hensch was an acknowledged master of his art, that difficult and faintly
unsavory art about which we knew very little, it was also true that he
bore with him certain disturbing rumors, which we reproached ourselves for having failed to heed sufficiently when they appeared from
time to time in the arts section of the Sunday paper.

Hensch, the knife thrower! Of course we knew his name. Everyone
knew his name, as one knows the name of a famous chess player or magician. What we couldn't be sure of was what he actually did. Dimly we
recalled that the skill of his throwing had brought him early attention,
but that it wasn't until he had changed the rules entirely that he was
taken up in a serious way. He had stepped boldly, some said recklessly,
over the line never before crossed by knife throwers, and had managed
to make a reputation out of a disreputable thing. Some of us seemed to
recall reading that in his early carnival days he had wounded an assistant badly; after a six-month retirement he had returned with his new
act. It was here that he had introduced into the chaste discipline of
knife throwing the idea of the artful wound, the mark of blood that was
the mark of the master. We had even heard that among his followers
there were many, young women especially, who longed to be wounded
by the master and to bear his scar proudly. If rumors of this kind were
disturbing to us, if they prevented us from celebrating Hensch's arrival
with innocent delight, we nevertheless acknowledged that without
such dubious enticements we'd have been unlikely to attend the performance at all, since the art of knife throwing, for all its apparent danger,
is really a tame art, an outmoded art—little more than a quaint old-
fashioned amusement in these times of ours. The only knife throwers
any of us had ever seen were in the circus sideshow or the carnival ten-
in-one, along with the fat lady and the human skeleton. It must, we
imagined, have galled Hensch to feel himself a freak among freaks; he

must have needed a way out. For wasn't he an artist, in his fashion? And so we admired his daring, even as we deplored his method and despised him as a vulgar showman; we questioned the rumors, tried to recall what we knew of him, interrogated ourselves relentlessly. Some of us dreamed of him: a monkey of a man in checked pants and a red hat, a stern officer in glistening boots. The promotional mailings showed only a knife held by a gloved hand. Is it surprising we didn't know what to feel?

At eight o'clock precisely, Hensch walked onto the stage: a brisk unsmiling man in black tails. His entrance surprised us. For although most of us had been seated since half-past seven, others were still arriving, moving down the aisles, pushing past half-turned knees into squeaking seats. In fact we were so accustomed to delays for latecomers that an 8:00 performance was understood to mean one that began at 8:10 or even 8:15. As Hensch strode across the stage, a busy no-nonsense man, black-haired and top-bald, we didn't know whether we admired him for his supreme indifference to our noises of settling in, or disliked him for his refusal to countenance the slightest delay. He walked quickly across the stage to a waist-high table on which rested a mahogany box. He wore no gloves. At the opposite corner of the stage, in the rear, a black wooden partition bisected the stage walls. Hensch stepped behind his box and opened it to reveal a glitter of knives. At this moment a woman in a loose-flowing white gown stepped in front of the dark partition. Her pale hair was pulled tightly back and she carried a silver bowl.

While the latecomers among us whispered their way past knees and coats, and slipped guiltily into their seats, the woman faced us and reached into her bowl. From it she removed a white hoop about the size of a dinner plate. She held it up and turned it from side to side, as if for our inspection, while Hensch lifted from his box half a dozen knives. Then he stepped to the side of the table. He held the six knives fanwise in his left hand, with the blades pointing up. The knives were about a foot long, the blades shaped like elongated diamonds, and as he stood there at the side of the stage, a man with no expression on his face, a man with nothing to do, Hensch had the vacant and slightly bored look of an overgrown boy holding in one hand an awkward present, waiting patiently for someone to open a door.

With a gentle motion the woman in the white gown tossed the hoop lightly in the air in front of the black wooden partition. Suddenly a knife sank deep into the soft wood, catching the hoop, which hung swinging on the handle. Before we could decide whether or not to applaud, the woman tossed another white hoop. Hensch lifted and threw in a single swift smooth motion, and the second hoop hung swinging from the second knife. After the third hoop rose in the air and hung suddenly on a knife handle, the woman reached into her bowl and held up for our inspection a smaller hoop, the size of a saucer. Hensch raised a knife and caught the flying hoop cleanly against the wood. She next tossed two small hoops one after the other, which Hensch caught in two swift motions: the first at the top of its trajectory, the second near the middle of the partition.

We watched Hensch as he picked up three more knives and spread them fanwise in his left hand. He stood staring at his assistant with fierce attention, his back straight, his thick hand resting by his side. When she tossed three small hoops, one after the other, we saw his body tighten, we waited for the thunk-thunk-thunk of knives in wood, but he stood immobile, sternly gazing. The hoops struck the floor, bounced slightly, and began rolling like big dropped coins across the stage. Hadn't he liked the throw? We felt like looking away, like pretending we hadn't noticed. Nimbly the assistant gathered the rolling hoops, then assumed her position by the black wall. She seemed to take a deep breath before she tossed again. This time Hensch flung his three knives with extraordinary speed, and suddenly we saw all three hoops swinging on the partition, the last mere inches from the floor. She motioned grandly toward Hensch, who did not bow; we burst into vigorous applause.

Again the woman in the white gown reached into her bowl, and this time she held up something between her thumb and forefinger that even those of us in the first rows could not immediately make out. She stepped forward, and many of us recognized, between her fingers, an orange and black butterfly. She returned to the partition and looked at Hensch, who had already chosen his knife. With a gentle tossing gesture she released the butterfly. We burst into applause as the knife drove the butterfly against the wood, where those in the front rows could see the wings helplessly beating.

That was something we hadn't seen before, or even imagined we might see, something worth remembering; and as we applauded we tried to recall the knife throwers of our childhood, the smell of sawdust and cotton candy, the glittering woman on the turning wheel.

Now the woman in white removed the knives from the black partition and carried them across the stage to Hensch, who examined each one closely and wiped it with a cloth before returning it to his box.

Abruptly, Hensch strode to the center of the stage and turned to face us. His assistant pushed the table with its box of knives to his side. She left the stage and returned pushing a second table, which she placed at his other side. She stepped away, into half-darkness, while the lights shone directly on Hensch and his tables. We saw him place his left hand palm up on the empty tabletop. With his right hand he removed a knife from the box on the first table. Suddenly, without looking, he tossed the knife straight up into the air. We saw it rise to its rest and come hurtling down. Someone cried out as it struck his palm, but

Hensch raised his hand from the table and held it up for us to see, turning it first one way and then the other: the knife had struck between the fingers. Hensch lowered his hand over the knife so that the blade stuck up between his second and third fingers. He tossed three more knives into the air, one after the other: rat-tat-tat they struck the table. From the shadows the woman in white stepped forward and tipped the table toward us, so that we could see the four knives sticking between his fingers.

Oh, we admired Hensch, we were taken with the man's fine daring; and yet, as we pounded out our applause, we felt a little restless, a little dissatisfied, as if some unspoken promise had failed to be kept. For hadn't we been a trifle ashamed of ourselves for attending the performance, hadn't we deplored in advance his unsavory antics, his questionable crossing of the line?

As if in answer to our secret impatience, Hensch strode decisively to his corner of the stage. Quickly the pale-haired assistant followed, pushing the table after him. She next shifted the second table to the back of the stage and returned to the black partition. She stood with her back against it, gazing across the stage at Hensch, her loose white gown hanging from thin shoulder straps that had slipped down to her upper arms. At that moment we felt in our arms and along our backs a first faint flutter of anxious excitement, for there they stood before us, the dark master and the pale maiden, like figures in a dream from which we were trying to awake.

Hensch chose a knife and raised it beside his head with deliberation; we realized that he had worked very quickly before. With a swift sharp drop of his forearm, as if he were chopping a piece of wood, he released the knife. At first we thought he had struck her upper arm, but we saw that the blade had sunk into the wood and lay touching her skin. A second knife struck beside her other upper arm. She began to wriggle both shoulders, as if to free herself from the tickling knives, and only as her loose gown came rippling down did we realize that the knives had cut the shoulder straps. Hensch has us now, he had us. Long-legged and smiling, she stepped from the fallen gown and stood before the black partition in a spangled silver leotard. We thought of tightrope walkers, bareback riders, hot circus tents on blue summer days. The pale yellow hair, the spangled cloth, the pale skin touched here and there with shadow, all this gave her the remote, enclosed look of a work of art, while at the same time it lent her a kind of cool voluptuousness, for the metallic glitter of her costume seemed to draw attention to the bareness of her skin, disturbingly unhidden, dangerously white and cool and soft.

Quickly the glittering assistant stepped to the second table at the back of the stage and removed something from the drawer. She returned to the center of the wooden partition and placed on her head a red apple. The apple was so red and shiny that it looked as if it had been painted with nail polish. We looked at Hensch, who stared at her and held himself very still. In a single motion Hensch lifted and threw. She stepped out from under the red apple stuck in the wood.

From the table she removed a second apple and clenched the stem with her teeth. At the black partition she bent slowly backward until the bright red apple was above her upturned lips. We could see the column of her trachea pressing against the skin of her throat and the knobs of her hips pushing up against the silver spangles. Hensch took careful aim and flung the knife through the heart of the apple.

Next from the table she removed a pair of long white gloves, which she pulled on slowly, turning her wrists, tugging. She held up each tight-gloved hand in turn and wriggled the fingers. At the partition she stood with her arms out and her fingers spread. Hensch looked at her, then raised a knife and threw; it stuck into her fingertip, the middle fingertip of her right hand, pinning her to the black wall. The woman stared straight ahead. Hensch picked up a clutch of knives and held them fanwise in his left hand. Swiftly he flung nine knives, one after the other, and as they struck her fingertips, one after the other, bottom to top, right-left right-left, we stirred uncomfortably in our seats. In the sudden silence she stood there with her arms outspread and her fingers full of knives, her silver spangles flashing, her white gloves whiter than her pale arms, looking as if at any moment her head would drop forward—looking for all the world like a martyr on a cross. Then slowly, gently, she pulled each hand from its glove, leaving the gloves hanging on the wall.

Now Hensch gave a sharp wave of his fingers, as if to dismiss everything that had gone before, and to our surprise the woman stepped forward to the edge of the stage, and addressed us for the first time.

"I must ask you," she said gently, "to be very quiet, because this next act is very dangerous. The master will mark me. Please do not make a sound. We thank you."

She turned to the black partition and simply stood there, her shoulders back, her arms down but pressed against the wood. She gazed steadily at Hensch, who seemed to be studying her; some of us said later that at this moment she gave the impression of a child who was about to be struck in the face, though others felt she looked calm, quite calm.

Hensch chose a knife from his box, held it for a moment, then raised his arm and threw. The knife struck beside her neck. He had missed—had he missed?—and we felt a sharp tug of disappointment, which changed at once to shame, deep shame, for we hadn't come out for blood, only for—well, something else; and as we asked ourselves what we had come for, we were surprised to see her reach up with one hand and pull out the knife. Then we saw, on her neck, the thin red trickle, which ran down to her shoulder; and we understood that her

whiteness had been arranged for this moment. Long and loud we applauded, as she bowed and held aloft the glittering knife, assuring us, in
that way, that she was wounded but well, or well-wounded; and we
didn't know whether we were applauding her wellness or her wound, or
the touch of the master, who had crossed the line, who had carried us,
safely, it appeared, into the realm of forbidden things.

Even as we applauded she turned and left the stage, returning a few
moments later in a long black dress with long sleeves and a high collar,
which concealed her wound. We imagined the white bandage under
the black collar; we imagined other bandages, other wounds, on her
hips, her waist, the edges of her breasts. Black against black they stood
there, she and he, bound now it seemed in a dark pact, as if she were
his twin sister, or as if both were on the same side in a game we were all
playing, a game we no longer understood; and indeed she looked older
in her black dress, sterner, a schoolmarm or maiden aunt. We were not
surprised when she stepped forward to address us again.

"If any of you, in the audience, wish to be marked by the master, to
receive the mark of the master, now is the time. Is there anyone?"

We all looked around. A single hand rose hesitantly and was instantly lowered. Another hand went up; then there were other hands,
young bodies straining forward, eager; and from the stage the woman
in black descended and walked slowly along an aisle, looking closely,
considering, until she stopped and pointed: "You." And we knew her,
Susan Parker, a high school girl, who might have been our daughter,
sitting there with her face turned questioningly toward the woman, her
eyebrows slightly raised, as she pointed to herself; then the faint flush
of realization; and as she climbed the steps of the stage we watched her
closely, wondering what the dark woman had seen in her, to make her
be the one, wondering too what she was thinking, Susan Parker, as she
followed the dark woman to the wooden partition. She was wearing
loose jeans and a tight black short-sleeved sweater; her reddish-brown
and faintly shiny hair was cut short. Was it for her white skin she had
been chosen? or some air of self-possession? We wanted to cry out: sit
down! you don't have to do this! but we remained silent, respectful.
Hensch stood at his table, watching without expression. It occurred to
us that we trusted him at this moment; we clung to him; he was all we
had; for if we weren't absolutely sure of him, then who were we, what
on earth were we, who had allowed things to come to such a pass?

The woman in black led Susan Parker to the wooden partition and
arranged her there: back to the wood, shoulders straight. We saw her
run her hand gently, as if tenderly, over the girl's short hair, which
lifted and fell back in place. Then taking Susan Parker's right hand in
hers, she stepped to the girl's right, so that the entire arm was extended
against the black partition. She stood holding Susan Parker's raised
hand, gazing at the girl's face—comforting her, it seemed; and we

observed that Susan Parker's arm looked very white between the black sweater and the black dress, against the black wood of the partition. As the women gazed at each other, Hensch lifted a knife and threw. We heard the muffled bang of the blade, heard Susan Parker's sharp little gasp, saw her other hand clench into a fist. Quickly the dark woman stepped in front of her and pulled out the knife; and turning to us she lifted Susan Parker's arm, and displayed for us a streak of red on the pale forearm. Then she reached into a pocket of her black dress and removed a small tin box. From the box came a ball of cotton, a patch of gauze, and a roll of white surgical tape, with which she swiftly bound the wound. "There, dear," we heard her say. "You were very brave." We watched Susan Parker walk with lowered eyes across the stage, holding her bandaged arm a little away from her body; and as we began to clap, because she was still there, because she had come through, we saw her raise her eyes and give a quick shy smile, before lowering her lashes and descending the steps.

Now arms rose, seats creaked, there was a great rustling and whispering among us, for others were eager to be chosen, to be marked by the master, and once again the woman in black stepped forward to speak.

"Thank you, dear. You were very brave, and now you will bear the mark of the master. You will treasure it all your days. But it is a light mark, do you know, a very light mark. The master can mark more deeply, far more deeply. But for that you must show yourself worthy. Some of you may already be worthy, but I will ask you now to lower your hands, please, for I have with me someone who is ready to be marked. And please, all of you, I ask for your silence."

From the right of the stage stepped forth a young man who might have been fifteen or sixteen. He was dressed in black pants and a black shirt and wore rimless glasses that caught the light. He carried himself with ease, and we saw that he had a kind of lanky and slightly awkward beauty, the beauty, we thought, of a water-bird, a heron. The woman led him to the wooden partition and indicated that he should stand with his back against it. She walked to the table at the rear of the stage and removed an object, which she carried back to the partition. Raising the boy's left arm, so that it was extended straight out against the wall at the level of his shoulder, she lifted the object to his wrist and began fastening it into the wood. It appeared to be a clamp, which held his arm in place at the wrist. She then arranged his hand: palm facing us, fingers together. Stepping away, she looked at him thoughtfully. Then she stepped over to his free side, took his other hand, and held it gently.

The stage lights went dark, then a reddish spotlight shone on Hensch at his box of knives. A second light, white as moonlight, shone on the boy and his extended arm. The other side of the boy remained in darkness.

Even as the performance seemed to taunt us with the promise of danger, of a disturbing turn that should not be permitted, or even imagined, we reminded ourselves that the master had so far done nothing but scratch a bit of skin, that his act was after all public and well traveled, that the boy appeared calm; and though we disapproved of the exaggerated effect of the lighting, the crude melodrama of it all, we secretly admired the skill with which the performance played on our fears. What it was we feared, exactly, we didn't know, couldn't say. But there was the knife thrower bathed in blood-light, there was the pale victim manacled to a wall; in the shadows the dark woman; and in the glare of the lighting, in the silence, in the very rhythm of the evening, the promise of entering a dark dream.

And Hensch took up a knife and threw; some heard the sharp gasp of the boy, others a thin cry. In the whiteness of the light we saw the knife handle at the center of his bloody palm. Some said that at the moment the knife struck, the boy's shocked face shone with an intense, almost painful joy. The white light suddenly illuminated the woman in black, who raised his free arm high, as if in triumph; then she quickly set to work pulling out the blade, wrapping the palm in strips of gauze, wiping the boy's drained and sweating face with a cloth, and leading him off the stage with an arm firmly around his waist. No one made a sound. We looked at Hensch, who was gazing after his assistant.

When she came back, alone, she stepped forward to address us, while the stage lights returned to normal.

"You are a brave boy, Thomas. You will not soon forget this day. And now I must say that we have time for only one more event, this evening. Many of you here, I know, would like to receive the palm mark, as Thomas did. But I am asking something different now. Is there anyone in this audience tonight who would like to make"—and here she paused, not hesitantly, but as if in emphasis—"the ultimate sacrifice? This is the final mark, the mark that can be received only once. Please think it over carefully, before raising your hand."

We wanted her to say more, to explain clearly what it was she meant by those riddling words, which came to us as though whispered in our ears, in the dark, words that seemed to mock us even as they eluded us—and we looked about tensely, almost eagerly, as if by the sheer effort of our looking we were asserting our vigilance. We saw no hands, and maybe it was true that at the very center of our relief there was a touch of disappointment, but it was relief nonetheless; and if the entire performance had seemed to be leading toward some overwhelming moment that was no longer to take place, still we had been entertained by our knife thrower, had we not, we had been carried a long way, so that even as we questioned his cruel art we were ready to offer our applause.

"If there are no hands," she said, looking at us sharply, as if to see what it was we were secretly thinking, while we, as if to avoid her gaze, looked rapidly all about. "Oh: yes?" We saw it too, the partly raised hand, which perhaps had always been there, unseen in the half-darkened seats, and we saw the stranger rise, and begin to make her way slowly past drawn-in knees and pulled-back coats and half-risen forms. We watched her climb the steps of the stage, a tall mournful-looking girl in jeans and a dark blouse, with lank long hair and slouched shoulders. "And what is your name?" the woman in black said gently, and we could not hear the answer. "Well then, Laura. And so you are prepared to receive the final mark? Then you must be very brave." And turning to us she said, "I must ask you, please, to remain absolutely silent."

She led the girl to the black wooden partition and arranged her there, unconfined: chin up, hands hanging awkwardly at her sides. The dark woman stepped back and appeared to assess her arrangement, after which she crossed to the back of the stage. At this point some of us had confused thoughts of calling out, of demanding an explanation, but we didn't know what it was we might be protesting, and in any case the thought of distracting Hensch's throw, of perhaps causing an injury, was repellent to us, for we saw that already he had selected a knife. It was a new kind of knife, or so we thought, a longer and thinner knife. And it seemed to us that things were happening too quickly, up there on the stage, for where was the spotlight, where was the drama of a sudden darkening, but Hensch, even as we wondered, did what he always did—he threw his knife. Some of us heard the girl cry out, others were struck by her silence, but what stayed with all of us was the absence of the sound of the knife striking wood. Instead there was a softer sound, a more disturbing sound, a sound almost like silence, and some said the girl looked down, as if in surprise. Others claimed to see in her face, in the expression of her eyes, a look of rapture. As she fell to the floor the dark woman stepped forward and swept her arm toward the knife thrower, who for the first time turned to acknowledge us. And now he bowed: a deep, slow, graceful bow, the bow of a master, down to his knees. Slowly the dark red curtain began to fall. Overhead the lights came on.

As we left the theater we agreed that it had been a skillful performance, though we couldn't help feeling that the knife thrower had gone too far. He had justified his reputation, of that there could be no question; without ever trying to ingratiate himself with us, he had continually seized our deepest attention. But for all that, we couldn't help feeling that he ought to have found some other way. Of course the final act had probably been a setup, the girl had probably leaped smiling to her feet as soon as the curtain closed, though some of us recalled unpleasant rumors of one kind or another, run-ins with the police, charges and countercharges, a murky business. In any case we reminded ourselves that she hadn't been coerced in any way, none of them had been coerced in any way. And it was certainly true that a man in Hensch's position had every right to improve his art, to dream up new acts with which to pique curiosity, indeed such advances were absolutely necessary, for without them a knife thrower could never hope to keep himself in the public eye. Like the rest of us, he had to earn his living, which admittedly wasn't easy in times like these. But when all was said and done, when the pros and cons were weighed, and every issue carefully considered, we couldn't help feeling that the knife thrower had really gone too far. After all, if such performances were encouraged, if they were even tolerated, what might we expect in the future? Would any of us be safe? The more we thought about it, the more uneasy we became, and in the nights that followed, when we woke from troubling dreams, we remembered the traveling knife thrower with agitation and dismay.

Questions for Discussion and Analysis

1. Why is the setting of the story not identified?
2. Why does the narrator use the first-person plural pronoun *we* to describe the audience that he is part of? Of what significance is this point of view?
3. How does the audience's view of the knife thrower and his performance change from the beginning of the story to the end?
4. Is the knife thrower really an artist, or does he perhaps stand for something else?
5. "The Knife Thrower" represents an allegory, a story that represents abstract ideas. What are some ways of interpreting the knife thrower's artistry and the audience's twin emotions of fascination and repulsion?

Selection 3   # Girl

Jamaica Kincaid

© Jerry Bauer.

Born in 1946 on the West Indian island of Antigua, Jamaica Kincaid is regarded highly as a short story writer. Her stories have been published in The New Yorker *and other literary magazines. "Girl" appeared in her first collection of short stories,* At the Bottom of the River, *which was nominated for the prestigious PEN/Faulkner Award. Her most recent book,* The Autobiography of My Mother, *was nominated for the National Book Critics Circle Award.*

Wash the white clothes on Monday and put them on the stone heap; wash the color clothes on Tuesday and put them on the clothesline to dry; don't walk barehead in the hot sun; cook pumpkin fritters in very hot sweet oil; soak your little cloths right after you take them off; when buying cotton to make yourself a nice blouse, be sure that it doesn't have gum on it, because that way it won't hold up well after a wash; soak salt fish overnight before you cook it; is it true that you sing benna in Sunday school?; always eat your food in such a way that it won't turn someone else's stomach; on Sundays try to walk like a lady and not like the slut you are so bent on becoming; don't sing benna in Sunday school; you mustn't speak to wharf-rat boys, not even to give directions; don't eat fruits on the street—flies will follow you; *but I don't sing benna on Sundays at all and never in Sunday school;* this is how to sew on a button; this is how to make a buttonhole for the button you have just sewed on; this is how to hem a dress when you see the hem coming down and so to prevent yourself from looking like the slut I know you are so bent on becoming; this is how you iron your father's khaki shirt so that it doesn't have a crease; this is how you iron your father's khaki pants so that they don't have a crease; this is how you grow okra—far from the house, because okra tree harbors red ants; when you are growing dasheen, make sure it gets plenty of water or else it makes your throat itch when you are eating it; this is how you sweep a corner; this is how you sweep a whole house; this is how you sweep a yard; this is how you smile to someone you don't like very much; this is how you smile to someone you don't like at all; this is how you smile to someone you like completely; this is how you set a table for tea; this is how you set a table for dinner; this is how you set a table for dinner with an important guest; this is how you set a table for lunch; this is how you set a table for breakfast; this is how to behave in the presence of men who don't know you very well, and this way they won't recognize immediately the slut I have warned you against becoming; be sure to wash every day, even if it is with your own spit; don't squat down to play marbles—you are not a boy, you know; don't pick people's flowers—you might catch something; don't throw stones at blackbirds, because it might not be a blackbird at all; this is how to make a bread pudding; this is how to make doukona; this is how to make pepper pot; this is how to make a good medicine for a cold; this is how to make a good medicine to throw away a child before it even becomes a child; this is how to catch a fish; this is how to throw back a fish you don't like, and that way something bad won't fall on you; this is how to bully a man; this is how a man bullies you; this is how to love a man, and if this doesn't work there are other ways, and if they don't work don't feel too bad about giving up; this is how to spit up in the air if you feel like it, and this is how to move quick so that it doesn't fall on you; this is how to make ends meet; always squeeze bread to make sure it's fresh; *but what if the baker won't let me feel the bread?;* you mean to say that after all you are really going to be the kind of woman who the baker won't let near the bread?

Questions for Discussion and Analysis

1. Who is the narrator in the story? Who is speaking in the sentences printed in italics?
2. What is the significance of the title? Why isn't the "girl" named?
3. From the many instructions given by the narrator, what conclusions can you draw about the role of women in her culture?
4. Of what particular significance are the instructions to set a table in five different ways?
5. What tension or conflict, if any, do you detect in the story?
6. What is the dramatic effect of the story's style—the fact that the entire story represents only a single sentence?
7. Comment on the final exchange between the two characters? What is the impact of the speaker's final question?

Selection 4

The Jilting of Granny Weatherall
Katherine Anne Porter

© Jerry Bauer.

One of America's most celebrated masters of the short story, Katherine Anne Porter was born in Texas and later lived in New Orleans. She has received numerous literary awards for her writing, and she has lectured and taught both in the U.S. and in Europe. Her major works are Flowering Judas and Other Stories; Pale Horse, Pale Rider; *and* Ship of Fools.

She flicked her wrist neatly out of Doctor Harry's pudgy careful fingers and pulled the sheet up to her chin. The brat ought to be in knee breeches. Doctoring around the country with spectacles on his nose! "Get along now, take your schoolbooks and go. There's nothing wrong with me."

Doctor Harry spread a warm paw like a cushion on her forehead where the forked green vein danced and made her eyelids twitch. "Now, now, be a good girl, and we'll have you up in no time."

"That's no way to speak to a woman nearly eighty years old just because she's down. I'd have you respect your elders, young man."

"Well, Missy, excuse me." Doctor Harry patted her cheek. "But I've got to warn you, haven't I? You're a marvel, but you must be careful or you're going to be good and sorry."

"Don't tell me what I'm going to be. I'm on my feet now, morally speaking. It's Cornelia. I had to go to bed to get rid of her."

Her bones felt loose, and floated around in her skin, and Doctor Harry floated like a balloon around the foot of the bed. He floated and pulled down his waistcoat and swung his glasses on a cord. "Well, stay where you are, it certainly can't hurt you."

"Get along and doctor your sick," said Granny Weatherall. "Leave a well woman alone. I'll call for you when I want you. . . . Where were you forty years ago when I pulled through milk-leg and double pneumonia? You weren't even born. Don't let Cornelia lead you on," she shouted, because Doctor Harry appeared to float up to the ceiling and out. "I pay my own bills, and I don't throw my money away on nonsense!"

She meant to wave good-by, but it was too much trouble. Her eyes closed of themselves, it was like a dark curtain drawn around the bed. The pillow rose and floated under her, pleasant as a hammock in a light wind. She listened to the leaves rustling outside the window. No, somebody was swishing newspapers: no, Cornelia and Doctor Harry were whispering together. She leaped broad awake, thinking they whispered in her ear.

"She was never like this, *never* like this!" "Well, what can we expect?" "Yes, eighty years old. . . ."

Well, and what if she was? She still had ears. It was like Cornelia to whisper around doors. She always kept things secret in such a public way. She was always being tactful and kind. Cornelia was dutiful; that was the trouble with her. Dutiful and good: "So good and dutiful," said Granny, "that I'd like to spank her." She saw herself spanking Cornelia and making a fine job of it.

"What'd you say, Mother?"

Granny felt her face tying up in hard knots.

"Can't a body think, I'd like to know?"

"I thought you might want something."

"I do. I want a lot of things. First off, go away and don't whisper."

She lay and drowsed, hoping in her sleep that the children would keep out and let her rest a minute. It had been a long day. Not that she was tired. It was always pleasant to snatch a minute now and then. There was always so much to be done, let me see: tomorrow.

Tomorrow was far away and there was nothing to trouble about. Things were finished somehow when the time came; thank God there was always a little margin over for peace: then a person could spread out the plan of life and tuck in the edges orderly. It was good to have everything clean and folded away, with the hair brushes and tonic bottles sitting straight on the white embroidered linen: the day started without fuss and the pantry shelves laid out with rows of jelly glasses and brown jugs and white stone-china jars with blue whirligigs and words painted on them: coffee, tea, sugar, ginger, cinnamon, allspice: and the bronze clock with the lion on top nicely dusted off. The dust that lion could collect in twenty-four hours! The box in the attic with all those letters tied up, well, she'd have to go through that tomorrow. All those letters—George's letters and John's letters and her letters to them both—lying around for the children to find afterwards made her uneasy. Yes, that would be tomorrow's business. No use to let them know how silly she had been once.

While she was rummaging around she found death in her mind and it felt clammy and unfamiliar. She had spent so much time preparing for death there was no need for bringing it up again. Let it take care of itself now. When she was sixty she had felt very old, finished, and went around making farewell trips to see her children and grandchildren, with a secret in her mind: This is the very last of your mother, children! Then she made her will and came down with a long fever. That was all just a notion like a lot of other things, but it was lucky too, for she had once for all got over the idea of dying for a long time. Now she couldn't be worried. She hoped she had better sense now. Her father had lived to be one hundred and two years old and had drunk a noggin of strong hot toddy on his last birthday. He told the reporters it was his daily habit, and he owed his long life to that. He had made quite a scandal and was very pleased about it. She believed she'd just plague Cornelia a little.

"Cornelia! Cornelia!" No footsteps, but a sudden hand on her cheek. "Bless you, where have you been?"

"Here, Mother."

"Well, Cornelia, I want a noggin of hot toddy."

"Are you cold, darling?"

"I'm chilly, Cornelia. Lying in bed stops the circulation. I must have told you that a thousand times."

Well, she could just hear Cornelia telling her husband that Mother was getting a little childish and they'd have to humor her. The thing that most annoyed her was that Cornelia thought she was deaf, dumb, and blind. Little hasty glances and tiny gestures tossed around her and over her head saying, "Don't cross her, let her have her way, she's eighty years old," and she sitting there as if she lived in a thin glass cage. Sometimes Granny almost made up her mind to pack up and move back to her own house where nobody could remind her every minute that she was old. Wait, wait, Cornelia, till your own children whisper behind your back!

In her day she had kept a better house and had got more work done. She wasn't too old yet for Lydia to be driving eighty miles for advice when one of the children jumped the track, and Jimmy still dropped in and talked things over: "Now, Mammy, you've a good business head, I want to know what you think of this? . . ." Old. Cornelia couldn't change the furniture around without asking. Little things, little things! They had been so sweet when they were little. Granny wished the old days were back again with the children young and everything to be done over. It had been a hard pull, but not too much for her. When she thought of all the food she had cooked, and all the clothes she had cut and sewed, and all the gardens she had made—well, the children showed it. There they were, made out of her, and they couldn't get away from that. Sometimes she wanted to see John again and point to them and say, Well, I didn't do so badly, did I? But that would have to wait. That was for tomorrow. She used to think of him as a man, but now all the children were older than their father, and he would be a child beside her if she saw him now. It seemed strange and there was something wrong in the idea. Why, he couldn't possibly recognize her. She had fenced in a hundred acres once, digging the post holes herself and clamping the wires with just a negro boy to help. That changed a woman. John would be looking for a young woman with the peaked Spanish comb in her hair and the painted fan. Digging post holes changed a woman. Riding country roads in the winter when women had their babies was another thing: sitting up nights with sick horses and sick negroes and sick children and hardly ever losing one. John, I hardly ever lost one of them! John would see that in a minute, that would be something he could understand, she wouldn't have to explain anything!

It made her feel like rolling up her sleeves and putting the whole place to rights again. No matter if Cornelia was determined to be everywhere at once, there were a great many things left undone on this place. She would start tomorrow and do them. It was good to be strong enough for everything, even if all you made melted and changed and slipped under your hands, so that by the time you finished you almost forgot what you were working for. What was it I set out to do? she asked herself intently, but she could not remember. A fog rose over the valley, she saw it marching across the creek swallowing the trees and moving up the hill like an army of ghosts. Soon it would be at the near edge of the orchard, and then it was time to go in and light the lamps. Come in, children, don't stay out in the night air.

Lighting the lamps had been beautiful. The children huddled up to her and breathed like little calves waiting at the bars in the twilight. Their eyes followed the match and watched the flame rise and settle in a blue curve, then they moved away from her. The lamp was lit, they didn't have to be scared and hang on to mother any more. Never, never, never more. God, for all my life I thank Thee. Without Thee, my God, I could never have done it. Hail, Mary, full of grace.

I want you to pick all the fruit this year and see that nothing is wasted. There's always someone who can use it. Don't let good things rot for want of using. You waste life when you waste good food. Don't let things get lost. It's bitter to lose things. Now, don't let me get to thinking, not when I am tired and taking a little nap before supper. . . .

The pillow rose about her shoulders and pressed against her heart and the memory was being squeezed out of it: oh, push down the pillow, somebody: it would smother her if she tried to hold it. Such a fresh breeze blowing and such a green day with no threats in it. But he had not come, just the same. What does a woman do when she has put on the white veil and set out the white cake for a man and he doesn't come? She tried to remember. No, I swear he never harmed me but in that. He never harmed me but in that . . . and what if he did? There was the day, the day, but a whirl of dark smoke rose and covered it, crept up and over into the bright field where everything was planted so carefully in orderly rows. That was hell, she knew hell when she saw it. For sixty years she had prayed against remembering him and against losing her soul in the deep pit of hell, and now the two things were mingled in one and the thought of him was a smoky cloud from hell that moved and crept in her head when she had just got rid of Doctor Harry and was trying to rest a minute. Wounded vanity, Ellen, said a sharp voice in the top of her mind. Don't let your wounded vanity get the upper hand of you. Plenty of girls get jilted. You were jilted, weren't you? Then stand up to it. Her eyelids wavered and let in streamers of blue-gray light like tissue paper over her eyes. She must get up and pull the shades down or she'd never sleep. She was in bed again and the shades were not down. How could that happen? Better turn over, hide from the light, sleeping in the light gave you nightmares. "Mother, how do you feel now?" and a stinging wetness on her forehead. But I don't like having my face washed in cold water!

Hapsy? George? Lydia? Jimmy? No, Cornelia, and her features were swollen and full of little puddles. "They're coming, darling, they'll all be here soon." Go wash your face, child, you look funny.

Instead of obeying, Cornelia knelt down and put her head on the pillow. She seemed to be talking but there was no sound. "Well, are you tongue-tied? Whose birthday is it? Are you going to give a party?"

Cornelia's mouth moved urgently in strange shapes. "Don't do that, you bother me, daughter."

"Oh, no, Mother. Oh, no. . . ."

Nonsense. It was strange about children. They disputed your every word. "No what, Cornelia?"

"Here's Doctor Harry."

"I won't see that boy again. He just left five minutes ago."

"That was this morning, Mother. It's night now. Here's the nurse."

"This is Doctor Harry, Mrs. Weatherall. I never saw you look so young and happy!"

"Ah, I'll never be young again—but I'd be happy if they'd let me lie in peace and get rested."

She thought she spoke up loudly, but no one answered. A warm weight on her forehead, a warm bracelet on her wrist, and a breeze went on whispering, trying to tell her something. A shuffle of leaves in the everlasting hand of God, He blew on them and they danced and rattled. "Mother, don't mind, we're going to give you a little hypodermic." "Look here, daughter, how do ants get in this bed? I saw sugar ants yesterday." Did you send for Hapsy too?

It was Hapsy she really wanted. She had to go a long way back through a great many rooms to find Hapsy standing with a baby on her arm. She seemed to herself to be Hapsy also, and the baby on Hapsy's arm was Hapsy and himself and herself, all at once, and there was no surprise in the meeting. Then Hapsy melted from within and turned flimsy as gray gauze and the baby was a gauzy shadow, and Hapsy came up close and said, "I thought you'd never come," and looked at her very searchingly and said, "You haven't changed a bit!" They leaned forward to kiss, when Cornelia began whispering from a long way off, "Oh, is there anything you want to tell me? Is there anything I can do for you?"

Yes, she had changed her mind after sixty years and she would like to see George. I want you to find George. Find him and be sure to tell him I forgot him. I want him to know I had my husband just the same and my children and my house like any other woman. A good house too and a good husband that I loved and fine children out of him. Better than I hoped for even. Tell him I was given back everything he took away and more. Oh, no, oh, God, no, there was something else besides the house and the man and the children. Oh, surely they were not all? What was it? Something not given back. . . . Her breath crowded down under her ribs and grew into a monstrous frightening shape with cutting edges; it bored up into her head, and the agony was unbelievable: Yes, John, get the Doctor now, no more talk, my time has come.

When this one was born it should be the last. The last. It should have been born first, for it was the one she had truly wanted. Everything came in good time. Nothing left out, left over. She was strong, in three days she would be as well as ever. Better. A woman needed milk in her to have her full health.

"Mother, do you hear me?"

"I've been telling you—"

"Mother, Father Connolly's here."

"I went to Holy Communion only last week. Tell him I'm not so sinful as all that."

"Father just wants to speak to you."

He could speak as much as he pleased. It was like him to drop in and inquire about her soul as if it were a teething baby, and then stay on for a cup of tea and a round of cards and gossip. He always had a funny story of some sort, usually about an Irishman who made his little mistakes and confessed them, and the point lay in some absurd thing he would blurt out in the confessional showing his struggles between native piety and original sin. Granny felt easy about her soul. Cornelia, where are your manners? Give Father Connolly a chair. She had her secret comfortable understanding with a few favorite saints who cleared a straight road to God for her. All as surely signed and sealed as the papers for the new Forty Acres. Forever . . . heirs and assigns forever.

Since the day the wedding cake was not cut, but thrown out and wasted. The whole bottom dropped out of the world, and there she was blind and sweating with nothing under her feet and the walls falling away. His hand had caught her under the breast, she had not fallen, there was the freshly polished floor with the green rug on it, just as before. He had cursed like a sailor's parrot and said, "I'll kill him for you." Don't lay a hand on him, for my sake leave something to God. "Now, Ellen, you must believe what I tell you. . . ."

So there was nothing, nothing to worry about any more, except sometimes in the night one of the children screamed in a nightmare, and they both hustled out shaking and hunting for the matches and calling, "There, wait a minute, here we are!" John, get the doctor now, Hapsy's time has come. But there was Hapsy standing by the bed in a white cap. "Cornelia, tell Hapsy to take off her cap. I can't see her plain."

Her eyes opened very wide and the room stood out like a picture she had seen somewhere. Dark colors with the shadows rising towards the ceiling in long angles. The tall black dresser gleamed with nothing on it but John's picture, enlarged from a little one, with John's eyes very black when they should have been blue. You never saw him, so how do you know how he looked? But the man insisted the copy was perfect, it was very rich and handsome. For a picture, yes, but it's not my husband. The table by the bed had a linen cover and a candle and a crucifix. The light was blue from Cornelia's silk lampshades. No sort of light at all, just frippery. You had to live forty years with kerosene lamps to appreciate honest electricity. She felt very strong and she saw Doctor Harry with a rosy nimbus around him.

"You look like a saint, Doctor Harry, and I vow that's as near as you'll ever come to it."

"She's saying something."

"I heard you, Cornelia. What's all this carrying-on?"

"Father Connolly's saying—"

Cornelia's voice staggered and bumped like a cart in a bad road. It rounded corners and turned back again and arrived nowhere. Granny stepped up in the cart very lightly and reached for the reins, but a man sat beside her and she knew him by his hands, driving the cart. She did not look in his face, for she knew without seeing, but looked instead down the road where the trees leaned over and bowed to each other and a thousand birds were singing a Mass. She felt like singing too, but she put her hand in the bosom of her dress and pulled out a rosary, and Father Connolly murmured Latin in a very solemn voice and tickled her feet. My God, will you stop that nonsense? I'm a married woman. What if he did run away and leave me to face the priest by myself? I found another a whole world better. I wouldn't have exchanged my husband for anybody except St. Michael himself, and you may tell him that for me with a thank you in the bargain.

Light flashed on her closed eyelids, and a deep roaring shook her. Cornelia, is that lightning? I hear thunder. There's going to be a storm. Close all the windows. Call the children in. . . . "Mother, here we are, all of us." "Is that you, Hapsy?" "Oh, no, I'm Lydia. We drove as fast as we could." Their faces drifted above her, drifted away. The rosary fell out of her hands and Lydia put it back. Jimmy tried to help, their hands fumbled together, and Granny closed two fingers around Jimmy's thumb. Beads wouldn't do, it must be something alive. She was so amazed her thoughts ran round and round. So, my dear Lord, this is my death and I wasn't even thinking about it. My children have come to see me die. But I can't, it's not time. Oh, I always hated surprises. I wanted to give Cornelia the amethyst set—Cornelia, you're to have the amethyst set, but Hapsy's to wear it when she wants, and, Doctor Harry, do shut up. Nobody sent for you. Oh, my dear Lord, do wait a minute. I meant to do something about the Forty Acres, Jimmy doesn't need it and Lydia will later on, with that worthless husband of hers. I meant to finish the altar cloth and send six bottles of wine to Sister Borgia for her dyspepsia. I want to send six bottles of wine to Sister Borgia, Father Connolly, now don't let me forget.

Cornelia's voice made short turns and tilted over and crashed. "Oh, Mother, oh, Mother, oh, Mother. . . ."

"I'm not going, Cornelia. I'm taken by surprise. I can't go."

You'll see Hapsy again. What about her? "I thought you'd never come." Granny made a long journey outward, looking for Hapsy. What if I don't find her? What then? Her heart sank down and down, there was no bottom to death, she couldn't come to the end of it. The blue light from Cornelia's lampshade drew into a tiny point in the center of her brain, it flickered and winked like an eye, quietly it fluttered and dwindled. Granny lay curled down within herself, amazed and watchful, staring at the point of light that was herself; her body was now only a deeper mass of shadow in an endless darkness and this darkness would curl around the light and swallow it up. God, give a sign!

For the second time there was no sign. Again no bridegroom and the priest in the house. She could not remember any other sorrow because this grief wiped them all away. On, no, there's nothing more cruel than this—I'll never forgive it. She stretched herself with a deep breath and blew out the light.

Questions for Discussion and Analysis

1. What is the occasion of this story?
2. What are the most important character traits that Granny Weatherall exhibits? How are these traits revealed? Is her name a "telling name," meaning does it shed any particular light on her character?

3. Why has she kept George's letters? What are her thoughts about George and his leaving her stranded at the altar?

4. What is suggested by the fog rising over the valley, "marching across the creek swallowing the trees and moving up the hill like an army of ghosts"? Look through the story and find instances of other natural phenomena. What do these suggest and how do their references help the reader understand the story?

5. How is time presented in the story? Besides her musings in her bed, how is Granny's past life revealed?

6. Explain Granny's thoughts toward the end of the story where she thinks, "I want you to find George. Find him and be sure to tell him I forgot him." To whom is she addressing these thoughts? In the same scene, what does Granny mean when she writes, "Oh, no, oh, God, no, there was something else besides the house and the man and the children. Oh, surely they were not all? What was it? Something not given back."

7. Explain this sentence at the story's end: "God, give a sign!" What is she asking of God?

8. Consider the dialogue in the preceding question. What meanings are suggested by the word "jilting" in the title?

Permissions Acknowledgments

Wiesenfeld, Kurt—"Making the Grade" by Kurt Wiesenfeld in *Newsweek,* June 17, 1996. Copyright © 1996 Newsweek, Inc. All rights reserved. Reprinted by permission.

Wilbon, Michael—"History in Black and White" by Michael Wilbon from *The Washington Post National Weekly Edition,* April 21, 1997. Copyright © 1997 The Washington Post. Reprinted with permission.

Winchester, Simon—Excerpts (pp. 58–59) from *The Professor and the Madman* by Simon Winchester. Copyright © 1998 by Simon Winchester. Reprinted by permission of HarperCollins Publishers Inc.

Wilson, Janet—"How to Tell if Political Polls Are About Truth, or Consequences" by Janet Wilson in *The Los Angeles Times,* January 30, 2000. Copyright © 2000. Reprinted by permission of The Los Angeles Times.

Woolf, Virginia—"The Death of the Moth" from *The Death of the Moth and Other Essays* by Virginia Woolf. Copyright © 1942 by Harcourt, Inc. and renewed 1970 by Marjorie T. Parsons, Executrix, reprinted by permission of the publisher.

INDEX